THE AZTEC IMAGE

in Western Thought

Benjamin Keen

THE AZTEC IMAGE
in Western Thought

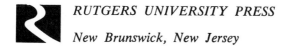

RUTGERS UNIVERSITY PRESS

New Brunswick, New Jersey

Library of Congress Cataloging in Publication Data
Keen, Benjmain, 1913–
    The Aztec Image in Western Thought

    Bibliographical references.
    Includes index.
    1. Aztecs—Historiography. I. Title. II: The Aztec Image in Western thought.
F1219.K43   972   74-163952
ISBN 0-8135-0698-0   MARC
ISBN 0-8135-1572-6 (pbk)

First paperback printing, 1990
Copyright © 1971 by Rutgers, The State University
Manufactured in the United States of America

TO BETTY

Contents

	Foreword	xiii
1	The People of the Sun	3
2	The Aztec World View	30
3	Europe Discovers the Aztecs	49
4	The Aztecs and the Great Debate: I	71
5	The Aztecs and the Great Debate: II	105
6	The Aztecs in Late Renaissance Thought	138
7	The Baroque Vision of the Aztecs	173
8	The Eyes of Reason: I	217
9	The Eyes of Reason: II	260
10	The Aztecs Transfigured: I	310
11	The Aztecs Transfigured: II	337
12	Montezuma's Dinner	380
13	Farewell to Fantasy: From Orozco y Berra to Seler	411
14	The Return of Cuauhtémoc	463
15	The Plumed Serpent	509
	Notes	569
	Index	619

List of Illustrations

FRONTISPIECE

Mask of Quetzalcóatl (?). Wood, with turquoise, jadeite, shell, and mother-of-pearl mosaic. Height: 9½ in. (24 cm.). Valley of Mexico (?). Aztec-Mixtec style, *c.* 1461–1521. Museo Nazionale Preistorico ed Etnografico Luigi Pigorini, Rome. Once in the collection of Cosimo de' Medici (Cosimo I).

PAGE 2

Relief slab of an eagle devouring a heart. Northern Veracruz. The Metropolitan Museum of Art, New York.

BETWEEN PAGES 12–13

Frescoes of the rain god Tláloc and his earthly paradise, Tepantitla, Teotihuacán.

Detail from the Codex Nuttall. British Museum, London. (After Zelia Nuttall.)

Sculptured stone slab from the Palace, Palenque.

Masks of Tláloc and Quetzalcóatl, Temple of Quetzalcóatl, Teotihuacán.

BETWEEN PAGES 34–35

Zapotec maize god. Valley of Oaxaca. Coll. Dr. and Mrs. Josué Sáenz.

The Aztec moon goddess Coyolxauhqui. Tenochtitlán. Museo Nacional de Antropología, Mexico.

The god-king Quetzalcóatl. Valley of Mexico. Musée de l'Homme, Paris.

Clay figurines in a ceremonial scene. Monte Albán. Museo Nacional de Antropología, Mexico.

BETWEEN PAGES 64–65

Portrait of Hernando Cortés by Christoph Weiditz (1529).

An Aztec juggler. Christoph Weiditz drawing.

An Aztec in mantle and feather apron, with jeweled face ornaments. Christoph Weiditz drawing.

Map of Tenochtitlán published with Cortés' Second Letter (1524).

BETWEEN PAGES 88–89

An Aztec shrine and its environs. Diego de Valadés, *Rhetorica Christiana* (1579).

The Great Temple of México-Tenochtitlán. Ignacio Marquina reconstruction (*c.* 1950).

BETWEEN PAGES 130–131

Scene of human sacrifice at the Great Temple. De Bry, *Grands Voyages* (1602).

The Great Temple Square of México-Tenochtitlán. Bernard Picart engraving (1722) for Bernard, *Cérémonies et coutumes religieuses.*

BETWEEN PAGES 162–163

Scenes by Iodocus a Winghe for the De Bry Latin edition (1598) of Las Casas' *Brevísima relación:* The massacre at Cholula. Torture of the King of the Province of Mechuaca.

View of Mexico by Joris Hoefnagel. Braun and Hohenberg, *Civitates orbis terrarum* (1576).

Title page of Ortelius, *Theatrum orbis terrarum* (1570).

Folio from the Codex Mendoza. Bodleian Library, Oxford. (After Paso y Troncoso.)

BETWEEN PAGES 204–205

Turquoise mosaic mask of the rain god Tláloc. Valley of Mexico. British Museum, London.

Mixtec gold lip plug. American Museum of Natural History, New York.

Ancient king of the Valley of Mexico. (After Gemelli Carreri, *Giro del Mondo* [1699–1700].)

Idols of southern Mexico. Bernard Picart engraving (1723) for Bernard, *Cérémonies et coutumes religieuses.*

Meeting of Cortés and Moctezuma. Jacob Schÿnvoet engraving for Solís, *Historia* (1724).

BETWEEN PAGES 248–249

Mexican greenstone mask incorporated in an eighteenth-century European niche figure. Schatzkammer der Residenz München.

Scenes by José Ximeno for the 1783–1784 Madrid edition of Solís, *Historia:* Moctezuma names the King of Spain as his successor. Moctezuma is wounded by his own vassals.

Rejoicing of the Mexicans at the beginning of a new century. Bernard Picart engraving (1721) for Bernard, *Cérémonies et coutumes religieuses.*

BETWEEN PAGES 302–303

Detailed measured drawing of the Coatlicue sculpture by León y Gama (1792; 1832).

Detail of the Stone of Tizoc. From a sketch by M. Dupré (1800).

BETWEEN PAGES 316–317

Tower in the Palace, Palenque. From a sketch by Jean-Frédéric Waldeck (*c.* 1832).

Mitla. From a sketch by Luciano Castañeda (1805–1808).

Xochicalco. From a sketch by Luciano Castañeda (1805–1808).

Sculptured wall panel, Temple of the Cross, Palenque. From a sketch by Luciano Castañeda (1805–1808).

BETWEEN PAGES 348–349

Monstrous carved head. From a sketch by Luciano Castañeda (1805–1808).

The Calendar Stone. From a sketch by Luciano Castañeda.

BETWEEN PAGES 444–445

Antonio Ruiz. *Sueño de la Malinche* (1939). Coll. Inés Amor.

Idealized representations of a young Toltec girl and an Indian king. Charnay, *Ancient Cities of the New World* (1887).

Mask of Xipe Totec, god of spring. Valley of Mexico. Ex coll. Henry Christy, British Museum, London.

BETWEEN PAGES 476–477

The Great Ball Court, Sculptured Chamber E, Chichén Itzá. From a drawing by A. Hunter in Maudslay, *Biologia Centrali-Americana* (1889–1902).

Mitla. Photograph Gordon F. Ekholm (1946).

Frank Lloyd Wright. Charles Ennis house, Los Angeles (1924).

BETWEEN PAGES 526–527

Eagle Knight. Valley of Mexico. Museo Nacional de Antropología, Mexico.

José Clemente Orozco. *The Departure of Quetzalcóatl* (1932–1934). Baker Library, Dartmouth College.

José Clemente Orozco. *Head of Quetzalcóatl* (1932–1934). The Museum of Modern Art, New York.

The Castillo, Chichén Itzá. Photograph Irmgard Groth (*c.* 1970).

Henry Moore. *Ideas for Metal Sculpture* (1938). Coll. Sir Kenneth Clark.

Henry Moore. *Reclining Woman* (1929). Leeds City Art Galleries.

David Alfaro Siqueiros. *Ethnography* (1939). The Museum of Modern Art, New York.

Man with canine headdress. Oaxaca. The Metropolitan Museum of Art, New York.

The earth goddess Coatlicue. México-Tenochtitlán. Museo Nacional de Antropología, Mexico.

LIST OF MAPS

PAGES XIV–XV

Principal Sites of Pre-Conquest Culture in Middle America.

PAGE XVI

Valley of Mexico in 1519.

Foreword

This book studies reflections of the Aztec civilization of ancient Mexico in Western social science, literature, and art over a period of four and a half centuries. It attempts to trace the rise of divergent interpretations of that vanished culture and to show how the resulting clash of views periodically produced new syntheses that incorporated the most valuable data and insights of the rival schools of thought. I have tried to show, too, how such intellectual or artistic movements as the Renaissance, the Baroque, the Enlightenment, Romanticism, and Positivism have shaped and colored the Western vision of Aztec society. Yet this book is more than a history of ideas in which theories generate, battle, and succeed each other. Throughout I have suggested or even affirmed (where the evidence seemed to warrant it) causal relations between the social and historical setting and the views of groups and individuals on Aztec civilization. I have tried, in short, to relate theoretical conflicts concerning the nature of Aztec society to underlying socioeconomic, political, and ideological struggles. In this respect, my book makes some contribution to the discipline known as "sociology of knowledge."

Two introductory chapters present a general, nontechnical account of Aztec life and thought, based on the findings of the best modern research. Because these chapters are designed to orient the nonspecialist, I have elected to avoid excessive use of "perhaps,"

PRINCIPAL SITES OF

PRE-CONQUEST CULTURE

IN MIDDLE AMERICA

Extent of the Aztec Empire in 1519
● Modern City

SCALE 0 ━━━━━ 100 MILES

N

24°

Mérida Aké Izamal
Acanceh△ △Chichén Itzá
Uxmal△ △Mayapán
Jaina Zayil△ △Kabah Cobá
△Labná
△Edzná
Champotón△ △Hochob
Río Bec
Gulf of
Campeche
Comalcalco△ Santa Rita△
La Venta Calakmul△ △Balakbal
Tortuguero Uaxactún△ Tikal
Palenque△ Holmul△ △Benque Viejo
Ocosingo△ Piedras Negras Gulf of Honduras
Yaxchilán Seibal Lubaantun
Tonalá Bonampak △Reforma
Quensanto△ Cancuén △Pusilhá
Chacula △Chamác
△Izapa Quiriguá△ Ulúa
Kaminaljuyú Copán
△Tiquisate
△Cotzumalhuapa

Usulután
△

Tulum

20°

16°

92°   88°

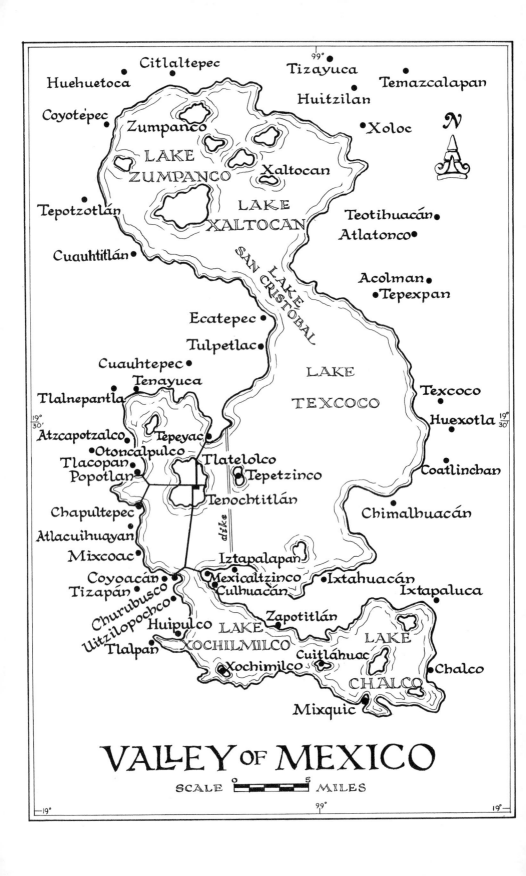

VALLEY OF MEXICO

SCALE 0 ⊢⊣⊢⊣⊢ 5 MILES

"possibly," and similar qualifiers, so that I may occasionally have stated conclusions more positively than the present state of our knowledge warrants. Readers of the chapters that follow will soon become aware of the tentative character of current opinion on many aspects of Aztec culture.

My basic method has been to outline the historical setting of each period, to describe the major schools of thought on Aztec culture in that period, and to analyze the ideas of leading exponents of each school, with a stress on the most original or distinctive facets of each man's thought. Specialists will undoubtedly note the omission of one or another favorite figure. I have sought to be instructive rather than exhaustive. Occasionally I may seem to have dealt at inordinate length with a minor figure. I have assigned more space, for example, to the obscure Father Diego Motezuma than to the celebrated mestizo chronicler Ixtlilxóchitl. The reason was precisely that Ixtlilxóchitl is a well-known writer whose idealized vision of ancient Texcoco is spread forth in the pages of countless works. On the other hand, Father Motezuma's bizarre reconstruction of ancient Mexico, combining fiction, political satire, and pride of race, seemed to me a true discovery that I wished to share with my readers. Similar considerations have governed my inclusion and treatment of other relatively obscure writers.

A word on the use of the term "Aztec" in this book. As R. H. Barlow showed a quarter of a century ago in his article "Some Remarks on the Term 'Aztec Empire,'" *The Americas*, I (1945), 344–349, the word is technically incorrect as applied to the people who expanded from their island redoubt of Tenochtitlán to form a great tribute empire in central Mexico. "Mexica" was the name by which they called themselves at the coming of the Spaniards. The name Mexica or Mexicans is not without ambiguity, however, whereas the word Aztec has the sanction of familiarity and long usage. I have therefore used it throughout this book. More loosely, I have sometimes applied it to other peoples of related culture within the confines of the Aztec Empire.

Numerous colleagues have aided me on points of fact, bibliography, and interpretation in letters and personal discussions. Two grants from the Social Science Research Council helped me to visit Mexico in the summers of 1963 and 1968 for library study and consultation with Mexican specialists. I recall with particular gratitude the generous assistance of Professor Wigberto Jiménez Moreno. Among the librarians who aided me, I owe a special debt to the staff of the Newberry Library in Chicago for unfailing courtesy, patience, and efforts to be helpful.

Benjamin Keen

DeKalb, Illinois
July 1970

THE AZTEC IMAGE
in Western Thought

Relief slab of an eagle devouring a heart. Limestone with traces of stucco and red orange, dark red, ocher, white, blue green, black, and light blue paint. Height: 27½ in. (70 cm.). Said to be from northern Veracruz, near Tampico. Early Postclassic, 1000–1200. The Metropolitan Museum of Art, New York, gift of Frederick E. Church. The motif is one that spread throughout Mesoamerican art. Photograph courtesy Museum.

CHAPTER ONE

The People of the Sun

The Aztec civilization of Mexico has a secure hold on the mind and imagination of Western man. The conqueror of the Aztecs, Hernando Cortés, was the first European to describe their society fully and precisely. His famous letters to the Emperor Charles V introduced Europe to the beauty and terror of Aztec life. Since Cortés' time scores of writers have attempted to capture the complex Aztec reality. Their judgments upon Aztec civilization are startlingly diverse. Where one has a vision of a tribal democracy in which "the Indians worked together for their common good, and no sacrifice was too great for their corporate well-being," another sees little more than "a band of pirates, sallying from their great city to loot and plunder." One discovers "a totalitarian state whose philosophy included an utter contempt for the individual"; another finds in Aztec political organization "a supreme achievement of humanity, full of happy inspirations that the present might well take into account." [1]

Since the contributors to this debate about the nature of Aztec civilization have drawn upon much the same sources of information, it is natural to ask how they arrived at such very different conclusions. Through what ideological prisms did these writers view their subject? What loyalties or interests influenced their judgments? How did such intellectual movements as the Enlightenment, Romanticism, Positivism, and Marxism color the interpretation of Aztec society over the centuries?

The intense interest that the Aztec theme has held for Western man from Cortés to D. H. Lawrence is attributable in part to the relative abundance of our sources of information about the Aztecs. A single body of documents—the monumental collection associated with the pioneer Spanish anthropologist Fray Bernardino de Sahagún—probably contains more information on Aztec life than is available for the Maya and Inca civilizations together. These copious materials have offered the possibility of re-creating Aztec society in rich, evocative detail. Consider, for example, the remarkable panorama of life in the Aztec capital of Tenochtitlán that unfolds in Diego Rivera's mural in the Palacio Nacional in Mexico City.

The contradictions in Aztec civilization, the cleavage in the Aztec soul, sharpened Western interest in Aztec culture. Aztec society presents intriguing paradoxes. The "Assyrians of America," whose great plunder empire rested on foundations of war and human sacrifice, were refined lovers of beauty. Their poets composed delicate verse filled with allusions to the scent and loveliness of flowers, to the brilliance of fine gems, to the brevity of life and its uncertain joys. Aztec parents admonished their children in speeches that breathe the tenderest affection and teach the purest precepts of charity and fair dealing. These paradoxes have naturally inspired not only curiosity but ambitious efforts to explain or resolve them.

The Aztecs were latecomers in a region that had been civilized for almost a thousand years before their arrival. As early as 900 B.C. the inhabitants of the Valley of Mexico were settled in small villages in the midst of their maize, bean, and squash fields. They cultivated the land with slash-and-burn methods, produced a simple but well-made pottery, and turned out large numbers of small clay figures that suggest a belief in fertility goddesses.

Advances in agricultural practices and the crafts, and in the organization of labor by priestly élites, led to an impressive upsurge of culture in Middle America in the first centuries before and after the opening of the Christian era. The great Olmec civilization of the Gulf coast lowlands, with its large ceremonial centers, monumental stone carving and sculpture, hieroglyphic writing, and a calendrical system, arose perhaps as early as 600 B.C. Very likely the Olmec culture was the "mother civilization" of Mesoamerica. In Mexico's central highlands the Classic period opened in splendor. Between the time of Christ and A.D. 250, at Teotihuacán, about twenty-eight miles from Mexico City, the mighty pyramids later given the names of the Sun and the Moon were completed. They towered over clusters of imposing temples and other buildings, forming the heart of a city that spread over an area of some nine square miles. The stone sculpture and the fresco work used in the decoration of the temples, and the cement work of the great structures, possess a marvelous grace and finish that testify to the high development of the crafts among the Teotihuacanos. The ancient water god, Tláloc, seems to have been their chief deity; but the feathered serpent with jaguar fangs, Quetzalcóatl, possibly a double of Tláloc, also appears prominently in the sculpture of their greatest temple. Of human sacrifice and ritual cannibalism there is some evidence. Whereas priests in benign poses, wearing the symbols of their gods, dominate most of the extant mural paintings, a certain number of works brought to light in recent excavations exude a more militaristic spirit.[2]

The great ceremonial center was sacred ground. Probably only the priestly nobility and their servants lived here. Further out were the residential sections, probably inhabited by officials, artisans, and merchants. On the outskirts of the great city lived a large rural population which supplied the metropolis with its food.

The walls of the houses of Teotihuacán were covered with a coat of very fine stucco that was frequently painted in fresco. Those scenes offer an insight into the tone of Teotihuacán life. Most breathe a serenity and a contentment at strong variance with the pessimism, the tragic sense of life, so characteristic of the later Aztec art. In one charming fresco, believed to depict the paradise of the god Tláloc, a multitude of little figures wearing loincloths divert themselves in a landscape of trees, beautiful flowers, delicious fruit, and butterflies. They sing, dance, play leapfrog, or bathe. Ignacio Bernal observes that "the Teotihuacán artist shows us what he considers to be the perfect life, the place of every pleasure, the location where everything highly esteemed in real life appears in abundance. . . . So this painting shows us something of the philosophy and aspirations, necessarily based on concrete reality, of the Teotihuacán people." [3]

Overshadowed by the great city, from which waves of influence radiated as far as Central America, other centers of Classic culture arose in Middle America. In the southwest, at Monte Albán, in the rugged mountains of Oaxaca, the people called Zapotecs erected a great ceremonial center; one of their achievements was a complicated system of ideographic writing. At approximately the same time the Classic Maya civilization flowered in the Petén region at the base of the Yucatán peninsula.

All the indications are that the Classic era at its height (A.D. 200 to 700) was basically peaceful and prosperous, an era of large-scale trade and exchange of ideas among the various regions of Middle America. The accumulation of costly produce as offerings to the gods in the temple centers made them veritable storehouses of the gods and laid the basis for wide regional trade. The Teotihuacanos, for example, carried on an active trade with the Maya, as shown by the finds of artifacts of this period in the two regions.

The Classic cultures of Middle America, it is now clear, sprang from a common seedbed of Formative culture and drew inspiration from one another; the traditional view of the primacy of Maya civilization is no longer tenable. Yet there were impressive differences between what may be called the Mexican and the Maya worlds; Teotihuacán, for example, did not have stone stelae bearing calendric notations, or the corbeled arch, or the zero of Maya mathematics. Equally notable were the differences between the artistic styles of the two worlds. Possibly, as Eric Wolf suggests, their art reflected the climatic differences between the high plains and the rain forest of the Maya. "The Mexican style is geometric, monumental. The Maya style, on the other hand, loves riotous movements, luxuriant form, flamboyance. Both styles are equally Classic. Yet their difference denotes in all probability a wide divergence in basic values and feeling-tones." [4]

By the end of the seventh century the Classic world had been shaken to its foundations by a crisis that spread from one Classic center to another and ended in the total collapse of that splendid era. Teotihuacán, Rome of the ancient Mexican world, perished at the hands of foes who burned the great city between A.D. 650 and 800. Toward the latter date the great ceremonial center at

Monte Albán was abandoned by its priests. And by the year 900 the process of disintegration had reached the Maya region of the Petén, whose deserted or destroyed centers were reclaimed one by one by the jungle. Long periods of decline certainly preceded these catastrophes, but there is little agreement among specialists as to the causes of the sequence of decline and fall. Among the suggested explanations are population pressure on deforested and exhausted soils; peasant revolts provoked by the excessive tribute demands of priestly rulers; conflicts between wealthy centers and exploited hinterlands. All led to the weakening of external defenses and the irruption of barbarian or semibarbarian tribes on the marches of civilization.

From the confusion of this Time of Troubles (approximately A.D. 700 to 1000), there emerged the outlines of a new order, sometimes appropriately called Militarist. Priests and kindly nature gods had presided over the hieratic societies of the Classic era; warriors and terrible war gods dominated the states that established themselves on the ruins of the Classic world. More and more, the spear and the club replaced religious awe and a sense of dependence as instruments for maintaining loyalty and the continued inflow of tribute. Chronic warfare and the fear of war led to the erection of more and more fortifications and fortified towns.[5] In central Mexico the loose imperium of Teotihuacán, which probably was based above all on its cultural and economic supremacy, gave way to the battering of new militarist states that were ruled by barbarian or semibarbarian leaders who warred with each other for land, water, and tribute.

The most important of these states, the successor to the imperium of Teotihuacán, was the Toltec Empire, with its capital at Tula, about forty miles north of Mexico City. Since it was situated on the periphery of the Valley of Mexico, Tula may once have been an outpost of Teotihuacán, guarding the frontiers of civilization against the hunting and gathering tribes to the north. In the period following the collapse of Teotihuacán, one such tribe, the Toltecs, swept down from the north by way of Jalisco and Guanajuato, entered the Valley of Mexico and swiftly overwhelmed the pitiful remnants of the Teotihuacán people. The Toltec leader was a great chief named Mixcóatl, who was later changed into a god.

Toltec power and prosperity reached its peak under the son of Mixcóatl, one Topiltzin, who seems to have absorbed the cultural heritage of Teotihuacán through relatives on his mother's side. About 980 Topiltzin moved the Toltec capital to Tula. He was renamed Quetzalcóatl in his capacity of high priest of the ancient god worshiped by the Teotihuacanos, and during the nineteen years of his rule he made his capital a center of such splendor that he and his city became legendary. The Song of Quetzalcóatl tells of the wonders of Tula, a true paradise on earth where cotton grew in colors, where the soil yielded fruit of such giant size that inferior grain was used only to heat steam baths. The legends of ancient Mexico invest the Toltecs with superhuman powers and talents. They are described as master artisans and scientists, as creators of culture. Over this Golden Age presided the great priest-king Quetzalcóatl, whose rule revived the glories of the Theocratic state of Teotihuacán.

Toward the end of Quetzalcóatl's reign, however, Tula became the scene of an obscure struggle between two religious traditions. One was associated with the worship of Tezcatlipoca, the Toltec tribal sky god who was pictured as an all-powerful and capricious deity who demanded human sacrifice; the other was identified with the cult of the ancient god Quetzalcóatl, a benevolent deity who had brought men maize and all learning and arts and who demanded of them only the peaceful sacrifice of jade, snakes, and butterflies. Very likely this religious conflict reflected a cleavage between "sacred rulers who continued the traditions of Theocratic society and the secular, militarily oriented groups which pushed and pulled in opposite directions." [6] This struggle found fanciful expression in the Náhuatl legend which tells how the enchanter Tezcatlipoca used black magic to make the saintly priest-king Quetzalcóatl fall from grace and go into exile from Tula. Evidence for the view that the defeat and exile of the historical Quetzalcóatl signaled the triumph of Militarist over Theocratic elements in Tula appears in Toltec art. Nearly all the art forms abound in representations of warriors, eagles eating hearts or drinking blood, and files of jaguars and pumas.

Whatever its factual basis or background, the legend of Quetzalcóatl made a profound impression on the folk culture of ancient Mexico and played its part in the destruction of the Aztec Empire.

The legend concluded with the promise that the Indian redeemer would someday return to his realm and resume his mild sway; and, by a singular coincidence, the year in which Quetzalcóatl was to return, Ce Acatl, One Reed, was the year in which Cortés landed at Veracruz. Aztec fears that the god-king had returned to reclaim his kingdom help to explain the vacillating and contradictory moves of Moctezuma.

Topiltzin-Quetzalcóatl was succeeded by lesser kings who vainly struggled to overcome a growing internal crisis of the Toltec Empire. The causes of this crisis are obscure. Severe droughts may have caused crop failures and famines, but these disasters were perhaps aggravated by Toltec neglect of agriculture in favor of the collection of luxury items as tribute from conquered peoples. The crisis within weakened the external defenses of the empire and led to a new irruption of barbarian tribes from the desert north. These were hunters and gatherers who may themselves have been seeking food and relief from the effects of drought by invading the lands of the agriculturists. A series of revolutions reflected the Toltec economic and social difficulties. The last Toltec king, Huémac, is thought to have committed suicide about 1174; with him the Toltec Empire disappeared. In the following years a general exodus or diaspora of the Toltecs took place. Tula itself fell into the hands of the barbarians about 1224.

The fall of Tula opened the way for a general invasion of the Valley of Mexico by the northern barbarians. These newcomers, generically called Chichimecs, bear comparison to the Germanic barbarians who broke into the dying Roman Empire. Like them, the Chichimec leaders, no doubt already partly acculturated, respected and tried to absorb the superior culture of the vanquished people; they were eager to intermarry with the surviving Toltec royalty and nobility.

In the period that followed the destruction of the Toltec Empire, a number of succession-states established themselves in the lake country at the bottom of the Valley of Mexico. Legitimately or no, the rulers of all these states claimed the honor of Toltec descent. First Culhuacán, then Atzcapotzalco, Texcoco, and Tenochtitlán, in succession, became the dominant city-state in the valley. Culhuacán, founded by refugees from Tula about 1207, appears to have had a real claim to Toltec descent. In point of artistic and industrial development, the Texcocan kingdom, organized by a Chichimec dynasty in 1260, easily excelled its neighbors. Excavations show that the rulers of Texcoco constructed one of the largest irrigation and terracing systems in ancient Middle America.

Texcoco illustrates the fusion of Chichimec military energy and Toltec civilization at its best. "Surrounded by the older sedentary peoples whom they had conquered without causing them to disappear, the Chichimecs gradually absorbed the old Toltec culture. It is the typical example of Greece and Rome." [7] Texcocan civilization was to reach its climactic moment two centuries later in the reign of the philosopher-king Nezahualcóyotl, perhaps the most remarkable figure to emerge from the mists of ancient America.

Among the last of the Chichimec tribes to arrive in the valley were the Aztecs or Mexica. The date of their departure from the north is given in their annals as 1168. They were led by four chiefs and a woman who carried a medicine bundle housing the spirit of their tribal god Huitzilopochtli. The god guided their steps, speaking in the strange twittering voice of a hummingbird, and after long wanderings they arrived in the Valley of Mexico about 1218. Finding the most desirable sites occupied by other tribes, they were compelled at last to take refuge on marshy lands in Lake Texcoco. Here, probably in 1344 or 1345, they began to build the town of Tenochtitlán. At this time the Aztec tribe seems to have been composed of five kinship groups or clans; later this number grew to twenty, organized in four territorial wards or quarters.

The patches of solid ground that existed in the Aztec territory were gradually built over with huts of cane and reeds; more ambitious structures of turf, adobe, and light stone belong to a later period. As population increased and tillable soil became scarce the Aztecs borrowed from their neighbors the technique of making *chinampas*. These artificial garden beds were formed as floats built up with masses of earth and rich sediment dredged from the lake bed and held in place by wickerwork; eventually reed and tree roots, striking downward, took firm hold in the lake bottom and created solid islands. On the *chinampas* the Aztecs grew corn, beans, and other crops.

For a long time the Aztecs lived under the tutelage of their powerful neighbors of Atzcapotzalco, the dominant power in the lake country in the late fourteenth and early fifteenth centuries. Tribute and military assistance were exacted from the Aztec vassals. A turning point in Aztec history came in 1427. Commanded by their new war chief, Itzcóatl, the Aztecs joined the rebellious city-state of Texcoco and the smaller town of Tlacopan to destroy the tyranny of Atzcapotzalco. Their joint victory (1430) led to the rise of a Triple Alliance for the conquest, first of the valley, then of much of the Middle American world. By degrees the balance of power shifted to the aggressive Aztec state; Texcoco became a junior partner, and Tlacopan was reduced to a satellite.

The strong position of the Aztec island redoubt, almost impregnable to the attack of rival tribes, together with the Aztecs' shrewd policy of forming alliances and sharing the spoils of conquest with strategic mainland towns that they later came to dominate, helps to explain Aztec success in gaining control of the Valley of Mexico. Conquest of the valley in turn offered a key to the conquest of Middle America. "The valley possessed all the advantages of short internal lines of communication surrounded by a mountainous perimeter of defense. Yet, through gateways leading to the north, east, west, and south, its traders had access to adjacent valleys." [8]

Conquest of Atzcapotzalco gave the Aztecs their first beachhead on the lake shore. Most of the conquered land and the peasantry living upon it were assigned to warrior nobles who had distinguished themselves in battle. Originally assigned for life, these lands tended to become fiefs, held in permanent inheritance. But, says an Aztec account, "to the common people they gave no land, save to those few who had shown spirit and courage." [9] Thus warfare created new economic and social cleavages within Aztec society, separating the warrior élite from the mass of the population.

Ideological change accompanied economic and social change. Miguel León-Portilla attributes a whole series of innovations or reforms in thought and religion to the Aztec general Tlacaélel. Tlacaélel headed the Aztec host in the battle of Atzcapotzalco and later acted as adviser and power behind the throne to Itzcóatl and several of his successors. These reforms included the elevation of the tribal god Huitzilopochtli to a position of equality with or actual supremacy over the great gods traditionally worshiped in the Valley of Mexico; a burning of the ancient picture writings, because these books slighted the Aztecs, and the fabrication of a "new history" that recognized the Aztec grandeur; and a revision of the ancient cosmogony to make it serve Aztec militarism. The new cosmogony incorporated the belief that the very existence of the universe and mankind was dependent on the continuous provision of victims taken in war for sacrifice on the altars of the sun god.[10]

The successors of Itzcóatl, sometimes individually, sometimes in alliance with Texcoco, extended Aztec rule over and beyond the Valley of Mexico. When the ill-fated Moctezuma II came to rule in 1503, the Triple Alliance levied tribute on scores of towns, large and small, from the fringes of the arid northern plateau to the lowlands of Tehuantepec, and from the Atlantic to the Pacific. Within this vast area only a few states or kingdoms, such as that of the fierce Tarascans and the city-state of Tlaxcala, retained complete independence; others, such as Cholula, were left at peace in return for their benevolent neutrality or cooperation with the Aztecs.

The Aztecs waged war with or without cause; refusal to pay tribute offered sufficient pretext. Injuries to the far-ranging Aztec merchants by people of the regions they visited sometimes provoked invasion. In fact, trading convoys may sometimes have been armed so that they could incite trouble in a rich area. Reversing the axiom that "trade follows the flag," Aztec merchants prepared the way for conquest by reporting on the resources and defenses of the regions in which they traded; sometimes they acted as spies in hostile territory. If they returned home safely, these worthy merchants were honored by the ruler with amber lip plugs and other gifts. If their enemies discovered them, however, the consequences were horrid. "They were slain in ambush and served up with chili sauce," says a Náhuatl account.[11]

The Aztecs waged war according to a complex ritual; successive embassies were sent to a recalcitrant people with warnings to submit within a specified period of time; these ambassadors brought symbolic gifts of war clubs and shields to the prospective foes and performed various ritualistic acts. If defiance continued, the Aztecs began preparations for war. Spies were sent to study the terrain

Frescoes of the rain god Tláloc and his earthly paradise. Tepantitla, Teotihuacán, Valley of Mexico. Indian red, salmon pink, gold ocher, light emerald green, and indigo blue. Classic period of Teotihuacán. (Copy, partially reconstructed by Agustín Villagra from murals found in situ.) Museo Nacional de Antropología, Mexico. Courtesy Instituto Nacional de Antropología e Historia, Mexico.

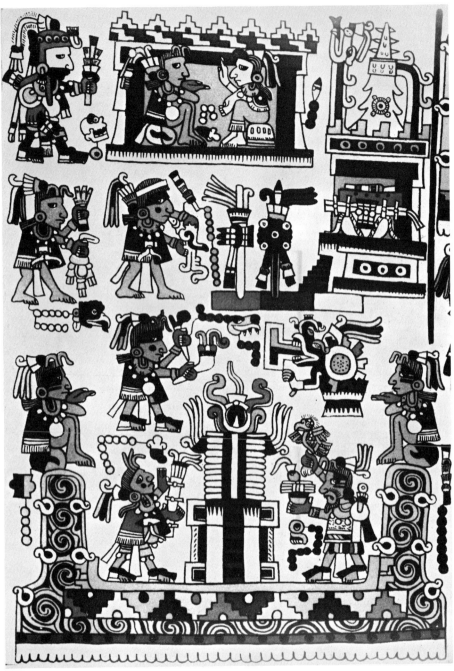

Detail from the Codex Nuttall. Mixteca-Puebla culture, 13th–16th centuries. Photograph after Zelia Nuttall (1902). This pre-Conquest historical and genealogical manuscript was one of two that Cortés sent to the Emperor Charles V. Presented as a gift to an unknown intermediary and then to a member of the Medici family, it was for a time in the Laurentian Library in Florence. From there it passed to an unknown Englishman and from him to Robert Curzon, 14th Baron Zouche, and finally to the British Museum, London.

Sculptured stone slab from the Palace, House E, Palenque, Chiapas. From Alfred P. Maudslay, *Biologia Centrali-Americana* (London, 1889–1902), Volume IV. Photograph courtesy American Museum of Natural History, New York.

Masks of Tláloc and Quetzalcóatl, Temple of Quetzalcóatl, Teotihuacán, Valley of Mexico. Teotihuacán II, Preclassic. Photograph courtesy Mexican National Tourist Council.

and ascertain the best invasion routes, and their maps were studied to determine the march of the armies. Clan leaders were ordered to muster their forces, majordomos and stewards to assemble arms and supplies. When all was ready, the Aztec war machine was set in motion.

At the head of the army went priests bearing idols of the gods. Behind them came the "valiant men," the warriors, wearing wooden helmets elaborately carved with the insignia of the orders of the Eagle, the Tiger, and the Arrow. Brilliant feathers fluttered on the warrior's head and shoulder-crest, and his body was covered with quilted cotton armor and a mantle of blue and green and yellow featherwork. These knights were followed by the rank and file of the Aztec tribe. One day's march behind came the men of Texcoco, followed one day later by the men of Tlacopan, with the auxiliaries of other allied or dependent towns coming after. Once in the vicinity of the enemy town, the Aztec host encamped. Nightfall was the time favored for attack. The priests gave the signal for battle by lighting a new fire and blowing on shell trumpets. Shrieking and whistling, dancing and singing, the Aztecs fell on their foes. Their chief offensive arms were wooden clubs edged with razor-sharp obsidian, and javelins, which they hurled with the aid of a dart-thrower. Bows and arrows were occasionally used. The besieged peoples usually made their last despairing stand on the heights of their temple pyramids.

Victory always had the same results: long lines of captives, wooden collars about their necks, made the long journey to Tenochtitlán to be offered up on the altars of the gods. In addition, periodic tribute payments of cotton, maize, cacao beans, cotton mantles, or other products—depending on the geography and resources of the region—were imposed on the vanquished. Certain lands were also set aside to be cultivated by them for the support of the Aztec crown, priesthood, state officials; or such land was divided into fiefs for warriors who had distinguished themselves in battle. A steward or tribute collector, sometimes assisted by a resident garrison, was stationed in the town. For the rest, the conquered people continued to enjoy complete autonomy in government, religion, and customs.

The mounting tempo of war, human sacrifice, and revolt in the Aztec Empire on the eve of the Spanish Conquest strongly suggests that a serious internal crisis was in the making. To supply the food needs of the enormous city of Tenochtitlán, not to mention the luxuries demanded in ever greater quantity by the Aztec ruling classes, must have placed a severe strain on an agriculture that in many areas was based on primitive slash-and-burn farming. Progressive soil erosion aggravated the problem. One modern student concludes that the peak of Aztec prosperity "had already been reached in the reign of Moctezuma II, or even perhaps earlier, that agricultural production had already begun to decline, and that population pressure was beginning to increase." [12]

The suggestion has even been made that wars and the monumental scale of human sacrifice in the last years of Aztec rule represented a group response to the problem of overpopulation.[13] Certainly the Aztecs had grown very hateful in the eyes of their vassals and even of their allies. Indeed the Texcocans wholeheartedly joined the Spanish invaders in wiping the arrogant Aztec power from the face of the earth.

In his history of the Conquest, Bernal Díaz del Castillo tells of the amazement of his comrades when they saw the shining white temples and palaces of Tenochtitlán rising out of the waters of its lake five miles away: "It is like the enchantments that are told of in the books of Amadís! . . . And some said: are not the things we see a dream?" And he recalled the palaces in which they had been lodged, "spacious and well built, the walls paneled with cedar and other scented woods," with great rooms and courts covered with awnings of cotton cloth, surrounded by gardens, lily ponds, bathing pools, and sculptured terraces. "Today," grieved the veteran conquistador, "all is overthrown and lost, nothing remains." [14] Sights that could inspire such feeling in hardened Spanish soldiers who had seen the architectural glories of Moorish Granada must have been wonderful indeed. Indian creative genius found its supreme material expression in the great city of Tenochtitlán, with its population of perhaps 300,000, its numerous and varied public structures, and its well-ordered life.

An Indian Venice, Tenochtitlán was an oval island connected with the mainland by three causeways that converged at the center of the city and served as the city's main arteries of traffic. There were few streets; however, numerous canals, thronged with canoes and bordered by footpaths, gave access to the thousands of houses that lined their sides. An aqueduct of solid masonry brought fresh water from the mountain springs of Chapultepec. The problem of sanitation was solved by keeping boats tied up at strategic points; their contents were sold to fertilize the fields. Urine, used by the Aztecs as a mordant in dyeing cloth, was preserved in pottery vessels in the home.

The architecture and furnishings of Aztec dwellings varied with the wealth and social position of their occupants. On the outlying *chinampas* the Aztec farmers who paddled their produce to town in tiny dugouts made their homes in huts with thatched roofs resting on walls of wattle smeared with mud; inside were a three-legged *metate* or grinding stone, a few mats that served as beds and seats, some pottery, and little more. The majority of the population—artisans, priests, civil servants, soldiers, and entertainers—possessed somewhat more imposing houses built sometimes of adobe, sometimes of the reddish tezontle lava, but always plastered and painted. Each house was placed on a raised platform faced with stone to protect against floods. Such houses were cool, windowless, no larger than a large modern room. With the addition of some wooden chests for clothing, and more, perhaps more finished pottery, the furniture here was much the same as in the humbler dwellings. The houses of clan leaders, rich merchants, and priests were far more pretentious. About a central court were arranged rooms for social purposes, sleeping, cooking, and quartering slaves. Here the furnishings were proportionately finer and more varied.

In dress, as in housing, the Aztecs differed according to their economic and social position. For men the essential garment was a loincloth with broad flaps at front and back, usually decorated with fringes and tassels as well as embroidery. A blanket about one yard wide and two yards long, hung under the left arm and was knotted on the right shoulder. Commoners wore plain blankets of maguey fiber or coarse cotton; rich merchants and nobles displayed very elaborate mantles adorned with symbolic designs. Women wore lengths of cloth as wraparound skirts of white cotton, tied with a narrow belt, and a loose, short-sleeved tunic, the whole costume being decorated with vivid embroidery. They did their hair in braids, interlaced with colored ribbons. Men wore sandals of leather or woven maguey fiber; women generally went barefoot.

The upper class of both sexes made lavish use of paint and ornaments; these refinements were strictly forbidden to commoners. Women's makeup consisted of yellow ocher face paint with a little pattern stamped in red on either cheek; from their ears dangled plugs of gold, silver, or white obsidian. They dyed their hair with indigo to make it glisten, stained their teeth scarlet with cochineal, and painted their bodies with designs. Servingwomen anointed their feet with a mixture of burned copal incense and dye.

Men painted their faces and bodies red, green, blue, or black (according to the occasion) in patterns of bars, stripes, and dots. When a youth first went to war at the age of fifteen, he indicated his status by putting a little tuft of white down with two crane feathers in his hair. Once he had captured his first enemy he drew his hair to the top of his head, tied a cord around it, and had it trimmed into a stiff brush on top. Distinction in war brought honors and rewards: the great Moctezuma himself presented the warrior with a lip plug of polished stone. As he rose in rank this stud also changed. Moctezuma wore a tube of crystal containing a blue hummingbird feather; a great captain wore a jaguar claw. Nobles also wore large ear plugs and displayed ornaments passed through the septum of the nose or suspended from a slit in the lip. Great feather headdresses and costumes modeled after the form of the ocelot or the eagle further distinguished the warrior nobility. As a member of this caste went about he might carry and occasionally sniff a bunch of flowers—a privilege reserved to the aristocracy.

The rich merchant was known by his staff and fan; the priest by his long, filthy blood-matted hair, by his black face paint, by his tattered ears, shredded from penitential blood letting, by the dress of the gods and goddesses that he wore on ceremonial occasions. The peasant, the commoner, was known by his bent back and docile air, by his bare feet and maguey fiber cloak.

As with dress, so with food; wealth and social position determined its abundance and variety. The fare of the ordinary Indian consisted then, as today, of ground cornmeal, beans, and vegetables cooked with chili. Meat was rarely seen on the commoner's table, but on festive occasions a dog might be served up. It was otherwise with the nobility. An Aztec account of the foods eaten by the lords includes many varieties of tortillas and tamales, roast turkey hen, roast quail, turkey with a sauce of small chilies, tomatoes, and ground squash seeds, venison sprinkled with seeds, many kinds of fish and fruits. Prized delicacies were maguey grubs with a sauce of small chilies, winged ants with savory herbs, and rats in sauce. The repast ended with chocolate, a divine beverage denied to commoners.

Education among the Aztecs was formal and highly developed, and served the dual role of preparing the child for his duties in the world and of indoctrinating him with the ideals of the tribe. At the birth of a child the parents consulted a priest who looked into a magic book of fate to see if the signs of the day were lucky or unlucky; according to these indications, he was given the name of that day or a more favorable one. If the child was a girl, a toy loom was placed in her hands; a noble's son was given a miniature bow and arrow; a craftsman's son received the implements he would probably use.

From the age of three the child was under the strict supervision of his father, if a boy, or of her mother, if a girl. Children were subjected to a rigorous training in which great emphasis was placed on careful performance of household chores and on filial obedience and courtesy to elders. When boys reached the age of ten or twelve, they were sent to school. Sons of commoners, merchants, and artisans attended the Telpochcalli, the House of Youth, where they received instruction in religion and good usage and were trained in the art of war. Their duties included collection of fuel for the temples and communal labor on lands set aside for the support of the school. Presumably they spent a part of the day at home, learning from their fathers the craft that they would practice in maturity. The Calmécac or priests' house, a school of higher learning, was reserved in principle for the sons of the nobility, but there is evidence that at least some children of merchants and commoners were admitted. Here, in addition to ordinary training, students received instruction that prepared them to be priests, public officials, and military leaders. The curriculum included what we would today call rhetoric, or a "noble" manner of speaking, study of religious and philosophical doctrines as revealed in the "divine songs," the arts of chronology and astrology, and training in history through study of the Xiuhámatl or Books of the Years. The *tlamatinime* (sages) who taught in the Calmécac were also concerned with the formation of "a true face and heart," the striking Náhuatl metaphor for personality. Self-restraint, moderation, devotion to duty, a stoic awareness that "life is short and filled with hardships, and all comes to an end," an impeccable civility, modesty: these are among the qualities and concepts that the Aztec sages sought to instill in their charges. A Náhuatl source describes the ideal man:

> The mature man
> is a heart solid as a rock,
> is a wise face.
> Possessor of a face, possessor of a heart,
> He is able and understanding.[15]

There were special schools for girls, where they were taught such temple duties as sweeping, offering incense three times during the night, and preparing food for the idols; weaving and other womanly tasks; and general preparation for marriage. Music was an important part of the education of children. From about the age of fourteen they were sent daily to an establishment called the House of Song to learn religious and secular songs and dances.

Men usually finished their education at the age of twenty or twenty-two, girls at sixteen or seventeen. These ages were also the usual ages for marriage. Elaborate negotiations on the part of parents and matchmakers, with considerable discussion of the size of the bride's dowry, attended the progress of the suit. On the evening of the wedding a feast was held in the new husband's house; on this occasion the newlyweds were subjected to long speeches and homilies by the father of the groom or the mother of the bride; the groom was admonished to work hard to support his family, obey his elders, be well-bred and civil, the bride was urged to be faithful, modest, and discreet. Polygamy existed among the Aztecs, but was reserved by law to nobles. Only the sons of the first wife could inherit; daughters did not inherit. Divorce was possible for cause, but was usually attended by great squabbling and heavy expense in returning presents. Adulterers were condemned to be stoned to death. Prostitution was prevalent, but most girls in the House of Joy were probably members of vanquished tribes.

In a society with such a complex economic and social life as the Aztec, disputes and aggressions were inevitable, and therefore an elaborate legal code was developed. A hierarchy of courts was topped by two high tribunals which sat in the royal palace in Tenochtitlán. One heard cases touching "princes and great lords. At once, swiftly, [it] passed judgment on their complaints or wrong doing." It was also a court of appeal from decisions of the court that heard cases involving commoners. Each tribunal had its clerks, who recorded in picture writings the causes of the dispute, the names of the contending parties, and the verdict. A Náhuatl account relates that the ruler chose the judges with great care, selecting "the wise, the able, the sage; who listened and spoke well; who were of good memory; who spoke not vainly or lightly; who did not make friends without forethought nor were drunkards; who slept not overmuch but rather rose early; who did nothing for friendship's or kinship's sake, nor for enmity; who would not hear nor judge a case for a fee." [16]

The punishments of the Aztecs were severe. Death was the penalty for murder, rebellion, wearing the clothes of the other sex, and adultery; thieves were consigned to slavery for the first offense, hanged for the second.

The Aztecs were very fond of games and gambling of every kind. The principal game throughout the empire, as in the Maya country, was a kind of basketball that was played on a court shaped like the letter I and flanked by two walls. The object of the player or players on each side was to drive a hard rubber ball through a stone ring set vertically in the middle of each wall; the ring was surmounted by an image of the patron god of the game. Winning strokes counted only when made by hitting the ball with the hips, buttocks, or elbows; to avoid injury the players wore leather gloves, and knees and hips were protected by leather guards. So furious was the pace of the game that players sometimes died of exhaustion. Professional ball players toured the country giving exhibitions of their skill; and the Aztec rulers and the great nobles maintained their own permanent teams. Frantic gambling attended the play; the nobility wagered precious stones, mantles, plumage, slaves, concubines, lands, and houses. Fray Diego Durán relates that commoners, having lost their mantles, household furniture, and maize and maguey fields, sometimes staked and lost the freedom of their children and their own persons.[17]

Another widely played game was *patolli*, which resembled our children's game of parchesi. It was a dice game played on a mat painted black, with the scoring board in the form of a cross. The counters were large black beans in which several holes had been made, and a numerical symbol painted on each. Durán cites a curiously familiar touch: before throwing the dice the players rubbed them between their palms, and in the act of throwing they called out the name of the patron god of the game.[18]

Division of labor and perfection in craftsmanship in ancient Mexico attained perhaps the highest point of development compatible with what was essentially an Upper Stone Age technology. The very large volume and variety of products, and the high development of regional specialization, were reflected in the existence of an extensive system of town markets, each of which featured some special product or products, and to which buyers came from great distances. The great market at Cholula, a leading industrial center, was famed for featherwork and precious stones. Texcoco specialized in fine textiles and in chocolate cups and other elaborate and delicately made earthenware. To Acolman men came from many places to buy or sell fat little castrated dogs, raised exclusively for eating.

For quantity and variety of products offered, none equaled the market of Tenochtitlán, which daily attracted more than 60,000 persons. Here, in a large square with a floor of polished pavement, surrounded by porticoes, an infinite variety of products and services could be found, each in its own section. Barter was the principal form of exchange; but a primitive money existed in the form of cacao beans and quills of gold dust (the ancient Mexicans had no system of weights and measured only by volume or quantity). The market was policed by inspectors who went about observing what was sold and the measures used by vendors. In a special building sat judges who heard and decided disputes in the market.

To this complex economic order corresponded a complex social organization. Among the Aztecs, as among many other peoples of ancient Mexico, the basic social unit was a kinship group called the *calpulli* (pl. *calpultin*), which was a territorial as well as a kinship organization. At the head of each *calpulli* stood a council of elders who administered the group's affairs; by the time of the Conquest these positions seem to have become hereditary in certain families. Each *calpulli* possessed a ceremonial center and council house where members gathered for communal activities. The men of each *calpulli* maintained a special school, the Telpochcalli, where boys were trained, among other things, in the art of war.

By the time of the Conquest a strong Aztec central government, superimposed on the old kinship organization, had sharply reduced the autonomy of the *calpulli*. Its influence, however, remained strong in economic life and the strictly internal affairs of the group.

Each farming *calpulli* held carefully mapped lands, some of which were set aside to be cultivated in common for the support of the group's officials, the temples, and the crown. The remainder was assigned in lots to the heads of families. Most accounts assert that these lots could not be transferred or sold.

The life of the Aztec free peasants who formed the rank and file of the *calpulli's* membership was probably a hard one. Besides working on communal lands, they had to labor on the construction and maintenance of dikes, fortifications, temples, and other public works.

Compulsory offerings to the gods placed a heavy burden on the peasantry. According to one Aztec account, the demands made in connection with the worship of Huitzilopochtli were particularly troublesome. For one whole year the families of two neighborhoods or subdivisions of a *calpulli* were made responsible for providing the enormous quantities of wood burned each night in honor of the god. The next year two new neighborhoods succeeded to the responsibility. To pay its share of the cost, each family had to contribute one large mantle and four small mantles, one small basket of dried maize kernels, and one hundred dried ears of maize. When all their possessions were gone, these commoners were reduced to pledging or selling their lands. The same source vividly depicts the plight of the Aztec peasant overwhelmed by the burdens of religious tribute. "This gave rise to much distress; it caused much anguish; it affected them. And some therefore fled; they went elsewhere. And many flung themselves in the midst of war, they cast themselves to their deaths." [19]

To the burdens imposed by tribal authorities one must add the hardships caused by the caprices of nature: droughts, hailstorms, and blight. The old communal spirit of mutual assistance was waning, and the unhappy *macehual* or peasant whose harvest had failed must beg for charity or even sell himself and his children into slavery to wealthy merchants. In time of famine the houses of the merchants were filled with the victims of economic disaster: "At this time one sold oneself. . . . Or else one sold and delivered into bondage his beloved son, his dear child. . . . Already they wielded the hoe, already they used the tump line,[20] already they were [like] someone else's dog, someone else's turkeys. For in truth slavery had come upon them; they had come against that which they could not leave, of which they could not be rid." [21]

By the time of the Conquest, division of labor among the Aztecs had so progressed that there existed a large class of artisans who no longer engaged in agriculture. These men pursued specialized activities and entered into exchanges with other persons to obtain foodstuffs and other articles that they did not themselves produce. This artisan class may have had its origin in the need of the temples and the priesthood for ritual objects, luxury ceramics, and architectural embellishments, but the growing complexity of Aztec society greatly broadened the scope of its activity. The artisans included carpenters, matmakers, potters, stonemasons, silversmiths, featherworkers, and the like. In the same general category belonged such specialists as fishermen, hunters, dancers, and musicians. Unlike the peasantry, these people performed no communal labor, paying tribute only in their special products or services when required by the crown or the temples. All these specialists were organized in guilds, each with its guild hall and patron god; their occupations were probably hereditary. Apparently these people were not attached to a particular quarter of the city, for they were free to go wherever they could earn most.

The artist, the craftsman, enjoyed a position of high honor and responsibility in Aztec society. Assigning the origin of all their arts and crafts to the Toltec period, the Aztecs applied the name "Toltec" to the master painter, singer, potter, and sculptor. A Náhuatl text describes the traits of such an artist:

> The artist: disciple, abundant, multiple, restless.
> The true artist, capable, practicing, skillful,
> maintains dialogue with his heart, meets things with his mind.

> The true artist draws out all from his heart:
> works with delight; makes things with calm, with sagacity;
> works like a true Toltec; composes his objects; works
>   dexterously; invents;
> arranges material; adorns them; makes them adjust.[22]

The *tlacuilo*, the painter of codices, enjoyed special respect not only because of the mystery that surrounded his work but also because of its importance as a vehicle for the transmission of tribal lore and religion.

> The good painter is a Toltec, an artist;
> he creates with red and black ink,
> with black water. . . .
> The good painter is wise,
> God is in his heart.
> He puts divinity into things;
> he converses with his own heart.
> He knows the colors, he applies them and shades them;
> he draws feet and faces,
> he puts in the shadows, he achieves perfection.
> He paints the colors of all the flowers,
> as if he were a Toltec.[23]

The same source contains a felicitous description of the good potter who "teaches the clay to lie," who creates images of reality.

> He who gives life to clay:
> his eye is keen, he molds
> and kneads the clay.
> The good potter:
> he takes great pains with his work;
> he teaches the clay to lie;
> he converses with his heart;
> he makes things live, he creates them;
> he knows all, as though he were a Toltec;
> he trains his hands to be skillful.[24]

Advances in regional division of labor and the increase in the market for luxury goods had also led to the emergence of a merchant class organized in a very powerful guild. The wealth of this class, and the important military and diplomatic services it rendered to the Aztec state, made the merchants a third force in Aztec society, ranking only after the warrior nobility and the priesthood. The secret of their wealth is suggested by the name they bore among the Aztecs: "The men who get more than they give." The chief lines of their trade radiated from the highlands to the Gulf lowlands. Exports from Tenochtitlán and the highlands included slaves, gold and precious stones, obsidian, herbs, red ocher, cochineal dye, copper bells, and rabbit pelts. From the Gulf lowlands came feathers, turquoise, jade, jaguar skins, feather cloaks, shirts, slaves, and cacao beans. In the pursuit of gain the Aztec traders, attended by long lines of carriers and armed guards, made hazardous journeys and dangerous sea voyages. They were also the bankers of their time, making loans of food and other articles on the basis of pledges of land and other possessions. In time of famine they took advantage of their poorer compatriots to acquire land and slaves.

The wealth and power of the merchants sometimes aroused distrust and hostility in the Aztec rulers and nobility. Popular hostility toward the traders is clearly evident from the words of a native informant of Sahagún: "The merchants were those who had plenty, who prospered; the greedy, the well-fed man, the covetous, the niggardly, the miser, who controlled wealth and family . . . , the mean, the stingy, the selfish." [25]

The Aztec priesthood was a most ancient class, with its roots in that remote period when the medicine man became a full-time cult specialist, wholly differentiated from his farming colleagues. The priesthood was the main integrating force in Aztec society. Through its possession of a sacred solar calendar that regulated the performance of agricultural tasks, it played a key role in economic life. The priest, by virtue of his special powers of intercession with the gods, was called upon in every private or collective crisis of the Aztec. Priests were also the repository of the accumulated learning and history of Aztec society, and very logically they served as the teachers of the young. Finally, as the ideologists of the tribe, they developed an elaborate theological explanation that made the life of gods and men hinge upon continued Aztec success in the hectic course of imperialism and human sacrifice. Celibate, austere, continuously engaged in the penance of bloodletting, the priests wielded immense influence over the superstitious Aztec masses.

In 1524 the Indian nobility of Tenochtitlán and neighboring cities offer an eloquent defense of their religion in a debate with the first twelve Franciscans in New Spain. The text, as preserved by Sahagún, enumerates the various categories of priests and their functions:

1. But, our lords,
2. there are those who guide us;
3. they govern us, they carry us on their backs
4. and instruct us how our gods must be worshiped;
5. whose servants we are, like the tail and the wing;
6. who make offerings, who burn incense,
7. those who receive the title of *Quetzalcóatl*.[26]
8. The experts, the knowers of speeches and orations,
9. it is their obligation;
10. they busy themselves day and night
11. with the placing of the incense,
12. with their offering,
13. with the thorns to draw their blood.
14. Those who see, those who dedicate themselves to observing
15. the movements and the orderly operations of the heavens,
16. how the night is divided.
17. Those who observe [read] the codices, those who recite [tell what they read].
18. Those who noisily turn the pages of the illustrated manuscripts.[27]
19. Those who have possession of the black and red ink [wisdom] and of that which is pictured;
20. they lead us, they guide us, they tell us the way.
21. Those who arrange how a year falls,
22. how the counting of destinies, and days, and each of the twenty-day months all follow their courses.
23. With this they busy themselves, to them it falls to speak of the gods.[28]

León-Portilla finds significance in the distinction between priests (nos. 2 to 13) and sages (astronomers, guardians of the codices and knowledge, experts in the calendars and chronology) (nos. 14 to 23). Basing himself on this and other texts, León-Portilla argues for the existence in ancient Mexico of a class of philosophers or sages (*tlamatinime*). To these men he assigns, by analogy, the roles of teachers, psychologists, moralists, cosmologists, metaphysicians, and humanists. More, he attributes to these sages a questioning of or skeptical attitude toward the ancient myths, and also the formulation of profound problems concerning the nature of truth, the hereafter, and the like. Such lines of thought are expressed in a large number of poems, and he feels that there is justification for calling the sages philosophers in the strictest sense. "This element of doubt attests to a divergence from religious thought. The priest, as such, believes. While he can systematize and study his beliefs, he cannot accept the existence of problems which conflict with the precepts of his religion. Therefore, although the *tlamatinime* might have belonged originally to the priestly class, as scholars they must have been something more than priests." [29]

The authority and prestige that the priesthood alone had once enjoyed, it came to share with a numerous nobility that arose in the processes of war, territorial expansion, and political centralization. Spanish and Indian accounts alike carefully distinguish between the commoners and the nobility. The nobility consisted of a large body of warriors and the many Aztec bureaucrats: tribute collectors, judges, ambassadors, and the like. As reward for their services, officeholders received the revenue from public lands assigned for their support. Although the offices as such were not hereditary, they normally were conferred on sons of men who had held the same positions.

The wealth of the warrior nobility consisted in the main of landed estates; and, with the expansion of the Aztec domain, the number of feudal estates steadily grew. The lands and peasantry assigned to valiant warriors following the conquest of Atzcapotzalco were originally granted for life, but these lands in time became private estates that were handed down from father to son and could be sold or exchanged. Meanwhile the free peasants on these lands in conquered territories were transformed into serfs (*mayeque*) tied to the land. Their number was augmented by landless peasants who had fled from other provinces, and who exchanged their freedom for the right to work or eat. These *mayeque* paid no tribute to the Aztec crown and did not belong to any *calpulli*.

The Aztec nobles did not pay tribute of any kind; moreover, they were set apart from the commoners by many special privileges, including the right to practice ceremonial cannibalism, drink pulque, keep concubines, dress in cotton garments, wear sandals in Tenochtitlán, and adorn themselves with plumes, ear plugs, and other ornaments.

On the margins of Aztec society was the large class of slaves. Slavery was the punishment for several offenses, including failure to pay legal debts, but the slavery sometimes assumed by poor people in return for food was supposedly voluntary. Slaveowners frequently sold their chattels in the great market at Atzcapotzalco. Some became personal servants to rich merchants or nobles; others lost their lives as sacrificial offerings to the gods. "They bought them there at the slave market of Atzcapotzalco; they sorted and arranged them, turning them around many times, examining them, buying the good ones—those of good bodies, without blemish, in good health." [30]

The Aztec political system on the eve of the Conquest was a mixture of royal despotism and theocracy with the scanty vestiges of tribal democracy. Political power was largely concentrated in an élite of warrior nobles and bureaucrats, priests, and merchants. The hereditary ruler possessed some of the attributes of an Oriental despot.

Originally, perhaps, the ruler had been chosen by the whole Aztec nation or tribe, assembled for that purpose. Later he was chosen by a tribal council supposedly representative of the *calpultin*. At the time of the Conquest this council was dominated by the highest nobility, including close relatives of the ruler. This council, in consultation with the kings of Texcoco and Tlacopan, selected the ruler from the brothers of the previous ruler, or, if he had none, from his sons or nephews. The new ruler was assisted by a council of four great nobles.

In theory, the authority of the ruler was limited by the tribal council, which could depose him at will, but the history of the Conquest shows that only the most severe crisis could shake the ingrained Aztec habits of reverence and obedience to the monarch.

A barbaric splendor, an intricate ceremonial, prevailed in the court of Moctezuma II. The great nobles of the realm took off their rich ornaments of feather, jade, and gold before entering his presence; barefooted, eyes to the ground, they approached the basketry throne of their king. Moctezuma dined in solitary magnificence, separated by a wooden screen from his servitors and the four great lords or councillors with whom he meantime conversed. From time to time, he would offer these councillors a favorite dish; this they must eat standing, never looking him in the face. After Moctezuma had eaten, it was proper for the rest of his household to dine in other parts of the enormous palace: his two wives and many concubines, and "the ambassadors, the war messengers, the princes, the judges, the high priests, the seasoned warriors, the masters of the youths, the rulers of the youths, the keepers of the gods, the priests, the singers, the ruler's pages, his servants, his jugglers, the various artisans, goldsmiths, featherworkers, cutters of precious stones, setters of mosaic, sandal makers, and the turquoise cutters." [31]

When Moctezuma would be amused, he summoned jesters to tell pleasantries and proverbs, jugglers who made logs dance with the soles of their feet while they lay on their backs, poor maimed dwarfs who performed droll leaps and dances, and singers and dancers who displayed their art to the accompaniment of an orchestra composed of drums, rattles, bells, and flutes.

When Moctezuma went out, he walked in great state, carrying a reed stalk which he moved in rhythm to his words; he was accompanied by great nobles who went before to clear the way. "None might cross in front of him; none might come forth before him; none might look up at him; none might come face to face with him." [32]

Sometimes it suited his pleasure to visit the royal aviary, where birds of many-colored plumage were bred amid the quiet beauty of pools, gardens full of sweet-scented flowers and trees, and sculptured walks and terraces; or to visit the royal zoo to watch fierce jaguars, ocelots, and rattlesnakes feed on the flesh of sacrificial victims. What Moctezuma and his suite loved best of all to watch was the ballgame, for which skilled professionals were attached to the court. Moctezuma and his nobles wagered all manner of costly goods on the outcome of the play: "gold, golden necklaces, green stone, fine turquoise, slaves, precious capes, valuable breech clouts, cultivated fields, houses, leather leg bands, gold bracelets, arm bands of quetzal feathers, duck feather capes, bales of cacao." [33] Sometimes Moctezuma himself donned leather gloves, girdle, and hip guards to play his royal cousins of Texcoco or Tlacopan.

All this show of wealth, luxury, and ceremonial testified to the profound social and economic change that had taken place in the small, despised Aztec tribe that had settled in the marshes of Lake Texcoco less than two centuries earlier. At the opening of the sixteenth century the Aztec Empire had reached a peak of pride and power. Yet the Aztec leaders displayed a deep insecurity; the Aztec annals reveal a pervasive mood of apprehension, of vague misgiving. The tributary towns seethed with discontent; revolts were quelled, only to erupt elsewhere. Portents of evil appeared on earth and in the troubled air. A child was born with two heads; the volcano Popocatépetl became unusually active; a comet streamed through the sky. The year 1519, Ce Acatl, One Reed, approached. The god-king Quetzalcóatl might return to claim his lost realm.

CHAPTER TWO

The Aztec World View

The Aztec world view reflected Aztec historical experience. It fused the martial ideals of a young warrior people not yet oblivious of its barbarian origins with the rich cultural heritage of the Classic or Theocratic world. The foundation of this world view was a very ancient cosmogony or collection of cosmic myths that the Aztecs altered to serve the ends of their militarism.

Long centuries before, priestly intellectuals, brooding on the catastrophes that overtook men, attempted to explain the origin of the universe and natural phenomena. The body of myths that they developed was imposing. These ancient theologians assumed the existence of a First Cause in the form of a supreme dual god, male and female, whose cosmic coupling gave rise to all that exists. The supreme being gave birth to the Tezcatlipocas, four creator-gods identified with the forces of earth, wind, rain, and fire. Their struggle for mastery constitutes the history of the universe. This history is the history of a succession of ages or "Suns," each culminating in the total ruin of earth and men. When the cosmic forces are in equilibrium, there exists an age or Sun; but at a preordained time this equilibrium is upset and sun, earth, and men are destroyed. Four ages existed before the present one. This, the age or Sun of Motion, is also destined to perish in great upheavals. As one modern writer suggests, "we seem to have a recapitulation of the great disasters from flood, eruption, hurricanes, and earthquakes that beset the communities of ancient Mexico." [1]

Aztec ideologists amended this tradition in a significant way. According to the ancient myth, the Fifth Sun, in which the Aztecs lived, had been created at Teotihuacán by the sacrifice of the creator-gods. In order to create the sun and moon and set them in motion, these gods cast themselves into a Divine Fire. A complementary myth told of the restoration of man on earth through the blood sacrifice of Quetzalcóatl, who quickened the ground bones of human beings from past ages by causing blood drawn from his penis to drip over them. According to the ancient tradition, however, nothing could avert another cataclysm that would destroy the new earth and the new race of men. Only in the mid-fifteenth century was this legend revised to serve the ends of Aztec imperialism. The new Aztec theologians maintained that the death of the sun could be averted by the sacrifice of captives taken in war. Each day the sun waged a struggle against the powers of darkness, the moon and the stars, and vanquished them. The sun was sustained in his struggle by blood, the same precious nutriment that kept men alive. The Aztecs, the People of the Sun, could collaborate with the god in his cosmic function by providing him with the miraculous substance. Yet even these devoted efforts could not forever put off the preordained catastrophe. Someday the sun would lose his daily struggle with his enemies; the earth would be destroyed by frightful earthquakes; and the forces of evil, descending from the skies in innumerable hosts of savage beasts, would put an end to humanity.

The scene of this perpetual strife was a universe divided into four quarters identified with the four cardinal directions. Over each of these directions presided a creator-god, and to each was allotted a space of years within the Fifth Age for domination or subordination. The east was the land of the color red, and its year sign was the reed, representing fertility and light; its governing deity was the Red Tezcatlipoca. The north, land of the dead, a cold and desert place whose year sign was a flint, had the color black; its presiding god was the Black Tezcatlipoca. The west, whose color was white and which was identified with the years bearing the sign "house," had a favorable significance, being the dwelling place of the White Tezcatlipoca or Quetzalcóatl, god of knowledge and benevolent creator of man. The south, region of the color blue, was identified with the Blue Tezcatlipoca, known in Tenochtitlán as Huitzilopochtli; it was associated with the years whose sign was the rabbit.

"Not only were colors and gods grouped in this manner," explains Alfonso Caso. "Animals, trees, days, and men, according to the day on which they were born, also belonged to one of the four regions of universal space. A man was given the name of the day of his birth within a ritual calendar of 260 days. . . . This calendar was divided into four parts of 65 days each, one part corresponding to the East, one to the North, one to the West, and one to the South, and these parts were infinitely repeated." [2]

The earth, a great disc, was situated in the center of the universe. Surrounding the earth was an immense ring of water, extending to the juncture of water with heavens. From the center of the earth issued the four directions that formed the quarters or quadrants of the universe. This horizontal division of the world, one writer suggests, "implied the association of divine powers with the phenomena of geography and climate." [3] The vertical universe, extending above and below the water-encircled earth, was probably a later concept that reflected the rise of social stratification in ancient Mexico. The vertical division of space consisted of thirteen heavens and nine underworlds. The heavens were the homes of the gods, ranged according to their rank in the divine hierarchy, with the highest heaven reserved for the supreme dual god who created the universe. The nine underworlds were successively lower planes through which the dead passed, enduring exhausting ordeals before achieving eternal rest in the ninth underworld.

In a universe pervaded with magico-religious content, time and space and events merged in predetermined patterns revealed by the sacred calendar (Tonalámatl). Jacques Soustelle lucidly explains the Aztec concept of spatialized time:

"Each 'place-moment' complex of location and time determines in an irresistible and foreseeable way (by means of the tonalámatl) everything existing within it. The world may be compared to a stage screen on which a number of different light filters of various colors are projected by a tireless machine. The color projections follow one another, overlap, and infinitely adhere to an unalterable sequence. In such a world, change is not conceived as a consequence of a 'becoming' which gradually develops, but as something abrupt and total. Today the East is dominant, tomorrow the North;

today we live in good times, and without a gradual transition, we shall pass into the unfavorable days (nemontemi). The law of the universe is the alternation of distinct qualities, radically separated, which dominate, vanish, and reappear eternally." [4]

The complexity of the Aztec pantheon at the time of the Conquest reflected, in part, the effort of Aztec religion to reconcile discordant or hostile elements of very different historical origins. In that crowded pantheon the ancient rain god, Tláloc, and the very old fire god, Huehuetéotl, who had been worshiped for centuries by the agricultural peoples of the central plateau, rubbed elbows with warlike sky gods brought from the northern plains by barbarian invaders. The duality of Aztec religion found expression in the great temple of Tenochtitlán, at whose summit the two sanctuaries of Huitzilopochtli and Tláloc, side by side on the same platform, "dominated the holy city, symbolizing the juxtaposition of the two fundamental religions: that of the stars, the religion of sun-worshipping warriors, and that of the earth and water, the religion of peasants and stationary, civilized people." [5] That duality was revealed again in the veneration accorded, on the one hand, to the dreaded sky god Tezcatlipoca, a protean figure taken over from the Toltecs, and, on the other, to the peaceful and benevolent Quetzalcóatl, who had been driven from Tula by Tezcatlipoca. From the host of deities, however, there emerged with ever growing stature the Aztec tribal god Huitzilopochtli. Gradually Huitzilopochtli absorbed the functions and attributes of other major gods, in a process that might have brought the Aztecs to monotheism. [6]

A supreme dual god, male and female, as conceived by ancient theologians in their search for a First Cause, was also recognized by the Aztecs, but this vast and shadowy being, known by many names and sometimes portrayed in Náhuatl poetry as passionless and indifferent to human needs or as toying wantonly with the fates of men, was chiefly of interest to the religious specialists of the tribe. To the Aztec commoner his local gods and goddesses were much closer and dearer.

In their efforts to systematize their pantheon, to define the relationships of their own gods to the gods they had adopted from other peoples, Aztec theologians initiated a process of synthesis in which each major god combined in himself a number of different and sometimes opposed forms. A partial listing of the aspects of the great god Tezcatlipoca will illustrate the point. He was conceived in quadruple form, and in this way absorbed other important gods. The Black Tezcatlipoca was a supreme, omnipotent god; one of his names, "He who is invisible and intangible," linked him to the supreme dual god, who also had that title. As the Red Tezcatlipoca, he was also Xipe Totec, god of spring. As the White Tezcatlipoca, he was sometimes Quetzalcóatl, god of knowledge. As the Blue Tezcatlipoca, he was identified with Huitzilopochtli, the Sun.

These blendings and interpenetrations of the Aztec gods, the frequent overlapping of their functions, have led some students to speculate that the Aztec sages and priestly initiates regarded the numerous deities as nothing more than the masks or aspects of an ubiquitous, multiform, supreme being. León-Portilla cites a statement by the seventeenth-century chronicler Juan de Torquemada that the Indians conceived of Nature as a divine couple, man and wife.[7] The German scholar Hermann Beyer was convinced that the Aztecs had attained a monistic-pantheistic vision of the cosmos. "When we penetrate more deeply into the metaphorical language of the myths and the figurative-symbolic representations of the manuscripts, we see that the crass polytheism that we find in ancient Mexico merely refers to *natural phenomena*, and that the priestly thinkers had developed much more elevated philosophico-religious ideas concerning the essence and interrelation of things. The two thousand gods of which [the chronicler] Gómara speaks were such only for the great masses; for the learned priests and the priestly initiates they were only so many manifestations of the One."[8]

In Beyer's judgment the pantheistic deity "who pervades and permeates everything" was Xiutecuhtli, god of fire. For León-Portilla, however, Xiutecuhtli himself was but one of the many masks or aspects of the supreme dual god. He points out that names for the supreme god included Ometéotl, God of Duality; Tloque Nahuaque, Lord of the Close Vicinity; Ipalnemohuani, Giver of Life; Yohualli-Ehécatl, "He who is invisible and intangible." León-Portilla recognizes that the masses of ancient Mexico worshiped a countless host of deities representing the forces of nature; but he insists that the sages, the *tlamatinime*, had transcended this poly-

Zapotec maize god, possibly Pitao Cozobi, Lord of the Fields of Maize. White-slipped gray clay. Height: 48¾ in. (1.24 m.). Valley of Oaxaca. Mid-Classic, Monte Albán transitional IIIa-b phase, 6th century A.D. Coll. Dr. and Mrs. Josué Sáenz, Mexico City. Photograph Irmgard Groth.

Colossal diorite head of the Aztec moon goddess Coyolxauhqui, half sister to Huitzilopochtli. Symbolizing the struggle between the forces of day and night, the goddess is shown decapitated. Height: 27.3 in. (70 cm.). Probably from México-Tenochtitlán, 15th century. Museo Nacional de Antropología, Mexico. Photograph Carlos Sáenz, courtesy Instituto Nacional de Antropología e Historia, Mexico.

The god-king Quetzalcóatl. Green porphyry. Height: 17⅝ in. (44 cm.). Aztec, Valley of Mexico, *c.* 1440–1521. Musée de l'Homme, Paris. Photograph Musée.

Clay figurines in a ceremonial scene possibly commemorating a ceremony to the dead. Solid brownish buff clay with red and blue paint; one stone image with red paint. Height of tallest: 7 in. (18 cm.). Patio over Tomb 103, Monte Albán, Oaxaca. Late Classic, Monte Albán IIIb phase, after A.D. 550. Museo Nacional de Antropología, Mexico. Photograph Irmgard Groth.

theism and reduced all the phenomena of nature to a single creative principle, the ubiquitous supreme dual god who created himself and all that exists. To this pantheism León-Portilla assigns the descriptive term "dynamic dualization of the universe," because the notion of ceaseless generation and conception, of an active masculine aspect and a conceiving feminine counterpart, is its very essence. He objects, however, to the use of the term pantheism because the Indian sages not only accepted the divine omnipotence but regarded the Giver of Life as distinct from the world and speculated poetically whether they would someday live in his presence, in his paradise, from which all truth and beauty came.

The concept of a supreme dual god or First Cause was doubtless of great antiquity in Mexico, going back to Toltec times or perhaps even to Teotihuacán. León-Portilla uses fascinating excerpts from Náhuatl poetry to illustrate the variety of postures assumed by Indian intellectuals toward this supreme being. The god was viewed sometimes as a benign creator in whose dwelling place one would find happiness, sometimes as an ironic divinity to whom we are but playthings, who laughs at us, who rolls us around endlessly like marbles. But the notion of such a supreme being is fully compatible with polytheism. As Edward Tylor pointed out long ago, "if the monotheistic criterion be simply made to consist in the Supreme Deity being held as creator of the universe and chief of the spiritual hierarchy, then its application to savage and barbaric theology will lead to perplexing consequences." [9]

Advocates of the "one god" position cite the statement of the chronicler Fernando de Alva Ixtlilxóchitl that the famous Nezahualcóyotl, king of Texcoco, "held to be false all the gods adored in this country, declaring that they were mere statues of demons, enemies of mankind. He said this because he was very wise in spiritual matters and more than any other was seized by doubts, wherefore he sought for light in order to know the true God." [10] This statement must be regarded with caution, for Ixtlilxóchitl was not an unbiased witness: he was a descendant of the royal house of Texcoco and was writing to exalt his country and his native ancestors. A recent study of the philosopher-king asserts that "to call Nezahualcóyotl a monotheist . . . is incorrect." [11]

A clear statement of the religious beliefs of the Aztec élite or educated class appears in the memorable defense of their faith made

by certain Aztec priests in debate with the first twelve Franciscans
in New Spain. Courteously but firmly, these priests replied to the
friars' attacks on their religion:

You said
that we know not
the Lord of the Close Vicinity,
to Whom the heavens and the earth belong.
You said
that our gods are not true gods.
New words are these
that you speak;
because of them we are disturbed,
because of them we are troubled.
For our ancestors
before us, who lived upon the earth,
were unaccustomed to speak thus.
From them have we inherited
our pattern of life
which in truth did they hold;
in reverence they held,
they honored, our gods.
They taught us
all their rules of worship,
all their ways of honoring the gods.
Thus before them, do we prostrate ourselves;
in their names we bleed ourselves;
our oaths we keep,
incense we burn,
and sacrifices we offer.

It was the doctrine of the elders
that there is life because of the gods;
with their sacrifice, they gave us life.
In what manner? When? Where?
When there was still darkness.

It was their doctrine
that the gods provide our subsistence,
all that we eat and drink,
that which maintains life: maize, beans,
amaranth, sage.

To them do we pray
for water, for rain,
which nourish things on earth.

They themselves are rich,
happy are they,
things do they possess;
so forever and ever,
things sprout and grow green in their domain . . .
there "where somehow there is life," in the place of Tlalocan.
There, hunger is never known,
no sickness is there,
poverty there is not.
Courage and the ability to rule
they gave to the people.

Even as the Aztec priests informed the friars, "we do not accept
your teachings as truth, even though this may offend you," they
closed on a note of dignified submission to fate:

Is it not enough that we have already lost,
that our way of life has been taken away,
has been annihilated.

Were we to remain in this place,
we could be made prisoners.
Do with us
as you please.

This is all that we answer,
that we reply,
to your breath,
to your words,
Oh, our Lords! [12]

From this document, so dramatically revealing of the conflict
between two worlds of culture, emerges the polytheistic essence
of Aztec religion. "It was their doctrine that they [the gods] provide our subsistence, all that we eat and drink. . . . To them do
we pray for water, for rain, which nourish things on earth." There
is no suggestion here that the Aztec sages regarded the other gods
as so many masks or symbols of the supreme dual god. On the

contrary, the gods are endowed with as much personality as the deities of pagan Greece or Norseland; they are rich and happy, and forever green and flowering is their paradise of Tlalocan.

Did the Aztecs possess a philosophy and philosophers? León-Portilla answers this question in the affirmative. He holds that the theological speculations of the *tlamatinime* ultimately led them "to question and to formulate problems in a philosophical manner about the very things the people accepted and believed." He finds proof for this contention in the skeptical or doubting spirit that pervades a number of surviving Náhuatl poems. These poems raise doubts concerning the possibility of attaining truth on earth and even concerning the Hereafter of Aztec theology.

An exceedingly common theme is that of "Vanity of vanities; all is vanity." A poem attributed to Nezahualcóyotl questions:

> Is it true that on earth one lives?
> Not forever on earth, only a little while.
> Though jade it may be, it breaks;
> though gold it may be, it is crushed;
> though it be quetzal plumes, it shall not last.
> Not forever on earth, only a little while.[13]

Confronting the transitory nature of all earthly things, aware that four worlds had come and gone and that the fifth or present age must also pass, another Náhuatl poet asks:

> Does man possess any truth?
> If not, our song is no longer true.
> Is anything stable and lasting?
> What reaches its aim? [14]

León-Portilla loads this little poem, whose generalized skepticism and despair seem commonplace enough, with an awesome burden of philosophical content, linking it to the speculations concerning the nature of reality of Scholastic philosophers, of Hegel, and of modern Existentialist thinkers.

The skepticism of the Indian intellectuals extended to existence after death:

> Do flowers go to the region of the dead?
> In the Beyond, are we dead or do we still live?
> Where is the source of light, since that which
> gives life hides itself? [15]

One poem suggests that the way of religious offerings, of sacrifice to the supreme dual god, may not open the door to truth:

> Perchance, oh Giver of Life, do we really speak?
> Even though we may offer the Giver of Life
> emeralds and fine ointments,
> if with the offering of necklaces you are invoked,
> with the strength of the eagle, of the jaguar,
> it may be that on earth no one speaks the truth.[16]

Doubt as to the destiny of man after death gave rise to an Epicurean, *carpe diem* trend in Náhuatl thought:

> For only here on earth
> shall the fragrant flowers last
> and the songs which are our bliss.
> Enjoy them now! [17]

Still others found escape from the sway of dream and illusion, from haunting uncertainty concerning the afterlife, in a doctrine seemingly analogous to that expressed in famous lines of Keats: " 'Beauty is truth, truth beauty'—that is all / Ye know on earth, and all ye need to know." The symbol of this teaching, which León-Portilla regards as the highest achievement of ancient Mexican thought, was the striking Náhuatl metaphor for poetry, "flower and song." Poetry, coming from above, "from the innermost part of heaven," is the only means of ensuring our immortality, of uttering inspired truth, of communicating with the divine. Such, at least, is the interpretation that León-Portilla places on verses like the following:

> Now do I hear the very words of the *coyolli* bird
> as he makes answer to the Giver of Life.
> He goes his way singing, offering flowers.
> Is that what pleases the Giver of Life?
> Is that the only truth on earth? [18]

I offer only a sampling from the broad range of philosophical speculations that León-Portilla attributes to the ancient Mexicans. He draws especially on the treasure house of Náhuatl texts collected by the distinguished scholar Ángel María Garibay K.[19] León-Portilla's works greatly enrich our vision of the intellectual panorama of the Aztec world on the eve of the Conquest. They make clear that in the half century or so before the Conquest there developed in certain circles a spirit of individualism, of skepticism, of philosophical inquiry, that strained the bounds of the traditional magico-religious view of the world. This climate of opinion flourished in such cities as Texcoco, Huexotzinco, and Chalco, enemies or doubtful allies of the Aztecs, in which the cultural traditions of the Classic or Theocratic period retained their vigor and influence. The courts of such rulers as Nezahualcóyotl of Texcoco, Tecayehuatzin of Huexotzinco, and Ayocuan of Tecamachalco became gathering places of sages, poets, and artists. Here, in an atmosphere of refinement and luxury comparable in some respects, perhaps, to that of the princely courts of Renaissance Italy, discussions of aesthetics and metaphysics were held.

One need not quarrel with the claim that the Aztecs and other Náhuatl-speaking peoples of ancient Mexico possessed philosophy and philosophers. The meditations of Nezahualcóyotl are as truly philosophic as the anguished questions of Job or the somber reflections of Solomon. On the other hand, León-Portilla appears to err in ascribing to the Nahua sages a level of conceptualization, of intellectual progress, comparable to that of the natural philosophers of ancient Greece, and even of Socrates and the sophists. To compare the highest thought achieved by an Upper Stone Age people whose known world was bounded by the waters of the Pacific, on the west, and those of the Gulf of Mexico, on the east, and whose destinies were governed by a divining calendar, with the climactic intellectual achievements of such a people as the ancient Greeks, appears an anachronism.

To make his comparison valid, León-Portilla must vest such elementary statements of philosophical skepticism as, "Does man possess any truth?" or "Is anything stable and lasting?" with a weight of sophisticated speculation that the original texts and contexts do not seem to justify. He also makes certain unproven assumptions, for example, that the great cosmological myths had merely symbolic significance for the ancient Mexican sages or that the sages constructed their complex mythological system "for symbolic explanation" of natural phenomena. Yet we have heard the Aztec *tlamatinime* bravely reaffirming their faith in their myths of origin in the very faces of the Franciscan friars sent to convert them: their faith in the life-sustaining action of the gods, in the divine dwelling place where "things sprout and grow green."

An element of ambivalence in Aztec civilization, "the cleavage in the Aztec soul," was reflected in the contrast between the ferocious cult of war and human sacrifice, on the one hand, and the celebration of the qualities of benevolence, humility, and mercy, so prominent in Aztec literature, on the other. This kind of duality was reflected again in the contrast between the rising supremacy of the vigorous young war god Huitzilopochtli in Tenochtitlán and the veneration accorded by Nezahualcóyotl of Texcoco to a supreme dual god who wished only the peaceful sacrifice of jade, snakes, and butterflies. The opposition of values is most evident in the tension between Tenochtitlán and the older cities of Texcoco, Chalco, and Huexotzinco; however, the conflict existed within Tenochtitlán.

Nahua literature offers many illustrations of this conflict of ideals. An Aztec song which compares the blood-stained battlefield to a vast plain covered with flowers and describes the good fortune of one who perished on it expresses in rich imagery the dominant mystico-militaristic view of life:

> There is nothing like death in war,
> nothing like flowery death
> so precious to the Giver of Life:
> Far off I see it: my heart yearns for it! [20]

Another war poem, celebrating the life-and-death struggle between the Aztecs and the Chalcans, clothes in a profusion of images the grim reality of battle:

> Now let Eagle Knights and Jaguar Knights embrace, oh princes!
> The shields make a great din,
> ready is the company that must make prisoners!
> Through our efforts alone are the flowers of war stained and
>   moved to and fro!
> It is time to give pleasure to the god.

The shields make a great din,
ready is the company that must make prisoners!
The fire blazes, the undulant flames leap up.
It is time to acquire glory,
time to make famous the shield!
Amid the jangle of bells bound to the ankle
the dust rises like smoke!

        *   *   *

Standards of Eagles mingle with banners of Jaguars,
standards of green and yellow plumage mingle with shields of
    quetzal plumes:
They undulate, they seethe.
Hastily comes the Chalcan,
the dweller of Amaquemecan comes!
Noisily echoes the war!
The arrows break with a clatter,
the obsidian points are shattered,
the dust of the shields rises above us.
Hastily comes the Chalcan,
the dweller of Amaquemecan comes!
Noisily echoes the war! [21]

By contrast, a plaintive mood dominates these lines by a Chalcan
poet who recalls the defeat that put an end to his city's independence:

Meditate, think upon it, oh princes of Chalco, oh men of Amaque-
    mecan!
A cloud of shields hangs over our homes, a rain of darts falls upon
    them!
What was the verdict of the Giver of Life?
Now the city of Chalco seethes in flames, thy vassals run about
    dispersed!
Enough of this, the sentence of the Giver of Life has been carried
    out!
May the god have pity!
In the field of the bells,
in the field of battle,
the shafts of the darts lie broken.
Here in Chalco the dust turns yellow,
the houses have begun to smoke.

Thy vassals of Chalco shed burning tears.
Never will the memory fade, never will we forget what the god did here.
All is destroyed, all is scattered, in the mountain of obsidian.[22]

An Aztec prayer addressed to the great god Tezcatlipoca presents the rationale of perpetual war and mass human sacrifice. A great war is about to begin, proclaims the priest. The gods hunger and thirst; their hunger and thirst must be sated with human flesh and blood. The Sun will receive the valiant dead who fall in this war into his House, where they will enjoy eternal pleasure and repose. An unexpected strain of tenderness, of pity for the parents of the dead warriors, is mixed with the matter-of-fact ferocity of this prayer:

The God of Earth opens his mouth, thirsty to swallow the blood of the many men who must die in this war.

It seems as if the Sun and the God of Earth named Tlaltecuhtli wish to rejoice; they want to give food and drink to the gods of heaven and hell, regaling them with the flesh and blood of the men who must die in this war.

The gods of heaven and hell keep watch to see who must conquer and who must be conquered, who must kill and who must be killed, whose blood must be drunk and whose flesh must be eaten.

The noble fathers and mothers whose sons must die do not know this, just as their kin and the nurses who reared them as children and gave them the milk that nourished them know nothing of it. Their parents suffered great hardships in order to provide them with whatever they needed, that they might eat and drink, and be clothed and shod, until they reached the age at which they are now.

Certainly their parents never foresaw the fate that the children they had reared with such pains must suffer, that they must be killed or made captive on the battlefield.

Grant, oh Lord, that the Sun and the Earth, who are the father and mother of all, receive with peace, joy, and love the nobles who must die in the strife of this war.

You know well what you do in wishing them to die in war, for your purpose in sending them into this world was that they might give the Sun and the Earth to partake of their flesh and blood.[23]

Meanwhile, in the older cities of the high plateau, where the humanist traditions of the Classic period remained strong, different notes were sounded. A poem sung at an assemblage of poets and sages in the court of King Tecayehuatzin of Huexotzinco, about 1490, proclaimed the peaceful character and artistic interests of that city-state and, by implication, denounced the militarist ideology of Tenochtitlán:

> Besieged, hated,
> would be the city of Huexotzinco,
> if it were surrounded by cactus,
> if it were ringed with thorny arrows.
>
> The kettledrum, the conch shell,
> are heard in thy house,
> they remain in Huexotzinco.
> There is Tecayehuatzin,
> there the Lord Quecéhuatl
> plays the flute and sings
> in his house of Huexotzinco.
> Harken:
> Hither descends our father the god.
> Here is his house,
> wherein is the jaguar drum,
> where the songs have endured
> to the sound of the kettledrums.[24]

The mystique of perpetual war and human sacrifice in order to maintain the life of the universe coexisted with more humane teachings in Tenochtitlán itself. The Huehuetlatolli or Speeches of the Ancients—didactic discourses or homilies pronounced on special occasions—offer an admirable code of conduct for the guidance of the young. The address of an Aztec noble to his son instructs him: "Revere and greet your elders; console the poor and afflicted with good works and words." "Be civil to others, for humility helps to attain the gift of God and one's elders." "When you eat, give part of your food to a needy person who comes to you, and you will win grace thereby." [25]

How can we account for the "disconcerting ambiguity of Aztec culture," for this "deep contradiction," as the archaeologist Laurette Séjourné calls it? Her answer is that the Aztec state was founded on a spiritual inheritance, the Toltec tradition of a mystical union with divinity, the teaching of Quetzalcóatl, which the Aztecs betrayed and transformed into a weapon of worldly power. The ancient tradition, expressed in prayers, homilies, poems, and myths, provided the spiritual framework of Aztec society, but it was constantly belied by reality, by the innumerable wars in the name of "the cosmic need for human sacrifice." Thus, according to Séjourné, two strong and opposed currents of thought coexisted in Aztec society: on the one hand, a degenerate mysticism supporting an ambitious strategy of conquest; on the other, the doctrine of Quetzalcóatl that inner perfection and spiritual sacrifice formed the only moral basis of life. She believes that a spiritual ferment caused by a rebirth of the Quetzalcóatl tradition developed in the Aztec Empire in the decades prior to the Conquest. This revival explains the teachings of King Nezahualcóyotl concerning a supreme creator-god and the Hamlet-like doubts and vacillations of Moctezuma II in his dealings with the Spanish invaders. For many years, according to this view, Moctezuma wavered "between the old, resurgent spirituality and the destructive concepts propping up his empire." [26]

León-Portilla offers a similar interpretation of the conflict within Aztec culture. He attributes the degradation of the Toltec spiritual heritage into a mystico-militaristic world outlook to the genius of the Aztec military leader Tlacaélel. It was this Aztec Alexander, according to León-Portilla, who fastened upon his people the cult of warfare and human sacrifice as a means of preserving the life of the sun. Nevertheless, the tradition of Quetzalcóatl was continued by many sages who sought a way of speaking the truth on earth and who finally found the answer in poetic inspiration, the way of "flower and song." These sages, who included princes, poets, and priests, may have outwardly accepted the bloody rites of the Aztec religion, but in their hearts of hearts they longed for the restoration of the old Toltec humanism and spiritualism. Following Séjourné, León-Portilla speculates that the wavering attitude of Moctezuma II may have reflected his doubts about the Aztec religion and his sympathy with the ancient Toltec traditions.[27]

The French scholar Jacques Soustelle offers a closely reasoned discussion of the same problem, but he limits himself to what can be inferred from the known facts. He assumes the existence of a duality in Aztec society from the time the Aztecs abandoned their nomadic life to settle in the Valley of Mexico and began to absorb the higher culture of the peoples about them. Two parallel hierarchies developed: one of military and civil dignitaries, the other of priests. Within Aztec religion itself an opposition developed. Side by side with the worship of the sky gods Huitzilopochtli and Tezcatlipoca—the cult of sun-worshiping warriors—flourished the cult of Tláloc, the ancient peaceful god of rain and vegetation, and of Quetzalcóatl, the Toltec god of knowledge and the arts.

This duality, observes Soustelle, extended into the decisive field of education. An antagonism developed between the Telpochcalli, the schools that trained children for the life of the average citizen and for war, and the Calmécac, higher schools that prepared young men for the priesthood or service to the state. Significantly, the child who entered the Telpochcalli was dedicated to Tezcatlipoca; the child who entered the Calmécac was dedicated to Quetzalcóatl. Behind these two divine personalities, suggests Soustelle, "were two opposing concepts of life and the world. . . . On the one hand there is the ideal of the warriors, deriving from the ancient nomadic life of the barbarians: a happy youth devoted to pleasures and to combat, war, death for the Sun, a happy eternity in the luminous sky. On the other hand there is the priestly ideal of self-renunciation, abnegation in favor of the gods or the State, contemplative study—in short, the 'Toltec' idea of the high pre-Aztec civilizations." [28]

Soustelle argues that the political and economic evolution of Aztec society over a space of two centuries tended to heighten the tension between these opposed ideals. Until the end of the fifteenth century the Aztecs were engaged in continuous struggle, first to survive in a very hostile environment, and later to establish and consolidate their hegemony in central Mexico. This situation gave primacy to the cult of war and human sacrifice, to military virtues. But by the end of the century the situation had fundamentally changed. The holy city of Tenochtitlán and its hinterland were now secure. Meanwhile, "the development of public and private wealth, the growth of the merchant class, the growing refinement of their way of life" had brought "a subtle but profound modification of the psychological climate and of the scale of values." [29]

Soustelle points to the tone of the Huehuetlatolli as evidence of such a change of values. The accent in these homilies is not on warlike virtues but on benevolence, compassion, humility, courtesy. "Note well, son," a ruler lectures his child, "that humility and abasement of body and soul, and weeping, tears, and sighing, are the true nobility, worth, and honor; consider that no haughty, presumptuous, or boisterous man has ever been chosen to rule." The same address condemns certain warriors who "were great killers but unfit for the tasks of governing." [30] In such statements Soustelle sees the influence of the priestly teachings of the Calmécac.

Soustelle does not speculate concerning a possible lapse from religious orthodoxy on the part of Moctezuma II. He is content to observe that one of the reasons for the easy success of Cortés and his men was "that they found in their way not a brutally courageous statesman and warrior like Motecuhzoma I, but his heir Motecuhzoma II: scrupulous and meditative, a studious pupil of the priestly college, very attentive to predictions, taking the Spaniards who landed in Mexico for the representatives of Quetzalcóatl announced by ancient prophecies." [31]

Was Aztec society going through a moral crisis, a *crise de conscience*, on the eve of the Conquest? Certainly the native chronicles reveal a state of jangled nerves, of profound insecurity on the part of the Aztec leadership. Economic and social factors undoubtedly contributed to this state of affairs: chronic discontent of conquered peoples under the mounting burden of tribute demands, perhaps population pressure on exhausted soils, dissension between warrior nobles and increasingly powerful merchants, a decline of tribal solidarity as a result of growing inequalities of wealth and status. Yet ideological factors also played their part. Here we note a certain paradox: predatory warfare poured into Tenochtitlán and its allied cities a mass of wealth, of luxury goods, that in time engendered milder manners and attitudes, a growth of refinement, a revival of the "Toltec" ideals of life. But these flowers grew on the soil of perpetual war that was sanctioned by the cosmic need for human sacrifice. No alternative to the Aztec devices for accumulating wealth in the hands of the ruling classes was in sight. Indeed, as Alfonso Caso points out, the Aztec religion had become a fetter on technical invention and cultural development in general. Aztec civilization had reached an impasse that perhaps could have been overcome only by a decisive advance in technology, of the kind that attended the invention of ironworking in the Old World. The Conquest, by interrupting the process of Aztec internal evolution, precluded the sixteenth-century Mexicans from achieving such an advance and attaining new levels of material, social, and intellectual greatness.

CHAPTER THREE

Europe Discovers the Aztecs

A disturbing report reached the Aztec capital of Tenochtitlán in 1518. The tribute collector Pínotl had hui   :d from the Gulf coast to tell King Moctezuma that winged towers containing men with white faces and heavy beards approached from the sea. After communicating with these men by signs, Pínotl had exchanged gifts with their leader. The mysterious visitors had departed, but Pínotl said that they promised to return soon and visit Moctezuma in his city in the mountains.

Indian accounts agree that the news filled Moctezuma with dismay. Were the visitors indeed heralds of the redeemer-god Quetzalcóatl? According to the Aztec account of Sahagún's Indian informants, Moctezuma exclaimed: "He has appeared! He has come back! He will come here, to the place of his throne and canopy, for that is what he promised when he departed!" [1]

The "winged towers" were the ships of the Spanish captain Juan de Grijalva, sent by Governor Diego Velásquez of Cuba to explore the coasts first reported by the slave-hunting expedition of Francisco Hernández de Córdoba in 1517. Córdoba had discovered the peninsula of Yucatán and encountered Maya Indians whose cotton cloaks and brilliant plumes, stone pyramids, temples, and gold ornaments revealed a native culture far more advanced than any previously seen by Spanish navigators in the New World. Córdoba had suffered a disastrous defeat at the hands of the Maya and returned to Cuba to die of his wounds. Encouraged by the gold and other signs of Indian wealth brought back by the expeditions, Velásquez outfitted a new venture and entrusted it to his kinsman Juan de Grijalva.

Grijalva sailed from Santiago in April, 1518, touched at the island of Cozumel on the northeastern corner of Yucatán, then coasted down the peninsula, following Córdoba's route. In June he reached the borders of Moctezuma's empire. At a river which Grijalva named the Banderas the Spaniards were greeted by natives waving white flags and inviting them by signs to draw near. Here the Aztec official Pínotl boarded Grijalva's flagship. A lively trade started up, with Indians bartering gold for Spanish green beads. Grijalva was now convinced that he had come to a wealthy kingdom with many large towns. Near the present port of Veracruz, Grijalva sent Pedro de Alvarado back to Cuba with the gold. Alvarado was to report to Velásquez what had been accomplished, request authority to found a colony, and seek reinforcements. Grijalva himself sailed on with three other ships, perhaps as far as the river Pánuco, which marked the northern limits of the Aztec Empire. Then he turned back and retraced his course, arriving in Cuba in November, 1518.

Velásquez was already planning a third expedition to conquer the Mexican mainland. Passing over his kinsman Grijalva, he chose as leader of the expedition the thirty-four-year-old Hernando Cortés, a native of Medellín in the Spanish province of Extremadura. Cortés was born in 1485 into an hidalgo family of modest means. At the age of fourteen he went to Salamanca, seat of the celebrated Spanish university, to prepare for the study of law. He left Salamanca two years later, determined on a military career. He had to choose between Italy, the battlefield of early sixteenth-century Europe, where Spanish arms were winning fame under the Great Captain, Gonzalo Fernández de Córdoba, and the Indies, lands of gold, Amazons, and El Dorados. In 1504, aged nineteen, he embarked for Hispaniola.

Soon after his arrival on the island he took part in his first military exploit, the suppression of a revolt of Indians made desperate by Spanish mistreatment. He was rewarded with an encomienda, a grant of Indian tribute and labor. In 1511 he served under Velásquez in the easy conquest of Cuba and was appointed alcalde of the new town of Santiago de Cuba. In 1518 he persuaded Velásquez to give him command of the new expedition to the Mexican mainland. At the last moment the distrustful governor decided to recall him, but Cortés simply disregarded Velásquez' messages. He sailed from Cuba in February, 1519, with a force of some six hundred men. Because Velásquez had not completed negotiations with the Emperor Charles V for an agreement authorizing conquest and settlement of the mainland, Cortés' instructions permitted him only to trade and explore.

Cortés' fleet first touched land at the island of Cozumel, where they rescued a Spanish castaway, Jerónimo de Aguilar, who had lived among the Maya for eight years. In March, 1519, Cortés landed on the coast of Tabasco, defeated the local Indians in a sharp skirmish, and secured from them a pledge of friendship. The Mexican girl Malinche was to be his interpreter, adviser, and mistress. In April he dropped anchor near the site of modern Veracruz. He now found a way to free himself from Velásquez' authority. Apparently yielding to the insistence of his followers that conquest and settlement would serve the royal interest better than mere trade, Cortés founded the town of Villa Rica de la Vera Cruz and appointed its first officials; into their hands he surrendered the authority he had received from Velásquez. These officials conferred on Cortés the title of captain general with authority to conquer and colonize the newly discovered lands. Cortés had skillfully drawn on Spanish traditions of municipal autonomy to give his disobedience a mask of legality.

Several days later Moctezuma dispatched ambassadors to the Spanish camp. He sent precious gifts, the garniture of the great gods Tláloc, Tezcatlipoca, and Quetzalcóatl. Reverently, the envoys arrayed Cortés in the finery of Quetzalcóatl. On his face they placed a serpent mask inlaid with turquoise, with a crossband of quetzal feathers and a golden earring hanging down on each side. On his breast they fastened a vest decorated with quetzal feathers; about his neck they hung a collar of precious stones with a gold disc in the center. They fastened a mirror encrusted with turquoise to his hips, placed a cloak with red borders about his shoulders, and adorned his legs with greaves set with precious stones and hung with little bells. In his hand they placed a shield with ornaments of gold and mother-of-pearl and a fringe and pendant of quetzal feathers. They also set before him sandals of fine soft rubber, black as obsidian.

The Aztec account relates that the "god" was not satisfied. "Is this all?" Cortés is said to have asked, "is this your gift of welcome? Is this how you greet people?"[2] The stricken envoys departed and returned with gifts more to the god's liking, including a gold disc in the shape of the sun, as big as a cart wheel, an even larger disc of silver in the shape of the moon, and a helmet full of small grains of gold.

The envoys reported to Moctezuma what they had heard and seen, supplementing their accounts with painted pictures of the "gods" and their possessions. They described the firing of a cannon, which Cortés had ordered to impress the Aztec emissaries. "A thing like a ball of stone comes out of its entrails; it comes out shooting sparks and raining fire. The smoke that comes out with it has a pestilent odor, like that of rotten mud. . . . If the cannon is aimed against a mountain, the mountain splits and cracks open. If it is aimed against a tree, it shatters the tree into splinters." Vividly they described other weapons, the armor, and the mounts of the Spaniards. "Their trappings and arms are all made of iron. They dress in iron and wear iron casques on their heads. Their swords are iron; their spears are iron. Their deer carry them on their backs wherever they wish to go. Their deer, our lord, are as tall as the roof of a house." Of the terrible war dogs of the Spaniards the envoys said: "Their dogs are enormous, with flat ears and long dangling tongues. The color of their eyes is burning yellow; their eyes flash fire and shoot off sparks. Their bellies are hollow, their flanks long and narrow. They are tireless and very powerful. They bound here and there, panting, with their tongues hanging out. And they are spotted like an ocelot."[3]

Moctezuma's envoys had assured Cortés that they would serve him in every way during his stay on the coast, but pleaded with him not to seek a meeting with their king. This fitted into Moctezuma's pathetic strategy of plying Cortés-Quetzalcóatl with gifts in the hope that he could be dissuaded from advancing into the interior and reclaiming his throne. Suavely, Cortés informed the ambassadors that he had crossed many seas and journeyed from very distant lands to see and speak with Moctezuma, and could not return without doing so.

Cortés became aware of the tributary towns' bitter discontent with Aztec rule and began to play a double game. He encouraged the Totonac Indians of the coast to seize and imprison Moctezuma's tax collectors, but promptly obtained their release and sent them to the king with expressions of his regard and friendship. Before marching on Tenochtitlán, he took two other steps. To Spain he sent a ship with dispatches for the Emperor Charles in which he sought approval for his actions and described the wonderful extent and value of his discoveries. To win the Emperor's goodwill, Cortés persuaded his men to send Charles not only the royal fifth but all the treasure received from Moctezuma. And to stiffen the resolution of his followers he cut off all avenues of escape by scuttling and sinking all his remaining ships, ostensibly because they were not seaworthy. Then Cortés and his small army began to march on Tenochtitlán.

Advancing into the sierra, Cortés entered the territory of the tough Tlaxcalan Indians, traditional enemies of the Aztecs. The Spaniards had to prove in battle the superiority of their weapons and their fighting capacity before obtaining an alliance with this powerful tribe. Then Cortés marched on Cholula, an ancient center of Indian cultural traditions and the cult of Quetzalcóatl. Here, claiming that the Cholulans were conspiring to attack him, Cortés staged a mass slaughter of the Cholulan nobility and warriors after they had assembled in a great courtyard. When news of this event reached Tenochtitlán, terror spread throughout the city. "The common people were terrified by the news; they could do nothing but tremble with fright. It was as if the earth trembled before them, or as if the world were spinning before their eyes, as it spins during a fit of vertigo." The Spaniards continued their inexorable advance. "They came in battle array, as conquerors, and the dust rose in whirlwinds on the roads. Their spears glinted in the sun, and their pennons fluttered like bats. They made a loud clamor as they marched, for their coats of mail and their weapons clashed and rattled. Some of them were dressed in glistening iron from head to foot; they terrified everyone who saw them." [4]

Moctezuma's fears and doubts had by now reduced him to a hopelessly indecisive state of mind. He wavered between submission and resistance, between the conviction that the Spaniards were gods and some half-formed suspicions that they were less than divine. He sent new envoys who brought rich gifts to Cortés but urged him to abandon his plan of visiting the Aztec capital. Moctezuma's naïve efforts to bribe or cajole the terrible strangers who "longed and lusted for gold," who "hungered like pigs for gold," in the bitter words of an Indian account, proved vain. As Moctezuma's doom approached, his own gods turned against him. A group of sorcerers and soothsayers sent by the king to cast spells over the Spaniards were stopped by the young god Tezcatlipoca, who conjured up before their terrified eyes a vision of Tenochtitlán burning to the ground. His forces spent, Moctezuma ended by welcoming Cortés at the entrance to the capital, receiving him as a rightful ruler returning to his throne. The Aztec king completed his degradation by allowing Cortés to kidnap him from his palace and take him to live as a hostage in the Spanish quarters.

The Aztec nation had not said its last word. In the absence of Cortés from the city, his lieutenant, Pedro de Alvarado, ordered an unprovoked massacre of the leading Aztec chiefs and warriors as they celebrated with song and dance a high religious festival in honor of Huitzilopochtli. The result was a popular uprising that forced the Spaniards to retreat to their own quarters. The tribal council deposed the captive Moctezuma and elected a new chief, Cuitláhuac, who launched heavy attacks on the invaders. Moctezuma died as the fighting raged: killed by stones cast by his own people as he appealed for peace, according to Spanish accounts; strangled by the Spaniards themselves, according to Indian sources. Cortés, fearing a long siege and famine, evacuated Tenochtitlán at a heavy cost in lives. The surviving Spaniards and their Indian allies at last regained friendly Tlaxcala.

Strengthened by the arrival of a Spanish contingent from Cuba and by thousands of Indians who joined the fight against their old masters, Cortés again marched on Tenochtitlán in December, 1520. A ferocious struggle began in late April, 1521. On August 23, after a siege in which the Aztecs fought for four months with extraordinary bravery, their last king, Cuauhtémoc, surrendered amid the laments of his starving people. Cortés took possession of the ruins that had been the city of Tenochtitlán. An Aztec elegy recalled the fate of the vanquished:

> Broken spears lie in the roads;
> we have torn our hair in our grief.
> The houses are roofless now, and their walls
> are red with blood.

Worms are swarming in the streets and plazas,
and the walls are splattered with gore.
The water has turned red, as if it were dyed,
and when we drink it,
it has the taste of brine.

We have pounded our hands in despair
against the adobe walls,
for our inheritance, our city, is lost and dead.
The shields of our warriors were its defense,
but they could not save it.

We have chewed dried twigs and salt grasses;
we have filled our mouths with dust and
bits of adobe;
We have eaten lizards, rats, and worms.[5]

The first European reactions to Aztec civilization appear in the accounts of the conquistadors. A society so strange and alien as the Aztec posed problems of understanding and interpretation for the Spanish invaders. The Church taught that all men were brothers, that the Indians were also descended from Adam and Eve. These teachings the conquistadors accepted in principle, but they had no historical or anthropological frame of reference, other than the vague category of "barbarians" (*bárbaros*), into which the exotic Aztec civilization could be fitted.

Some conquistadors may have been acquainted with the concept of a primeval Golden Age of innocence and simplicity, a notion descended from classical antiquity and blended in medieval and Renaissance times with the Christian tradition of an Earthly Paradise. Columbus seemed to have found that Edenic abode in the West Indies, the original home of the American Noble Savage. The advanced, warlike Aztecs, however, had little in common with the primitive and peaceful Arawaks of Haiti, of whom Columbus wrote that "they love their neighbors as themselves, and their speech is the sweetest and gentlest in the world, and always with a smile." [6] Nor was there an affinity between the Aztecs and the fierce but primitive Caribs who inhabited some of the West Indies and mainland shores of the Caribbean.

The conquistadors were acquainted with one infidel civilization that offered a clue to the posture they should assume toward the

Aztecs. This was the advanced Moslem culture, known to the Spaniards through centuries of contact in war and peace. That contact had produced a cultural rapprochement, each side adopting some ways of the other; it had bred in the Spaniard an attitude compounded of a firm belief in the superiority of his faith and acceptance of his foe's superiority in technology, science, and art.[7] As Moorish military power declined and Spanish complacency grew, the Castilians became even more disposed to acknowledge Moslem cultural superiority. Consequently the Moor entered Spanish literature in the late Middle Ages as the representative of "a brilliant and refined but decadent civilization which the Christians admire in its external aspects but never cease to combat, firmly believing in the superiority of their faith." [8]

A similar attitude toward Aztec civilization appears in the writings of some of the conquistadors. Occasionally they compare Moslem and Aztec cultural achievements, to the advantage of the latter, in order to demonstrate the high level of civilization attained by the Aztecs.

More commonly, however, the conquistadors defined Aztec society in Spanish terms and measured Aztec civilization with Spanish yardsticks. They observed the pomp and ceremony that surrounded the person of Moctezuma and concluded with considerable logic that he was a king in the European sense, a sovereign personage like their own Emperor Charles V. They compared the great lords of Moctezuma's court with Spanish grandees, and the Aztec warrior nobility with the hidalgo class of Spain. They found parallels between the Aztec priesthood and the clergy of Spain, between the docile Aztec *macehuales* or commoners and the semiservile peasantry of Castile. On the whole, the conquistadors saw in the Aztec realm a well-ordered state on the European model, with a smoothly working machinery of government and justice that aroused their admiration.

We possess at least six Spanish eyewitness accounts of the Conquest of Mexico. Three of these accounts—the *Relaciones* of Andrés de Tapia, Francisco de Aguilar, and Bernardino Vásquez de Tapia—are essentially recitals of military events and offer little description or assessment of Aztec civilization. A fourth narrative, the relation of the Anonymous Conqueror, first published in Italian in 1556, contains a summary account of Aztec institutions and customs. Its authority has been seriously weakened by recent studies that suggest the work was compiled in Italy by a free-lance writer who never set foot in America.[9] These minor sources supplement the basic eyewitness reports on the Conquest and Aztec civilization: the *Cartas de relación* sent by Cortés to Charles V; and the *Historia verdadera de la conquista de la Nueva España* by Bernal Díaz del Castillo.[10]

The letters of Cortés were written in the intervals of respite from battle and difficult marches, or amid political storms. This makes all the more remarkable their serene, unhurried flow and their wealth of precise observations. For our purposes the most important of these letters is the Carta segunda, which covers the period July, 1519, to October, 1520. This dispatch pays glowing tribute to the Aztec cultural and political achievement. Cortés naturally wished to impress Charles V with the value of his discoveries and conquests, but his eulogies have the ring of sincerity.

The Second Letter gave a quite detailed account of the things Cortés saw on the march from the coast to Tenochtitlán. Having left the coastal province of Cempoala, the Spanish army ascended the sierra and entered the independent state of Tlaxcala. Cortés found the city of Tlaxcala "so large and admirable that the little I shall say is almost incredible." He declared that Tlaxcala was not inferior to Granada in size, beauty, or population, and was much better supplied with provisions. The city displayed all the comforts and refinements of European life, including barbershops and bathhouses. The people were superior in intelligence and understanding to the best that the Moslem states of North Africa could show. Cortés compared the form of government to that of Genoa, Venice, or Pisa, because there was no one supreme ruler.

From Tlaxcala the conquistadors marched on the ancient city of Cholula. Cortés related that the city was surrounded by very fertile fields, in large part irrigated; it was more beautiful than Spanish cities because it lay on very level ground and contained many temples; from the summit of a pyramid Cortés counted more than four hundred such structures. Everywhere on the march Cortés found a dense population and the familiar contrasts between rich and poor, including beggars in the streets. "Such is the multitude of people who live in these parts, that there is not a palm of land which is not cultivated, and even then there are many places in which they suffer for lack of land, and there are many poor who beg among the rich in the streets, and in the marketplaces, just as the poor do in Spain and other civilized places." [11]

Evidence of a luxurious, refined civilization accumulated as Cortés and his army approached the Aztec capital of Tenochtitlán. On the shores of Lake Texcoco lay the city of Iztapalapan, ruled by a brother of Moctezuma. Cortés found this ruler's palace as good as the best in Spain. He described its "refreshing gardens, with many trees and sweet-scented flowers," and its "bathing places of fresh water, well constructed, with steps leading down to the bottom." Iztapalapan had a botanical and zoological garden stocked with many kinds of fish and fowl. "Within the garden, is a great pool of fresh water, very well built with sides of handsome masonry, around which runs an open walk with well-laid tile pavements, so broad that four persons can walk abreast on it, and four hundred paces square, making sixteen hundred paces in all. On the other side of this promenade, toward the wall of the garden, it is all surrounded by a lattice walk of canes, behind which are arbors planted with fragrant shrubs. The pool contains many fish, and waterfowl such as ducks, cranes, and other kinds of water birds, in such numbers that the water is covered with them." [12]

The climactic experience of the march was the first sight of Tenochtitlán. As he began to describe what he saw there, Cortés' serene, detached manner—almost the manner of a tourist leisurely recording his observations of a foreign country—gave way to excitement. "I know very well," Cortés informed his royal master, "that what I shall say, although imperfectly told, will appear so wonderful that it will hardly seem credible, for even we, who see with our own eyes the things I describe, are unable to comprehend their reality." He proceeded to give a methodical description of the setting of Tenochtitlán; of the three great causeways that connected it with the mainland and converged at the center of the city, serving as its main arteries of traffic; of its many squares where markets were held; of the numerous temples where sacrifices were offered to the Aztec gods. The great market at Tenochtitlán, "twice as large as that of Salamanca," impressed Cortés with its immense activity and display of material wealth, all under the careful supervision of special officers and mercantile courts; and he listed in detail its varied offerings.

Cortés' comments on the gifts that Moctezuma and his lords heaped upon him reveal an unexpected artistic sensitivity in the great soldier. "What greater grandeur can there be than that a barbarian monarch such as Moctezuma should have imitations in gold, silver, stones, and featherwork of all the things existing under heaven in his dominion? The gold and silver things are so like to nature that there is not a silversmith in the world who could do better; and as for the stones, there is no imagination which can divine the instruments with which they were so perfectly executed; and as concerns the featherwork, neither in wax nor in embroidery could nature be so miraculously imitated." [13]

When he turned to describe Aztec political and social institutions, Cortés followed the testimony of his eyes, which suggested parallels with the political and social arrangements of sixteenth-century Spain. Cortés described Moctezuma as an absolute ruler who inspired an incredible dread and veneration among his subjects. "He was so feared by the present, as well as the absent, that there was never prince more so. He had many pleasure houses, within and outside the city, each as well constructed for its particular pastime as could be desired for so great a lord. Within the city he had residences so marvelous that it is almost impossible to speak of their excellence and grandeur. So I limit myself to saying that there is nothing comparable to them in Spain." [14] Cortés viewed the Aztec nobles as Moctezuma's feudal vassals; like the court nobility of Spain, these lords resided the greater part of the year in the royal court and gave their first-born sons to the service of the king.

The Aztec priests, who were dressed in austere black, given to prayer, penance, and fasting, recalled the clergy of Spain. Yet Cortés found the manners and morals of Spanish prelates less commendable than the behavior of the Aztec priests. He accused the former of "disposing of the gifts of the Church, wasting them in pomps and other vices, leaving family estates for their children," whereas the latter "were so strict in composure and honesty, and also in chastity, that if one was discovered violating his vows, he was punished with death." [15]

Cortés concluded his description of Tenochtitlán with the remark that "the mode of life of its people was about the same as in Spain, with just as much harmony and order; and considering that these people were barbarians, so cut off from the knowledge of

God, and of other civilized people, it is wonderful what they have attained in every respect." [16]

Cortés' judgment on Aztec civilization, taken in the large, is highly favorable. If Columbus created the image of the American Noble Savage, technologically backward but generous, mild, and just, Cortés created the other ideal Indian type which "Europe received and incorporated in its repertory of human figures: the 'clever and discreet' Indian, educated in his own complex and exquisite civilizations, singularly well endowed for art and industry." [17]

The *Historia verdadera* of Bernal Díaz del Castillo, composed half a century after the Conquest, re-creates the vanished Aztec world with equal power, thanks to the warmth and spontaneity of the book and its natural, unpolished style. Bernal Díaz vividly remembered the splendors of Tenochtitlán. He recalled the sublime perfection of Aztec silverwork and goldwork, "which excited the admiration of the great silversmiths of Spain," and compared the genius of Aztec painters and carvers to that of the greatest Greek, Italian, and Spanish artists. "We can form some judgment of what they did then from what we can see of their work today. There are three Indians now living in the city of Mexico, named Marcos de Aquino, Juan de la Cruz, and El Crespillo, who are such magnificent painters and carvers that, had they lived in the age of the famous Apelles of old, or of Michelangelo or Berruguete in our own day, they would be counted in the same rank." Of the great marketplace he recalled that he and his comrades were astounded by "the great number of people and the quantities of merchandise, and at the orderliness and good arrangements that prevailed, for we had never seen such a thing before." [18]

Bernal Díaz's deep horror at Aztec human sacrifice and ritual cannibalism did not extend to the Aztec people. He ascribes complete humanity to both the Aztecs and their Indian foes. They reason, feel grief and joy, and weep under the stress of great emotion; they display dignity in debate and bravery in war. When Bernal Díaz recalled how the Tlaxcalans rejected Cortés' request that they abandon their gods in favor of Christianity, he noted their "honest and fearless reply." In telling an anecdote about a Spanish guard who treated the captive Aztec king rudely, Bernal

Díaz assured his readers that "it was not necessary to instruct many of us who did guard duty about the civility that was due this great cacique." He added, "I used to doff my helmet very respectfully every time I went on guard or walked by him." The Moctezuma that Bernal Díaz knew was very different from the irascible and bloodthirsty despot described in some Indian chronicles. He was a prince of great dignity and refined manners who possessed a good sense of humor and was so kind that "he gave us all jewels, and to some of us he gave cloaks and beautiful girls." He inspired such affection in the Spaniards that Bernal Díaz and "some of the others who knew Moctezuma and had dealings with him, mourned his death as if he had been our father." [19]

In a closing chapter which is in jarring contrast to the sympathetic portrayal of the Indians in most of the book, Díaz heaps them with abuse. They were guilty of committing human sacrifice and cannibalism on a horrendous scale; most of them were sodomites, "especially those who lived on the coasts and in the *tierra caliente*"; and incest was a common practice among them. They were also great drunkards; among the Indians of Pánuco such was the passion for drink that when one could no longer stand he lay down and had it injected by a squirt into his breech! [20]

Note, however, the context in which Bernal Díaz makes these charges. He has come to the self-serving point of his book; he wishes to impress the Spanish king with the great services that the conquistadors rendered him and all Christendom by abolishing all those evils and bringing the Indians to a knowledge of God. Surely such great services should be rewarded by the king! The Bernal Díaz who itemized Indian vices was not the chronicler of penetrating vision but the petitioner who wrote, "And I say with sadness in my heart, because I am an old man, poor and with one daughter to be married off, many sons already grown men with beards and others still to rear, I cannot go to Castile to plead for those things which I need and for those favors which His Majesty might grant me and which are truly due me for the service I have given him." [21]

The generous acknowledgment of Aztec creative capacity and achievement made by Cortés and Bernal Díaz is missing from other reports of the Conquest. Instead these accounts lay stress on the horrors of Aztec religion or on the bestial practices of the Indians. Typical of their tone is the letter sent to Charles V by the town council of Villa Rica de la Vera Cruz on July 10, 1519. It conceded that the Mexican Indians "live civilly and reasonably, better than any of the other peoples found in these parts," but quickly added the sweeping statement that "they are all sodomites, and practice that abominable sin." [22]

Francisco de Aguilar, a conquistador who later turned friar and wrote his *Relación* when he was more than eighty years old, declared roundly that "there is no other kingdom on earth where such offense and disservice have been rendered Our Lord, or where the Devil has been more honored and revered."

Aguilar emphasized the awful power of the Aztec priests and religion over the minds of the Indians. So great was this authority that Indian sacrificial victims cooperated with their slayers. "They had large towers with a house of worship at the top, and close to the entrance a low stone, about knee-high, where the men or women who were to be sacrificed to their gods were thrown on their backs and of their own accord remained perfectly still. A priest then came out with a stone-knife like a lance-head but which hardly cut anything, and with this knife he opened the part where the heart is and took out the heart, without the person who was being sacrificed uttering a word." Aguilar drew a striking word picture of the Aztec priests. They went about "very dirty and blackened, and wasted and haggard of face. . . . At night they walked like a procession of phantoms to the hills where they had their temples and idols and houses of worship."

Yet the diabolic cult and priesthood commanded such loyalty that all the people, "whether noble or plebeian, removed their sandals in the courtyard before they entered to worship their gods; and at the door of the church they all squatted on their heels and very reverently sobbed and wept, asking forgiveness of their sins." Now, lamented Fray Francisco, now that they are Christians, "as though in retaliation for our sins, most of them come to church by force, and with very little fear or reverence; they gossip and talk, and walk out during the principal parts of the Mass and the sermon. In their time . . . great strictness was observed in the ceremonies to their gods, but now they feel neither fear nor shame." [23]

The relation of the so-called Anonymous Conqueror made its concessions to Aztec achievements. "Many of their cities were better laid out than those of Spain, with very handsome streets and squares where they have their markets." Indeed, the Aztecs were the cleverest and most industrious people in the world. "Among them are masters of all kinds of trades, and they need to see a thing only once to be able to make it themselves." The general tendency of the relation, however, is to reduce the Aztecs to the level of ferocious, brutish savages. The writer distorts the significance of Aztec ritual cannibalism, explaining that it arose from a taste for human flesh, "which they value more than any other food, so much so that many times they go to war and risk their lives only in order to kill someone to eat." They were commonly sodomites and drank without moderation. The worst offenders were the men of Pánuco; here the men were great sodomites, idlers, and drunkards. The sensationalist tendency of the relation is illustrated by the absurd tale, clearly designed to amuse Italian readers, that Indian women urinated standing up and the men sitting, like women.[24]

Two visions of Aztec society thus emerge from the accounts of the conquistadors. Where one sees a gifted people whose mode of life "was about the same as in Spain, with just as much harmony and order," another sees a race guilty of the blackest crimes against God and nature. All the sources mingle praise and criticism, but in each a favorable or unfavorable viewpoint clearly predominates.

The ship sent by Cortés to report his activities to the Emperor Charles V anchored in the port of San Lúcar below Seville in early October, 1519. Aboard were the procurators of the new town of Villa Rica de la Vera Cruz, Alonso Hernández Portocarrero and Francisco de Montejo. They brought the Emperor a dispatch from Cortés (the lost First Letter); another from the magistrates of the new town; and the treasure obtained from Moctezuma. In the ship also came six Totonac Indians, four men and two women, sent by Cortés as presents to the Emperor. From Bernal Díaz and other sources we learn that the men had been rescued at Cempoala from cages where they were being prepared for sacrifice; the two women had been assigned for their service.

The arrival of a ship bringing news of a fabulously wealthy empire and a rich store of treasure for the Emperor created a sensation in Spain. The letters of Peter Martyr, Italian humanist and member of the Spanish Council of the Indies, revealed the impression made on a cultivated Renaissance mind by the first Mexican Indians and artifacts to reach the Old World. These Latin letters, addressed to high prelates of the Church and great nobles, and quickly published in the form of *Decades* (groups of ten letters), offered a running account of the events of the New World by an informed, urbane commentator who was privileged to read the dispatches of Columbus, Cortés, and other discoverers and conquerors. Peter Martyr supplemented these sources of information by personal contact with some of these men, and himself was at the very center of Spanish decision-making. These qualities give Martyr's *Decades* an immense authority. Of particular value for the subject of Mexico are the Fourth and Fifth Decades.[25]

One of the last Books of the Fourth Decade describes in some detail the Aztec objects sent by Cortés to Charles V. Among these objects were a number of Aztec codices, and Martyr gave a long and remarkably precise account of the materials and construction of these picture writings. He noted that "the characters are entirely different from ours, and are in the form of dice, dots, stars, lines, and other similar signs"; it seemed to him that they almost resembled the hieroglyphs of the ancient Egyptians. It was believed, he wrote, that these books contained "their laws, the ritual of their sacrifices and ceremonies, astronomical observations, and the precepts of agriculture."

The art objects filled Martyr with genuine enthusiasm. "I am at a loss," he wrote, "to describe the aigrettes, the plumes, and the feather fans. If ever artists of this kind have touched genius, then surely these natives are they. It is not so much the gold or the precious stones I admire, as the cleverness of the artist and the workmanship, which much exceed the value of the material and excite my amazement. I have examined a thousand figures which it is impossible to describe. In my opinion, I have never seen anything which for beauty could more delight the human eye." [26]

The distinguished humanist Gaspar Contarini, Venetian ambassador to Spain, shared Martyr's pleasure in the Aztec art. In 1522 Martyr invited his friend Contarini and other members of the diplomatic corps to view a second collection of Aztec objects sent by Cortés to the Emperor. Contarini described these objects in a

Portrait of Hernando Cortés made in 1529 by the German medal-maker
Christoph Weiditz, who visited the Spanish Court in 1529. From Weiditz'
Trachtenbuch. Photograph courtesy Howard F. Cline, Hispanic Foundation,
The Library of Congress, Washington, D.C.

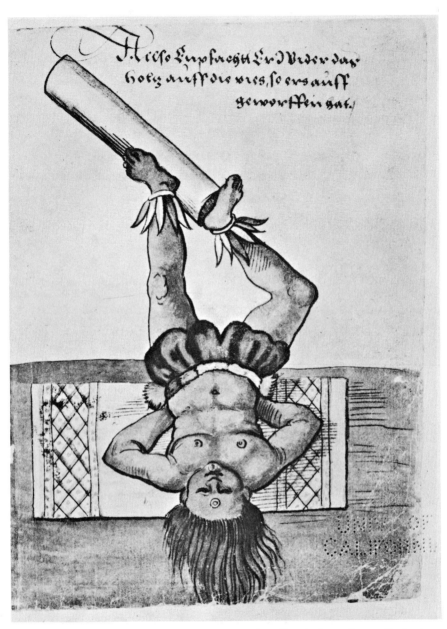

Weiditz sketches of two of the Aztecs that Cortés brought to Spain in 1528 to show the Emperor and the Spanish Court. Left, a juggler with wooden block. Right, a man clad in a mantle and feather apron and with

costly jewels let into his face. From Weiditz' *Trachtenbuch*. Photographs courtesy Howard F. Cline, Hispanic Foundation, The Library of Congress, Washington, D.C.

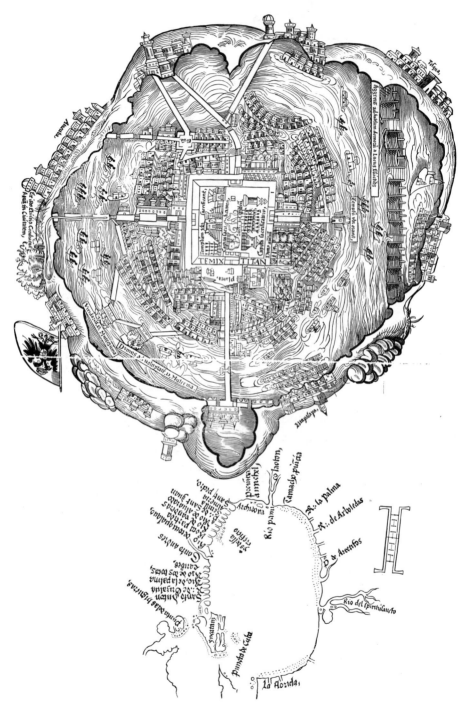

Map of Tenochtitlán based on the lost sketch sent by Cortés to the Emperor Charles V. From the Latin translation of Cortés' Second Letter published in Nuremberg in 1524.

report on his diplomatic mission, read to the Senate of the Venetian Republic on November 15, 1525. Contarini praised the Aztec gold and silver objects and the obsidian mirrors. The featherwork he found miraculous. "Never," he declared, "have I seen embroidery so lovely and delicate as some examples of this work." [27]

Martyr's description of the first Mexican visitors to Europe [28] illustrates his marked objectivity, an objectivity that disposed him to regard with philosophic calm all Aztec customs except human sacrifice and cannibalism.

"These natives," he wrote, "are of brownish color. Both sexes pierce the ears and wear golden pendants in them, and the men pierce the extremity of the underlip, down to the roots of the lower teeth. Just as we wear precious stones mounted in gold upon our fingers, so do they insert pieces of gold the size of a ring into their lips. This piece of gold is as large as a silver Carolus, and thick as a finger."

Introspectively, Martyr noted that these bizarre pendants and plugs inspired repulsion in him. He analyzed his reactions in words that recall the skepticism of Montaigne. "I cannot remember ever to have seen anything more hideous; but they think that nothing more elegant exists under the human circle. This example proves the blindness and the foolishness of the human race; it likewise proves how we deceive ourselves. The Ethiopian thinks that black is a more beautiful color than white, while the white man thinks the opposite. A bald man thinks himself more handsome than a hairy one, and the man with a beard laughs at him who is without one." [29]

On another occasion a young Mexican slave brought to Spain by Juan de Ribera, an envoy of Cortés, staged a dramatic performance for Martyr and other notables of the court. Martyr's description of this performance illustrates the precise, ethnographic quality of his reportage on Indian culture:

In his right hand he carried a simple wooden sword without the stones which ordinarily decorate this weapon, for the battle swords have their two edges hollowed out and filled with sharp stones fastened in with solid bitumen, so that these swords are almost as stout in battle as our own. The stone is that used for the razors of which I have spoken. In his other hand he carried a native shield, made of stout reeds covered with gold. The lower extremity of this shield is decorated with a feather fringe, a cubit long. The shield was lined with tiger skin, and the center of the exterior had colored feathers resembling our raw silk. Armed with his sword, the slave advanced. He wore a robe of woven feathers, half blue and half red, and cotton trousers, a handkerchief was suspended between his hips and his leggings were fastened to his garments like a cuirass which is taken off without undoing the strings that fasten the leggings. He wore beautiful sandals. He then gave an exhibition of a battle; first hurling himself upon his enemies, then retreating; then he engaged another slave who served with him and was trained to these exercises. He seized him by the hair, as they do their enemies whom they capture with weapons in their hands, dragging them off to be sacrificed. After throwing the slave on the ground, he feigned to cut open his breast above the heart, with a knife. After tearing out the heart, he wrung from his hands the blood flowing from the wound, and then besprinkled the sword and shield. This is the treatment they show prisoners.

Rubbing two sticks together he lighted a new fire, in which he burned the heart, for the sacrificial fire must never have served any other purpose, as they believe the smoke of this sacrifice pleases the tutelary gods of their country. The rest of the body is cut to pieces, as the gestures of the slave showed, but the belly and entrails are untouched; no doubt for fear of corruption. The head of the enemy sacrificed in this way is stripped of its flesh and set in gold, after which the victor keeps it as a trophy.[30]

From Spain, news of the discovery of Moctezuma's empire spread through Europe by word of mouth, by means of letters, but especially through books and newsletters. The published letters of Peter Martyr and Cortés played a key role in the diffusion of information about the Aztecs. The first printed book dealing with the subject was an epitome of Martyr's Fourth Decade, written by Martyr himself, entitled *De nuper sub D. Carolo Repertis insulis* (Basel, 1521). The Fifth Decade, which contained a description of Tenochtitlán based on Cortés' Second Letter, did not see the light until the appearance of the first complete edition of Martyr's eight decades under the title *De Orbe Novo* (Alcalá de Henares, 1530). Between 1530 and 1550 French, German, and Italian translations or summaries of Martyr's decades made them better known outside of Spain.[31]

Juan Cromberger, a leading German printer in Seville, published Cortés' Second Letter on November 8, 1522, more than two years after it was written.[32] Its publication may have been delayed by the hostile influence of Juan de Fonseca, Bishop of Burgos, and of Benito Martín, agent in Spain for Governor Velásquez of Cuba.[33] The immediate success of the book spurred publication of a second edition the next year by another German printer in Seville, Jorge Coci. The lengthy title announced sensational news:

"Epistolary relation sent to his Sacred Majesty the Emperor, our Lord, by the Captain General of New Spain, called Fernando Cortés, wherein is an account of the lands and provinces innumerable, newly discovered in Yucatán, from the year XIX to the present; and which he subjected to the Royal Crown of his Sacred Majesty. There is an especial mention of a very extensive and rich province called Culua; and of large cities and marvelous edifices, and of great trade and wealth, among which there is one richer and more wonderful than all, called Temixtitan, which with astonishing skill, is built on a large lake, of which city and province the king is a great lord called Muteccuma, where happened to the Captain and the Spaniards things astounding to hear. With a full account of the great estate of the said Muteccuma, of his rites and ceremonies, and how he is attended." [34]

Translations, extracts, and summaries soon made the Second Letter known to readers in Italy, France, the Lowlands, and Germany. A Latin translation of the Second and Third Letters by Pietro Savorgnani appeared in Nuremberg in 1524 and introduced Aztec civilization to the brilliant artistic and humanist circle of that city. In his introduction Savorgnani praised the feats of Cortés and his small army, comparing them favorably with those of Hannibal and Alexander.

A notable feature of this book was a map of Tenochtitlán, evidently based on the lost sketch sent by Cortés to Charles V sometime between 1520 and 1522. The engraver, who may have taken considerable liberties with the original, gave his work the conventional aspect of island-city plans of that period. The total effect is unreal, even dreamlike. The city and the lake both have a circular form; the houses, European in style, are tightly packed together; canoes swarm on the lake; on the shores appear other towns dominated by buildings of European architectural style. This plan, freely altered according to the caprice of engravers, became the basis of successive representations of the Aztec capital in the *isolari* of the sixteenth century, which described and depicted the most celebrated islands of the world. We find it, for example, together with a lengthy account of Tenochtitlán based on Cortés' Second Letter, in the *Libro di Benedetto Bordone* (Venice, 1528), "in which is told of all the islands of the world with their ancient and modern names." [35]

Between 1520 and 1522 at least three newsletters informed German readers of the discovery of the Aztec Empire.[36] Their sources of information appear to have been correspondents of German firms in Spain. One such newsletter, published in Nuremberg, March 17, 1520, described the Mexicans as being of medium height, with well-formed bodies, and pretty faces. "However, they make themselves ugly for they bore holes in nose, ears, and lips and hang jewels and gold rings in them. The stones which they put in their lips force their mouths wide open so that it is horrible to see." There followed a description of their human sacrifices, ending on a hopeful note. "Inasmuch as these islanders are so assiduous in their service of the gods whom they believe to be divine, one may expect them to be very devout when they are taught the divine creed." [37]

We possess three contemporary private letters telling of the discovery of the Aztec Empire.[38] One, written from the shores of the present state of Veracruz by a soldier in Cortés' army, presented the country as a Land of Cockaigne. The writer informed his correspondent in Seville that gold, silver, and precious stones abounded. "One can hardly tell what wonderful things one finds in their houses. Their bedsteads are covered with canopies and other costly cloths. The people of this land are honest, and have extraordinarily beautiful women. . . . The cities are larger than Seville, more than half of them have five miles of roads in length and breadth, wondrously beautiful with splendid streets, all of them paved." The natives were beautiful of body, very wealthy, and circumcised. "It is believed that these natives peopled the land originally when Rome was destroyed." The letter closed on a cheerful note. "It is very friendly people, and they have manifested great joy that they have seen Christians, and they themselves have brought the Christians among their people, and shown them the land." [39]

Another letter, written by one Diego Dienz from Seville to a correspondent in Burgos on November 7, 1519, two days after the arrival of Cortés' dispatch ship, had the same exuberant tone. It reported the discovery of the richest land that ever existed. "And the houses are of stone, and the land is very beautiful, and rich in grazing, mountains, and game as in our countries, also exceedingly fertile, especially in gold." [40]

On July 12, 1520, Albrecht Dürer set out from Nuremberg on a journey to the Netherlands. The great painter hoped to be received there by the new Emperor, Charles V, and to obtain confirmation of the pension granted Dürer by the late Emperor Maximilian, who had died on January 12, 1519. From August 26 to September 3, 1520, Dürer stayed at Brussels, scene of festivities celebrating the election of the young Charles as Holy Roman Emperor. In the great Townhall, Dürer visited an exhibition of the Aztec treasure sent to Spain by Cortés. "I saw," Dürer wrote in his journal, "things which have been brought to the king from the new land of gold, a sun all of gold a whole fathom broad, and a moon all of silver of the same size, also two rooms full of the armor of the people there, and all manner of wondrous weapons of theirs, harness, and darts, very strange clothing, beds, and all kinds of wondrous objects of human use, much better worth seeing than prodigies. These things are all so precious that they are valued at 100,000 florins. All the days of my life I have seen nothing that rejoiced my heart so much as these things, for I have seen among them wonderful works of art, and I marvelled at the subtle intellects of men in foreign parts. Indeed, I cannot express all that I thought there." [41]

Four years later (1524) Pietro Savorgnani's Latin translation of the Second and Third Letters of Cortés was published in Nuremberg. The book contained the map of Tenochtitlán mentioned above. It seems more than likely that Dürer, member of a coterie of brilliant intellectuals with the most far-ranging interests, knew this book. One student reports internal evidence in an architectural sketch by Dürer, a project for an ideal city, that he was influenced by the plan of Tenochtitlán. Erwin Walter Palm finds striking affinities between the ideal city of the German master, with its enormous central square dominating the residential area, and the sketch of Tenochtitlán, in which the central precinct, surrounded by the Coatepantli (Wall of the Snakes), similarly dominates the residential area. This central precinct may have suggested to Dürer "the idea of the internal defense which preoccupied all the urbanist theoreticians of the sixteenth century." [42]

By the third decade of the sixteenth century Aztec civilization had entered the consciousness of many cultivated Europeans, if not of the masses. The accounts of Cortés and Peter Martyr (the work of Bernal Díaz remained in manuscript until 1632) had created an image of a complex, refined society, of a people equal in intellectual and artistic capacity to Europeans, although blemished by the vices of paganism, human sacrifice, and cannibalism. The genius of Aztec artists and craftsmen had aroused the enthusiasm of conquistadors, of humanists of the stature of Peter Martyr and Gaspar Contarini, of a giant of Western art, Albrecht Dürer. The Aztec capital of Tenochtitlán, made visually known through the map sent to Spain by Cortés, had entered as a second Venice into the list of celebrated islands and great cities depicted in the atlases of the sixteenth century. In short, a new ideal Indian type, the creator of splendid empires and high civilizations, had joined the Noble Savage first announced by Columbus.

The discovery of the Aztec Empire offered Europe new evidence of the enormous diversity of customs and opinions among the nations of the earth. By revealing the extraordinary creative capacity of a distant people who knew not the Word of God it helped to widen the mental as well as the geographical horizons of Europe, weakened faith in old certainties, and supplied new ammunition for Renaissance critics of the philosophic premises on which the European Old Order rested.

CHAPTER FOUR

The Aztecs and
the Great Debate: I

The dispute begun by the conquistadors over the nature of Aztec civilization merged with a larger controversy over the American Indians and the relations that Spain should establish with them. What was the essential nature of the Indians? What cultural level had they achieved or were they capable of achieving? Were they the "slaves by nature" described by Aristotle, a race of subhuman beings who might properly be conquered and made to serve the Spaniards? What rights and obligations in regard to the Indians were implicit in the Papal grant of America to the Spanish monarchs? Such questions inspired a battle of books in which the opponents supported their positions with citations from Aristotle, the Church Fathers, and Scholastic philosophers and, less frequently, with ethnographic material obtained by direct observation or from written accounts of Indian life and manners.[1]

For reasons deeply rooted in Spain's past, Spanish thought of the sixteenth century had a strong legalistic and Scholastic cast. In no other European land did Scholasticism retain so much vitality as a philosophic method and as an instrument for the solution of public and private problems.[2] The need "to discharge the royal conscience," to make the royal actions conform to the natural and the divine law, explains official preoccupation with the moral foundations of Spain's Indian policy. Behind the subtle disputations of theologians and jurists, however, there developed a complex struggle of groups and institutions which had large stakes in the Crown's decisions on Indian policy. The Spanish colonists and their allies in Spain, the Church, and the Crown itself were the main parties to this struggle. The central issue was the question of who should control Indian labor and tribute, the material foundations of the Spanish Empire in America.

The question had several facets. How could the demand of the colonists for cheap Indian labor be reconciled with the Crown's interest in preserving a large tribute-paying native population? There was a political issue, for excessive concentration of land and Indians in the hands of colonists might lead to the rise of a class of great feudal lords independent of royal authority. Such a development the Spanish monarchs were determined to prevent. The Church also had a major interest in the Indian problem. If the Indians perished as a result of Spanish mistreatment, the great task of saving pagan souls would remain incomplete and the good name of the Church would suffer. Besides, who then would construct churches and monasteries and support the servants of God in the Indies?

The question of Indian policy assumed a crucial character with the discovery and conquest of the rich Indian empires of Mexico and Peru. Spanish colonial experience had demonstrated that Indians who were left to the tender mercies of the conquistadors might become an extinct race. This had happened on the once densely populated island of Hispaniola. The most elementary interests of the Crown and its colonial enterprise demanded that the same disaster should not occur in the newly conquered lands.[3]

The focal point of the struggle over Indian policy, at least until after mid-century, was the encomienda. This system, first established in the West Indies, consisted in the assignment to a Spanish colonist of a group of Indians who were to serve him with tribute and labor. He in turn assumed the feudal obligation of defending the country, of protecting his Indian charges, and of instructing them in the Christian religion. In practice, the encomienda in the West Indies became a hideous slavery. Bent on preventing a repetition of the West Indian catastrophe, Charles V in 1523 sent Cortés an order forbidding the establishment of the encomienda in New Spain, "because God created the Indians free and not subject." Cortés, who had already assigned encomiendas to himself and some of his comrades, refused to obey the order. Backed by the strength and needs of the hard-bitten conquistadors, he argued so persuasively for the encomienda system, declaring it necessary for the security and welfare of the colony, that the royal order was revoked. The lines of battle over the encomienda had been clearly drawn.

The colonists—more precisely the *encomenderos* or those who aspired to become such—had well-defined objectives. They sought not only to preserve the encomienda but to make it perpetual or hereditary. They urged that perpetuity would make *encomenderos* more solicitous for the welfare of their Indian charges and thus avert the evils associated with the encomienda in the West Indies. Even the suggestion of a lapse of their rights caused uneasiness among the *encomenderos*. Recalling their services in the Conquest, they threatened the Crown with loss of its American empire through Indian revolt or foreign invasion if they quit the country because their privileges had been revoked.

The Church did not speak with one voice on Indian policy. The religious who came to Mexico in the first decades after the Conquest were, on the whole, an élite group. Products of one of the periodic revivals of asceticism and discipline in the medieval Church, and of the reform of the orders instituted in Spain under the Catholic Sovereigns and carried out with implacable energy by Cardinal Jiménez de Cisneros, this vanguard group of Dominicans, Franciscans, and Augustinians combined a sensitive social conscience with missionary zeal. Some religious, filled with millenarian fervor, believed that "the friars were given the unique opportunity of creating, on the eve of the end of the world, a terrestrial paradise where a whole race of men would be consecrated to evangelical poverty." [4] These men were virtually unanimous in denouncing the cruelties and tyrannies used by Spaniards against the Indians. They found it easier to denounce, however, than to agree on a solution for these evils.

A handful of priest reformers reached the conclusion that the welfare of the Indians was incompatible with the encomienda. The Dominican Bartolomé de Las Casas was the spokesman for this group. Las Casas ultimately advanced a program calling for the suppression of the encomienda, liberation of the Indians from all forms of servitude except a small tribute to the Crown, and the restoration of the ancient Indian states and rulers, the rightful owners of those lands. Over these states the Spanish monarch would preside as "Emperor over many Kings" in order to fulfill his sacred mission of bringing the Indians to the Catholic faith and the Christian way of life. Las Casas' ideal was a theocratic state in which the clergy should enjoy special jurisdiction over the Indians, and the natives should be completely separated from the corrupting and oppressive presence of lay Spaniards.[5]

The majority of the clergy, both regular and secular, including such bitter critics of Spanish mistreatment of the Indians as Bishop Juan de Zumárraga and Fray Toribio de Benavente, known as Motolinía, disagreed with Las Casas. These "realists" adopted a compromise position; they argued that the encomienda, regulated to safeguard Indian welfare, was necessary for the prosperity and security of the Indies. As early as 1529, Zumárraga spoke for the encomienda, carefully regulated, as indispensable to the collective interest of Spaniards and Indians.[6] With the passage of time, clergy and colonists moved toward a unity of views. During the crisis caused by the issue of the New Laws of 1542, which doomed the encomienda, the provincials of the Augustinians, Dominicans, and Franciscans journeyed to Spain to plead for the revocation of the laws and to demonstrate "that the highest dignitaries of the missionary orders in closest contact with the Indians were solidly behind the conquistadores." A memorial presented to the Emperor by representatives of the town council of Mexico City emphasized the mutual interests of clergy and colonists, noting that "Spaniards, not Indians, supported the ecclesiastics, and that those who proposed to support the conquistadores by paying them pensions instead of granting them encomiendas did not suggest where the necessary money was to come from."[7]

By mid-century a yawning gulf separated Las Casas from the great majority of his clerical brethren. At the time of his debate of 1550 and 1551 with the Spanish jurist and theologian Juan Ginés de Sepúlveda over the justice of Spain's wars against the Indians, Las Casas had the chagrin of knowing that Bishop Vasco de Quiroga of Michoacán, who was famed for his benevolence toward the natives, supported Sepúlveda's position. Quiroga also favored the perpetual encomienda. Four years later Motolinía sent Charles V a letter in which he bitterly denounced Las Casas as an ignorant, arrogant troublemaker. In the same letter Motolinía expressed an unjustified optimism concerning the improvement that had taken place in the condition of the Indians.[8]

The evolution of the Crown's Indian policy reflected pressures from different quarters, its political and economic needs at a given moment, and the views of the reigning monarch. Under Ferdinand the Catholic, whose Castilian and Aragonese favorites shared with him as absentee *encomenderos* in the merciless exploitation of the Indians of Hispaniola, little or no change for the better took place. The famous Laws of Burgos (1512), for all their humane provisions, remained almost entirely on paper. Under Charles V, who took a larger view of the imperial interest in the Indies, the pro-Indian party headed by Las Casas met with more favor at court.

It was in the New Laws of 1542 that the efforts of Charles and the reformers to prevent a repetition of the West Indian tragedy in Mexico and Peru and to check the rise of a colonial feudalism reached their climax. These laws looked to the ultimate extinction of the encomienda. They prohibited the enslavement of Indians in the future, ordered the release of Indian slaves to whom title could not be proved, abolished compulsory personal service by Indians, regulated tribute, and provided that existing encomiendas were to lapse on the death of the holder.

The New Laws caused a great revolt in Peru; in New Spain they provoked a storm of protest by the *encomenderos* and a majority of the clergy. Under this pressure the Crown retreated and finally agreed to a compromise. The laws forbidding enslavement and forced personal service were reaffirmed, but the right of inheritance by the heir of an *encomendero* was recognized and was extended by stages to a third, fourth, and sometimes a fifth life. Thereafter, or earlier, in the absence of an heir, the encomienda reverted to the Crown. In the natural course of events, the number of private encomiendas steadily diminished and that of Crown towns increased. A system of tribute assessment by Audiencias, royal courts which sought to adjust tribute to the fluctuation of population and harvests on appeal from the Indians, further curbed the power of the *encomenderos*. The Crown also attempted to control and rationalize the use of an ever diminishing supply of Indian labor by means of the *repartimiento*, a system under which all adult male Indians were required to give a certain amount of time to work in mines and factories, on farms and haciendas, and on public works.

These changes failed to bring any significant or enduring relief to the Indians. The Crown magistrates (*corregidores*) exploited the Indians of the towns in their charge as severely as the *encomenderos*. Forced labor under the *repartimiento* was as great a scourge to the Indians as had been compulsory personal service under the encomienda. To make matters worse, the dominant motive of Spain's Indian policy from the accession of Philip II (1556) was to augment the royal revenues in order to overcome the Crown's desperate financial crisis. The royal commissioner Jerónimo Valderrama, sent to New Spain in 1563, gained the title of *afligidor de los indios* for his efforts to squeeze more tribute from the Indians. These efforts drew a collective protest from the heads of the Franciscan Order in New Spain. They refused to give their approval to the new assessments, declaring that they imposed intolerable burdens on the rapidly declining Indian population and must lead to the total destruction of the natives.[9] Valderrama countercharged that the religious themselves were taking advantage of the Indians. In one monastery alone, "and that not the largest," he found more than one hundred and ninety Indian servants.[10] The chorus of charges and countercharges documented the fact that Crown officials, colonists, clergy, and Indian chiefs were making intolerable demands for tribute and labor on a rapidly shrinking Indian population. Simultaneously the influence of Las Casas and his Indianist movement virtually disappeared from the Spanish court. Valderrama's venomous comment to the king that certain Dominicans who objected to his tribute proposals had suckled their doctrine at the pap of Las Casas suggests the new political climate.[11]

In the long run, the colonists won the struggle over Indian policy. If they lost the battle of the encomienda, which the Crown finally tamed and put in the way of extinction, they won victories elsewhere. Indian forced labor, although separated from the encomienda, became available to them in the form of the *repartimiento*. The rise of the hacienda, the large landed estate, confirmed the victory of the creoles, the American-born Spaniards. The catastrophic decline of the Indian population of New Spain in the second half of the sixteenth century caused a labor crisis and sharply reduced the flow of foodstuffs to the Spanish colonial cities;

moreover, it stimulated a rapid expansion of the hacienda. The hacienda grew at the expense of the pueblo, leaving the Indian town without enough land for its people; the hacienda lured laborers from the pueblo, making it difficult for the Indian town to meet its tribute and *repartimiento* obligations. The hacienda was practically free from royal control; over its broad expanse the *hacendado* was supreme. The emergence of a hereditary creole aristocracy, ever richer in land and peons, signified a defeat both for the Crown and for the Indian community.[12]

A survey of the literature on Aztec themes composed in Spain and America between 1530 and 1600 suggests a link between the positions of Spanish writers on Indian policy and their attitudes toward Aztec civilization. Three well-defined viewpoints on Aztec society emerge from this literature.

One group of writers, closely tied to the *encomendero* and conquistador interest, displayed a fixed hostility toward the Aztecs and Indians in general. In effect, these writers documented the thesis of Sepúlveda, that the Indians were slaves by nature whose best interests were served by their conquest and subjection to Spanish rule. Writers of this school generally disparaged Aztec cultural achievements, stressed the misery of commoners under Aztec rule, and praised the Conquest as a liberation of the Indian from abject material and spiritual slavery. Francisco López de Gómara brilliantly expounded the viewpoint of this group.

A smaller group of writers, foes of the encomienda and violently opposed to wars of conquest against the Indians, rallied to the defense of the Aztecs. These humanists replied to charges of Indian inferiority by arguing that Aztec cultural achievements equaled or surpassed those of the ancient Greeks and Romans. The writings of these men embellished the Indian past, depicting a pagan Golden Age in which obedient commoners lived happily under the mild sway of enlightened kings. Human sacrifice and other major blights on Aztec civilization they minimized or rationalized. Las Casas was the group's major theoretician and publicist.

A third group of Spanish writers occupied an uncertain middle ground. These men were working clergy who had little patience with what they regarded as the extravagances of Las Casas. They accepted as self-evident the proposition that the maintenance of

Spanish rule and Christianity in the Indies required the presence of Spanish laymen and that these must be supported by Indian labor, assuming that such labor was carefully regulated in order to safeguard the health and lives of the natives. The logic of such a position disposed these moderates to accept the view of the Sepúlveda school that the Conquest was just, that it was a divine chastisement of the Aztecs for their sins of idolatry and human sacrifice. Yet the moderates agreed with Las Casas in condemning Spanish excesses toward the Indians; they also regarded the natives with protective tenderness, finding in them the traits of simplicity, humility, and innocence that they associated with the founders of primitive Christianity. Duality marked the writings of the moderates. When they viewed Aztec Mexico through the lenses of religion, they saw a realm of Satan, an accursed people wallowing in crimes of every sort. On the other hand, Aztec achievements in education, child rearing, jurisprudence, and other fields of culture inspired their highest admiration. The moderates included such great students of Aztec civilization as Motolinía, Bernardino de Sahagún, and Diego Durán.

A fourth group of writers was composed of Indian and mestizo descendants of pre-Conquest rulers and nobles. These men wrote their histories from a variety of motives: local patriotism, the desire to keep alive the memory of their forebears, or the wish to strengthen their claims to lands and titles. The ambivalence of their works reflected the ambiguous social and political situation of the authors. Pride in their pagan ancestors and resentment over their loss of property and privilege to the Spaniards struggled with a fervent Catholicism and a general tendency to identify with the dominant Spanish culture. They manifested these sentiments in efforts to find anticipations of Christianity in the thought of ancient Indian kings and to shift responsibility to some other Indian group for the rise of human sacrifice in Aztec Mexico. One Indian, Fernando Alvarado Tezozómoc, and two mestizo chroniclers, Diego Muñoz Camargo and Juan Bautista Pomar, may be taken to represent this group of writers.

The line of anti-Indian chronicles was initiated by the *Historia general y natural de las Indias* of Gonzalo Fernández de Oviedo. Oviedo, born into an Asturian hidalgo family, passed his youth in the service of Spanish princes in Spain and Italy. In 1514 he sailed for the Indies in the expedition of Pedrarias Dávila with the title of *veedor* (overseer) of gold smelting in Tierra Firme (the coasts of Venezuela and Panama), and held this post until 1532. He took part in Indian wars and used Indian slaves in mining and other enterprises. In 1552 the Emperor Charles named him royal chronicler and he retired to Santo Domingo on Hispaniola, where he combined work on his history with the duties of governor of the fortress of Santo Domingo and the care of his large economic interests. The first part of the *Historia general* was published in 1535; the second part appeared in Valladolid in 1557, shortly after Oviedo's death.[13]

Oviedo may have been stimulated to write his history by a visit he paid to Peter Martyr in 1516 and by reading the first three *Decades* of Martyr, published in the same year.[14] According to Eduard Fueter, Oviedo's work marked an advance over Martyr's in the use of an ethnographic approach. In his *Historia* Oviedo frequently described Indian customs in an objective manner and sometimes compared them with those of such prestigious cultures as the Roman and the Greek. Although such a comparative method implicitly recognized Indian membership in the family of men, Fueter's judgment that Oviedo regarded the Indians "without hatred or scorn," that he viewed them primarily as interesting objects of natural history, is untenable. Alberto M. Salas more correctly describes Oviedo's posture toward the Indians as identical with "the biased attitudes of the conquistador and the colonist, with the most widespread and most vulgar prejudices of the colonial world." Oviedo's Indians are "dirty, lying cowards who commit suicide out of sheer boredom, just to ruin the Spaniards by dying; they have no liking or capacity for work." Oviedo's callous contempt for the Indians is typified by his statement that the idea of making Christians of them was like "pounding on cold iron"; their skulls were so thick that when the Spaniards fought with them they took care not to strike them on the head, lest their swords should break.[15]

Oviedo displayed the same implacable hostility toward the relatively primitive Indians of the Caribbean area, whom he knew at firsthand, and toward the advanced Aztec civilization, which he knew not at all. His *Historia general* described conditions in Aztec Mexico on the basis of what he had learned from "reliable persons

who fought with Hernando Cortés in the conquest of that land."
He drew a picture of abysmal poverty and oppression. The Indian
lords had no mercy or charity; fear, not virtue, was the driving
force of their actions. They worshiped the Devil, not from love
but from fear of him. "They said that if they failed to offer
sacrifices and festivals in his honor, he would send hail to destroy
their grain and fields." The Mexican Indians were great loafers
and drunkards, giving themselves up to drunken orgies while they
sent their wives to dig, sow, and harvest, and perform all other
tasks.

Oviedo depicted in darkest colors the life of Aztec commoners
under the tyranny of their kings and lords. "In their homes they
had no furnishings or clothing other than the poor garments that
they wore on their persons, one or two stones for grinding maize,
some pots in which to cook the maize, and a sleeping mat. They
ate little—not that they would not eat more if they could get it,
for the soil is very fertile and yields bountiful harvests, but the
common people and plebeians suffered under the tyranny of their
Indian lords, who taxed away the greater part of their produce."
If sickness or poverty kept some poor Indian from paying his
tribute, he was sent to a slave market to be sold, and the proceeds
of the sale were applied to payment of his tribute.[16]

Oviedo's history immediately became an authoritative source-
book for the colonialist party in Spain and America. He was the
only writer on American affairs mentioned by the party's leading
ideologist, Sepúlveda, during his debate with Las Casas. Sepúlveda
cited Oviedo, whom he described as "a grave chronicler who has
lived for many years in the islands and Tierra Firme," in support
of his thesis of the essential depravity and inferiority of the
Indians.[17]

Sepúlveda was one of Spain's most distinguished classical scholars,
historians, and theologians. Erasmus honored him with the title of
the "Spanish Livy." He had close links with *encomendero* and conquistador circles and enjoyed the friendship of Cortés. At the time
of the crisis caused by the passage of the reform laws of 1542,
Sepúlveda was urged by highly placed friends to write a paper
against the ideas of Las Casas. Sepúlveda complied by writing a
Latin treatise, *Democrates alter, de justis belli causis apud Indos,*
which sought to prove the justice of Spanish wars against the
Indians by demonstrating that the Indians fitted Aristotle's defini-

tion of slaves by nature.[18] The influence of Las Casas, supported by liberal-minded professors at leading Spanish universities, was strong enough to prevent publication of Sepúlveda's treatise; however, in 1550, in an atmosphere of retreat from the reform laws of 1542, the Emperor Charles summoned a junta of theologians to consider the question of the justice of Indian wars, with Las Casas and Sepúlveda as the disputants. In his debate with Las Casas in Valladolid during 1550 and 1551, Sepúlveda summarized the main points of his treatise.

Sepúlveda chose the advanced Aztec civilization as the touchstone in elaborating his argument. He noted that the Aztecs were considered the wisest, most refined, and most powerful of all Indian peoples. Moctezuma ruled over a great empire from a strongly defensible capital situated, as was Venice, in a large lake. Yet this cowardly monarch made no effort to destroy the small Spanish force, but instead attempted to dissuade them from advancing on Tenochtitlán. When this tactic failed, Moctezuma admitted Cortés and his army into the capital without a show of resistance. So cowardly and passive were the Aztec barbarians that Cortés imprisoned Moctezuma without an effort on their part to free their king.

Having demonstrated the Aztec lack of spirit, Sepúlveda went on to prove the "rudeness, barbarism, and inherently slavish nature of these people." True, they had cities, kings, and carried on trade in the manner of civilized people, but Sepúlveda brushed aside this evidence of a higher culture. "The possession of dwellings, of a fairly rational mode of life, and a kind of commerce," he declared, "is something that natural necessity itself induces, and only serves to prove that they are not bears or monkeys and are not completely devoid of reason." On the other hand, they lacked all learning, had no written language, and preserved no other record of their history than some vague and obscure recollections of past events which they represented by means of pictures. They had no written laws, only barbaric customs and institutions. What was worse, they had no private property. Their heirs could not inherit their houses and fields, for all was in the power of their lords, whom they improperly called kings. That they submitted peacefully to this state of affairs and did not have to be coerced by arms only confirmed the base, servile spirit of these barbarians.

Aztec human sacrifice and ritual cannibalism offered easy targets for Sepúlveda. He worked up a calculation to show that the advantages of the Conquest to the Indians far exceeded its evils. Assuming that twenty thousand persons had been sacrificed each year on the Aztec altars, he reckoned that six hundred thousand lives had been saved in the thirty years since the Conquest. As the Conquest could not have taken more lives than the number annually put to death by the Aztec priests, the net gain in Indian lives was clear. "How can we doubt," he asked, "that these people, so uncivilized and barbarous, contaminated by so many infidelities and vices, have been justly conquered by such excellent and pious kings as Ferdinand the Catholic and the present Emperor Charles, and by a nation that is most humane and excels in every virtue?" Sepúlveda concluded that the encomienda system was just and worthy of support, because the *encomenderos* would instruct the Indians in civilized ways and the Christian religion.[19]

The colonists of New Spain showed their gratitude to Sepúlveda for his efforts in their behalf. The town council of Mexico City voted on February 8, 1554, to send Sepúlveda "some jewels and clothing from this land to the value of two hundred pesos" in recognition of his services and "to encourage him in the future." [20]

Francisco López de Gómara excused himself from justifying the Conquest in his *Historia de las Indias* (1552) because Sepúlveda had written so well on the subject.[21] Gómara was too modest; his artistry put flesh and bones on Sepúlveda's abstract debater's points. Only the second part of the *Historia*, which deals with the conquest of Mexico, interests us here. Gómara served as Cortés' private secretary and chaplain from 1541 to 1547 and received five hundred pesos from Don Martín Cortés, son of the conquistador, for his literary services.[22] From first to last, the *Conquista de México* is a celebration of the man whose genius and heroism made it possible for a small band of Spaniards to conquer a vast empire.

Gómara's power lay chiefly in his style, a trenchant, chiseled style sometimes acid with irony, sometimes racy and sprinkled with homely Castilian proverbs, sometimes rising to a lofty eloquence. Unfortunately, Gómara followed classical models in the use of long, made-up speeches which he assigned to Cortés and other personages. In one such speech Cortés lectured a group of patient Indians on the advantages of the Christian faith. Naturally he reiterated Sepúlveda's thesis of the superiority of Spaniards over Indians. "We were all given the same kinds of bodies, souls, and senses, wherefore we are all equal, not only in body and soul, but are kindred in blood. It happens, however, that by an act of the same God some are born beautiful and other ugly, some wise and discreet, other foolish and without understanding, judgment, or virtue. It is just, holy, and in conformity with the will of God, therefore, that the wise and virtuous should teach and indoctrinate the ignorant, guide the blind and erring, and place them upon the way of salvation, by the path of the true religion. This is the great boon and blessing that I and my companions strive and desire to attain for you, and the more we strive the closer become the bonds of friendship." [23]

Gómara supplemented the story of the Conquest with considerable material on Aztec history, society, and religion, drawn principally from Motolinía's *Memoriales*. He edited this material with admirable skill, compressing and rewriting Motolinía's rough text into a smoothly flowing account; however, he used this material for his own anti-Indian ends, adding crudely prejudiced comments not found in Motolinía. Gómara declared that the Mexicans were liars, thieves, drunkards, and loafers; they were very lustful; the men had relations indifferently with women or other men, without any sense of shame. "Motolinía stressed the virtues of the Indians," observes Ramón Iglesia, "Gómara their defects." [24]

"Never," wrote Gómara, "was there a more idolatrous people, or one so given to the killing and eating of men." He went on to contrast the somber past with the shining present. Under Aztec domination, the commoners paid excessive tribute. If they could not pay their tribute obligations, they were sacrificed and served up at the Aztec banquets. Their lords used them as beasts of burden on the roads and in construction. They dared not wear a decent cloak or even look at their king. "Now through the grace of God they are Christians and free from the sacrifice and eating of men. The idols have been overthrown; an end has been put to the drunken orgies that befuddled men's minds. The horrid sin of sodomy has been stamped out. For these favors the Indians owe much to the Spaniards who conquered and converted them. Now they are masters of their property; indeed, they enjoy an excessive, harmful freedom. They pay so little tribute that they live at their ease, for the Emperor Charles regulates their tribute. No one can compel them to bear burdens or to work for him; they are paid well for all they do. . . . God truly did them a great service by entrusting them to the Spaniards who converted them and treated them so well." [25]

Gómara stressed Spain's civilizing mission, the gifts she sent to relieve the poverty of Indian Mexico. Before the Conquest the Indians had no weights, for they did not know that God made all things by count, weight, and measure. Some said that it was to avoid frauds the Aztecs did not use weights; ignorance was the more likely reason. They lacked money, although they had plenty of gold, silver, and copper, and knew how to smelt ore and to work these metals. The Spaniards gave them money so they might know what they bought, sold, and owned. The Spaniards gave them beasts of burden, and wool, and the use of iron and lamps, all to ease and brighten their lives. The Spaniards also brought the Indians the gift of Latin and the sciences, more valuable than all the gold and silver taken from them, for learning alone makes a man truly a man.[26]

Gómara's book was highly readable and informative; moreover, it radiated a fervent Spanish nationalism and a proud conviction of the superiority of European Renaissance civilization over American barbarism that was satisfying to most Western minds. Las Casas denounced it as slanderous and mendacious. The Crown, still fearing the rise of a powerful colonial feudalism, sought to suppress the book because of its frank sympathy with the conquistadors and its implied criticism of the Emperor's policies.[27] But the Indianist movement headed by Las Casas had lost its momentum and was in retreat; Lascasian ideas were becoming suspect at the Spanish court. Under these conditions the anti-Indian current of thought brilliantly represented by Gómara soon gained the ascendancy in Spain. By the last decades of the sixteenth century Gómara's view of the Indian had become the dominant viewpoint of Spanish writers dealing with America.

The section on the discovery and conquest of America in the *Historia de España* by the Jesuit Juan de Mariana illustrates this ideological shift. The book, written in the 1590's and published in 1601, enjoyed great popularity in Spain. Mariana's treatment of the Indian reflects the strong influence of Gómara. No trace remains here of the Noble Savage of Columbus or of the talented, artistic Indian admired by Cortés and Peter Martyr. Mariana presents a stereotype abysmally backward in moral and material culture.

"The customs of all the peoples discovered in these parts," wrote Mariana, "were strange. . . . They lacked the use of letters, a notable deficiency. They used neither money nor weights. They did not know how to make ships with sails, tackle, rigging, and cordage, and how to steer them; they navigated in boats like troughs, dug out from a single timber, which they call canoes. They made their clothing and fabrics of cotton, which grows well in those lands, in different colors, without the need of dyeing it. They lacked iron and the weapons and tools which are made from it; they also lacked wheat and mills with which to grind their maize, the grain they eat. They had no olive oil or wine, although the earth produced both olives and grapes naturally; they used other drinks for their drunken orgies, to which they were much given. They did not know how to make candles from wax and tallow for lighting. They had no beasts of burden for riding or for drawing carts or litters. They sacrificed war prisoners and slaves in such great numbers that in Mexico City alone they are believed to have sacrificed more than twenty thousand persons each year, and they ate their flesh without repugnance. They had intercourse with many women and practiced sodomy without shame, so filthy and indecent were they. Their dress varied greatly; the majority went naked. God did them a great favor to bring them under the power of Christians. . . . It had been a greater kindness to subjugate them than to allow them their liberty." [28]

New Spain had its own Gómara in the person of Francisco Cervantes de Salazar, whom the provincial aristocracy delighted to honor for his services to their cause. Cervantes de Salazar came to Mexico in 1551, perhaps at the urging of Cortés himself. He had behind him a career as a professor of rhetoric at various Spanish universities and was the author of several philosophical tracts. He began his career in New Spain as a teacher of Latin in a private school; later he rose to become professor of rhetoric in the newly founded Real y Pontificia Universidad de México (1553). In 1567 he was named rector of the university. A perfect type of academic opportunist, he seems to have been chiefly concerned with gaining

the favor of the leading personages of colonial society. His friendship with Don Martín Cortés, in whose house he lodged, may have
aided his rapid rise.

In January, 1558, the *cabildo* or town council of Mexico City
voted to support Cervantes' project for a book in which he proved
"the just and rightful title of his Majesty to this New Spain." [29]
It is not clear whether this was his *Crónica de la Nueva España*,
the manuscript of which the royal commissioner Valderrama took
to Spain on his return in 1566, or another work that Cervantes did
not complete. In any case, the manuscript of the *Crónica* gathered
dust until its discovery and publication in 1914.

A Mexican scholar, Jorge Hugo Díaz-Thomé, has destroyed the
pretensions of the *Crónica* to be an original historical work based
on serious scholarship.[30] Cervantes de Salazar took from Gómara
not only the general plan of his work but much of his text as well.
As a plagiarist, Cervantes botched his job, making errors in copying and sometimes distorting the meaning of Gómara's text. Díaz-
Thomé believes that the manuscript sources cited by Cervantes
were chiefly padding designed to offset the impression of total
dependence on Gómara. On the other hand, the *Crónica* contains
much valuable material on natural history, native medicine, and
Indian genealogical and divinatory lore.

If the *Crónica* sheds little new light on the Conquest, it does
illuminate the mentality of Cervantes de Salazar and the colonial
aristocracy with which he identified himself. A rabid hatred for
the Indian pervades the book. Cervantes goes beyond Gómara in
the process of degrading the Indian, of reducing him to a beast.

In describing pre-Conquest Mexico in his opening chapters, Cervantes made some concessions to Aztec success in social and political organization. He admitted that the Aztecs had had some wise
and energetic kings, otherwise they could not have established and
maintained such a powerful state. "Their laws severely punished
offenses; all lived peacefully and told the truth; they greatly respected their kings." Among the Aztecs, as among other peoples,
some men were made to govern, and the majority were made to
obey; the latter were the men Aristotle called slaves by nature.
Cervantes insisted nonetheless that both groups were barbarians,
because they committed many offenses against the natural law
that even beasts instinctively respect. The Aztecs adored stones

and animals, sacrificed human beings, and engaged in the abominable sin of sodomy. They committed these crimes until God was pleased to send the Spaniards to wage just war against them, until such time as they should voluntarily accept the Christian faith.[31]

Frozen fast in his anti-Indian position, Cervantes sometimes contradicted his own principal source, Gómara. Gómara, following Motolinía, had carefully described the Aztec system of law courts and the penalties meted out for various offenses.[32] Yet Cervantes declared that nothing in the Indian picture writings showed that the Aztecs had "judges to govern and keep them in justice." From a denial that the Aztecs lived under the reign of law he moved on to attack Aztec despotism. "Nothing argues more cogently for the barbarous and uncivilized state of these people than the fact that they obeyed their ruler without question, carrying out his most unjust orders without appeal or other recourse; this was truly a great tyranny."[33]

Cervantes also deviated from Gómara's treatment of the last Aztec king, Cuauhtémoc. Gómara, closely following the text of Cortés' Third Letter, assigned to Cuauhtémoc a dignified, knightly speech of surrender. For Cervantes this would not do. Wishing to diminish the stature of the Aztec hero, he described him as "inconstant and changeable, like the rest of his nation"; when he appeared before Cortés, he was "very fearful and timid, which are natural traits of the Indians." And Cervantes replaced Cuauhtémoc's laconic speech as given by Gómara with an insipid address in which the Aztec king greeted Cortés as "Invincible and most fortunate Captain."[34]

Cervantes showed even less mercy to the contemporary Indians than to their pagan forebears. They were cowardly and had no sense of honor. They were extremely vindictive and could not keep a secret. They were ungrateful and changeable. The majority were dull of wit; some had learned Latin, but made no progress in fields of knowledge requiring reasoning power. They were so lazy that if necessity did not force them to work, they would squat the whole day on their haunches, never speaking to each other. They were false swearers and even in confession rarely told the truth. They had plenty of land, yet preferred to sow next to Spanish pastures in order that cattle might damage their crops and give them a pretext for complaining to the judges and getting the

land away from the Spaniards. What they got for their labor (and
it was more than they were worth), they spent on wine or their
own evil-smelling drink, pulque, which they preferred because it
made them drunk more quickly. There was nothing they would
not steal, given the chance.[35]

The same implacable hostility to the Indian appears in the
Noticias históricas de la Nueva España of Juan Suárez de Peralta.
Fernando Benítez has drawn a diverting sketch of this eccentric
figure, who combined elements of the feudal hidalgo and the *pícaro*.
A son of the *encomendero* Juan Suárez and thus a nephew of that
Catalina who was Cortés' first wife, Suárez was a *segundón*, a
younger son with limited prospects at a time when royal efforts to
liquidate the encomienda were creating panic in the colonial aristocracy. His efforts to better himself included an unsuccessful attempt at blackmail and an equally fruitless bid to curry favor with
the Cortés family by blackening the reputations of his own father
and aunt. In 1579, despairing of the situation in Mexico, Suárez
departed for Spain in the hope of being taken under the wing of
a prosperous branch of his family. "The creoles," remarks Benítez,
"had lost a great historical battle"—the battle of the encomienda—
"and the paradise of the Indies became a miserably uncomfortable
spot." [36]

In 1580, moved by nostalgia for his distant *patria*, Suárez began
to write a history of the colony. Its chief historical value lies in
its eyewitness account of the atmosphere and events of the abor-
tive conspiracy (1565) to establish an independent monarchy
headed by the son of Cortés, and of its ferocious suppression.
Suárez introduced the book with a description of the Mexican land
and its natives. He offered some piquant variations on the theme
of Indian vices. Cervantes had already cited the Indian lack of
filial feeling; Suárez gave an example of this heartlessness. He had
known an Indian, Suárez assured his readers, who regularly beat
his unruly father and reported that the beatings greatly improved
the erring parent's behavior. Suárez also illustrated the Indian flair
for deceit by describing how Indian traders regularly adulterated
cacao beans, cochineal, and other products.

Just as Cervantes went one step beyond Gómara in his anti-
Indian passion, so Suárez went a step beyond Cervantes. Cervantes
had affirmed that Aztec Mexico had no judges who punished of-

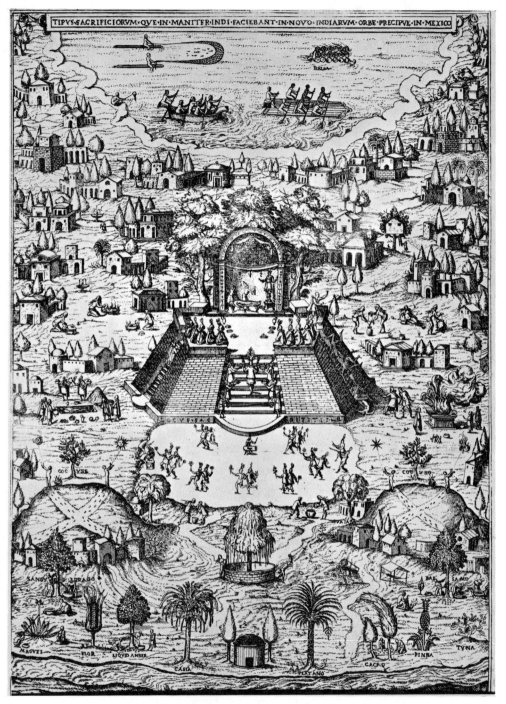

Imaginative drawing of an Aztec shrine and its environs by the Mexican Fray Diego de Valadés for his *Rhetorica Christiana* (Perugia, 1579). Courtesy Rare Book Division, The New York Public Library.

The Great Temple of México-Tenochtitlán as reconstructed by the twentieth-century pre-Conquest architectural historian Ignacio Marquina, according to the plans of Bernardino de Sahagún and Diego Durán. Photograph courtesy American Museum of Natural History, New York.

fenders and kept the peace. Suárez elaborated on this theme. Because there was no law among the Indians, injured parties had to avenge themselves or bear their wrongs in silence. He had heard that in some regions individuals who owed debts to many persons were torn into pieces which were divided among their creditors.

Like Gómara and Cervantes, Suárez stressed that the Indians were far better off than their forebears as a result of the Conquest. The Aztec lords used to take for themselves the best land in conquered provinces and make the inhabitants plant it to maize, cotton, and other crops. The Indians had to carry tribute produce on their backs to the Aztec garrisons and to the Aztec court at Tenochtitlán. An Indian had to trudge eight or more leagues with his burden. Since he received no food or pay for his labor, he must take along some tortillas or gather wild fruit or roots along the way. Now the Indians paid a moderate tribute in their own towns and carried nothing but their own supplies, for horses were used to carry heavy burdens.

Brooding over the injustices of Spain's Indian policy, Suárez asked why no tender-hearted defenders of the Negro slave arose to plead for his freedom. Every argument advanced in favor of the Indian applied to the Negro. Aside from one being darker than the other, they were not different from each other. Both were idolaters. Both ate human flesh (but here the advantage was with the Negro, for the Indians sacrificed their victims before eating them). Both Indians and Negroes sold themselves and each other into slavery. Las Casas' argument that it was unjust to enslave Indians because they had not made war on the Christians or attempted to destroy their religion also applied to the Negroes; both races had lived peacefully in their own lands until the coming of the Christians. Yet Spaniards of every condition—bishops, priests, even friars—held Negro slaves. By what argument of morality or conscience, asked Suárez, could an ordinary Spaniard be required to give up his Indian or Negro slaves, as the laws freeing all Indian slaves in America had done? [37] To Suárez' malicious question the defenders of the Indian could offer no satisfactory answer.[38]

The case of Baltasar Dorantes de Carranza illuminates the changing creole mentality of the twilight years of the sixteenth century. A son of Andrés Dorantes, conquistador, Dorantes de Carranza held important official posts in the colony; "the noble conquista-

dors and settlers of New Spain" designated him their procurator
to go to Castile in order to plead for relief of their poverty. Both
Suárez and Dorantes belonged to the decaying creole aristocracy
which saw its world collapsing in ruins as the Crown pressed its
program of liquidating the encomienda. Dorantes and his friends
lamented the ingratitude of the mother country toward the conquistadors and their sons; they viewed with spite the swarm of
peninsular newcomers who competed with creoles in the scramble
for *corregimientos* and other government appointments. A gifted
poet, Francisco de Terrazas, gave voice to the black mood of his
class:

> "Spain: to us a harsh stepmother you have been,
> a mild and loving mother to the stranger.
> On him you lavish all your treasures dear,
> with us you only share your cares and danger.
> Ungrateful Fatherland, Adieu! With
> your adopted sons live long and well,
> while we, consumed by unrelenting spite,
> departing one by one, from this sad world take flight." [39]

The generation of Dorantes and Terrazas knew that the battle
of the encomienda had been lost. A melancholy, resigned spirit
succeeded to the combative spirit of the *encomenderos* who had
dallied with the idea of deposing the viceroy and establishing an
independent Mexican kingdom. The passions of the encomienda
struggle were not entirely dead, but they had subsided sufficiently
to allow the colonists to view the Indians and their past with a
certain objectivity. Besides, the creoles were second or third
generation Mexicans who had a feeling of identity with the land
and its people that the conquistador could not know. They had
been suckled by Indian nurses, were familiar with the fluid music
of Náhuatl speech, and relished native dishes. Constant contact
between the two races produced some cultural rapprochement and
a literary sympathy on the part of the creole for the Indian,
together with an increased respect for his past. The first dawning
of Baroque sensibility in New Spain contributed to a growing
appreciation of things Indian.

These tendencies are apparent in the *Sumaria relación de las cosas
de la Nueva España* (1604) of Dorantes de Carranza. The practical

core of this chaotic work is a mass of genealogical data designed to assist the viceroy, the fountainhead of all favors, in distinguishing between legitimate sons of conquistadors and their bastards, between hidalgos and commoners, between Johnnies-come-lately and oldtimers in the land. Thrown in haphazardly are historical accounts, descriptions of Indian customs, and even specimens of colonial poetry, such as the poem by Terrazas given above.

By contrast with Cervantes and Suárez, Dorantes is a veritable model of fairness and objectivity in his comments on the Aztecs. Naturally he denounced their human sacrifice, but he stressed that it was a late development, that when the Aztecs first came into the Valley of Mexico their religion and sacrifices were extremely simple. By comparing Aztec divinities to Greek and Roman deities, Dorantes raised Aztec religion to the prestigious level of the great classical cults of Europe. He defended the Indians against the charge of being "barbarians" because they wore ear plugs and similar ornaments. After all, he argued, the Mexicans were not the only people who pierced their ears and inserted gold ornaments in them. Spanish women liked drop earrings, a mode "the French ridicule and mock, regarding these women as most barbarous." [40]

Dorantes praised the bravery and tenacity of the Aztecs in the Conquest, both the men and the women. Almost alone among the writers of this period he noted the unequal nature of a struggle between Spaniards armed with cannon, armor, pikes, and swords, and a people fighting with the primitive weapons of the Aztecs. "They fought valiantly, but after all they were a naked and unarmed people. To be sure, some knights, princes, and lords wore tiger, jaguar, or eagle headdresses as symbols of their bravery and prowess, with much featherwork on the head and arms, but these things served more for display and appearance than for defense; they offered no more protection than a linen shirt." [41]

Dorantes' uncertain attitude toward the Conquest sets him sharply apart from the Sepúlveda-Gómara school of thought. He conceded that the ends were good but the means dubious, "for to preach the Evangel with sword in hand and by shedding blood is a fearful thing." He surmised that divine displeasure with such conduct was behind the present poverty of the sons of the conquistadors. "It seems that their descendants atone for this arrogance, for hardly will one find a man of that stock who does not go about

with hand outstretched at the stranger's door." Yet, he mused,
"we know that the Saints aided the conquistadors in their battles,
and even the most holy Queen of the Angels came to their defense."
He ended on a note of perplexity. "It is impossible to grasp the
theology of this business, for the secrets and judgments of God are
inscrutable." [42]

Dorantes displayed considerable sympathy with the contemporary Mexican Indian. He did not catalogue Indian vices in the
manner of Cervantes de Salazar or Suárez. He described the natives
as "great cultivators of the soil." They were peaceful by nature
and did not covet the goods of others or seek to hurt their fellows.
He painted an idyllic picture of Indian women going to the river
for water: "One could paint them as images of Charity, each
holding two or three children in front, and another pressed to her
stomach, so that the mother cannot clasp the water jar, which she
carries on her head." [43]

Dorantes typifies the *Conquistador conquistado*, or rather the
conquistador's son conquered by his Mexican milieu. His detached
view of Aztec civilization, his doubts concerning the justice of the
Conquest, his favorable portrayal of ordinary Indian men and
women, reflect the dying down of the struggle over the encomienda, the first stirrings of Baroque sensibility, and the influence
of an incipient Mexican nationalism.

Las Casas was unquestionably the principal organizer and ideologist of the sixteenth-century Spanish movement in defense of
the Indians. His blazing militancy, his exalted humanism, continue
to arouse the admiration and affection of liberals and radicals and
the dislike of many conservatives.[44] To Sepúlveda's thesis of the
Indians' natural inferiority and depravity Las Casas opposed the
view that the Indians were completely rational beings, equal or
superior in capacity to all other races, and thus eminently qualified
to lead the good Christian life. The Aztec civilization of Mexico
was the prime exhibit in the Indian showcase that Las Casas
assembled to prove his argument.

The studies of Manuel Giménez Fernández have dispelled much
of the obscurity surrounding Las Casas' early life. The tradition
linking him to the great noble house of Casas or Casaus has no basis
in fact; his father was a modest merchant, his sister married a

carpenter. He did not study or graduate from the University of Salamanca, although he studied Latin and the humanities at Seville. The facts of his life after 1502 are well known. In that year Las Casas sailed for Hispaniola with the expedition of Nicolás de Ovando. In the islands he acquired land and slaves, prospered, and apparently felt no serious qualms concerning the morality of his mode of life, although he had become a priest. Not until his fortieth year did he experience a conversion, apparently the awakening of a dormant sensitivity and gentleness as a result of the horrors he saw about him. The *encomendero* Las Casas became a passionate foe of the encomienda and all its works. Henceforth, says Lewis Hanke, the story of the struggle of justice for the Indian became "to a considerable extent the story of his life." [45]

The character of Las Casas' thought remains a subject of dispute. Eduard Fueter scornfully disposed of Las Casas as a man of typically medieval mentality "who possessed a great mass of dead erudition and never lost an opportunity to overwhelm the reader with proofs of his Scholastic-theological learning." The truth is that Las Casas had an immense fund of classical and medieval learning and was a master of the Scholastic method of disputation. These weapons he employed in debate with deadly effect. Sepúlveda himself described Las Casas as "most subtle, most vigilant and most fluent, compared with whom the Ulysses of Homer was inert and stuttering." [46]

Certainly Las Casas was a spiritual son of Thomas Aquinas and Aristotle. But he was also a child of the Renaissance. This was the Las Casas who rested his case on the Indians on experience and observation above all, offered an environmentalist interpretation of cultural differences, and regarded with scientific detachment such deviations from European norms of conduct as human sacrifice and cannibalism. [47] This was the Las Casas who, speaking of geography, said of the ancients that, after all, they "did not know very much." [48] Alberto Pincherle observes that the medieval and Renaissance-humanist elements in Las Casas' thought blend into an indissoluble and complex unity. Some strands in the fabric of Las Casas' ideas appear to link him with even more modern currents of thought. Juan Friede, for example, speaks of the materialist tendency of Las Casas' philosophy, as illustrated by his stress on the economic roots of the colonialist ideology and by his insistence that the survival and material welfare of the Indians take precedence over all other interests, even those of their conversion.[49]

Las Casas discussed Aztec civilization most extensively and methodically in his *Apologética historia*, composed between 1527 and 1550, but not published until 1909. For the writing of this work he drew on half a century of American experience, including residence in Mexico and Guatemala, on letters from a network of correspondents throughout the Indies, and on many manuscript and printed scores. The *Historia* is, in essence, an immense accumulation of ethnographic data used to demonstrate that the Indians fully met the requirements laid down by Aristotle for the good life.[50]

Las Casas applied a rudimentary theory of cultural evolution in considering all Indian societies. This theory viewed all peoples as being in different stages of development, ranging from the stage of very primitive beginnings to the highest stage attained by fully civilized nations illuminated by the Evangelical Law. Progress from the first savage state common to all nations to a higher stage was made through the agency of great teachers who emerged within a group, or came from other lands, and taught men the art of living in houses, social intercourse, the utility of laws and government, and other civilized ways. All mankind was one; all peoples, no matter how barbarous or savage they might be, were capable of advancing along the road to civilization, "provided that the method that is proper and natural to man is used; namely, love and gentleness and kindness." [51] Las Casas' theory of cultural evolution enabled him to examine the customs and beliefs of an Indian people dispassionately and within the framework of its own culture. The theory also suggested comparison of Indian cultures with civilizations of other times and places that appeared to represent about the same stage of development. Las Casas used this approach to demonstrate the superiority of Aztec civilization over such cultures as the Greek and the Roman.

Las Casas devoted many pages to the material achievements of Aztec civilization. Aztec technology attracted his special attention. His account of the Aztec craft of featherwork illustrates his ethnographic precision and his pride in the creative capacity of his beloved Indians:

The activity in which they seem to excel over all other human intellects and which makes them appear unique among the nations of the earth is the craft they have perfected of representing with real feathers, in all their natural colors, all the things that they and other excellent painters can paint with brushes. They used to make many things of feathers, including animals, birds, men, cloaks or mantles, apparel for the priests, crowns or miters, shields and flyswatters, and a thousand other things. The feathers they used were green, red, golden, purple, crimson, yellow, blue or pale green, black and white, and all other colors, mixed and pure. None was tinted by human industry, but all were natural, taken from different birds. For this reason these people greatly valued all sorts of birds and made use of every variety; they kept the feathers of even the smallest birds found on land or in the air for their special hues and blended them to beautify their work. They set the feathers on a cotton cloth placed on a frame. Just as their painters took paint from different shells or containers in which they kept their colors, so the featherworker had his little boxes or jars in which he kept these feathers, each kind or color being kept separate from the others. Let us say that he wished to represent a man's face, the figure of an animal, or some other thing. If he needed a green or red feather, he would take that from its box, and so on. He fastened these feathers to the cloth with a certain paste. If the artist wished to show the eyes of a man or an animal, he used black and white feathers to show the pupil of the eye, and with these feathers he distinguished the various parts of the eye with all the delicacy of a great painter using an extremely fine brush. Surely this is a wondrous thing.

Before the coming of the Spaniards they used this art and craft to make marvelously perfect things: a tree, a rose, a blade of grass, a flower, an animal, a man, a bird, a tiny and delicate butterfly, a hill, a stone or cliff, all so natural or lifelike that if they represented a living thing the work seemed alive, and if they represented an inanimate object the copy seemed natural. They showed thereby how subtle were their intellects, how great their ability. After the Spaniards came, the Indians had incomparably greater scope and opportunity for demonstrating the quickness of their intellects, the purity and unobstructed nature of their internal and external senses and powers, and their great capacity. Our religious images and *retablos* being large and well painted in different colors, the Indian featherworkers could give larger play to their talents and distinguished themselves even more in their subtle and novel art by copying our things. One of the greatest beauties of their featherwork, especially in an object of large size, is the placing of the feathers in such a way that, viewed from one direction, the object looks golden although there is no gold in it; viewed from another direction it appears iridescent, though green is not its principal color, and so on, all with marvelous luster and grace. To achieve this, an artist will spend a whole day without eating or drinking, arranging and removing feathers to see what combination of colors looks best. In order that his work may possess great variety of luster and color and appear more beautiful, he will look at it from different directions and under different conditions, now regarding it in sunlight, now in shadow, sometimes at night or twilight, sometimes by a weak light and again by a strong light, sometimes athwart and from the corner of the eye, sometimes from the opposite direction.[52]

Las Casas never denied himself an opportunity to compare Aztec civilization with the great civilizations of the antique world. In a discussion of Aztec warfare, he cited a statement of Moctezuma that the Aztecs permitted the enemy state of Tlaxcala to survive for fear that their warriors might become soft, lazy, and cowardly if they lacked enemies on whom they could practice the art of war. A most prudent reply, observed Las Casas, one that recalled the advice of Scipio Africanus Major to the Romans not to destroy the city of Carthage lest the Roman people, deprived of the opportunity to make war, lose their soldierly virtues and become degenerate.

Las Casas used his comparative method to equate the Aztec orders of knighthood with the Spanish military orders of Santiago, Alcántara, and Calatrava. Like these orders, he noted, the Aztec societies admitted only sons of lords of very noble descent. Las Casas described with relish the medieval cast of Aztec ceremonies of investiture, in which the new knight would stand with head bent, displaying great devotion and humility. In such matters, "these people surpass many other nations, for they possess from birth the innate qualities of humility and meekness." [53]

Las Casas' comparative method yielded large gains in the field of religion. Las Casas had no difficulty in demonstrating that the Aztecs excelled over all the peoples of the ancient world in the number and splendor of their temples. Mexico had more major temples than all the great cities of the Roman Empire, Egypt, and Greece combined. The city of Cholula alone had more than three hundred principal temples! In the number, variety, and value of their sacrifices the Aztecs were obviously superior to their counterparts of the ancient European world. Citing the fertility rites, temple prostitution, and Priapic festivals of that world, Las Casas argued for the relative purity of the Aztec religion.

Las Casas' handling of the thorny problem of Aztec human sacrifice in his debate with Sepúlveda shows him at his most ingenious and resourceful. To begin with, he minimized the extent of the practice. He denied Sepúlveda's claim that the Aztecs sacrificed more than twenty thousand persons a year. He insisted that the number must have been less than one hundred or even less than fifty a year. Otherwise the land could not have been so densely populated as it was at the coming of the Spaniards. Turning the tables on Sepúlveda, Las Casas asserted that more human victims had been sacrificed by the Spaniards to their beloved Goddess of Greed every year since the discovery of America than by the Indians to their gods for a century before that event.[54]

Las Casas' second argument was notable for its daring. Almost every nation on earth, reasoned Las Casas, had practiced human sacrifice at some time in its history. Human sacrifice, although contrary to the Evangelical Law and an aberration in Christian eyes, was not evidence of depravity on the part of the people who practiced it. On the contrary, it argued for a profound religious feeling and a most elevated conception of God, because the peoples who offered the most precious sacrifices to God (whether the true or a false god) could be regarded as the most religious of all. He concluded that since "the peoples of New Spain offered the most costly, painful, and horrendous sacrifices, they surpassed all other peoples in their esteem and natural understanding of God, and consequently in clear understanding, sound judgment, and the use of reason." [55] The horrified Sepúlveda denounced Las Casas' position as "impious and heretical." We have no record of the reaction of the judges, since they made no final report.

The Aztec homilies in which Aztec parents urged honesty, obedience, charity, and other exemplary traits upon their children, proved to Las Casas the excellence of the Aztec system of rearing children. Again he compared the Aztec achievement with Greek and Roman models, to the advantage of the former.

"Did Plato, Socrates, Pythagoras, or even Aristotle leave us exhortations to the virtuous life that were better or more natural

or more necessary than those these barbarians delivered to their
children? Does the Christian religion teach us more, save the Faith
and what it teaches us of invisible and supernatural matters?
Therefore, no one may deny that these peoples are fully capable
of governing themselves and of living like men of good intelligence
and, more than others, of being well ordered, sensible, prudent,
and rational." [56]

Note that Las Casas agrees with Sepúlveda in calling the Aztecs
"barbarians." In his *Apologética historia*, however, Las Casas subjected the term to an elaborate semantic analysis that robbed it
of most of its sting. The Aztecs were not the barbarians of
Sepúlveda, brutish and irrational slaves by nature. Las Casas denied
that such individuals existed anywhere except as freaks of nature,
defectives such as were found in Spain itself. Nor were they
barbarians in the sense of being marked by a special ferocity,
cruelty, or perverse nature. On the contrary, they were the meekest
and mildest of men, assured Las Casas, and obeyed their kings with
a wonderful humility. They were barbarous only in one major
sense; they lacked the Christian religion. The Romans and Greeks
and other advanced peoples of antiquity were also barbarians, for
no people could be free from grave flaws in laws, customs, and
way of life before it accepted the Catholic religion. The Aztecs
were barbarians in some other special and secondary senses of the
word. They lacked letters and did not speak or understand Spanish.
In this last sense, commented Las Casas, just as they seem barbarians
to us, so we seem barbarians to them.[57]

Las Casas rarely criticized specific aspects of Aztec culture.
An instance of such criticism occurs in his *Tratado sobre los indios
que se han hecho esclavos*, written to prove that all Indian slaves
held by the Spaniards were held unjustly. Many of these slaves
had been bought or obtained in other ways from Indian slaveowners, and Las Casas undertook to show that the Aztecs had
many unjust ways of making slaves, "because they lacked knowledge of the true God and the Evangelical Law." They committed
these injustices because they were not restrained from evil by a
salutary fear of Hell or encouraged to practice virtue by the hope
of gaining eternal bliss in Paradise. Injustice tainted their wars for
the same reason, and therefore the slaves they made in war were
often unjustly acquired. This criticism of Aztec slavery and war

of course served Las Casas' overriding purpose of defending the Indian.

Even as he denounced Aztec slavery as unjust, Las Casas hastened to assure his readers that Indian slavery was very mild, very different from the European institution. "The term *slave* does not mean for the Indian what it means to us; it means nothing more than servant, a person who has a special obligation to serve me in some ways. For an Indian, being another's slave was much the same as being his son. The slave had his own home and hearth, his land and property, his wife and children. He enjoyed the same liberty as his free neighbors, save for the times when his master needed his assistance in the construction of a house, or for work in the field, or the like. The slave did his work at the time he chose, frequently in the intervals in his own business; the rest of the time he had for himself, as did a free person. The owners treated their slaves very gently and mildly, as if their slaves owed them nothing." [58]

The Spanish lawyer and royal official Alonso de Zorita went beyond Las Casas in expressing enthusiasm for Aztec institutions. Zorita wrote his *Breve y sumaria relación de los señores de la Nueva España* in retirement, between 1566 and 1570, in delayed response to a royal order requesting information on the Indian tribute problem. His sources on Aztec life and manners included manuscript treatises prepared by such notable scholars among the regular clergy as Motolinía and Andrés de Olmos. Zorita's work sheds important light on Aztec social organization and tribute systems. Even his warmest admirers, however, must agree that Zorita bathes Aztec society in an unreal rosy glow. As I have written elsewhere, "His frequent contrast of an idealized past with a somber present makes the *Breve y sumaria relación* a study in unrelieved whites and blacks. . . ." [59]

Zorita, no less than Las Casas, brought to the writing of his book a vibrant social passion. His sympathy for the oppressed Indians, his indignation at the charges of Indian inferiority and wickedness made by men of such high standing in sixteenth-century scholarship as Sepúlveda, help to explain the vehemence with which he defended the Indian character and achievement. To these sources of his attitude we may add the conviction, shared by many religious reformers and intellectuals of the Renaissance, that Europe was

in moral decline. Disturbed by the decay of medieval standards
and values, by the fever of money-making that had seized on
European society, sensitive spirits began to question the value of
civilization and learning, to eulogize simplicity and innocence. The
discovery of America and the Noble Savage of the West Indies
gave a stimulus to this "disillusioned recoil from the civilized
world." These humanists, however, were eminently civilized men,
and they were inherently proud of the material and cultural
achievements of the Western societies whose values they doubted.
Thus they were delighted when there came into view a civilization
like the Aztec, at once simple and complex, unspoiled and refined,
childlike yet capable of majestic achievements in political and
social organization, in art and technology. As Hoxie N. Fairchild
shrewdly observes, "they are uncertain whether to admire the
Indian because he is so civilized or because he is so savage." [60]
Zorita, a true son of the Renaissance, reflects both the disillusionment of many humanists with the fruits of civilization and their
somewhat discordant attitudes toward the high Indian civilizations:
now Zorita eulogizes the simplicity and innocence of the Mexican
Indians, now he compliments them on their polish and refinement,
on their intricate political and social order.

Zorita early set the tone of his book with an account of the
Aztec rules of succession to the crown. He noted that these rules
stressed capacity to govern rather than close relationship to the old
ruler. "Like the great Alexander, the rulers were more concerned
with leaving a successor capable of governing their lands and vassals
than with leaving their inheritance to sons or grandsons." He
described an investiture ceremony in which the people tested the
ruler-elect by hurling insults at him and otherwise trying his
patience. This led Zorita to praise the Indian character as molded
by their ancient institutions:

"These people are by nature very long-suffering, and nothing
will excite or anger them. They are very obedient and teachable;
if you blame or scold them for some negligence or vice, they
display great humility and attention, and their only reply is, 'I
have sinned.' The more noble they are, the more humility they
display. . . . I speak of those who are in the state of their natural
simplicity, for those who have been made slaves or deal with the
Spaniards are greatly changed." [61]

Zorita ascribed to Nezahualcóyotl and Nezahualpilli, rulers of Texcoco, the wisdom of Solomon and Solon. Aztec justice was swift and exact. Judges were never moved by influence and displayed great rectitude in their judgments. Rulers and judges imposed the penalty of the law strictly, making exception of none, and did not even spare their own guilty children. Zorita quoted approvingly an Indian chief who said to him: "When we were pagans, there were very few lawsuits, men told the truth, and cases were decided very quickly. There was no difficulty in determining which party had justice on its side, and today's snares and delays were unknown." [62]

Zorita took particular care to refute the charge of writers of the Sepúlveda-Gómara school that the Indians were guilty of sodomy. He declared that Aztec judges diligently sought out sodomites and punished their offense by death, for they held it a grave sin and one seen only among beasts. He also exonerated the Indians of the charge of chronic drunkenness. "No one could drink wine without permission from the lords or judges, and its use was allowed only to the sick and to persons more than fifty years of age." Spaniards were much mistaken if they believed that the Indians had been free to drink as they pleased. On the contrary, the drunkard was punished very severely by having his hair cropped publicly in the marketplace, after which his house was razed.[63]

Only one oblique reference to such blots on the Aztec record as human sacrifice and cannibalism interrupted Zorita's flow of eulogy. "To be sure, they had some unjust and wicked laws, some cruel, tyrannical, and most mistaken laws; for they were like blind men in that they lacked the Evangelical Law. But the same is and has been true of other infidels." [64]

Zorita approvingly quoted from Cortés' glowing description of Tenochtitlán and other Indian cities. Yet Zorita's vigilant eye caught a flaw in the conqueror's view of Aztec civilization. Cortés had fallen into the same snare of prejudice and ignorance that held fast those Spaniards who allowed the Indians "no human trait other than the shape of men." Immediately after praising the admirable good order displayed by the Aztecs in all their affairs, Cortés had called them a barbarian, uncivilized people. In contrast with Las Casas, Zorita would not admit the use of this word in reference to the Aztecs in any sense whatever. To prove Cortés' fallacy, Zorita launched on a careful analysis of the term.

Men commonly made the mistake of calling infidels "barbarians," observed Zorita. The ancient Egyptians and Greeks, infidels all, were very wise peoples, as Zorita proved with a wealth of pedantic citations. Sometimes men followed the example of the Romans and the Greeks, who called peoples of different speech, customs, and idolatry "barbarians." Zorita cited Saint Paul to make short shrift of this error: "Therefore if I know not the meaning of the voice, I shall be unto him that speaketh a barbarian, and he that speaketh shall be a barbarian unto me." Again, some Spaniards called the Indians "barbarians" on account of their great simplicity, for they were by nature free of duplicity and cunning; this made them easy game for Spaniards who sold these simple trusting people all kinds of baubles in exchange for very valuable objects. "But we could also call the Spaniards barbarians in this sense," remarked Zorita, "for at the present day, even in the best-governed cities, little toy swords and horses, and brass whistles, and little wire snakes, and castanets with bells, are sold in the streets. . . . Many foreigners come with this stuff from their lands; they also bring merry-andrews, puppets, tumblers, acrobats, and dancing dogs. . . . With these and other childish tricks these jugglers gain much money. . . . If this can happen among such enlightened folk as ourselves, in such well-ordered commonwealths, why should we wonder at the innocence of the Indians?" [65]

Zorita ended his discussion of the term "barbarian" by asking his readers to judge whether these Indians, "who observed their laws so strictly as to impose the most rigorous penalties on their own sons, were at all inferior to the famous Romans and other ancient peoples in justice and government, or less ingenious in justifying their wars. Whoever considers the question maturely must conclude that they were the equals of the ancients in all respects, or fell but little short of the ancients in their achievements." Unfortunately, unlike the ancients, the Indians did not have many excellent historians to record their exploits. Regretfully, Zorita noted that the picture writings in which the Indians recorded their history were either badly damaged or lost; the only persons who had seriously attempted to study these writings were a few friars. [66]

Zorita's romanticism reached its climax in his account of the manner in which the Aztec peasantry performed their communal tribute labor. By subtle touches he built up an image of slight, delicate creatures gaily trooping to their light collective labors, and returning to domestic warmth and comfort in their small, cozy homes.

In the old days they performed their communal labor in their own towns. Their labor was lighter, and they were well treated. They did not have to leave their homes and families, and they ate food they were accustomed to eat and at the usual hours. They did their work together and with much merriment, for they are people who do little work alone, but together they accomplish something. Six peons will not get as much done as one Spaniard, for since they do not get much food they have little stamina and do not do as much work.

The building of the temples and the houses of the lords and public works was always a common undertaking, and many people worked together with much merriment. They left their houses after the morning chill had passed, and after they had eaten what sufficed them, according to their habits and means. Each worked a little and did what he could, and no one hurried or mistreated him for it. They stopped work early, before the chill of the afternoon, both winter and summer, for they all went around naked or with so few clothes it was like wearing none. At the slightest rainfall they took cover, because they tremble with cold when the first drops fall. Thus they went about their work, cheerfully and harmoniously.

They returned to their houses, which, being very small, were cozy and took the place of clothing. Their wives had a fire ready and laid out food; and they took pleasure in the company of their wives and children. There was never any question of payment for this communal labor.[67]

To the small number of ardent defenders of Aztec civilization we may add the Augustinian Jerónimo Román y Zamora, who composed a work on the antiquities of Mexico and Peru about 1573. Román drew heavily on the writings of Motolinía and Las Casas. Using the comparative method of Las Casas, Fray Jerónimo easily demonstrated that the religious rites and ceremonies of the "barbarian" Aztecs were not as cruel or impure as those of the Romans, for example. The excellent laws and chastisements of the Aztecs showed that they did not live in disorderly bands (*behetrías*), as some supposed. Indeed, they displayed very good judgment in all their affairs, and discerned through the use of natural reason all that rational men needed to know. With saintly anger, the good friar broke out:

"I cannot bear it when I hear men say that the Indians were and are bestial and of mean understanding. The people who say this think that if a man is not malicious, frightful, and does not have the Devil in him (as they say), he is not a man. These people forget that pity, meekness, and humanity are God-given virtues and are more in conformity with the natural law than the qualities of cruelty, harshness, and terror. When I consider the good regimen of those Indians, it seems to me that they lacked naught of what is required for a goodly commonwealth, for they had natural order in all things and were highly civilized." [68]

CHAPTER FIVE

The Aztecs and the Great Debate: II

The vision of Aztec society in the writings of the Spaniards who may be called moderates reflected their views on the larger question of Spain's Indian policy. Men of goodwill all, the moderates sought to reconcile the interests of the colonists with the welfare of the Indians. Motolinía and others dreamed of a fruitful fusion of the two races and cultures under the sign of a Christianity restored to its original purity.[1] The position of the moderates required them both to defend the Indians against those colonists who, blind to their own interests, made excessive demands upon the natives and to defend the colonists against radicals like Las Casas who denied that the settlers had any just claim to Indian tribute and labor. This struggle on two fronts helps to explain the dualism of the moderate attitude toward Aztec civilization. The case of Vasco de Quiroga, humanist, judge, and bishop, illustrates the confusion this attitude sometimes introduced into the thought of the moderates.

Quiroga, born into a Spanish noble family about 1477, belonged to that class of legists (*letrados*) on whom the Catholic Sovereigns and their successors largely relied to achieve and maintain their goal of royal supremacy. Before coming to Mexico, he had seen colonial service in the Spanish possession of Oran in North Africa. In 1529, "in a spirit of dedication," he accepted a position as *oidor* or judge on the Second Audiencia sent by Charles V to replace the totally discredited First Audiencia in the government of New Spain. Together with his colleagues, Quiroga wrestled with the problems of Indian slavery, tribute, and the encomienda, seeking to bring order out of the chaos left by the Conquest. The sufferings and virtues of the Indians deeply touched his sensitive spirit.

In a letter to the Royal Council of the Indies of August 14, 1531, he advocated bringing the scattered and needy Indians together in villages under the tutelage of friars. Here "by working and tilling the soil, they may maintain themselves with their labor and may be ruled by all good rules of polity and by holy and good and Catholic ordinances." In the same letter he stressed the plasticity of the Indian character and the fitness of the natives for Christianity. "Anything can be done with these people; they are most docile, and, if we proceed with due diligence, they can easily be taught Christian doctrine. They possess innately the instincts of humility and obedience, and the Christian impulses of poverty, nakedness, and contempt for the things of this world; they go barefoot and bareheaded with the hair long like the Apostles; in fine, they have very tractable minds, void of error and ready for impression." [2]

Later, influenced by a reading of Thomas More's Utopia, Quiroga proposed to the Spanish Crown the establishment of Indian cities, organized on the lines of More's ideal commonwealth, in which the natural virtues of the Indians would be preserved and perfected by training in the Christian religion and polity. Impatient with the Royal Council, which ignored his proposals, Quiroga used his own resources to found the pueblo-hospitals or refuges of Santa Fe. In his communities Quiroga established, among other features, collective ownership of property; systematic alternation between agricultural and craft labor; work for women; the six-hour working day; distribution of the fruits of collective labor according to need; and the shunning of luxuries and of all occupations that were not useful. [3]

Quiroga's fervent piety drew him into the priesthood. In 1538 Archbishop Zumárraga consecrated him Bishop of Michoacán, an office he held until his death in 1565. The Indians of Michoacán still revere "Tata Vasco." He is one of the most attractive figures among that vanguard group of humanist clergy who worked for the material and spiritual redemption of the Mexican Indians in the sixteenth century.[4]

The principal source for Quiroga's ideas on Aztec society is his *Información en derecho* or legal brief of July 24, 1535. This long, rambling document had its origin in a dispute over Indian slavery. The Second Audiencia had brought a royal order forbidding further enslavement of Indians. To this, the colonists reacted with angry protests; and the Crown, yielding to pressure, reversed its stand in February, 1534. The members of the Audiencia, collectively and individually, denounced this retreat on legal, moral, and social grounds.

Quiroga's memorial answered the argument of the colonists that they held their slaves legally by purchase from Indian slaveowners. To admit the legality of such transactions, Quiroga wrote, was to open the door to innumerable evils. The Indian lords would sell their subjects to the Spaniards for profit or to revenge themselves upon commoners who had denounced their idolatries and drunken sprees to the authorities. Like Las Casas, who wrote a treatise on the same subject, Quiroga stressed the differences between Aztec and European slavery. He had made a careful study of this question, obtaining information from native elders. Indian slaves rendered only a few light services to their masters and owned their own homes and other property; their condition, in short, differed little from that of their masters. Theirs was not the harsh chattel slavery of Europe but recalled rather the patriarchal relationship between master and servant in the Golden Age as described by the Roman poet Lucian in his *Saturnalia*.

Quiroga's mind insensibly wandered from the subject at hand to dwell on the Indian character and way of life in their pagan state. His musings reflected the characteristic Renaissance disillusionment with European civilization and the humanist yearning for a return to the presumed simplicity and innocence of the world's childhood. Quiroga saw the Indians as living in that Golden Age which in the Old World had been turned into an age of iron by the greed of men. The Indians' behavior was similar in all respects to that of the happy subjects of King Saturn described by Lucian. They were given to "the same customs and manners, the same equality, simplicity, goodness, obedience, and humility, the same festivities, games, pleasures, drinking, idling, pastimes, and nudity, and lacked any but the poorest of household goods nor had any desire for better, and had the same clothing, footwear and food, all such as was provided free by the fertility of the soil, and almost without labor, care, or seeking on their part."

The lives of the Indians were peaceful and free of care for the morrow. They had no affinity with the turbulent world of Europe, with its pomps and vainglory, its restless strivings and discontents. Even the songs, dances, and entertainments of the Indians reminded Quiroga of those of the Golden Age; he mentioned the graceful *volador* ceremony in which performers who had been attached to ropes wound around a platform at the top of a high pole leaped off into space and circled the platform like birds until they reached the ground.

These gentle, peaceful, and humble people needed only to be taught the pure doctrines of Christianity and a fully civilized way of life. The Holy Spirit had inspired an Englishman of super-human genius, Thomas More, to show how this could be done without loss of the natural Indian virtues of innocence and sim-plicity. Although he had never seen an Indian, More had written a book in which he described a people amazingly like the Indians in character and customs. The Utopian commonwealth seemed to Quiroga to offer a perfect instrument for the formation of an ideal human type possessed of both the virtues of the unspoiled child of nature and the principles of primitive Christianity.[5]

So far we are on Lascasian ground. Quiroga also delighted in the exquisite manners and polished speech that formed part of the Indians' pagan heritage. In his memorial he gave an example of this Indian refinement and civility. A group of Indian nobles from the town of Otumba appeared before the Audiencia to request the court to confirm the election of one of them as governor. "They notified us of his election with incredible harmony and order and excellent reasoning. They said they had unanimously chosen one man as chief because he could govern them best (the man was there, wearing a mantle different from those worn by the others) and said they would regard it as a favor if we would confirm him. After the Audiencia had confirmed him in the name of His Majesty, they took leave with the same ceremony and stately speech. Each thanked us in turn, followed at the last by the elected chief who addressed us as eloquently as if he had studied oratory all his life." [6]

These eulogies of the Indian character and culture vanish abruptly, disconcertingly, when Quiroga, moving freely from point to point, addresses himself to the question of the justice of the wars waged by Spain against the Indians. Quiroga sharply rejected the argument of those who invoked the authority of Thomas Aquinas and other theologians to denounce such wars on the grounds that the Indians had never done any injury to the Christians. Quiroga averred that this doctrine applied only to pagans who observed the natural law, led a civilized, orderly life, and did not worship many gods. It did not apply to barbarous peoples such as the Aztecs, who lacked good polity and were savage, bestial, and ignorant. "To this day," declared Quiroga, "they are barbarian nations, and their chiefs are tyrants who oppress the weak and humble mace-huales." Quiroga regarded as irrelevant the argument that the Indians had never invaded Spain or attacked the Christian faith. War was a justified means of breaking the irrational Indian resistance to the spread of the superior Spanish culture and the Christian religion. To be sure, once Indian resistance had ended the Spaniards should go about the work of conversion in a Christian spirit, "going among them as Christ came to us, doing good, not evil, showing pity, not cruelty, preaching to them, healing the sick, and performing all other Christian works of mercy, goodness, and pity." [7]

Bent on proving the barbarous character of Aztec civilization, Quiroga argued that the Aztec political system did not conform to any of the three ideal forms described by Aristotle (monarchy, aristocracy, and constitutional government) but represented the perversions of those forms (tyranny, oligarchy, and democracy), none of which had in view the good of all the people. Aztec rule was a tyranny because Moctezuma so oppressed his people that they dared not raise their eyes to look at him or wear fine mantles or footwear in his presence. He was not respected as a mortal king by a free people, but adored and feared as the god of a captive nation. The Aztec system was an oligarchy because the Indian nobles did not seek the common good but pursued their private advantage by exploiting the commoners. Even now the Indian chiefs collected more tribute from the commoners than was due to the Crown or their *encomenderos* and pocketed the difference;

and they hired the Indians out as carriers, and practiced other abuses. Finally, in regions such as Jalisco where there were no rulers or lords, there prevailed the worst of all political systems, democracy. In those parts the Indians lived in complete ignorance and bestiality, without law, order, or good customs of any kind.[8]

The contradictions in Quiroga's views on Aztec civilization arose from the clash within the man himself, from the duel between the intellectual and the worker in the Indian vineyard who must come to terms with a stubborn reality. The Quiroga who flagrantly idealized the pagan past was the Christian humanist, heartsick at the desolation wrought by the Conquest, the dreamer of Utopian dreams who founded islands of charity and cooperative life in a sea of exploitive encomiendas, *corregimientos*, and haciendas. The Quiroga who denounced Aztec rule was the judge who knew at firsthand the oppressive ways of Indian nobles and defended the Conquest, with all its cruelties, in the name of Spain's civilizing and Christianizing mission. This was the Quiroga who supported the encomienda as necessary for the maintenance of the Spaniards, upon whose presence depended the success of that mission.[9]

The ambivalence of Quiroga reappears in the writings of Motolinía. Motolinía was one of the famous "Twelve," that pioneer group of Franciscan missionaries who landed in New Spain in 1524. A vision of multitudes of Indian souls waiting to be saved "even as the day of the world declined unto the eleventh hour," in the words of their leader Martín de Valencia, inspired the Apostolic Twelve. With their missionary activity Motolinía and his brethren combined an energetic defense of the Indians that aroused the wrath of the colonists and caused them to protest against the friars' meddling and ambition to rule. By the middle decades of the century, however, many of the friars were of a different mind. Royal intervention had partially stabilized the labor and tribute situation, the worst abuses against the Indians had been corrected, and the majority of religious assumed positions more favorable to the encomienda. By 1555 Motolinía was assuring the Emperor that the condition of the Indians had greatly improved, and he was making bitter attacks on Las Casas.

Motolinía was a diligent student of Indian languages and antiquities. His major published works are the *Historia de los indios de la Nueva España*, written in 1541, and the *Memoriales*, a work composed about 1542 and left in draft state. The *Memoriales* is especially valuable for its rich store of ethnographic material, obtained from Indian informants and picture writings. Motolinía's writing was usually clear and vigorous but unpolished. He collected and collated large amounts of data and recorded his findings in a careful, impartial manner (when not carried away by religious fervor or other partisanship).

Alternation of praise and censure and carefully qualified judgments characterize Motolinía's approach to Aztec civilization in the *Memoriales*. His caution sometimes led to such strange involved passages as the following: "Blinded by their idolatry, these natives frequently took light for shadow and often chose evil over good. Because their palate was deranged they took the sweet to be sour, and the sour to be sweet. Yet they had some praiseworthy laws and customs by which they were governed, though not all their laws were so just and equal as to give each man his due according to the requirements of true justice." [10]

Motolinía's comment on the controversial subject of sodomy among the Indians illustrates his careful weighing of evidence. "I know," he wrote, "that in two or three provinces far from the province of Mexico sodomy was tolerated, and the reason why they permitted this wicked, abominable sin was that they lacked the Divine Law and that the Devil, wishing to increase his mastery over them, deluded them into believing that their gods had this custom and that therefore it was licit: this their histories show. However, since it is a vice most repugnant to nature, the Indians always regarded it as an evil, a great dishonor and infamy. In the provinces of Mexico and Texcoco, together with the towns subject to them, sodomy was punished with death." [11]

In the *Memoriales*, Motolinía acquitted the Indians of the charge that they were greatly given to drinking in pagan times. "Having informed myself fully of the use they made of wine [pulque], I find that these natives condemned drunkenness as a very evil thing and denounced it just as the Spaniards do. They used wine only with the permission of their lords and judges." [12]

Realism characterized Motolinía's discussion of Aztec economic and social institutions. Where Zorita saw patriarchal relationships between benevolent lords and obedient commoners, Motolinía perceived marked inequalities of wealth, and much poverty. "Not all nations are so just that they equalize and divide their lands with string and measuring rod, as did the tribes of Israel. Everywhere some have more and others less. The earth is large enough for all to have a share in it, if properly distributed. But this is not done, with the result that some feast while others fast. So it was among these Indians of New Spain." [13]

A comparison of two versions of a traditional speech made by the Aztec high priest to the ruler-elect clearly reveals Motolinía's superiority over Zorita in this matter of realistic reporting. The texts of the two men correspond closely until the subject of human sacrifice is reached. Zorita's *Breve y sumaria relación* presented the high priest's remarks in an obviously bowdlerized form: "You must give special care to the service of God and his temples, so that there will be no lack of what is needed for the sacrifices." Motolinía's text brought out more directly the pagan essence of the speech. "You must see to it that the sun and earth continue on their courses; (which means, in plain speech), consider, Lord, that you must toil in order that the sun god may not lack his sacrifice of blood and food that he needs in order to continue on his course and shed his light on us; you must do the same for the earth goddess, that she may give us provisions." [14]

Despite Motolinía's habitual caution, some aspects of Aztec social life won his unqualified approval. The strict discipline that Aztec parents used in rearing their children he cited as a model that Christians could well follow. He praised the Aztec marriage rules as conforming fully to the Evangelical Law. He admired the obedient, submissive bearing of Aztec wives toward their husbands, remarking that they were not like many Spanish women, "who think the wife instead of the husband should be master of the house; what is even more monstrous, they order their husbands about!" [15]

God, Motolinía believed, had endowed these Indians with an intelligence superior to that of many other nations, as shown by the incredible speed with which they had mastered many Spanish crafts and arts. Their minds were not slow or diffuse in operation, like those of some other nations, but quick, yet composed and serene. [16]

The rigorous Aztec discipline and laws had formed a character that recalled to Motolinía the traits of the founders of the primitive Church. "They are incredibly patient and long suffering, and meek as sheep. I do not once remember having seen one of them nurse a grudge. They, the humble and scorned, live only to serve and work. Great is their patience and endurance in time of sickness. They sleep on the ground, with an old mat for a bed, at best, with a stone or piece of wood for a pillow. Their houses are very small, some being of thatch. The saints sought such a life, and we read about it for our instruction and wonder thereat. Now we may read about it in the book of life and see it with our own eyes, and what we see is more than we have read and learned, indeed more than we could believe." [17]

Motolinía agreed with the view commonly held among the Mendicants that the Indian character and behavior had suffered as a result of the Conquest and its aftermath. "The Indians," he observed, "say that the coming of the Spaniards and their wars caused a great upheaval in the land. As a result (they say) they have lost their old justice and punishments, their order and harmony, their authority to punish and put down offenders. That is why lying, perjury, and adultery are no longer punished as they once were." [18]

Yet Aztec civilization appeared in a very different light when Motolinía viewed its sway in its religious or supernatural aspect. Then it assumed a dark and sinister hue. Motolinía compared the rulers of Tenochtitlán not to Alexander or Scipio Africanus, as did Las Casas and Zorita, but to the ferocious Assyrian despots. "So strong was this city that it seemed no human power could take it. It dominated the whole land, and its lord Moctezuma gloried in his throne and the multitude of his vassals and the strength of his city, just as Aphahad gloried in his city of Ecbatana. He sent his messengers throughout the land and they were well served and obeyed; from afar came messengers sent by other rulers who had heard of his power and came to bring him gifts and render obeisance. Against the people who rebelled or disobeyed he sent his captains, even to many distant lands, and he showed himself a most severe avenger, another Nebuchadnezzar of Assyria." [19] With Oviedo and Gómara, Motolinía regarded the Conquest as a divine chastisement of the Indians. God, he wrote, delivered the great city into the hands of His people because of its many sins.[20] After the destruction of "the tyrannical reign of the Devil," the reign of Jesus Christ began in New Spain.

By 1555, when Motolinía wrote his famous letter to Charles V, all trace of sympathy with Aztec civilization had vanished. "Your Majesty should know," Motolinía wrote, "that when the Marqués del Valle entered this land, Our Lord God was much offended, men suffered very cruel deaths, and the Devil, our adversary, was served with the greatest idolatries and slaughters of men that the world had ever known." [21]

The work of Bernardino de Sahagún was the supreme achievement of the Franciscan ethnographic school that Motolinía helped to found. Fray Bernardino came to New Spain in 1529. He was a founder of the famous Colegio de Santa Cruz de Tlatelolco, established by the Franciscans in 1536 for the education of boys of the Indian upper class. In 1557 he was ordered by his provincial, Fray Francisco de Toral, to compile in Náhuatl all the information needed by the missionaries in their work of converting the Indians. This project grew into the monumental *Historia de las cosas de la Nueva España*. In effect, Sahagún created an encyclopedia of Mexican culture, with a structure closely resembling that traditionally given medieval encyclopedias. Before beginning his work, Sahagún drew up a series of questions covering the subjects on which he sought information. The answers that he obtained from carefully selected Indian informants were written down in Latin letters by young Indians trained in the Colegio de Santa Cruz. Sahagún pursued, unknown to himself, "the most rigorous and demanding method of the anthropological sciences." [22] The Spanish version that he prepared later was a paraphrase rather than a translation of the Náhuatl text.

Sahagún's practical motive was to arm the missionary with the knowledge he needed to discover the presence of pagan religious rites and practices, and to combat them. To this practical motive he soon joined a humanistic purpose. As he discovered the rich world of Aztec culture, with its treasures of poetry, science, and lore of every kind, he fell under its spell.

Luis Villoro has made a penetrating analysis of Sahagún's attitude toward Aztec civilization. [23] For Sahagún that civilization had two aspects or profiles, one natural, the other supernatural. The angle from which it was viewed determined whether the culture or one of its elements had a negative or positive aspect. An Aztec prayer, for example, might illustrate the elegance and subtlety of Aztec literary expression, or it might be viewed as a cunning snare set by Satan to entrap the Indians.

For the missionary, the supernatural aspect of Aztec civilization was of course decisive. The first books of Sahagún's Spanish version of his *Historia* dealt with the world of Aztec gods, festivals, temples, and rites. This was a veritable realm of Satan, seething in the lurid glow of unimaginable sins. Lucifer, father of all wickedness and lies, presided over this realm; he wore the mask of the supreme god Tezcatlipoca. In their blindness the Mexicans accepted the rule of the Father of Lies and of his many servants, devils large and small, adoring them in the form of idols. At the instigation of their evil demons the Mexicans offered them their own blood and that of their sons, and also the hearts of their neighbors, for it was foolishly believed that these demons had the power to grant men's wishes and free them from all ills.[24]

Satan intervened in all the acts of this fallen people. Under his influence they adopted the abominable practice of cannibalism. At the end of every cycle of fifty-two years the Aztecs renewed their collective pact with the Devil. "When they lighted a new fire and performed this solemnity, they renewed the pact they had made with the Devil to serve him." [25]

Satan had inspired the Aztecs to deify not only the forces of nature but even mere mortals. Thus they raised to godhood a man named Huitzilopochtli, "a sorcerer and friend of the Devil, an enemy of mankind, ugly, frightful, cruel, turbulent, an inventor of wars and enmities, responsible for many deaths and riots." They did the same with a man named Quetzalcóatl, "a great sorcerer and friend of the devils," who now burned in the perpetual fires of Hell.

Viewed from this supernatural perspective, the Conquest was a decisive turning point in the history of Mexico and this whole American continent. For Sahagún, the Conquest, instrument of God and vehicle of conversion, was the punishment imposed on the Indian for his sins; he could achieve total purification only by the destruction of his civilization and the death of his gods.[26] With the Conquest the reign of Satan ended in New Spain; the Kingdom of Christ began. Sahagún then sounded a recurring theme in the writings of the Mendicants: "It seems that in our time the Lord God has been pleased to return to the Church what the Devil stole from her in England, Germany, and France, in Asia and Palestine." [27]

Aztec civilization had another facet, its natural aspect. Denied divine illumination because of their culpable, stiff-necked rejection of God's grace, the Indians, guided only by natural reason, had established a civilization superior to the cultures of Greece and Rome.

Both Sahagún and Las Casas rejected the notion of an innate Indian inferiority. Spaniards were wrong to judge the Indians by what they now were. The Conquest had destroyed their culture so completely that they were but a shadow of the people they once had been. Some Spaniards called them barbarians, but in fact they surpassed some nations that were considered highly civilized. "We may judge what they once were from what we see of their present capacity for all the mechanical arts; they show ability to learn all the liberal arts and even theology, as experience has shown; they are able to endure hunger and thirst, cold and lack of sleep. They are equally capable of becoming good Christians if properly instructed in the faith." [28]

Sahagún took pleasure in drawing parallels between episodes of ancient Mexican history and incidents in Greek and Roman history. Tula, "that great and famous city, very rich and refined, wise and powerful, suffered the fate of Troy." Sahagún compared the Cholulans, refugees from Tula, to the Trojans who fled from the destruction of Troy and founded Rome. "Just as the Romans built the Capitoline for their fortress, so the Cholulans built by hand the great mound that stands near Cholula and resembles a mountain or large hill." The Tlaxcalans, sworn enemies of the Aztecs, were the Carthaginians of the ancient Mexican world.[29] Sahagún drew similar comparisons in the religious field, comparing Huitzilopochtli to Hercules, Tezcatlipoca to Jupiter, and the goddess Chicomecóatl to Ceres.

Sahagún asserted that the ancient Mexicans surpassed the Greeks and Romans in material achievements, in political and social organization, in the arts and sciences. The Aztecs had "perfect philosophers and astrologers, and were very skillful in all the mechanical arts." [30] These achievements were all the more remarkable in view of the Indian inclination toward vice, sensuality, and indolence. These tendencies were not caused by organic defects or infirmities but were traceable to the baneful influence of the American climate and constellations. The unfavorable American environment operated upon the Spaniards who came there, and still more upon American-born Spaniards or creoles. "They are Spanish in appearance, but not in temper and character; I believe that this is due to the climate or to the constellations of this land." [31]

Sahagún attributed the Aztecs' success in checking or repressing these evil inclinations to their excellent educational system. Training in the home, in the school, and in the temples combined to produce an austere youth, hard of body, profoundly moral and religious, and filled with a high sense of duty to family, state, and the gods. With more than a trace of regret, Sahagún observed that the Spaniards had destroyed not only the Aztec religion but their whole way of life in the belief that it was idolatrous and barbarous. Along with idolatry they destroyed the educational system that restrained the natural sensuality and other evil impulses of the Indian. For this reason drunkenness and other vices were now rampant among the Indians.[32]

Sahagún related how the friars attempted to revive the Aztec system of education in the early years. "When we learned that in the old days they reared the boys and girls in the temples, where they taught them discipline and the cult of their gods and loyalty to the state, we adopted this method of training in the monasteries. The children slept in a house built just next to ours. We taught them to rise at midnight and recite the matins of Our Lady, and the hours in the morning; we even taught them to flog themselves at night and to say mental prayers. But they were not obliged to perform physical labor as they once were and as their fiery sensuality required, and they ate better than they had been accustomed to eat in the old days, for we used with them the mild and charitable ways that we use among ourselves. Consequently they began to feel sensual passions and to give themselves to the pleasures of the flesh." The friars had to dismiss the children from the monasteries. After that they slept in their parents' homes and came to school mornings to learn reading and writing; this was the system presently in use.[33]

When the aged Sahagún wrote these words in 1576, he could

look back on an apostolate of forty-five years in New Spain. A profound pessimism filled his review of the state of the Indians. Pestilence was wiping them out. The survivors were tainted with moral and religious decay; they boldly celebrated their ancient festivals at which they sang songs and danced dances with a hidden pagan meaning. The vice of drunkenness daily grew worse. The pride of the Franciscans, the Colegio de Santa Cruz, was also in full decline. Pestilence had nearly emptied its halls of Indian students; those who remained were demoralized. Sahagún bitterly complained that neither "laymen nor churchmen were disposed to favor or assist the Colegio, not even with a penny." [34] The Indian ship and its rich cargo of culture seemed to be going down; Sahagún had the consolation of knowing that he had made a careful inventory of its contents. Dispersed and largely forgotten for centuries, the immense corpus of Sahagún manuscripts was gradually re-discovered and partially published in the course of the nineteenth and twentieth centuries.

The Dominican Diego Durán shared Sahagún's dualistic view of Aztec civilization. Durán was born in Seville, and was brought to Mexico as a child of seven or eight. He passed his childhood in Texcoco, the cultural capital of the Aztec Empire, and became thoroughly steeped in Indian ways. In 1556, aged about nineteen, he entered the monastery of Santo Domingo in Mexico City. He was active in missionary work but also devoted himself to the study of Aztec antiquities. His affection for the Indians, despite his occasional scolding tone, shines through the pages of his *Historia de las Indias de Nueva-España e islas de tierra firme*.

Durán also wrote his book with the practical motive of helping other priests to combat the concealed pagan elements in native life. He warned his colleagues that Christianity could not be firmly established in New Spain until all superstitions and pagan rites were erased from the memory of the Indians. He chided those early friars who, "with much zeal but little wisdom," destroyed the Indian picture writings. The result of this folly was that the clergy did not recognize idolatry practiced before their very eyes. Durán saw the persistence of paganism in every aspect of Indian life, "in their dances, their markets, their baths, in the songs that mourn the loss of their ancient gods and lords, in their meals and banquets." The same idolatry could be observed at their burials, weddings, and birth ceremonies, and even "in their sowing and reaping, the storing of their grain, the cultivation of the earth, and the building of their houses." Since the Indians practiced their pagan rites in secrecy, these abominations eluded the clergy.[35]

Durán composed his history with the aid of Indian picture writings, glossed for him by native informants, and of written accounts. The abundance of his sources and the Indian point of view that dominates his work rank it with Sahagún's *Historia* as "one of the most serious and truthful documents available for the reconstruction of the history of the ancient Mexicans." [36]

Durán also took a providential attitude toward Aztec history and the Conquest. Mexico before the coming of the Spaniards was under the direct sway of Satan; the Conquest was a divine chastisement of the Indians for their sins. Although the origin of the Indians was hidden in mystery, Durán inclined toward the theory, also favored by Motolinía, of their Jewish origin, for God had promised to punish the ten lost tribes of Israel severely for their sins. Durán could say nothing good of the Indians in their character of an accursed race. Like the Jews, they were timid and cowardly, as shown by the way great numbers of them fled before Cortés and his few hundred Spaniards. Like the Israelites, the Aztecs were much given to ceremony, burned incense, slew their own children as sacrifices to the gods, and ate human flesh.[37]

If the Conquest was of divine inspiration, Durán could not say the same of the methods of the conquistadors. He described Alvarado's massacre of the Indian nobility of Tenochtitlán as "an atrocious, tyrannical cruelty" and implicated Cortés in its planning. He tended to accept the Indian assertion that Moctezuma's death was caused by the Spaniards. Telling of a hermitage, called "of the Martyrs," erected by the conquistadors in memory of some comrades who had been slain by the Indians, Durán observed wryly that God alone knew if He accepted that martyrdom. "I hold it a fearful thing to preach with sword in hand, taking by force what belongs to another." He even denounced the actions of the famous chaplain of Cortés, Fray Bartolomé de Olmedo. Olmedo should have been suspended and excommunicated, wrote Durán, for "I understand that he washed his hands in innocent blood more often than Pilate washed his hands with water at Christ's death." [38] These remarks reveal Durán's ideological kinship with Las Casas.

As his work progressed and he immersed himself more deeply in Indian sources, Durán's attitude toward Aztec civilization perceptibly changed. The disparaging comments of his opening pages gave way to more respectful views and eventually to frank eulogy. Durán's special enthusiasm was reserved for the Aztec political and social order. Possibly reflecting his own hidalgo background, Durán praised highly the hierarchical, class-conscious spirit of Aztec society. He observed that in Mexico, as in Spain, there had been three careers open to those who sought advancement. The first was war, the second was the Church, and the third and least honorable was trade. Aztec rulers properly rewarded the brave and virtuous in order to spur others to follow their example. Royal palaces and temples had different accommodations for individuals of different classes, in order that "men of good blood might not be placed on a level with others of low extraction." Durán cited this fact to prove that the Indians "were not so brutish and barbarous as we make them out to be." Quite the reverse. In their pagan state they had as good a government and way of life as any nation in the world could have, "especially in distinguishing the *caballero* from the *hidalgo*, and the *hidalgo* from the *escudero*, and the *escudero* from artisans and plebeians of base birth." In his own time, Durán lamented, things had come to such a pass that one could not tell a *caballero* from a muleteer, or an *escudero* from a sailor, for embroidery and fine dress made all men equal.[39]

Durán scaled the heights of eulogy with a series of rhetorical questions. "What land ever had such just and righteous ordinances for the commonwealth? What land had kings who were so much feared and so well obeyed? What land had grandees and lords who were so much respected or so well rewarded for their exploits? What land had more caballeros, hidalgos, and valiant soldiers who sought to distinguish themselves in the service of their king? What land had priests and ministers of the gods who were accorded such great reverence, respect, and fear, not just by the common sort but by kings and princes?"

With Sahagún, Durán recommended the strict discipline the Aztecs used in bringing up their children as a model for Spaniards to follow. Movingly he described the grief of aged Indians as they commented on the demoralized Indian youth of the present time, "lost, shameless, drunkards, murderers, evildoers, and thieves who ran about with their concubines." These ancients declared that in pagan times young people were not so bold. None dared drink pulque except very old men, and these were allowed to drink to warm their blood and relieve the infirmities of their age. Rulers who were found drunk were stripped of their office or even slain; drinking was permitted only at certain festivals. Adulterers and men who kept concubines were punished with the same severity.[40] Durán's manuscript gathered dust for centuries; it may be doubted whether the Spanish political climate in 1581, when Durán wrote the last lines of his book, would have tolerated publication of his blunt criticism of the Conquest or his extravagant praise of Aztec political and social institutions.

The Jesuit José de Acosta was more cautious on both counts. His *Historia natural y moral de las Indias*, which appeared in 1590, immediately achieved popularity.[41] Acosta attended Jesuit schools and entered the Company of Jesus at an early age; in 1571 he sailed for Peru as one of the first Jesuit missionaries in the New World. He held high offices in the Company and wrote, in addition to the *Historia*, a Latin work entitled *De procuranda Indorum salute* which discussed, among other matters, the question of just wars, the encomienda, and other aspects of the Indian problem. His position on Indian policy was that of a typical moderate, combining support for the encomienda with earnest appeals to the *encomenderos* to perform their Christian duty toward the Indian. Acosta even regretfully accepted as a harsh necessity the notorious *mita* or system of Indian forced labor in the mines.[42]

Acosta's writings reveal a distinct advance in methodology over previous studies of Indian history and civilization. Without deviating one iota from the orthodox Catholic and Scholastic world view, his work reflected the new rationalist and critical currents of thought of the late sixteenth century. His commonsensical approach to some problems of American history is shown both by his rejection and easy demolition of the myth claiming a Jewish origin for the Indians and by his suggestion, based on reasoning from analogy, that the first men and animals in the New World came over a strait or land bridge linking Asia and America. The many precise observations in the *Historia* on plants, animals, minerals, and atmospheric and climatic conditions indicate his scientific interests and temper. He does not hesitate to point out Aristotle's errors when the philosopher's statements contradict Acosta's own experience.[43]

Previous writers on the Indians tended to ignore the great cultural differences between native groups, treating all as though they were a single nation. Acosta seems to have pioneered in the classification of Indian societies according to their cultural level. He distinguished three classes of barbarians, a category which for Acosta included all pagan nations on the face of the earth. The first class, illustrated by the Chinese, differed little in their way of life from the civilized peoples of Europe. The second class comprehended those nations who possessed governments, magistrates, armies, and organized religions, but lacked letters and a body of scientific and philosophic knowledge. The Aztec and Inca civilizations belonged to this class. Barbarians of the third class were savage peoples like the Caribs, who were hardly human, since they had no laws, kings, or magistrates. Aristotle had such people in mind when he spoke of barbarians who could be hunted down and tamed like beasts.[44]

In the *Historia* Acosta gave two principal reasons for having written on Indian religion and political and social institutions. First, he wished to provide other clergymen with the information necessary for the work of conversion. Second, he believed it important to know the political and social institutions of the Indians and to govern them according to their ancient laws and customs wherever these did not contravene the teachings of the Church. Ignorance of those institutions was responsible for the widely held opinion that the Indians were a bestial people, so dull of wit that they scarcely merited the name of men. "I see no better way of dispelling this pernicious error than to show the excellent order and polity under which they lived when they governed themselves. Certainly their way of life had many barbarous and irrational features, but there were many others, truly admirable, that show their natural capacity to be taught." Acosta's principal source for Inca history and culture was a relation by the lawyer Juan Polo de Ondegardo; his chief source of information on the Aztecs was a work by the Jesuit Juan de Tovar, who by order of Viceroy Martín Enríquez had "made a diligent and copious inquiry into the ancient histories of that nation." Acosta also used other "grave authors who in writing or by word of mouth informed me adequately concerning all that I report."[45]

An all-encompassing providential interpretation guided Acosta in his final judgment of the high Indian civilizations. The rise of the Inca and the Aztecs from their first humble and primitive condition to mastery over great empires formed part of a divine plan. By no accident, Christianity passed over to America precisely when the Aztec and Inca Empires had reached the peak of their growth and power. The unity and internal peace imposed by those empires greatly aided the work of conversion. These empires also aided the missionary efforts by bringing formerly dispersed peoples together into sedentary communities and by promoting the use of a common language, such as the Mexican or Náhuatl, spoken throughout the Aztec Empire. Equally providential were the great factional struggles and civil wars that weakened the empires on the eve of the Conquest. Acosta also saw God's hand in the fact that Moctezuma and Atahualpa admitted the Spaniards into their lands without offering resistance.

Even the snares by which Satan held the Indians captive led mysteriously to the same great objective of their conversion. Tenochtitlán and Cuzco were Satan's cities, his Rome or Jerusalem, until ejected therefrom by the Spaniards. Satan had cleverly imitated the usages of the Church, establishing his own hierarchy of pontiffs, priests, acolytes, and deacons; he even had communities of monks and nuns of a sort. In his great presumption the Devil went so far as to steal the names used in the Church of Christ, for the name the Mexicans assigned to their high priest was *papa*. But the very arms that Satan stole from the arsenal of God—the ceremonies of communion, confession, baptism, and the like—God turned against him, for knowledge of these rites served to prepare the Indians for the acceptance of Christianity.

The bad as well as the good features of the Indian empires served God's great design. Even before the coming of the Spaniards the Indians were weary of the intolerable burden of tribute and sacrifices, but fear and awe of their priests made the Indians continue to obey them and execute their demands. The discontent of the natives with the heavy Aztec and Inca yoke caused them to welcome the Spaniards as liberators and gladly accept the mild law of Christ.

In conformity with his general position, Acosta accepted the justice of the Conquest. But he had difficulty fitting the methods of Cortés and Pizarro into the divine plan. He expressed his misgivings in a cautiously worded passage that trailed away into a statement of the inscrutable ways of God and the heavy burden of guilt borne by both the Spanish and the Indian sides.[46]

The Franciscan Gerónimo de Mendieta spoke his mind with greater candor. His *Historia eclesiástica indiana* documents for New Spain the collapse of the premises on which the moderates rested their solution for the Indian problem. The partial stabilization achieved by royal intervention in the Indian labor and tribute question soon ended; in the 1560's the situation began to deteriorate sharply. From the accession of Philip II, the Crown, caught up in its own acute financial crisis, made mounting tribute demands on a shrinking Indian population. The great epidemic of 1576 to 1581 seriously aggravated food and labor shortages and increased the burdens imposed on the surviving Indians. Meanwhile the Mendicants, the sole remaining defenders of the natives, lost parishes and influence to the secular clergy, the latter being firmly supported by the Crown. Within the orders themselves, affluence and routine had corroded the high ideals of the first missionaries. The apocalyptic gloom that pervades portions of Mendieta's book reflected his awareness of these conditions.[47]

Mendieta, having entered the Franciscan order in Spain at an early age, came to New Spain in 1554 and was assigned to the monastery at Xochimilco. He studied Náhuatl under Fray Andrés de Olmos and achieved such mastery of the language that it is said he preached in it with greater fluency than in his native Castilian. In 1575 he was appointed guardian of Xochimilco. He began his *Historia* in 1573 at the orders of superiors in Spain, but did not complete the work until 1596. It was published in 1870 by the Mexican scholar Joaquín García Icazbalceta, who suggested that its bitter denunciation of the *encomenderos* had prevented publication of Mendieta's book. John L. Phelan cites another possible reason: Mendieta's outspoken criticism of the Indian policies of Philip II, whose reign he characterized as a "Silver Age," or worse, by contrast with the Golden Age of Charles V. Mendieta's primary aim was to record the Franciscan missionary achievement in New Spain, but he introduced this historical account with a lengthy account of Aztec religion, government, and way of life, remarking that this material contained many salutary lessons. The reader would learn how low the human understanding could sink without the illumination of faith and grace; he should also feel remorse that these Indians, of less capacity and intelligence than ourselves, had a better way of life under their pagan government and institutions than under Christian rule.[48]

Mendieta's views on Aztec civilization so closely resemble those of the other writers whose work has been surveyed in this chapter that a detailed analysis is unnecessary. He shared the admiration of those writers for Aztec education, jurisprudence, and government. The Indians, who had never heard of Aristotle, followed his rules for the education of children better than any other people in history, declared Mendieta. To prove this, he included in his *Historia* copious selections from the remarkable Aztec Huehuetlatolli or Speeches of the Ancients. As early as 1562 he indicated his preference for the Aztec social order in remarkably bold language. "Anyone who compares the two regimes," he wrote a Franciscan official, "must conclude that their condition and way of life, with the religion and rites that they had, were better than their state today." Formerly, he asserted, the Indians were free not only of the vice of drinking but also of the rage for litigation in which they now consumed their energies and estates.[49]

Ultimately, as Phelan has shown, Mendieta broke with the basic premise of the moderate school, that "Spanish laymen were entitled to a decent standard of living in a manorial economy based upon Indian labor." He proposed instead a program of total segregation of the Indians from the Spaniards. Mendieta would banish all Spanish officials from his Indian commonwealth, except an all-powerful viceroy who should be a father to his people and give the friars a free hand in governing the natives.[50] These proposals fell on completely deaf ears.

In a document entitled "Consideraciones de Fray Hierónimo de Mendieta cerca de los indios de la Nueva España," Mendieta presented his credo on the Indian character and capacity before and after the Conquest. The document is undated, but appears to be a definitive statement of his views.

I believe [wrote Mendieta] that the Indians are rational men, descended like ourselves from Adam and Eve; this is an article of faith with us. Consequently they are capable of being converted, without which they must inevitably go to Hell.

I believe that they are not wild or savage, but excessively mild and meek, friendly and docile, as experience has shown.

I believe that they displayed great wisdom, good order, and prudence when they governed themselves. In pagan times they observed the commandments of their religion (granted that it was an evil religion) very strictly, punished offenses very severely, and managed their political affairs with great good order and foresight. As a result they multiplied marvelously, as the first Spaniards in the land could see.

I believe that under Spanish rule their spirits were totally broken; they lost their old way of life without learning that of the Spaniards. As a result they were reduced to the state, capacity, and intelligence of children of nine and ten who need to be ruled as minors by tutors, and they should be regarded as such. . . .

I believe that these Indians whom we scorn as being so dull and wicked show in their works (and these are the only things by which they can be judged) more signs of virtue and Christianity than are found in many of our own nation.

Finally, Mendieta gave his explanation of the causes of the great epidemics that seemed to threaten the extinction of the Indian race. Some Spaniards, "who take little note of their own sins," argued that God sent these plagues to punish the Indians. Mendieta offered a very different explanation: God showed his mercy to the Indians by removing them one by one from an evil world before their faith weakened under the intolerable burdens to which they were subjected.[51] Mendieta's unrelieved pessimism underlines the total collapse of the moderate dream of harmonious coexistence or even fusion of Spanish and Indian communities united by common Christian, Hispanic, humanist ideals.

Before that vision failed, the friars scored some important if short-lived cultural successes. The Mendicants assigned a special role in their program of social reform to the creation of educational institutions in which Indian upper class boys could receive instruction in the humanities, including Latin, logic, and philosophy, as well as Christian doctrine. Before the most important of these centers, the Franciscan Colegio de Santa Cruz de Tlatelolco, suffered its sharp decline in the 1560's, it produced a harvest of graduates who were devout Christians and competent Latinists, yet took pride in their Indian cultural heritage.[52] These students of Tlatelolco were the collaborators of Sahagún, Olmos, Motolinía, and other Mendicant scholars in the enterprise of preserving for posterity the history and culture of the ancient Mexican world. Exposure to Plutarch and Livy, to the whole Greco-Roman tradition, heightened the Indian students' historical awareness, awoke in them the desire to preserve the glories of their own pagan past, and provided them with models to imitate. Some of these men, as well as other educated Indians and mestizos who did not attend the Colegio de Santa Cruz, wrote important histories which, in common with the writings of the friars, display an ambivalent attitude toward Aztec civilization.

The mestizo chronicler Diego Muñoz Camargo wrote a *Historia de Tlaxcala*, composed between 1576 and 1595 but not published until 1870. Son of the conquistador Diego Muñoz and an Indian woman, he was probably of illegitimate birth. Muñoz Camargo married an Indian noblewoman of Tlaxcala, where he acquired extensive properties through inheritance and purchase. His involvement in the factional struggles of the Indian community resulted in a royal order (1589) demanding the expulsion from Tlaxcala of Muñoz Camargo and some other mestizos "for their abuse of the Indians and for setting a bad example," but evidently this order was not carried out.[53]

Thanks to its services to the Spanish cause in the Conquest, Tlaxcala enjoyed, for a time, a privileged position among the provinces of New Spain. The desire to defend the privileges of Tlaxcala and its native nobility certainly figured among Muñoz Camargo's motives for writing his book. His work resembles some other Tlaxcalan writings of this period in that it tends "to misrepresent certain features of the Tlaxcalan past, to dignify the local historical narrative, and to suggest greater and earlier degrees of accord between Tlaxcalans and Spaniards."[54] For his information Muñoz Camargo relied on Gómara and some Sahagún manuscripts; he also drew on the memories of native informants.

Muñoz Camargo left no doubt that he considered himself first of all a Spaniard. In his account of the Conquest he consistently spoke of the Spaniards as "los nuestros" (our people); he referred to the Tlaxcalans as "nuestros amigos" (our friends). To the Indians, regarded by Muñoz Camargo as an alien race, he assigned negative traits in the manner of Gómara or Cervantes de Salazar. The Indians were great liars, vainglorious and jealous, especially over women; this jealousy was the cause of many deaths. They were very cowardly when alone, but regular demons when accompanied by Spaniards. The majority were very simple-minded people and lacked all reason and honor as "we" (the Spaniards) understand those terms. Muñoz Camargo conceded that Indian morality had been much better before the Conquest. "In the old days they told the truth, especially to their lords . . . , they kept their word with each other on pain of death. Now, because of the excessive liberty they enjoy, they are great liars and cheats. To be sure, there are all kinds among them, and many of their merchants are truthful and very dependable, and have learned many of our ways." [55]

Muñoz Camargo denounced the pagan religion of his Indian forebears in the strongest terms. As one might expect, Muñoz Camargo assigned the origin of human sacrifice to the ancient tribal enemy of the Tlaxcalans, the Aztecs or Mexicans. In this connection he made a statement that his nineteenth-century editor, Alfredo Chavero, dismissed as a vulgar canard. Muñoz Camargo explained that the Mexicans first ate human flesh to revenge themselves on their enemies, but their "ravenous appetites grew until it became customary for them to eat each other, like demons; they even had public slaughterhouses in which human flesh was cut up just as beef and veal are cut up today." [56]

Muñoz Camargo emphasized that the Indians had some glimmerings of light that enabled them to discern, however darkly, the truths of Christianity. They had some inkling of a Supreme Being in Whom all things had their beginning and some notion of an afterlife. They even had a confused idea of angels inhabiting the sky whom they called gods of the air. In this manner Muñoz built a bridge between the pagan faith of his Indian ancestors and the Catholic religion.

Muñoz Camargo was at his most tendentious in relating the events of the Conquest. He had the Tlaxcalan Indians invoking the Spanish Saint James in the heat of the struggle with the Aztecs. He invented other imaginary events. One was the baptism of Moctezuma; another was an attack by the Cholulans on an embassy sent to them by Cortés, a fiction needed by Muñoz to justify Cortés' massacre at Cholula. Finally, Muñoz distorted the whole course of Spanish-Tlaxcalan relations by wiping from the pages of history the resistance initially offered to the Spaniards by Tlaxcala.

Muñoz Camargo was eager to identify himself fully with the victors, but did not completely deny his Indian heritage. A certain nationalism emerges from his enthusiastic description of the beauties of the Tlaxcalan landscape. But there was more; Muñoz felt himself part of a larger community of Náhuatl speech and culture. He described the excellencies of the Náhuatl tongue, spoken the length and breadth of New Spain before the Conquest; even barbarian tribes prided themselves on their ability to speak it. "This is the most ample, copious language ever spoken, suave and tender, yet dignified and stately, rich in words, easy and flexible; one can easily compose verses in Náhuatl according to the rules of meter and scansion." [57]

Muñoz again showed his Tlaxcalan nationalism in his rejection of the claim of some "speculative writers" that Moctezuma could have destroyed Tlaxcala had he wished, but preferred to leave the Tlaxcalans "like quails in a cage" in order to give his warriors exercise in war and keep a source of sacrificial victims. Muñoz retorted that were this true the Tlaxcalan lords would not have been so eager to join the Christians in war against the Mexicans. In fact, he wrote, there was such mortal enmity between the Tlaxcalans and the Aztecs that they never contracted marriages or entered into other close relations such as they maintained with other peoples of the region. In this fixed enmity Muñoz saw the hand of God, who wished to preserve the Tlaxcalans as his instrument for the achievement of the Conquest.[58]

Muñoz Camargo's nostalgic description of the life of the Tlaxcalan nobility before the Conquest suggests his ties of blood and sentiment with the Indian upper classes. The Indian lords delighted in the pleasures of the bath, hunted, and took their ease in delightful woods and groves. They kept jesters, jugglers, and dwarfs in their courts for their amusement. They feasted and drank; "they adored the god Bacchus, god of wine and all intoxicating drinks, under the name Ometochtli, and held a festival for him once a year." [59]

In the last analysis, Muñoz Camargo's position on the Mexican pre-Conquest cultures identifies him with the moderates rather than with writers of the anti-Indian school. A typical moderate effort at balance appears in his summing up: "Among these barbarian nations were many good customs and many evil, tyrannical, and irrational customs." [60]

Texcoco, cultural capital of the Aztec Empire, produced a gifted chronicler in the mestizo Juan Bautista Pomar, son of a Spanish conquistador and an Indian noblewoman. On his mother's side he was descended from the philosopher-king Nezahualcóyotl. Pomar prepared his *Relación de Texcoco* in response to a royal request for information on political and social organization in ancient Texcoco. He completed the work in March, 1582, but it remained in manuscript until Joaquín García Icazbalceta published it in 1890.[61] It is written in excellent Castilian by an obviously well-educated, thoughtful, and humane individual. Immediately apparent, however, are the tendencies common to all the productions of the Indian and mestizo school of writers on Aztec themes: the spirit of local patriotism, the search for Christian antecedents in the pagan past, and stern denunciation of paganism qualified by nostalgic references to the advantages of the old order.

Pomar's account of his research methods stressed the thoroughness of his preparation. To make the work as truthful as possible, he wrote, he had consulted knowledgeable Indian elders and collected ancient songs and picture writings. If there were gaps in his information concerning the ancient rites and customs, one reason was that all the best-informed persons, the priests and the children of King Nezahualpilli, were dead. Another reason, he observed with a trace of bitterness, was that the picture writings in which the Indians used to record their history, were lost. During the Conquest the picture histories stored in the royal archives of Nezahualpilli had been burned, "a thing that his descendants continue to mourn, having been left in ignorance of the deeds of their ancestors." The noble owners of other picture writings had destroyed them in the time of Fray Juan de Zumárraga, first Archbishop of Mexico, for fear of being charged with heresy and sent to the stake, as had happened to a son of Nezahualpilli, Carlos Ometochtzin.[62]

Pomar's *Relación* reflects an intense pride of race and lineage, his conviction of the cultural and moral superiority of the Acolhuas or Texcocans over all other Náhuatl-speaking peoples. His historical account concentrated on the two illustrious rulers Neza-

Scene of human sacrifice before the shrines of Tláloc and Huitzilopochtli in Part IX of the De Bry *Grands Voyages* (Frankfurt am Main, 1602). Courtesy Rare Book Division, The New York Public Library.

Le Grand Temple de VITSLIPUTSLI dans la Ville de MEXIQUE

The Great Temple Square of México-Tenochtitlán. Engraved by Bernard Picart in 1722 for J.-F. Bernard's *Cérémonies et coutumes religieuses des peuples idolâtres* (Amsterdam, 1735). Courtesy Department of Rare Books and Special Collections, Princeton University Library.

hualcóyotl and Nezahualpilli, father and son, "because they were very virtuous and taught their subjects good customs and a proper mode of life." These kings treated their subjects so well that their reigns were a Golden Age. Pomar remarked with some boldness that the Indians continued to remember and speak well of those kings, "especially now when they suffer oppression and affliction." These kings wielded absolute power of life and death, but ruled with such even-handed justice that the laws they framed were adopted by Tenochtitlán and Tlacopan. Indeed, it was a common saying throughout the land that Texcoco gave the law to all the other provinces, that the Indians learned from Texcoco how to live like civilized men, not beasts. In Texcoco, even slaves were accorded humane treatment; a slave whose master treated him cruelly could win his freedom by fleeing to the royal palace, and the king gave the master a small payment for his loss.[63]

Like Muñoz Camargo, Pomar ascribed the "diabolical invention" of human sacrifice to the Aztecs of Tenochtitlán, who introduced it after the conquest of Atzcapotzalco. Believing that no sacrifice could be more pleasing to the gods than the flesh and blood of men, the Aztecs offered to the gods the prisoners made in the war of Atzcapotzalco. At first they practiced this custom moderately, but as their power grew so did the number of their victims. From Tenochtitlán the practice was extended to Texcoco, Tlacopan, Chalco, Huexotzinco, and Tlaxcala.[64]

Having established Aztec responsibility for human sacrifice, Pomar went on to show that his Indian forebears had certain intimations of Christianity. Nezahualcóyotl and Nezahualpilli offered sacrifices to the gods, but they doubted that they were truly gods, suspecting them to be only objects of wood and stone. Nezahualcóyotl felt the strongest doubts on this score. Searching for light, he found it in the ancient songs and prayers of his ancestors. These songs, of which only fragments remained, contained many beautiful names and titles for God. Their sense was that there was only one God, the Maker of Heaven and Earth, who supported all things and dwelled in a place above the nine celestial tiers, who was invisible and never appeared in human or any other form. Pomar also insisted that the Texcocoans never addressed the idols representing their many gods by their individual names, but by the name *in Tloque in Nahuaque,* meaning "Lord of Heaven and

Earth." This proved their belief in only one God. They also had some knowledge of the immortality of the soul.[65]

With a muted sadness, Pomar compared the material and moral conditions of the Indians before and after the Conquest. Before the Conquest the Indians enjoyed excellent health; pestilence was unknown. Death came only to the very old or to very young infants. If an Indian died between those extremes of infancy and old age, it was taken as a very strange, evil omen. Their forebears had never seen such epidemics as had struck them since their conversion to Christianity. It was commonly said that the Indian population was only a tenth as large as it had been at the time of the Conquest.

Pomar declared that considerable inquiry into the subject had not given a completely satisfactory answer to the question of why the Indians formerly enjoyed such good health and why they suffered so much from disease at present. But all who gave the matter thought were agreed that a principal cause was the excessive labor performed by the Indians on Spanish farms and haciendas and in the mines. Hunger and fatigue weakened the Indians to the point where the slightest illness carried them away. Lack of will to live contributed to their debility. Pomar referred to the "affliction and fatigue of their spirits because they had lost the liberty that God had given them; for the Spaniards treat them worse than slaves." [66]

An authentic native voice sounds in the *Crónica mexicana* of Fernando Alvarado Tezozómoc, the only full-blooded Indian among the three chroniclers considered here. Tezozómoc was the son of Diego de Alvarado Huanitzin, who served as *tlatoani* or lord of Tenochtitlán under the Spaniards, and of Francisca de Moctezuma, daughter of Moctezuma II. Tezozómoc had access to a rich hoard of picture writings, oral information, and written narratives. The distinguished historian of Náhuatl literature, Ángel María Garibay, stresses the value of its peculiarly Indian point of view: "I do not have in mind the many Indian words or the equally numerous Indian phrases that give color to his relation. I speak rather of the inner, underlying spirit of the account." Tezozómoc's nineteenth-century editor, the Mexican historian Manuel Orozco y Berra, compared it to the great sagas and epic poems of Europe. "The chronicle of Tezozómoc presents the Aztec legend in all its pristine simplicity; it has the flavor of the relations preserved by savage peoples from remote times and transmitted from generation to generation, with all the fabulous and fantastic aspects of such accounts; Tezozómoc depicts the exploits of his heroes with a certain elevation, joined with that rusticity which is so attractive in the personages of the *Iliad*." [67]

Writing at the turn of the sixteenth century, Tezozómoc took care not to appear lukewarm in his Christian faith or in his loyalty to Spanish rule. He denounced the great devil and deceiver Huitzilopochtli; he expressed a proper horror at the cruelty of human sacrifice. "Such great cruelty toward one's neighbors was a monstrous thing to see," he exclaimed as he described the gladiatorial sacrifice. Yet one senses a grim pride in Tezozómoc when he portrays the fear that the Aztec armies on the march inspired. "When the army marched along the roads and through the towns, all shut themselves up in their houses from fear of the soldiers. If these soldiers came across traders or farmers on the road, they stripped them of all their possessions and left them naked. If the townspeople did not come out to receive them, they destroyed and robbed everything, destroying their bins of maize and killing their turkeys and even their dogs." [68]

Pride turned into exultation when Tezozómoc described the great victory won by the Aztecs over Atzcapotzalco in 1430 and the ensuing sweep of Aztec power over central Mexico. He described the fruits of victory in a rush of words, interspersed with Indian terms and phrases, that faithfully conveyed the spirit of the tribal history. "All these towns and lands the valorous Mexicans gained and conquered in a short time. From these lands the people brought the most precious and valuable objects as tribute: precious stones, jade, gold, plumage of different colors and kind, the valuable birds called *Xiuhtototl, Tlauhquechol, Tzinitzcan*, cacao of different kinds and colors, and embroidered mantles of every kind, some twenty brazas long, some ten, eight, and less, which they gave to the *principales* as tribute, and the valuable birds called *Tozneuc*, which are parrots of many kinds, and *Ayocuan*, which are eagles brought by the people who live on the shores of the sea, and all sorts of snakes and provisions. . . . All this the Mexicans deserved for having conquered so many large towns of this New World with valiant spirit and exertion of their persons." [69] In such passages the descendant of Aztec warrior kings triumphs over the graduate of the Colegio de Santa Cruz de Tlatelolco.

The great debate over the American Indian found few echoes in Spanish belles-lettres of the sixteenth century. In general, American themes did not stimulate the Spanish literary imagination to the degree that might have been expected. The conquest produced only one work of outstanding literary merit, the virile *La Araucana*, composed between 1555 and 1590 by the soldier-poet Alonso de Ercilla. This epic poem, dealing with the Spanish struggle against the Araucanian Indians of Chile, helped to create an influential literary image of the Indian, combining bravery, ferocity, stoicism, and nobility of character.

The justice of the Conquest, however much it preoccupied the jurist-theologians of the period, seems to have troubled its poets very little. The only extant work to deal directly with the problem is the *auto* or mystery play *Las Cortes de la Muerte*, begun by Micael de Carvajal and completed by Luis Hurtado de Toledo and published in Toledo in 1557. The cast included the World, the Flesh, the Devil, Saint Augustine, Saint Francis, Saint Dominic, and an Indian cacique. In the manner of Las Casas (whose *Brevísima relación de la destruición de las Indias* had been published a few years before) the cacique depicted the Indians as living in a pagan Golden Age of peace and plenty before the coming of the Spaniards. Now that the Indians were Christians, they lived in misery. In their greedy pursuit of wealth the Spaniards had drowned the New World in blood and corrupted the Indians' wives and daughters. In a final scene, Death and the saints comfort the Indians, assuring them that their sufferings will gain them eternal rewards in heaven. A Mexican scholar argues that this play implies a certain knowledge of the facts of the Conquest on the part of its peasant audiences and that it suggests the existence of a strong current of popular sympathy with the ideas of Las Casas.[70]

In the historical poems that compose the so-called "cycle of Cortés," the Aztecs appear in their own right, but only as a supporting cast for the heroic figure of the conqueror. The first effort to describe the conquest of Mexico in verse was made by Luis Zapata in his *Carlos famoso*, published in Seville in 1566. The work is totally lacking in literary merit. Zapata faithfully followed

Gómara in his description of the Aztecs. He depicted them as war-like people who sacrificed great numbers of victims, ate human flesh, and had up to a hundred wives each. Their arms were the lance, the bow, and the club; they also hurled stones with their hands and with slings. They defended themselves with cotton armor, helmets of bark, and large round shields. They wore cotton mantles and feathered headdresses, hung pearls and gold pendants from their ears and noses, and painted themselves to appear brave and fierce in war.[71]

Two Mexican poets tried their hands at celebrating the deeds of Cortés and his comrades. Francisco de Terrazas, whose poem on Spain's ingratitude to her Mexican sons was cited in a previous chapter, began an epic poem entitled *Nuevo Mundo y Conquista* which he did not complete before his death in about 1600. In fact, the poem never arrives at the Conquest proper. The model for this as for other efforts of the same character was Ercilla's *Araucana*. Terrazas' modern editor, conceding that he had a certain descriptive power and facility, concludes that "the epic was not the field in which his talents shone." [72] One idyllic episode tells of the loves and misfortunes of the Indian prince Huitzol, king of Campeche, and the beautiful maiden Quetzal. Spanish slave hunters abduct the happy pair and embark for the West Indies, but Huitzol and his Indian comrades overpower the brutal Spaniards, fling them overboard, and sail their bark to the province of Champotón, where the lovers receive the hospitality of the friendly king Mochocoboc. Terrazas assigns to the Indian lovers an exquisite sensibility; he places in their mouths the most elevated sentiments. But this is all artifice and literary convention; nothing, except perhaps their names and the locale, would indicate that we have to do with Indians, much less Mexican Indians.

Antonio de Saavedra Guzmán wrote *El peregrino indiano*, a life of Cortés in more than sixteen thousand lines, during the seventy days he spent on shipboard on a voyage to Spain. The work was published in Madrid in 1599. Saavedra had none of Terrazas' lyrical and descriptive talent; the eighteenth-century historian Clavigero summed up the poem's literary merits in the comment that its only relationship to poetry was its meter. It is Gómara's history of the conquest of Mexico put into verse.

A Spanish gentleman named Gabriel Lasso de la Vega, inspired like the others by the example of Ercilla, published in 1588 the first part of a long poem entitled *Cortés valeroso;* six years later he published an expanded version under the name of *La Mexicana.* Unlike Ercilla, Lasso de la Vega could not breathe life into his Indian characters; the work is a versified version of Gómara's history, interspersed with allegorical and mythological interludes.

A greater interest attaches to a spirited defense of the Aztecs appended to Lasso de la Vega's poem. Its author was Gerónimo Ramírez, secretary of Cortés' grandson. His apology for the Aztecs represented an effort to answer the claim that Cortés had won an easy victory over a cowardly, superstitious, and backward people.

Certain individuals envious of Cortés' glory, began Ramírez, wished to diminish his fame by alleging that the Mexican Indians were cowardly, ignorant, and lacked all polity; such people sought to reduce the Indians to pygmies or satyrs. To begin with, the Indians were men and displayed the valor that men naturally display in defense of their homes, religion, fatherland, children, and wives. In actual fact, the Indians were second to no other nation on earth in valor, understanding, and capacity for reasoning. Certainly the Europeans were more civilized, more advanced in letters and the arts, and had better customs. If the Indians had studied in proper schools and learned the liberal arts that correct and perfect nature, they too would have produced many individuals eminent in every kind of learning. Distinguished intellects are born in the most remote and barbarous lands.

By their natural intelligence and experience alone, the Indians had penetrated great secrets of nature, of stones, roots, herbs, minerals, and plants. They had gained understanding of the qualities of animals and, like the Egyptians, could represent whatever they wished and preserve the memory of the important events in their history. Their architectural skill was such that they seemed to have read Vitruvius, for they built houses and other structures marvelously well, with such mastery of perspective that they rivaled the Roman Capitol. The fine coloring of their paintings would have inspired admiration among the Greeks of the time of Apelles. The Indians achieved artistic masterpieces in featherwork, mixing feathers of the most varied colors to represent objects of every kind. The Indians were also devoted to music, dancing, games, and the hunt; they were skillful in the use of the bow, swam like dolphins, and their sports included wrestling, long races, and the hurling of weights: these were their Olympic games.

Their political life proved that they were not barbarians: they had governors, elders, kings, caciques, captains, and many other officials who served in peace and war. Ramírez condemned their paganism, but with remarkable mildness, remarking only that they were "excessively superstitious" in the construction of sumptuous temples to their gods and in the sacrifices that they offered to their gods; they walked in blindness because the Evangel had not yet come to those parts. Withal they had some notion of a Supreme Being and First Cause; unlike some atheist philosophers, they did not deny the existence of God and the immortality of the soul. These things testified to their natural intelligence.

Some Spaniards ridiculed the Indians because the latter, never before having seen men on horses, thought rider and steed were one. But they were soon undeceived and bravely met the Spanish horsemen in the field, frequently severing a horse's neck with a single blow of their obsidian-bladed clubs. What was more remarkable, they fought to the end with desperate fury, although they had had many portents of the destruction of their empire before the coming of the Spaniards. Whoever considered these things dispassionately, concluded Ramírez, must conclude that Cortés performed prodigies of valor in the service of God and the Crown of Castile in the conquest of Mexico.[73]

By an intriguing paradox, in a time of strong anti-Indian reaction, a spokesman for the house of the conqueror had risen to defend the people that Cortés vanquished.

CHAPTER SIX

The Aztecs in Late Renaissance Thought, 1550–1600

The debate over the Indian and the Spanish Conquest spread from Spain to other lands. Between 1550 and 1600 translators introduced the major published Spanish writings on America to readers in Italy, France, Germany, the Netherlands, and England. Envious of the Spaniards' good fortune in winning the treasures of Peru and Mexico, Europeans generally could begin to sit in judgment on Spain's work in America as recorded by Spanish pens. Foreign writers joined in the dispute that Spain herself had begun. Inasmuch as their opinions usually reflected their own political, religious, and philosophical premises, Catholics were inclined to defend the Spanish colonial record, Protestants to attack it. A lonely voice, the voice of Montaigne, pronounced a bitter judgment, not against Spain but against European civilization for its failure to approach the Indians in a spirit of "brotherly fellowship and understanding," for not respecting the rights of weaker peoples to life and liberty.

One of the neglected episodes in the intellectual history of Renaissance Europe is the debate the Spanish Conquest inspired beyond the Pyrenees.[1] In this new debate over the justice of the Conquest and the nature of the Indian, the Aztec civilization served as a prime exhibit for both defenders and detractors of the Indian. Europeans of this period, however, often ignored the cultural differences between the various Indian peoples and based their judgments on the Indian considered as a universal type.

Italy contributed relatively little to the critique of Spain's Indian policy in the second half of the sixteenth century. The political conditions of the Apennine Peninsula had much to do with the restraint of Italian writers. By the Treaty of Cateau-Cambrésis (1559), France effectively abandoned her Italian ambitions and recognized Spanish hegemony over the peninsula. Only the Venetian Republic and the Duchy of Savoy escaped direct or indirect Spanish control. Under the shadow of Spanish absolutism and the Inquisition, Italian intellectual life stagnated; Italy, in the words of Henri Hauser, suffered a sort of asphyxia.[2] A deferential tone characterized Italian discussion of Spanish affairs. Since the pro-Indian movement in Spain was under an official cloud, prudence counseled restraint in the discussion of Spain's colonial policies. It was no accident that Italy was the only major country of Western Europe in which no translation of Las Casas' *Brevísima relación de la destruición de las Indias* had appeared by 1600.

By contrast, only four years elapsed between Spanish publication of Gómara's *Conquista de México* and its appearance in Rome in 1556 in a translation by Agostino de Cravaliz. This first Italian version had no prefatory comment or notes. A new translation by Lucio Mauro appeared in Venice in 1566. The publisher, Giordano Ziletti, explained in his dedication of the book to a Church dignitary that he intended to publish a series of works dealing with "the wonderful deeds of the Spaniards in the discovery and conquest of the new lands rightly called the New World because of their vast extent and number." Ziletti declared that the Spaniards had shed their blood in the conquests for the sole aim of converting the Indians to Christianity. He ascribed to Providence the victory of a small force of Spaniards over an Aztec host of more than a million, and compared Cortés' feat to the recent exploit of the outnumbered defenders of Malta in holding off their Turkish besiegers until relief came (1565). Ziletti closed with compliments to Cortés, "discoverer of New Spain and the great city of Mexico, now called New Venice because it greatly resembles Venice in location, buildings, and wealth."[3]

In 1556 the Venetian official and humanist Giovanni Battista

Ramusio published the third volume of his great compilation *Delle navigationi e viaggi*, the first of the monumental travel collections published in Venice, London, and Frankfurt am Main in the second half of the sixteenth century. He devoted this volume almost entirely to the New World. It contained summaries of some of Peter Martyr's *Decades* and Oviedo's *Historia general y natural de las Indias*, translations of Cortés' Second, Third, and Fourth Letters, and a full-length new work, the relation of the Anonymous Conqueror.[4] Ramusio's publication of this last narrative had a special significance. Widely read, copied, and believed, it helped to establish an image of the Aztecs as a brutal people with the most depraved customs. Finally, Acosta's *Historia natural y moral de las Indias* became available to Italian readers in a translation by Giovanni Paolo Galucci published in Venice in 1596.

Italian writers on geography drew their picture of the American Indian with the aid of these materials. The unfavorable tone of their accounts reflected the strong influence of Oviedo, Gómara, and the Anonymous Conqueror. In his adaptation of Ptolemy's *Geography*, Giovanni Antonio Magini devoted some pages to the American Indians. He reported that the Indians were swarthy, rather ugly, and had fierce and almost bestial customs. The majority went nude. They were excellent runners and swimmers, clean of body, but very lascivious and given to sodomy. The majority were cannibals and worshiped evil demons and idols. But since the coming of the Spaniards and Christianity among them, their customs and manners had improved.[5]

Another writer, Michele Zappullo, mourned the long reign of the Devil in the New World, with the consequent loss of millions of Indian souls. Zappullo charged the Indians, both men and women, with being cruel, bestial, treacherous, senseless, ignorant, inconstant, and thievish; buggers, drunkards, cannibals, epicureans, poltroons, and vagabonds; ungrateful, faithless, changeable, malignant, and shameless. He offered graphic descriptions of the various Aztec modes of human sacrifice, but did not indicate that these practices were limited to Mexico. Zappullo claimed that sodomy was so common among the Indians that men married other men, with the one who played the part of wife performing the tasks usually assigned to women. In close imitation of Gómara, Zappullo scornfully depicted the poverty of Indian life. The Indians lacked all things necessary for human comfort, such as wheat, wine, and the olive; mills, beasts of burden, and iron. They had no weights, measures, or numbers; no music or letters; indeed, none of the liberal arts.[6]

The same bias pervades the section on America and the Indians in the *Relationi universali* (1596) of the eminent Jesuit social scientist Giovanni Botero. Regarding the spread of the Faith as the principal result of the discovery of the New World, Botero devoted the Fourth Part of his book to the missionary enterprise in the Indies. In addition to using older sources such as Gómara and Oviedo, Botero borrowed extensively from Acosta's recent *Historia*, but ignored the Spanish Jesuit's pro-Indian comments.

Gómara had insisted on the overwhelming superiority of European culture over the most advanced Indian civilizations; Botero, expanding this idea, argued the general inferiority of the New World to the Old. Thus he anticipated the campaign of systematic disparagement of the New World waged by certain eighteenth-century *philosophes*. Botero asserted that the reason America had a smaller population than Europe was partly that mountains, swamps, and deserts covered a large part of its surface. He also explained the relative absence of cities and a civilized way of life by America's lack of such staples as wheat, rice, and melons, and of domesticated animals. Botero conceded that the New World had been more densely populated before the coming of the Spaniards, but denied that Spanish mistreatment of the Indians was the principal cause of this decline. Botero pointed out that the introduction of such Spanish victuals as beef, mutton, pork, and wine gave the Indians a more substantial diet than they had been accustomed to, and he claimed that the change was injurious to their health. He also cited the ravages of epidemics of smallpox and the plague called *cocoliztli* in New Spain.

Botero inclined to the belief that a principal cause of the great decline of the Indian population was the addiction of the natives to drinking, gluttony, and lechery. The severe and burdensome rule of their pagan kings kept the Indians in check, but the mild Spanish yoke brought them too much freedom and leisure. "As a result of excessive eating and drinking, with all their train of harmful consequences, the parents are short-lived and the children acquire frail constitutions." A Spaniard who had spent a quarter of a century in Peru and New Spain assured Botero that if the Spaniards quit the Indies the Indians would die off faster than before, "because the Indians have such weak natures, and are so given to gluttony, lechery, and idleness, that if the Spaniards (especially the religious) did not restrain them, they would wallow in their vices." [7]

An occasional Italian geographical work gave special attention to the Aztecs. Thomaso Porcacchi included "the great city and island of Temistitan" among the celebrated island-cities of the world in his *L'isole più famose del mondo*, published in 1572 and reprinted several times. The book contained a drawing of the city and its environs based on the map that first appeared in the Nuremberg (1524) edition of Cortés' letters. Porcacchi appended a description of Tenochtitlán that opened with the conventional comparison of the city with Venice. His relation drew heavily on Gómara, Cortés, and especially the Anonymous Conqueror. As did his principal source, Porcacchi's account gave a general impression of a warlike, cruel people who possessed certain talents and industry, but were afflicted with incredible blemishes. Porcacchi closed on a cheerful note. Thanks to the Conquest and to contact with the Spaniards, the Indians had shed their barbaric customs and adopted the civilized way of life of Christians.[8]

The celebrated *Historia del Mondo Nuovo* of Girolamo Benzoni, published in Venice in 1565 and reprinted in 1572 with the addition of line drawings by the author, dissented from this conventional view of the Spanish Conquest and the Indian. Benzoni supplied almost all the information we have about his life. In a dedication addressed to Pope Pius IV, Benzoni wrote that he was born in Milan, left his native city as a youth to travel in France, Germany, and Spain, and in 1541 sailed from Seville for the Indies in search of fortune. After passing fourteen years in America, chiefly in the Caribbean area, he had returned home to write a book telling of "the strange and rare things" he had seen in the New World.

The historical criticism of the late nineteenth century dealt harshly with Benzoni. He was accused of padding out his own scanty account with materials taken without acknowledgment from Peter Martyr, Oviedo, and Gómara, all available to Benzoni in Italian translations. Marco Allegri concluded after an intensive study of the book and its sources that Benzoni was a plagiarist whose travels were completely unimportant. Allegri also asserted that Benzoni's principal object was to vent his anti-Spanish spite.[9]

A new look at Benzoni's book suggests that the older judgment was too harsh. Granted the offenses of padding and plagiarism, the book nevertheless contains a substantial body of eyewitness testimony on Spanish dealings with the Indians in the Caribbean area. The assertion that Benzoni displayed a violent hostility toward Spain and the Spaniards also appears excessive. Benzoni praised the Dominicans in the Indies for their efforts in behalf of the natives. He called one of the New Laws, prohibiting Indian slavery, "a most holy and glorious law, vouchsafed by a divine emperor." He spoke warmly of Alonso López de Cerrato, president of the Audiencia of Guatemala. "I can testify that throughout the Indies there never was a better judge, nor one who practiced the royal precepts more strictly, obeying the royal commands, always endeavoring that the Indians should not be ill-treated by any Spaniard." Benzoni even complimented Viceroy Antonio de Mendoza of New Spain for his prudence in not attempting to enforce the New Laws amid the overwhelming opposition of the colonists. Curiously enough, Benzoni appears poorly informed concerning Las Casas. Following Gómara, Benzoni criticized Las Casas' efforts to establish a colony on the coast of Venezuela as a scheme to fish for pearls.[10]

Benzoni's book does not possess great documentary value. Its importance consists above all in the effect made on European minds by its heart-rending descriptions of Spanish cruelty to the Indians, illustrated by Benzoni's own artless line drawings. A simple style, much anecdotal detail, and a general effect of candor and compassion contributed to the book's popularity. Numerous translations and editions were issued in the sixteenth and seventeenth centuries. According to Rómulo Carbia, Benzoni's *Historia* and Las Casas' *Brevísima relación* were the cornerstones of the so-called Black Legend of Spanish inhumanity to the Indians.[11]

The writings of the radical wing of sixteenth-century Italian thought reveal traces of interest in the American Indian and the Spanish Conquest. Tommaso Campanella, a rebel against religious and philosophical orthodoxy who spent the last twenty-five years of his life in various prisons, denounced the Spaniards in his utopian socialist work, *La Città del Sole*, for seeking new regions out of lust for riches. Yet he also regarded the conquistadors as God's instruments, working unknown to themselves for a higher end, the gathering of all nations under a single law, the purified Christianity of the future.[12]

The philosopher Giordano Bruno, who was burned at the stake for heresy, may have used an Aztec intellectual achievement to deride the Judeo-Christian chronology. In Bruno's satirical allegory, *Spaccio de la bestia trionfante* (1584), Jove informs the assembled Greek gods that Aquarius is to visit men and inform them that "a new part of the earth, called the New World, has been recently discovered, that there they have memorials of ten thousand years and more, which years are . . . whole and round." This is perhaps a reference to the circular Aztec Calendar Stone. The gods fear this discovery will unsettle men's minds. In a pointed reference to doctrines of Indian inferiority, Bruno has the god Momus offer a solution: let it be explained to mankind that "those of the new land are not of the human generation, because they are not men, although they are very similar to them in members, shape, and brain and, in many circumstances, show themselves wiser, and not even ignorant in dealing with their gods." [13]

In France, the Indian question provoked a battle of the books. The Protestant physician and pastor Urbain Chauveton became his party's specialist on American affairs. In 1578 he published a Latin translation of Benzoni's *Historia del Mondo Nuovo*, which he dedicated to the Protestant theologian Théodore de Bèze. The next year he published a French translation of the same work, dedicated to Henry III. The lengthy title summarized Chauveton's propagandist message: "New History of the New World, briefly relating what the Spaniards have done to the present in the West Indies, and the harsh treatment they have given to the poor people there." [14] Chauveton was more than a propagandist. His copious notes give evidence of wide and careful reading in published sources. He was well informed on the course of events in the New World and praised the efforts of Spanish friars like Bernardino de Minaya and Las Casas in behalf of the Indians.

In his preface and notes Chauveton accused Gómara of historical falsehoods and distortions. Chauveton warned his readers that the greater part of Gómara's book was based on hearsay and that he was excessively partial to the Spaniards. According to Chauveton,

Gómara had said that the Indians were descended from Ham and had inherited the curse laid by God on Ham and his descendants. Employing a combination of Biblical learning and common sense, Chauveton neatly disposed of this and of another widely held theory that the Indians were descendants of the Canaanites. He offered his own view, which anticipated by ten years the position of José de Acosta in his *Historia natural y moral de las Indias* (1590). Chauveton suggested that the Indians had come to the New World from "East India" (Asia) over a land bridge connecting the two continents where they approached each other in the north; if they were separated, it must have been by a very narrow strait that could easily be navigated.

Chauveton also criticized Gómara's suggestion that the Indian servitude and sufferings were divine punishment for their sins. The Indians, argued Chauveton, no more deserved God's wrath than did the pagan ancestors of the present Christians of Europe. Their nudity and lack of shame merely proved their innocence and simplicity. The Indians worshiped the Devil, true, but so did the people of India, Japan, Guinea, and all others who prostrated themselves before images. They practiced human sacrifice, but so did the ancient Germans and Franks until God was pleased to enlighten them by sending Christ to earth.

Chauveton perceived a divine purpose in the discovery of America and the Indians. God wished to show Europeans the variety and grandeur of His terrestrial riches in a completely new setting, because they had become too familiar with their own. He also wished to show Europeans in the persons of the American savages what a poor thing was corrupt human nature without God. He wished the Europeans to see themselves as if in a mirror. "What they are, so were we when deprived of the light of God: poor, blind, naked idolaters, lacking all virtue and filled with all the vices."

Would to God, exclaimed Chauveton, that "Messieurs les Espagnols" had understood this divine purpose. Instead of attracting the Indians to the Faith by mild and merciful means, they had cruelly abused those poor barbarians. To the Indian vices they had added their own. They had brought from the New World diseases hitherto unknown to Europe (a reference to syphilis). To America they took iron; from America they took gold, the cause of a thousand evils. As the gold amassed in Europe, so did men's greed, the worship of Mammon.

Chauveton was confident that the French could manage the business of Christianizing the Indians better than the Spaniards or Portuguese. It was in the nature of men to prefer persuasion by reason to being forced by violence. The Indians preferred the French to the Spaniards because the former sought to gain their ends by amicable means, while the latter relied on blows and kicks.[15]

Chauveton's relativist comments on Indian human sacrifice suggest that he was familiar with the arguments of Las Casas on the same subject. If Chauveton did not read the summary of the dispute between Las Casas and Sepúlveda that Las Casas published in 1552, he may have read a French translation of the *Brevísima relación* with which were joined excerpts from two other Las Casas tracts in a volume published in Antwerp in 1579. An English version of the lengthy title would read as follows: *Tyrannies and Cruelties of the Spaniards, Perpetrated in the West Indies, Called the New World; Briefly Described in the Castilian Language by Bishop Don Fray Bartelemy de Las Casas or Casaus . . . Faithfully Translated by Jacques de Miggrode to Serve as an Example and Warning to the Seventeen Provinces of the Low Countries.*[16]

In his preface the Fleming Miggrode informed the "friendly Reader" that he would behold "as many millions of men put to death as there had been Spaniards born into the world since their first fathers, the Goths, settled Spain or since their second progenitors, the Saracens, expelled and murdered the greater part of the Goths." The Spaniards had destroyed in the Indies three times as many people as were found in all Christendom together. They had invented such tortures, their treachery was so great, that posterity would not believe so cruel and barbarous a nation had ever existed in the world.

Miggrode confessed that he had never loved the Spanish nation because of its intolerable pride, but he assured his readers that he could not but "commend and love certain persons among them." He called on God to witness that hatred did not prompt him to write what he did. After all, the author of the book was himself a Spaniard, and "writes with far more bitterness than I myself." Miggrode closed with a generous tribute to Las Casas, whom he called "a grave author and deserving of immortal praise for having dared to oppose his own cruel and barbarous nation." [17]

Miggrode's translation of Las Casas went through at least three more editions in the sixteenth century, two in Paris in 1582 and one in Lyon in 1594.[18] However, neither Benzoni nor Las Casas approached the popularity enjoyed by Gómara in sixteenth-century France. A translation of the first part of his book, the *Historia general de las Indias*, appeared in Paris in 1568; the translator, Martin Fumée, promised a separate publication of the second part, the *Conquista de México*. After Fumée's translation of the *Historia general* had gone through five editions, it was published in 1584 with the addition of the second part. New editions of the complete work appeared in that same year, in 1587, 1597, and 1605.

The lively interest in Gómara's book inspired a new French translation in 1588. The translator, Guillaume le Breton, took note of Chauveton's criticism of Gómara. Without naming the Protestant writer, Breton observed in his foreword that such illustrious chroniclers as Peter Martyr and Oviedo could also be charged with having written from hearsay. Most classical historians had done the same. As for the charge of partiality directed against Gómara, the Greek and Roman historians had also heaped praise on their national heroes and called their enemies barbarians. The claim that Gómara had written that the Indians were descended from Ham was a distortion of Gómara's text. What Gómara actually wrote was that "God may have permitted the servitude and labor of these people to punish them for their sins, for Ham sinned less against his father than those Indians against God, and God laid the curse of slavery upon Ham's children and descendants." [19]

America and the Indians first drew the attention of French historians in this period. The learned Jacques-Auguste de Thou, author of a universal history completed about 1595, made a brief reference to the discovery and conquest of the New World. De Thou, a moderate Catholic who favored toleration for Protestants, believed that God had raised Spain to a peak of power so that she might undertake long and difficult voyages, illuminating with the light of truth "an infinite number of barbarian nations buried in the darkness of ignorance and error." Events had demonstrated that self-interest and thirst for plunder were more important Spanish motives than piety or love of religion, which the

Spaniards had disfigured with a thousand superstitious practices. Yet it was good that the name of Christ had been announced to so many nations who previously knew Him not, "although there is something reprehensible about the manner in which it was announced." De Thou hoped that someday the Indians would shake off the Spanish domination and be ready to receive a purer light,[20] presumably from French hands.

François de Belleforest, who turned out with equal facility histories, cosmographies, funeral elegies, and tracts of every description, devoted the last part of his *Histoire universelle du monde* (1572) to the New World. This section included a lengthy survey of Aztec civilization. Belleforest's account is a patchwork of excerpts from various sources, with no effort at synthesis; however, his confused, contradictory portrait of Aztec society has some value, for it suggests the mixture of admiration, revulsion, and puzzlement that the exotic Aztec culture inspired in most educated Europeans of the time.

Cortés' description of Tenochtitlán, of its elaborate system of dikes and aqueducts, the large and spacious streets and canals crossed by bridges, the teeming markets carefully regulated by judges who decided all controversies between sellers and buyers, moved Belleforest to exclaim at "the polity and refinement of these people, called savages and barbarians by men who cannot see civilization beyond the borders of their own countries." He would not attempt to describe the beauty of their houses and gardens, or to explain the great skill with which they conducted the sweet water by subterranean channels and aqueducts into their city, and similar achievements. "Let it suffice to say that although they were barbarians, they were better governed and trained than any people discovered to the present time; for the rest, they were valiant, ingenious, hardy, courageous, and most devoted to their prince." Belleforest accepted Cortés' view of the Aztec political system as an analogue of the European monarchical system. "These people were ruled by a great monarch who was supreme (before the Spaniards deprived him of his authority) and had under him a number of kings, dukes, counts, and barons, as well as knights and soldiers, all ready to march to war the moment he gave the word of command." [21]

Belleforest's reading of the Anonymous Conqueror gave him a

very different picture of Aztec society. In war, "the Aztecs are the cruelest people imaginable, for they spare no one, not even their closest relative, and they respect neither age nor sex; they kill and eat all their enemies if they cannot take them into captivity." After describing the various Aztec modes of human sacrifice, one more horrifying than the other, Belleforest concluded with an indictment lifted almost word for word from the Anonymous Conqueror. "In fine, however gentle they may have been in their own society, they were so cannibalistic, so greedy for human flesh, that they disdained all other food in comparison with this meat, and frequently went to war and risked their lives to satisfy their gluttonous appetites. For the rest, they are all sodomites and drunkards." [22] Observe that Belleforest improved on the Anonymous Conqueror, who had charitably asserted, "the majority . . . are sodomites and drunkards."

Three years later Belleforest published a translation of Sebastian Münster's *Cosmography*, considerably revised and enlarged by himself. His viewpoint and sources of information on Aztec society were the same as in the *Histoire*. At one point, however, Belleforest had a new thought; he wondered how this people, "so distant from knowledge of God, having no contact with other civilized nations, surrounded by an infinite number of bestial and almost irrational peoples, could be so civilized and enlightened that if they had only possessed Christianity, one might call them the most accomplished and sagest people in the universe." Belleforest found the answer to this riddle in Cortés' report of a speech in which Moctezuma allegedly claimed descent for his people from strangers who came from distant lands. "These remarks of Moctezuma prove to me that the Mexicans are descended from Europeans. The civilized way of life of the Mexicans, so different from their neighbors in customs and refinement, gives sufficient reason to believe that they are descended from either the Europeans or the Africans" (by which Belleforest meant the advanced Moslem cultures of North Africa). Belleforest explained Aztec human sacrifice as a borrowing from the sanguinary religion of the primitive inhabitants of the country, imposed on the milder worship brought by immigrants from the Old World.[23]

The Franciscan André Thevet may be called the first true French Americanist and collector of Aztec antiquities. This adventurous, insatiably curious friar traveled to Italy, Spain, North Africa, Egypt, and Brazil before settling down in Paris to devote himself to research and writing. From his travels he brought back rare objects ranging from antique medallions and coins to Indian featherwork, skins of American fauna, and a portrait of Cortés allegedly done from life. His manuscript collection included a number of American items. One was the Codex Mendoza, a written and pictorial document dealing with Aztec history, tribute, and customs, prepared by Indian scribes and Spanish friars by command of Viceroy Antonio de Mendoza of New Spain. A French corsair seized the ship that carried this document to Spain, and the corsair presented it to the King of France. Thence it passed to Thevet. It bears his signature and the date 1553. Another jewel of Thevet's collection was a translation, presumably made by himself, of a now missing Spanish document dealing with Aztec religion, history, and customs. Garibay has tentatively assigned a part of this document to a lost work by the Franciscan scholar Andrés de Olmos; another part he has ascribed even more tentatively to Fray Marcos de Niza. Garibay regards the section ascribed to Olmos as a precious source for the religious and literary history of Mexico.[24]

Thevet's major work was his *Cosmographie universelle* (1575), a rival of the *Cosmographie* of Belleforest, to whom Thevet referred in most uncomplimentary terms. Thevet also wrote a *Cosmographie du Levant* (1554), an account of his travels in the Mediterranean and the Middle East, *Les Singularitez de la France antarctique* (1558), a report on his brief stay in Brazil, and a biographical encyclopedia, *Les Vrais Pourtraits et vies des hommes illustres grecz, latins, et payens* (1584). He accorded two American Indian worthies—Moctezuma and Atahualpa—the honor of inclusion in this work. Large engraved portraits, of course done from the artist's imagination, accompanied these biographical sketches. Thevet's scholarly achievements, combined with an unsullied orthodoxy, brought him offices and titles; he was named almoner to the Queen Mother Catherine de Médicis and was later appointed royal historiographer and cosmographer.

In his own time Thevet's veracity and scholarship came under attack. The Protestant writer Jean de Lery, sent by Calvin to Brazil to protect the Reformed interest in the French colonial

project there, charged that Thevet's account of Brazil was a far-
rago of wild, unlikely tales based on the briefest of stays. Gómara's
translator, Martin Fumée, called Thevet's Brazilian narrative a
"mess of lies" ("farci de mensonges"). Thevet's unhappy reputation
clung to him to the end of the nineteenth century. In 1911 Gilbert
Chinard wrote charitably of Thevet: "A poor writer, a geographer
devoid of all critical sense, he unquestioningly accepted the worst
legends and invented new ones. He is nevertheless of interest to
us; with Rabelais, he seems to be one of the last representatives of
medieval science." In recent decades Thevet's scholarly stock has
risen. The author of an intensive study of early ethnographic
sources relating to North America observes that of the French
cosmographers contemporaneous with Cartier, "the most important, the most misread, and the most condemned is André Thevet."
For this condemnation he blames not only "Thevet's somewhat
unfortunate attempts at historical fiction, possibly an attempt to
enlarge the marketing possibilities of his book," but "careless, hasty,
biased scholarship on the part of various students." He concluded
that "whether we consider his voyage accounts as valid, or as being
fictional adventure, we must give him credit for using the best
factual materials available." [25]

A reading of the chapters dealing with the Aztec region in
Thevet's *Cosmographie* inspires mixed feelings. Sometimes Thevet
prattled artlessly in the spirit of the medieval *Travels of Sir John
Mandeville*. In the fresh water part of the Lake of Mexico lived a
fish as large as a seal, said Thevet. Its head and ears resembled
those of a pig; its flesh was as tasty as that of an albacore. Thevet
had once had a skin of this animal in his collection, but it rotted
and he had to throw it away. In the lake also lived a large and
hideous serpent, so venomous that the man or beast bitten by it
could hardly recover. To the legends surrounding the Conquest
of Mexico Thevet added one of his own invention. He told how
a certain Cudragni predicted the fall of the Aztec Empire. This
was a great physician who knew the nature of simples, had the
power of prophecy, and had books full of signs dealing with these
things. He lived very soberly, eating only once a day, one hour
after noon, and lived one hundred and thirty-seven years. He used
to take a certain herb in his mouth to comfort his stomach. He
died two years after the fall of Tenochtitlán and was accorded as

great honors as if he had been a king. Thevet's carelessness in regard to some well-known facts of Aztec history is also disturbing. Thus he called Cuauhtémoc Moctezuma's son, although Gómara, one of Thevet's sources, specified that Cuauhtémoc was Moctezuma's nephew, "and not, as some say, his brother."

Yet Thevet's survey of Aztec civilization is in some respects the most original and valuable of all those written outside Spain and the Indies. If he invented fairy tales and used published sources carelessly, he drew extensively on two valuable manuscripts, the Codex Mendoza and the relation tentatively ascribed to Olmos and Niza. This last document, containing creation myths, tribal history, and other lore, Thevet incorporated with some changes, chiefly in the order of its contents, in the chapter of his *Cosmographie* entitled "The Province of Mexico and its first inhabitants, whence it got its name, and how they sacrifice men." Thevet repeatedly cited his manuscript sources. He based his account of the Aztec manner of counting the years on "what I have been able to learn from one of their books called Xehutonali, that is, their count of years." He compared the elements in Aztec picture writing to the hieroglyphs he had seen on Egyptian obelisks and columns, and offered a specimen of such writing (part of the Codex Mendoza) "which I obtained by the taking of a ship coming from that country." He described some of the signs, "drawn in the shape of toads or frogs, and other animals, terrestrial and aquatic." [26]

Thevet paid tribute to the Aztec achievements. He proclaimed the beauty and greatness of Tenochtitlán, "second neither in wealth nor in traffic to the two ornaments of the East and royal seats of the Grand Tartary, namely, Cambaluc in the Kingdom of Cathay and Quinsay in the Kingdom of China." Indeed, Tenochtitlán surpassed Venice in size and splendor, for around its lake were other large towns joined to it by bridges, the whole forming one great city. But in an access of patriotism Thevet immediately declared that Tenochtitlán was not as large as Paris or so well governed; and he scolded Sebastian Münster for calling Tenochtitlán the premier city of the world. [27]

Thevet occasionally defended the Aztecs against the disparaging comments of other writers. He took a special pleasure in hunting down humbugs in Belleforest's revision of Münster, punningly styled by Thevet "the forest of Münster." He denied that among the Mexicans a father would not scruple to sacrifice his son, or a son his father. This, exclaimed Thevet, borrowing a phrase from his friend Rabelais, was "to pantagruelize too much." Thevet also denied that the Aztecs tolerated incestuous unions, "for there are no people in the world, among the many I have seen, however barbarous they may be, in which the men marry or have relations with their mothers, much less their sisters." [28]

The pessimistic, *memento mori* cast of Aztec religion appealed to Thevet's Catholic soul. He noted with approval the elegant symbolism of the childbirth ceremony in which the knees of the newborn child were rubbed with earth, signifying, according to Thevet, "that with which we are covered after the soul is separated from the body." The Aztec greeting to the newborn, "Oh little creature! Have patience, you are born to suffer," moved him to exclaim: "Behold the grand philosophy of a people that knew not God!" [29]

For Thevet, however, the evils of Aztec life far outweighed its virtues and refinements. He had no patience with the humanitarian critique of the Spanish Conquest. "We know very well," he wrote, "that sodomy, idolatry, and other enormous impieties were the fashion in those regions before the Spaniards set foot there. Today, by the grace of God and their ministry, the light of Christianity has penetrated there and chased away those pernicious corruptions, which were enough to engulf those poor barbarians in the deepest recesses of Hell." [30]

Thevet angrily rejected the charges of certain writers that the Spanish conquistadors aimed only at enriching themselves by pillage. Benzoni, whose wholesale borrowings from Gómara he correctly noted, aroused Thevet's suspicions. He wondered how Benzoni's French translator, the good Sieur Chauveton, had been so easily taken in. This Benzoni passed himself off as a traveler in lands where he had never set foot; indeed, Thevet doubted that the man existed at all! Thevet turned the same suspicious eye on the Miggrode translation of Las Casas. He described both works as "little tracts of falsehood used by men who would not dare to say these things for fear of losing their skins, and so pass off these impostures under the names of men who supposedly had traveled in those countries in order to give weight, color, and authority to

their own ridiculous fooleries." Thevet found especially incredible
the story told by the "supposed Las Casas" in the *Brevísima relación* of the Indian chief who, informed that the Spaniards went
to Heaven, declared his preference for Hell. It seems strange that
the well-traveled Thevet should not have known of Las Casas'
activity in defense of the Indians.

Thevet did not deny Spanish mistreatment of the natives, but
opined that the facts had been greatly exaggerated. He assumed a
hard-nosed attitude toward Spain's Indian wars. The Spaniards
had to use force to break the resistance of a stubborn, stiff-necked,
savage people who refused to accept the rule of Spanish kings.
Thevet asked why the critics of Spain did not protest the cruelties
committed by the Indians against the Spaniards, for the Spaniards
had brought the Indians a greater good than all the treasure that
was taken from their lands. He fired a parting shot that revealed
the underlying political and religious issues in the controversy.
Spain's enemies charged that the conquistadors were moved, not
by zeal for spreading the Faith, but by lust for riches. Thevet
asked why these critics did not make the same reproach against
the English explorer Martin Frobisher, whose voyages in search of
the Northwest Passage were related in a book recently published
in a French translation. Did they believe that Frobisher risked his
life in the frozen North to bring Christianity to the natives of that
region? He sought no other end, said Thevet, than "to gain the
riches of his northern mines." [31]

Thevet, in his biographical sketch of Moctezuma, poured scorn
on the humanitarians, "the crack-brained men who in their count-
inghouses and studies give themselves up to the contemplation of
Platonic ideas." Thevet rudely swept aside the image projected by
Las Casas and Benzoni of a simple-hearted Moctezuma whose hospitality and friendship Cortés basely abused. Thevet's Moctezuma
was a Renaissance ruler, scheming, conniving, abounding in ruses,
who sparred and dissembled with Cortés, seeking by every possible
means to keep him from coming too near. This was the meaning
of his offers, embassies, and gifts. Cortés' vigilant eye penetrated
these stratagems; relentlessly he advanced toward a meeting with
Moctezuma in Tenochtitlán. When the time was ripe, Cortés seized
Moctezuma as a potential source of danger, finding an excuse for
his act in the murder of some Spaniards by order of Moctezuma.

"I know," wrote Thevet, "that some maintain that Cortés' avarice and ambition made him invent this crime, and that Moctezuma displayed all possible humanity and courtesy toward Cortés and the Spaniards. . . . But they do not know the temper of this Mexican, who had to do with one more cunning than himself, and hence was miserably outwitted and so abased that his own people, who once dared not look him in the face because of the great respect they bore him, killed him with showers of stones." [32]

"Geography," wrote the great Flemish mapmaker Abraham Ortelius, "is the eyes of history." Frenchmen could study the geographic setting of Aztec history and civilization in the remarkably accurate and detailed map of New Spain first published in the 1579 Latin edition of Ortelius' world atlas, *Theatrum orbis terrarum*, and reprinted in the French edition of 1587.[33] Copied from a Spanish map of unknown authorship, or perhaps drawn by Ortelius himself, this map identified a large number of pre-Conquest settlements by their Náhuatl names. Together with its companion maps depicting the Culiacán area, Nueva Galicia, and the Huaxteca region, this map marked a major cartographic advance over the map of New Spain drawn by Girolamo Ruscelli (1561), which had corrected an error of long standing by connecting the Yucatán peninsula to the mainland rather than showing it as an island.

The note that Ortelius appended to his map showed some acquaintance with the facts of Aztec history. Ortelius wrote that the Spaniards conquered Tenochtitlán in about 1518, one hundred and forty years after its founding (modern works usually give the date 1325 or 1345 for the founding of Tenochtitlán). Moctezuma, ninth of the line of Aztec kings, ruled Tenochtitlán at the time of its fall. Ortelius marveled that the city had attained such magnitude and magnificence in so short a time. He referred readers who desired more information about the city and the customs of its people to the letters of Cortés. Ortelius' correspondence gives another indication of interest in ancient Mexico; on April 26, 1597, the Spanish scholar Arias Montanus sent him a "very sharp flint fragment which the Mexicans use as knives or razors." [34]

The title page of Ortelius' atlas shows four female figures representing the four continents. At the top sits Europe, depicted as a queen with crown and scepter, enthroned upon the world. In one hand she holds the orb, symbol of the sway of Catholic Europe over the world. To the left stands Asia, a richly dressed oriental princess; to the right Africa, a humbly dressed Negress. At the bottom is an allegorical representation of America, perhaps the first in history.[35] Lovely but unabashedly naked, gorged with human flesh, she reclines drowsily upon the ground. In one hand she holds a thyrsus, in the other a severed human head. Beside her lie her hunting equipment, a bow and arrows. A sonnet by Gérard du Vivier explained the symbolism of the four figures. The lines dealing with America dwell on cannibalism, savagery, and infinite treasure. To the map of Europe Ortelius appended a note proclaiming Europe's historic mission of world conquest, in process of fulfillment by Spain and Portugal, "who between them dominate the four parts of the globe." Ortelius declared that the inhabitants of Europe had always surpassed all other peoples in intelligence and physical dexterity. These qualities naturally qualified the Europeans to govern the other parts of the world." [36]

The lovely, sulky savage on Ortelius' title page may be regarded as a fitting symbol of the Indian as conceived by the majority of French writers of this period. Protestants and Catholics might dispute the morality of Spanish conduct toward the Indians, but they were as one in regarding the Indians, whatever their cultural level, as tainted with vices, as "poor barbarians." "Poor, blind, naked idolaters," the Calvinist Chauveton called them, "lacking all virtue and filled with all the vices." "Sodomy, idolatry, and other enormous impieties," explained Thevet, "were the fashion in those regions before the Spaniards set foot there." These writers showed little tendency to idealize the Indians; certainly they did not think of the Indians as existing in a state of natural perfection to be envied by Europeans.

For a more favorable view of the Indian, we must turn to French belles-lettres. In the poetry of Pierre de Ronsard and the essays of Michel de Montaigne we again meet both the Noble Savage introduced to Europe in the letters of Columbus and the creator of splendid civilizations first made known by Cortés and later eulogized by Las Casas and other Mendicant writers. A fundamental difference, however, separates Las Casas and Montaigne in their approach to the Indian. Montaigne was not greatly interested in the Indians in themselves; the true focus of his interest always remained Europe, with its follies, corruptions, and injustices. For Montaigne and other French humanists, the Indian served primarily as an instrument of criticism of European civilization; and America, whose vast, vague contours the literary imagination could people with ideal societies of every kind, became a geographical symbol of the generous aspirations of these humanists for a better world.

America had already served as such a symbol in the *Gargantua* and *Pantagruel* of François Rabelais. Chinard and others have shown that this work contains New World elements drawn from the letters of Columbus, Peter Martyr, Vespucci, and Cartier. Rabelais sent Pantagruel sailing westward in order to consult the oracle of the bottle. The priestess of the bottle proclaimed a message as Utopian as that of Thomas More, who also drew inspiration from early American travel accounts: "Down here, in these circumcentral regions, we place the supreme good, not in taking or receiving, but in giving and bestowing." [37] The poet Ronsard depicted an Indian Utopia on the shores of Brazil. In his *Discours contre Fortune* (1559), he appealed to Nicholas Durand de Villegagnon, an explorer of Brazil, not to carry the evils of European civilization to those blessed shores where men lived free from kings, Senates, private property, and lawsuits.[38]

The French literary apotheosis of the New World reached its climax in Montaigne, who held up both the cannibals of Brazil and the Aztecs of Mexico to the admiration of decadent Europe, the first for their simplicity and innocence, the second for combining natural virtue with great cultural attainments. Montaigne also used the Indians for a special purpose: to attack the philosophical foundations of Western civilization, to deepen the skeptical crisis of late Renaissance Europe. Beyond the Atlantic, he seemed to say, lay another cultural universe, with different values and ideals. How could one tell whether European religious practices, manners, and customs were better than those of the Indians? [39]

Montaigne read widely in the available literature on the Indians and the Spanish Conquest. He knew the cosmographies of Belleforest and Thevet; he incorporated in his own writings material from Chauveton's translation of Benzoni; from Jean de Lery's account of Brazil he drew the literary profile of the innocent cannibal, illustrating a type of moral perfection free from the vices of civilization. The work that seems to have most profoundly influenced Montaigne's thought on the Indians was Gómara's *Conquista de México*. He knew the work both in the Italian version of Cravaliz and the French version of Fumée. Between 1580 and 1592, as Montaigne polished and added to the successive editions of his *Essais*, he incorporated many passages from Gómara's book in his own work.[40]

What attracted Montaigne most in Gómara's book, according to Pierre Villey, was its revelation of the infinite variety of Indian beliefs and customs. "Montaigne had never seen assembled in so brief a compass such a diversity of moral and political concepts and opinions. He amused himself by making collections of these traits, of those which recalled Europe and of others which had absolutely nothing in common with our own. And his aim was always the same: to show that no universal reason presides over the birth of these traits, that they arise and flower by chance; he wished to show our folly when we seek to erect our opinions and habits into intangible beliefs and absolute rules." [41]

Aztec civilization, combining culture traits that appeared to parody or imitate those of Europe with others that were totally alien, offered Montaigne abundant materials with which to play his impish game. In the following list of Indian customs, cited by Montaigne in his *Apology for Raymond Sébond*, the great majority are of Aztec origin:

"In one place they came across a belief in the day of judgment, so that the people were strangely shocked by the Spaniards for scattering the bones of the dead while searching the tombs for riches, saying that these scattered bones could not easily come together again; traffic by exchange, and none other; fairs and markets for that purpose; dwarfs and deformed persons to adorn the table of princes; the practice of falconry according to the nature of their birds; tyrants' subsidies; refinements in gardening; dances, tumbling; instrumental music; coats of arms; tennis games, games of dice and of chance in which they grow so heated as to stake themselves and their liberty; no medicine other than that of charms; the system of writing in pictures; belief in a single first man, father of all nations; worship of a god who once lived as a man in perfect virginity, fasting, and penitence, preaching the law of nature and religious ceremonies, and who disappeared from the world without a natural death; the belief in giants; the custom of getting drunk on their beverages and of competition in drinking; religious ornaments painted with bones and death's-heads; surplices, holy water, sprinklers; women and servants competing in offering themselves to be burned or buried with the dead husband or master; a law that the eldest succeed to all the property, and no portion is reserved for the youngest but obedience; a custom, upon promotion to a certain office of great authority, that he who is promoted takes a new name and abandons his own; the custom of sprinkling lime on the knee of the newborn child, saying to him: 'You have come from dust and will return to dust'; the art of augury." [42]

The folly of killing men in the name of religion weighed heavily on Montaigne's spirit. Sardonically, he referred to the very old belief that "we gratify heaven and nature by committing massacre and homicide, a belief universally embraced in all religions." Even in the New World, "still pure and virgin compared with ours, this practice is to some extent accepted everywhere: all their idols are drenched with human blood, often with horrible cruelty. They burn the victims alive, and take them out of the brazier half roasted to tear their heart and entrails out. Others, even women, are flayed alive, and with their bloody skins they dress and disguise others. And there are no fewer examples of constancy and resolution. For these poor people that are to be sacrificed, old men, women, children, themselves go about, some days before, begging alms for the offering at their sacrifice, and present themselves to the slaughter singing and dancing with the spectators." Montaigne went on to describe the Aztec Flowery Wars that were fought to obtain prisoners of war for sacrifice. Fascinated by the subject, Montaigne declared he could go on endlessly, but must stop; he would tell only "this one story more." And he told with relish Gómara's anecdote about a message sent by one Mexican tribe to Cortés. "Some of these people, having been beaten by him, sent to acknowledge him and seek his friendship. The messengers offered him three sorts of present, in this manner: 'Lord, here are five slaves; if you are a cruel god that feeds on flesh and blood, eat them, and we will bring you more. If you are a good-natured god, here are incense and plumes. If you are a man, take these birds and fruits.' " [43] How ingenious in reasoning, how fluent of speech, were these barbarians!

A serene disenchantment, tinged with subtle mockery or playful wit, is more characteristic of Montaigne's philosophic and literary style than moral indignation or reproof. His reading of Gómara's *Conquista de México* touched off one of Montaigne's few explosions of wrath. Chinard notes the contrast between the playful spirit of the essay *On Cannibals*, written in 1580, and the bitter anger of the essay *On Coaches*, composed in 1588. What happened between 1580 and 1588? "In the interval Montaigne has read Gómara and could see, through the eyes of a Spaniard, the methods employed by Pizarro and Cortés in their conquests." [44]

Hoxie N. Fairchild calls attention to another difference between the two essays. The spirit of the essay *On Cannibals* is completely primitivist: the Brazilians live an idyllic existence because they are so close to nature, because their state is based on natural goodness. But by 1588 Montaigne had become well informed, through reading Gómara, about the advanced Aztec and Inca civilizations. Hence in the essay *On Coaches* he wavers between two points of view; he is "uncertain whether to admire the Indian because he is so civilized or because he is so savage." [45] Fairchild notes a curious discordance of ideas in the following passage, in which the reference to a world so childlike that it "lived only on what its nursing mother provided" is contradicted by the reference to "the awesome magnificence of the cities of Cuzco and Mexico":

Our world has just discovered another world . . . no less great, full and well-limbed than itself, yet so new and infantile that it is still being taught its ABC; not fifty years ago it knew neither letters, nor weights and measures, not clothes, nor wheat, nor vines. It was still naked at the breast, and lived only on what its nursing mother provided. . . .

I am much afraid that we shall have very greatly hastened the decline and ruin of this new world by our contagion, and that we will have sold it our opinions and our arts very dear. It was an infant world; yet we have not whipped it and subjected it to our discipline by the advantage of our natural valor and strength, nor won it over by our justice and goodness, nor subjugated it by our magnanimity. Most of the responses of these people and most of our dealings with them show that they were not at all behind us in natural brightness of mind and pertinence.

The awesome magnificence of the cities of Cuzco and Mexico (and, among many similar things, the garden of that king in which all the trees, the fruits, and all the herbs were excellently fashioned in gold, and of such size and so arranged as they might be in an ordinary garden; and in his curio room were gold replicas of all the living creatures native to his country and its waters), and the beauty of their workmanship in jewelry, feathers, cotton, and painting, show that they were not behind us in industry either. But as for devoutness, observance of the laws, goodness, liberality, and frankness, it served us well not to have as much as they; by their advantage in this they lost, sold, and betrayed themselves.[46]

Montaigne continued in this vein of eulogy. In courage, endurance, patriotism, the Indians surpassed "the most famous ancient examples that we have in the memories of our world on this side of the ocean." Montaigne stripped every shred of glamor from the conquistadors. Eliminate the disparity in armaments between the victors and the vanquished, take away the ruses used by the Spaniards against the Indians, remove the surprise and fear caused by the sight of strange bearded men mounted on large unknown monsters and by the lightning and thunder of European cannon and muskets, and you deprive the conquerors of the whole basis of their victories.

Montaigne's critique of the Spanish Conquest differs from that of all other critics of the period, Catholic or Protestant, in its completely secular tone. Whereas others debated the efficacy of Spain's proselytizing methods, Montaigne was silent on the subject of conversion; indeed, he applauded the struggle of the Indians in defense of their gods and altars. If the Indians had to be conquered, Montaigne would have preferred it done by other pagan peoples. He grieved that "such a noble conquest" had not fallen to Alexander or to the ancient Greeks and Romans:

Why did not such a great change and alteration of so many empires and peoples fall into hands that would have gently polished and cleared away whatever was barbarous in them, and would have strengthened and fostered the good seeds that nature had produced in them, not only adding to the cultivation of the earth and the adornment of cities the arts of our side of the ocean, insofar as they would have been necessary, but also adding the Greek and Roman virtues to those originally in that region? What an improvement that would have been, and what an amelioration for the entire globe, if the first examples of our conduct that were offered over there had called those peoples to the admiration and imitation of virtue and had set up between them and us a brotherly fellowship and understanding! How easy it would have been to make good use of souls so fresh, so famished to learn, and having, for the most part, such fine natural beginnings! On the contrary, we took advantage of their ignorance and inexperience to incline them the more easily toward treachery, lewdness, avarice, and every sort of inhumanity and cruelty, after the example and pattern of our ways.

As he warmed to his subject, the genial philosopher was transformed; the fire of his denunciation recalls the wrathful chapter on "Primitive Accumulation" in Marx's *Capital:*

Who ever set the utility of commerce and trading at such a price? So many cities razed, so many nations exterminated, so many millions of people put to the sword, and the richest and most beautiful part of the world turned upside down, for the traffic in pearls and pepper! Base and mechanical victories! Never did ambition, never did public enmities, drive men against one another to such horrible hostilities and such miserable calamities.[47]

Montaigne's Indians are products and parts of nature. Their culture, their customs and practices, good or bad, obey the laws of their natural environment, for "the air, the climate, and the soil where we are born" determine "not only the complexion, the stature, the constitution and countenance, but also the faculties of the soul." The obligation of technologically advanced peoples toward the primitive was neither conquest nor conversion, but the establishment of "a brotherly fellowship and understanding" for the purpose of gently clearing away "whatever was barbarous in them," preserving meanwhile their "fine natural beginnings." More closely even than Las Casas, Montaigne approached the modern anthropological viewpoint on the Aztecs and other Indian societies.

Religious and political issues strongly colored attitudes toward the American Indian and the Spanish Conquest in the Netherlands and in German-speaking lands. The Dutch, locked in a prolonged, exhausting struggle with Spain, quickly seized on the writings of Las Casas and Benzoni to prove to their people the merciless and unjust nature of the enemy. The first translation of Las Casas'

Scenes by Iodocus a Winghe for the De Bry Latin edition of Las Casas' *Brevísima relación de la destuición de las Indias* (Frankfurt am Main, 1598): Above, the massacre at Cholula. Below, torture of the King of the Province of Mechuaca. Courtesy Rare Book Division, The New York Public Library.

View of Mexico by the Flemish artist and geographer Joris Hoefnagel, in Georgius Braun and Franz Hohenberg, *Civitates orbis terrarum* (Cologne, 1576). Courtesy Rare Book Division, The New York Public Library.

Title page of Abraham Ortelius' *Theatrum orbis terrarum* (Antwerp, 1570). Courtesy Department of Rare Books and Special Collections, Princeton University Library.

Folio from the Codex Mendoza. Bodleian Library, Oxford. Photograph after Francisco del Paso y Troncoso. Courtesy Department of Rare Books and Special Collections, Princeton University Library.

Brevísima relación into any foreign language was a Dutch version printed in Antwerp or Brussels in 1578. A second edition in 1579 had a significantly altered title. Rendered into English, it reads: *Mirror of Spanish Tyranny, in Which Are Told the Murderous, Scandalous, and Horrible Deeds Which the Spaniards Have Perpetrated in the Indies.* Two more editions of Las Casas' book appeared in Amsterdam in 1597. A Dutch translation of Benzoni's book was issued in 1579, a second edition following in 1582.

Absorbed in a life-and-death struggle with Spain, the Netherlands could give little attention to publishing or literary activity. More favorable conditions for such activity existed in Germany. The Peace of Augsburg (1555) temporarily solved the religious problem by permitting each German prince to choose Lutheranism or Catholicism as the faith of his people. As a result, Protestantism gained the ascendancy over most of northern Germany and even made inroads in the south. The distinguished artistic and industrial traditions of certain German cities also helped to make Germany a major center for the publication of finely printed and illustrated works dealing with America. Some of these works had a distinct anti-Spanish tendency.

The first German translation of Benzoni's *Historia del Mondo Nuovo* was issued in the staunchly Protestant city of Basel. The translator, Nicolaus Hoeniger, identified himself with the views of Benzoni. In dedicating the book to the Margrave of Baden, Hoeniger lamented that the Spaniards had not reduced the Indians to obedience and Christianity by the methods of love and friendship. Instead they had imposed a dreadful tyranny, driving the poor Indians, old and young, men and women, to labor in gold mines until the poor creatures fled in despair into remote forests and caves where they died of hunger. Hoeniger also accused the Spaniards of the most complete sexual license, as a result of which Indian venereal diseases had been introduced into all the nations of Europe.[48] A second edition appeared in 1582.

No publisher did more to popularize the so-called Black Legend in Germany and throughout Europe than Théodore de Bry and his sons Jean Théodore and Jean Israel. A Walloon, born in Liège, the elder De Bry left Flanders about 1570, probably to escape the "Spanish Fury," and settled in Frankfurt in the domain of the Calvinist Frederick III of the Palatinate. A distinguished engraver, De

Bry established in Frankfurt a publishing house that specialized in handsomely made, profusely illustrated books. De Bry became interested in the subjects of discovery and travel primarily for their pictorial value. In the 1580's he developed a plan for a new travel collection in four languages. In pursuit of his plan he visited England in 1587 and received encouragement from Richard Hakluyt. The principal result, as it concerned America, was the series known as the *Grands Voyages,* produced by De Bry and his successors in thirteen parts between 1590 and 1634. In this series De Bry included two editions of Benzoni's book: first Chauveton's Latin translation, in three parts between 1594 and 1596, and then Hoeniger's German version in 1597.[49]

Curiously enough, De Bry omitted Las Casas' *Brevísima relación* from the *Grands Voyages.* The first German translation of the work, based on Miggrode's French translation, was published in 1597 without indication of publisher or place. The following year Jean Théodore and Jean Israel de Bry issued a Latin translation also based on the French translation; as usual, the book also contained excerpts from the summary of the dispute between Las Casas and Sepúlveda and from another of Las Casas' Indian tracts. Of special importance were the seventeen illustrations, drawn by Iodocus a Winghe, that accompanied the text of Las Casas' *Brevísima relación.* Their clarity and beauty of line, the graceful postures struck by the Indian figures, to whom the artist gave a minimum of clothing, heightened the horror of the scenes of massacre and outrage that they depicted. In 1599 the plates were published as a separate with a title that would translate as *Brief Explanation of the Horrible Deeds Done by the Spaniards in Various Parts of the New World.* A simply worded legend underneath each plate summarized the event with which it dealt. Of these hair-raising illustrations Rómulo Carbia complained: "Reproduced various times in different editions of the pamphlet, they and their content became so familiar that men came to believe that these pictures summed up the whole work of Spain in America." [50]

Three of the seventeen illustrations depicted scenes in the conquest of Mexico. One portrayed the massacre at Cholula, another showed Moctezuma's messengers bringing gifts to Cortés, and the third presented the agonized Moctezuma as he watched the slaughter of his nobles by Alvarado's soldiers. Many of the Aztecs display the scanty attire of plumage around the head and waist assigned by European artists to the Indians; none is given the characteristic Aztec dress of a loincloth and a mantle knotted over one shoulder.

In dedicating the book to the Count Palatine of the Rhine, Frederick IV, Jean Théodore and Jean Israel de Bry expressed a pious hope that the book would show honest men the evil fruits of avarice. They recalled that their father had already published Benzoni's book, which dealt with the same subject but not so thoroughly as did Las Casas' work. The brothers declared that the Spaniards had committed such cruelties that they could more fittingly be called lions and tigers than men. Their actions exposed their specious claims that they had conquered the Indies for the conversion of the heathen. God Himself had inspired the Spanish author of this book to publish the deeds of the Spaniards for their eternal ignominy and disgrace. The brothers went on to commend the efforts of this *bonus vir* and of the Spanish monarchs in behalf of the Indians. They disavowed any desire to defame Spain or the Spanish nation. Their sole desire was to enable men to understand the terrible fruits of the root of all evils, love of money, and eradicate that passion from their hearts. Whoever searched his conscience seriously would find it rooted in his heart as well. Magnanimously the brothers affirmed that "if we enjoyed the same freedom and license that the Spaniards gained for themselves in America, having no superior magistrate to fear and hold them in check, we would doubtless be equal to the Spaniards in savagery, cruelty, and inhumanity." [51]

A fine engraving of Tenochtitlán appeared in the magnificent pictorial atlas, *Civitates orbis terrarum*, compiled by Georgius Braun and Franz Hohenberg and published in Cologne in 1572. The full-page scene was made by the Flemish artist and geographer Joris Hoefnagel on the basis of the so-called Cortés map first published in 1524. Three Indian figures in graceful poses stand in the foreground. One, a half-naked savage, carries a bow and has a quiver of arrows slung over one shoulder; another wears a modified Aztec dress including a mantle correctly knotted over one shoulder; the third is clad in a robe of European style. A page of description taken chiefly from Cortés' Second Letter accompanied the map. Reprinted in many editions in the sixteenth and seventeenth centuries, the *Civitates* helped through its picture of Tenochtitlán to spread the fame of the Aztecs and their great city.

A pragmatic spirit marked English discussion of the American Indian and the Spanish Conquest in the last half of the sixteenth century. One looks in vain for an authentic concern for Indian welfare or a strong interest in Indian civilization. English praise and disparagement of the Indian were equally perfunctory; sentiment was subordinated to whatever was the current English interest. As the period opened, the marriage of Spanish Prince Philip to Mary Tudor gave Spain a decisive influence in English affairs; understandably enough, a respectful, admiring tone dominated English comment on Spain's work in the New World. By 1570, however, English strategists had begun to see in the New World a solution for the problems of unemployment and overproduction. English as well as French pirates were harrying the Indies. The rising antagonism between Spain and England was soon to flame up in open war. By the 1580's the great publicist of England's overseas expansion, Richard Hakluyt, was denouncing the Spaniards for their "strange slaughters and murders of these peaceable, lowly milde, and gentle people," the Indians.

Before 1550 English printers had produced almost nothing on overseas travel. The government official and scholar Richard Eden broke this silence with publication of his *Treatyse of the Newe India* (1553), a translation of material dealing with the voyages of Columbus, Vespucci, and Magellan from Sebastian Münster's *Cosmography*. Two years later Eden published a second volume of translated materials dealing with the Spanish discoveries and conquests, *The Decades of the New Worlde* (1555). Eden, it seems, had two objectives in mind. He wished to ingratiate himself with the new queen, Mary Tudor, by flattering her husband, Prince Philip, to whom he dedicated the book; he also wanted to stimulate English interest in colonial expansion. The first Four Decades of Peter Martyr occupied about one third of the book. The Fourth Decade (given in abridged form) introduced English readers to Aztec civilization. Eden's version, when compared with the modern translation of MacNutt, contains some errors and distortions, but in general it is sound. Seeking to make his work up-to-date, Eden included a brief description of Tenochtitlán and the resources of the Aztec Empire based on Gómara's recently published *Conquista de México*. We do not know how many copies of Eden's book were published, "but the considerable number extant today and the fact that the edition was handled by four publishers instead of one suggest that it was large." [52]

In his preface Eden praised the Spanish conquistadors for their "mercyfull warres," notable because "greater commodities hath thereof ensewed to the vanquished than to the victourers." The Spaniards had taken from the Indians only what they were willing to part with as of no consequence: gold, pearls, precious stones, and the like, and had compensated them with wares they much preferred. Eden stoutly defended the work of Spain in the New World against its critics. "But sum wyll say, they possesse and inhabite theyr regions and use them as bondemen and tributaries, where before they were free. They inhabite theyr regions indeed; yet so, that by theyr diligence and better manurynge the same, they maye nowe better susteyne both, than one before. Theyre bondage is suche as is much rather to be desired than theyre former libertie which was the cruel Cannibales rather a horrible licentiousness than a libertie, and to the innocent as terrible a bondage, that in the myddest of theyr ferefull idlenesse, they were ever in daunger to be a pray to those manhuntynge wolves. But nowe thanked be God, this devilyshe generation is so consumed partely by the slaughter of such as could by no meanes be brought to civilities, and partely by reservynge such as were overcome in warres, and convertynge them to a better mynde."

Eden called on the English to emulate Spain's example. Blithely ignoring Spanish claims to monopoly of America, he asserted that to the north of the regions of Spanish occupation there remained a vast portion of mainland "not yet knowen but onely by the sea coastes, neyther inhabyted by any Christiane men." In this area there were "many fayre and frutefull regions, hygh mountaynes, and fayre ryvers, with abundaunce of golde and dyvers kyndes of beastes. Also cities and towres so wel buylded and people of such civilitie, that this parte of the worlde seemeth lyttle inferiour to oure Europe, if the inhabitauntes had receaved owre religion. They are wyttie people and refuse not barterynge with straungers." Sebastian Cabot, that "woorthy owlde man yet lyving," had touched only in the north corner and "most barbarous parte thereof." The western and southern part of those regions were inhabited by civilized peoples. The chief city here was Temistetan or Mexico. It stood in a very great lake and had about it innumerable bridges and buildings "to be compared to the woorkes of Dedalus." The inhabitants could read and write. Although the Spaniards had certain colonies in the part called New Spain, the majority of the natives were idolaters awaiting conversion. Eden reproached the English, who were much closer to this region than the Spaniards, for not having attempted "summe vyages into these coastes, to doo for our partes as the Spaniardes have doone for theyrs, and not ever lyke sheepe to haunte one trade." [53]

The only additions made by Eden to Peter Martyr's text consisted of marginal summaries or comments meant to enlighten the reader. Beside Martyr's glowing description of the Aztec presents sent by Cortés to Charles V, Eden entered the query: "How then can we call them [the Indians] beastly or barbarous?"

Eden died in 1576 before completing an expanded second edition of the *Decades*. Richard Willes, an employee of the Muscovy Company, finished the work, which he published in 1577 under the title *The History of Travayle in the West and East Indies*. New material dealing with the Aztecs included Peter Martyr's Fifth Decade, describing the conquest of Mexico and the grandeur and riches of Tenochtitlán. Like its predecessor, Willes' book was meant to stimulate English interest in exploration and colonization, and especially in the search for the Northwest Passage, which "be it never so full of difficulties, will become as plausible as any other journey, if our passengers may returne with plentie of silver, silkes, and pearle."

The tide of interest in the New World was now beginning to run strong. In 1578 Thomas Nicholas, an employee of the Levant Company, published a translation of Gómara's *Conquista de México* under the title *The Pleasant Historie of the Weast India, Now Called New Spayne*. Although Nicholas abridged some parts and completely omitted others, including the last chapter on the character of Cortés,[54] he supplied Englishmen with the most accurate and comprehensive account of Aztec civilization then available. Here, put into florid Elizabethan prose, English readers could read Gómara's picturesque description of the splendors and terrors of Aztec life.

The translations of Peter Martyr, Gómara, and other Spanish chroniclers, including Oviedo, helped to whet English appetites for the exploration and colonization of America. If gold and silver abounded in Mexico and Peru, why not in Virginia and Newfoundland? Publication in 1583 of a translation of Las Casas' *Brevísima relación*, together with abstracts of two other tracts by Las Casas, served the same practical purpose; it inspired a virtuous hatred for Spain, the chief obstacle to England's expansion. A certain "M. M. S." translated the work from the French version by Jacques Miggrode (here named "James Alligrodo"), and entitled it *The Spanish Colonie or Briefe Chronicle of the Acts and Gestes of the Spaniardes in the West Indies, Called the Newe World, for the Space of XL Yeeres.*

By the early 1580's English readers had access to at least partial translations of the major published Spanish sources on America and the Indian, except for the letters of Cortés. In a pamphlet published in 1583, Sir George Peckham, a Catholic promoter of English colonization who sought to rouse his countrymen out of the "drowsie dreame, wherein we have so long slumbered," wrote that he would not describe the Spanish exploits in America because all "their discoveries travells, and conquests, are extant to be had in the English tongue." [55]

Peckham wrote to drum up support for Sir Humphrey Gilbert's project for a Newfoundland colony. His discourse presented an exotic image of the Indian, confusedly combining notions derived from Spanish sources and the patently fabulous relation of one David Ingrams, who in 1582 gave Sir Francis Walsingham and Peckham an account of a prodigious trek from Mexico to Cape Breton. Following Ingrams, Peckham distinguished between the savages and the cannibals. The former were "poore Pagans, so long living in ignourance and idolatry," and also given to human sacrifice. These savages waged continual war "wyth their next adjoining neighbours, and especially the Cannibals, being a cruell kind of people, whose foode is mans flesh, and have teeth like dogges, and doo pursue them with ravenous myndes to eate theyr flesh, and devoure them."

Peckham pictured the spiritual and cultural advantages that would accrue to the Indians from the Newfoundland project. They would not only receive the inestimable boon of Christianity but would be taught "how to tyll and dresse their grounds," and "shalbe reduced from unseemly costumes, to honest maners, from disordred riotous rowtes and companies, to a wel governed common wealth, and withall shalbe taught mechanicall occupations, artes, and lyberal sciences." Best of all, "they shalbe defended from the cruelty of their tyrannical and blood sucking neighbors, the Canniballes, wherby infinite numbers of their lives shalbe preserved." Recalling descriptions of Aztec human sacrifice in Spanish sources, Peckham gratuitously ascribed the same practice to the blameless Indians of Newfoundland: "And lastly, by this meanes many of their poore innocent children shalbe preserved from the bloody knife of the sacrificer, a most horrible and detestable custome in the sight of God and man, now and ever heertofore used amongst them." [56]

In Gómara's *Conquista de México*, Peckham and other Elizabethan promoters of overseas expansion found evidence to buttress English claims to the New World. Peckham cited a speech made by Moctezuma to his lords, an apparent reference to the Quetzalcóatl legend, to prove an early English presence in America. Peckham asserted that the prince who had departed from Mexico with a promise to return was no other than the Welsh prince Madoc, who allegedly sailed away from England about 1170, planted a colony on the shores of Mexico, and then returned to England. The Welsh antiquary David Powell developed the Madoc-Quetzalcóatl theme in his partly original *Historie of Cambria*, published in 1584. On the strength of Moctezuma's speech and other evidence, this writer pronounced it certain that New Spain or Mexico "was long afore by Brytaines discovered, afore either Columbus or Americus Vespatius lead anie Spaniards thither." [57]

The work of Eden, Willes, Nicholas, Peckham, and others culminated in the propagandist efforts of Richard Hakluyt. For a space of almost fifty years Hakluyt pursued with single-minded energy the goal of English overseas expansion. As a collector and compiler of documents dealing with America, he made at least one major contribution to the field of Aztec studies. From 1583 to 1588 Hakluyt resided in Paris as chaplain to the English ambassador, Sir Edward Stafford. Here he made the acquaintance of André Thevet. Their common interest in exploration and travel drew the two men together. During his stay in Paris, Hakluyt purchased the Codex Mendoza from Thevet, paying the equivalent of £5 for the manuscript. At the suggestion of Sir Walter Raleigh, to whom he showed the document, Hakluyt hired the English merchant and translator Michael Lok to prepare an English version of the Spanish text of the Codex, with a view to its publication. On Hakluyt's death in 1616 this translation, together with the Codex itself, passed into the hands of Samuel Purchas, a clergyman who continued Hakluyt's work of collecting and publishing travel materials. The fortunes of the Codex Mendoza are discussed in later chapters.

Hakluyt's great collection of English travels, *The Principall Navigations, Voiages and Discoveries of the English Nation* (1589), included several accounts by English travelers in Mexico. The report of the merchant Henry Hawks, who spent five years in Mexico and wrote his narrative at Hakluyt's request in 1572, presented his views on the Indians and recorded the persistence of pagan ways and beliefs among them. Hawks had apparently imbibed the prejudices of the Spaniards among whom he lived, for he charged the Indians with great crimes against nature. He declared that as a result of drinking pulque the Indians "are soone drunke, and given to much beastlines, and void of all goodnes. In their drunkennes, they use and commit sodomie, and with their mothers and daughters have their pleasures and pastimes." They were also "of much simplicities, and great cowards, void of all valour, and are great Witches. They use divers times to talke with the Devill, to whome they doe certaine sacrifices and oblations: many times they have been taken with the same, and I have seene them most cruelly punished for that offence."

The memory of Moctezuma's splendor still lived in the minds of the natives. Aged Indians described Moctezuma to Hawks in terms that made him proclaim the Aztec ruler "one of the richest princes which have bene seene in our time, or long before. He had all kinde of beasts which were then in the countrey, and all maner of birds, and fishes, and all maner of wormes, which creepe upon the earth, and flowers, and herbes, all fashioned in silver and gold, which was the greatest part of all his treasure, and in these things had he great joy, as the old Indians report. And unto this day, they say that the treasure of Moctezuma is hidden, and that the Spaniards have it not." [58]

Hakluyt himself seems to have given little thought to the nature of Indian civilization. His comments on the Indian and the Spanish Conquest have a clearly opportunistic ring. In a discourse in favor of English colonization that Hakluyt presented to Queen Elizabeth in 1584, he discussed the question of Spain's military reaction to English efforts to plant colonies in America. In order to strengthen the prospects of English success, Hakluyt drew a picture of masses of Indians who, disaffected by Spanish cruelty, would rise in revolt at the first English landing. He sounded the theme of Spanish barbarity again when he argued that Spain had not complied with the terms of the Papal donation of America to the Crown of Castile. Instead of converting the Indians as the Papal grant required, the Spaniards had destroyed these "peacable, lowly milde, and gentle people." With relish, Hakluyt cited Las Casas in proof of his contention that "the kings of Spain have sent such bloodhounds and wolves thither as have not converted but almost quite subverted them, and have rooted out alone fiftene millions of reasonable creatures." Hakluyt also cited statements by Oviedo and Benzoni.[59]

Yet Hakluyt could eulogize the conquistadors when it served his purposes. In dedicating to Raleigh a new Latin edition of Peter Martyr's *Decades* (Paris, 1587), Hakluyt urged Raleigh to follow the example of Cortés: "Let the doughty deeds of Ferdinand Cortés, the Castilian, the stout conqueror of New Spain, here beautifully described, resound ever in your ears." And Hakluyt assured Raleigh that he would find, if not a Homer, a second Peter Martyr to rescue from oblivion Raleigh's heroic deeds.[60]

A word of summary. A negative stereotype dominated European thought and writing on the Indian, Aztec or any other, in the second half of the sixteenth century. The epithet "poor barbarian" or "poor savage," conveying a mixture of commiseration and scorn, was the phrase most widely applied to the Indian by European writers. The stereotype ignored not only the cultural differences between the various Indian groups but also the outstanding achievements in art, industry, and social and political organization of the most advanced Indian peoples; moreover, it attributed to all Indians the aberrations, real or imaginary, that Europeans found most objectionable: human sacrifice, cannibalism, sodomy. Only a few Europeans of progressive outlook, such as Bruno and Montaigne, utterly rejected the notion of the Indian's inferiority and depravity and admitted him to equal membership in the family of man. Aztec civilization supplied both Bruno and Montaigne with proofs of the equality and creative capacity of the Indian.

CHAPTER SEVEN

The Baroque Vision
of the Aztecs

The seventeenth century added new dimensions to the European image of the Aztecs. Although European writers continued to treat the subject in accordance with their backgrounds and philosophies, some stressing the virtues of Aztec society, others its vices, the artistic and intellectual styles of the age lent a distinctive coloring to their handling of the Aztec theme. Mannerism touched it with fantasy; classicism gave it a new dignity; rationalism caused Moctezuma to assume the skeptical tone of Montaigne or the scientific accents of Descartes.

Hostility dominated the Spanish attitude toward the Indian in this period. This hostility reflected the triumph of the anti-Indian reaction that began in the Spanish court under Philip II. By 1600 the indigenist movement identified with Las Casas had disappeared as a political force; the memory of the Protector of the Indians had fallen under a cloud. Only one edition of Las Casas' *Brevísima relación de la destruición de las Indias* appeared in Spain during the seventeenth century; appropriately enough, that edition was published in Barcelona in 1646 during the Catalan revolt against Castilian imperialism. In 1659 the Aragonese Inquisition banned the *Brevísima relación*, and the ban was later extended to all Spain. Typical of the contemporary Spanish comment on the book was the observation of the jurist and bibliographer, Antonio de León Pinelo, who declared that foreigners valued the *Brevísima relación* not for its learning or information but for the severity with which it treated the conquistadors, "diminishing and annihilating their exploits, exaggerating and elaborating their cruelties with a thousand synonyms; this delights foreigners." [1]

Meanwhile the doctrines of Sepúlveda, once repudiated by Spain's leading theologians and jurists, gained increasing approval. The authoritative *Política indiana* (1647) of Juan de Solórzano y Pereira, a work written under royal auspices, endorsed Sepúlveda's argument that the natural inferiority of the Indians required their subjection to Spanish tutelage and supported his view that the bestial customs of the Indians provided a just cause for war against them. Solórzano rejected Las Casas' claim that Spanish tyranny had destroyed a multitude of Indians; he attributed the Indian population decline rather to "their own vices and drunkenness or the earthquakes and repeated epidemics of smallpox and other diseases with which God in His mysterious wisdom has seen fit to reduce their numbers." León Pinelo, a disciple of Solórzano, stated, as a fact requiring no further proof, that the Indians were slaves by nature. [2]

Spain's progressive economic, military, and political decline in the seventeenth century tended to harden these anti-Indian attitudes and to discourage criticism of the Conquest and Spain's Indian policy. On the defensive or in retreat in the Old World and the New, an anachronism among Western nations in its stubborn resistance to change, Spain grew increasingly intolerant of dissent. For the later Hapsburgs to allow, as had Charles V, a domestic debate on Spain's Indian policies in the full sight and hearing of Europe was unthinkable. Such a debate would have had little point, in any case, for the Hapsburgs could not seriously undertake a program for lightening the burdens of their Indian subjects. Chronically faced with bankruptcy, Spain's rulers instead increased tribute demands on the Indians; they connived with the colonial aristocracy in its usurpation of Indian lands through the device of *composición*, royal confirmation of title to such lands in return for a stipulated fee. In an atmosphere of financial crisis, corruption, and cynicism at the Spanish court, the highest colonial offices were sold to great nobles who expected to recover their investment and make a profit at the expense of the Indians. In 1695, for example, the viceroyships of Peru and Mexico were in effect sold to the highest bidders. [3]

These realities made it difficult if not impossible for seventeenth-century Spanish historians of the Conquest to write about the Indians and their civilizations in an objective manner. Moreover, all these historians were official chroniclers whose writing constituted an instrument of Spanish state policy. Their aim was to justify Spain's work in America, to refute foreign fault-finders, and to revive the drooping national spirit by evoking the brilliant exploits of the conquistadors. Consequently, if they acknowledged Aztec bravery in the defense of Tenochtitlán, it was to throw into bolder relief the heroism of Cortés and his men; if they praised the splendor of Tenochtitlán, it was to enchance the value of Cortés' conquests. They did not regard Indian life and manners as worthy of study for their own sake; moreover, they were rather contemptuous of the Mendicant tradition of careful inquiry into Indian antiquities.

The work of Antonio de Herrera y Tordesillas illustrates these attitudes. Herrera received his appointment as royal chronicler of the Indies in 1596 and promptly began to compose a general account of the Spanish discoveries and conquests in America. By 1615 he had completed his vast enterprise. In his dedication of the *Historia general de los hechos de los castellanos en las islas y tierra firme del Mar Océano* to Philip III, Herrera stressed the motive of defending the injured Spanish honor. Certain writers had abandoned the impartial spirit proper to history in order "to diminish the piety, valor, and constancy shown by the Spanish nation in the discovery, pacification, and settlement of many new lands." These writers had made more of the evil acts of a few Spaniards than of the good done by many; they had not understood that even the evils of the Conquest were divine retribution for the many sins of the Indians.

Herrera's official position gave him access to a wealth of manuscripts in the Spanish archives; copyists and research assistants were placed at his disposal. He had a clear and fluent style. With these advantages he could have written a superior new account of the Conquest of Mexico and its native civilizations. Unhappily, he did nothing of the kind. Carlos Bosch García has shown that Herrera lifted whole chapters from the manuscript history of Cervantes de Salazar, who himself had plagiarized extensively from Gómara.[4] Herrera did the same with Muñoz Camargo's history of Tlaxcala and the *Breve y sumaria relación* of Alonso de Zorita, often without changing a comma, and never identifying his source. It cannot be denied that he rendered his contemporaries a service by publishing the contents of these manuscript works. His book stands as a veritable mine of historical and ethnographic information. Nonetheless, his account of ancient Mexican civilization lacks originality or a distinctive viewpoint.

The *Historia de la conquista de México* of Antonio de Solís offers much more interest. Solís, a talented poet and playwright, was named royal chronicler of the Indies by Philip IV in 1661. His history, published in 1684 as a fruit of his old age, reveals a haughty aristocratic spirit, a fervent piety, and the same sombre *desengaño*, disillusionment with the things of this world, that pervades the plays of Calderón. Over the work broods an unspoken awareness of Spain's melancholy plight in the reign of the imbecile Charles II. In a letter to his friend Alonso Carrera, Solís gave voice to that awareness: "A fine time we have come to! May God look after us, for our poverty and misery give us a just claim on His mercy." [5]

Regarding his subject with the eyes of a skilled playwright, Solís gave his history the form of a heroic drama. He omitted from his narrative all that he considered unessential or derogatory to the high dignity of the theme. The work proceeded with rising tension to a climax and resolution. The hero, Cortés, was an instrument of Divine Providence; the Indians were the hosts of Satan, who personally intervened to prevent the light of the Faith from flooding the New World. Following his historical model, Livy, Solís assigned to his Indian as well as his Spanish figures formal speeches that sometimes create an effect of incongruity and fantasy. The style is grave and mannered, but free of Gongorist obscurity and bombast. Although he criticized Bernal Díaz' homely speech and plebeian fractiousness, Solís made large use of his *Historia verdadera;* he also drew on such well-known sources as Herrera's work, the letters of Cortés, and the histories of Gómara and Acosta.

Solís declared that a strong motive in his work was the desire to defend Spain's honor against foreign detractors. Foreign writers, he complained, had written whole volumes to obscure the glory of the conquistadors. He listed Benzoni, De Bry, and Jean de Laet among the principal offenders. Solís bitterly criticized Las Casas for supplying ammunition to these enemies of Spain, and charged that he "showed more zeal for his cause than regard for the truth." [6]

Solís' unwavering partiality for the Spanish side went hand in hand with systematic disparagement of the Indian character and actions. On the other hand, the need to make the Indian foe worthy of the Spanish hero compelled Solís to make concessions to Aztec valor and intelligence. Solís asserted that certain foreign writers had depicted the Indians as brutes, incapable of reasoning, in order to diminish the importance of the Conquest. As proof of Indian ability to plan and organize, he cited the careful preparations of Cuauhtémoc for the defense of Tenochtitlán against the Spaniards. Solís even allowed the Aztecs the glory of having defended their city and king to the last ounce of spirit and endurance.[7]

Yet Solís' bias repeatedly transformed a Spanish virtue into an Indian flaw. Describing the intensity of the Indian attacks on the Spanish garrison in Tenochtitlán, Solís exclaimed: "Notable examples of daring, which might pass for gallant actions had they been the work of true valor rather than of ferocity." In another place, Solís observed that although the Indians lacked valor, "which is proper to men, they did not lack ferocity, of which brutes are capable." [8]

Just as the interests of his hero required Solís to make the Aztecs formidable foes, so the conventions of humanist historiography required him to assign to the leading Indian personages of the story both a large dignity and loftiness of expression and an appropriately advanced cultural setting. Solís furnished the Tlaxcalans and the Aztecs with a council of state and a senate. In these bodies Indian tribunes rose to speak with an eloquence that Solís compared to that of Appius Claudius in the Roman Senate. In the case of Moctezuma, Solís went further and fabricated a speech for the Aztec ruler in which he casually discussed the climatic basis of racial differences and the laws governing the firing of projectiles. The effect is one of mannerist fantasy.

"I see," said Moctezuma to Cortés, "that you are of the same composition and form as other men, although you are distinguished from us by some accidents which the differences of climate occasion among men. Those beasts which obey you I know to be large deer which you have tamed and trained in that imperfect knowledge which the instincts of animals can attain. Your arms, which resemble lightning, I also understand to be tubes of an unknown metal whose effect, like that of our blowguns, proceeds from compressed air which seeks a vent and casts out the impediment. The fire which your tubes discharge with greater noise is at most some supernatural secret of that same science which our magicians understand." [9]

The abundant testimony of Spanish sources obliged Solís to acknowledge the excellence of Aztec political and social organization. "The Mexican government," he observed, "displayed a remarkable harmony between the parts that composed it." Aztec justice "paid equal attention to the assignment of rewards and punishments." He especially commended the Aztec educational system. "One of the principal and most laudable features of their government was the education of children, and the great industry with which they sought to discover and encourage their inclinations. They had public schools for the instruction of the plebeians, and colleges and seminaries, very well endowed, where the sons of nobles were reared from infancy, and where they continued until they were able to make their fortunes or follow their inclinations."

Solís admired above all the feudal-militarist features of Aztec society: the knightly orders of Jaguars and Eagles, each with its special insignia and dress, and the honors of fringes and pendants accorded to warriors as they rose in their profession. "We must praise the Mexicans for the ardor with which they aspired to such honors, and Moctezuma for having introduced them; this money, being most easily coined, holds the first place among the treasures of a king." [10]

Yet all these virtues failed to lessen the detestable nature of the Aztec religion. Following Acosta, Solís ascribed the similarities between Christian and Aztec religious ceremonies to the wiles of the Devil. It was the Devil who introduced among the Aztecs infant baptism, confession of sins, and even "a kind of ridiculous communion that the priests administered on certain days of the year, dividing into small portions an idol made of flour mixed with honey which they called God of Penitence." Solís closed the subject, which he found distasteful, by observing that the Mexican religion "was a detestable compound of all the errors and abominations found among pagans in the different parts of the world."

He would not go into detail about their superstitions, "not only because we meet them at every step, with tedious repetitions, in all the histories of the Indies, but because it is our opinion that we cannot be too cautious about how we write upon a subject of this nature, and at best we look upon it as an unnecessary lesson, affording the reader little pleasure and much less profit." [11]

Solís was the last notable representative of the militant anti-Indian school of historians that had begun with Oviedo and Gómara. In Spain his book scored an immediate success. It was presently translated and published in France (1691), Holland (1692), Italy (1699), and England (1724). Nevertheless, the historiographic conventions to which Solís adhered were already becoming obsolete; half a century later those conventions, coupled with Solís' implacable partiality for the Spanish side, would inspire amusement or satirical jibes beyond the Pyrenees. In the Peninsula his book continued to be a perennial favorite, as shown by the twenty-five editions published in the eighteenth century.

Spanish literature of the Golden Age almost completely ignored the Conquest of Mexico and the Aztec theme. Not that the New World was absent from the Spanish consciousness. The writings of Lope de Vega, Tirso de Molina, Cervantes, and lesser literary lights reveal the existence of a body of attitudes and images relating to America. To begin with, the New World was associated in the Spanish mind with gold, silver, precious stones, all kinds of riches. It was a land of hope to which Spaniards dreamed of escaping from the poverty and misery of Castile; we know that the great Cervantes aspired to end his days in some sinecure in New Spain or Peru. Yet strong disapproval tempered this favorable view of America. Spaniards tended to believe that American wealth was typically obtained by fraud and cruel exploitation and had corrupted the severe old Castilian manners; it had transformed Seville into a "New Babylon." Hence the literary portrait of the Indiano, the nouveau-riche returned from America, often featured qualities of ostentation, vulgarity, and low cunning.[12]

The Indian fared no better at the hands of Spanish writers. The composite portrait of the Indian drawn by the Spanish literary imagination assigned him great strength, ferocity, and the practices of cannibalism and human sacrifice, dressed him in a feathered headdress and a belt of feathers, and placed a bow and arrows in his hands. Lope de Vega illustrates the total indifference of the Spanish literary guild to the reality of Indian life; in one play he speaks of "the naked Mexicans dancing their *areitos.*" In fact the Aztecs wore clothes and the *areitos* were West Indian dances. To complete the effect of incongruity, Lope sometimes made his Indians speak like "the shepherds of pastoral novels, polished courtiers disguised behind masks . . . who know their mythology to the last letter and allude to it with great propriety." [13]

No surviving Spanish play or novel of the seventeenth century deals with the conquest of Mexico. We know that Lope wrote a play with the title of *La conquista de México,* but it is not certain that it centered on events in America. Lope occasionally refers to Cortés, and the Cortés in his play *La mayor desgracia de Carlos V y hechicerías de Argel* defends the valor of the Aztecs to disprove the suggestion that he won an easy victory against naked foes who were frightened of a horse and the sound of a musket.[14] In sum, however, we cannot speak of a Spanish literary image of the Aztecs in this period.

The Mendicant tradition of intensive and respectful study of the Indian past was in full decline by 1600. The waning of the influence of the orders, their growing materialism, and the estrangement of the Indians from the friars as the latter drew closer in outlook and way of life to Spanish laymen, discouraged investigations of the kind made by Olmos, Motolinía, Sahagún, and Mendieta. In this time of abandonment of that great tradition, Fray Juan de Torquemada began to write his *Monarchía indiana,* capstone and epitome of the Franciscan scholarly enterprise in New Spain.

Born in Spain about 1557, Torquemada came to Mexico as a child and in time assumed the Franciscan habit. From his teachers, who included the distinguished Indian Latinist Antonio Valeriano, and Sahagún and Fray Juan Bautista, Torquemada acquired a deep interest in Mexican antiquity. In 1603 he became guardian of the monastery of Santiago de Tlatelolco. Knowing his interest in Indian topics, his superiors ordered him to write a history that should celebrate the first century of Franciscan missionary activity in New Spain. By 1613 Torquemada had completed the *Monarchía indiana.* Approved by his superiors and the Council of the Indies, it was published in Seville in 1615 in three stout volumes. Most of the copies of this edition were lost at sea; a second edition appeared in Madrid in 1723. In his prologue, Torquemada explained that he had written the book at the command of his superiors and in a spirit of affection for the Indians, whose errors he wished to excuse. He had sought to make known "all the things by which they preserved their pagan republics—things that refute the name of beasts which the Spaniards have given them."

John L. Phelan suggests that another motive underlay the publication of the *Monarchía indiana*. He speculates that permission to publish Gerónimo de Mendieta's *Historia eclesíastica* was denied because of his militant criticism of the Indian policies of Philip II, and that Torquemada's book, which incorporated most of Mendieta's work while "omitting and suppressing all that seemed offensive and critical of Spanish action in America," represented a Franciscan effort to salvage Mendieta's great history. It is a fact, however, that Torquemada also engaged in sharp criticism of Spain's Indian policy. He frequently cited the abuses he had observed during his many years of ministry among the natives. He compared favorably the mild Aztec slavery with the intolerable conditions of Indian workers in Spanish *obrajes*, and described the ruses by which Indian women and children were enslaved for life in these establishments. He complained that his reports to the viceroy on these conditions had not brought action. "May God provide a remedy, for the state of the Indies is beyond remedy. They are so distant from their king that even if he provides ways of correcting the situation, they are never used." One recent study characterizes Torquemada's attitude toward the colonial administration as "open rebellion." [15]

Torquemada constructed his monumental work around three major themes. The first was the historical development of the principal Indian cultures of Central Mexico from their remote beginnings to the Conquest, followed by an account of events during the first century of colonial life. The second was pre-Hispanic Indian culture, conceived in the broadest possible sense. The third was the history of the conversion of the Indians, naturally featuring the Franciscan missionary labors. The printed work consists of some two thousand folios. Torquemada's sources included Indian picture writings and texts in Spanish; the manuscripts of other scholars of his order, especially Mendieta; and such printed works as the history of Acosta, whose statements he sometimes corrected.

Torquemada applied the comparative method of other Mendicant writers to the study of ancient Mexican civilization, but raised that familiar method to a higher level of generalization. Las Casas, Sahagún, and Mendieta had stressed the similarities between Indian practices and beliefs and those of the ancient European world, principally to show that Indian cultures were not inferior to the most prestigious Old World civilizations. Torquemada had a higher aim. He wished to show that natural reason, searching for God but led astray by Satan, produced similar religious developments in widely separated parts of the world.

Pagan man everywhere first worshiped those forces and objects of nature that were most prominent and most visible, such as the sun, the moon, and the stars. In time a complex pantheon arose; the gods were grouped into classes and orders, superior and inferior, with their respective duties and prerogatives. There were supreme gods, demigods, and gods representing natural objects. "This error, so common among the ancient pagans, prevailed as well among the Indians of New Spain. They had certain gods whom they regarded as wholly spiritual and incorporeal, such as Tezcatlipoca, whom they called Soul of the World; these were the select gods, so to speak, whom they regarded as primary and supreme. Other gods, of inferior rank, they held in less esteem; to still lesser gods they ascribed divinity, although they were mere men." [16]

The operation of this law of religious development, as we would call it today, meant that the Aztec divinities did not merely resemble the Greco-Roman gods; they were precisely the same, "with the same names, although their names sounded different, since all men did not have the same languages." [17] Tezcatlipoca was Jupiter, Huitzilopochtli was Mars, Tláloc was Neptune, and so on.

Natural reason, groping in search of God but led astray by Satan, produced a similar developmental pattern in the history of religious sacrifice. Pagans first offered flowers to their gods, later animals, and finally other human beings. Like Las Casas, Torquemada stressed that Spaniards had also practiced human sacrifice at one time. "We who preen ourselves on having the noblest blood in the world and being superior to other nations . . . cannot deny that our forebears were guilty of the same barbaric ignorance." [18]

By explaining the similarities in the religious practices of widely separated groups by the operation of natural reason, one and the same in all men, Torquemada seems to have anticipated the anthropological view that explained such regularities by the "psychic unity" of mankind.

Aztec political and social institutions elicited from Torquemada the warm approval characteristic of Mendicant writers. Guided by that natural reason which God implanted in all nations of the earth, the ancient Mexicans established excellent laws for their preservation and governance. They did not have to learn from Greek or Roman annals; they could read in the books of sound reason. "You will see, reader," wrote Torquemada, "laws so wise and conformable to sound reason that they do not seem to have been made by men without knowledge of the True God." Because they lacked the divine law the Indians erred in many things, especially in the excessive rigor with which they enforced their laws. But their pagan way of life might serve as an example to Christians. They held one principle inviolable: that the public good and interest always came before the private good.[19]

In a nostalgic spirit, Torquemada recalled that King Nezahualpilli of Texcoco ordered the execution of judges who ruled unjustly in favor of nobles against plebeians. "God knows," he commented, "there is not much of this sort of justice today; men who in the old days would have been punished do not even suffer a rebuke." Loss of the old severe discipline and collective spirit was responsible for the decline of Indian morality and morale. "The Indians of the present time, reared among Spaniards and suffering under immense oppression and labor, are the most mean-spirited people in the world; they want only to live their lives and shun work, for they are oppressed like the children of Israel in Egypt."[20]

Torquemada offered the conventional Mendicant eulogy of Aztec cultural achievements. The temples of Tenochtitlán and Texcoco were larger than the Egyptian temple of Busiris; and were ornamented with paintings that made the whole "appear the work of a very subtle, delicate brush." Torquemada especially admired the technical finish of Aztec sculpture, citing two bas-reliefs of Mexican kings still standing in the Chapultepec woods. These portraits were sculptured in virgin rock. So smooth and clean was the work that it seemed done in wax rather than stone.[21]

Aztec literature, whose beauties he illustrated by including in his book a number of the Speeches of the Ancients, inspired Torquemada with enthusiasm. "Neither Fray Olmos nor the Bishop of Chiapas, Las Casas, who got those speeches from him, nor I who now have them in my possession, and made the most diligent efforts to comprehend them and their metaphors, could turn them into Castilian with the sweetness and suavity they possess in the Indian language." Nature, not the precepts of Quintilian, taught the Indians to become expert rhetoricians. "I feel much envy for the style in which they are written, and dearly wish that I could translate them with the grace and elegance with which they are recited in the Mexican language." [22]

When Torquemada turned to the story of the Conquest, the other side of Franciscan dualism emerged. Now Torquemada, closely following Mendieta, set his face like flint against the Indians. The Conquest, made by fire and sword (*tan a fuego y sangre*), was divine punishment for their sins of idolatry, incest, fornication, and mass killings. Cortés was God's instrument, appointed to open the way for the entrance of the Gospel into the New World. His cruelties were unavoidable, given the circumstances of that time and place.

Torquemada was frequently credulous and uncritical in his use of Indian histories (he accepted without question reigns of eighty and even two hundred years for Indian rulers). Nineteenth-century historical criticism charged him with pedantry and especially with plagiarism because he incorporated in his own work the writings of others, especially of members of his own order. Only recently have historians begun to appreciate the individuality of the work, the value of its insights in such areas as Indian religion, and the modernity of its broad vision of history, which for Torquemada comprehended all the works of man, from his gods to his agricultural techniques. It represents, in the words of León-Portilla, "the richest and best synthesis of what was known about the Indian past at the beginning of the seventeenth century." [23]

Torquemada had few disciples among the clergy, either secular or regular. In this time of anti-Indian reaction, the clergyman who wrote a book excessively favorable to the natives or excessively critical of the conquistadors ran certain risks. The story of the

Dominican Antonio de Remesal is a case in point. With the encouragement of Torquemada, Remesal completed a large work which combined a religious and political history of the province of Guatemala with a eulogistic biography of Las Casas. In 1619, having received the approval of ecclesiastical and royal censors, the book was published in Spain. On Remesal's return to Guatemala, however, a storm broke over his head. His enemy Ruiz de Corral, Dean of the Cathedral of Guatemala City and *comisario* of the Holy Office, ordered all copies of Remesal's book seized, confined Remesal in his monastery cell, and charged him before the Inquisition of Mexico City with various offenses. Ruiz accused Remesal of defaming Cortés, Pedro de Alvarado, and other distinguished conquistadors and their descendants; he also objected to Remesal's statement that "the encomiendas and *repartimientos* of which the New Laws treat were always against the wishes of the kings of Castile." [24]

Remesal eventually gained his release and also dismissal of the charges against him, but his priestly career was finished. His own Dominican chapter repudiated him and his provincial exiled him to New Spain, where he was again denied permission to preach. His pleas for redress went unheard, and he died in obscurity, probably in 1627.[25]

A Spanish statesman and ecclesiastic of rare ability and integrity, Juan de Palafox, espoused the Indian cause that the orders had almost abandoned. Of illustrious birth, Palafox made a brilliant record at the University of Salamanca and went on to serve the government of Philip IV, first on the Council of War and later on the Council of the Indies. Having entered the Church, he was in 1639 appointed Bishop of Puebla in New Spain. In these various offices he offered the king excellent advice but was rarely heeded. Palafox shared the agony of those thoughtful and responsible Spaniards who perceived their country's drift toward disaster but were unable to halt it. "So wretched is the state of Spain," he wrote in 1642, "that only the grace of God and the zeal and valor of the king, aided by his good ministers and vassals, can return it to its former credit and splendor." [26]

Palafox developed his interest in the Indian problem during a stay of nine years (1639 to 1648) in Mexico. To his office of Bishop of Puebla he briefly joined that of viceroy. His Indianism reflected a sincere desire to relieve the misery of the wretched natives. "The Indians," he wrote in a report to his successor as viceroy, the Conde de Salvatierra, "are so miserable that nothing deserves more attention on Your Excellency's part than their protection; for the outrageous profits of the alcaldes mayores, parish priests, caciques, and governors are made from their sweat, with the use of all the ruses that greed can invent to exploit the nakedness and misery of these unfortunates." Palafox gave a practical demonstration of his interest in Indian welfare and the cause of education by founding in 1648 the Colegio de San Pedro de Puebla, where Indian children studied side by side with the children of Spaniards, and Indians were admitted to competitions for teaching posts and scholarships.[27] The magnificent Biblioteca Palafoxiana, still standing in Puebla, testifies to his love of books and learning.

In an eloquent memorial, later entitled *De la naturaleza de los indios,* Palafox attempted to move Philip IV to action in behalf of the Indians. Viceroys and other high officials, he wrote, did not understand the sufferings of the Indians, because between them and the Indians stood the very men who exploited the Indians, men who did all in their power to conceal from the viceroy the true situation of the natives. Prelates like himself were closer to the Indians and their problems. In order to prove the Indians' claim to royal protection, Palafox proposed to speak of the character and virtues of these "most useful and loyal vassals of the Indies."

Thoroughly Lascasian was Palafox's first argument in defense of the Indians. In Europe, Asia, and Africa, idolatry had resisted the entrance of the Faith, sword in hand. Not in America, where the Indians had accepted the Catholic religion like "meek lambs," erecting temples to God and tearing down the temples of Belial. Palafox cited the ready submission of Moctezuma. Persuaded by the words of Cortés and the Quetzalcóatl legend, Moctezuma together with his lords took an oath of obedience to the Emperor Charles V. True, Moctezuma's vassals had for various reasons become disaffected and had rebelled against the Spaniards, but the former, having once been conquered, never again sought to throw off the Spanish rule. Comparing Indian docility with the rebellious spirit of the Dutch and Portuguese, Palafox commented that the king had good reason to favor subjects who were so loyal and who had been acquired with so little bloodshed.

Palafox stressed that the swift submission of the Aztecs was not due to lack of valor. He cited their expulsion of Cortés and his large Spanish force of sixteen hundred men and two hundred horses from Tenochtitlán, a rout that caused such heavy losses that the shattered Spanish army had to retreat to Tlaxcala. To be sure, the Indians were frightened at first by the sight of strange bearded men mounted on horses and of their ferocious dogs, and by the sound of their guns, which made a fearsome noise and killed people who could not see the objects that slew them. Imaginatively, Palafox suggested that Europeans would be just as terrified if their continent were invaded by people of strange aspect, borne by squadrons of ferocious birds, who fought from the air with weapons against which European arms were powerless.

The Indians soon threw off their fears and attacked the Spaniards with great resolution, despite the unequal nature of a struggle between men armed with sticks and stones on one side, and swords and muskets on the other. Four or six unarmed Indians sometimes joined to stop a horse at full gallop, pull off the armed Spaniard, and carry him off. Among other instances of Aztec heroism, Palafox cited the warrior who, having been transfixed and mortally wounded by a Spanish lance, still advanced toward his foe and wrested the lance from his hands.

To his valor the Indian joined the virtues of patience, generosity, and modesty. Indeed, Palafox maintained that the Indian was prone to only two of the seven capital sins, gluttony and laziness. Gluttony he exhibited only in drinking. Laziness went naturally with his mild, easygoing temper, but there was no need to exhort the Indians to be diligent and work hard. "They have spiritual and secular physicians aplenty to cure them of that vice, such as parish priests and *alcaldes mayores* who keep them busy at weaving and other tasks which are the source of their profits; as a result Indians who are not naturally diligent soon have that vice of laziness knocked out of them." [28]

Palafox's pro-Indian views were not typical of the clergy of his time, either regular or secular. The gulf between the early Mendicants and their brethren of the end of the seventeenth century is suggested by a reading of the *Teatro mexicano* (1696) by the Franciscan Agustín de Vetancurt, who drew much of his material on Indian history and culture from Torquemada's book. The two men differed most obviously in their attitude toward the contemporary Indian. Vetancurt had little sympathy for the Indians and rarely criticized Spanish mistreatment of the natives. Indeed, he wrote in the manner of Gómara or Cervantes de Salazar that the burdens of the Indians were much lighter than they had been before the Conquest. Were the Indians not so lazy and given to drink, they would be rich, better off than the Spaniards. God intended the Indians to be poor, that they might remain humble, for an Indian who grew rich became intolerably arrogant. Spanish judges protected the Indians so well that they were insolent. "His Majesty's desire to protect them is very good, that they may know how different is the gentle treatment they now receive from what they had in pagan times, but we must have a care, for they are very malicious." [29]

Torquemada and Vetancurt also had different motives for studying the Indian past. In the traditional Mendicant way, Torquemada sought evidence of Indian creative capacity in culture and government in order to refute the charge that the Indians were mere beasts. Vetancurt's interest in Indian antiquity seems to have been rather an expression of incipient creole nationalism. The tension between creoles and peninsulars, already visible in the sixteenth century, grew more acute in the following century; it penetrated not only lay society but even cathedral chapels and cloisters. Mexican creoles such as Vetancurt became increasingly conscious of themselves as a class and of Mexico as their *patria*. Creole intellectuals began to search for origins, for a classical antiquity other than the European, to which the peninsulars could lay better claim.

In the largest sense, the creole *patria* was all America. Vetancurt proclaimed that the New World was superior to the Old in natural beauty and resources. New Spain and Peru, he wrote in florid prose, were two breasts from which the whole world drew sustenance, drinking blood changed into the milk of gold and silver. In a change of imagery, he compared America to a beautiful woman adorned with pearls, emeralds, sapphires, chrysolites, and topazes, drawn from the jewel boxes of her rich mines. [30]

For Vetancurt Mexico held the center of the American stage. In his survey of Indian history he stressed those episodes and aspects which provided Mexico with a suitably dignified and heroic past. Hence his obsession with the monarchical and aristocratic

features of Aztec society. After describing the splendors of Moctezuma's court, he carefully traced the descendants of "this great
emperor" down to his own time, using manuscripts by the Indian
writer Chimalpahin in the library of Vetancurt's "good friend and
compatriot," Don Carlos de Sigüenza y Góngora. Vetancurt noted
that Sigüenza had demonstrated the venerable antiquity of this
noble house in great detail in an unpublished work entitled *Genealogía de los emperadores mexicanos*. He had pursued Moctezuma's
progenitors back to Atoloztli, mother of Acamapichtli, first king
of Tenochtitlán-México, and her husband Opochtli, "a very important knight among the Aztecs or Tenochca, later called Mexicans or Culhuas." [31]

Vetancurt's respectful references to Sigüenza testify to the authority that this creole scholar enjoyed in the field of Mexican
antiquities. Carlos de Sigüenza y Góngora was born in Mexico City
of noble Spanish parents. At the age of fifteen he entered the Jesuit
order as a novice, but in 1668 a breach of discipline caused him
to be expelled from the Jesuit colegio in Puebla. Although his repeated efforts to gain readmittance to the order were rebuffed,
Sigüenza remained loyal to the Jesuits, and by his will left them
his precious collection of books, manuscripts, and instruments.

Sigüenza early displayed a prodigious intellectual capacity and
an insatiable curiosity; his restless mind probed the secrets of
mathematics, astronomy, history, archaeology, and the applied sciences. At the age of twenty-seven he won in competition the post
of professor of mathematics at the University of Mexico. With an
impeccable religious orthodoxy he combined a questioning, experi-
mentalist spirit that brought him into collision with the prevailing
neomedieval climate of thought. In his famous polemic with Father
Eusebio Francisco Kino over the significance of comets, Sigüenza
upheld the modern astronomical view of their nature against Kino's
traditional view of comets as portents of divine wrath. Kino rested
his case on tradition and authority, Sigüenza on observation and
experience. In his treatise on comets Sigüenza revealed his familiarity with the most advanced European scientific and philosophical
thought, citing Descartes, Gassendi, Copernicus, Galileo, and
Tycho Brahe. [32]

Sigüenza cited "the great love that I bear my country" as the
chief spur to his researches in Mexican history. He mastered the

Mexican or Náhuatl language, he excavated at Teotihuacán in the vain hope of proving that the Mexican pyramids were hollow like those of Egypt, and he collected books, Indian codices, and maps relating to ancient Mexico. The son of the mestizo chronicler Fernando de Alva Ixtlilxóchitl, grateful to Sigüenza for his assistance in saving a family estate from the greed of Spanish officials, presented him with his father's large collection of manuscripts and codices.

Few of Sigüenza's many writings on Mexican antiquities saw the light; most are known only through the use made of them by writers such as Vetancurt and Clavigero. Perhaps the most important of these lost works is the *Ciclografía mexicana*, dealing with chronology, and written, according to Clavigero, "after diligent study of the Mexican paintings and after a great many calculations of the eclipses and comets shown in those paintings." [33] Lack of funds to cover the heavy costs of publication kept these works from appearing in print. Sigüenza had to content himself with smuggling some of this material into the commissioned works that he wrote from time to time.

Sigüenza lamented his countrymen's indifference to Mexico's history. "We compliment ourselves on our great love for our *patrias*," he wrote, "but what we know of them we owe to foreign pens." He praised the Englishman Samuel Purchas for having published the collection of picture writings known today as the Codex Mendoza. Sigüenza scolded persons who considered Indian hieroglyphs "a contemptible triviality unworthy of their sublime studies." Mexicans had only themselves to blame if foreign writers fell into error, as had happened with the German Jesuit Athanasius Kircher when he tried to interpret certain Mexican codices in the Vatican Library. Mexicans rarely visited Europe, and their scholarly works remained unpublished, and as a result foreign students had no one to help them.[34]

Sigüenza never lost an opportunity to compare Indian achievements with those of the Greco-Roman world, to the advantage of the former. There was no novelty in this approach, long used by Mendicant writers. What was novel was the motive, which was to show that the Mexican fatherland had an antiquity as dignified, as honorable, as that of Europe. In his *Paraýso occidental*, a commissioned history of a Mexican nunnery, Sigüenza inserted much information about the vestal virgins of ancient Mexico, assigned like those of Rome to guard the sacred temple fire. Sprinkling his text with sonorous Aztec words, Sigüenza pointed with relish to the analogies between the Mexican and Roman vestals. He cited the elegant speech with which the parents of the prospective vestals presented them to the superintendents of the Aztec convents; he had found this oration among the speeches that the "Cicero of the Indian language," the noble Fernando de Alva Ixtlilxóchitl, had from the lips of ancient natives and preserved among his manuscripts:

"Lord, invisible God whose light hides among the shadows of the nine compartments of Heaven, cause of all things, defender and protector of the Universe: we, the father and mother of this girl, this precious stone which we value most highly, this resplendent torch which lights up our house, come with humble hearts to offer her to you, for she is your creation and the work of your hands, that she may live and serve in this sacred house and place of penitence. We supplicate you, Lord God, to receive her into the company of the other well-bred and discreet virgins, and to favor her, that she may be of good life and do what you wish of her."

Sigüenza asserted that oral tradition and the native picture writings yielded no instance of impropriety on the part of these virgins. Why, then, should not Indian as well as Roman vestals be held up as examples for pious Christian maids? The only reason was the common disdain for all that was Mexican and native as opposed to what was European and Roman.[35]

Sigüenza held up the ancient Mexicans as models of all the virtues in his *Theatro de virtudes políticas* (1680), written in connection with ceremonies celebrating the arrival of a new viceroy, the Conde de Paredes. Assigned by municipal authorities the task of constructing a triumphal arch in honor of the new governor, Sigüenza had the happy inspiration of having the panels of the arch painted with portraits of the Aztec kings; appropriate legends attributed to each king the virtue that most distinguished his life. Sigüenza was also commissioned to write a book describing the triumphal arch. The Aztec tribal god Huitzilopochtli appeared on the first panel. Acamapichtli, first Aztec ruler, elected in the time of the Tepanec tyranny, served as a symbol of patience and endurance. Successive rulers offered examples of valor, self-sacrifice, wisdom, and so on. The procession of Aztec kings ended with Cuauhtémoc, "that invincible youth" whose deeds vied with the most heroic exploits known to the history of the world.[36]

Sigüenza took greatest pride in a work, now lost, that was baroque alike in its lengthy title and the spirit of fantasy that pervaded it. This was his *Phoenix of the West, the Apostle Saint Thomas, Found in the Name of Quetzalcóatl Among the Ashes of the Ancient Traditions Preserved in Stones, in Toltec Teoamoxtles, and Teochichimecan and Mexican Songs.* Not content with drawing analogies between Mexican and Old World civilizations, Sigüenza proceeded to link them organically, assigning Hebraic, Egyptian, and even Christian antecedents to ancient Mexican culture. He believed that the first Mexicans were descendants of Nephtuhim, son of Mezrain and nephew of Chaim, who was no other than the Neptune of Greek mythology. The first Mexicans passed over to America by way of the continent or group of islands called Atlantis. Their Old World homeland was Egypt, from which they departed shortly after the construction of the Tower of Babel. The first contingents of invaders were the Olmecs, who built the great structures of Teotihuacán. Sigüenza found evidence of the Egyptian origins of Mexican civilization in its pyramids, computation of time, hieroglyphic writing, and in alleged verbal similarities. His major thesis, however, was that the god Quetzalcóatl was no other than the Apostle Saint Thomas, who had visited Mexico long ages before and introduced the Christian faith by his preaching. This Sigüenza demonstrated by explication of the Apostle's name, garments, doctrine, and prophecies.[37] Sigüenza had now created a most venerable and honorable antiquity for his Mexican fatherland.

Sigüenza's aristocratic *patria* obviously did not count the Indian and mestizo masses among its sons. Walls of prejudice and distrust divided the creole aristocracy from the native proletariat. On occasion Sigüenza wrote with generous appreciation of the Indian commoners, "a people who surpass all others in patient endurance of suffering, trampled underfoot by all, endlessly waiting for relief from their miseries." [38] Yet when Indian discontent, raised to intolerable pitch by famine conditions, burst forth in the great riots in Mexico City of June 6–9, 1692, Sigüenza turned in cold anger against a people no longer patient. In a memorial to the viceroy he recommended ouster of the Indians from the center of the city and the permanent separation of the Spanish and Indian quarters. In the manner of that other creole *aficionado* of Indian antiquities, Vetancurt, Sigüenza spoke of the "inherent malice" felt by the Indians toward Spaniards, "even those who do most for them." [39] Put to the test, Sigüenza's sympathy for the living Indians of his own time proved more rhetorical than real.

Mexican literature of the seventeenth century only faintly reflected its Indian milieu. Indicative of the poverty of ideas and imagination of most colonial literature is a long, dreary poem by Arias de Villalobos which traces the history of Mexico City from its founding to 1623.[40] The only authentic native elements in the poem are the Náhuatl words that Villalobos sprinkled through his text and whose meaning he carefully explained in footnotes.

Among a multitude of colonial poetasters towered a strange and rare genius, the nun Juana Inés de la Cruz. Sor Juana dealt delicately and perceptively with a difficult theme drawn from Aztec religion in the *loa* or prologue that introduces the mystery play *El divino Narciso*.[41] The *loa*, itself a short mystery play, opens with two royal Indian figures presiding over a festival in honor of the god Huitzilopochtli. Occident, the West, is adorned with a crown; beside him sits his consort, America, wearing native dress, a mantle and a huipil. Indians, men and women, dance about them, holding plumes and rattles in their hands, "as is the custom in this dance." Meanwhile a figure symbolizing Music sings that on this festive day the Mexicans celebrate the great god Huitzilopochtli by eating portions of a paste statue of the god, made of a mixture of crushed maize and human blood. America explains that the god sustained Indian life by assuring that their fields yielded abundant harvests. He provided spiritual as well as material protection, for eating the flesh of the god cleansed Indian souls of sin. Sor Juana thus established the Aztec communion as a pagan forerunner of the Eucharist.

Now Religion, in the person of a Spanish lady, and Zeal, shown as a Spanish captain, appear and listen to the Indian song. Zeal grows furious and wishes to attack the Indians with his soldiers, but Religion restrains him and proposes to try persuasion. An argument between Religion and the Indian rulers ensues. They spurn the pleas of Religion; angry Zeal sounds a call to arms; the Indians, stricken with panic by the strange aspect and weapons of their foes, flee, leaving their rulers defenseless. America exclaims: "What are these lightnings that Heaven hurls against me? What fiery globes of lead hail upon me? What monstrous centaurs fight my people?"

Furious Zeal wishes to slay Occident and America, but Religion restrains him; she must have the Indians alive. In the next scene a lively debate takes place. Religion asks Occident what god the Indians adore. He replies with a spirited defense of the cult of Huitzilopochtli:

> He is a god who makes our fields bear fruit,
> Before him the Heavens bow,
> The rains obey him,
> He cleanses our sins and then turns into food which
> we may eat.

Enumerating these benefits, Occident asks Religion: "Can your Christian God do as much?" In an aside, horrified Religion marvels at the ruses by which Satan, that "crafty serpent," imitates the sacred truths of the Catholic faith. Patiently she explains to the Indians that these blessings flow not from the idol but from the True God who makes the rains to fall and plants to grow, giving them "vegetative soul." America is impressed, but would know if the Christian divinity will allow himself to be touched by mortal hands, "like this idol that my own hands create from seeds and blood." Told by Religion that only priestly hands can touch the Divine Essence, made flesh and blood in the Eucharist, America exclaims: "Then are we agreed, for only the hands of his priestly servants can touch this idol, and laymen may not even enter his chapel."

Religion explains to America the mystery of the Eucharist, in which wheat is converted into the Savior's flesh and blood. The dialogue boldly elicits the analogies between Christian and Aztec rites. America asks if the Christian God will allow Himself to be eaten, as does the kindly pagan god. Religion says yes, if America will wash in the fount of baptism. She replies that it was ever the

Indian custom to wash before partaking of their sacrament, and the *loa* ends with America's acceptance of Christianity.

Sor Juana returned to the same delicate topic in the *loa* which introduces the mystery play *El cetro de José*.[42] It opens with Faith accepting the congratulations of Nature on the conversion of the Indians, "whose sacrilegious altars . . . stained with human blood, showed that men are more barbarous than the cruelest beasts." But Idolatry enters and boasts that her customs are too deeply rooted to be eradicated all at once. She proposes a compromise to Faith: Let the Indians adore but one God, but allow them to sacrifice men to that God. Idolatry's reasoning recalls the argument with which Las Casas sought to mitigate Indian guilt for the offense of human sacrifice. If the Supreme Being merited the choicest of sacrifices, why should He be denied the most precious sacrifice of all? Faith has won so many victories that she can surely allow this small concession; let her at least allow the sacrifice of "the captives that Tlaxcala yields to the Aztec Empire."

Faith asks why Idolatry is so tenacious on this point. She cites two reasons. First, Divinity is placated by the sacrifice of such noble victims; second, the flesh of sacrificial victims is the most savory dish of all and gives long life to those who eat of it. Faith offers to satisfy all of Idolatry's demands. "I will place on my altars a holocaust so pure, a victim so rare, an offering so supreme, that it is not only human but divine; it not only placates the Deity but appeases Him completely; it not only pleases the taste but gives infinite delight; it offers not only a long life but Life Eternal." This is the Sacred Eucharist.

If the subject matter of these *loas*, imposing a didactic and expository style, hampered Sor Juana in the display of her lyrical talent, her audacious play on the similarities between Christian and Aztec religious rites and beliefs, her profound insight into the rational basis of Aztec religion, and her sympathetic, even affectionate attitude toward the Indian characters, testify to the penetrating vision and humanism of the glorious nun.

The position of the Indian and mestizo nobility steadily deteriorated in this period as Spanish landlords and officials encroached on its lands and appropriated for themselves the various sources of revenue enjoyed by the Indian aristocracy.[43] Some nobles re-

sponded to this crisis by writing historical works in Spanish or
Náhuatl that were designed to prove to the king and his agents
the antiquity of their houses and the large services their forebears
had rendered to the Conquest. Ambivalence continued to mark the
work of the native chroniclers. Thinly disguised or open rancor
over Spanish injustice and nostalgia for the pre-Conquest social
order battled with their fervent Catholicism and sense of guilt for
the pagan sins of idolatry and human sacrifice.

An occasional work seems to have had no other purpose than
to preserve the fading tribal record by the use of the Latin alphabet. Such may have been the aim of Cristóbal del Castillo, who in
1599 completed a brief account of Aztec history from the migration from the legendary homeland of Aztlán until the Conquest.
According to its modern editor, Francisco del Paso y Troncoso, the
work is written in purest Náhuatl. Despite his Spanish name, Castillo was probably of Indian descent on both sides. He most probably was educated in a monastery school, and his fortunes illustrate the unhappy lot of most Indian *principales*, the lower nobility
who in post-Conquest years lost their lands and tenants and were
reduced to the condition of tribute-paying commoners.

Castillo movingly described himself as "a poor needy person who
arouses compassion," who in his declining years must earn his bread
by labor in the fields and forests. He freely expressed his hatred
of the conquistadors, calling them "crafty killers" and "murderous
robbers." Unlike the mestizo historians, Castillo identified himself
not with the conquerors but with the vanquished. Yet his values
were basically Spanish and Catholic. After a passage, clearly part
of the tribal record, which described with magnificent coloring
the rewards of conquest and its aftermath of human sacrifice, Castillo entered an apologetic comment that the early Aztecs did not
practice human sacrifice and cannibalism, but offered instead the
blood of animals and especially quails to their "false gods"; it was
the great sorcerer Tezcatlipoca who taught the Mexicans "all that
was perverse, all that was evil." [44]

Indian and European historiographic traditions were fused in the
Relaciones originales de Chalco Amaquemecan of Francisco de San
Antón Muñón Chimalpahin. A descendant of the ancient kings of
the province of Chalco, conquered by the Aztecs in the middle of
the fifteenth century, Chimalpahin received an excellent monastery

education and became warden of the Church of San Antonio Abad in Mexico City. His work represented a long-delayed compliance with the request of Viceroy Mendoza in the sixteenth century for a history of the province that would guide Spanish officials in the grant of posts and privileges to members of the Chalca nobility. Chimalpahin began writing in 1620, at the age of forty-one. He based his work on picture histories of Chalco, supplemented by glosses of the pictographs by knowledgeable descendants of the ancient nobility. Silvia Rendón remarks that the *Relaciones* are not, properly speaking, the history of a people but of "a privileged class within the pre-Columbian social organization, an educated class, exquisitely refined, firmly in power." [45]

The work followed the Indian annalistic form, giving for each year the Indian name followed by the Christian date. Chimalpahin incorporated Indian history in world history by associating Old and New World events. Thus the year Eleven House, A.D. 73, marked the destruction of Jerusalem by Vespasian as vengeance on the Jews for the death of Christ; it also marked the twenty-third year of the Aztec stay in Aztlán. Chimalpahin interlarded the Indian history with Christian moralistic judgments. Tula, for example, was destroyed by the will of Jesus Christ for its great sins and perversities.

Sometimes a passage suggests the author's internal conflict: Chimalpahin evokes the flourishing state of ancient Chalco and simultaneously recalls pagan vices over which he prefers to cast a veil. "It is necessary that you should know, beloved elder brothers, beloved younger brothers, that in ancient times there were many more people than there are today, so are we told and I shall show, for there were people in every place that one can mention. And my heart knows one thing more, how the ancients conducted themselves before they received the word of God. But this I certainly keep to myself, my heart guards this story." Once again Chimalpahin reassures the descendants of the Chalca nobility in whose interests he writes his history. "All is told and said here. But do not be disturbed on that account. Are you not perchance Christians? Let not what is told here confound you, for you need only believe in the one True God." [46]

As one might expect, the work has a bitterly anti-Aztec tone. Chimalpahin described the heavy tribute of labor on Aztec temples imposed on the Chalca; he mentioned, among other curious details, the fact that the laborers sent by the tributary towns received only one meal a day. An extreme pro-Spanish bias features Chimalpahin's account of the Conquest; thus, he assigns the origin of the war not to Alvarado's massacre of the Aztec nobility but to Cortés' pious zeal in destroying the paste idol of Huitzilopochtli. "This caused the war, because the priests and the youths of the College of Warriors grew furious. But Captain Don Pedro de Alvarado knew how to master them; and he mastered them by killing and destroying them to the point that it is said there remained not a single Mexican warrior of high rank." [47]

The work of Fernando de Alva Ixtlilxóchitl bears comparison with that of his contemporary, the Peruvian mestizo historian Garcilaso de la Vega, author of the celebrated *Comentarios reales de los Incas*. Ixtlilxóchitl displays the same mastery of European historical technique; the same massive base of information obtained from native sources; the same tendency to embellish the tribal record; the same ambivalent outlook on the pagan past and the Conquest.

A descendant of the last king of Texcoco, cultural center of the Aztec Empire, Ixtlilxóchitl studied at the Franciscan Colegio de Santa Cruz at Tlatelolco. His many classical allusions and references to European history reflect a broad humanistic training. Although he held various posts under the Spanish colonial administration, including the office of Indian governor of Texcoco and that of royal interpreter, he complained pitifully of his poverty and the indignities suffered by himself and other members of the royal house of Texcoco. He and his kinsmen not only had lost their patrimony of land and vassals but were reduced to the condition of tribute-payers; the descendants of Nezahualcóyotl and Nezahualpilli must plow and dig the ground like common *macehuales* in order to earn their bread and pay the personal tribute of ten silver reales and half a fanega of maize.[48] Possibly Ixtlilxóchitl exaggerated his family's poverty and sufferings. Certainly the hope of securing restitution of land and other favors encouraged him to write his histories and gave his writings their strong flavor of *probanzas de méritos*, proofs of meritorious service to the Spanish kings. Clearly, an authentic pride in his Indian heritage also inspired his efforts.

In the dedication of one of his *Relaciones* to Bishop García Guerra, Ixtlilxóchitl explained his motives and his research methods. From youth, he wrote, he had had a great desire to know the things that had been done in the New World, "things not at all inferior to the deeds of the Romans, Greeks, Medes, and other pagan peoples famed throughout the world, although the passage of time and the destruction of my forebears' states has buried their history in obscurity. For this reason I sought with much labor, diligence, and travel to collect the paintings and the songs with which they preserved their histories and annals. In order to understand them, I summoned many *principales* of this New Spain, men famed for their knowledge of those histories. Among all these men, I found only two who had a complete understanding and knowledge of the paintings and signs, and who could correctly interpret the songs, which are very obscure, being allegorical in form and adorned with metaphors and other figures of speech. With the help of these men I learned to understand the paintings and histories, and to translate the songs accurately, in order to satisfy my wish to attain the truth. Therefore I decided not to use the existing histories that deal with those matters, because the false relations and contradictory interpretations their authors obtained made their accounts confused and contradictory." [49]

Ixtlilxóchitl's historical writings, most of which remained unpublished until 1891, fall into two parts. One consists of a number of short relations that are basically Spanish versions of Náhuatl documents. The other is Ixtlilxóchitl's major work, the *Historia chichimeca*. His chief source for both the *Relaciones* and the *Historia* was the Codex Xólotl, painted after the Conquest but based on pre-Conquest codices, and offering the Texcocan version of the history of the Valley of Mexico. Although written from this and other Indian sources, the *Historia* clearly reveals the influence of European models and the contemporary European tendency to regard history as a branch of literature. "It has the air of a novel," remarks Garibay.[50]

The *Historia* nonetheless possesses immense factual value, especially in regard to the political and social organization of the Texcocan state. At the same time it is thoroughly tendentious, displaying an intense anti-Aztec bias that was natural enough in view of the strained relations between the two states on the eve of the

Conquest. Ixtlilxóchitl's version of the overthrow of the Tepanec tyranny is entirely different from that of the Aztec chronicles. According to Ixtlilxóchitl, King Nezahualcóyotl of Texcoco responded to an Aztec appeal for aid in throwing off the Tepanec yoke by marching on Tenochtitlán and expelling the Tepanecs from the city; he then drove on the Tepanec capital of Atzcapotzalco, routed its defenders, and slew the tyrant Maxtla. The Aztec chronicles, on the other hand, denied Nezahualcóyotl any role in the battle of Atzcapotzalco.

The many fictional touches in the *Historia* suggest Ixtlilxóchitl's reading of Spanish medieval chronicles, romances of chivalry, and pastoral romances. His legend-making propensities flowered in his account of the life of an ancestor of the same name, that Ixtlilxóchitl who took the side of the Spaniards against his own brother, King Cacama, and treacherously seized and turned over .this brother to Cortés. The chronicler assured his readers that many signs and portents had accompanied the birth of this prince. The royal astrologers and soothsayers informed the king his father that the Infante would embrace new laws and customs and would ally himself with the enemies of his own people. "They said that he would avenge the blood of the many captives who had been slain, and would be a total enemy of his own people's gods, religion, rites, and ceremonies. Saying these things, they sought to persuade the king to take the Infante's life. He replied that this would be against the will of the God Who Created All Things, for it was not without mystery and God's secret judgment that this son was born to him as the time drew near for the fulfillment of his forebears' prophecies that new people would come to possess the land." [51]

The *Historia* terminates abruptly with the Spanish attack on Tenochtitlán on June 9, 1521, and contains no criticism of the Conquest or its aftermath. In the *Relación décimotercera*, on the other hand, an immense bitterness wells up and overflows. This *Relación* included an account of the expedition Cortés made to Honduras (1525), during which, on suspicion of a conspiracy, he executed Cuauhtémoc and other Mexican princes who accompanied him. One of the executed princes was a brother of Cortés' Indian ally, Ixtlilxóchitl. From an indictment of this action the mestizo chronicler moved to a general attack on Spanish conduct in the

Indies. There is an astounding boldness about his comment on Spanish treatment of the Indians. "So great is their misery that I have read in many books which treat of the tyrannies and cruelties of other nations that neither separately nor all together can these tyrannies compare with the toil and slavery imposed on the Indians. The Indians themselves say that they would prefer to be branded slaves, and not live as they do today, for if they were slaves the Spaniards would show some mercy toward them in order not to lose their money. These Indians are so miserable that if one stumbles and falls and complains of his hurt, the Spaniards are as happy as they can be; and on top of that they rain every imaginable curse on him. If an Indian dies, the Spaniards say the Devil should have carried them all away. I say these things because they happen every moment and I hear them said, but since God permits it, His Majesty must know the why thereof. Therefore let us thank Him for it." [52]

With the curious *Corona mexicana, o Historia de los nueve Motezumas* by the Jesuit Pedro Diego Luis de Motezuma, we leave sober history completely behind. The author, descended from the marriage of a son of Moctezuma with a Spanish noblewoman, was born and lived all his life in Spain. He completed the writing of his history in 1686, two years after the publication of Solís' *Historia*, whose anti-Indian tone may have provoked Father Motezuma to write a refutation. Whatever his intention, the *Corona mexicana* remained unpublished and finally passed into the manuscript collection of the Biblioteca Nacional in Madrid, where it slept until Lucas de la Torre discovered it and published it in 1914.

The "history" of Father Motezuma does not in the least fit the ordinary meaning of the word. It is a curious blend of heroic romance, political satire, and pro-Indian polemic with a small portion of historical facts. The story is told in an inflated, precious style that reflected the influence of Góngora.

In Father Motezuma's imaginary history there is no development. As the story opens, México-Tenochtitlán is what it always had been, "the capital city and Court of all America." Aided by their strategic situation in the midst of a lake, the Mexicans had from the first been the dominant people of the region and had extended their boundaries at the expense of their neighbors. Aztec pride and presumption at last provoked a rebellion of Texcoco, Tlaxcala, and other tributary states. "The cloud of this general revolt broke on all the frontiers in a deluge of armies, hailing not lead but balls of flint, with which they reinforced the edges of their swords and pikes. So great a quantity of blood was shed that it transformed the lake into a red sea." The struggle went badly for the Aztecs; their enemies threatened to break into the city. At this desperate hour a company of warriors led by an unknown captain arrived from the East and relieved the beleaguered Aztecs. To the unknown hero they gave the name of Huitzilopochtli, son of the Sun. The grateful Mexican Senate at first heaped him with honors; then, fearful of the power of the strangers, it considered attacking and expelling them. A venerable senator dissuaded his colleagues from their unworthy purpose. "Unsound foundations have brought the collapse of magnificent structures, and lack of good faith in Senates has ruined many republics." Moved by this oration, the Senate invited the stranger to mount the Mexican throne. He married a princess descended from the first kings of Mexico and founded the dynasty of Motezumas, which, the author assured his readers, was a title corresponding to that of Caesar.

The strange tale soon took on the aspect of a political satire, with transparent allusions to the weakness and corruption of government under Charles II. The first Motezuma banished job-seeking from his court. He declared that the state needed, "not memorials, but deeds, not outstretched hands but clenched fists; more swiftly than the heart learns of the functioning of every part of the body does the emperor learn of merits and demerits of his soldiers." The fruits of this policy soon became apparent. "Gone was the loathsome business of kissing the hands of ministers, the superstition of bending the knee, the futile waiting for the arrival of ministers, the humiliation of receiving rewards as alms, the tricks and deviousness of intermediaries, and the need to steal in one position the money required to buy a promotion to another. Men knew that posts would come to them if they proved in battle against the enemy that they deserved them." To perpetuate his wise policies, the emperor had certain maxims carved in hieroglyphics. One showed a lion battening on a tiger, signifying that a prince should drink not the blood of the poor but that of the haughty and powerful men who preyed like tigers on the weak and innocent. The boldness of the satire suggests one reason why

Father Motezuma's work did not see the light during his lifetime.

No conditions in Hapsburg Spain provoked more criticism than the excessive number of clergy, the relaxation of their discipline, and the wealth of the Church.[53] The fifth Motezuma confronted the same problem; from all parts of the empire came memorials protesting the licentious life of the *bonzes* (the name Father Motezuma gave to the Aztec friars) and demanding an end to their meddling in affairs of state. The emperor hit on the statesmanlike solution of issuing a general dispensation to all *bonzes* who wished to change their vocation. Immediately innumerable friars threw off their habits. "As a result, the countryside filled up with soldiers, the workshops with artisans, and the highways with robbers. Thus the monasteries were purged of those wayward, immodest, and vicious persons, almost all of plebeian origin, who, having been born with few obligations, did not know how to adapt to their state."

There remained the problem of the noble clerics who had introduced into the cloister "pleasures, gradations of rank, and conduct better suited to lords than to friars." These nobles fell into another trap prepared by the emperor. He established a military order, entitled the Order of the Maguey, and invited them to leave their cells and assume its habit. He assigned to these knights "the defense of the two lakes and the coasts of the South Sea, and vested them with salaries, encomiendas, and privileges, awarding honors, not on the basis of the antiquity of their houses or noble titles, but according to the number of enemy heads each lopped off." The emperor stopped the mouths of those influential clergy who were inclined to protest the destruction of their order with the grant of high offices and dignities, which healed their wounds and put their pastoral zeal to sleep.

Father Motezuma was at his most inventive in dealing with the last Motezuma's relations with the Spaniards. He insisted that contrary to Solís, "that consistent maligner of Motezuma's intentions," the Aztec monarch never engaged in double-dealing, never attempted to trap the Spaniards or bar their way to Tenochtitlán. There was no conspiracy of Cholula, nor any massacre there; this "ridiculous fable" was based on a trivial incident—a brawl in a Cholulan inn between some peasants overheated in their cups—of which incident the prudent Cortés took no account. Equally ridic-

ulous were the old wives' tale of enchanters sent to conjure away
the Spanish invaders or that other tale that Motezuma had ordered
the royal roads blocked with stones and tree trunks.

According to Father Motezuma, the Aztec king persuaded his
council to accept the course of admitting Cortés to his royal court.
"If the parting of the curtain of the seas exposes us to the fire of
that other world whose greed and ambition already take aim at
our riches, if the removal of that veil of gulfs and waters exposes
us to fatal blows, no better remedy exists than to welcome these
Spaniards and naturalize them in my empire." The Mexicans would
derive large advantages from contact with the strangers. They
would learn the use of gunpowder, guns, swords, and horses.
Moved by greed, other European nations would seek to compete
with Spain in the markets of Mexico; the Aztecs could play upon
this rivalry to gain foreign aid and weaken the influence of Spain.

Father Motezuma added other romantic touches to his version
of the Conquest. Cortés, fearing that his forces, even if they were
swelled by Indian auxiliaries, would prove no match for the power
of Motezuma, secretly sent the famous Malinche to the capital. She
visited the empress (whom she had previously served as lady-in-
waiting) at her palace in Tula, and won favor for the Spaniards
by describing the good treatment she had received at their hands.
Malinche then had an audience with Motezuma and convinced
him of Cortés' honorable intentions. Assured of Motezuma's goodwill, the Spaniards made a peaceful entry into the Aztec capital
and were received as honored guests by the Aztec ruler.

Cortés' chaplain easily convinced Motezuma of the truths of the
Christian religion, but the seasoned statesman restrained Father
Olmedo's missionary zeal and asked for time to prepare his people's
minds for acceptance of the new doctrines. "Let us make haste
slowly, Father Olmedo, let time and skill bring the business to
maturity, diligence will do more than violence. A king can do
much, but not everything; he can imprison bodies, not minds;
speculative ideas do not always correspond to reality. You are
guided by theory, I speak from experience."

Father Motezuma scoffed at the notion that his royal forebear
was a prisoner in Spanish hands when he took an oath of allegiance
to Charles V. The last Motezuma voluntarily renounced his throne,

Turquoise mask of the rain god Tláloc(?). Height: 7 in. (17.8 cm.). Aztec civilization, from the Valley of Mexico, early 16th century. Probably Mixtec workmanship. British Museum, London. One of Moctezuma's gifts to Cortés for the Emperor Charles V, it may have been transmitted to one of the Medici Popes and placed for a time in the private museum of the Medici family in Florence. Photograph courtesy Museum.

Gold lip plug cast by the cire perdue process. Height: 2¾ in. (7 cm.). Mixtec style. Ingeniously crafted so that the forked tongue moves freely within the jaws of the serpent. American Museum of Natural History, New York. Photograph courtesy Museum.

European three-dimensional representation of an ancient king of the Valley
of Mexico as reproduced by Lord Kingsborough in Volume IV (London,
1831) of his *Antiquities of Mexico* from Francesco Gemelli Carreri's *Giro
del Mondo* (Naples, 1699–1700). Gemelli Carreri seems to have adapted it
from an illustration in the Codex Ixtlilxóchitl supplied to him by his friend
Carlos de Sigüenza y Góngora. The Codex figure is identified as Nezahualpilli of Texcoco, instead of Tizoc of Mexico. Courtesy Department of
Rare Books and Special Collections, Princeton University Library.

IDOLES de CAMPÉCHE et de IUCATAN.

IDOLES de TABASCO.

Idols of southern Mexico. Engraving made in 1723 by Bernard Picart for J.-F. Bernard's *Cérémonies et coutumes religieuses des peuples idolâtres* (Amsterdam, 1735). Courtesy Department of Rare Books and Special Collections, Princeton University Library.

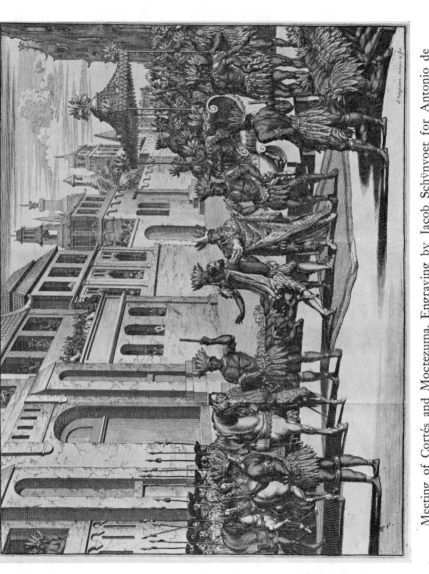

Meeting of Cortés and Moctezuma. Engraving by Jacob Schÿnvoet for Antonio de Solís' *History of the Conquest of Mexico* (London, 1724). Courtesy Department of Rare Books and Special Collections, Princeton University Library.

principally on the basis of sober calculations. With Spanish aid, King Motezuma had studied maps of Europe and the world; he was well informed of the relative power of European kings; he was aware of the superiority of European arms. "The walls of the sea that had long guarded his empire had fallen; across that sea new armadas would soon fly in chase of their American prey." Prudence dictated that Motezuma prepare for this contingency by becoming a feudatory and ally of Europe's most powerful king, whose protection would preserve Motezuma on his throne and shield the Mexicans against foreign attack while they mastered the use of European weapons and their art of war. Father Motezuma thus completed the transformation of the Aztec king into a European prince, knowledgeable in the arts of diplomacy, familiar with such concepts as balance of power, commercial warfare, and reason of state.

Cortés, returning to Tenochtitlán after defeating Pánfilo de Narváez on the Gulf coast, found the Aztec people increasingly resentful of the Spaniards' presence and of Motezuma's favors toward them. Cortés became unjustly suspicious of Motezuma and made him prisoner. The Aztecs rose in revolt, and Motezuma was killed by his own people as he tried to put an end to the strife. The Spaniards broke out of the city and made their way to Tlaxcala, whence they returned to lay siege to Tenochtitlán. As if weary of his subject, Father Motezuma hurried the story to a close. He ended on a note of complete approval of the Conquest and of identification with the conquerors. "God miraculously aided our men, who were so few, to resist an infinite number of infidels who had to be reduced to Christ."

This descendant of the last Aztec king felt keenly Spanish ingratitude toward his forebears. He devoted the closing pages of his book to the text of a memorial addressed to Philip II by Don Diego Luis de Moctezuma, grandson of the last Mexican emperor, a memorial overflowing with implied reproach. "Today Your Majesty receives from Motezuma's Empire infinite millions in gold and silver. . . . The grandson of one who gave Your Majesty so much can ask but little of Your Majesty." [54] That little was admission to the magic circle of the grandees of Spain and an annual income of 100,000 pesos. Father Motezuma does not say what reply the Prudent King made to this request.

Beyond the Pyrenees, cultivated Europeans displayed a growing respect for the Aztecs and their achievements. With the growing volume of geographic and ethnographic information came advances in the mapping and classification of Indian cultures which gradually dispelled the blurred, confused vision that reduced all Indians to the category of "poor savages." By 1622 Francis Bacon was challenging the view that the natives of Peru or Mexico were mere "brute savages," noting that the Inca government had "many parts of humanity and civility" and that the Mexicans had a well-ordered state with an elective monarchy.[55] An outpouring of translations of Spanish works that were largely favorable to the Indians and critical of Spanish conduct in America contributed to this change of opinion. The writings of Las Casas led the list with an impressive total of editions,[56] but Acosta's *Historia natural y moral de las Indias* and Garcilaso de la Vega's immensely popular *Comentarios reales de los Incas* also helped to neutralize or cast doubt on the older, virulently anti-Indian writings such as those of Oviedo, Gómara, and the Anonymous Conqueror.

An idea of the variety of pro-Indian materials available to European readers in this period may be obtained from the fourth volume of the great travel collection, *Hakluytus Posthumus, or Purchas, His Pilgrimes*, compiled and published in 1625 by the Anglican clergyman Samuel Purchas.

In addition to the second English edition of Las Casas' *Brevísima relación*, supplemented by excerpts from his terrible denunciation of Spanish cruelty, *Entre los remedios*, and the summary of his dispute with Sepúlveda, *Aquí se contiene una disputa*, Purchas included in this volume selections from or abstracts of Benzoni's *History of the New World*, Acosta's *Historia*, and Garcilaso de la Vega's *Comentarios reales de los Incas*. The great novelty of the volume was the Mexican picture writing now known as the Codex Mendoza. It will be recalled that Richard Hakluyt, having purchased this document from André Thevet, planned its publication and had the Spanish text translated. As Purchas told the story, "It seems that none were willing to be at the cost of cutting the Pictures, and so it remained amongst his papers till his death, whereby according to his last will in that kinde, I became possessor thereof, and have obtained with much earnestnesse the cutting thereof for the presse." [57]

A slim volume of seventy-one folios, the original *Codex Mendoza* [58] consists of three parts: a historical section dealing with the rise of the Aztecs and the conquests of the Triple Alliance; a record of the tribute paid to the Aztec Confederacy, with place signs recording the tributary towns; and a pictorial account of daily life among the Aztecs. Each section was accompanied by a Spanish text or gloss based on interpretation of the signs by knowledgeable Indian elders. Although the woodcuts Purchas used were so crude as to be "mere bibliographical curiosities" today, and there were numerous errors in transcription and translation, publication of the Codex opened a new era in the appreciation and study of ancient Mexican civilization.

Purchas recognized the value of his "Mexican History in Pictures." "Reader," he wrote, "I here present unto thee the choicest of my jewels." He had previously introduced his readers to the "hierographicall mysticall pictures" in which "the ancient Aegyptians and Ethiopians, have by way of Emblemes obscurely and darkly delivered their obscure mysteries, uncertaine, waxenly, pliant conceits to the world. . . . But a Historie, yea a Politicke, Ethike, Ecclesiastike, Oeconomike History, with just distinctions of times, places, acts, and arts, we have neither seene of theirs, nor of any other Nation, but of this, which our light and slight apprehensions terme not barbarous alone, but wilde and savage." [59]

The Codex Mendoza gave impressive evidence of the high state of Aztec culture: here was a people with writing, numerical notation, a chronology, and an elaborate machinery of government and justice. Most impressive of all, perhaps, was the third section, with its pictorial demonstration of the care with which the ancient Mexicans reared their children, of the high development of their military art, of the strict and efficient Aztec justice, and of the complex division of labor in Aztec society. The Codex soon became widely known in Western Europe. It was included in a Dutch edition of Purchas' book (1651); the travel compiler Melchisédec Thévenot published a French version, with woodcuts, in Paris in 1696. In far-off Mexico City, Sigüenza knew it and praised Purchas for his service to Mexican scholarship.

Publication of the Codex inspired scholarly interest in the relation of Aztec writing to the hieroglyphic systems of the Old World. The learned Jesuit Athanasius Kircher devoted a chapter to this subject in his immense study of hieroglyphic writing, the *Oedipus Aegyptiacus*. Because of the importance of the Mexican or Náhuatl language as the *lingua franca* of ancient Mexico, Kircher compared it to Latin, the common language of Europe, and to Arabic, the common language of the East. Lacking characters or letters, the Mexicans expressed ideas with pictures, depicting in this manner their history, the revenues of their empire, the education of their children, and the like. He denied, however, that this was hieroglyphic writing, arguing that the Mexican signs, unlike the true hieroglyphs of the Egyptians, lacked a secret or hidden meaning.[60] His conclusions drew a rebuke from Sigüenza, followed in the eighteenth century by a barrage of retorts from such creole enthusiasts for Aztec antiquity as Juan José de Eguiara y Eguren and Clavigero.

The Aztecs and their language also figured in the contemporary controversy over the origin of the American Indians. The famed Dutch scholar Hugo Grotius published a treatise in 1642 proving that Norsemen coming by way of Iceland and Greenland first settled North America. He asserted that all the lands stretching south to the Isthmus of Panama had German name endings: Cimatlan, Coatlan, Tenochtitlán, and so on; they lacked only the last letter *d*, which the Spaniards had dropped. Was not the name of the Germanic god Teut also the Mexican word for god? Grotius alleged other similarities between the Aztecs and the ancient Germans; they included such traits as the habit of nudity, a passion for gambling, and human sacrifice. America south of the Isthmus of Panama, however, had been settled from Asia rather than from Europe, said Grotius. "The more highly refined minds of the Peruvians, their capacity for just and extended government testify to another origin, which, if I see anything, can be no other than from the Chinese, a race of equal elegance and equal imperial ability."[61]

The Flemish geographer and philologist Jean de Laet answered Grotius in a Latin tract that easily demolished his frail arguments. Laet, who had studied Náhuatl, noted that the place names cited by Grotius, such as Tenochtitlán, were not of regions but of towns and cities; he went on to explain the meaning of the Náhuatl suffix *lan*. Laet remarked that he had diligently sought in a vocabulary of Mexican words published in Mexico City (probably the *Vocabulario* of Alonso de Molina, published in 1571) for words that resembled those of any European language known to him, but without success. As concerned the alleged similarity of customs between the Aztecs and the Germans, Laet demonstrated that many of the traits cited by Grotius were common to many barbarian peoples; others, like nudity, were not found among the Mexicans. Indeed, the Aztecs paid much attention to dress and had names for different articles of clothing. Laet was also the author of an *Histoire du Nouveau Monde* which contained perhaps the best brief survey of ancient Mexico then available to European readers. Laet made ample use of that "rich treasure of strange things," the Codex Mendoza, in addition to such standard sources as Gómara and Acosta. A unique feature of the book was the set of vocabularies of Náhuatl words Laet included in his chapter on Mexican language, writing, and chronology.[62]

As the century drew to a close, an Italian traveler brought Europe new evidence of the intellectual progress made by the ancient Mexicans. When the Neapolitan jurist Francesco Gemelli Carreri landed at Acapulco in January, 1697, he was on the last leg of a voyage round the world that had been marked by many strange adventures.[63] In Mexico City he met Sigüenza y Góngora, and the two men, drawn together by their common interest in science and antiquities, became close friends. During the year he spent in Mexico, Gemelli made a careful study of the history and civilization of ancient Mexico. Sigüenza, generous to a fault, made available to his Italian friend native writings that Gemelli had copied. When his *Giro del mondo* was published in Naples in 1700, the book introduced to European readers two new examples of Mexican picture writing. One was a map depicting the early migrations of the Aztecs; costumes and other details of this map had clearly been retouched by a later artist. The other was a representation of the so-called calendar wheel, showing how the Aztecs computed and marked their age or cycle of fifty-two years. From Sigüenza, Gemelli also obtained the drawings of Mexican kings and gods that adorned his book.

Gemelli devoted several chapters of his book to Aztec history, religion, and chronology. His discussion of "the months, years, and age of the Mexicans, with their hieroglyphics," was the most detailed survey of the subject to appear to date, and owed much to Sigüenza's now vanished work, *Ciclografía mexicana*. Gemelli commended the elegance and skill with which the Mexicans avoided error in their count of months, years, and fifty-two-year cycles. "They therefore who know how much almost all the Eastern Nations err'd in this particular, may be Judges of how much the Wit of the Mexicans deserv'd to be commended, and look'd upon, for inventing so Artificial and regular a circle." Gemelli warned that this praise did not extend to the present-day Indians, who were neither astronomers nor mathematicians, but "very great Thieves, Cheats, and Impostors." Tribute was due rather to their forebears and their ancient teacher Neptune, "as is learnedly observ'd by D. Carlos de Sigüenza y Góngora, Professor of Mathematicks in the University of Mexico, in his *Cyclographia*." [64] Gemelli also visited the pyramids and ruins of Teotihuacán. He wrote that the journey cost him dear, for his horse died from fatigue. Following Sigüenza, Gemelli assigned the building of the pyramids to the legendary Olmecs, supposedly come from Egypt by way of the lost island of Atlantis. With better reason, Gemelli observed that the extensive ruins surrounding the pyramids proved that a great city had once stood on the site. Strangely enough, in view of the abundant internal evidence in Gemelli's book of his stay in Mexico, suspicions of its authenticity arose in the eighteenth century; for this reason the cautious Scottish historian William Robertson did not use Gemelli's book in writing the section on ancient Mexico in his *History of America*.

In the seventeenth century, literature outside of Spain began to exploit the possibilities of the Aztec theme. Moctezuma, whose kingly office and pathetic fate suited the contemporary taste for heroics and sensibility, now entered the European novel, play, and dialogue.

Moctezuma occupied only a minor role in the sentimental romance *Polexandre*, which scored an immense success in the France of Louis XIII. Its author, Marin Le Roy de Gomberville, had the inspiration of placing his work in the exotic setting of the New World. In Gomberville's fanciful geography, the Kingdom of the

Amazons adjoins the Inca Empire, which has communication with the Aztec Empire by land and by sea. The extravagant tale centers about the adventures and tragic love of Zelmatida, a son of the Inca Emperor Gascar. Zelmatida comes to Mexico in search of another prince, Xaire, who has been kidnapped by Mexican raiders. In Mexico he rescues Xaire; he also saves Moctezuma (depicted as a weak and cowardly ruler) from being sacrificed by his enemies, and breaks a siege of Tenochtitlán by killing a giant in single combat. He falls in love with the beautiful Mexican princess Izatide. After being forced to depart from Mexico because of her father's enmity, he returns with royal rank only to learn that she has died. The heart-broken Zelmatida becomes an aimless wanderer of the seas, and is picked up by the pirate Bajazet (a European prince in disguise), to whom Zelmatida's faithful servant Garxuca relates his master's misfortunes.

Gomberville assigned the Incas a higher level of morality and civilization than the Aztecs; Inca mildness and benevolence contrasted with Aztec ferocity. In an effort to give some air of authenticity to his Mexican episodes, Gomberville introduced references to Aztec religion, dress, and other customs; he also sprinkled his narrative with genuine or made-up Aztec words. The Mexicans refer to the Inca hero as "the eye of Vitcilopuchtli, which is the God of Providence, and the right arm of Tezcatlipuca, which is the God of Battles." Zelmatida wears a Mexican cuirass of quilted cotton, and a head piece covered with feathers which comes down over his shoulders and covers part of his face. There is considerable stress on Aztec human sacrifice. The rebel cacique of Thevic, having laid siege to Tenochtitlán, raises a great scaffold in the middle of the lake; on this scaffold the captured Aztecs are sacrificed, in full view of the city. In a letter written to Moctezuma by the high priest Mirzenia, "unworthy archiculti of the sacred Ziamacazques, and least servant of the gods," Gomberville seems to have imitated the florid style of Aztec oratory, of which Acosta had given some examples in his *Historia*. "After the sacrificing the three hundred Panucien slaves which thy sovaraigne valour destinated for the Gods on the day of thy triumph, after the besprinkling their holy images, bathing the feete of their Altars, and washing the tyles of their chappells, with so much blood as was conse-

crated to them. After the filling the Censers royall with the precious gumme of Copalli, and perfumed the heavenly nostrils with
so sweete an odor; I have poured out mine owne blood from all
parts of my body, and by my purification I have merited the sight
of the great Tezcatlipuca, whose providence watches alwaies over
the Empire of Mexico." The god had rent the veil that hid from
Mirzenia the shape of things to come. "I see comming from another
world, Monsters, that fly on the sea, and throw fire everywhere.
They shall disgorge on the shoares unknowne men, who by their
presence alone shall destroy those people that obey thee; and thy
selfe consenting to thy losse, shalt suffer one of those men to take
thee prisoner in thine own Pallace, and to lead thee in triumph
through proud Mexico." [65]

By such artificial means Gomberville attempted to evoke the
reality of ancient Mexico. What he achieves, with his giants and
Amazons, is an atmosphere as dreamlike as that of the romances of
chivalry; the language of its characters is as stilted and inflated.
For these faults one must blame not Gomberville but the tastes of
his time.[66]

The characters in John Dryden's heroic play *The Indian Emperor*, first performed to great applause in London in 1665, and
printed in 1667, inhabit the same unreal world. Like the romantic
novel, the heroic play demanded of its characters a uniform loftiness of sentiment and expression. In the case of Dryden's hero,
Moctezuma, whose conduct at the coming of the Spaniards was
not precisely heroic, conformity to the convention required wholesale juggling of history. Thus, in the fifth act, Dryden substituted
Moctezuma for Cuauhtémoc on the Spanish torture rack, and gave
Moctezuma the stoic behavior and sentiment that legend ascribes
to Cuauhtémoc. In a prefatory note to the printed play, Dryden
asked his readers to imagine that about twenty years had elapsed
since the coronation of Moctezuma, "who in the truth of history
was a great and glorious prince, and in whose time happened the
discovery and invasion of Mexico by the Spaniards under the conduct of Hernando Cortés, who, joining with the Taxallan Indians,
the inveterate enemies of Montezuma, wholly subverted that flourishing empire." Somewhat disingenuously, Dryden asserted that he
had neither wholly followed the historical record nor varied from
it: he had attempted to show "the native simplicity and ignorance

of the Indians in relation to European customs—the shipping, armour, horses, swords, and guns of the Spaniards being as new to them as their habits and their language were to the Christians." Typical of Dryden's effort to capture the Indian perception of European objects is this description of Spanish ships by Mocte-zuma's son Guyomar:

"The object, I could first distinctly view,
Was tall straight trees, which on the waters flew;
Wings on their sides, instead of leaves, did grow,
Which gathered all the breath the winds could blow:
And at their roots grew floating palaces,
Whose outblowed bellies cut the yielding seas." [67]

The intricate plot, in which Moctezuma dies a suitably heroic death by his own hand, need not detain us; its conventions, absurd to the modern reader, were the conventions of its time. Of greater interest is the drama's character of a play of ideas, with Moctezuma as spokesman for those ideas which intrigued Dryden most. Although Dryden was a political and religious conservative, convinced that King and Church provided the only firm foundations for a stable social order, he was also of a skeptical and inquiring bent, with a deep aversion for fanaticism of every kind, a man "whose intellectual biography consists of his ardent and curious examination and testing of those ideas which were current in his age." [68] In the fifth act of *The Indian Emperor*, Dryden arranged a debate between a fanatical Spanish priest and Moctezuma, presented alternately as a convinced pagan and a skeptic or deist. The second scene of the act opens with Moctezuma and his high priest fastened to the rack. The Christian priest exclaims:

"Mark how this impious heathen justifies
His own false gods and our true God denies.
How wickedly he has refused his wealth
And hid his gold from Christian hands by stealth.
Down with him. Kill him. Merit heaven thereby."

As the cords of the rack are pulled tighter, the priest threatens Moctezuma with eternal damnation, but the king dismisses his threats:

"Thou art deceived. For whenso'r I die,
The sun, my father, bears my soul on high,
He lets me down a beam, and mounted there,
He draws it back and pulls me through the air.
I in the eastern parts and rising sky,
You in Heaven's downfall and the west must lie."

Urged by the Spanish priest to change his faith, and by the Aztec high priest to hold fast, Moctezuma voices his uncertainty:

"In seeking happiness you both agree,
But in the search the paths so different be,
That all religions with each other fight,
While only one can lead us in the right.
But till that one hath some more certain mark,
Poor human kind must wander in the dark,
And suffer pain eternally below,
For that which here we cannot come to know."

Informed by the priest that they worship the same Supreme Being under different names, Moctezuma proposes that they remain in this comfortable middle way of agreement.

"Where both agree, 'tis there most safe to stay,
For what's more·vain than public light to shun,
And set up tapers, while we see the sun?"

The priest indignantly rejects this deistic compromise. Heaven's beam, he says, sheds a brighter light than Nature. To prove the superiority of his religion, he points to the willingness of Christians to suffer martyrdom for their faith. Moctezuma has a ready answer:

"You do no more than I for ours do now.
To prove religion true —
If either wit or sufferings would suffice,
All faiths afford the constant and the wise:
And yet even they, by education swayed,
In age defend what infancy obeyed." [69]

The debate ends with the appearance of Cortés, who virtuously denounces the priest and the greedy soldiers, and releases Moctezuma from the rack.

The French writer Bernard de Fontenelle made Moctezuma voice an even more corrosive skepticism when he confronted Cortés in one of the *Dialogues des Morts* (1684). Over these sparkling dialogues there plays "the smile of reason." The conversation between Cortés and Moctezuma opens with the conqueror asking Moctezuma to confess that the Indians were very stupid in imagining that the Spaniards "were descended from the Region of Fire, because of their Cannon, and thought their Ships vast Birds that flew upon the sea." Moctezuma concedes the point, but immediately cites examples to prove that the Athenians, who were the teachers of the rest of mankind, committed even greater follies. He would not speak of the Romans, "of their inviting the Gods to eat with 'em on their Festival Days; nor of the Holy Chicken, whose appetites decided everything in the Capital City of the whole Earth."

True, admits Cortés, but "the Greeks and Romans invented all Arts and Sciences, of which you had not the least idea." So much the better, counters Moctezuma, or Indians might not have had the wisdom to avoid becoming learned. America had found ways to shift without the arts, ways more wonderful than the European arts themselves. " 'Tis easy to compose Histories, when you can write, but we did not know how to write, and yet made Histories. You can make bridges well enough, when you can build in the water; but the difficulty is to be wholly ignorant of building, and yet make bridges. You ought to remember too, that the Spaniards found some riddles in our Country, which they were at a loss to expound; for example stones of a prodigious magnitude, rais'd to such an amazing height as they could not conceive possible without machines. What do you say to all this? I do not see yet that you have very clearly prov'd the advantages which Europe has above America."

Cortés falls back on the most traditional of arguments: the superiority of European civilization over Indian barbarism. "Civility reigns among us. Force and violence are banished; all the powers are moderated by justice; all wars are founded upon lawful causes; and to show you how nicely scrupulous we are, we did not move a step in that descent upon you, till we had critically examined whether your Country belonged to us or no, and decided the question in our favor."

This, Moctezuma ironically comments, "was a Civility which we Barbarians could never merit. But I fancy you are just as civil among one another in the same manner as you were scrupulous in regard to us. Whoever should strip Europe of her formalities, would render her very much like America. Civility measures all your steps, dictates all your speech, intricates all your discourtesies, but does not enter your hearts; and all the justice which should be in your designs, is found only in your pretexts."

The dialogue ends with Moctezuma lamenting that "we had no ships to go and discover your lands, and that we had not determined that they belonged to us! We should have had at least as much right to conquer them, as you had to conquer us." [70]

How great was the intellectual alienation of Spain from northern Europe is suggested by the fact that Fontenelle's light-hearted, iconoclastic piece was published in the same year as Solís' *Historia*, that perfect incarnation of the implacable orthodoxy that dominated Spanish thought. Chronologically, Fontenelle's dialogue is of the seventeenth century, but in spirit it belongs rather to the eighteenth century.

CHAPTER EIGHT

The Eyes of Reason: I

The Age of Enlightenment, according to a common view, idolized the primitive, and especially the American Indian, as a prime example of unspoiled humanity in the state of nature.[1] In fact, intellectuals of the Enlightenment wrangled bitterly about the capacity, character, and achievement of the Indian. The eighteenth-century "Dispute of the New World"[2] rivaled in intensity the debate between Sepúlveda and Las Casas and between their followers. In this new debate, a writer's general ideological position, the degree to which he was "enlightened," offered no certain clue to his position on the Indian question. Some freethinkers and skeptics made ferocious attacks upon the Indian; some Jesuit scholars of impeccable orthodoxy defended him, with equal passion and superior learning.

What is certain is that the leading *philosophes* did not assume fixed, principled positions on each side of the debate over the Indian. Although reformers such as Voltaire and Diderot sometimes used the Indian to attack the follies and frailties of European civilization, just as they sometimes employed fictional Persian, Chinese, or Turkish visitors to Europe for the same purpose, they no more regarded the savage state as ideal than they seriously proposed Turkish or Persian society as a model that Europeans should adopt. Most *philosophes* conceded that the savage possessed certain virtues, but they were aware of the material and cultural poverty associated with his condition. A typical Enlightenment view described the savage state as the childhood of the race. The savage might display an admirable simplicity, candor, courage, and nobility of spirit, but he was prey to deplorable passions, and his lack of control over his environment exposed him to terrible miseries and privations.

The creators of the great *Encyclopédie*, that monument to the advance of the arts and sciences, could have no serious doubts concerning the superiority of civilization over savagery. Voltaire wrote in 1766 that life in eighteenth-century Paris, London, or Rome was infinitely more amusing than in the Garden of Eden. "Ah! What a fine time is this Age of Iron!" he exclaimed in a mocking allusion to primitivists who condemned the contemporary rage for pleasure and luxury. The Abbé Guillaume Raynal even argued, perhaps with some truth, that the cult of the Noble Savage and return to nature represented a "dangerous illusion" employed by the aristocracy to embellish the hard life of their peasantry and relieve their own consciences.[3]

If most *philosophes* rejected the Noble Savage idea, they also rejected its opposite. Enlightenment psychology, stressing the plasticity of a universal human nature, saw no impassable barrier separating the primitive from the civilized man. The strong environmentalist bias of the Enlightenment, although sometimes used to the prejudice of the Indian, chiefly operated in his favor. The causes of the defects in the Indian character were now found, not in an innate sinfulness, perversity, or diabolic possession, but in climatic and other environmental factors whose effects could likely be overcome by instruction and efforts to change the environment. "The savage man and the civilized," wrote the Baron d'Holbach, "the white man, the red man, the black man, Indian and European, Chinaman and Frenchman, Negro and Lapp, have the same nature. The differences between them are only modifications of the common nature produced by climate, government, education, and the various causes that operate on them. Men differ only in the ideas they form of happiness and the means they have imagined to obtain it."[4] Most *philosophes* neither idolized the savage nor branded him with the stigma of an inherent inferiority.

The savage Indian posed one problem, the barbarian or semi-civilized posed another. Outside Spain, Enlightenment writers consistently distinguished between the true savages of America and members of the advanced societies of Mexico and Peru. How to evaluate these societies, to what rung on the scale of progress they should be assigned, were among the questions asked by European social scientists. The material and intellectual progress of these peoples inspired admiration in some students, contempt in others. The supposed "welfare state" aspects of the Inca and Aztec Empires drew warm praise from reformers bent on correcting the immense social evils and disorders of contemporary Europe. For others, however, those empires served as object lessons of a different kind, illustrating the disastrous fate that awaited peoples ruled by those *bêtes noires* of the Enlightenment, despotism and priestcraft. Thus Enlightenment writers tended to focus attention on those aspects of the Aztec and Inca civilizations that supported their analysis of and solutions for the problems of European society. In the many comparisons made between the Aztec and Inca states, the latter almost invariably came off better, thanks above all to the golden haze in which Garcilaso de la Vega had enveloped the Inca realm.

The Indian, after all, had only a marginal interest for European writers: Europe was surely the center of the world stage. Very different was the view of Mexican creole intellectuals. More and more self-conscious, filled with a growing pride and optimism concerning the prospects of their *patria*, they responded to the new barrage of European attacks on the New World with remarkable research and literary efforts. The depth of their feeling was partly attributable to the fact that European attacks linked Indians and creoles in a common condemnation.

The Enlightenment entered and diffused its influence in Spain with the cautious, qualified approval of a new dynasty begun by a grandson of Louis XIV. The Bourbons undertook to raise the country from its miserable decadence, to arm it with the weapons needed to win the economic and military struggles of the eighteenth century. Under Philip V and his two sons, Ferdinand VI and Charles III, a major movement of reconstruction took place. It was not enough to build factories and ships and make government more efficient; the Spanish Bourbons must also modernize the mind of Spain. Their aim was to banish Scholasticism from the schools and promote science and all the useful arts, without encouraging the growth of materialism; to curb the power of the Church and the Inquisition, without permitting the rise of heresy. In short, they set themselves the delicate task of naturalizing the Enlightenment in Spain without stimulating a dangerous radicalism or giving offense to the feelings of a people as ferociously devout, superstitious, and peninsular, as hostile to foreign ideas, as the Spaniards. The channels of enlightenment included the reformed universities and the economic societies of the Amigos del País, as well as the printing press.[5] All helped to spread the spirit of inquiry, of generous aspirations for the improvement of the condition of the masses, among the nobility, the clergy, and the small middle class. The new intellectual climate also produced a certain thawing of the Spanish attitude of hostility toward the Indian; a minor revival of the spirit of Las Casas and Palafox took place.

These changes were reflected in the writings of a remarkable Benedictine monk, Benito Gerónimo Feijóo y Montenegro. In 1726 Feijóo began to publish an encyclopedic series of essays in which he gave his opinions on a multitude of topics. Feijóo aimed to familiarize Spanish readers with the new world view created by Bacon, Descartes, and Newton. He fought an unyielding battle against superstition, prejudice, and folly of every kind. Yet he never voiced an opinion that went counter to Catholic doctrine. "He united a strong devotion to his faith with a sincere desire to see his country enter the world stream of thought." [6]

Feijóo's comments on the Indian illustrated the characteristic Enlightenment stress on environmental influences within the context of a belief in a universal human nature. He conceded that climate influenced the character of man as well as of plants and animals, but denied that on this account one nation was inherently more intelligent than another. "If asked what peoples have the sharpest wits, I must candidly reply that I cannot give a certain judgment. I perceive that the sciences at one time flourished among the Phoenicians, at another among the Chaldeans, at still another among the Egyptians, then among the Greeks, later among the Romans, and still later among the Arabs. Eventually the sciences spread to almost all the European nations. Each people was regarded as uncouth until its turn came. Later it became clear that that people was not at all inferior to those who had the good fortune to be first. Perhaps, if the world lasts long enough and there are great revolutions of empire (for Minerva wanders over the earth in response to the impulses she receives from the violent agitations of Mars), the Iroquois, the Lapps, the Troglodytes . . . and other peoples whom we admit with disdain and repugnance into the family of man will cultivate the sciences in eminent degree." [7]

Feijóo applied this generous conception of the unity of mankind to the American creoles and the Indians, defending both against the charge of inferiority. Ever since the Discovery, he complained, Spaniards, especially those of the common sort, had believed that the Indians were governed not by reason but by instinct, "as if some Circe, wandering through those vast regions, had changed all the men into beasts." Feijóo cited the testimony of Bishop Palafox and the chroniclers of the Indies to prove the contrary. The conquest of Mexico offered examples of Indian military strategy not inferior to the exploits of the Carthaginians, Greeks, and Romans. It was a vulgar error to scorn the Indians because they gave gold in exchange for glass beads. The Spaniards who expressed such scorn were duller of wit than the Indians whom they abused. Viewed objectively, glass beads are prettier than gold; offer a man two things that are equally beautiful, and he will choose that which is rarer. The Indians behaved as did the rest of the world. They had gold, but lacked glass beads; therefore they regarded a small bead necklace as a worthier adornment for a princess than a large gold chain.[8]

Withal, Feijóo displayed the traditional Spanish sensitivity to criticism of the Conquest and offered the traditional defense that cited Indian misdeeds to justify Spain's work in the New World. Even here, however, a new rationalist spirit was reflected in the reasonable tone of his argument, in the concessions he made to the critics, and in the virtual absence of the appeal to religion.

In his essay on the "Glorias de España," Feijóo conceded that the crimes of the conquistadors were great and numerous. Given the frailty of human nature, however, such excesses were inseparable from war. Indeed, Spanish cruelties were more excusable than others, for the Spaniards fought with men whose deeds gave some color to the allegation that they were brutes rather than men. Feijóo listed the customary charges against an undifferentiated

Indian type: they were cannibals, tortured prisoners to death, practiced sodomy, were given to perfidy, deceit, and theft. He argued that these barbarous deeds and proceedings had inspired such horror and disgust in the Spaniards that they were seized by an uncontrollable wrath. Other nations had done the same in the lands they colonized; Feijóo recalled the cruelties of the German Welsers in Venezuela. If Spanish crimes were better known, it was because Spaniards had risen to condemn and publicize those outrages; among foreigners, on the other hand, not a voice was raised to accuse or censure the crimes of their countrymen.[9]

Another reformer, the economist José del Campillo y Cosío, also challenged the stereotype of the brutish and stupid Indian. His argument wove together the familiar Enlightenment strands of social utility and faith in reason. In a long essay, probably written in 1743 but not published until 1789, Campillo proposed a sweeping reform of Spain's colonial policy. As part of this reform, he proposed that tax-free grants of land be made to the Indians and that they be trained as farmers and artisans. The Indian would thus become the active instrument of an economic transformation that would benefit Spain as well as the colonies.

Campillo rejected the time-honored view that American gold and silver were the chief sources of Spain's wealth. He proclaimed that the Indian masses were "the great treasure of Spain. They are the true Indies and the richest mine in the world, a mine which should be worked with scrupulous economy." The notion that the Indians were incapable of becoming efficient producers was the fruit of ignorance and malice. "If we consider what the Indians were before they met the Europeans, we must confess that they displayed remarkable talents and rationality. This is clearly shown by the immense and excellent structures they built, their orderly mode of life under civil and military laws, their divine cults, and the dexterity with which they practice all European arts and crafts, even painting, music, and the like, having learned them by imitation of the most skillful European craftsmen." If the Indians now appeared dull the cause, he daringly suggested, might be that a long course of oppression had reduced them to barbarism, as had happened to the modern Greeks, descendants of those great statesman and philosophers of antiquity who were teachers to the world.[10]

The enlightened views of Feijóo and Campillo cannot be regarded as typical of Spanish opinion of the Indian in this period. Fray Pedro Murillo Velarde doubtless expressed a more popular view when he wrote in his *Geographía histórica* (1752) that the Indian character was childish; the Indians were greatly excited by trivial things, but important matters moved them not at all. "Their capacity is limited, their ignorance great; this is especially true of those in a barbarous state." Like the Filipinos, whom Fray Pedro knew best, the Indians were uncouth, crafty, stubborn, and distrustful; moral weakness was a trait common to all.

Fray Pedro touched a delicate colonial nerve when he mentioned a popular tendency to assume that the creoles had the same failings as the Indians. He recalled that a certain Fray Juan de la Puente, in a work published in 1612, had claimed that the American constellations bred inconstancy, lasciviousness, and lying, "vices proper to the Indians," and that these vices also appeared in Spaniards who were born and reared in the Indies. The same Fray Juan also asserted that the soil of the Indies was better for producing weeds and metal than men; men degenerated there like seeds planted in sterile soil. Murillo also cited a statement of the famous Father José de Acosta to the effect that the creoles resembled the Indians in character and customs because they were suckled on Indian milk and reared in Indian ways. For this reason, commented Murillo, some Spaniards jestingly called the creoles "white Indians"; others said that the creoles were Indians in substance and Spaniards in nonessential things. Murillo took care not to identify himself with these views. From personal experience, he wrote, he knew that such generalizations contained a grave injustice; he was himself acquainted with many creoles of distinguished talents. He was personally inclined to attribute creole failings to poor upbringing and education, and excessive idleness and freedom in youth.[11]

Creole sensitivity to Spanish imputations of inferiority found expression in a book by the Mexican professor of theology Juan José de Eguiara y Eguren. Eguiara began to write his *Bibliotheca mexicana* by way of answer to a slighting comment on the state of letters in America by the Spanish priest Manuel Martí. Martí had written to a young friend of scholarly inclinations to dissuade him from going to the New World. "Whither," he asked, "will you turn your eyes in that horrid intellectual desert that prevails among the

Indians? What students, not to speak of teachers, will you find there? What libraries will you frequent there?" Martí closed by advising his friend to go to Rome.[12]

This "tremendous and atrocious injury to our *patria* and our people," published in a volume of Latin letters by Martí, stirred Eguiara to a high pitch of patriotic anger. He undertook to vindicate the capacity and learning of the Mexicans, both Indians and creoles, by compiling a bibliography that would prove Martí's disparaging comment to be the fruit of complete ignorance. In a series of prologues to the first and only volume of his work (1755), Eguiara attempted a point-by-point refutation of Martí's charges. He began with a defense of the ancient Mexicans. Eguiara's work displayed a profound acquaintance with the Spanish and Indian literary production on the subject, both printed and manuscript.

Eguiara declared that the Indians possessed sciences, books, and libraries. Their writing, which was both hieroglyphic and pictorial, was entirely adequate to transmit to posterity all the things they regarded as worthy of being remembered, "including the day, month, and year of their origin and of their emigration to America." Like the Chaldeans, the Indians had books of divination called *tonalámatl*, which they used to predict future events. They had innumerable volumes containing their sacred calendars, festival days, the gods associated with those days, and the like.

Eguiara lamented that at the time of Conquest most of these books had been destroyed by certain saintly men who did not know their significance and considered them works of the Devil. Fortunately, the loss was not irreparable, for some Indians had secretly preserved a few of these books and presently revealed them to learned friars who used them to write their chronicles. Eguiara greatly honored the Indians who preserved the codices, calling them new Oedipuses who solved the riddles posed by the hieroglyphs of their forebears. Their aid had made possible the monumental history of Sahagún, consisting of twelve large folio manuscript volumes, the great *Monarchía indiana* of Torquemada, and similar works.

Another prologue celebrated "the love of the Mexicans for poetry and oratory, their skill in medicine, and their laws, together with other proofs of their intelligence." Eguiara recalled

the literary achievements of Kings Nezahualcóyotl and Nezahualpilli, and their efforts to promote the arts. These and other
Indian rulers, priests, and sages composed long epic poems that
were taught to children in their schools; in this way they transmitted to posterity, clothed in the attractive garb of poesy, the
most important events of their history. Thus the Indians possessed
two instruments for the preservation of their history: the system
of pictorial and hieroglyphic writing and the songs that were mem-
orized and passed on from generation to generation. In the face
of this evidence of Indian abilities and achievement in the sciences,
arts, and government, what right, asked Eguiara, had Martí to blot
them from the list of cultured nations and deny them the capacity
to teach or even learn? [13]

Eguiara ably continued the nationalist historical tradition of
Sigüenza y Góngora, whose writings he often cited with respect.
The sharpness of his counterattack on Martí, its rationalist tone,
the passionate Americanism that pervades his work, and his remarkable erudition foreshadow the crowning work of creole colonial scholarship, Clavigero's *Historia antigua de México*.

As the battle lines began to be drawn in the new "dispute of
the New World," an obscure professor of law at the University
of Naples, Giambattista Vico, published a book that marked an
epoch in the philosophy of history and gave a radical new direction to study of ancient Mexico. Vico's *Nuova scienza* (1725)
offered a view of history that clashed sharply with the prevailing
faith in reason and mathematics. [14] As the starting point for his
reconstruction of the early history of man, Vico substituted for
the abstract state of nature posited by the modern philosophers
(who incorrectly extended backwards to the first men the rational
thought of their own time) a purely "bestial" condition to which
all the non-Hebraic descendants of Noah had degenerated after
the flood. To this first bestial condition or prehistory succeeded
a divine age or "age of the gods" in which men were driven by
superstitious fear of thunderbolts to give up their wandering and
anarchical life and institute religion, marriage, and burial of the
dead. In this stage the folk mind, as yet incapable of reflective
thinking, created myths and fables about the gods that were fantastic renderings of actual events and individuals. The divine age

gave way to a heroic age, in which the patriarchal king-priests of the preceding period were transformed into a feudal aristocracy; the Homeric epic illustrates the mythological thought and barbaric manners of this period. Then followed a "human" age of civilized men, of fully developed rationality, prose, and science.

After attaining a peak of humanization, a softening of laws and manners attended by a growing corruption, society suffered internal collapse or conquest from without. This brought a return to barbarism and the start of a new cycle that repeated the trends of the previous one, perhaps on a higher level. The motor of this social evolution was the dialectical opposition between classes, between feudal lords and serfs, between patricians and plebeians. In Vico's view, Europe had passed through the second divine age (the age of faith of the early middle ages) and the second heroic age (the age of chivalry), and now found itself in the tail end of the second human age (the age of rationalism and bureaucratic monarchies). Corrupted by an excess of refinement and civilization, society was ready for a breakdown, the emergence of a new barbarism, and an eventual upward swing.

Vico believed that these stages of development were the same for all the peoples of the world. If Europeans had not discovered the New World, the American Indians would now be following the same course. The similarity of customs of the peoples of ancient Europe and Mexico was due to the operation of the same universal primitive imagination. Thus the human sacrifices of the Aztecs exemplified the ferocious religions created by the fears and credulity of the people of the divine age, the age mistakenly called "golden" by the poets. Just as the Greeks had as many as thirty thousand gods, so the American Indians made a god of everything that surpassed their limited understanding. The ancient Mexicans, like the ancient Germans and Greeks, preserved in verses the beginnings of their history, for poetry was the spontaneous mode of expression of the folk mind in the divine period. Moved by the same superstitious ideas, not by abstract reason but by fanciful imagination, the Indians of Peru and Mexico, like the people of Guinea, buried the dead because of the belief that the souls of the unburied roamed restlessly over the earth.[15]

An original and striking feature of Vico's historical method was his use of mythology and poetry to reconstruct the history of the early societies. For Vico these fables and songs represented the "poetic wisdom" or knowledge of the ancient pagans, their perception of the world, not as seen through the eyes of reason but as felt by "robust sense and vigorous imagination." These myths held for Vico the content of primitive economics, politics, theology, and science. Such ancient poets, heroes, and sages as Homer, Romulus, Lycurgus, and Zoroaster he regarded as symbols or types of social classes and institutions, created by the poetic imagination of early man.

A disciple, the Italian nobleman Lorenzo Boturini Benaducci, attempted to apply Vico's novel theories to the history of ancient Mexico.[16] Born in Lombardy, Boturini studied in Milan, and in 1735 went to Madrid. Here he met the Condesa de Santibáñez, a descendant of Moctezuma II, who urged Boturini to visit Mexico and gave him a power of attorney to collect a stipend payable to her from the royal treasury of Mexico City. The next year Boturini was in New Spain, engaged in collecting the pension. A man of ardent piety, Boturini became interested in the tradition of Our Lady of Guadalupe and began research designed to authenticate the Virgin's apparition to the Indian Juan Diego two centuries before. Gradually his interest broadened to take in all of the Indian past. In search of native documents he journeyed over rough roads and trails to villages in every part of Mexico, living for whole days on wild fruit or toasted maize, and sleeping in Indian huts, frequently "with fear and danger of his life because, distrusting his intention, they suspected him of coming to rob them or do some other evil thing." [17]

In the course of years of assiduous searches he assembled some five hundred documents, including many of pre-Columbian origin, as well as a large number of Indian and Spanish manuscripts written after the Conquest. With this mass of materials he returned to Mexico City, convinced that he had sufficient evidence to authenticate the Virgin's apparition. Having secured a papal bull authorizing the coronation of the Virgin's image at the Guadalupe shrine, he began to collect funds for this purpose. At this point the Spanish authorities intervened, ever suspicious of foreigners and jealous of any infringement on the royal prerogative in ecclesiastical affairs. In 1743 Boturini was arrested, his precious collection of manuscripts was seized, and after a preliminary investigation he was sent to Spain under special guard.

Spain was then at war with England, and the sea swarmed with English corsairs. In mid-ocean the ship carrying Boturini was captured by an English privateer; he was robbed of the few remaining manuscripts he had preserved and was finally set ashore in Spain almost penniless. Fortunately, he carried a letter of introduction from Don José de Veytia, *oidor* of the Audiencia of Mexico, to his son Mariano, who resided in Madrid. The younger Veytia opened his house and heart to Boturini, and soon became infected with his enthusiasm for Mexican antiquities. While the Council of the Indies considered the charges against Boturini and the vigorous memorial in which he set forth his grievances and requested redress, he had begun to write his *Idea de una nueva historia general de la América septentrional*, which was published in Madrid in 1746.

As the title indicated, this book was a sketch of a much larger projected history of ancient Mexico. Since it was largely based on Boturini's recollections of the contents of his archive in Mexico, the *Idea* must rank among the most prodigious *tours de force* of memory in the history of scholarship.

The book represents the first and only known effort to apply Vico's theory to the early history of a people. Oddly enough, Boturini nowhere mentions Vico in the *Idea*, merely stating that he proposed to divide Mexican history into three stages, "Divine, Heroic, and Human, which is the same division to which the most learned Varro gave the names, Obscure, Fabulous, and Historical." That Boturini did not mention his debt to Vico even in conversation with his close friend and disciple Veytia, with whom he lived during the time of the writing of the *Idea*, is clear from the fact that Veytia did not refer to Vico in his extensive discussion of Boturini's plan and method. The omission of Vico's name from the *Idea* is perplexing. Was Boturini attempting to claim credit for the development of the theory for himself? Or did he hesitate to mention Vico because the Neapolitan had already come under attack for advancing views regarded by some as incompatible with Scripture and with Catholic doctrine? [18] Whatever the reason, Boturini's debt to Vico was not to pass unnoticed.

In the dedication of his book to Philip V, Boturini told how his search for materials to authenticate the apparition of the Virgin had led to his discovery that "the history of paganism clamored for one who would rescue it from the tomb of oblivion." He proceeded to describe the "excellencies" of the history of ancient Mexico. It surpassed all others in the variety and interest of its sources. These included pictures, symbols, and hieroglyphs; songs of lofty conception, containing exquisite metaphors; and manuscripts of post-Conquest composition in both the Indian and Spanish languages. Boturini also ascribed to the Mexicans, on very doubtful evidence, the knotted cords used as memory aids (*quipu*) by the Incas.

Lauding the cultural achievements of the ancient Mexicans, Boturini noted that they had developed a chronology more exact than that of the Egyptians and Chaldeans. Their year was a lunisolar year of 365 days, like that of the Egyptians. Boturini declared that Toltec mathematicians, noting the excess of six hours over the civil year, assembled in the city of Huehuetlapan shortly before the birth of Christ and adjusted civil to solar time by intercalating one day every four years. No less admirable was the Mexican knowledge of geography; Boturini described the delicate precision and detail with which the Indian maps showed the bounds of empires, provinces, cities, and the lands belonging to each town, as well as hills, rivers, and other features. The ancient Mexicans were also models of virtue; they loved truth so much that they punished the liar by slitting his lower lip, and greater offenders paid with their lives.

All these things and many more Boturini had learned from his study of the manuscripts and maps in his lost Museo, "the only estate I possess in the Indies, one so precious that I would not trade it for gold and silver, for diamonds and pearls."

Boturini shared with Sigüenza y Góngora and Sor Juana Inés de la Cruz the belief that the first Indians emigrated to America at the time of the confusion of tongues and dispersion of peoples from the Tower of Babel. He suggested that they had crossed over to the New World from Asia by way of the "straits of California." These pioneers were the famous Toltecs. Under the patriarchal leadership of clan fathers, the Indians trekked over the American continent until they reached the land of Anáhuac.

The migration and the period following their arrival composed the first or divine stage of Vico's scheme. In this stage the Indian imagination, confounding secondary and first causes, created thirteen major gods and a multitude of other divinities who embodied natural forces or symbolized important events of this obscure time. In his discussion of these deities, Boturini followed undeviatingly Vico's interpretation of the origins of the Greek and Roman gods. The great god Tezcatlipoca, the Indian Jupiter, reflected Indian consciousness of a supreme providence that ruled the world from an abode in the sky. His thunderbolts and lightning frightened the Indians into abandoning their wandering, animal-like existence and forming families and civil societies. The fire god, Xiuhtecuhtli, recalled the accidental discovery of this element by the rubbing together of two pieces of wood. The god Océlotl, represented as a man-beast, recorded the triumphs of men over the animals they killed in the process of clearing the fields with fire. Huitzilopochtli, the war god, symbolized the bloody struggles between the first Indian farmers and the lawless vagrants who roamed about and tried to steal their harvests. Boturini described the mode of government in this stage as theocratic, with power vested in the hands of the "fathers," patriarchal priest-kings who ruled over their families and over dependents who entered their service to save themselves from the violence of their lawless fellows.

According to Boturini, the heroic age dawned in Mexico when the threat of servile uprisings and invasions by outlaws forced the fathers to form "heroic states." These states were marked by a sharp division between the patrician element and the plebeians, or serfs, who worked the fields. Indian fables that told of the origin of the heroes preserved the history of this period. These heroes the plebeian imagination transformed into gods. Boturini cited the myths of the creation of the sun and the moon and the birth of Huitzilopochtli as examples of the transformation of heroes into divine beings. He promised to bring many such fables together in his projected history of ancient Mexico. "Someday these fables may challenge the abundant talents of the two Spains to reveal to the world, in glorious competition with Ovid, the Indian Metamorphoses." [19]

Closely following Vico's evolutionary scheme, Boturini saw the heroic age of ancient Mexico as a period of notable expansion of agriculture through the burning and clearing of large forests and jungles. Vico had assigned an economic significance to Greek myths that told of the exploits of Hercules. Boturini declared that Indian mythology contained thousands of Hercules who "burn down the forests and tear into pieces the snakes of the earth, who cut off the head of the Hydra, symbol of the earth which, deprived of its head (trees), casts out new shoots; there are thousands of Bellerophons who slay an infinite number of Chimeras, comprising different kinds of beasts, *all symbols of agriculture.*" [20]

In the heroic age, as in the divine, the Indians used two languages to preserve the memory of past events and to communicate with each other. One was the symbolic or pictorial, which employed such signs as the bow and arrow, animals, birds, and other objects to record the exploits of heroes, identify heroic lineages, and the like. The Indians also used this symbolic language to record titles to the lands they occupied. The other language was the spoken, used by hero-poets to create songs in which they celebrated the origin and ministry of the gods and the military and political exploits of other heroes. By way of example of these songs, Boturini cited an epic poem in his archive that glorified the victory of Moquihuix, king of Tlatelolco, over the men of Cuetlaxtla.

In this period, wrote Boturini, Toltec poets fashioned the Náhuatl language into an exquisitely refined instrument of literary expression. Because of this superiority of the Náhuatl, the peoples who succeeded to the Toltecs, such as the Chichimecs and the Mexicans or Aztecs, gave up their own tongues and adopted Náhuatl, which became the common language of the Indian courts. Pursuing Vico's theory that the language and culture of a people always evolved in accordance with its own experience and needs, Boturini rejected the possibility of kinship between Náhuatl and Hebrew, Egyptian, or some other language. For the same reason he denied any trace of foreign influence on Indian customs and laws. The Apostle Saint Thomas, he insisted, was the only visitor from the Old World to the New before the coming of the Spaniards. [21]

Boturini saw the transition from the heroic to the human stage in ancient Mexico as resulting from the growing pressure of the commoners for civil equality with the nobles, for admission to the rights of land ownership, legal marriage, and citizenship. Gradually the plebeians came to recognize that they were not inferior to the heroes, that the latter were not of divine origin; they demanded that the laws be made plainly known and not expressed in the esoteric language of "heroic symbols." As a result, the aristocratic government of the nobles fell and gave way to monarchy, which, according to Vico, "is the form of government best adapted to human nature when reason is fully developed." The age of reason began in Indian Mexico, in a strict sense, in A.D. 660. In that year the Toltec astronomer Huemantzin summoned a congress of sages in Tula. With the approval of the king this asembly drew up the Teoamoxtli (the Divine Book), containing the history, calendrical lore, and the laws and customs of the Toltecs.

Boturini swiftly sketched the rise and fall of Indian states in the third age. The Toltec Empire collapsed amid the disasters of war and famine, and the remnants of the Toltec nation abandoned their land, some migrating to Guatemala, others to Campeche, only a few remaining to preserve the memory of their vanished greatness. On the ruins of the Toltec Empire the warrior-king Xólotl, leader of the "most numerous and very refined Chichimec nation," founded a new state that vied with the Toltec in brilliance. The seat of this new empire was first Tenayuca, later Texcoco. Here, said Boturini, there flowered a famous university to which all the lords of Anáhuac sent their sons to study the most polished Náhuatl, poetry, philosophy, theology, astronomy, medicine, and history, and to be taught those exquisite speeches that were delivered on various ceremonial occasions.

Boturini closed his survey of the history of ancient Mexico with an account of the rise of the Triple Alliance of Tenochtitlán, Texcoco, and Tlacopan, "which represented the majesty and grandeur of the Empire in its last days." For Boturini, therefore, Mexico had enjoyed an imperial unity since Toltec times. He limited himself to a few laudatory remarks about the Spanish Conquest, but made a point that reveals the modernity of his historical outlook: the historians who had written on that subject could not do it justice, "because it is impossible to write accurate history without having examined the contemporary materials of the land in which the events took place, especially when the historian is separated from those events by the distance between two worlds." [22] Boturini emphasized his own qualifications to deal with the subject, noting that his Museo contained manuscript histories of the Conquest by the Indian chroniclers Chimalpahin and Ixtlilxóchitl, in addition to many manuscript fragments in Indian and Spanish.

Boturini added a prospectus or summary of the contents of a proposed general history of New Spain, of which the *Idea* was a mere foretaste. His program, with its heavy stress on economic, social, and intellectual topics, richly merited the name of the "New History" which he gave it. In order to gain the interest and support of the king and his ministers for the project, Boturini emphasized its practical value. Royal officials in the colonies frequently had to decide rival claims to land and other privileges presented by descendants of Indian nobility. Boturini promised to shed light on the ancient hierarchies of the Indian nobility, now "badly confused under the term cacique." He would explain the types of land tenure and entailed estates in ancient Mexico, distinguishing among the various titles by which land was held. He would also interpret the land measures and maps continually used by Indians in His Majesty's courts to authenticate their titles. Because of the ignorance of the official interpreters, they frequently distorted the facts in many cases involving title to land.

Boturini's book would also delight the scholar, eager only to know and understand man's early past. His book would show from the example of ancient Mexico that the beliefs, customs, and laws of the first or divine age were always linked to religion and human needs. It would illuminate the primitive beginnings of the sciences, "whose architect was Divine Providence, whose builder was the human understanding." Boturini's interpretation of the metamorphosis myths would make plain to philosophers the morality of that remote time. Poets would find in the songs he had collected "the nectar of the Indian Parnassus." Philologists would find instructive his study of the origins and the metaphors of the Náhuatl language, a language that surpassed Latin in beauty, declared Boturini. To prove the abundance and value of his sources, Boturini appended to the *Idea* a Catálogo of the contents of his Museo.

Meanwhile the Council of the Indies had rendered a judgment in Boturini's favor; it absolved him of any intentional violation of the law and praised his pious and scholarly zeal. A further sign of favor followed; on July 10, 1747, Boturini was appointed royal historiographer of the Indies. But the salary of 1,000 pesos a year was too small to enable him to return to Mexico. According to the historian Juan Bautista Muñoz, a royal order of December 19, 1746, ordered immediate restitution to Boturini of his confiscated collection, "without any delay or reply." [23] But if the order was given, it was not carried out. The collection continued to lie in the damp basement of the viceregal palace in Mexico City, utterly neglected and steadily diminished by pilfering.

By the middle of 1748, Boturini had submitted to the Council of the Indies a detailed outline of his projected *Historia general*. The Marqués de Ensenada, a distinguished reformer, friend of education and culture, and the most powerful figure in Spanish politics in this period, interested himself in the affair. Apparently rumors circulated that Boturini's *Idea* not only drew inspiration from Vico's work but shamelessly copied from it. Ensenada directed a letter to the naval officer and scientist Jorge Juan, asking his opinion of the value of Boturini's project. Juan in turn sought the advice of the Jesuit archaeologist Andrés Marcos Burriel. Having reread the *Idea*, Burriel wrote Juan on September 26, 1748, that Boturini's project seemed good to him. He confirmed that Boturini's treatment of the Indian fables closely paralleled Vico's interpretation of Greek myths, but cleared him of the charge of plagiarism. Boturini himself had given Burriel a copy of Vico's work "to convince [Burriel] that he was innocent of the calumny that his book was a sort of translation of Vico's." [24]

In February, 1749, Boturini put finishing touches to the manuscript of the first volume of his *Historia general de la América septentrional*, which he entitled *De la cronología de sus principales naciones*. He dedicated the book to Ferdinand VI. Boturini explained that he had decided to write first on chronology, because it was the torch required "to light up the dark labyrinth of paganism," for without it one could not set events in the proper order of their occurrence. Moreover, certain learned men of Madrid, having read his *Idea*, could not believe that Indian minds were capable of creating such a wealth of scientific knowledge. He had determined, therefore, to present them with this evidence of what "Nature can achieve, and what human intelligence can achieve for the satisfaction of the common needs." In this work Boturini made generous acknowledgment of his debt to Vico, "eagle and immortal honor of the sciences," the man who had blazed a trail into "the thick wood of paganism," and who had shown that "the order of the ideas of men corresponded to the order of human things." [25]

This first volume of the *Historia*, profusely illustrated with tables, is a largely technical study of Indian calendrical systems. Boturini planned to follow this with a volume containing a "vocabulary of the gods," a study of the Náhuatl language, and all the material that he could bring together on Mexican astronomy and geography. Separation from his Museo, despite an apparently prodigious memory, created almost insuperable problems for Boturini. On March 6, 1755, he wrote Crown officials requesting an increase in salary to 5,000 pesos yearly so that he could return to Mexico. No further reference to Boturini or his work appears in the official correspondence; and we must assume that he died shortly after writing this letter.

Neither Boturini's contemporaries nor his successors in the field of Mexican studies understood or appreciated the significance of his work. These writers paid tribute to Boturini's erudition and his industry as a collector of documents, but accompanied this praise with slighting comments. Clavigero commended this "studious and erudite *caballero*," but at the same time expressed skepticism about some of his statements, flatly denied others, disputed the authenticity of some of the documents he cited, and found that "the historical system he had formed was too magnificent and consequently somewhat fantastic." Prescott, usually inclined to be more generous, described Boturini as "a man of zealous temper, strongly inclined to the marvelous, with little of that acuteness requisite for penetrating the tangled mazes of antiquity, or of the philosophic spirit fitted for calmly weighing its doubts and difficulties." Of the *Idea*, Prescott said that "with abundant learning, ill-assorted and ill-digested, it is a jumble of fact and puerile fiction, interesting details, crazy dreams, and fantastic theories." [26]

The perplexity and lack of comprehension of contemporaries and even later generations of scholars who examined Boturini's *Idea* are understandable. To begin with, his failure to mention Vico and to explain the master's system and strange vocabulary left readers almost completely at a loss as to what Boturini was about. The eighteenth century received Vico's work with massive indifference. His creative dream, clothed in a peculiarly obscure style, employing a strange terminology, and stressing imagination and symbolism in an age of reason and mathematics, made little impact on his own time. Finally, Boturini's insistence on forcing all his

facts into the rigid mold of Vico's theory, the obvious inadequacy
of his data to support his imposing scheme, the sweeping generalizations and occasional contradictions of the work, and a style
somewhat baroque, febrile, and sometimes incoherent, were bound
to damage him in the eyes of scholars as cautious, learned, and
influential as Clavijero and Prescott. Boturini was doomed to be
known above all as a collector of manuscripts; his *Idea* fell into the
limbo of forgotten things.

The very obvious flaws of Boturini's work concealed and still
conceal from view its considerable theoretical importance. The
fact that it represents the only known effort to apply Vico's ideas
to the history of an ancient people would in itself seem to lend it
a certain interest. Yet M. H. Fisch and Thomas G. Bergin, in their
survey of Vico's reputation and influence, do not mention Boturini's name or book.

Apparently the first scholar to assess Boturini's contribution
fairly was the French anthropologist E.-T. Hamy, curator of the
Musée d'Ethnographie of Paris, who wrote in 1885: "The *Idea* of
Boturini truly opened the modern period of Mexican studies. It is
indeed the précis of a New History, *Nueva historia*. This book
partly strips primitive times of their mysteries; it presents the successive migration of the peoples in their natural connection; in
fine, the religious beliefs, astronomical knowledge, etc., are set
forth with a certain clarity in this book." [27]

Boturini's book does strip away almost all supernatural mystery
from the history of ancient Mexico. Boturini ridiculed the notion
that Mexican religion or customs reflected diabolical influence.
Human fear and credulity, not the Devil, created the Mexican
gods. God Himself does not directly intervene in the affairs of
men. To paraphrase Boturini, God is the architect of the house
of man, the human understanding is its builder. Boturini, like Vico,
may have seen connections where none existed in his efforts to
explain the Mexican myths and fables as reflections in the folk
mind of natural phenomena and social and political developments,
but the approach was a potentially fruitful one, often used by
modern students of the origins of gods and myths.

There is more: Boturini's *Idea* represents the first effort to construct a developmental sequence for the history of ancient Mexico,
a history viewed as a succession of stages, with movement from

one stage to the next caused by internal changes and struggles. It is of interest that the term "theocratic," applied by Boturini to the first or divine stage, continues to be used as a synonym for what scholars now prefer to call the Classic period. The extraordinary modernity of Boturini's historical vision is also apparent in his program for the projected *Historia general*, with its stress on such topics as land tenure, social organization, religion, and intellectual life.

The "unfortunate Boturini," as more than one writer has called him, left a disciple who attempted, in his own fashion, to complete his master's unfinished work. The paths of Boturini and Mariano Veytia first crossed, it will be recalled, when the Italian knocked on Veytia's door in Madrid after a disastrous voyage from Mexico. During the almost two years that he lodged in Veytia's house, Boturini imparted to his young friend his own passion for Mexican antiquities and shared freely with him his great store of learning. "His friendship," Veytia later recalled, "kept back nothing of what he had learned; indeed, he regretted that he did not have his papers so that he might instruct me in full detail about certain matters on which his memory failed him. In order to assist me he jotted down certain notes, which I still have and which he later used to write the book he published in Madrid in 1746." [28]

When family business called Veytia to Mexico in 1750, Boturini requested him to have copies made of certain documents in his archive. In Mexico Veytia obtained permission from Viceroy Revillagigedo to examine the collection and make the requested copies. He had just completed this long task when news reached him of Boturini's death. Finding himself in possession of a considerable mass of rare documentary material, Veytia determined to use this material to write his own history of ancient Mexico.

Veytia knew that Boturini had planned to write his *Historia general* in conformity with a theory that Veytia supposed had been originated by Varro or the ancient Egyptians. Despite an almost filial show of respect and admiration for Boturini, Veytia neither fully understood nor sympathized with this theory, for it clashed with his own conception of the course of Indian history. Declaring himself unequal to Boturini in talents and learning, Veytia professed to have a more modest plan. He intended to write "a simple historical narrative, faithfully drawn from the manuscripts I have collected, subjecting this narrative as best I can to the laws and precepts that a sincere, impartial historian should observe." [29] At the time of his death, Veytia had only reached the middle of the fifteenth century. His work remained unpublished until 1836, when C. F. Ortega issued it with a biographical introduction, notes, and his own supplement that continued the story to the completion of the Conquest. Veytia's "Discurso preliminar," apparently missing from Ortega's copy of the text, was published by Lord Kingsborough in the eighth volume of his *Antiquities of Mexico*.

Like Boturini, Veytia began his history with the dispersion of peoples from the Tower of Babel and the departure of the Indians on their long journey to America. Significant divergences between the two accounts soon appeared. For Boturini the religion of the first stage of Indian history was a polytheism that reflected superstitious fear of the forces of nature. For this view the creole historian substituted one more flattering to the founders of the Mexican nation. Following the tradition of Ixtlilxóchitl and other Texcocan writers, Veytia declared that the early Toltecs believed only in a Supreme Being whom they called "Creator of all Things." Even after their monotheism was corrupted by the introduction of idolatry, they continued to regard this Supreme Being as superior to all the other gods. Veytia also dissented from Boturini's view that the metamorphosis myths were products of the second or heroic age. Veytia insisted that they arose much later, for the Indian relations proved that the Indians of the first period and for a long time thereafter worshiped only one Supreme Being. Thus Veytia substituted for the complex Vico-Boturini conception of a paganism evolving in conformity with the changing conditions of Indian life the naïve conception of a long fall from grace, a progressive retreat from monotheism toward full paganism.

The creole historian's desire to assign a venerable antiquity to Christianity in Mexico was reflected in the enormous amount of space he assigned to the theme of Saint Thomas-Quetzalcóatl. Veytia believed that the Apostle had arrived in New Spain shortly after a great eclipse and earthquake announced the death of Jesus Christ to its inhabitants. The Indians saw the saint in the appearance of a bearded white man dressed in a white robe with red crosses, barefoot, and carrying a staff in one hand. It was Saint

Thomas who, under the name of Quetzalcóatl, taught the Indians all the virtues and all the doctrines of the Church. Veytia hotly rejected Torquemada's hostile account of Quetzalcóatl. He was no sorcerer or magician, "but a venerable, just, and holy man who with works and words showed the Indians the road of virtue by the conquest of one's passions, by mortification, fasting, and penance." [30] Among other wondrous deeds, before his departure Quetzalcóatl prophesied the coming of the Spaniards and the destruction of the great tower of Cholula (built in imitation of Babel!) on account of the stiff-necked idolatry of its people.

Toltec history proceeded in an atmosphere of omens and miracles. By advice of the astrologer Huemantzin, the Toltecs left their first place of arrival and finally reached the land of Anáhuac, where they founded the city of Tula. For Veytia, Indian accounts of life spans of one hundred fifty years and more for the Toltec kings were plausible. The Divine Providence, which had given such long lives to the patriarchs of the Bible, could have easily done the same for the men it guided in their long journey to the promised land of Anáhuac. The venerable Huemantzin died, leaving behind him portentous prophecies and the Sacred Book called Teoamoxtli, which contained an account of the creation of the world, the deluge, the Tower of Babel, the dispersion of the peoples, and all the Toltec history and lore. Veytia grieved that this sacred book had been lost.

After founding Tula, the Toltecs also founded Teotihuacán, the City of the Gods, whose very name revealed that the Toltecs had by now fallen into the darkness of idolatry. Teotihuacán vied with Tula in splendor, especially in the magnificence of its temples. Veytia portrayed the Toltec realm at this period, despite the deplorable growth of idolatry, as having achieved a peak of prosperity. Agriculture was highly developed, with cultivation of maize, cotton, chile, beans, and *chía*. Wise and prudent monarchs ruled the land; and so perfect was the unity of its subjects that they were entirely free of envy or rivalry, all "regarding as their own the increase and happiness of each individual and each seeking the greater glory and exaltation of the realm." [31]

This state of felicity ended in the reign of Emperor Topiltzin; Heaven, fulfilling the prophecies of Huemantzin, punished the sinful Toltecs with disorders and plagues, and finally collapse. On the ruins of the Toltec Empire, Chichimec invaders, a people "rude and rustic," but valorous and advancing in culture, established a new state and dynasty. Their second capital, Texcoco, would give the law to the Mexican world in all that concerned civilized conduct and refinement.

Veytia, closely following the lead of Ixtlilxóchitl, developed a fundamental opposition between Texcoco, last stronghold of the pure ancient worship of the Supreme Being and of a humane way of life, and the warlike Mexicans or Aztecs, late arrivals whose bloody religion gained increasing numbers of converts among peoples already corrupted by the growth of idolatry. Veytia portrayed the Texcocan ruler Techotlalatzin as firmly resisting the entreaties of his ministers that he abandon the ancient faith and follow the Mexican way. Veytia's idealizing tendency reached a climax in his account of the romantic adventures and wise policies of King Nezahualcóyotl. Veytia was still recording the exploits of his hero when death interrupted his work.

Veytia not only rejected Boturini's historical theory but on occasion criticized Boturini's facts and especially his chronology. As Víctor Rico González has shown, Veytia was himself guilty of gross errors, uncritical use of sources, and speculation without a documentary base.[32] In all these respects he was old-fashioned by contemporary standards, as comparison of his work with that of Clavigero reveals. The Enlightenment had not seriously touched the spirit of this pious and romantic creole, who never understood the ideas of the man who awoke his interest in ancient Mexico. The baroque spirit of fantasy that pervades Veytia's work links him in the past to Sigüenza y Góngora, founder of the creole nationalist school of history; and in the future to Fray Servando Teresa de Mier, whose heated imagination would create even more bizarre effects with the theme of Saint Thomas-Quetzalcóatl and the planting of Christianity in New Spain.

In France, as the eighteenth century opened, the Indian basked in the sun of a warm literary approval. Several traditions, whose beginnings went back to the seventeenth and even the sixteenth century, converged in this period to form a strong favorable current of opinion.

One group of pro-Indian writings was composed of relations by French Franciscans and Jesuits who reported on their experiences with the Indians in New France, the Antilles, and South America. Influenced by their classical humanist training, by nostalgia for the Christian socialism of the early Church, and by their eagerness to demonstrate the fitness of the natives for conversion, the good Fathers were delighted to discover in the New World men who combined the beauty of Greek gods with the primitive Christian virtues of frugality, poverty, and brotherhood. "They are all equal," wrote the Franciscan Jean-Baptiste du Tertre of the natives of the West Indies, "without any special sign of respect, even among relations, as between father and son. None is richer or poorer than his fellow, and they all limit their wants to their needs." [33]

French colonists or promoters of colonization in New France contributed another group of writings of similar tendency. An influential early work in this group was the lively *Histoire de la Nouvelle France* (1609) of Marc Lescarbot, who assured his countrymen that the Canadian savages "have as much humanity and more hospitality than we." [34] Like the missionaries, Lescarbot was deeply impressed by the resemblance in customs and manners between the Indians and such models of heroic virtue as the ancient Spartans.

Finally, a closely related group of writings consisted of fictional or semifictional travel accounts that employed the Indian as a mouthpiece for a destructive critique of European institutions and beliefs. Of these, none was more corrosive in spirit than the *Dialogues curieux entre l'auteur et un sauvage de bon sens* (1703) of the Baron de Lahontan, particularly in the 1705 revision by the Huguenot exile Nicolas Gueudeville. The exchanges between Lahontan (who had lived among the Indians of New France) and the fictional Huron savage Adario reveal the existence of a perfect Indian society without kings, laws, or priests. Chinard observes that the book contains not only the whole reform program of the Enlightenment but a defense of anarchy and a call for revolution. "The savage Adario announces not only Jean-Jacques Rousseau but Père Duchesne and the modern revolutionists—and that ten years before the death of Louis XIV." [35]

Jesuits and rebels against society thus joined in a chorus of praise of the Indian, but for very different reasons. Whereas Lahontan and Gueudeville had their exemplary Huron criticize religion and the extablished order in the name of natural reason, the Jesuit Joseph-François Lafitau wrote his *Mœurs des sauvages américains comparées aux mœurs des premiers temps* (1724) to defend religion against the attacks of deists and atheists. In his dedication to the Duke of Orléans, Lafitau immediately struck the note of eulogy. He declared that the Indians displayed all the qualities that the noble prince possessed: "love for country, a natural passion for glory, a greatness of soul superior to all the trials of danger and misfortune, an impenetrable secrecy in their deliberations and, when it comes to action, an innate scorn for death that is fortified by education."

Lafitau complained that some missionaries, "who wrote too precipitately about things of which they had too little knowledge," had depicted the Indians as brutes without religious feeling, laws, or any form of government. These missionaries unwittingly played into the hands of atheists. Lafitau proposed to prove that the Indians, in common with primitive men of all times and places, possessed an inherent religious sense; that no people on the face of the earth was without God and morality. "One of the strongest proofs that we have against [the atheists] of the necessity and existence of God is the unanimous acknowledgment by all peoples of a Supreme Being." [36]

Not only did the Indians possess religions, but these offered so many striking parallels with the cults of ancient Europe and Asia that Lafitau was convinced that they all sprang from a single pure natural religion, more ancient than Moses or even the Deluge. God gave this religion directly to man, and it attained its perfection in Christianity. The resemblances between the Indians and the ancients were not limited to religion. Lafitau had discovered that just as his reading of Greek and Roman authors shed much light on Indian customs and manners, so a knowledge of Indian traits helped him to understand many obscure aspects of Old World antiquity. By observing the life of the American savage one could better understand the life of ancient Sparta; by studying the customs of an advanced barbarian people such as the Aztecs, a European might obtain insight into the thinking of his medieval forebears. The initiation ceremonies of the Aztec orders of knighthood, for example, closely resembled those of "the ancient chivalry of our Europe." [37]

Lafitau's comparative method, by stressing the common savagery or barbarism of Indians and the ancients, tended to place them on the same level. In Lafitau, "Penelope howls like an Indian woman when she believes her son to be dead; the Greek heroes fight like ferocious beasts; and Achilles displays all the barbarity of an Iroquois." [38] In his emphasis on the unitary character of primitive culture, Lafitau showed his affinity with his contemporary Vico, another pioneer of the science of anthropology. Unlike Vico, however, Lafitau explained the similar customs of widely separated groups, not by the workings of a universal law, but by transfer of traits from one people to another. In one particularly wild stab he suggested that the widespread practice of couvade was brought to Spain from Asia by the Iberians, who then brought it back to Asia, whence it was transported to America.[39]

Few French voices were raised against the early eighteenth-century apotheosis of the Indian. One dissenter was the philosopher Pierre Bayle. In his *Dictionnaire historique et critique*, he devoted an entry to the Spanish chronicler of Peru, Pedro Cieza de León. Remarking on Cieza's discussion of the sexual deviations of the coastal Moche Indians, Bayle ostensibly defended Christians against the charge that they had corrupted the Indians. According to Bayle, almost all the Indians were incredibly brutal and vicious before the coming of the Europeans. Chastity was unknown over entire regions. "What the author says in regard to sodomy is frightful; it was practiced publicly and on a large scale . . . there were even temples where it was practiced as an act of piety."

The subtle antireligious point of this attack on the Indians soon emerged. Bayle, who regarded ethics as completely independent of faith and revelation, and who believed in the possibility of a just, well-ordered community of atheists,[40] wished to show that the Indians were immoral despite their religious feelings. "Observe that this frightful depravity, which had extinguished all humanity and sense of shame, which plunged those peoples into all the cruelty and ferocity of cannibalism . . . , had not suffocated religious ideas. They believed in the immortality of the soul, offered sacrifices to the idols, and did not even spare their own blood." [41]

Bayle's subterranean methods of warfare against religion were peculiar to himself. The same Gueudeville who had sharpened the satirical cutting edge of Lahontan's *Dialogues* used the Aztecs for more direct attack on Church and State in a "dissertation" on ancient Mexico, one of a number he wrote to accompany the great historical atlas of Henri-Abraham Châtelain. Gueudeville based his survey on Gómara, Acosta, Purchas, and Solís, among other sources. His glowing picture of Aztec judicial and educational excellence made an unspoken point concerning European backwardness in these regards; however, the irrepressible Gueudeville could not refrain from using the facts of Aztec history for broad satire at the expense of the Catholic Church. For this end he lifted from Solís his account of the means by which the second Moctezuma came to the throne, but gave the story a scandalously anticlerical point. Like Solís, Gueudeville portrayed Moctezuma as a scheming, cunning man who concealed his vast ambition under a mask of false modesty and piety:

This young lord, in order to assist fortune and help to make his way, employed all his skill to make friends. . . . In this he followed the maxim of politics, which, great art that it is, does not scorn to make its home among barbarians; or rather degenerates into ferocity when the so-called Reason of State takes precedence over sound and rightful reason. Moctezuma on all occasions affected as much obedience as veneration for his king. His conduct was sage and modest; his actions and words composed; his conduct always uniform.

He employed still another ruse in his machinations, and one no less effective; I mean the outward aspect and mask of religion. Our ambitious prince, knowing this was the surest and most effective means of impressing superficial minds, and wishing to gain ascendancy over the foolish and credulous mob, omitted nothing to acquire a reputation for zeal, of a man attached to the support of religion, in short to secure the reputation and don the respected cloak of the devotee. To this end the *good apostle* (for hypocrisy makes its home in all lands) selected the most stylish Church and one reputed to be the site of the greatest number of miracles. In this church he set up an apartment, in the form of a tribune; there, exposed to the view of the multitude, ingenuously reports the historian, he passed hours in receiving the true, the sincere applause for his false piety and in consecrating among his gods the idol of his ambition. This pagan Tartuffe has imitators of every rank and condition in Christendom!

Gueudeville related how these stratagems succeeded and Moctezuma was unanimously chosen king.

On this important occasion, the impostor played his role of hypo-
crite like a skillful comedian; he hid for a long time, trembling for
fear of being found; and yielded only after having made all the
grimaces necessary to make himself more ardently desired. Do we not
seem to see a Court Abbé who has been named to a big fat bishopric,
and who, just before his coronation, protests before God and men
that he does not wish to be bishop? What mummery!

Having used Solís for his own ends, Gueudeville cautioned his
readers that other historians spoke much more favorably of Moctezuma. "They depict him as displaying an extravagant, and unheard-
of pride, I agree; but they endow him with greatness of soul and
love of justice, two essential qualities in a monarch."
Gueudeville also derided Solís for taking seriously the native
accounts of the omens that foretold the fall of the Aztec Empire.
He suggested that the Mexicans, wishing to make excuses for the
weakness and quick collapse of their empire, had fabricated these
fairy tales for the benefit of their conquerors, who, being the pious
men they were, took these stories of miracles and prodigies at face
value. "Hear what the grave historian of the conquest of Mexico
has to say on this subject: this devout Spaniard is persuaded that
Heaven and Hell, God and the Devil, were extraordinarily active
in this affair!" [42]
Between 1723 and 1743 the learned Dutch bookseller J.-F. Bernard published his *Cérémonies et coutumes religieuses des peuples
idolâtres*, a veritable *machine de guerre* against Christianity. The
American Indians greatly interested Bernard. He included in his
work a "dissertation" with a title curiously reminiscent of that of
Lafitau's work (published in 1724): "Concerning the Peoples of
America and the Conformity of their Customs with Those of Other
Peoples, Ancient and Modern." He also devoted a section to the
religious beliefs and practices of each of the major American Indian
groups, including one on the Aztecs.
The tone of the book is consistently rationalist and relativist.
Bernard used the comparative method to expose the folly of Euro-
pean claims of religious or cultural superiority over other peoples.
The pro-Indian literature of two centuries provided him with

abundant ammunition for his attacks on such prejudices. He cited with approval a statement by Lescarbot that "the savages observe that mutual love and charity to one another, which we laid aside the moment the words *meum* and *tuum* were known among us." He praised in those savages the absence of that "showy politeness, which custom obliges the modest Europeans to observe toward one another," and from which flowed "all the mistaken judgments we are apt to make with regard to the character of those we converse with."

In words that reveal the influence of Locke, he dismissed the suggestion that the Indians were morally inferior to Europeans. "The Savages have the same principles of virtue and vice as we. This is an incontestible proposition. No one doubts but that an *American* infant, and that of a European, when just born, are directly upon the same level, and that God design'd 'em equally for reasonable beings." The Indians had the same love of country, the same spirit of bravery, as Europeans. "Born as free as ourselves, they were not under any obligations to deliver up their liberty and properties into our hands. Could it be possible for us to be so unjust as to ascribe to a savage brutality, the glorious actions which the Americans perform'd for the good of their country?"

Yet Bernard was no sentimental devotee of the Noble Savage cult. He carefully distinguished between the savages, "who may be justly compared to children," and the advanced Inca and Aztec societies. "We don't pretend to comprehend the Mexicans and Peruvians under the general character we have here given of the rest of the Americans. The history of those two nations furnishes us with many shining instances of their politeness, which, tho' it be different from ours, is yet not less valuable upon that account, since 'tis founded on the same rules on which our boasted *good breeding* is established. The Mexicans used to soften the rusticity which is so natural to children, by education; they fashion'd their inclinations, taught them modesty and civility, and even the very gait they should have in walking; they used to correct the errors and lapses of youth, and check the progress of the infant passions." Filled with admiration, Bernard exclaimed: "If we except what Christianity rectifies by the purity of its morals, can we affirm that our method of education is much superior to theirs? And can the Europeans justly boast that they make their youth more upright, or more useful to the state; that they make the heart less corrupt, or form more sprightly genius?"

Bernard conceded that it would be difficult to reconcile the high civilization of the Mexicans with the bloody character of their religion, but he observed that it was equally difficult to reconcile the mild and humane teachings of the Christian religion with the barbarity of the Spanish Conquest.[43]

Two French priests, the Abbés Antoine Banier and Jean-Baptiste Le Mascrier, undertook to transform Bernard's *machine de guerre* against Christianity into an apologia for the Faith. They republished the work, slightly changing its title, radically revising its text and spirit. They left intact and even added to the pro-Indian material. Rising to heights of eulogy in their discussion of Aztec jurisprudence, they wrote that the Aztecs knew nothing of the snares of European justice. They had no need for notaries, lawyers, and prosecutors, those miserable agents of injustice. A court from which there was no appeal terminated all civil cases. All judgments were summary. The plaintiff and the defendant presented their arguments and witnesses, after which the verdict was handed down. The only possible cause of delay was an appeal to a superior court over which the king himself presided. "Happy land," exclaimed the Abbés, "where a man who defended his property against a ravisher did not risk losing it through the chicanery of his own lawyers! In that land you would not find a family ruined by twenty successful lawsuits!" [44]

The pro-Indian current appeared to sweep all before it; however, the Dominican Antoine Touron, in his lengthy ecclesiastical history of America, sounded a note of caution. Some authors, he observed, depicted the Indians as stupid, almost imbecile people, little better than beasts and given to every sort of vice. Other authors, no less learned, were favorably inclined and stressed the mildness, justice, and wisdom of the peoples among whom they had long lived. Touron concluded that both groups had exaggerated the good or bad qualities of Indians in general. Yet all may have told the truth with reference to particular peoples. It was a mistake to ascribe to the civilized Indians the wickedness and cruelty properly assigned to the Caribs and other savages who wandered about through the forests without fixed dwellings or organized society. Life in the Aztec and Inca Empires, and above all in their capitals, obviously was very different from the way of life of the savages of Florida.

Although Touron paid his respects to Aztec achievements in such fields as education, jurisprudence, calendrical science, and the like, he left no doubt that for him the evils of the bloody Aztec religion nullified all these advantages. Touron saw ancient Mexico as a field of battle between the forces of God and Satan. In the manner of some Spanish Mendicant writers, he explained that the Devil had taught the Mexicans to imitate certain ceremonies of the Church and even some sacraments of the Christian religion. God had sent the omens seen by the Indians in the years before the Conquest, "in order to diminish the ferocity of those barbarians and make easier the great work of the Spaniards." By abolishing the cruel human sacrifices of the Aztecs, the Conquest had saved many innocent lives. Touron's Providential interpretation of the Conquest, his belief in omens, set him completely apart from the prevailing rationalist and skeptical intellectual climate of France in his time.

Yet Touron, faithful to a tradition of his order, denounced the crimes of the conquistadors and warmly praised the apostolic labors of Las Casas. Touron's defense of Las Casas, against the charge that his *Brevísima relación* had supplied propaganda ammunition to Dutch rebels against Spain, has lost none of its cogency. "It is impossible to believe," he wrote, "that the outrages of which Las Casas complained were not known in the Netherlands before the appearance of his book. The tyranny of the conquerors had been too widely bruited in both the Old and the New Worlds, men of good will had complained too loudly for thirty or forty years before the publication of that book, for the Dutch to be unaware of facts so generally known throughout Europe. Given this notoriety, it is the crimes of the conquerors and the impudence of those who dared defend them, and not the writings of a Bishop who only spoke up to condemn them, that one must regard as the cause or pretext of the revolt of the people of the Low Countries." [45]

Finally, among the works on history and geography that helped to shape French opinion of the Aztecs in this period, brief mention must be made of the great *Histoire générale des voyages*, edited by the Abbé Antoine-François Prévost, better known as the author

Mexican greenstone mask incorporated in an eighteenth-century niche figure. Silver gilt, gilt bronze, gold, enamel, greenstone, onyx, cabochon and faceted rubies, and rose-cut diamonds. Height: 23⅝ in. (60 cm.); mask, 4⅜ in. (11 cm.). Munich, 1720. Schatzkammer der Residenz München. Originally a fine bib-head pendant fashioned probably during the first centuries of the Christian era, the mask was recut by an Aztec lapidary to suit the prevailing mode. After reaching Europe and the collection of Albrecht V of Bavaria, perhaps within a century of the Conquest, it inspired a European craftsman to provide a body with enameled arms, golden horns, a jeweled diadem, and a rich Oriental costume and shawl. The niche itself is of still different workmanship and style and probably was intended for another figure. Courtesy Bayerische Verwaltung der staatl. Schlösser, Gärten und Seen, Munich.

Nombra Motezuma al Rey de España por sucesor de su Impe-
rio: le da la obediencia y tributo.

Scenes made by José Ximeno for the sumptuous 1783–1784 Madrid edition
of Antonio de Solís' *Historia de la conquista de México*. Left, Moctezuma
names the King of Spain as successor to his imperial crown. Right, Moc-

Reprehende Motezuma à sus Vasallos desde el alojamiento de Cortés, y estos, perdiendole el respeto, le apedréan, y queda herido.

tezuma reproves his vassals from Cortés' quarters, and they, losing respect for him, cast stones at him and he is wounded. Courtesy Department of Rare Books and Special Collections, Princeton University Library.

Rejouissances des MEXICAINS, au commencement du SIECLE.

Rejoicing of the Mexicans at the beginning of a new century or cycle of years. Engraved from a drawing made in 1721 by Bernard Picart for J.-F. Bernard's *Cérémonies et coutumes religieuses des peuples idolâtres* (Amsterdam, 1735). Courtesy Department of Rare Books and Special Collections, Princeton University Library.

of such popular sentimental novels as *Manon Lescaut*. The project began as a simple translation of a contemporary English collection of travels, but starting with the eleventh volume, Prévost began to condense his sources into smoothly written narratives. Volume XII (1754) was devoted principally to Mexico. Prévost introduced his account of the conquest with a bibliographical essay that competently evaluated the principal sources. Drawing on Gómara, Herrera, Acosta, Purchas, and Gemelli Carreri, Prévost offered his readers a reasonably thorough survey of Aztec history, institutions, and cultural achievements. His illustrations included a rather fanciful view of Tenochtitlán, the Mexican "Calendar Wheel," taken from Gemelli Carreri, and several plates from Purchas. Although Prévost noted and condemned the immense scale of human sacrifice among the ancient Mexicans, he left no doubt that they had attained a very respectable level of culture.

At mid-century, a shadow fell over the bright French image of the Indian. In 1749 the eminent Comte de Buffon began publication of his *Histoire naturelle*, a monumental survey of animate and inanimate nature, of their history, and of the history of the earth itself. Although the work dealt only marginally with Indians, a hypothesis of Buffon, presented in sweeping form and vested with all the authority of the renowned scientist, appeared to condemn the Indian to physical, mental, and moral inferiority. In spite of the fact that Buffon qualified his own pessimistic statements and later protested against the misuse of his ideas, his protests were in vain. The harm had been done. The irony was that Buffon, an enlightened man who separated science and religion, who was denounced by the Sorbonne for heresy, appeared to provide serious scientific support for the ancient doctrine of Indian inferiority. Up to this point the doctrine had rested largely on the discredited concepts of God's curse upon the Indians and medieval astrology, or on vague speculations.

The heart of Buffon's doctrine in regard to America was the theory that it was a young world, much younger than the Old. Until recently America had been covered by a sea which once submerged the entire earth, and it had not yet dried out. This fact explained its dense jungles and swamps, sources of disease and breeding places of innumerable small noxious animals. All the animate nature of the New World, both animal and human, displayed the harmful effects of the frigid, humid American climate.

That climate not only diminished the number of animal species in America but made them incomparably smaller than those of the Old World. Thus the New World lacked the elephant, the rhinoceros, the camel. Those animals which had been transported from Europe to America—the horse, the ass, cattle in general—grew smaller there, and those that were common to both, such as the wolf, the fox, and the stag, were considerably smaller in America.

Man was no exception to the general rule of the diminution of species in the New World. "The American savage's organs of generation are small and feeble; he lacks hair, beard, and sexual ardor for his female. He is swifter of foot than the European, but much weaker in body; he is less sensitive, but at the same time more fearful and cowardly. Take away hunger and thirst and you remove the active principle of all his movements; he will remain stupidly in repose, standing or sleeping, for two whole days. Nature has denied him the most precious spark of the fire of nature; the Indians lack ardor for their females and consequently love for their fellows. Since they lack the most tender, the liveliest passions of all, their other sentiments of this kind are cold and languishing; their love for their parents and children is feeble. This indifference for the female sex is the original taint that withers Nature, prevents it from flowering, and, even as it destroys the germs of life, simultaneously severs the roots of society." [46]

From what sources did Buffon derive this appalling indictment of the Indian? Certainly one finds in it echoes of the Spanish colonialist stereotype of the Indian as weak in body, character, and mind. Oviedo, Gómara, Botero, to mention only three authors of that school, could have supplied Buffon with materials for his thesis. Las Casas himself had unknowingly contributed to the making of the stereotype by depicting the Indian as a frail, delicate being in special need of protection against the excessive demands of the Spaniards.[47] Among more recent works of anti-Indian tendency, probably the most important was Charles-Marie de La Condamine's account of a French scientific expedition to South America.[48] La Condamine had returned disillusioned with the Indians, whose indolence, passivity, and stupidity he described in language very similar to that of Buffon.

Whatever Buffon's sources, the categorical character of his indictment of the Indian, couched in that "grand," rhetorical style that was a hallmark of his writing, sprang from his desire to prove beyond all doubt the truth of his discovery—one of which he was very proud—that the animal species of the New World were in many cases not only different from but weaker than those of the Old.

Yet Buffon was too much a man of his time—a time of considerable optimism about mankind and its prospects—to abandon the Indian to the mercies of a rigorous climatic determinism. Another of Buffon's theories taught that climate had a less decisive influence on man than on animals. "Man, white in Europe, black in Africa, yellow in Asia, red in America, is everywhere the same man, tinged with the color of his climate. Because he was made to rule over the earth, because the whole globe is his domain, it seems that his nature has adjusted to all situations. Under the hot sun of the South, amid the frozen wastes of the North, he lives and multiplies; he is to be found everywhere from a time of such remote antiquity that he does not seem to fancy one climate more than another." [49]

The Indian, then, is a member of that species which Providence has destined to reign over Nature, and is not doomed to perpetual inferiority. He will escape the prison of climatic determinism by changing his climate. Someday, "when the soil has been cleared, the forests cut down, the streams channeled, the waters controlled, America will become the most fertile, the healthiest, the richest of all lands, as it already seems to be wherever man has worked the soil." [50] Buffon was no doubt thinking in particular of the English and other foreign colonies in America, but he explicitly recognized that some Indian groups had already made large strides toward control of their environment. "If in North America we encounter only savages, in Mexico and Peru we find civilized men, cultured peoples, subject to laws and governed by kings." [51]

Thus Buffon rejected his own stereotype of the spiritless and stupid Indian. But to no avail. His qualifications and corrections were generally overlooked, and his indictment of the Indian, erected into a dogma, soon precipitated one of the stormiest episodes in the history of the "Dispute of the New World."

Among the major *philosophes*, only Montesquieu and Voltaire wrote about the Indians at sufficient length to permit an assessment of their views on Aztec civilization. The case of Montesquieu illustrates how a *philosophe's* preoccupation with European problems could color and restrict his vision of Indian society. Franz Neumann describes two schools of thought that were locked in bitter struggle in the ideological conflicts of the eighteenth century.[52] One saw the solution of France's problems in an enlightened despotism; the other saw the salvation of France in a balance of power between the king and an autonomous nobility and other privileged bodies which should limit the sovereignty of the king and protect against royal infringement the fundamental laws of France and the rights of citizens. Montesquieu supported the aristocratic or conservative solution of France's political problems. On the other hand Montesquieu was a thoroughgoing Cartesian and rationalist who identified religious fanaticism and clerical influence with absolutism. For this aristocratic liberal, therefore, the fate of the great Indian empires offered proof positive of the disastrous effects of the sway of despotism and priestcraft.

As early as 1725, in an address to the Academy of Bordeaux, Montesquieu ascribed the ease of Spanish conquests to Indian ignorance of the laws of nature, an ignorance abetted and maintained by priestly rulers. Had Descartes arrived in Mexico a hundred years before the arrival of Cortés and taught the Indians that the effects of nature are a consequence of laws of movement, Cortés and his few followers would never have conquered the Aztec Empire. "Who could believe that this disaster, the greatest history has ever known, was nothing more than the simple effect of ignorance of a philosophical principle?"

Montesquieu proceeded to prove his point. The Mexicans lacked firearms, but they had bows and arrows, the weapons of the Greeks and Romans; they had no iron, but they had stones as sharp as iron with which they edged their swords; they even had an excellent military tactic which consisted in fighting in close order, so that as soon as one soldier fell he was replaced by another; they had an intrepid nobility, educated in the same principles as the nobility of Europe, which aspired to die for glory. The vast extent of their empire also gave the Mexicans ample means of destroying the foreigners, even if they could not conquer them. Why, then, were the Mexicans so easily defeated? Because every new thing that they saw—a bearded man, a horse, a firearm—represented an invisible power that they could not resist. The Indians never lacked courage; they lacked hope of success.[53]

Montesquieu also used the Aztec and Inca experience to make the point that kings who ruled with the aid of superstition undermined the basis of their own power. The superstition that made possible their absolute rule was also the cause of their destruction. "The mere arrival of the Spaniards discouraged Atahualpa's subjects and Atahualpa himself, because he regarded it as a sign that the Sun was angry and abandoning his nation." The superstitious Moctezuma, who could have wiped out the Spaniards on their arrival if he had had the courage, or who could have let them die of hunger without running any risk to himself, only resisted them with sacrifices and the prayers he caused to be said in all the temples. He even sent the Spaniards every kind of provisions and sat idly by while they formed alliances with other Indian states against him and subjugated his vassals. Montesquieu noted that whereas the Spaniards encountered savage resistance from small barbarian tribes who sometimes forced the invaders to retreat, they met with no resistance in Peru and very little in Mexico, "where superstition deprived the empires of all the advantage they could have derived from their large extent and their civilization. In order to be revered like gods, the kings had rendered their peoples as stupid as beasts, and perished because of that same superstition which they had sanctioned for their advantage."

Montesquieu made an even more pointed allusion to the dangers of despotism. "It is very dangerous for a prince to have subjects who obey him blindly. . . . If Moctezuma, a prisoner in Spanish hands, had been respected merely as a man, the Mexicans would have destroyed the Spaniards. If the captured Cuauhtémoc had not brought the war to an end with a single word of command, his capture would not have been the signal for the fall of the empire and the Spaniards would have been afraid to anger his subjects by torturing him." [54]

Clearly, Montesquieu saw the Aztec and Inca Empires in no ideal light; ignorance, the fruit of despotism and priestcraft, nullified for him all the beneficial aspect of their civilization. He had even harsher words for the Spanish conquerors. He charged Cortés with perfidy and barbarism. "It moves one to anger to see Cortés speak endlessly of his justice and moderation to peoples against whom he commits a thousand barbarities. . . . By an unheard-of audacity he makes the abolition of an established religion the object of his embassy. When he endlessly repeats his peaceful intentions, is he not really seeking a conquest without resistance?" [55]

Voltaire saw the Indian empires in a more favorable light and in a larger perspective.[56] Our chief source for his opinions on this subject is the celebrated *Essai sur les mœurs*, begun about 1740 and published in 1756. In this work, based on a radically new conception of history, Voltaire undertook to tell the story of the development of the human spirit, or culture, and included in his vast panorama the distant civilizations of China and America. His sources for the Indians included Herrera, Las Casas, and Garcilaso de la Vega.

Voltaire paid his respects to the authority of Buffon in his comments on the American climate and population. "In general," he wrote, "America has never been as densely populated as Europe and Asia; it is covered by immense swamps that make the air very unhealthy; the earth there produces a prodigious number of poisons. . . . In fine, Nature has given the Americans much less diligence than she gave the men of the ancient world." [57] Yet Voltaire did not surrender to a narrow climatic determinism. "The climate," he wrote, "has some power, government a hundred times more, and religion joined to government, still more." [58]

Voltaire carefully distinguished between the "large and populous nations of America," the Aztec and Inca Empires whose accomplishments he regarded with much respect, and the *petits peuples*, the small savage tribes of which, in general, he took a very dim view. He recognized the admirable qualities of these savages, whom he compared favorably with "our savages," the dull, mean-spirited, cowardly peasants of France who had no idea of liberty and lacked the courage to rise up against their oppressors. "By contrast, the so-called savages of America are sovereigns who receive ambassadors from the colonies that our greed and light-mindedness established in their territory. They know honor, of which our European savages have never heard. They have a fatherland which they love and defend; they make treaties, fight with courage, and often speak with a heroic energy."

The *petits peuples* of America he placed on a very low stage of social development, on a level with the Kaffirs of Africa. Their industry did not go beyond the satisfaction of their essential needs. They had no notion of a Supreme Being, for this demanded a cultivated reason. Of these *petits peuples*, the highest in the scale of progress were the Canadian Indians. Lowest on that scale was the Brazilian Indian, to whom Voltaire assigned none of the virtues depicted by Montaigne. "The naked Brazilian is an animal who has not yet attained the full complement of his species." [59]

Very different from these primitives were the Peruvians and Mexicans, whom Voltaire described as semicivilized. Greatly influenced by Garcilaso's *Comentarios reales*, of which he had two copies in his library,[60] Voltaire showed a clear preference for the Incas. Theirs was the only American religion not repugnant to reason, for they worshiped the sun, a cult that appeared more rational than any other in a country denied the light of revelation. Voltaire proclaimed the Peruvians to be the most civilized and industrious people in the New World, and perhaps the most gentle in the entire world. Some writers maintained that the Incas, like the Aztecs, stained the cult of the sun with human sacrifices, but Voltaire believed that the Spaniards had fabricated this charge in order to justify their own barbarities. He appeared to contradict himself a few lines later, declaring that the ancient peoples of the Old World and the most civilized peoples of the New resembled each other in their barbarous practice of human sacrifice.

Voltaire thus gave the palm to Inca civilization, but he accorded almost equally high praise to the Aztecs. The Aztec political system moved him to admiring comment. "The Mexican king had thirty vassal kings under his command, each of whom could take the field at the head of ten thousand men armed with bows and arrows, and with those sharp stones which they used instead of iron. Who would expect to find a feudal government established in Mexico?" Voltaire appeared to commend the feudalism he found so hateful and oppressive in Europe. The reason, probably, is that feudalism in Mexico represented for Voltaire a sign of progress from a primitive to a higher stage of social development. Besides, feudalism in Mexico was associated with the existence of a strong central government of whose enlightened social policies Voltaire approved.

Voltaire pronounced Tenochtitlán to be one of the noblest monuments of American industry. He described the splendors of the city, taking special note of the marketplaces, whose shops were "full of the most curious pieces of workmanship, carved and engraved in gold and silver; rich vessels of painted porcelain; cotton stuffs; and ornaments of feathers which formed the most beautiful patterns with the variety of their colors and shades." He was also impressed by the royal botanical gardens, "wholly devoted to the raising of medicinal plants, which special officers distributed to the sick, giving an account of the success attending their use to the ruler; these physicians also kept a register of cases, after their fashion, since they were not acquainted with writing." Thus the ancient Mexicans offered an example of enlightened benevolence to the kings of Europe. "Their magnificent articles prove only the progress of the arts in that kingdom; this latter shows the progress of humanity."

How to reconcile the humanity of this institution with "those barbarous sacrifices in which human blood was poured in torrents before their idol Huitzilopochtli"? Voltaire answered that "human nature combines the best things with the worst; the religions of most nations had something bloody about their institutions." Besides, the Spaniards had greatly exaggerated the number of Aztec human sacrifices in order to cover up their own injustices; Voltaire cited Las Casas to the effect that no more than one hundred fifty prisoners were annually sacrificed in the great temple of Mexico. Voltaire showed the impartiality of his skepticism by noting that Las Casas had occasionally exaggerated the outrages of the Spaniards.

For the rest, Voltaire found the domestic policy of the ancient Mexicans both sage and humane. Education of the youth formed a principal object of the government, which maintained public schools for the young of both sexes. The Aztecs were not at all behind the Egyptians in astronomy. They had reduced warfare to an art; this was the secret of their superiority over their neighbors. A careful order in their finances maintained the grandeur of the empire, which their neighbors regarded with fear and envy. Voltaire praised the valor that the Aztecs displayed in confronting Spanish cannon and firearms in the conquest of Mexico. He rebuked Solís for calling the Mexican resistance a revolt, and their valor, brutality. "So easily do writers catch the spirit of injustice from conquerors." [61]

The articles on Mexico City and the Mexican Empire in Volume X of the *Encyclopédie* took their viewpoint and most of their facts from Voltaire's book. The author, identified only as "D.J.," was Louis de Jaucourt, physician, savant, and Diderot's principal collaborator in the preparation of the *Encyclopédie*.[62] Borrowing freely from Voltaire's text, Jaucourt described Aztec rule as "sage and humane, excepting only the barbaric custom of immolating their prisoners to Huitzilopochtli, chief of the gods; but this custom, after all, formerly prevailed among many peoples." Jaucourt also warned his readers against forming their idea of the Conquest from the history of Solís.[63] On the other hand, a series of unsigned articles on Aztec religion and culture, ascribed to the atheist Baron d'Holbach, painted a dark picture of barbaric human sacrifices and crafty priests who exploited the blind superstition of the masses for their own profit.[64]

English writing on the Indians in this period reveals little tendency to embellish the Aztec and Inca societies or to offer their institutions as models for the courts of Europe. The reason, perhaps, is that English intellectuals, unlike the French, were on the whole satisfied with the workings of the English political and economic system and felt less need to use exotic peoples and states as instruments of satire or reproach against established order. It is true that Anglo-Spanish commercial rivalry continued to inspire pamphlets that condemned Spain's actions in the New World and expressed pity for her victims. An occasional example of the same anti-Spanish tradition appeared in English belles-lettres. Thus Lord Lyttleton's *Dialogues of the Dead*, a mediocre imitation of Fontenelle, contained a dialogue between Cortés and William Penn in which Penn accused the conquerors of having turned a "fertile and populous Region into a Desert, a Desert flooded with Blood." [65] On the other hand, the most serious English works on America in this period, such as John Harris' great travel collection, John Campbell's *The Spanish Empire in America* and Edmund Burke's *An Account of the European Settlements in America*, reveal no special pro-Indian bias.[66] Indeed, Harris' work, which was extensively used by both Campbell and Burke, displays a marked partiality for the Spaniards and a definite coolness toward the Indian side.

Harris' account of the conquest of Mexico relied heavily on Solís. The illustrations included one fanciful drawing that showed Moctezuma, dressed in a rich mantle and crown, receiving Cortés in a setting of buildings of European and Oriental architectural style, and surrounded by attendants wearing plumed headdresses and the conventional girdle of feathers around the waist. Harris offered a skillful defense of Cortés. He partially disarmed Cortés' accusers by admitting that some of his actions were not altogether justifiable. "But this is far from being a new thing in a Hero . . . I believe it may be fairly said, there is scarce a Character of this kind in ancient or modern history, in which more immoral and more outrageous Actions do not frequently occur."

Taking his cue from Solís, Harris defended Cortés against the charge that he fought with regular, well-trained troops against "a barbarous and uncivilized People, unskilled in the arts of Policy or War. . . . The measures taken by the Indians, to drive him out of Mexico, and the manner in which they acted in the execution of those Measures, very plainly prove that the Suggestion was ill grounded." The Aztecs lacked neither skill as politicians nor discipline as soldiers. Had they come up against a lesser man than Cortés they would certainly have driven him out of Mexico; indeed, they might have preserved their empire down to the present time. "Had they once acquired a thorough knowledge of the Artillery and Powder, they were ingenious enough to have acquired the use of them; which if they had done, there is no reason to doubt that they would have kept their Ground, and have preserved, at least, the interior Part of their Country; though, by dint of their naval power, the Spaniards had made themselves Masters of their Coasts."

Harris declared that Aztec barbarity had inflamed the Spaniards and provoked them to cruelty against the Indians. He was skeptical of Las Casas' figures concerning the number of Indians slain by the Spaniards. Anyway, "a Monk is not by any Means a fit person to decide on the Behavior of a Statesman and a General." And finally, if there was no excuse for the ambition and acts of Cortés, "why should we have more Indulgence for the Pride and Tyranny of Motezuma, who certainly had no better title than he to trample upon the rights of Mankind, and to make so many Millions miserable as he did." [67]

Campbell and Burke stated, somewhat more moderately and at less length, the same pro-Spanish views. These works help to correct the widely held notion that the so-called Black Legend of Spanish cruelty and injustice had an almost absolute sway over the European mind outside Spain until the dawn of the twentieth century.

CHAPTER NINE

The Eyes of Reason: II

A new stage in the "Dispute of the New World" opened with the publication in 1768 of the *Recherches philosophiques sur les Américains* of the Dutch-born Cornelius de Pauw.[1] This philosophic cleric transformed Buffon's thesis of America's immaturity and imperfection into a thesis of America's decrepitude and hopeless inferiority. Whereas Buffon's judgment was tempered by the belief that the works of man would eventually make the New World equal to the Old, no gleam of light relieved the darkness of America's prospects for De Pauw.

Great natural catastrophes, including a second Deluge, had caused the "grand and terrible spectacle" of America's degeneracy, said De Pauw. Because of the cool and humid climate, the atmosphere of the New World was oppressive and unhealthy; the sun's rays never penetrated dense, gloomy forests. The rampaging waters of America's rivers flooded the land, which swarmed with insects and serpents. America did not have nearly as many quadrupeds as the Old World, and these were diminutive as well as timid.

Man in America was even less numerous than the animals, but equally weak and cowardly. The Indian lacked virility; pederasty was the style in the West Indies, Peru, and indeed throughout the New World. Not only the natives, but children born in America of European parents, felt the pernicious influence of the American climate. De Pauw cited the common Spanish belief that creoles had less capacity for learning than the true Europeans. None disputed this belief, he wrote, until Fray Feijóo, "well known for the monstrous paradoxes in his *Theatro crítico*," attempted to defend the American creoles against the charge of degeneracy. In vain, declared De Pauw; and he asserted that the American universities had not produced a single creole scholar of reputation. As for the mixed bloods, although they were inferior to the creoles, they were greatly superior to the natives without mixture of European blood. "From this one may infer that these last hardly merit the name of rational men." [2] Across the centuries, the Aristotelian Sepúlveda and the admirer of Voltaire joined hands!

De Pauw did not exempt the most advanced Indian peoples from his indictment. Those peoples also bordered on savagery, for they did not possess the distinguishing traits of civilization: coined money, iron, ships, arches, and letters. We must not take seriously the exaggerated descriptions of the Inca and Aztec Empires by Spanish writers.

Having demolished their claims about Peru to his satisfaction, De Pauw turned upon ancient Mexico. He sought to shake the foundations of the traditional accounts of Mexican history by showing how doubtful were their sources. He scolded historians who assigned the name "hieroglyphics" to the drawings the Mexicans were supposed to use to record the past. Like the seventeenth-century Jesuit Athanasius Kircher, De Pauw argued that these drawings were not hieroglyphics proper, that is, symbols, but merely copies of the objects they designated. The Mexican painters lacked signs to represent moral and metaphysical ideas. As a result, their work had very limited scope and significance.

De Pauw subjected the Codex Mendoza to a disdainful examination. He professed to have studied those drawings very carefully. Never had he seen clumsier or cruder drawings, without a trace of chiaroscuro, with no idea of perspective or imitation of nature, with the objects completely out of proportion. He concluded that the Mexicans had made almost no progress in the art of recording the past.

Using the method of systematic doubt, De Pauw questioned all dates, reigns, and other facts contained in the Spanish portion of the Codex. Indeed, he doubted whether the Codex dealt with any of the things it was supposed to deal with; the alleged list of the

eight kings who had preceded Moctezuma II might in fact be a
list of the king's mistresses!

With the same ferocity, De Pauw attacked the reliability of the
Mexican calendar as interpreted by Francesco Gemelli Carreri.
Gemelli, wrote De Pauw with a breathtaking impudence and ignorance, had followed the explanation of a certain creole professor
named "Çongara" [Góngora], "who had not dared to publish a
work he had written on the subject because his friends and relatives assured him it abounded in absurdities." De Pauw could not
believe that the Mexicans recorded the passage of centuries by the
use of "calendar wheels"; such reckoning supposed a long series
of astronomical observations and the possession of very precise
data, things incompatible with the prodigious ignorance of those
people. How could they have perfected their chronology if they
did not have words enough to count to ten?

De Pauw found the history of ancient Mexico as fabulous as
that of Peru, filled with the same uncertainties and shadows. He
denied the Mexicans any great antiquity. "The extreme rudeness
of their language, which no European has ever been able to pro-
nounce, and which lacks an infinite number of words needed to
express ideas; their lack of iron; the imperfection of their implements; the few mechanical discoveries they had made; the atrocity
of their bloody cult; the anarchy of their government; the paucity
of their laws; none of these things points to a people formed before
the Deluge."

Cortés and Solís had distorted the reality of Aztec life, charged
De Pauw. "The so-called palace occupied by the Mexican kings
was a hut; Cortés could not find a dwelling suitable for him to
occupy in the capital of the realm he had just conquered. These
things make clear the extravagant and fantastic character of the
portrait that has been drawn of this American city."

We may leave De Pauw with a quotation that illustrates both
the depth of his anti-American passion and his lordly pride in the
superiority of European civilization. "Is it not astounding to find
half the world occupied by men without beards, without intelligence, tainted by venereal disease, and so debased that they are
incapable of being trained—a defect that goes hand in hand with
stupidity? The inclination the Americans have always had for the
savage life proves that they hate the laws of society and the re-

straints of education, which, by dominating the most immoderate passions, are the only means that can raise man above the animal." [3]

In France, De Pauw's book quickly achieved a large popularity and influence. It appeared to support the prestigious Buffon, and displayed on every page that historical skepticism which Voltaire had helped to make fashionable. It was also fashionably anti-Spanish, anticlerical, and anticolonialist. In vain did Buffon protest against De Pauw's extravagances, in partial retraction of his own views. In 1777 Buffon wrote that many of the things said by De Pauw directly contradicted well-known facts. "I shall cite here only the monuments of the Mexicans and the Peruvians, whose existence he denies, but the remains of which exist to demonstrate the grandeur and genius of the people whom he regards as stupid beings, degenerates from the human species in body and mind." Buffon accused De Pauw of selecting and manipulating all his facts to suit his point of view. Buffon now wrote that in some parts of America, such as Guiana and the Amazon region, the natives appeared to be less robust than the Europeans, but this could be attributed to local and particular causes. In short, "the imperfection of nature that he [De Pauw] ascribes gratuitously to America in general should be applied only to the animals of the southern part of the continent, which have been found to be much smaller and very different from those of the southern parts of the Old World." [4]

Buffon's protest and partial retreat from his own positions seem to have gone unnoticed; the views of De Pauw continued to gain favor. The famous Abbé Raynal made those views his own in his *Histoire philosophique et politique des établissements et du commerce dans les Deux Indes*. Hans Wolpe has called this book a *machine de guerre* of the Enlightenment against colonialism, tyranny, superstition, and ignorance. [5] The work went through more than seventy editions in some twenty years and was translated into more than a dozen languages. Conservatives understood the subversive tendency of Raynal's book; in 1781 it was burned in Paris by the hand of the public executioner and Raynal had to flee to Belgium.

First published anonymously in Amsterdam in 1770, Raynal's *Histoire philosophique* was extensively revised in 1774 and again in 1780. A comparison of the discussion of Aztec society in the first edition with that of later editions, revised in the light of De Pauw's book, shows how strong the influence of that book was. In the first edition of the *Histoire philosophique*, Raynal included the familiar brilliant description of Tenochtitlán found in Gómara and other classic Spanish chroniclers of the Conquest. He closed with the favorable comment: "When we consider that these people were of no very remote antiquity, that they had no intercourse with any enlightened nation, no iron, writing, or any of those arts which assist us in the knowledge and exercise of others, and that they lived in a climate where the invention of man is not stimulated by necessity, we must acknowledge them to be one of the most ingenious peoples in the world."

In the 1774 edition Raynal here inserted a devastating paragraph that began: "The falsity of this pompous description may easily be made evident to every man's capacity," and went on, in the manner of De Pauw, to impugn the sincerity and motives of the Spanish chroniclers. In the same spirit, Raynal entered a new harsh judgment on Aztec civilization: "Were it possible to form a proper judgment of a people that exists no more, it might possibly be said that the Mexicans were subject to a despotism as cruel as it was ill concerted; that they rather conceived the necessity of having regular tribunals of justice, than they could feel the advantage of them; that the small number of arts they followed were as defective in execution as they were rich in materials; that they were farther distant from a savage than they were near to a civilized people; and that fear, the chief spring of all arbitrary governments, served them instead of morality, and principles." [6]

Even before he made these revisions, however, the tone of Raynal's book was on the whole unfriendly to the Aztecs. For Raynal, as for Montesquieu, the history of the Conquest offered object lessons in the evil effects of despotism and priestcraft. "In arbitrary states, the fall of the prince, and the reduction of the capital, usually bring on the conquest and subjection of the whole realm. The people cannot preserve their attachment to an oppressive government, or to a tyrant who thinks to make himself more respectable by never appearing in public. Accustomed to acknowledge no right but that of force, they never fail to submit to the strongest party. This was the case in the revolution in Mexico."

Moreover, the magnificence of the Aztec court only masked the bitter poverty and misery of the masses. "We should be very much deceived if we should judge of the ancient prosperity of the inhabitants of Mexico by what has been said of its emperor, its court, its capital, and the governors of its provinces. Despotism had there produced those fatal effects which it produces everywhere. The whole state was sacrificed to the caprices, pleasures, and magnificence of a small number of persons." Raynal declared that a multitude of tribute payments weighed down the commoners, who went naked, lived in poor huts, and ate scanty repasts.[7]

Raynal praised the Aztec law that prescribed merit as the only title to the crown, but noted that the sway of superstition gave the priests considerable influence in the selection of the ruler. As for the Aztec system of religion, this was "in every view odious and terrible." In short, the Aztecs were bowed "under the double yoke of tyranny and superstition." Raynal even declared that the condition of the Mexicans had improved under Spanish rule—a surprising conclusion for a writer usually identified with the Black Legend tradition. "The Mexicans are now less unhappy. Our fruits, our corn, and our cattle have rendered their food more wholesome, agreeable, and abundant. Shoes, drawers, shirts, a garment of wool or cotton, a ruff, and a hat constitute their dress." [8]

The role of Tlaxcala in the conquest of Mexico allowed Raynal to draw another political moral. He explained the stubborn resistance of the Tlaxcalans to the Spaniards by their supposedly "republican" form of government and resulting love of liberty. Though mountainous, Tlaxcala was "well cultivated, very populous, and very happy." Raynal concluded that in many respects the Tlaxcalan form of government could serve as "an excellent model." [9]

If the great Raynal so meekly followed the line laid down by De Pauw in American matters, lesser writers must follow suit. One or two examples will suffice to make the point.

Antoine Hornot, author of a short history of America, assured his readers that Spanish chroniclers had greatly exaggerated the size of the population of the Aztec Empire, which they set at thirty million, in order to enhance the importance of the Conquest. Yet, after their victory, the Spaniards had to bring laborers to Mexico from the West Indies. How could twelve hundred Spaniards slaughter such a multitude of souls? Hornot's skepticism extended to every aspect of the traditional picture of Aztec society.

"When the historians of the Conquest of Mexico seriously tell us that there were degrees of jurisdiction, judges or provosts, and sentences which could be appealed to a supreme council, when they tell us that denials of justice or wrongdoing on the part of judges were severely punished or suppressed, they assume a level of rationality more highly developed than was the case at that period." Hornot asserted that the Aztec orders of knighthood described by Solís were also the fruit of his imagination, borrowed from the military orders existing in Spain in his time. "We perceive that Solís was more interested in embellishing his narrative than in relating things as they really were."

Were one to believe what the Spanish historians reported, declared Hornot, he must conclude that ancient Mexico was one of the most civilized and happiest countries known to history. All that admirable legislation, unhappily, was a mere figment of those writers' imagination. Hornot found decisive proof for his statement in the fact that a handful of adventurers had overthrown the Aztec Empire. "This event was a result of the ignorance and weakness of the people, of the abuse of authority and the divisions that such abuse engendered; it could not have happened under a government in which morality and legislation were as perfect as has been supposed." [10]

Another French writer, Louis Genty, began his survey of the American scene by presenting a somber picture of ignoble savages who inhabited a brooding wasteland. Genty concluded his discussion of the American savage with the tart remark that "only love of paradox and novelty has made some ingenious writers believe that savage life is preferable to the social state. . . . The savage is an imperfect being, useless to his fellows, the plaything of the elements and all Nature."

Turning to the more advanced Indian societies, Genty appeared to waver between the climatic determinism of De Pauw and a more hopeful evolutionist viewpoint. Genty took Raynal to task for his embellishment of Mexican reality in the first edition of the *Histoire philosophique*. He had taken too seriously the exaggerated reports of Cortés and the imaginative descriptions of Solís, whose falsehoods included the statement that Tenochtitlán alone contained two hundred temples. Fortunately Raynal had changed his views, and the new editions of his book spoke a different language.

In the debunking vein of De Pauw, Genty declared that Aztec agriculture was very backward. Its yield could not have supported a large population had it not been for the extreme frugality of the people, a frugality that kept them in a state of weakness. All the other arts among the Mexicans were in a state of infancy. The vaunted cities were mere collections of huts; the supposed palaces and temples were only enormous piles of earth of which no vestige remained. The so-called masterpieces of goldwork and painting were crude essays and daubs, unworthy of attention save as they marked the progressive advance of human industry.

More generous than De Pauw, however, Genty recognized that Aztec civilization had made certain strides in morality, reason, the arts, and industry. To be sure, the Aztecs had kept certain vices of the savage state and added to these the vice of servitude, which subjected them to a despot. Yet "justice was administered with admirable wisdom for those times of ignorance and barbarism; their cities were very large and had large markets. Their progress was truly remarkable for a state barely one century old, and must have communicated itself to its neighbors." The Incas offered a much more striking example of progress. Their empire, founded on wise laws and a mild religion, "must sooner or later have led that immense peninsula to the highest degree of power and prosperity." [11]

The Incas, thanks to the invincible bright image created by Garcilaso de la Vega and the lachrymose historical novel *Les Incas* (1777) of Jean-François Marmontel, fared much better than the Aztecs under the furious onslaught of De Pauw. Thus Raynal, who accepted unquestioningly De Pauw's revisionism in regard to the Aztecs, protested in the 1774 edition of his book against a similar attitude toward the Incas. "A Pyrrhonism, which hath succeeded to a blind credulity, hath for some time endeavoured to throw a cloud over what has just been related of the laws, manners, and happiness of ancient Peru. This picture hath appeared to some philosophers as chimerical, and formed only by the naturally romantic imagination of a few Spaniards. But among the destroyers of this distinguished part of the New World, was there a single ruffian capable of inventing a fable so consistent in all its parts? Was there any among them humane enough to wish to do it, should he have been capable of the task? Would he not have been restrained by the fear of augmenting that hatred, which so many devastations had brought on his country throughout the world? Would not the fable have been contradicted by a multitude of witnesses, who would have seen the contrary of what was published with so much pomp? The unanimous testimony of contemporary writers, and of their immediate successors, ought to be regarded as the strongest historical demonstration that can possibly be desired." [12] Raynal seems curiously blind to the fact that his powerful argument applied with even greater force to the copious Spanish documentation on Aztec material and social culture.

By and large, the school of De Pauw had much the better of it in the French debate over the American Indian in the 1770's and 1780's.[13] During these years, of course, political and economic clouds were gathering over France. In the hardening French attitude toward Aztec despotism, in the consistently favorable attitude taken by French writers toward "republican" Tlaxcala, one is tempted to see signs of a leftward political evolution, portents of the coming revolutionary storm.

In Italy, by contrast with France, the ideas of De Pauw found little support. One Italian scholar, Paolo Frisi, demolished the geophysical bases of De Pauw's theories of American inferiority.[14] Another, the nobleman Gian Ricardo Carli, refuted De Pauw's charges against the Indians in his *Lettere americane* (1780). Carli's book slighted the genuine savages (for whom he had scant sympathy), but warmly defended the Aztecs and the Incas, above all the latter. An economist and ardent reformer, a collaborator of the enlightened despot Emperor Joseph II and the author of important economic reforms in the Duchy of Milan, Carli evidently saw in the Aztec and Inca states proof of the advantages of a directed economy, of a state concerned with the economic welfare of its people. Once again, a passion apparently inspired by American themes seems to have been rooted in European problems.

In the letters devoted to the Aztecs, Carli systematically refuted De Pauw's arguments against them. De Pauw had charged the Aztecs with cowardice. Carli did not hesitate to compare the Aztec valor to that of the Greeks at Thermopylae and Marathon. The Mexicans deserved even greater credit because of the inferiority of their weapons. The Spaniards thundered against them with their cannon and their guns, death-dealing arms unknown to the Indians. The horses were a frightening novelty. Yet the famous Medes and the Persians never resisted Alexander with the courage shown by the Aztecs.[15]

Carli drew a glowing picture of Aztec political and social institutions. In the Aztec Empire, merit, not birth, was the basis for appointment to high political office. The monarchy was elective rather than hereditary. The oath taken by the Aztec emperor that the rains would fall in his reign, often cited as a sign of Aztec simplicity, proved only that the Mexicans were aware of the importance of agriculture and (like good physiocrats!) knew it to be the only true source of wealth. The first care of the paternal Aztec government, Carli stressed, was to maintain commerce in a flourishing state, keep the markets well supplied, and carefully regulate the terms and enforcement of contracts.

The priesthood was in charge of education; the priests' judgment determined whether their pupils should be inscribed as nobles or commoners. A heraldic tribunal pronounced on the quality of individuals, without regard to the status of their forebears. In Europe, bitterly commented Carli, such a tribunal must often deplore the idleness, folly, and arrogance of the persons who claimed nobility by hereditary right. Among these so-called savages only a man's inherent worth mattered. A dishonorable or immoral act entailed instant loss of the title of nobility.

Carli conceded that the Aztec government grew despotic under the second Moctezuma, whom he described as a sort of Asiatic voluptuary, given to luxury, and as a cowardly man without thirst for glory. This despotic tendency antagonized the nobility and grandees and hastened the downfall of the state. Yet Carli perceived a division of powers within the Aztec government, for there existed a number of independent tribunals. Carli also cited Herrera on the point that the emperor could not rule on important matters without approval of the royal council. He must also defer to the wishes of the high priest, for the grandees and the people were blindly obedient to theocratic authority. Thus in Aztec Mexico two powers disputed for despotic control, forming a kind of check-and-balance system.[16]

By comparison with the ideal Inca state, the Mexican political system did appear in a darker light. In the Aztec Empire, where the monarchy was elective and private property existed, Carli remarked that an ambitious man might be motivated to seek to rise ever higher on the ladder of state, until he ascended the throne. Under the second Moctezuma this evil spirit of ambition achieved a despotism that enslaved and oppressed the people, causing widespread discontent. Moreover, Aztec Mexico had a religion that supported despotism and sanctioned the most frightful cruelties.

By contrast, the absolute, hereditary Inca kings presided over a simple and humane religion. Regarded as the true descendants of the sun which they adored, as the fathers of their people, they maintained a benevolent sway, punishing idleness, watching over morals, and eradicating from the hearts of their people the spirit of interest, of property and ambition, so general elsewhere. As a result, every individual was content with his lot and loved his sovereign. Carli challenged De Pauw to show a code of law or plan of government as just, as harmonious as that of the Incas.[17]

Carli revealed his reformist zeal by stressing the welfare aspects of the Indian empires. In their attention to public needs the Aztecs were clearly in advance of Europe. Military hospitals, for example, were unknown in Europe until the eighteenth century. Yet Moctezuma, Carli claimed, had constructed a hospital that provided medical care not only to soldiers but to private citizens as well.[18]

The Italian economist also challenged De Pauw's statement that the Indians' lack of coined money proved their savagery. The Aztecs traded in the great market of Mexico as did the Greeks in the time of Homer, using barter; and no one calls the Greeks of the Homeric age savages. Besides, the Mexicans did possess a common measure of the value of things. This was not a metal without intrinsic value, as was the European medium of exchange, but the healthful cacao bean, whose alloy was unalterable and did not lend itself to the fraud of the counterfeiter. Carli gave examples: a pair of sandals cost so many cacaos, a measure of grain so many more. Since the consumption of cacao corresponded to the annual production of the product, the value of this money remained relatively stable. Such was the manner of carrying on commerce in Mexico, where private property and trade existed. In the happier realm of the Incas, where private property was unknown and the government provided for the needs of every family, there was no trade.[19]

Finally, Carli defended Aztec cultural achievements against De

Pauw's attacks. He insisted that the Mexicans possessed a system of writing as refined, as capable of conveying distinct meanings, as the Egyptian. He also upheld their mathematical attainments. De Pauw had alleged that the Aztecs could not count beyond ten. Citing Herrera, Laet, and Prévost's *Histoire générale des voyages*, Carli showed that the Aztecs had terms for units of twenty, thirty, and up to a thousand. As for astronomy, the Mexicans had a calendar more exact than that of present-day Europe. "A calendar which is based on the annual revolution of the sun, not only by the addition of five days every year, but also by the correction of the bisextile, must be regarded as an operation resulting from reflective study and large calculations. We must therefore assume that these peoples made a series of astronomical observations, that they had a definite idea of the sphere, of the declination of the ecliptic, and calculated the days and hours of the solar appearances." [20]

Carli's book represented the first large-scale counterattack on the anti-American current of thought identified above all with De Pauw. New editions and translations soon made the book well known in Europe. The Jesuit historian Clavigero, who received a copy of the *Lettere americane* when his own great work was in press, inserted a note describing Carli's book as "most novel and full of erudition" and one that gave "a true though incomplete idea of the culture of the Mexicans." Clavigero dedicated his *Disertaciones* to Carli, paying him graceful tribute, "in the name of the Americans," for having had the courage "to defend these scorned peoples against so many renowned Europeans, their declared enemies and persecutors." [21]

In the British Isles the anti-Indian ideas of Buffon and De Pauw met, on the whole, with a favorable reception. The prestige of Buffon, the skeptical, critical tradition of British historiography, and Scottish efforts to develop a "sociology of progress" stressing the distance that separated primitives from the good life of civilized societies,[22] help to explain this reception. One may also cite again the relative absence of the tendency, so prominent on the Continent, to idealize the advanced Indian societies. English intellectuals, on the whole content with the existing social order, felt little need to extoll Inca statism or Aztec paternalism. Insofar as there was a cult of the Noble Savage, this did not generally operate to the advantage of a people like the Aztecs. The philosopher Adam Ferguson, for example, regarded the Aztecs with stern disapproval because of their lack of savage virtues. "The Mexican," he wrote, "like the Asiatic of India, being addicted to pleasure, was sunk in effeminacy; and in the neighborhood of the wild and the free, had suffered to be raised on his weakness, a domineering superstition; and a permanent fabric of despotical government." [23]

In his *Wealth of Nations* (1776), Adam Smith measured Indian achievements with an economic yardstick and found even the most advanced Indian societies wanting. Toward Spanish accounts of Indian magnificence he displayed a skepticism that suggested familiarity with De Pauw. "After all the wonderful tales which have been published concerning the splendid state of those countries in ancient times, whosoever reads, with any degree of sober judgment, the history of their first discovery and conquest, will evidently discover that in arts, agriculture, and commerce, their inhabitants were much more ignorant than the Tartars of the Ukraine are at present." The Indians did not have coined money, carried on all their commerce by barter, and had almost no division of labor. The few artisans among them were probably slaves or servants in the service of the sovereign, the nobles, and the priests.

In evident imitation of De Pauw, Smith found proof of Indian agricultural backwardness in the experience of Cortés and his men. "The Spanish armies, though they scarce ever exceeded five hundred men, and frequently did not amount to half that number, found almost everywhere great difficulty in procuring subsistence. The famines which they are said to have occasioned almost wherever they went, in countries, too, which are represented as very populous and well cultivated, sufficiently demonstrate that the story of their populousness and high cultivation is in a great measure fabulous."

Smith asserted that the Spanish Conquest had led to major advances in American productivity and population. Mexico City, with its population of one hundred thousand, was probably more than five times greater than in the time of Moctezuma. "Before the Conquest of the Spaniards, there were no cattle fit for draught either in Mexico or Peru. . . . The plough was unknown among them. They were ignorant of the use of iron. . . . A sort of wooden spade was the principal instrument of agriculture. Sharp stones served them for knives and hatchets to cut with; fish bones and the hard sinews of certain animals served them for needles to sew with, and these seem to have been their principal instruments of trade. In this state of things, it seems impossible that either of those empires could have been so much improved or so well cultivated as at present, when they are plentifully furnished with all sorts of European cattle, and when the use of iron, of the plow, and of many of the arts of Europe have been introduced among them." Since the population of a country must be in proportion to its agricultural productivity, Smith suggested that the two empires were more populous now than they ever had been before.[24]

The learned Henry Home, Lord Kames, shifted uneasily from position to position on the Indian question in his voluminous *Sketches of the History of Man* (1778). He appeared to accept the thesis of Indian inferiority when he cited the remark of "Mr. Buffon, a respectable author, and for that reason often quoted," to the effect that the Indian males "are feeble in their organs of generation, that they have no ardor for the female sex, and that they have few children; to enforce which remark he adds that the quadrupeds of America, both native and transplanted, are of a diminutive size, compared with those of the old world."

Some pages later, however, Kames discovered that these inadequate beings were capable of notable things. "America," he exclaimed, "is full of political wonders. At the time of the Spanish invasion, the Mexicans and Peruvians had made great advances toward the perfection of society; while the northern tribes, separated from them by distance only, were only hunters and fishers, and continue so to this day." Why, asked Kames, were the Mexicans and Peruvians, who lived in the torrid zone, more civilized, whereas in the Old World the inhabitants of the torrid zone were for the most part little better than savages? "We are not sufficiently acquainted with the natural history of America, nor with that of its people, to attempt an explanation of these wonders."

Kames' generally favorable view of Aztec technical attainments contrasted sharply with the disparaging comments of Adam Smith. Kames declared that the ancient Mexicans were skillful in agriculture. By intensive cultivation they produced high yields of maize, their chief crop. They practiced gardening and botany as

well as agriculture. Nor did they lack the refinements of civilization. "The art of cooking was far advanced among them. Montezuma's table was for ordinary covered with two hundred dishes,
many of them exquisitely dressed in the opinion even of the
Spaniards." Kames again differed with Smith when he wrote that
"the populousness of Mexico and Peru affords irrefragable evidence that the arts of peace were there carried to a great height."
Music, poetry, and astronomy were among the arts and sciences in
which the Aztecs excelled.

Curiously enough, Kames considered the Mexicans most deficient
in a sphere that is usually considered peculiarly their own: the art
of war. Kames contended that the Aztecs would have been invincible had they understood the order of battle; lack of such
understanding caused their empire to fall prey to a handful of foreigners. Kames disagreed with the view that imputed the Aztec
collapse to Spanish firearms and horses. After all, the horses could
not have been more terrible to the Mexicans than elephants first
were to the Romans; but familiarity with those beasts soon rid
them of their terror. The Mexicans would probably have acted
like the Romans, had they only equaled them in the art of war.
Kames found only one serious stain upon the Aztec record, and he
wondered that good and evil should be so strangely intermingled.
"When that illustrious people, by their own genius, without borrowing from others, had made such proficiency in the arts of
peace, as well as of war; is it not strange that with respect to religion they were no better than savages?"

Kames made the usual comparison between the Inca and Aztec
empires, and found that each enjoyed a certain superiority over
the other. The Mexican government, he suggested, was supported
by arms, that of Peru by religion. The Aztec monarchy was elective, the Peruvian hereditary, yet, contrary to what might be expected, the government of Peru was by far the milder. Even so,
Kames disputed Montesquieu's assertion that the Aztec monarchy
was despotic, for was not the king's power limited to a royal council whose members, hereditary princes, were independent of him?
Kames reserved his warm praise for the Incas. Montesquieu was
again wrong to term the Inca regime despotic. "An absolute monarchy it was, but the farthest in the world from being despotic:
on the contrary, we find not in history any government so well

contrived for the good of the people. . . . Upon the whole, comprehending king and subject, there perhaps never existed more virtue in any other government, whether monarchical or republican."

If the Incas excelled over the Mexicans in political science, the latter had the better of it as concerned economic life. "In Mexico, arts and manufactures were carried to a surprising height considering the tools they had to work with: in Peru they had made no progress, every man, as among savages, providing the necessities of life for himself."

The balance of favor again shifted to the Incas in point of religion. "The religion of the Peruvians, considered in a political light, was excellent. The veneration they paid their sovereign upon a false religious principle was their only superstition; and that superstition contributed greatly to improve their morals and their manners; on the other hand, the religion of Mexico was execrable." [25]

Fresh from his resounding triumph in the field of European history, the *History of the Reign of the Emperor Charles V* (1769), William Robertson turned to write his masterpiece, the *History of America*, published in London in two volumes in 1777. Professing a severe objectivity and a preference for facts instead of "systems," Robertson dissociated himself both from the doctrines of Indian inferiority proposed by Buffon and De Pauw and from the Noble Savage ideas identified with Rousseau. In fact, Buffon and De Pauw made a strong impact on Robertson; it was especially apparent in his unflattering description of the American savages as feeble, indolent, lacking in sex drive, and incapable of forming abstract ideas.

Yet the work is a monument to Robertson's immense industry and careful scholarship, to his fine critical spirit, and to the breadth of his historical vision. Lafitau and Adam Ferguson, among others, had already suggested that American Indian civilization afforded European philosophers an opportunity to study the same archaic social formations through which the civilized peoples of Europe had once passed. Robertson elaborated and stated this view with great clarity and precision. Going beyond this, he offered a theory of social evolution through stages defined in terms of technology and division of labor, a theory particularly associated in our times with the American evolutionist Lewis Morgan, whose anthropology, indeed, Robertson anticipated "at many points." [26]

"In order to complete the history of the human mind, and attain to a perfect knowledge of its nature and operations," wrote Robertson, "we must contemplate man in all those various situations wherein he has been placed. We must follow him in his progress through the different stages of society, as he gradually advances from the infant state of civil life toward its maturity and decline." The Greek and Roman historians had been handicapped in the study of the early stages of society because civil society had already made considerable advances in all the regions with which they were acquainted. Not so in America. Here "man appears under the rudest form in which we can conceive him to subsist. We behold communities just beginning to unite, and may examine the sentiments and actions of human beings in the infancy of social life. . . . That state of primeval simplicity, which was known in our continent only by the fanciful description of poets, really existed in the other. The greater part of its inhabitants were strangers to industry and labor, ignorant of arts, and almost unacquainted with property, enjoying in common the blessings which flowed spontaneously from the bounty of nature. There were only two nations in this vast continent which had emerged from this rude state, and had made any considerable progress in acquiring the ideas, and adopting the institutions, which belong to polished societies." [27]

Robertson examined Aztec society within an evolutionary framework of three stages: savagery, barbarism, and civilization. His criteria for civilization are basically technological: an industry so regular as to render subsistence secure, "the arts which supply the wants and furnish the accommodations of life," and the "various institutions requisite in a well-ordered society." From the viewpoint of these criteria, the Aztecs, as well as the Incas, belonged at most on the higher levels of barbarism, or "in the first stages of transition from barbarism to civilization." "Without knowledge of the useful metals, or the aid of domestic animals, [they] labored under disadvantages which must have greatly retarded their progress, and in their highest state of improvement, their power was so limited, and their operations so feeble, that they can hardly be considered as having advanced beyond the infancy of civil life." [28]

Robertson does not express this disparaging view of Aztec society consistently; he wavers time and time again between the scornful attitude of a De Pauw and the glowing accounts of the classic Spanish chroniclers. If his anthropological theory, his scholarly caution, and the influence of De Pauw weighed against the Aztecs, the source materials spread before him argued for a civilization of much greater splendor. Never before had a European historian assembled such an immense store of materials on ancient Mexico. His bibliography cites not only such rare printed items as Torquemada, Boturini, and Eguiara y Eguren but also invaluable manuscript sources, such as Zorita's *Breve y sumaria relación* and Motolinía's *Historia de los indios de la Nueva España*. Robertson's persistent search for manuscripts brought to light in the Imperial Library of Vienna a copy of the letter sent to the Emperor Charles V by the town council of Veracruz and a copy of Cortés' so-called Fifth Letter dealing with the expedition to Honduras.

Not satisfied with this mountain of sources, Robertson mourned the defective and incomplete state of information on Aztec society. Upon the conquistador chroniclers he turned a sternly suspicious and doubting eye. "Cortez and the rapacious adventurers who accompanied him had not leisure or capacity to enrich either civil or natural history with new observations." "The inquiries of illiterate soldiers were conducted with so little sagacity and precision that the accounts given by them of the policy and order established in the Mexican monarchy are superficial, confused, and inexplicable." He echoed De Pauw's indictment of Zumárraga and other monkish destroyers of Indian documents. As to the surviving Indian picture writings (Robertson appears to have coined this phrase), which were supposed to contain the annals of the empire, he complained that they were few in number and ambiguous in meaning.[29]

As did De Pauw, Robertson posed the problem of reconciling the short life of the Aztec Empire with the high level of Aztec civilization depicted in the Spanish chronicles. "The infancy of nations is so long, and, even where every circumstance is favourable to their progress, they advance so slowly toward any maturity of strength or policy that the recent origin of the Mexicans seems to be a strong presumption of exaggeration in the splendid descriptions of their government and manners." On the other hand, if the Mexican state was of greater antiquity than the three hundred years allowed by their annals, Robertson found it difficult to

conceive how, "among a people who possessed the art of recording events by pictures, and who considered it an essential part of
their national education to teach their children to repeat the historical songs which celebrated the exploits of their ancestors, the
knowledge of past transactions should be so slender and limited." [30]

A tone of perplexity continued to mark Robertson's discussion
of Aztec society. Some of the facts suggested that the Mexicans
had made considerable progress in civilization; others indicated that
they had advanced but little beyond the savage tribes around them.
To assist his readers in determining where the evidence pointed,
Robertson drew up a balance sheet of the facts supporting one
position or the other.

The first and strongest claim to civilization that Robertson made
for the Aztecs was the existence of the right of private property.
By contrast with the communalism that he found to characterize
savage tribes, both real and personal property existed among the
Aztecs, and both could be transferred from one person to another
by sale or barter and descend by inheritance. Drawing on Zorita's
manuscript relation, Robertson distinguished between the various
types of Aztec land tenure, noting that only nobles possessed land
with full right of sale or inheritance; commoners held land through
the *calpulli*, a landowning kinship group whose members could
not alienate or subdivide their plots of land, which were assigned
for the support of their families. Interestingly enough, Robertson
found admirable this Aztec communalism. "In consequence of this
distribution of the territory of the state, every man had an interest
in its welfare, and the happiness of the individual was connected
with the public security."

Robertson cited the number and size of the Aztec cities as another index of progress toward civilization; however, he suggested
that the surprise of the Spaniards at finding that the Indians lived
in towns resembling those of Spain led them, by a natural impulse,
to exaggerate their population and size. The desire to enhance the
importance of their conquests may also have tempted them to
magnify what they saw. For these reasons Robertson proposed to
fix the size of the Aztec population at a much lower level than had
the Spanish chroniclers. Even so, "they will appear to be cities of
such consequence, as are not to be found but among people who
have made some considerable progress in the arts of social life."

Robertson found equally remarkable the trend toward division of labor ("separation of professions") in Aztec society. "Among the Mexicans, the separation of the arts necessary to life had taken place to a considerable extent. The functions of the mason, the weaver, the goldsmith, the painter, and of several other crafts, were carried on by different persons. Each was regularly interested in his calling." This specialization, assisted by "the persevering patience peculiar to Americans," made it possible for Mexican artisans to achieve a perfection in workmanship far beyond what might have been expected of the primitive tools with which they worked. The flow of these productions into commerce, and their exchange in fixed markets held in the cities, made possible the satisfaction of mutual wants "in such orderly intercourse as characterizes an improved state of society."

To this division of labor corresponded a complex class structure that Robertson contrasted with the equality and absence of subordination characteristic of "the infancy of civil life." Robertson painted a dark picture of the condition of the Mexican commoners. A large number were *mayeque*, peasants who were attached to the soil as mere instruments of labor, attached to the soil like the serfs of medieval Europe. More wretched still was the plight of the slave, treated, according to Robertson, with utmost rigor. And even the free commoners were treated by the haughty nobles as "beings of an inferior species." The nobility itself was divided into a series of classes with unequal privileges, titles, and wealth. The structure was topped by a monarch who enjoyed extensive power and was surrounded by an immense pomp and reverence. "Thus the distinction of ranks was completely established, in a line of regular subordination, reaching from the highest to the lowest member of the community." For Robertson this complex and carefully graded social organization proved that Mexican society had considerably advanced toward civilization.

Robertson found the Spanish descriptions of Mexican political organization contradictory and often inaccurate. Sometimes the monarch depicted by the chroniclers was hedged about with limitations on his power, sometimes he reigned absolute and decided all things according to his pleasure. The contradictions, Robertson suggested, arose from a failure to take account of the revolution worked in Mexican politics by Moctezuma, whose "aspiring ambi-

tion subverted the ancient system of government, and introduced
a pure despotism."

The original "form and genius of Mexican policy" as they existed from the foundation of the monarchy to the ascent of Moctezuma were rigidly feudal. The three distinguishing characteristics
of the traditional Mexican constitution were "a nobility possessing
almost independent authority, a people depressed into the lowest
state of subjection, and a king entrusted with the executive power
of the state." Originally the whole body of the nobility participated
in the election of the monarch; later this function was assigned to
six electors, of whom the chiefs of Texcoco and Tacuba always
formed two. As the power of the monarch grew, the original simplicity of his state and retinue gave way to a growing ostentation,
which in the time of the last Aztec ruler seemed to resemble "the
magnificence of the ancient monarchies in Asia, rather than the
simplicity of the infant states in the New World."

Yet Robertson had to confess that even under the despotism of
Moctezuma Mexican potentates wielded their power beneficially
"in the order and regularity with which they conducted the internal administration and police of their dominions." If the accounts
of the Spanish chroniclers might be believed, "justice was administered in the Mexican empire with a degree of order and equity,
resembling what takes place in societies highly civilized." No less
sagacious was the Aztec tax system. Taxes were considerable, but
neither arbitrary nor unequal. The system of payment in kind filled
the public storehouses with the natural products and manufactures
of all the different provinces of the empire. From these storehouses
the emperor supplied his attendants, officials, and armies with food,
clothing, and ornaments. Tribute labor was used to cultivate crown
lands, carry on public works, and build and repair houses that
belonged to the emperor.

In certain refinements of public order and management, wrote
Robertson, the Mexicans displayed a degree of development that
"even polished nations are late in acquiring." Such a refinement
was the public courier system used to convey messages from one
part of the empire to the other, a device unknown to Europe in
that period. Equally admirable was the planning of the capital city,
with its water conduits and long causeways, which served as
avenues linking the city to the mainland. The employment of

persons to clean the streets, of night watchmen, of street lighting, were so many proofs of the advances made by the Aztecs in the arts of life.

On the other hand, Robertson reacted with skepticism to the rapturous descriptions of Aztec art by Cortés and other early Spanish authors. He suggested that a psychological factor operated here. "In examining the works of people whose advances in improvement are nearly the same with our own, we view them with a critical, and often with a jealous eye. Whereas, when conscious of our own superiority, we survey the arts of nations comparatively rude, we are astonished at works executed by them under such manifest disadvantages, and in the warmth of our admiration, are apt to represent them as productions more finished than they really are. To the influence of this illusion, without supposing any intention to deceive, we may impute the exaggeration of some Spanish authors, in their accounts of the Mexican arts."

Robertson cited the opinions of persons "on whose judgment and taste I can rely," who had examined examples of Aztec gold, silver, and other ornaments and utensils deposited in the museum recently opened by Charles III of Spain; these persons reported that the "boasted efforts of their art are uncouth representations of common objects, or very coarse images of the human and some animal forms, destitute of grace and propriety." Robertson had confirmed the correctness of these observations by inspecting the woodcuts or copper engravings of Aztec paintings as published by Purchas and other compilers. "In them every figure of men, of quadrupeds, or birds, as well as every representation of animated nature, is extremely rude and awkward. The hardest Egyptian style, stiff and imperfect as it was, is more elegant. The scrawls of children delineate objects almost as accurately."

Robertson assigned considerable importance to Mexican paintings as historical records. He adhered to the common view that Mexican writing had in general not gone beyond the pictographic form, that is, the depiction of objects. These picture writings were "the most curious monuments of art brought from the New World," the collection published by Purchas (the Codex Mendoza) being the most valuable. He believed that if the Conquest had not intervened, "and the human mind holding the same course in the New World as in the Old," the Aztecs might have made the transi-

tion from picture to hieroglyphic writing and ultimately to alphabetic writing: "the short duration of their empire prevented the
Mexicans from advancing farther in that long course which con-
ducts men from the labour of delineating real objects to the simplicity and ease of alphabetic writing."

Robertson found a more decisive evidence of their progress in
their calendrical and chronological science. In their calendar of
365 days, including five intercalary days, with its near approach
to scientific accuracy, he saw a remarkable proof that "the Mexicans had bestowed some attention upon inquiries and speculations,
to which men in a very rude state never turn their thoughts."

These facts demonstrated the Aztecs to be "a people considerably refined." Others, however, indicated that "their character, and
many of their institutions, did not differ greatly from those of
the other inhabitants of America." In the first place: like their
savage neighbors, the Mexicans constantly engaged in war, for the
same motives. Those sentiments of humanity which temper the
horrors of war among civilized people were unknown among them.
The ferocity with which they treated their enemies forced Robertson to suspect "their degree of civilization to have been very
imperfect."

Robertson also insisted that Aztec agriculture was not highly
developed. This deficiency was reflected in their scanty and poor
diet, a diet capable of preserving life but not of imparting bodily
vigor. Hence the Spanish observation that the strength of one
Spaniard exceeded that of several Indians. That Cortés had difficulty supplying his small body of soldiers with food pointed to a
low level of cultivation in the Aztec Empire. The fact that Mexican women took measures to prevent pregnancy also suggested an
agriculture of limited productivity.

Robertson was skeptical of the claims made for the extent of the
Aztec Empire. Seeking to magnify the valor of their countrymen,
Spanish historians had depicted Moctezuma's power as extending
over all New Spain, from the Atlantic to the Pacific. In fact much
of the area was occupied by fierce hunting tribes, such as the
Otomí and the Chichimeca, which did not recognize Moctezuma's sovereignty. Even in the interior there were cities, such as
Tlaxcala, only twenty-one leagues from the capital, and Tepeaca,
thirty leagues distant, which were independent and hostile states,

and a powerful kingdom, Michoacán, which successfully repelled the Aztec onslaughts. The Aztec Empire, surrounded on all sides by hostile powers, was far from being the universal master depicted in the Spanish chronicles.

The relative lack of intercourse between the various provinces of the empire, reflected in the total absence of roads, and the lack of coined money, were evidence of Mexican backwardness. On the other hand, the use of cacao beans as an instrument of commerce was "an evidence, no less satisfying, of the superior progress which the Mexicans had made in refinement and civilization."

Robertson renewed his criticism of Spanish accounts of the splendor of the Aztec cities. To prove his contention that those cities were rather "the habitation of men just emerging from barbarity, than the residence of a polished people," Robertson cited Herrera's description of Tlaxcala as "a number of low straggling huts, scattered about irregularly, according to the caprice of each proprietor, built with turf and stone, and thatched with reeds, without any light but what they received by a door, so low that it could not be entered upright." Robertson believed that the construction of the majority of the houses of Tenochtitlán was equally humble. The vaunted temples of Mexico were nothing more than solid masses of earth of square form, partly faced with stone, and topped by a platform housing the shrine of the god and altars on which victims were sacrificed.

Robertson cast the same skeptical eye on Spanish accounts of the splendor of Moctezuma's palaces and other public buildings. Assuming the total destruction of such structures in the siege of Tenochtitlán, why did they not survive in those cities which had not experienced the hardships of warfare? He concluded that those buildings were neither "so solid or magnificent as to merit the pompous epithets which some Spanish authors employ in describing them."

From this enumeration of facts Robertson concluded that Aztec society was considerably advanced beyond that of the savage tribes of North America, but that "with respect to many particulars the Spanish accounts of their progress appear to be highly embellished." He ascribed this not to willful deceit but to semantic confusion caused by the mistaken terminology employed by the Spanish conquistadors.

"There is not a more frequent or more fertile source of deception in describing the manners and arts of savage nations, or of such as are imperfectly civilized, than that of applying to them the names and phrases appropriated to the institutions and refinements of polished life. When the leader of a small tribe, or the head of a rude community, is dignified with the title of king or emperor, the place of his residence can receive no other name but that of his palace; and whatever his attendants may be, they must be called his court. Under such appellations they acquire an importance and dignity which do not belong to them."

By such a process Europeans acquired a distorted image of Aztec society. Later writers, such as Solís, adopted the viewpoints of the early chroniclers, and further embellished them. "The colours with which De Solís delineates the character of Montezuma, the splendor of his court, the laws and policy of his empire, are the same that he must have employed in exhibiting to view the monarch and institutions of an highly polished people."

Having warned against the embellishments in the portrait of ancient Mexico drawn by Cortés and the Spanish chroniclers, Robertson expressed just as strong objections to the claims of such writers as De Pauw that the Spanish accounts were "the fictions of men who wished to deceive, or who delighted in the marvelous." On the contrary, declared Robertson, "there are few historical facts that can be ascertained by evidence more unexceptionable than may be produced in support of the material articles in the description of the Mexican constitution and manners." There was available the eyewitness testimony of men who had resided in Mexico before and after the Conquest, soldiers, priests, and lawyers, all concurring in their testimony. Robertson cited with approval and applied to the Mexican case Raynal's vigorous defense of the traditional account of Inca political and social institutions.

Had Cortés attempted to deceive his sovereign by presenting to him a picture of imaginary institutions and manners, would not his many rivals and enemies have quickly exposed the imposture? Who among the conquistadors was so learned, so close a student of society and politics, as to fabricate a "factitious system of policy," so intricate and so well integrated as that which they portrayed in their descriptions of the Aztec government? Where could they have borrowed the idea of institutions completely foreign to their experience, and indeed in advance of the most civilized European states, such as the municipal regulations of Tenochtitlán or the courier system for conveying messages from one end of the empire to the other? Had Cortés been capable of such a deception, what reason would the writers who followed him—such men as Zorita, Motolinía, or Acosta—have had for continuing the deceit?

Robertson closed his survey of Aztec civilization with a comment on the genius of Mexican religion, whose influence on the character of the Aztecs, he declared, "produced an effect that is singular in the history of the human species. The manners of the people in the New World who had made the greatest progress in the arts of policy were the most ferocious, and the barbarity of some of their customs exceeded even those of the savage state." [31]

Robertson's survey of Aztec society displays some obvious weaknesses. The excessive brevity and resulting superficiality of some of the description flowed inevitably from the fact that the subject formed only a small part of a much larger theme. More difficult to understand is why Robertson did not make larger use of the rich hoard of printed and manuscript materials available to him; why, for example, he did not exploit the rich mine of information that is Torquemada's *Monarchía indiana*. Prescott caught him in a number of errors and inconsistencies, and the list of errors could now be made longer. Like most of his contemporaries, Robertson was totally blind to the aesthetic value of Aztec art.

Yet Prescott's description of Robertson as the "illustrious historian of America" remains as valid as ever. In some respects he marks the brilliant climax of Enlightenment writing on the Aztecs. His anthropological approach, his freedom from theological bias, his careful weighing of the evidence, his acute analysis of the psychological and semantic factors that made for distortion of what they saw on the part of Spanish observers, testify to the modernity of the historian who "gave the world its first comprehensive ethnology of the Americas and, at the same time, laid a number of solid foundation piers for later development of anthropology." [32]

Spain, whose conquistadors and chroniclers had created the classic vision of splendid and populous Indian empires, offered little resistance to the efforts of De Pauw and the many writers he influenced to discredit that vision. Instead some Spanish apologists incorporated the anti-American arguments in the Spanish defense against charges of genocide and other cruelties in the Indies.

The *Reflexiones imparciales sobre la humanidad de los españoles en las Indias* (1782) of the Spanish Jesuit Juan Nuix illustrates this shift in strategy. On the one hand, Nuix bitterly denounced De Pauw's accusations of Spanish atrocities against the Indians. On the other hand, he willingly followed De Pauw and Robertson in their drastic reduction of the pre-Conquest population of Mexico, since this removed from the Spaniards the onus of guilt for the disappearance of great numbers of natives.

Citing the support of many foreign writers for his position, Nuix disputed the claim of the classic Spanish chroniclers that Cortés had an army of one hundred fifty thousand Indians at the siege of Mexico, and that there was an equal number of Indians inside the city. It would have been impossible, argued Nuix, in a country whose agriculture was so backward, where the people were so improvident and incapable of such a complicated plan of operations, to assemble the quantity of foodstuffs needed to maintain such a large number of men in one place for three months. In its march through the supposedly flourishing republic of Tlaxcala, Cortés' little army suffered such shortages that the soldiers had to eat tuna, a kind of wild fruit. "Who will believe that a country inhabited by millions could not provision a small detachment of four hundred soldiers?"

Nuix observed that this shortage of foodstuffs was understandable, for Mexican agriculture was inadequate to fill the needs of the native population. The frail constitution of the Mexicans was due to the meagerness and poor quality of their diet, sufficient to preserve life but not to impart vigor. Nuix explained the backwardness of Mexican agriculture by the lack of domestic animals, useful metals, and efficient implements: all these things America received as gifts from Spain.[33] If the stress on Indian weakness and backwardness inevitably diminished the glory of the Conquest, it reinforced the case for Spain's civilizing mission in the New World.

The poet and essayist José Cadalso, an ardent defender of that mission, combined old and new arguments in his defense of Spain's work in America. He turned their own weapons against foreign critics by denouncing the cruelty of the slave trade. He chided the English and other nations who engaged in this trade for their hypocrisy. The same people who shed tears for the fate of the unhappy Indians sailed their ships to the coast of Africa, purchased slaves of both sexes, carried them thousands of miles to America, and sold them in public markets like animals; and with the proceeds of their sale they published in their own humanitarian lands books full of invectives and insults against Cortés because of what he had done. What, in fact, had Cortés done? He had torn down the idols, saved innocents from a cruel death, brought peace to a strife-torn land.

In the tradition of Solís, Cadalso asserted that it was the revolt and treason of the Aztecs, who slew their own king and sacrificed captured Spanish soldiers on their altars, that compelled the Spaniards to harden their hearts and wage an unequal battle of one thousand men against an incredible multitude of wild beasts. Traditional, too, was Cadalso's accent on the courage and military skill of the Indians. A friend, well versed in the military science of the Romans and the Greeks, had assured him that in the War of Tlaxcala the Indians had employed all the maneuvers, tactics, and ruses described in the writings of Xenophon and other chroniclers of antiquity. Yet foreigners continued to speak of the Indians as barbarians, with the design of diminishing the glory of Cortés.[34]

The Spanish writer Juan Pablo Forner, champion of Spanish traditional values and foe of French influences in the national life, used the unfamiliar weapon of satire to defend the Spanish record in the New World. In his brilliant *Exequias de la lengua castellana* (1792), Parnassus became the scene of a new debate between Las Casas and Sepúlveda. Plato, Aristotle, Zeno, Grotius, and Locke rallied to the side of Sepúlveda; the shades of Francisco de Vitoria, Melchor Cano, José de Acosta, with a number of foreigners, including Robertson and Raynal, supported Las Casas.

Raynal, "lying shamelessly," proclaimed the Spaniards savages and the Indians highly cultured and of irreproachable customs. The seventeenth-century poet Francisco de Quevedo, angry at these calumnies, urged Apollo to send Raynal to occupy a chair of philosophy among the Caribs, with the proviso that he must teach stark naked and join in the cannibal hunt for European victims.

Bernal Díaz, joined by Oviedo and Gómara, entered the debate; Díaz swore, "with that plain soldierly directness of one who had fought the Indians in one hundred nineteen battles," that he would teach the little Frenchman to respect the memory of his comrades, almost all of whom had died in the Conquest. "The Conquest," proclaimed Bernal with an eloquence that Forner ascribed to daily communication with the sages of Parnassus, "was what all conquests have been and are: killing, burning, destruction, robbery; but in this respect America displayed nothing that had not been done for ages past in Europe itself, where not a year passes without the sight of the destruction wrought by fire and sword, a thing that Spanish America last saw for a few years during the Conquest." Thanks to Spain, America had long enjoyed a profound peace. Europe, by contrast, had seen endless fighting, "for the same ends and with the same results as in the battle of Otumba and the siege of Mexico."

In the matter of just wars, Bernal wished to know whether there was more justice in a war launched to avenge an insult to a ship laden with sarsaparilla, or in one waged to subdue men who hardly lived for any other end than to eat each other. Were the European wars really more profitable to mankind than the Conquest of America? Was it really more harmful to abolish barbarism than to slaughter civilized men in the interests of ambition, profit, or vanity?

The dispute produced such an uproar that Apollo had to call for silence, and finally settled the argument with this statement:

"Europe today is cultured because the Romans, who slaughtered and enslaved her ancient savages, adopted those arts, sciences, and mild manners which they had acquired by intercourse with Greece and through their conquests in the East. To improve the lot of mankind is always praiseworthy, even at the cost of a temporary affliction. To compel the barbarian to end his barbarism, when it is pernicious or degrading to mankind, only the friend of barbarism will regard as a crime. The principal law of human nature is its physical and moral preservation; this law could not operate if men were forbidden to cure the errors of other men who had degenerated from their species to the injury of their fellows." [35]

Forner's stress on improving "the lot of mankind," his reference to the "law of human nature," the omission of theological or religious justifications from his argument, suggest that Enlightenment ideas had penetrated even conservative Spanish circles. For the rest,

his argument did nothing to rescue the Indian from the doom pronounced by De Pauw. Forner's Indian, whether Aztec or Carib,
is a stereotype tainted with crimes against human nature. Indeed,
the reference to "men who had degenerated from their species"
has a definite De Pauwian tonality. Clearly, a Spain preoccupied
with defending her colonial record against foreign attack could not
be expected to reject the charges leveled against the Indian by the
Buffon–De Pauw school. The New World must conduct its own
defense before the tribunal of world opinion.

In the last third of the eighteenth century, at the height of the
reform movement initiated and supported by Bourbon enlightened
despotism, a modest revival of the pro-Indian tradition of Las Casas
and Palafox took place among members of the Mexican clergy.
To that tradition belongs the *Tardes americanas* (1778) of the
Franciscan Bishop Joseph Joaquín Granados y Gálvez, a book
which combined eulogy of the Indian past with protest against the
misery of the modern Mexican Indian.

In the baroquely worded dedication of his book to his kinsman
José de Gálvez, Secretary of the Indies, Granados explained that
his object was to "bring out of the dust of ignorance and the
obscure chaos of confusion many precious documents of Indian
antiquity which time has greedily kept entombed amid the ruins
of oblivion." The introductory matter included the customary
encomiums of the book by ecclesiastics and scholars. These efforts
in verse and prose revealed a strong sensitivity to the "calumnies"
written about the Indians by "impious philosophers." An anonymous poet proclaimed in a sonnet that the Indians were members
of the human race and possessed all the abilities of other men.
According to Fray Joseph Arias, the book proved that the ancient
Mexicans were adorned with all the moral virtues and that their
political, economic, and cultural achievements rivaled those of the
Greeks and Romans.

Granados cast his book in the form of a series of conversations
he held day after day on the pleasant banks of the Alaja River in
Spain with a Spanish friend and an Indian who turns out to be
astonishingly fluent and learned, familiar not only with the history
of his own people but with that of European antiquity, of Spain,
with science, medicine, and so on.

In response to a question from the Spaniard, the Indian proceeded to lead him through the mazes of ancient Mexican history. The narrator transformed some of the ancient Mexican rulers into demigods. The Indian's account of the laws of Nezahualcóyotl moved the Spaniard to exclaim in breathless admiration: "What measures! What laws! What just and commendable provisions! What excellent customs and maxims for securing and making perpetual the existence of a state!" [36]

The Indian went on to describe the Aztec theogony, the calendrical system, and other Indian cultural achievements. He interrupted these accounts with eulogistic descriptions of the Indian character in the manner of Palafox. The Indians were long-lived and largely free from that "tyrannical domination of vice which irritates and upsets the concert and harmony of men." Granados or rather his Indian spokesman explained this equanimity by the simple and scanty Indian diet. This was always the same: twenty-five to thirty thin, delicate maize tortillas with a little chile and salt. The Indians were also free from the passions of wrath, vengeance, fear, gluttony, and intemperance; free even from the immoderate use of strong liquors (a curious statement in view of the well-attested plague of alcoholism among the colonial Indians). Contributing to the Indians' buoyant health was the fact that their arteries, tendons, nerves, and skin were tougher and more solid than those of other men, either because such was their nature or because exposure to the open air in all seasons had hardened them.[37]

If ancient Mexico had not been sunk in the darkness of paganism, proclaimed the Indian, one could speak of their antiquity as a golden age, and of the present as one of iron, for in those days the Indians lived in conformity with the laws of reason; greed had no place in their society; they had attained the summits of culture and science. They had even mastered the science of philosophy. If they lacked the subtleties of Aristotle, they were wise in that moral science that teaches men to think and know good and to distinguish truth from falsehood. They knew of hell and its punishments, of purgatory, and of paradise, which they called Tlalocan. Indeed, their doctrines might serve to convince the impious Helvetius and other atheist philosophers of their errors.[38]

The ancient Indians also knew the rules of rhetoric and the science of music. They produced great poets whose verses combined the tragic spirit of Seneca with the sweetness of Euripides. The philosopher-poet Nezahualcóyotl had composed sixty such verses in iambic meter. In a footnote Granados offered a translation of the Otomí text of a poem, allegedly by the royal bard. (Not many years ago Ángel María Garibay exposed the poem as a hoax, perhaps the work of some creole Chatterton who gave it to the trusting Granados. The poem, wrote Garibay, "is not authentic; it is not in ancient Otomí and cannot be by Nezahualcóyotl.") [39]

The ancient Mexicans, declared Granados' Indian, were also masters of mathematics, mechanics, and medicine. So excellent was their educational system that the same methods were utilized in the Franciscan Colegio de Santa Cruz, founded after the Conquest for the training of Indian youth, with the approval of the Spanish Crown. The Indian even had praise for the pagan religion of the ancient Mexicans. It was purer than the pagan creeds of the Old World; no other pagan faith imitated so closely the rites and customs of the Catholic Church. "They frequented the temples with profound devotion, paid tribute incessantly to their idols, and observed inviolably their ecclesiastical laws, rites, and ceremonies." Nowadays no people equaled the Indians in Catholic piety. Of all that they gained during the year by their labor, they kept only a third for food, tribute, and comforts; the rest they consecrated to the Church. Citing the authority of Boturini and Sigüenza, the Indian believed it likely that the Apostle Saint Thomas, aided by four disciples who imitated his perfection and virtue, had implanted this piety in the hearts of the Indians.

The Spaniard, impressed by these glowing accounts but noting that now a visitor to the same land saw only poverty, disorder, and ignorance, asked a pertinent question: What has happened to all that former grandeur and ability? "Either you are not the descendants of these people, or we must do violence to our reason, by accepting what is written in your books, forcing ourselves to believe what our eyes deny."

The Indian had a ready answer. What remains of the grandeur and beauty of Carthage, Thebes, Tyre, and Babylon? Within the small space of six hundred rods that the Spanish laws assigned to an Indian town of eight hundred or one thousand families, the Indians must find room for their fields, homes, and possessions, for themselves and their descendants. "Our ancestors worked under

conditions of an ample freedom to expand; we work under conditions of having barely enough room to live; they worked magnificently because of the happiness they enjoyed; we work meanly
because of our confined state, abasement, and poverty." The Indian
pursued the contrast between the splendid past and the miserable
present. The ancient Indians wore rich garments of cotton and on
festive days adorned themselves with plumage of variegated colors;
their descendants wore garments of coarse wool. "Does this mean
that we are not the descendants of those men?" [40]

The implied protest against Spain's Indian policy grew sharper
when the Indian discussed the contrast between the royal protective
legislation and the reality of progressive usurpation of Indian land
by Spanish *hacendados*. Bitterly he complained of owners of haciendas who pushed their landmarks up to the very edge of the
Indians' houses, "leaving us hardly an inch of land for rest from
our labors, closing off the roads and paths so that we cannot even
take a stick of wood from the hills and forests, although the laws
expressly grant us that privilege." Meanwhile the tribute burdens
of the Indians had steadily risen; the quota for heads of families,
originally set at 4 reales, now stood at 17 reales plus a hen worth
3 reales.[41]

Yet when Granados related the story of the conquest of Mexico,
he sided completely with the conquerors, in the tradition of the
Mendicant moderates. He accepted without question the Spanish
version of such disputed episodes as the affair of Cholula and the
death of Moctezuma. He put in the mouth of his Indian spokesman
a eulogy of Cortés: "What can I and all my countrymen say, we
who owe to his heroic valor the banishment of our ignorance and
unhappiness, and the gift of the treasures of the Faith and the
Evangel?" [42] Granados appeared oblivious of the contradiction between this statement and his references to the lost pagan Eden.

No authentic Indian voice was raised in this period to protest
against European charges of Indian inferiority and degeneracy.
The majority of the native aristocracy, having been ruined by
debt and loss of their lands as a result of Spanish usurpations and
a variety of other pressures, had sunk into the commoner class.
Those who survived the storm, fusing with the creole aristocracy,
had become totally hispanicized in culture and outlook and showed

little interest in the preservation of their native heritage. It was the creole élite who felt a fervent nationalism and optimism concerning the future of their *patria*, and it was they who responded most sharply to the European challenge. For these men the anti-American charges of a De Pauw not only reflected an exasperating ignorance of American reality but a willful malevolence.

Among these creole defenders of Mexico a group of Jesuit scholars stand out by their sincerity and learning. Suppressed and banished from the New World by order of Charles III in 1767, these men felt a profound nostalgia for Mexico, a wound in the heart that time never healed. Nostalgia deepened their bitterness over the anti-American charges of De Pauw and his school. In their Italian exile some filled their idle hours with scholarly work and writing whose aim was to correct the fantastic ideas held of America by a deluded Europe. Among the most important such Jesuits were Francisco Javier Clavigero and Pedro José Márquez.

The Jesuits combined an impeccable fidelity to Catholic doctrine with efforts to renovate Scholasticism by assimilating all those modern rationalist ideas and scientific findings that were compatible with Catholic dogma. Consequently, in their colegios Clavigero and his colleagues cultivated the new mathematical sciences, taught the doctrines of Bacon and Descartes, and elevated physics above metaphysics and the experimental method above abstract reasoning and speculation.[43] The *Historia antigua de México* of Clavigero illustrates the Jesuit fusion of old and new approaches in the field of history.

In his prologue Clavigero stated that his aim was "to restore the truth to its splendor, truth obscured by an incredible multitude of writers on America." He would employ a plain, unadorned style, for "truth is more beautiful when naked." To make known his sources, and to "honor the memory of some illustrious Americans whose works are entirely unknown in Europe," Clavigero introduced his history with a bibliographical survey of the printed and manuscript sources on Mexican history.

Clavigero devoted the first book of his work to a loving description of the land of Anáhuac, of its soil, climate, other geographical features, of its animals, plants, and people. He indignantly denied the charge of Indian inferiority. False was the allegation that the Indians were able imitators but lacked the capacity for invention.

The originality of their featherwork, goldwork, and silverwork revealed their capacity for invention. False too were the charges with respect to their moral character. They were long suffering, laborious, and responded with gratitude to favors received; however, a long course of insults and mistreatment at the hands of Europeans had bred a habitual mistrust of the white people. This mistrust was frequently expressed, Clavigero sorrowfully admitted, in lying and perfidy. His discussion of the causes of Indian alcoholism contained a strong implied criticism of the colonial regime. In pagan days severe laws against drunkenness kept the Indians temperate; now half the nation went to bed in a drunken state. This alcoholism, joined to misery that weakened their resistance to disease, was the principal cause of the ravages that epidemics caused among them. Clavigero concluded that the Indian character, like that of other men, was compounded of good and evil, but experience had shown that the greater part of the evil could be eradicated by education.[44]

Later books traced the history of the peoples of Anáhuac from the arrival of the first inhabitants to the eve of the Spanish Conquest. Clavigero described in rich detail the religious, political, social, and cultural life of the ancient Mexicans, and told the story of the Conquest. To the main body of his history he added nine *Disertaciones* which addressed themselves directly to the refutation of the anti-American arguments, above all those of De Pauw, "the principal target of my shots."

The history of ancient Mexico took on an epic, heroic character under Clavigero's pen. The annals of the Toltecs, the Texcocans, the Aztecs, offered as many examples of valor, patriotism, wisdom, and virtue as the histories of Greece and Rome. Mexican antiquity displayed such models of just and benevolent rule as the wise Chichimec king Xólotl, and philosopher-kings such as Nezahualcóyotl and Nezahualpilli.

Clavigero's historical method represented a fusion of the providential interpretation of history with a cautious rationalism. His opening lines sounded the characteristic Enlightenment note of skepticism. The history of the first peoples of Anáhuac was so obscure, distorted by so many fables, that it was impossible to ascertain the truth. Toward Boturini's "anecdotes" about the early history of the Toltecs, supposedly based on their sacred book, the

Teoamoxtli, he displayed a polite neutrality. He demonstrated that Boturini's statement that the Toltecs had constructed the pyramid of Cholula in imitation of the Tower of Babel was based on modern forgery containing falsehoods, anachronisms, and nonsen He applied the same critical treatment to the "extravagant" c nology of Torquemada, whose account of ten Totonac lord h of whom ruled for exactly eighty years, "was fit only t use children." And he dissented, despite his great respect fo denza, from a tradition dear to that famous scholar and othe cole historians, that Quetzalcóatl and Saint Thomas were on d the same person.[45]

Clavigero's history is, generally speaking, a "r al history" in which supernatural powers do not intervene, which the great majority of events have natural causes. Yet. en his formation and solid Catholic orthodoxy, Clavigero cc not dispense with the supernatural view of the world and h ry. Suggestive is his discussion as to whether the Devil guided Aztecs in their migrations. Clavigero flatly denied that th migrations were made, "as authors commonly say," by the press order of Satan. He commented sarcastically on Solís' a unt of the numerous visits made to Moctezuma by the Devil The Devil must have been pretty stupid to favor in this way whom he despised so much." Clavigero conceded that evil spir sometimes appeared to men in visible form in order to seduce them, especially to such as had not yet entered the body of the Church, but he insisted that such events must be rare, for God could not allow these enemies of mankind license to inflict injury.

Yet supernatural interventions occur with a fair frequency in Clavigero. He agreed with the traditional view that the Aztec ceremony of communion, in which the people ate portions of a statue of Huitzilopochtli made of blood and maize, represented the Devil's striving to caricature the rites of the Church. Clavigero found it likely that Satan had sent the omens that foretold the fall of the Aztec Empire, but did not exclude the possibility that those omens were the work of God. He allowed the truth of the story that the princess Papantzin, sister of Moctezuma, had been resurrected from the grave to announce to the king the coming of the Christians and the Evangel.[46]

If for Clavigero most events had natural causes, the same was not true of the larger movements of history. He gave unqualified approval to the providential view of the older chroniclers. Like Motolinía, Sahagún, and Acosta, he regarded the Conquest and its aftermath as the price the Mexicans must pay for their sins; and he closed the story of the Conquest on a curiously ambivalent note that appeared to make Spanish cruelty and mistreatment of the Indians an instrument of God's avenging hand. "The Mexicans, with all the other nations which assisted in their ruin, were abandoned, despite the Christian and prudent laws of the Catholic Monarchs, to misery, oppression, and scorn, not only by the Spaniards but even by the vilest African slaves and their infamous descendants. Thereby God avenged upon the miserable posterity of those nations the cruelty, the injustice, and the superstition of their forebears." [47]

Despite his condemnation of Aztec religion as "an aggregate of errors and puerile, cruel, and superstitious practices," Clavigero insisted on a comparative approach by which he established the clear superiority of Mexican paganism over that of the ancient European world. Clavigero affirmed in the traditional manner of the Mendicant chroniclers that the Mexican religion was less superstitious, less indecent, less childish, and less irrational than the pagan creeds of the Old World. As for its cruelty, examples of even more atrocious cruelty abounded among all the peoples of the world. In the process of the development of natural reason, Aztec religion represented a higher stage than the religions of the ancient world, for it had a higher conception of divinity. The Aztec gods were less numerous than those of the Greeks and Romans, and more virtuous. "The Mexicans honored virtues, not vices, in their divinities: in Huitzilopochtli, valor; in Centéotl, Tzapotlaténan, Opochtli, and others, beneficence; and in Quetzalcóatl, chastity, justice, and prudence."

Turning to the most vulnerable aspect of Aztec religion, its human sacrifices, Clavigero stressed that this was a trait of almost all the peoples of antiquity. Even with respect to cannibalism, the Aztecs were not alone in their guilt: it had existed among the Scythians, the Carthaginians, and even the Greeks.[48]

Aztec political institutions also drew Clavigero's praise. He denounced De Pauw's reference to the "anarchy" of the Mexican government. The great authority of Moctezuma and the respect his subjects displayed for him were well known: "If this is anarchy, then all the states of the world are anarchical." Until the time of the second Moctezuma, despotism was unknown in Mexico, for its monarchs religiously respected the limits set on their power by established laws. The penalties prescribed by Aztec justice were severe, true, but not more so than among other peoples of antiquity. Aztec justice was swift and scrupulously fair to all parties, regardless of their social status. Only the testimony of witnesses was admitted. The barbarous device of torture to compel testimony, or the equally barbarous proofs of the duel, fire, or boiling water, so frequently used in Europe, were unknown to the enlightened Mexicans. They also possessed a law of nations and laws of war to which they strictly adhered; war could not be declared until the matter had been carefully examined in full council and approved by the high priest, and repeated efforts made to secure a peaceful adjustment of the quarrel. In fine, at every point where Clavigero compared Aztec political and social institutions with those of peoples at more or less the same stage of development, the Mexicans had the better of it.[49]

Clavigero strongly objected to De Pauw's claim that the Aztecs and the Incas were on about the same level of cultural development as the Caribs or the Iroquois. He recalled the advanced state of Aztec agriculture, as evidenced by the fertile *chinampas* or floating gardens, which foreign observers had so often eulogized. He systematically refuted De Pauw's assumption that the Aztecs fell far short of attaining civilization because they did not have coined money, iron, ships and bridges, writing and the arts. In regard to money, he evidently borrowed from Carli the argument that the Aztecs were no worse off than the Homeric Greeks who used sheep and cattle as a medium of exchange; cacao beans were a much more efficient medium of exchange than cattle! If the Aztecs did not work iron, they produced tempered copper of very high quality. They had no need of seagoing ships, canoes being sufficient for their coastwise trade. In point of fact, the Indians had bridges of stone. If their architecture was inferior to that of Europe, it was superior to that of most Asiatic and African peoples. They had mastered the use of the arch and the vault, the grounding of structures on piles, and the use of lime. If their painting was primitive, their sculpture was highly developed; their silver and goldwork aroused the admiration of contemporary European artisans.

Turning momentarily from De Pauw, Clavigero trained his fire on Robertson's suggestion that the old Spanish chroniclers had unwittingly exaggerated the quality of Aztec artwork. "A fine solution, indeed," exclaimed Clavigero. "So we have all been deceived, including the famous Acosta, the learned Hernández, the silversmiths of Seville, King Philip II, and Pope Sixtus V, all admirers and eulogists of those Mexican artifacts! Yes, all! Only the Scot Robertson and the Prussian De Pauw have had the mentality needed to form a correct judgment of things, perhaps because the chill of their lands has moderated the warmth of their imagination." [50]

Clavigero insisted that De Pauw, like Kircher and others before him, were wrong in saying that Mexican writing was limited to the crude representation of objects. He cited the Aztec signs for night, day, year, age, heaven, earth, water, and the like, to prove that they had arbitrary or conventional characters to represent abstract ideas and objects, making their writing truly hieroglyphic. With equal warmth, Clavigero cited the Náhuatl language to refute De Pauw's charge that the poverty of Indian languages made it impossible to express metaphysical concepts or even to count beyond three. "One might think," exasperatedly wrote Clavigero, "that De Pauw had traveled the length and breadth of America, had dealt with all its peoples, and studied their languages. Without ever having left his study in Berlin, De Pauw knows the affairs of America better than the Americans themselves and understands their languages better than the men who speak them."

Clavigero, who knew Náhuatl and had heard it spoken for many years, offered proof that the Mexicans had the means to express figures of 48 million and beyond, and to express a wide range of metaphysical concepts. They did lack words for "matter, substance, accident," and the like, but the same was true of the Romans when they began to philosophize; Cicero often struggled to find words corresponding to Greek metaphysical ideas. Clavigero also cited Boturini and other witnesses to the effect that no language compared with the Mexican in urbanity, elegance, and sublimity of expression. [51]

The cultural inferiority and degradation of the modern Indian

Clavigero attributed basically to one cause: ignorance. This inferiority was therefore an accidental, historical fact, easily remedied by education. In words that recalled Voltaire's stress on the importance of the religious and political systems, Clavigero wrote: "For the rest, it cannot be doubted that the present Mexicans are not entirely like the ancient Mexicans, just as the modern Greeks under Turkish rule are not like those who existed in the time of Plato and Pericles. Such was the influence of the political and religious constitution of a state on the spirit of a nation. In the souls of the ancient Mexicans there was more fire, and ideas of honor had greater weight. They were more intrepid, more able, more industrious, and more active, but more superstitious and inhumane." [52]

First published in Cesena in a four-volume Italian version prepared by Clavigero himself (1780–1781), the *Storia antica del Messico* was quickly translated into other languages. The first English edition appeared in London in 1787, a second edition in Richmond, Virginia, in 1806, a third in Philadelphia, in 1817. A German version of the English text was published in Leipzig in 1789 and 1790. In 1789 the Spanish government approved publication of the book with revisions that would eliminate Clavigero's criticism of Spanish colonial policy, but nothing came of the project.[53] The first Spanish edition, a translation from the Italian, appeared in London in 1826. The original Spanish text was first published in Mexico City in 1945, in an edition by Father Mariano Cuevas.

Despite its patent idealization of ancient Mexican society, Clavigero's book represented a superb synthesis of the best available information on its subject. Its clear, unassuming style, devoid of flourish or affectation, increased its effectiveness. Prescott declared that the book created something like a "popular interest" in Mexican antiquities. In his debate with De Pauw and Raynal, Clavigero was "perfectly successful," according to the careful Prescott.[54] He had met his Encyclopedist foes on their own ground, the ground of reason, and had soundly beaten them. His crushing refutation of De Pauw, in particular, helped to liquidate the influence of the *Recherches philosophiques*.

A notable aspect of Clavigero's book is its contribution to what has been called "neo-Aztecism." [55] Clavigero was not the first to relate the "cult of Aztec antiquity to the social problems of the

contemporary Indians" and thus bring out its anti-Spanish implications. Besides the older Mendicant chroniclers, Bishop Granados
had compared the past and present state of the Mexican Indian in
a way that was most uncomplimentary to Spanish rule, only two
years before the appearance of Clavigero's book. However, Clavigero's book, modern in spirit and method, favored by the approval
of cultured Europe, did incomparably more to provide patriotic
Mexican creoles with a glorious native past.

Another Jesuit exile, Father Pedro José Márquez, wrote the first
work on Mexican archaeology to be published in Europe. His *Due
antichi monumenti di architectura messicana* (1804), proposed to
publicize the archaeological finds recently made at Tajín and
Xochicalco and described by the illustrious Mexican scientist José
Antonio Alzate in the pages of his *Gazetas de Literatura* and in a
pamphlet. The homesick Jesuit dedicated the book to Mexico City,
"which gave its name to a vast empire where once flowered the
remarkable civilization of its founders, and where today flower
letters and every kind of European learning."

Stung by European attacks on the character and capacity of the
Indian, Márquez took the occasion to proclaim the equality of all
races and his belief in the transforming power of education. To
his creed, Enlightenment radicals like the atheist Baron d'Holbach
could have subscribed without a murmur. "All nations," wrote
Márquez, "believe themselves superior to each other; all men laugh
when they hear a language not their own. But the true philosopher
is a cosmopolitan; he holds all men to be his countrymen, and
knows that every language, however exotic it may seem, can with
increasing culture become as learned as the Greek, and that by
means of education every people can become as civilized as the
people which considers itself superior. True philosophy does not
care whether a man is born white or black, or whether he was
educated under the Poles or in the torrid zone. Given the requisite instruction (this is what the true philosophy teaches), man in
every climate is capable of everything." [56]

Márquez introduced his summary of Alzate's writings on archaeology with a sketch of Mexican history. He wrote that the Aztecs
were the most cultured people of ancient America; into their capital flowed the wealth and commerce of their subject towns and
even of other kingdoms. And there were other cities, the homes

of an equally high civilization, such as Tlaxcala and Texcoco. These peoples had governments and laws that maintained internal stability and order; commerce flourished among them; they conducted scientific studies, both theoretical and practical.

Turning to the problem of human sacrifice among the ancient Mexicans, Márquez assured his readers that the Aztecs had not practiced it on the extravagant scale supposed by some writers. Besides, they also offered to their gods rabbits, quails, and other animals, and flowers in abundance. For the rest, every nation on earth had used human sacrifice at one time or another.

The body of Márquez' book was devoted to a summary of Alzate's description of the ruins of Tajín and Xochicalco. Márquez promised that he would soon make available the "learned dissertation" of another Mexican savant, Antonio de León y Gama, dealing with the calendrical lore derived from a large stone recently unearthed in Mexico City.

The two scholars cited by Márquez—Alzate and León y Gama—were central figures in the scientific movement that developed in Mexico in the last third of the eighteenth century as a result of the impulse given by Bourbon enlightened despotism, the diffusion of Enlightenment ideas, and the desire of patriotic creoles to know and exploit the material and cultural resources of their country.[57]

Alzate, whose astronomical studies gained him the title of corresponding member of the Academy of Sciences of Paris, began publication in 1788 of a *Gazeta de Literatura* which aimed to inspire interest in the natural and social sciences among the Mexican reading public. He hoped thereby to promote the economic and intellectual welfare of Mexico. In 1791 he published, as a supplement to the *Gazeta*, a *Descripción de las antigüedades de Xochicalco, dedicada a los señores de la actual expedición alrededor del orbe*.

Like Clavigero and Márquez, Alzate displayed a marked concern with the "dark and vile colors" in which foreign writers had systematically painted the Mexican Indians. On various occasions, he recalled, he had challenged these libels in the pages of the *Gazeta*, but had wished to obtain more convincing evidence of the greatness of the ancient Mexicans. Upon learning, therefore, of the discovery in 1784 of the ruins of an ancient palace at Xochicalco, southwest of Cuernavaca, he had journeyed there and found "a work of such precious architecture" that he determined to offer the public a detailed description. His findings fully corroborated the observations of the "sage Clavigero."

Alzate opened his pioneering archaeological study with the luminous observation that an edifice reveals the character and culture of a people, for the progress made in the sciences and arts discloses that people's state of civilization or barbarism. He repeated Clavigero's analogy between the Indians and the Greeks. As a result of the Spanish Conquest, the Indians had lost their distinctive traits, becoming in respect to their forebears what the modern Greeks are to the ancient. It was unfair, therefore, to describe the ancient Mexicans as "uncultured," simply because the modern Indians were such. The contemporary Indians made up the humblest plebeian element of the population. "In what land were the plebeians ever educated?"

Alzate regretted that "the indiscreet zeal of some, and the avarice of others, had destroyed the Mexican monuments." Had they survived, it would have been possible to establish the origin of the Indians and to reconstruct their customs, legislation, and the character of their monarchs. Even in their ruined state, the structures of Xochicalco—a complex of five terraces faced with stone leading to a low, profusely decorated pyramid—provided Alzate with evidence of the high civilization of the ancient Mexicans, "for the science of architecture embraces many others that are necessary to it," including sculpture and astronomy. Moreover, such stupendous constructions required the labor of a multitude of Indians, clear evidence of the existence of a powerful monarch with unlimited authority over his subjects.[58]

The discovery in 1790 of two massive monoliths during the paving of what had been Tenochtitlán's central square and ceremonial center opened up new perspectives on Mexican antiquity. One was the statue of the earth goddess Coatlicue, the other the twenty-four-ton Stone of the Sun, now known as the Calendar Stone.

One year after the appearance of Alzate's essay, Antonio de León y Gama published a much more detailed study of the two sculptures and of the more recently discovered Sacrificial Stone or Stone of Tizoc. León y Gama declared that the discovery of the Stone of the Sun had brought him special satisfaction, for in its inscriptions he found confirmation of the conclusions he had reached about the Mexican calendrical system. Fearing that the

Measured drawing of the Coatlicue sculpture made by Antonio de León y Gama for his *Descripción histórica y cronológica de las dos piedras que se hallaron en la Plaza Principal de México* (Mexico, 1792; reprinted 1832). Courtesy Marquand Art Library, Princeton University.

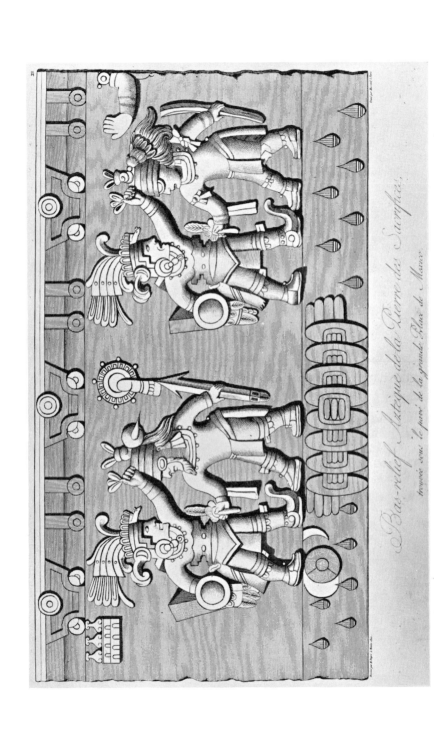

Bas-relief Aztèque de la Pierre des Sacrifices.

Trouvée sous le pavé de la grande Place de Mexico.

Detail of the Stone of Tizoc or Sacrificial Stone, another monolith discovered on the
site of the Great Square of México-Tenochtitlán. Engraved from a drawing made by
M. Dupré in Mexico in 1800. Published by Alexander von Humboldt in his *Vues des
cordillères et monumens des peuples indigènes de l'Amérique* (Paris, 1810). Courtesy
New York Public Library.

stone might suffer injury from the curiosity or fanaticism of the people, Gama hastened to have an exact copy made; and at the instance of friends resolved to publish a description and analysis of both monuments. The *Descripción* of 1792 contained only the first part of his lengthy essay; the second part remained in manuscript until Carlos María Bustamante published the entire work in 1832. León y Gama's essay, in the words of a French scholar, "founded the science of Aztec archaeology." [59]

León y Gama cited among the reasons for writing his study a now familiar motive: the wish to show how falsely the enemies of Spain described the ancient Mexicans as "irrational or simple-minded beings, in order to tarnish the glorious deeds of the Spaniards who conquered these kingdoms." He proposed to show the great ability of the artisans who so perfectly engraved the inscriptions on these stones, although they did not have tempered steel chisels or points, but only other, harder stones.

His analysis of the Calendar Stone would reveal the Indians' remarkable mathematical knowledge. Its volume and weight would show their knowledge of mechanics, for without knowledge of its fundamental principles they could not have cut the stone and brought it from its place of origin to its resting place. The perfection and uniformity of the circles, the exact division of the stone's parts, and other features proved that the Indians had a clear understanding of geometry. He would also show, declared León y Gama, that the Indians made observations of the sun and stars, and that the stone was a true calendar, representing the Aztec hours, days, weeks, months, years, and cycles of fifty-two years.

Gama devoted the body of his essay to an attempt at explication of the symbolism of the Coatlicue, the Calendar Stone, and the Sacrificial Stone, principally with a view to reconstructing the Aztec calendrical, mathematical, and writing systems. Concerning the calendrical system he derived from the Calendar Stone, a modern scholar writes that "with all its errors, it marked a notable advance." [60]

As a scientist, León y Gama took pleasure in noting the remarkable results achieved by the ancient Mexicans with very limited means. The beautiful simplicity of Aztec mathematical operations inspired his high praise. "We must admire the supreme skill with which, using only nine terms, they were able to express immense quantities." The same simplicity and economy of means marked and continued to mark all their work. "One wonders to see them split a log with such precision and so finely that one can hardly see the divisions, using only one stone as a wedge and another as a hammer." [61]

The creole defense of the ancient Mexicans took a fantastic turn when the Dominican Servando Teresa de Mier rose in his pulpit in the town of Guadalupe on December 12, 1794, to announce in his sermon that the famous image of the Virgin of Guadalupe had not been presented to the Indian Juan Diego by Our Lady in colonial times, as tradition had it, but had resulted from a meeting in America, long ages before, between the Virgin and Saint Thomas, known to the Mexicans as Quetzalcóatl and to the Incas as Viracocha. St. Thomas had come with four disciples to preach the Gospel in the New World. In this the Apostle had succeeded, and at the time of the Conquest Christianity, somewhat deformed, to be sure, reigned in Mexico.

As Mier successively revised his version of these interesting events, the legend assumed an ever more bizarre character. The war god Huitzilopochtli became the form under which the Aztecs worshiped the Redeemer. After all, Huitzilopochtli was a man-god born of a virgin, and one of his names was "Lord of the Crown of Thorns." Tezcatlipoca became the Supreme Being; the fearsome Coatlicue the Virgin Mary. Thus, with a wave of his magic wand, as Villoro observes, Mier transformed the whole Indian world. "In all of Mexican historical bibliography," less tolerantly writes Edmundo O'Gorman, "it would be difficult to match this in the category of nonsense and absurdity." [62]

Villoro sees in Mier's fantasy a reaction to European scorn for the creole, an effort to establish the equality of America with Europe by wresting from Spain her best claim to dominion over America: the conversion of the Indians. If Mier was right, America owed nothing to Spain, not even her Christianity. No doubt this helps to explain the swift punitive action taken against Fray Servando, his arrest and exile to Spain. Fray Servando himself thus explained the Spanish reaction to his sermon.

More than the creole-peninsular cleavage was involved in the making of this legend. On both sides of the Atlantic, a wayward and imaginative romanticism was challenging the sway of rationalism. The Aztecs were to be the beneficiaries of this process. The welter of illusion and fantasy that surrounds Mier's Aztecs suggests the romantic apotheosis to come, the Aztecs transfigured.

Eighteenth-century literary portrayals of the Aztec and the conquest of Mexico lack both artistic and intellectual value. We look in vain for poetry or prose containing the well-made verse of Dryden's *Indian Emperor* or the cheerful iconoclastic sparkle of Fontenelle's dialogue between Moctezuma and Cortés.

The numerous Spanish plays and poems dealing with the conquest of Mexico reveal peninsular sensitivity to foreign criticism of the Conquest. The Indian portrayed in these plays and poems is the Indian of Solís: a formidable fighter, but ferocious, cruel, superstitious, and barbarous.[63] Typical of the outpouring of writings of this kind is the long heroic poem *México conquistada* (1798), by the Zaragoza priest Juan de Escóiquiz. The author's polemical intent is broached in a prologue in which Escóiquiz attacked foreign detractors of Spain and sorrowfully criticized "the indiscreet exaggerations of one of our bishops, named Fray Bartolomé de Las Casas, whose zeal would have been very laudable if accompanied by sound judgment, and if he had not gone beyond the bounds of truth."

Although Escóiquiz rang the changes on the familiar Spanish rebuttals of the foreign critique, Enlightenment influence was evident in the tone of reasonableness and in the concessions he made to the critics. Spain had introduced "rationality, civilization, and the true religion" into the New World. To portray the Mexicans as beings of dove-like simplicity and mildness was a classic piece of nonsense—these people, who had built a vast empire by force of arms, were continually at war with their neighbors, and not only sacrificed their prisoners but ate their flesh. As for Spanish cruelty, did not the great Charlemagne commit equal cruelties in his campaign to convert the Saxons? In an unexpected admission, Escóiquiz conceded that there might have been more cruelty in the Spanish Conquest than in others; but he said that this was natural, for, excepting some young noblemen, the majority of the conquistadors were a mass of illiterate adventurers, greedy and audacious men whose hard and dangerous life disposed them to barbarity of every sort. Their barbarities would have not become known, had it not been for the outcry of other Spaniards. Could other peoples, guilty of the same crimes, say the same? The mild spirit of the Laws of the Indies reflected the true spirit of the Spaniards; the misdeeds of a few should not be used to dishonor a whole nation, for great rascals could be found in every land.

The poem drags its weary length through three volumes. It is little more than a rendering in rhymed verse of Solís' *Historia de la conquista de México*, with borrowing of whole phrases and words, and is totally without literary merit.

French contributions to the theme of the Conquest included a curious production by one Boesnier, a "heroic poem" in prose entitled *Le Mexique conquis* (1752), whose tone was unctuously pious and pro-Spanish. In his dedication the author declared that the sole purpose of the Conquest was to spread the Evangel; it had ended with "the overthrow of the visible throne of Satan." Equally pro-Spanish was Alexis Piron's play, *Fernand Cortez ou Moctezuma* (1776), whose ideological posture led to publication of a Spanish version. The play portrays Moctezuma as a repentant convert to Christianity who regrets having reigned over "such an uncivilized people, a people so vile and perverse." The extravagant plot contains an inevitable love intrigue; the Spanish heroine, Elvira, loves Cortés but has been promised to Moctezuma by her father, Don Pedro, in the belief that "thy happy union will extinguish the horrible paganism that reigns here." However, all ends well; Moctezuma is slain by rebellious Indians and in his dying speech yields Elvira up to Cortés.

The Aztec theme enjoyed a certain popularity among English poets and playwrights of the last third of the eighteenth century. In English literary circles, sensibility and the Noble Savage were the fashion—to the vast disgust of such champions of civilization as Samuel Johnson. English pre-romanticism sentimentalized Rousseau's complex notion of the natural man, injecting color and enthusiasm into what had been in Dryden a polite literary convention. Typical of the Aztec plays and poems of this period were Henry Brooke's *Montezuma* (1778), which unblushingly copied from Dryden's *Indian Emperor* its theme, ideas, and even the names of the characters, and Edward Jerningham's *The Fall of Mexico* (1775), whose major characters included Cuauhtémoc and Las Casas. One critic's description of Jerningham's poem as "hopelessly dull" hits the mark, but it is a good early example of the romantic apotheosis of the Aztec. Cuauhtémoc, subjected to torture by fire, responds to the groans of his companion in suffering:

> Amidst the raging flames that round him blaz'd,
> The royal chief his martyr'd figure rais'd,
> Cast on the youth a calm-reproaching eye,
> And spoke—oh eloquent, sublime reply!
>   Oh heav'n! oh earth! attend "Do I repose
>   All on the silken foliage of the rose?"
> He ceas'd—and deep within his soul retir'd
> To honour firm, triumphant he expir'd.

The Inca theme, thanks to the influence of Garcilaso de la Vega and *Les Incas, ou La Destruction de l'Empire du Pérou* (1777) [64] of Marmontel, enjoyed greater favor among the literati of the time.

The American poet Joel Barlow glorified the Inca state in his epic poem *The Vision of Columbus* (1787) and made the Inca monarch and lawgiver Manco Capac one of the great figures of American history. In a "Dissertation on the Genius and Institutions of Manco Capac," which he inserted in the poem, he unfavorably compared the Aztec system of government and religion with that of the Incas. "The Mexican Constitution," he wrote, "was formed to render its subjects brave and powerful; but while it succeeded in this object, it tended to remove them farther from the real blessings of society, than they were while in the rudest state of nature. The history of the world affords no instance of men whose manners were equally ferocious, and whose superstition was more bloody and unrelenting. On the contrary, the establishments of Manco Capac carry the marks of a most benevolent and pacific system; they tended to harmonize the world and render his people happy; while his ideas of the Deity were so perfect, as to bear a comparison with the enlightened doctrines of Socrates or Plato." [65]

Barlow, true to romantic literary convention, depicted Tenochtitlán and Moctezuma in most attractive colors, as they appeared to Columbus in a prophetic dream. Observe how he endows Tenochtitlán with walls, towers, and turrets that turn it into a medieval city:

Fair on the north, bright Mexico, arose,
A mimic morn, her sparkling towers disclose,
An ample range the opening streets display,
Give back the sun and shed internal day;
The circling wall with sky-built turrets frown'd,
And look'd defiance to the realms around;
A glimmering lake, without the walls, retires,
Inverts the trembling towers and seems a grove of spires.
Bright, o'er the midst, on columns lifted high,
A rising structure claims a loftier sky;
O'er the tall gates sublimer arches bend,
Courts larger lengthen, bolder walks ascend,
Starr'd with superior gems, the porches shine,
And speak the royal residence within.
        There, robed in state, high on a golden throne,
Mid suppliant kings, dread Montezuma shone;
Mild in his eye, a temper'd grandeur sate,
Great seem'd his soul, with conscious power elate;
In aspect open, haughty, and sincere,
Untamed by crosses and unknown to fear,
Of fraud incautious, credulous and vain,
Enclosed with favorites and of friends unseen.

Columbus rejoices at the smiling aspect of the Mexican landscape and expresses the hope that this "happy land" may remain safe from foreign foes. But the angel who guides his vision disillusions him, foretelling the desolation to be wrought by Cortés, "the blackest of mankind." [66]

Whereas the Jeffersonian Barlow, the "warm-hearted humanitarian," as Parrington called him,[67] viewed pre-Columbian America through romantic eyes and saw smiling lands, the Federalist Timothy Dwight, a stiff-necked foe of infidelity and democracy, saw a very different state of affairs. In his poem *America* (1780), he exempted no people from his indictment of Indian America before Columbus:

O'er all, the impenetrable darkness spread
Her dusky wings and cast a dreadful shade;
No glimpse of science through the gloom appeared;
No trace of civil life the desert chear'd;

No soft endearments, no fond social ties,
Nor faith, nor justice calm'd their horrid joys.

Sentiments, these, of which De Pauw could well have approved. Thus, in the New World as in the Old, political ideologies and artistic canons colored men's vision of the peoples and institutions of ancient America.

CHAPTER TEN

The Aztecs Transfigured: I

The Age of Romanticism [1] brightened the Indian image in Western eyes. The Indian was linked to other groups of the disinherited and the vanquished—peasants, artisans, small nations struggling for their freedom—whose sorrows and virtues commanded the sympathy of the romantic heart. Among the Indians, the Aztecs formed a singularly proper object of romantic interest. They belonged to a remote past, a past which the romantic saw blazing with color or shadowed with attractive mystery. The exoticism of Aztec civilization, its ambiguous blend of refinement and barbarism, satisfied the romantic taste for the fantastic and bizarre. If some romantic poets and novelists sought escape from a humdrum present in Xanadu, ancient Rome, or medieval England, others took the road to Tenochtitlán.

Ambivalence marked the romantic attitude toward the Aztec. The romantic admired Aztec bravery, stoicism, and eloquence. He might rejoice in the Aztec's cultural achievements, which enhanced his other ornaments with the fine flower of civilization. These achievements, in their parallelism with the works of ancient Egypt and China, demonstrated the unity of mankind and its upward-striving spirit. Conversely, since the romantic usually subscribed to the liberal creed of individualism and progress, he generally abhorred not only the sanguinary Aztec religion but Aztec despotism and theocracy. The nineteenth-century liberal regarded all three as insuperable obstacles to progress. An occasional romantic historian, such as Charles-Etienne Brasseur de Bourbourg, argued that Aztec civilization at the time of the Conquest was in rapid forward movement, advancing toward a freer society and a purer religion. More typical was the view of Alexander von Humboldt, who seemed to look upon Aztec society as a fossil civilization, frozen in its tracks by the repressive influence of a despotic, theocratic government hostile to the development of the mind.

Equally pessimistic about the potential for Aztec progress was William H. Prescott, who proclaimed the essential Aztec nature to be that of children of the wilderness, doomed like their more primitive kinsmen of the northern forests and plains to melt away on contact with the higher European culture. "The American Indian has something peculiarly sensitive in his nature. He shrinks instinctively from the rude touch of a foreign hand. Even when this foreign influence comes in the form of civilization, he seems to sink and pine away beneath it. It has been so with the Mexicans. . . . Their civilization was of the hardy character which belongs to the wilderness." [2]

Romantic interpretations of Aztec society presented considerable variation from country to country. In Mexico the War of Independence fostered the growth of the nationalist cult of Mexican antiquity, which reached its climax in the emotional effusions and the valuable though defective editorial labors of Carlos María Bustamante. Once the goal of independence had been attained, Mexican fervor for the Indian past subsided, although some liberals continued, more or less sincerely, to invoke the shades of Cuauhtémoc and Moctezuma as part of their struggle against a neocolonial society and mentality.

On the Continent, leadership and interest in ancient Mexican studies passed definitively from Spain to other lands. As the nineteenth century opened, the young Prussian nobleman Humboldt, who combined the philosophical idealism of Herder and Kant with a Renaissance thirst for knowledge and a rigorous scientific method, began the comparative study of the ancient civilizations of the Old and the New Worlds. The monumental documentary publication of Humboldt, followed by those of the Abbé Jean-Henri Baradère and Edward King, Viscount Kingsborough, quite destroyed the surviving influence on the Continent of the skeptical ideas identified with De Pauw and Robertson. In France there arose a genuine school of ancient Mexican studies under the leadership of J.-M.-A. Aubin, author of the first true monograph on Aztec picture writing, and of his self-avowed disciple, Brasseur de Bourbourg, who was immensely learned but unhappily given to extravagant speculation.

In the British Isles, the French enthusiasm for Mexican antiquity was tempered by English caution and by the influence of classical economics, which found Aztec civilization seriously wanting when measured by the yardsticks of technology and productivity. In the United States, Prescott's *Conquest of Mexico* appeared to give firm scholarly support to the romantic vision of Aztec magnificence; however, discerning critics perceived that Prescott's air of scholarly impartiality concealed a strong anti-Indian prejudice. Other writers, such as Lewis Cass and Albert Gallatin, who knew at first hand the modest cultural level of the Indian tribes of the United States, displayed a radical skepticism about the claims made for the ancient civilizations of Mexico. These men were the first skirmishers in the revisionist campaign that Lewis H. Morgan and Adolph F. Bandelier were soon to launch against what the latter called the "Romantic School of American Archaeology."

Archaeological investigations played a key role in the romantic rediscovery of the past. Such activity had a special importance for the rehabilitation of the high Indian cultures. De Pauw and his disciples had attempted to discredit them by insisting that impressive ruins were almost nonexistent in the New World. The pioneering archaeological studies of Alzate, León y Gama, and Márquez had proved otherwise. Even earlier (1786), Charles III of Spain, who as King of Naples had shown strong interest in the study of Greek and Roman ruins, ordered a systematic exploration of the architectural remains at Palenque, in the province of Chiapas, whose existence had been known from about 1750. Captain Antonio del Río, dispatched by the governor of Guatemala to execute the royal order, arrived at the site on May 3, 1787. Del Río summarized his research (he stayed at Palenque all of three weeks) in a report which slept in the colonial archives until it was smuggled out of the country and published in English translation in London in 1822.[3]

At the opening of the nineteenth century, Charles IV continued the admirable initiative of his father by extending the field of archaeological inquiry to all Mexico. An officer of French descent, Captain Guillermo Dupaix, was placed in charge of this reconnaissance. Accompanied by a troop of cavalry and a competent illustrator, Luciano Castañeda, Dupaix made three expeditions between 1805 and 1808. Xochicalco, Monte Albán, Mitla, and Palenque were among the sites he visited. Dupaix, whom the French editor of his relations described as "a simple and truthful man," and as "adequately educated in history and archaeology," wrote a number of detailed reports, accompanied by numerous illustrations by Castañeda.

The outbreak of the Mexican War of Independence in 1810 halted preparations to send these documents to Madrid. They remained in the possession of the artist Castañeda, who deposited them in the Museo de Historia Natural in Mexico City, from which they were later transferred to the Museo Nacional that was established in 1825. There the Abbé Baradère found them in 1828. After delicate negotiations he secured permission to take them to Paris, where they were published in 1834 in a sumptuous edition.

Dupaix's observations, the observations of a professional soldier with no special training in archaeology, displayed an unexpected sensitivity and sympathy with his subject. Like Alzate and León y Gama, Dupaix stressed the broad importance of architectural remains as indicators of the cultural level of ancient societies. Reflecting on the Zapotec ruins of Monte Albán, he wrote: "This ancient and original American school [of architecture], these and many other structures strewn throughout the New World, demonstrate increasingly a body of knowledge that one would not expect to find in a people that has always, though unjustly, been regarded as barbarian. Their surviving works offer a better apology for this people than the words of their defenders; they show that theory must have preceded practice and that, far from constructing in a mechanical way, this people worked from carefully thought-out plans. There is no doubt that this people had its own geometry, consisting like ours in invariable rules and calculations." [4]

Dupaix used an analogy previously employed by such writers as Granados and Clavigero to explain the apparent intellectual inferiority of the modern Mexican Indian. "The Indians," he wrote, "cannot be today what they once were. The ancient Egyptians, so highly praised by the historians of former times, produced in the days of their glory pyramids and columns; now they produce only huts and pygmies. The point is that the arts require a large and free field of action to prosper. The beautiful Greece of antiquity offers another example." [5]

However elementary or naïve, Dupaix's comments on Mexican architecture represent the first efforts to distinguish the various art styles of ancient Middle America. He was of the opinion that the Aztecs were deficient in art as in all other fields of culture; they learned all they knew from the Toltec nation, "the Attica of these ancient lands." The pyramids in the Aztec territory were distinguished by a massive base and a severe aspect, said Dupaix. They were not merely ornamental in purpose, for they were consecrated to the cult of the gods. Each pyramid had one to seven platforms that diminished in area as the structure rose. Dupaix called the pyramid of Papantla (Tajín) "an admirable structure, comparable to the celebrated pyramids of Egypt." [6]

He repeatedly called attention to analogies between the Egyptian and Mexican pyramids; these similarities might be accidental or the result of communication. Very different were the structures of the "Zapotec Empire" in the Oaxaca area. In solidity they resembled those of the Aztec territory; however, the walls of the "palaces" of Mitla, with their mosaics of geometric figures in bas relief, seemed to Dupaix to breathe a Greek spirit. Finally, the ruins of Palenque impressed Dupaix with their originality. This ancient people, he wrote, borrowed nothing from any other nation of the earth. He suggested that the builders of Palenque either had developed their architectural and art style in the long centuries that followed their arrival from the Old World, or had brought them from their Old World home. [7]

The *Cartas mejicanas* of Fray Benito María de Moxó, Bishop of Mexico, reflected the upsurge of interest in Mexican archaeology. This work, written at the end of 1805, was the swan song, as it were, of the Mendicant school of writers on ancient Mexico. Fray Moxó defended the Indians against the aspersions of De Pauw, Robertson, and Raynal, but simultaneously upheld the legitimacy of the Conquest and of Spanish rule in the Indies. Much of the work rings changes on the familiar arguments of Clavigero and

Carli against the charges of Indian inferiority made by De Pauw and Robertson. Moxó also cited Aztec mathematics, astronomy, industry, writing, and other cultural achievements. Yet Moxó was not an unqualified apologist for Aztec customs. Fighting a battle on two fronts, he rebuked Voltaire and other impious *philosophes* for having minimized the extent of human sacrifice and cannibalism among the Aztecs.[8]

In agreement with the older Mendicant chroniclers, Moxó was alternately repelled and attracted by the Indians. In the manner of Durán and Sahagún, he complained of the firm hold that idolatry had on the natives. They continued to worship their idols in the mode of their ancestors; they had priests who did penance by drawing blood from their bodies with maguey thorns and obsidian knives. "Will you believe that I have in my collection many of these lancets and even a piece of paper stained with countless drops of blood offered by these priests a few months ago to two ugly idols? Such is the cunning with which these natives seek at any risk to preserve what they call *the immemorial custom of their forebears.*"[9]

The most original aspect of the *Cartas mejicanas* is their defense of ancient Mexican art. Bishop Moxó recalled that in Spain he had read Clavigero's contention that the ugliness and lack of proportion in the figures of Mexican idols were due not to ignorance of the rules of drawing but to religious requirements, but Moxó was not convinced, "for I, like most Europeans, had a very low opinion of the intelligence and ability of the ancient Mexicans in the fine arts."[10] Now, however, he was persuaded that the misshapen aspect of the Aztec deities was caused by the many hieroglyphs with which the native artist burdened the figures in order to represent all their divine attributes.

Moved by enthusiasm for Mexican antiquities, Moxó had formed his own collection. The Indians of Tlatelolco, knowing of his interest in these matters, had presented him with various figurines that they had found in the ruins of the ancient town. These figurines proved to Moxó that the ancient Mexicans, like the Egyptians, surrounded the mysteries of their religion with an infinite number of symbols and hieroglyphs.

Moxó had discovered that Mexican sculptors were capable of creating figures with correct proportions and even beauty of line.

Recently the Indians had brought him a sculptured head found in a site being excavated for the construction of a water channel. It was made with a precision, fineness, and simplicity that would do credit to a Greek or Roman artist. Moxó vowed that he would guard this "precious monument of Mexican antiquity" for the rest of his life as one of the rarest and most exquisite objects of his collection. He assured his readers that if the collection of Mexican antiquities being formed by "the industrious Monsieur Dupaix" were ever published, it would utterly dispel any doubts that Europe's savants might have concerning Indian artistic ability.[11]

The *Cartas mejicanas* continued the Mendicant tradition of defending the Indian against Spanish mistreatment. Pointing to the miserable shacks inhabited by the Indians of Tlaxcala, "a city to which Spain and Religion owe so much," Moxó complained that among those huts there rose the stately dwellings of a few moneybags "who could easily improve the commonweal by distributing equitably the surplus of their wealth; instead they burden the commonweal by the enormous weight of their usury." And he appealed to the Spaniards to deal kindly with "those poor laborers [*gañanes*]" to whom they owed their wealth.[12]

As Bishop Moxó soon discovered to his sorrow, the day was late for appeals for reforms of any kind in the management of the Indies. In December, 1805, he departed from Mexico to assume the office of Archbishop of Chuquisaca in Upper Peru (Bolivia). Three years later a creole revolt deposed the Audiencia's president and set up a governing junta dominated by creoles. The revolt was crushed, but in 1815 a revolutionary army led by the Argentine General José Rondeau invaded Upper Peru, arrested Archbishop Moxó, and deported him to Salta. On his way to exile the Archbishop wrote a "letter to the Americans" in which he cited his manuscript *Cartas mejicanas* as proof of his affection and loyalty to his American *patria*. He died in captivity some six months later. His book remained in manuscript until 1837, when it was published in Genoa through the good offices of some friends and admirers.[13]

The Mexican struggle for independence, begun by the priest Miguel Hidalgo in 1810, continued by another revolutionary priest, José María Morelos, and brought to a successful conclusion under conservative auspices in 1821, completed the building of that ro-

Tower in the Palace, Palenque, Chiapas. Lithographed from a sketch by
Jean-Frédéric Waldeck *c.* 1832. From C.-E. Brasseur de Bourbourg, *Monu-
ments anciens du Mexique* (Paris, 1866). Courtesy Marquand Art Library,
Princeton University.

Mitla, Oaxaca. Lithographed from a sketch by Luciano Castañeda in the Guillermo Dupaix expeditions of 1805–1808. From Lord Kingsborough's *Antiquities of Mexico,* Volume IV (London, 1831). Courtesy Department of Rare Books and Special Collections, Princeton University Library.

33.

Xochicalco, Morelos. Lithographed from a sketch by Luciano Castañeda in the Guillermo Dupaix expeditions of 1805–1808. From J.-H. Baradère, *Antiquités mexicaines* (Paris, 1834). Courtesy Marquand Art Library, Princeton University.

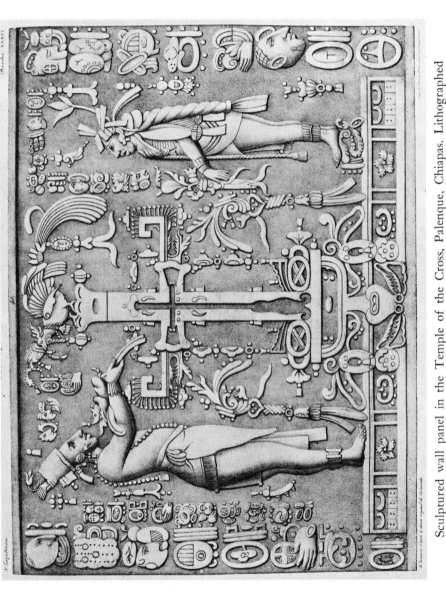

Sculptured wall panel in the Temple of the Cross, Palenque, Chiapas. Lithographed from a sketch by Luciano Castañeda in the Guillermo Dupaix expeditions of 1805–1808. From J.-H. Baradère, *Antiquités mexicaines* (Paris, 1834). Courtesy Marquand Art Library, Princeton University.

mantic cult of ancient Mexico whose principal architects were Ixtlilxóchitl, Sigüenza y Góngora, Boturini, Veytia, and Mier. In patriot propaganda, identification of the revolutionary Fatherland with ancient Mexico became total. Morelos, in his speech to the Congress of Chilpancingo, summoned in 1813 to proclaim the independence of Mexico, invoked the shades of the Indian kings martyred by the Spaniards and called on them to celebrate with song and dance the opening of the assembly, "even as you danced and sang the *mitote* in the fiesta at which you were perfidiously attacked by Alvarado." Morelos joined in mystical union the dates August 12, 1521, the day on which Tenochtitlán fell, and September 8, 1813, the opening day of the Congress of Chilpancingo. "On the former day the chains of our servitude were fastened in México-Tenochtitlán; on the latter, they are broken forever in the fortunate town of Chilpancingo." [14]

Revolutionary spokesmen attempted in every way possible to establish the continuity of Mexican history and nationality from Aztec times to the present. They revived a Náhuatl geographical term of uncertain meaning, Anáhuac, and applied it to the immense territory of New Spain. [15] The fiery Mier, having learned of the outbreak of the Hidalgo revolt, went from Spain to England and published there his *Historia de la revolución de Nueva España, antiguamente Anáhuac* (1813). In this book Mier extended the anti-Spanish polemic that he had begun in 1794 with his sermon linking the appearance of the Virgin of Guadalupe to the missionary activities of Saint Thomas. In 1794 Mier had denied, in effect, that Spain brought the gift of Christianity to Mexico. In his new book, Mier denied Spain any civilizing mission in America. He dismissed the subject of human sacrifice by greatly minimizing its extent, on the authority of Las Casas. He cited Cortés to prove that ancient Mexico had magnificent cities, temples, and palaces, without their like in Europe, an immensely productive agriculture, markets teeming with goods of notable fineness and quality. There were parliaments, councils, courts, academies, libraries, schools. Mier compared the strict justice and integrity of the Aztec courts of Mexico with the corruption allegedly rampant in Spanish courtrooms. Among the Texcocans, he declared, even the historian who lied was put to death. "How many Spanish historians of the Indies would have suffered death had that law been in force!"

Mier threw out a challenge to all civilized Europe. Citing the African slave trade, the miseries inflicted by commercial wars, the evil of dueling, the high rate of suicide, Mier compared the unhappy state of contemporary Europe with the idyllic condition of Aztec Mexico, where, he insisted, warfare was restricted to prescribed fields of battle to avoid injury to populated centers, where war was never allowed to interfere with the peaceful activity of merchants, where challenges were only made to test valor in battle, where suicide was unknown. "Pardon me if I tell you that this very day I find you less civilized in many respects than the ancient Nahuatlaca or Aztecs." [16]

A disciple of Mier's, Carlos María Bustamante, likewise a veteran of the struggle for independence, devoted himself to giving the Mexican people, in his words, some idea of its origin. He edited and published important manuscript works, including Sahagún's *Historia general de las cosas de la Nueva España* and the second part of León y Gama's *Descripción histórica y cronológica de las dos piedras*. His original writings included the *Galería de los príncipes mexicanos* and the curious *Mañanas de la alameda de México*, in which a señorita of singular erudition day after day expounded the principal events of ancient Mexican history to some foreign visitors.[17]

Ideologically Bustamante was in direct line of descent from Boturini, Veytia, and especially Mier, whom he greatly admired, remarking that he was "an extraordinary man, whose like does not occur in a century." Bustamante accepted implicitly Mier's teaching concerning the apostolic activity of Saint Thomas–Quetzalcóatl in America and the establishment of Christianity in Mexico before the coming of the Spaniards. Bustamante also saw in the complex of Aztec rituals and beliefs a corrupt version of the Christian mysteries. He speculated that Indian foes of Christianity had maliciously worked this corruption following the departure of Saint Thomas and his disciples.[18]

In Bustamante, as in Mier, the cult of ancient Mexico developed a strain of fantasy and even absurdity. An example is Bustamante's invocation of the Virgin of Guadalupe, patron saint of Mexican independence, by the name of Tonantzín, Aztec mother of the gods: "O Tonantzín! O blessed and most lovely creature! We prostrate ourselves at your feet and bless you, because your delicate hands, purer than light and more aromatic than balsam and cinnamon, broke our chains forever." Other examples are Bustamante's reference to the ancient Mexicans as "our fathers" (Bustamante was of pure Spanish stock on both sides) and his complaint that the weakness of Moctezuma has "undone us." [19]

For Bustamante, the history of ancient Mexico was a great source of lessons for the present. He wrote a brief history of ancient Tlaxcala to prove the evils of Mexican disunity. Exhortations, warnings, reflections, gushed out of his writings in an endless stream. According to a modern Mexican historian, Bustamante completely lacked historical spirit or objectivity. His grand object was to create a myth that should justify Mexican independence and grant him a "spiritual consistency." [20] Inevitably the effort involved him in inconsistencies arising from the elementary historical facts and from the clash of loyalties within Bustamante himself.

The myth required Bustamante to picture ancient Mexico as a political and cultural unity whose power was usurped by the Conquest and restored by Independence. "Ashes of Ferdinand, Charles, and Philip," exclaimed Bustamante in 1821, "return to life and behold the spectacle presented by that Anáhuac which you chained! Know that three centuries later this precious patrimony has been restored to its sons, for Heaven is just and sooner or later avenges the offenses done to the people." [21]

Five years later, however, Bustamante offered a very different view of the Conquest in a note appended to his edition of the Chimalpahin-Gómara life of Cortés. Conceding that Cortés' record was marred by various cruelties, he nevertheless insisted that Cortés was "the best, the wisest, and most humane of all the conquistadors of America. . . . Humanity lost much through his aggressions, for he almost caused the loss of a world, but how great was the gain for the moral world! Huitzilopochtli is adored no more; men's blood no longer flows on the infamous altars of the Devil; the people no longer march in the ranks of the armies to die in defense of their lords or to be sacrificed to the war gods. What a gain for mankind! Oh Cortés! To you the world owes this happy change! Would that Heaven had allowed you to achieve it by other means than aggression and robbery." [22] The confusion of thought in such passages needs no comment.

Such inconsistencies make Bustamante an easy target for critics.

His work contained other serious flaws. He was credulous, accepting at face value the fantasies of Mier about Saint Thomas–Quetzalcóatl and the Spanish chroniclers' stories of Satan's visits to Moctezuma. His sentimentality, his rhetorical, high-flown style, make parts of his work difficult to read. As an editor, Bustamante was guilty of crimes against scholarship: he freely altered, omitted, and introduced irrelevant glosses that were usually designed to point some contemporary moral.

Still one must view these faults in proper perspective. They derive largely from Bustamante's colonial background, the background of a creole aristocrat from Oaxaca whose home was governed like a religious house by a strict Spanish father, whose education at the hands of priests reinforced the piety and conservatism learned at home, who was only lightly touched by Enlightenment influences. His experiences in the War of Independence, including narrow escapes from death and imprisonment at Spanish hands, helped to give his historical writing its emotional, partisan tinge. To expect this veteran of revolutionary struggles to display the serenity and historical method of a Prescott is to expect too much.[23]

On the other hand, it is only fair to admit that Bustamante's knowledge of Mexico's Indian past and its documentary sources was broad and deep, that his works, along with much irrelevancy, contain varied and useful information, and that he was capable of making realistic and penetrating judgments on conditions in pre-Conquest Mexico. His attachment for the Indians was genuine. "I know the Mexican Indians," he once wrote in a reference to *chinampa* agriculture, "they are natural farmers and gardeners; they study the seasons with the greatest care; they know when it is time to sow and can say with the greatest accuracy when the fruit will be ripe." He was realistic enough to perceive what some liberals did not, that independence had not broken the chains of the Indians. "They still drag the same chain," he wrote, "although they are flattered with the name of freemen." Characteristically, he offered a religious explanation for this fact: the Indians were atoning their crimes of human sacrifice, which "covered with blood, mourning, tears, and abomination this beautiful continent." [24]

Against his editorial aberrations, we must balance his services of bringing to light and publishing such valuable sources of information on ancient Mexico as the second part of León y Gama's study of the Calendar Stone and Sahagún's great history, whose importance he was among the first to recognize. "To make this and other works public," notes Jiménez Moreno, "he made great personal sacrifices." [25]

Bustamante was also the first Mexican public figure to raise a cry of alarm over the flow of Mexican antiquities abroad. Although he took pride in the growing number of foreign visitors to Palenque, Mitla, Xochicalco, and other sites, he complained that foreigners were removing maps, codices, and other documents, some stolen from archives and others acquired from private individuals who could be bilked because they were ignorant of their value. In order to halt these depredations, Bustamante, then deputy from Oaxaca, introduced a bill in the Chamber of Deputies forbidding the export of ancient manuscripts or other antiquities before the government had exercised its option of previous purchase; both houses of Congress approved this measure in 1829.[26] Unfortunately, Bustamante complained, gold was more powerful than laws or love of country, and antiquities continued to leave the country. Bustamante also lamented that a Mexican who wished to study his country's ancient history was regarded as a madman by his countrymen. "The present generation is incapable of appreciating the value of such labors." [27]

The efforts of Bustamante and another scholar profoundly interested in Mexico's past, Isidro R. Gondra, led to the establishment (1822) of a Museo de Antigüedades housed in the university library. To this museum were brought such important monoliths as the Stone of Tizoc.[28] In 1825 a Presidential decree renamed the institution the Museo Nacional. Even before its formal establishment, it was proposed that the museum initiate a publication program, to begin with the publication of Castañeda's illustrations for Dupaix's archaeological reconnaissance. The Mexican Congress assigned responsibility for the project to Bustamante and Lucas Alamán, "who began to work with enthusiasm," but obstacles, presumably financial, prevented its realization. In 1827, however, the museum began publication of a series of lithographs of various objects in its collections. The artist was Jean-Frédéric-Maximilien, baron de Waldeck, who later acquired fame as an illustrator and student of Maya ruins.[29] Three fascicles, containing twelve plates and six pages of text, were published before the series was suspended, presumably for lack of public support.

A flier announcing the series spoke hopefully of satisfying "the universal interest in Mexican antiquities," an interest which had greatly increased since Mexico had assumed its rightful place among the nations of the earth. The commentary on the artifacts and pictures was in the eulogistic vein of the Bustamante school. According to one note, the plates demonstrated the great knowledge and perfection attained by the ancient Mexicans in geometry, architecture, and sculpture, and indicated the magnificence of their buildings, whose design and execution were worthy of comparison with the most admired ruins of Asia and Europe.

Other comments reflected the diffusionism run wild that dominated the archaeological thought of the period. A note by Waldeck on a clay jar reported that the museum possessed pottery that was certainly Etruscan in form, confirming "the judicious idea of a distinguished savant who assigns a Carthaginian origin to the Mexicans." The imaginative Waldeck reported that he had been able to distinguish three epochs in the pottery, very different in form and style. The first stage represented the infancy of the art, the second the progress resulting from the intrusion of a foreign style with Egyptian and Etruscan elements, and the third reflected imitation of the Japanese style.[30]

In 1829 the Museo Nacional proposed to publish the manuscript works of Ixtlilxóchitl and Sahagún. Although the government found the museum's publication program "useful to history and the Mexican nation," it limited its assistance to a subsidy to Bustamante for the publication of Sahagún's *Historia*.

By the 1830's creole ardor for the ancient Mexicans had cooled. The Aztec cult had served its purpose of providing a historical rationale and rhetoric for the generation of Morelos, Mier, and Bustamante. The new generation of Mexican politicians, whether liberal or conservative, viewed pre-Conquest Mexico with attitudes varying from indifference to hostility. Serious writers ceased to invoke the shades of Cuauhtémoc and Moctezuma, leaving such activity to the poets. The new attitude can be studied in the works of three of the major figures in Mexican political life of this period, José María Luis Mora, Lorenzo de Zavala, and Lucas Alamán.

Mora, the most creative thinker in the liberal camp during the three decades following independence, was in no sense hostile to the Indian race as such.[31] He roundly rejected the concept of an inherent Indian inferiority, believing that "with both races and individuals, education can accomplish everything." For Mora, however, the communal traditions inherited by the Indians from their past constituted as much of an obstacle to progress as the system of caste and special privilege established by Spain. Significantly, in discussing the colonial era in his major work, *Méjico y sus revoluciones*, Mora attacked neither Cortés nor the *encomenderos*, but rather Las Casas, Vasco de Quiroga, and other clerical defenders of the Indians. Mora held these men responsible for the disabling tutelage imposed by Spain on the natives. By their insistence on the physical weakness and simplicity of the Indians, by regarding them as minors who must be segregated from the Spaniards for their own protection, these well-meaning friars were in practice "nothing less than enemies of the Indians." [32]

The economic and social liberation of the Indian could only come through education, the growth of his wants, and his entrance into the modern world of industry and trade. Given these premises, Mora saw no reason to idealize the social order of ancient Mexico. He referred to Bustamante's writings on this subject as "insipid and irrelevant fables"; and he regretted that Congress had subsidized his works instead of providing for publication of records of the colonial era, which Mora regarded as far more important for an understanding of Mexican history.[33]

What little space Mora gave to ancient Mexico in his work was clearly intended to dispel the effect of Bustamante's "fables." Returning to the viewpoint of De Pauw and Robertson, Mora rejected the large population estimates assigned to pre-Conquest Mexico by the Spanish chroniclers. A country with an agriculture as backward as that of the Aztecs could not support a large population. For these fantastic estimates of millions of inhabitants and thousands of soldiers, Mora blamed the missionaries' desire to enhance their spiritual conquests and the conquistadors' tendency to magnify their exploits. Mora believed that the Indian population of Mexico was much larger in 1810 than it had been in 1519.[34]

Lorenzo de Zavala, Mora's comrade-in-arms in the reform movement of 1833, concurred in general with Mora's assessment of the Indian past in his *Ensayo histórico de las revoluciones de Mégico*.

Zavala scornfully dismissed the authority of Bustamante, asking, "What should one think of a man who seriously declares in his writings that devils appeared to Moctezuma; that the Indians had warlocks and sorcerers who made pacts with the Devil?" He treated with equal derision Cortés' description of Aztec civilization in his letters to Charles V. Zavala accused Cortés of painting pictures so glowing and poetic that one "might believe himself transported to a new world, a land equal and even superior to the fabled Atlantis. . . . Magnificent palaces covered with gold and silver; kings and emperors richer than the most powerful potentates of Europe." [35]

Zavala drew a picture of Indian material and cultural poverty on the eve of the Conquest. The languages spoken by the Indians, including the Náhuatl, "about which some romantics have written pompous eulogies," were poor and lacked words to express abstract ideas. The speeches placed in the mouths of Xiconténcatl and other Indian heroes by historians and poets were no more authentic than the orations assigned by Homer, Virgil, and Livy to Greek and Roman heroes. "Those Indian chiefs were as barbarous or even more barbarous than the Greek and Roman heroes, and their language could not lend itself to such oratorical beauties, which suppose long centuries of civilization and regular government."

Zavala did make some concessions to the ancient Mexicans. He differed with Mora on the subject of pre-Conquest populations, declaring that Spanish America was more densely populated before the Conquest than at present. He also acknowledged that the Indians had made some intellectual progress under their native governments. "They had confused notions about the immortality of the soul, they had made a small number of extremely imperfect observations of the movement of the stars, and were not wholly ignorant of metallurgy. But all these arts were in their cradle. . . . The Conquest destroyed completely the incipient flight of the spirit of invention among those natives." [36]

Lucas Alamán has been depicted with good reason as a Mexican Metternich, a champion of the conservative landowning aristocracy, the military, and the clergy.[37] Yet his views on the Indian, past and present, did not differ significantly from those of the liberal leaders. Of pure Spanish descent, intensely proud of his Hispanic heritage, Alamán found the true origins of the Mexican nation in the Conquest; like his modern disciple, José Vasconcelos, he regarded Cortés as the creator of Mexican nationality. Yet he was in no sense systematically or consistently anti-Indian. He rejected more categorically than Mora the notion of Indian racial inferiority, and he objected to the title of *gente de razón* the Spaniards assigned to themselves, "as if the Indians lacked reason." [38] He vigorously dissented from the epithet of "barbarians" applied by Prescott to the Aztecs.

Not since Gómara, however, had a writer presented the thesis of Spanish cultural superiority so forcefully as did Alamán in his *Disertaciones sobre la historia de la República Mejicana.* Alamán renewed the ancient debate and enriched it at a number of points. He began with an attack on Aztec religion, citing the description of the bloody Aztecs rites in Sahagún's *Historia general.* "A religion which sanctioned such sacrifices was certainly an insuperable obstacle to all true advance of civilization, for there cannot be a society among people who eat each other."

Alamán asked his readers to consider the way of life to which they would be reduced without the conveniences brought by the Conquest. They would have no beef or pork, chicken or eggs, butter, milk, or oil. They must do without bread, flour, rice, peas, lentils, most of their fruits, sugar, coffee, and tea. Even chocolate, despite its Mexican origin, would be an unpalatable drink without the addition of sugar and cinnamon. Their nights would pass in darkness, for the torch was the only illumination known to the Indians. The houses of Mexico would lack doors, windows, and furniture. They must forego all clothing made of wool, linen, or silk. A multitude of other conveniences, including all articles of leather, iron, and steel, would vanish from their homes. "Amid our privations we would finally grant that the venerable Bishop Zumárraga had good reason to say to Charles V that the Indians, who lacked all these things, were the most miserable beings on earth; and in their lack of all these conveniences we may find a plausible explanation for their horrible practice of eating human flesh."

Alamán sent a strong shaft in the direction of the *indigenistas.* "Those who found the justice of Independence on the injustice of the Conquest, without reflecting on the results of the latter, fail to see that they thus deprive of a *patria* two-thirds of the present inhabitants of the Republic; and that they deprive the Republic itself of its rights to all those immense territories that were not subject to the Aztec Empire and were added to New Spain by Spanish military occupation, those rights being defined and acknowledged by the treaties that the Spanish government made with various powers."

Alamán also censured the *indigenistas* for depriving the Mexican nation of "its noble and glorious origins." His argument paid artful tribute to both Spanish and Indian heroism, and appeared to approve race mixture. Alamán recalled Livy's endorsement of "mythological fictions" to ennoble national origins. The Mexican people, declared Alamán, had no need of such fictions. "Formed by the mixture of the conquerors and the conquered, it owes its being to a nation which was then the first in Europe, a nation whose arms were respected by all other nations, in all the splendor of its literature and arts; and to warlike peoples who defended their liberty with heroism and whose defeat was more the result of their own divisions than of foreign power. Their fall was honorable; nothing about it detracts from our glory." To these noble beginnings, continued Alamán, Mexico owed a history full of interest, a history that was worthy of the attention of the most distinguished writers of Europe and America. Yankee writers had to search in foreign lands for topics with which to occupy their pens; Mexican writers found in their own history ample material for poetry, history, and the study of antiquities.[39]

It would be incorrect to say that the cult of Aztec antiquity disappeared from Mexico in the period under discussion. The very vigor of Alamán's attack upon it and the graceful homage he paid to Aztec valor proves the contrary. The fact remains that no serious Mexican writer of this period endorsed the idealizing Mier-Bustamante interpretation of pre-Conquest Mexico. There was a general decline of interest in the subject.

A lone figure, José Fernando Ramírez, continued to cultivate the field and rendered inestimable service to history with his editorial and bibliographical labors.[40] Ramírez was certainly a defender of the achievements of the ancient Mexicans, but his work was free of the sentimentality and the extravagant claims of Bustamante. Indeed, his strictly secular, sociological approach anticipated the scientific, positivist method of the next generation of

Mexican historians. His only important original writing, his notes to the second Mexican edition of Prescott's *Conquest of Mexico*, can best be considered in connection with that work.

What remained of the cult proper was a vogue of sentimental, bombastic evocation of Aztec glory and Spanish cruelty by public speakers and journalists of the liberal persuasion. "Cortés crossed the waters of the sea," proclaimed one such orator at a commemoration of the Grito de Dolores in Mexico City on September 16, 1851, "and beheld a New World, whose innocent inhabitants peacefully enjoyed in their homes the excellent fruits of their soil. . . . Over the roofs of the simple habitations of our forebears the Indians, the beautiful sun sent its resplendent rays. . . . All was happiness! Parents instructed their children in the precepts of the Natural Law, carefully fed, clothed, and adorned them, as the dearest objects of their affections."

A defender of Spain's work in America responded to this effusion in *El Universal* of September 31, 1851. He wondered what was the "Natural Law" to which the orator referred. Surely he could not have in mind "the most atrocious and sanguinary idolatry in the history of the world." He must therefore have been influenced by the poetic pictures of life on the island of Tahiti drawn by "impious French philosophers" of the last century with the intention of convincing men that in order to be happy they must live by "the law of nature," free from the superstitions of revealed religion.[41] On this level, too, the debate over the nature of Aztec society continued.

Whereas Mexicans neglected the Indian, past and present, Europeans displayed an ever growing interest in Mexican antiquity. Bustamante wrote with a mixture of pride and alarm about a stream of travelers who "devotedly study our history and origins, buy up the scanty remains of our antiquities, sketch our landscapes, and inspect with the greatest care the celebrated ruins of Palenque, Mitla, Xochicalco, and Uxmal."[42] An archaeological mania, a passion for collecting ancient Mexican manuscripts and other relics, appeared among these travelers.

Thus the Italian traveler Giacomo Beltrami, with no evident background of interest in the subject, boasted of having acquired an ancient picture writing drawn by Indian scribes under the direction of Motolinía. "This is the only work of this kind, so far as I know, that has triumphed over time and vandalism; and I have the happiness of possessing it. In it is shown the history of the Mexican monarchy." With romantic passion, Beltrami also defended the Indians against the charges of slothfulness and laziness. He cited the immense industrial, agricultural, and commercial activity of pre-Conquest Mexico, and the perfection of its products, achieved with such limited means. "Are these the products of sloth and indolence? Is it not rather in their spiritual and material debasement by the Spaniards that we must look for the sources of the vices with which they are reproached?" [43]

In this period the German intellect began to concern itself with the place of the Indian in world history. A member of the brilliant Weimar circle over which Goethe presided, Johann Gottfried von Herder, provided a theoretical framework for studying the Indian in his *Outlines of a Philosophy of the History of Man* (1784). Herder's essentially religious view of history accepted the historical process as the unfolding of a divine plan, as a cosmic, teleological evolutionary process that encompassed in its chain of being both inorganic and organic nature. An Enlightenment figure in his stress on environment, his empiricism, and his reforming zeal, Herder rose in romantic revolt against the fatuous complacency and optimism of the Enlightenment, against its frequent assumption of the superiority of the civilized over the savage. A forerunner of historical relativism, Herder insisted on the unique quality and innate validity of each civilization. Its achievements and its errors must not be evaluated by current standards or in the light of historical absolutes. In his belief in the potentiality for growth of every group and in the essential goodness of man, Herder was, as Gerbi notes, the antithesis of De Pauw. [44]

In his chapter on the American Indian in his *Outlines*, Herder described a universal Indian character, unique in its virtues and vices, fashioned by environment and history. "They came over [from Asia] hardy, uncultivated nations, fashioned amid mountains and storms. . . . Their healthy air, the verdure of their fields and woods, and the invigorating waters of their lakes and woods, have infused into them the spirit of liberty and property in this land." Their character consisted in that "firm health and permanent strength, that proud savage love of liberty and war which their mode of life and domestic economy, their education and government, their customs and occupations both in peace and war, equally tend to promote." Other traits common to the Indians were their "goodness of heart, and infantile innocence, a character which their ancient establishment, their habits, their few arts, and above all their conduct toward the Europeans, confirm."

Yet Herder cautioned that "we should speak generally of the nations of a quarter of the globe, which extends through all the different zones, as seldom as possible. Whoever says America is warm, healthy, wet, low, and fertile, says truly, and if another should say the reverse, he would equally speak truth, that is, with different seasons and places. So it is with the American nations, for these are men of a whole hemisphere, and of each of the zones. At one extremity and the other are dwarfs, and close by the dwarfs are giants; in the midst inhabit nations of intermediate and more or less well-formed proportion, gentle and warlike, indolent and active, of all the various ways of life, and of every cast of character."

To Mexico, Herder devoted only a few lines, based on Clavigero, comparing the miserable lot of its natives with their happy condition before the Conquest. "Mexico is now a melancholy picture of what it was under its own kings. Scarcely a tenth part of its inhabitants remain: and how is their character changed by the most unjust of oppressions! I do not believe there exists on the face of the earth a more deep, inveterate hatred, than that the suffering American cherishes against his oppressors, the Spaniards. . . ." True to a venerable tradition, Herder depicted the Peruvian Indians in a still more idyllic light. "All the powers of these tender children of Nature, who once lived so happily under the Incas, are now compressed into the single faculty of suffering and forbearing with silent hatred." [45]

Herder's idealism and passion for humanity were wedded to a rigorously scientific, empirical method in the American studies of the German nobleman Alexander von Humboldt. "Humboldt's romantic sentimentality materially reinforced his idealism," observes Juan A. Ortega y Medina, "but his undeviating scientific empiricism protected him from mere scientific speculation." [46]

Humboldt visited Mexico in 1803 on the last lap of his scientific reconnaissance of the Spanish possessions in America (1799–1804), a reconnaissance which in due time yielded thirty volumes, twenty folio, ten quarto, accompanied by 1,425 illustrations and maps. Two books of this vast set relate particularly to our subject. One is the *Essai politique sur le royaume de la Nouvelle Espagne* (1810), an intensive study of the physical and human geography of Mexico, based on Humboldt's own investigations and on a wealth of statistical data generously furnished to him by colonial officials and Mexican savants. More important for our purposes is the *Vues des cordillères et monuments des peuples indigènes de l'Amérique* (1810), a pictorial atlas with sixty plates and an accompanying volume of text which discussed, often in monographic detail, the subjects of the plates. Mexican codices, monoliths, and other artifacts formed the largest single group of *monuments* with which the book dealt. Humboldt incorporated in the work the results both of his Mexican investigations and of his search for codices in European museums and libraries.

Two sets of guiding ideas influenced Humboldt's interpretation of his data and his assessment of Aztec civilization. One, favorable to the Aztecs, reflected Herder's stress on the uniqueness and worth of every age and culture, his insistence that cultures that belonged to different stages of human progress must not be evaluated in terms of each other, and his rejection of the eighteenth-century rationalist disdain for the works of the savage or barbarian. The other, unfavorable to the Aztecs, reflected Humboldt's laissez-faire liberalism, his hatred of all despotic, theocratic, and feudal governments.

The first set of premises led Humboldt to condemn the scorn that De Pauw and his disciples used in treating Aztec civilization. "A people who regulated its festivals according to the motion of the stars, and who engraved its fasti on a public monument, had no doubt reached a degree of civilization superior to that which has been allowed by De Pauw, Raynal, and even Robertson, the most judicious of the historians of America. These writers consider as barbarous every state of society that did not have the type of civilization which they, according to their systematic ideas, had formed. We cannot admit these abrupt distinctions into barbarous and civilized nations." [47]

Humboldt repeatedly attacked the rationalist historiography for its "absolute skepticism," for its refusal to study Indian civilization in the objective spirit of the natural scientist. Fortunately, continued Humboldt, a revolution had taken place in historical viewpoints since the close of the eighteenth century. The progress of archaeology in several continents had revealed societies "the customs, institutions, and arts of which differ almost as widely from those of the Greeks and Romans as the primitive forms of extinct races of animals differ from those of the species which are the objects of descriptive natural history." In this striking analogy, comparing such civilizations as the Aztec with the fossil remains of ancient animal life, Humboldt revealed his evolutionist point of view. He drove home the point that a society such as the Aztec was no less interesting as an object of study because it differed from the Greek or Roman models. "My own recent investigations on the customs of America appear at an epoch in which we no longer deem unworthy of attention whatever is not conformable to that style, of which the Greeks have left such inimitable models." [48]

The comparative method, Humboldt appeared to say, should not be used to assign of good or bad marks to civilizations, but to establish broad lines of social development and distinguish the local variations caused by environment and history. He repeatedly expressed misgivings about the difficulty of comparing nations, "who have followed different roads in their progress toward social perfection." If comparison must be made, it should be of peoples in about the same stage of social evolution. "The Mexicans and Peruvians must not be judged according to the principles laid down in the history of those nations which are the unceasing objects of our studies. They are as remote from the Greeks and the Romans as they bear a near affinity to the Etruscans and the people of Thibet." [49]

Despite his own warning, Humboldt did in fact compare the Inca and Aztec civilizations with the Greek. The results turned out, on the whole, badly for the former. True to his laissez-faire views, Humboldt criticized the supposedly paternalistic Inca state as harshly as the Aztec despotism. "Among the Peruvians, a theocratic government, while it favoured the growth of industry, the construction of public works, and whatever might be called general civilization, presented obstacles to the display of the faculties of the individual. Among the Greeks, on the contrary, before the time of Pericles, the liberal and rapid progress of individual talents outstripped the tardy steps of general civilization. . . . The Peruvian theocracy was, no doubt, less oppressive than the government of the Mexican kings; yet both contributed to give the monuments, the rites, and the mythology of the two nations that dark and melancholy aspect which forms a striking contrast with the elegant arts and soothing fictions of the people of Greece." [50]

Humboldt, that "bourgeois, evolutionary liberal," as Ortega y Medina calls him, states that on the arrival of the Spaniards the Mexican people was "in that state of abjection that everywhere accompanies feudalism and despotism. The emperor, the princes, the nobility, and clergy (the *teopixqui*) exclusively possessed the most fertile lands; the provincial governors committed the worst exactions with impunity; the farmer was debased, the principal roads swarmed with beggars; the lack of large domestic animals forced thousands of Indians to serve as beasts of burden, and to transport the maize, cotton, skins, and other articles of consumption that the more distant provinces sent as tribute to the capital." [51]

Even the Codex Mendoza, that vivid pictorial demonstration of the complexity and good order that marked Aztec political and social organization, only proved to Humboldt the oppressive and paralyzing effects of Aztec despotism and theocracy. "Fettered by the yoke of arbitrary power, and the barbarism of civil institutions, without freedom of will in the most indifferent actions of domestic life, the whole nation was reared in a languid uniformity of customs and of superstition. The same causes have produced similar effects in ancient Egypt, in India, in China, in Mexico, and in Peru; wherever men were merely masses animated by a sameness of will; wherever laws, religion, and custom have placed barriers to the progress of intellectual improvement and individual happiness." [52]

Despite his caution about cross-cultural comparisons, Humboldt did not hesitate to deny to the sculpture, architecture, and painting of the ancient Mexicans and Peruvians the very name of art. "The works of art," he wrote, "belonging to a people highly advanced in civilization, excite our admiration by the harmony and beauty of their forms, and by the genius with which they are conceived. . . . The monuments of those nations, on the contrary, which have attained no high degree of intellectual cultivation, which either from religious or political causes have never been affected by the beauty of forms, can be considered only as memorials of history."

In this category Humboldt included all the ancient sculpture found from the banks of the Euphrates to the shores of eastern Asia, as well as the "feeble remains of the skill, or rather industry, of the nations of the New Continent." From this category he exempted only one American "monument," the so-called "palace" of Mitla, "a building constructed by the Tzapotecs, anciently inhabiting Oaxaca, and covered with ornaments remarkable for their elegance." [53]

For Humboldt, however, the imperfect works of half-civilized nations had an interest other than the purely historical. Humboldt called this interest "psychological," in that they presented "a picture of the uniform progress of the human mind," revealing so many way stations on the road of that progress. In the scale of intellectual progress, the monuments of ancient Mexico "hold an intermediary place between those of the Scythian tribes and the ancient monuments of Hindustan. What a striking spectacle does human genius present, when we survey the immense disparity that separates the tombs of Tinian and the statues of Easter Island from the monuments of the Mexican temple of Mitla; and compare the shapeless idols of this temple with the masterpieces of the chisels of Praxiteles or Lysippus!" [54]

The precise reasons for what he called "the rude style and incorrect expression of the monuments of the nations of America" caused Humboldt not a little perplexity. He advanced a variety of explanations. One stressed the isolation of the American peoples from the rest of mankind, and the difficult and intractable nature against which they had to struggle. Another called attention to the harmful effect on Mexican artistic taste of their system of writing, which familiarized them with the "aspect of the most hideous figures, and of forms the most remote from correctness of proportion." Once the representational forms of a divinity, a temple, or some other thing became fixed, it was extremely difficult to change them without upsetting the whole system of writing. In summary, "a warlike nation, living on mountains, robust but extremely ill-favoured according to the European principles of beauty, degraded by despotism, accustomed to the ceremonies of a sanguinary worship, is but little disposed to raise itself to the cultivation of the fine arts; the habit of painting instead of writing; the daily view of so many hideous and disproportionate figures, the obligation of preserving the same forms without change, these various circumstances must have contributed to perpetuate a bad taste among the Mexicans. . . ." [55]

Humboldt's statements about the origin of ancient Mexican civilization are sufficiently vague and even contradictory to allow extremely diverse interpretations of his position. Ignacio Bernal says that Humboldt, "generally speaking, has only one point of view: diffusionism," but adds that Humboldt "was too intelligent and possessed too much scientific sense not to see the other side of the problem." Paul Kirchhoff, on the other hand, views Humboldt as engaged in a pioneering comparative study of the antique civilizations of the Old World and the New that looked for similarities and differences without commitment to a diffusionist or antidiffusionist thesis. Miguel León-Portilla describes Humboldt as the "initiator" of the diffusionist concept (upheld today by Robert Heine-Geldern and Gordon Ekholm) that "establishes a very ancient relation of dependence between the high American cultures and those of the Far East," but concedes that Humboldt's cautiously scientific attitude sometimes makes him appear to think in the opposite sense. Finally, Justino Fernández flatly denies that Humboldt subscribed to the theory today called "diffusionist." [56]

By selecting appropriate passages from Humboldt's books, one could easily prove Humboldt a disciple of either the diffusionist or the antidiffusionist school. The nearly absolute hold of diffusionism over the archaeological thought of his time made it inevitable that his writings should reflect its influence. That influence is particularly evident in his somewhat sketchy remarks on the origins of Mexican civilization in the *Essai politique*. If we take into account only the more careful, detailed, and analytical studies of specific resemblances between Old and New World culture traits in the *Vues des cordillères*, it becomes clear that the main thrust of Humboldt's thinking on the subject is not diffusionist, that he believed most of the similarities to which he himself called attention resulted from parallel evolution:

"Notwithstanding these striking analogies existing between the nations of the new Continent and the Tartar tribes who have adopted the religion of Buddha, I think I discover in the mythology of the Americans, in the style of their proceedings, in their languages, and especially in their external conformation, the descendants of a race of men which, early separated from the rest of mankind, has followed for a lengthened series of ages a peculiar road in the unfolding of its intellectual faculties; and in its tendency toward civilization." [57]

Humboldt's characteristic method was to note apparent similarities between Old and New World culture traits and then subject them to close analysis which made the supposed similarities break down. Thus he called attention to certain resemblances between the headdress of Isis and a Mexican goddess, between Egyptian and Mexican pyramids, between the writing and calendrical systems of the two peoples. These things, wrote Humboldt, "exhibit very remarkable points of comparison between the people of the Old and the New Continent." Whereupon Humboldt proceeded to demonstrate that "these analogies for the most part disappear when the facts are examined separately." Having noted some formal resemblances among the pyramids of Egypt, Asia, and America, he promptly destroyed the implied common origin by showing that their purposes were altogether different. Old World pyramids were designed as tombs of illustrious dead, whereas the Mexican *teocallis*, claimed Humboldt, served as both temples and tombs.[58]

Again, speaking of the geometric patterns that covered the walls of Mitla, he remarked that they offered "a striking analogy with those of the vases of lower Italy," but discounted the value of this analogy as proof "of the ancient communication of nations." He advanced instead an explanation that appeared to anticipate the doctrine of "psychic unity" of Adolf Bastian, who explained cultural similarities wherever found by the claim that the human mind was everywhere essentially similar. "Under every zone," wrote Humboldt, "men are pleased with a *rhythmic repetition* of the same forms, a repetition which constitutes the principal character of what we vaguely call Grecques, meanders, and arabesques." Humboldt's use of the concept of "psychic unity" was natural enough, since, as Marvin Harris says, "some form of psychic unity is also implied whenever there is emphasis upon parallel evolution, for if the different peoples of the world advanced through similar sequences, it must be assumed that they all began with essentially similar psychological potentials." [59]

The importance of Humboldt's *Vues des cordillères* can hardly be stressed sufficiently. Not only did it greatly increase European interest in Aztec civilization but it raised study of the subject to a higher scientific level. Of the splendid variety of "monuments" or cultural documentation contained in the book, four-fifths related to Mexico. Most significant of all was Humboldt's methodological contribution: his empirical, rigorously scientific, yet generalizing approach that sought to avoid the two reefs of "brilliant hypotheses founded on frail bases" and the sterile accumulation of data. The very structure of the work, composed of a series of monographs on various subjects (writing, religion, architecture, and the like), each of which took as its point of departure a specific artifact, provided a model for future scholars. Despite his harsh verdicts on Aztec government, society, and religion, the intensity of his research effort indicates the high value Humboldt placed on Aztec cultural achievements.

Paul Kirchhoff writes that Humboldt launched a program for the comparative study of the ancient civilizations of the whole world whose completion remains "a challenge to the historian, the ethnologist, the Orientalist, and all those who dedicate themselves to the investigation of the *disjecta membra* of that great assembly of data and problems that constitute the ancient civilizations of the world." In Bernal's opinion, the great result of Humboldt's stay in Mexico was to diffuse an interest in Mexican archaeology among Europeans. That interest, Bernal correctly notes, was particularly strong in France; here Humboldt's books were first published, with the result that the institutions and individuals most interested in the archaeological exploration of the New World in the first half of the nineteenth century were formed in France. León-Portilla stresses the importance and permanent value of Humboldt's comparative studies of Mexican and Far Eastern calendrical and astrological systems, and points out that Humboldt discovered in advance of many others the profound universal and human meaning of the cultures of ancient Mexico. [60]

CHAPTER ELEVEN

The Aztecs Transfigured: II

"After two centuries of obliviousness and indifference," exulted the French Americanist Brasseur de Bourbourg in 1864, "science in our own time has at last effectively studied and rehabilitated America and the Americans from the viewpoint of history and archaeology. It was Humboldt . . . who woke us from our sleep." In 1885, however, E.-T. Hamy, curator of the Musée d'Ethnographie of Paris, minimized Humboldt's contribution to the rediscovery of ancient Mexico. Hamy acknowledged the scientific value of Humboldt's work but argued that it had not stimulated any significant research, that it had had almost no repercussions. It was the publication of the *Antiquités mexicaines* in 1834 by the Abbé Baradère, declared Hamy, that gave Mexican archaeology its rightful place in the history of man's past.[1]

Jean-Henri Baradère was one of a group of colorful figures of the first half of the nineteenth century—a group including Frédéric Waldeck, Lord Kingsborough, Brasseur de Bourbourg—who were attracted by the romance of ancient Mexico as the flame attracts the moth. Baradère first visited Mexico in 1828 as agent for a company formed to establish a French colony on the Isthmus of Tehuantepec. Going to the Museo Nacional in Mexico City, he drew from the boxes in which they had reposed for twenty years, Dupaix's reports on his archaeological reconnaissance and the accompanying illustrations of Castañeda. Excited by his discovery,

Baradère obtained official permission to carry out archaeological investigations in the Maya area visited by Dupaix, with the understanding that he might retain half of the objects that he should collect.

Perhaps Baradère's success was beyond expectation, for on his return to the capital he had to surrender his finds, accepting in exchange the original illustrations of Castañeda and an authentic copy of the journals of Dupaix. These documents aroused considerable scholarly interest in France. With the aid of a subsidy from the French government, they were issued in a superb edition of two folio volumes by the renowned publishing house of Didot. In addition to the Dupaix-Castañeda collection, the work contained a number of other travel accounts bearing on American archaeology, and two studies, one dealing with Indian origins, the other with parallels between the Mexican monuments and those of the Old World, both written from a diffusionist point of view.

The *Antiquités mexicaines* also presented testimonials to its value from leading figures of the French learned world. A Discours préliminaire by Charles Farcy of the Royal Society of Antiquaries of France proclaimed that the book opened immense new fields to scholarly investigation. Foreign notables also lent their endorsements. A letter from Humboldt attested to the authenticity and accuracy of Castañeda's drawings. Another letter, from President Antonio López de Santa Anna of Mexico, expressed confidence that the book would prove to the world that the ancient Mexicans were not sunk in the abysmal ignorance to which some assigned them. The French literary lion Chateaubriand added his voice to the chorus of praise and proposed that a company of savants depart for Mexico to study the ruins of Mitla and Palenque. He hoped that this expedition would supply answers to the questions inspired by the sight of "those pompous monuments which once dominated the forests and now support forests upon their fallen roofs." [2]

The French archaeological conquest of Mexico had begun. In 1835 the Abbé Baradère, abandoning his priestly duties, vanished from Paris and sailed for America; there he disappeared mysteriously, perhaps in the wilds of Mexico, where he was last seen in 1839. Like that other colorful scholar-adventurer, Frédéric Waldeck, whose *Voyage archaeologique et pittoresque dans la Province de Yucatan* was published in Paris in 1838, Baradère belongs "among the semilegendary figures who, early in the nineteenth century, gave some form and substance to scientific investigation of American antiquity chiefly by calling attention to it and providing some sincere and important results of research. . . ."[3]

The work of J.-M.-A. Aubin has more substantial interest. A physicist, Aubin came to Mexico in 1830, attached to the scientific expedition of François Arago. Deprived by accident of his scientific instruments, he turned his attention to the antiquities of the country. He was surprised by the profusion of archaeological remains; in the collections of the capital alone he found three to four thousand pieces: idols, animal figures, pottery, and busts of divinities. "Some of these pieces," he wrote in retrospect, "comparable in execution to the most perfect examples of European medieval art, completely contradicted the generally held opinion respecting the static state of native art; at the same time a multitude of unpublished documents seemed to demand a total revision of our ideas about Mexican history and geography."[4]

To earn his living, Aubin obtained a position as a tutor in a rich Mexican family; later he opened a French school that was very successful. According to Auguste Génin, many Mexican youths learned from Aubin "the language of Auguste Comte and the antireligious ideas of Comte as well." Aubin's ruling passion, however, was the collection and study of ancient documents; to this pursuit he devoted all his spare time and his growing wealth. His grand object was to restore the scattered collection of Boturini and to add to it the materials collected by Boturini's testamentary legatee Veytia, by the astronomer León y Gama, "the indefatigable explorer of the archives of the royal Audiencia," and by Father José Antonio Pichardo, described by Humboldt as "that learned and industrious man whose collection was the richest in the capital." Aubin found that the trail of many of these documents led to the monasteries of Mexico City, and especially to the Convento de San Francisco. There he found the famous Tonalámatl, the Aztec ritual calendar of 260 days, a treasure of the Boturini collection. The friars, asked by Aubin what they wanted for it, replied that they would take a Spanish edition of Chateaubriand's *Génie du Christianisme*, priced at 8 pesos.[5]

In 1840 Aubin returned to France with his hoard of manuscripts.

According to one writer, Aubin, fearing seizure of his collection by Mexican customs officials, dispersed its contents throughout his baggage to avoid calling attention to it. In Paris he continued to add to his collection through purchase. He wrote in his old age that "sixty years of research and sacrifices of every kind have been consecrated to this difficult task." [6]

Aubin was not a mere dilettante or collector of rarities for the sake of their rarity. He mastered Náhuatl, the language in which many of his documents were written. With its aid he went on to attack the problem of deciphering his Mexican codices. Torquemada and Acosta, followed by Boturini, León y Gama, and Humboldt, among others, had recognized the presence of phonetic elements (rebus writing) in the codices. Aubin, however, left these pioneers far behind by his success in segregating, classifying, and explaining over a hundred of the syllabic glyphs. Too optimistically, as it turned out, his disciple Brasseur de Bourbourg declared that after twenty years of difficult labors Aubin had reconstructed almost the entire system of ancient Mexican writing and gave hope of discovering the key to the characters and inscriptions on the monuments of Palenque, Yucatán, and Central America.[7]

Aubin's studies not only demonstrated the rich expressive resources of Aztec writing but also contributed to a growing appreciation of Aztec civilization. Yet appreciation of Aztec art lagged behind that of other aspects of the culture. Almost simultaneously with the publication of Aubin's most important *Mémoire* on Mexican writing (1849), the Louvre published (1851) the first monograph on Aztec archaeology issued by an European museum, the *Notice des monuments exposés dans la Salle des Antiquités au Musée du Louvre* by Adrien de Longpérier. A deprecatory tone marked Longpérier's discussion of the Mexican objects in the collections of the Louvre.

Taking his cue from Humboldt, he wrote that the organization of Aztec and Inca society "barred the quest for beauty that comes only with progress. Because they could not see Nature in its most noble aspect, they employed all their wits in the effort to create bizarre combinations; and thus, perhaps by chance, acquired a common style with the peoples of the Far East." In an apologetic vein, Longpérier remarked that "the antiquities of America do not possess the same strong interest that the Egyptian monuments owe to their intimate ties with our history; they are not yet classic . . . and have not yet aroused the zeal of numerous collectors." [8] For Longpérier, as for Humboldt, the interest of Aztec art was historical and sociological rather than aesthetic.

A self-proclaimed disciple of Aubin, the Abbé Brasseur de Bourbourg in time surpassed his master in knowledge of the history of ancient Mexico and its sources. At the age of seventeen Brasseur read in the *Journal des Savants* a précis of Antonio del Río's report on the ruins of Palenque. "It is impossible for me to describe the impression of wonder mixed with pleasure that my reading produced in me; it decided my future career of archaeology. A vague presentiment showed me, in the distance, I know not what mysterious veils that a secret instinct incited me to lift. On hearing the name of Champollion, whose fame had begun to penetrate even the colleges of our province, I dreamily asked myself whether the Western continent would not one day figure in the great scientific work then taking place in Europe." [9] At last, in 1848, prepared for his work by an immersion of two years in the rich manuscript and codex resources of the Vatican libraries, Brasseur de Bourbourg visited Mexico. His post of almoner of the French legation in Mexico City left him ample time for study of Mexican antiquity. The erudite director of the Museo Nacional, Isidro Rafael Gondra, befriended him and guided him in his search for rare manuscripts. He learned Náhuatl from a descendant of the Indian nobility, Faustino Chimalpopoca Galicia, professor of law at the Colegio de San Gregorio.

In the course of this and four subsequent visits to Mexico, Brasseur discovered a number of highly important documents which he later published. They included the Codex Chimalpopoca (the Anales de Cuauhtitlán), a basic source for the history of the Aztec area; two precious Maya texts, the Popol Vuh and the work called Anales de los Cakchiqueles; and the indispensable *Relación de las cosas de Yucatán* by the Spanish Bishop Diego de Landa.

Unhappily, Brasseur's writing on American subjects displayed from the first a tendency to unfounded speculation that grew ever more unrestrained. In 1869, convinced that he had found the key to all the Mexican Indian characters, he offered the scholarly world an incoherent translation of a Maya codex, the Manuscrit Troano, which he believed to be a record of ancient geological cataclysms that had torn the Old World away from the New. Six years before his death in 1874 he published his *Quatre Lettres sur le Mexique*. Here he maintained that the Egyptian and other great civilizations of the Old World were established by migrants from America; he also believed that the accounts of historical events, dynasties, and movements of peoples in the Mexican codices were actually an allegorical record of "the history of the geological formation of the Gulf of Mexico and the surrounding lands, a formation which took place as a result of a cataclysm caused by volcanic movements." [10]

Brasseur's tendency to regard all mythological references as clues to actual events and to build towering structures on these frail foundations was already apparent in his masterwork, the *Histoire des nations civilisées du Mexique et de l'Amérique centrale* (1857–1859). In its opening pages Brasseur stated his point of view, which clearly owed much to Boturini and perhaps to Vico. "Since the gods, that is, the divinized heroes, are always the point of departure for a people or tribe, we shall present them as they appear in history, allowing them the roles that the Indians assign them in their traditions; we shall develop the cosmogonic systems of which these personages form part . . . , since these cosmogonies, it is well known, constitute the base for the national institutions of ancient peoples. In general, we shall limit ourselves to reproducing these systems, without other commentary than that which is necessary to elucidate obscure points." [11]

For Brasseur, such figures as Quetzalcóatl had a real existence; they were the hero-priests and legislators from whom Middle America received the elements of civilization. Native traditions transformed these civilizers into gods. At the time of the Conquest, all the civilized nations of Mexico acknowledged the existence of a Supreme Being, but the priesthood had created a number of inferior gods who were no other than the divinized heroes and primitive legislators of Indian America. "In the mysterious obscurity of the Quiché and Mexican texts, we catch a glimpse of the hands of the ancient priests lowering the veil of symbolism over the sacred origins from which they derived their power." [12]

According to Brasseur, in Central Mexico it was Quetzalcóatl who led the Nahua tribes to the shores of Pánuco and established a mighty empire before he mysteriously disappeared. The famous

Huémac, who guided the Toltecs in their migrations, was for Brasseur the "symbol of the religious authority that the chiefs obeyed: he represents the priesthood which seems to have directed the supreme government, and which remained at its head until the moment when it became necessary to separate the religious and secular powers and when the king, impatient of the priestly yoke, sought to subordinate the priests to royalty by making the supreme sacrificer a member of his family."

In agreement with some modern viewpoints, Brasseur declared that the Theocratic period was a peaceful one. "If the city of Tula may be considered the cradle of the civilization of Anáhuac, it certainly owed its predominance to the ruling theocracy. Huémac, symbol of wisdom and prudence, personified this power." Brasseur speculated that the supposed sacred book of the Toltecs, the Teoamoxtli, was merely a symbol of the learning vested in the priesthood.

For Brasseur, as for some modern scholars, the story of the famous Topiltzin-Quetzalcóatl (not to be confused, according to Brasseur, with the first Quetzalcóatl who brought civilization to central Mexico) represented the crisis of the Theocratic order and the transition to a militarist state. Brasseur rejected the view that this Quetzalcóatl was a mere allegorical figure symbolizing certain divine attributes. "The special study that we have made of the American histories and traditions proves the contrary. A contemporary of Charlemagne and Harun al-Rashid, Quetzalcóatl summed up in himself all the splendors of the civilization of his time and place; he was the instrument and most august personification of that civilization, just as the two princes were in Europe and Asia." According to Brasseur, "far from being a personified symbol, he identified in himself preexisting symbols and prepared the apotheosis of his family by personifying in them the ancient myths." [13]

On the fragile foundations of Indian traditions and legends, Brasseur constructed an account of the reign of Quetzalcóatl almost as circumstantial and detailed as if he were writing the life of a contemporary European statesman. According to Brasseur, Quetzalcóatl crowned his glorious reign by abolishing the practice of human sacrifice. "This law made Quetzalcóatl a hero and a martyr." Against the reformer-king rose the priests of the immense and wealthy city of Teotihuacán, where human sacrifice was widely practiced; the revolt spread to Tula itself, where it was led by the noble Tezcatlipoca. True to his peaceful creed, Quetzalcóatl abandoned Tula and departed for Cholula, a town founded by his disciples; then, learning that his enemies planned to attack Cholula, he determined to spare his beloved city the calamities of war and sallied for the coast, whence he sailed away "on a ship ornamented at the poop with two intertwined wooden serpents," presently to reappear as king in Yucatán. His triple rule in the Valley of Mexico, Cholula, and Yucatán, declared Brasseur, "is not the least remarkable thing in the life of this extraordinary personage." [14]

Brasseur told how natural disasters, followed by civil war, brought the collapse of the Toltec Empire. From the north came barbarian invaders who "merged themselves with the remains of the vanquished people and sought to restore on its ancient foundations the structure of the fallen monarchy." Brasseur hailed Texcoco as the most brilliant of the succession-states that rose on the ruins of the Toltec Empire. Brasseur's inflated style made Texcoco appear a veritable Athens of the Mexican plateau. "In the fourteenth century Texcoco was the principal city of Anáhuac; its population, boasting a multitude of illustrious notables who sought refuge in its bosom from the disorders that afflicted neighboring lands, was the most active, industrious, and polished in Mexico. Through the wisdom of its kings, it had peacefully succeeded to all the advantages, all the prerogatives in arts and letters, on which the ancient Toltec cities had once prided themselves." Brasseur declared that complete religious toleration prevailed within Texcoco's borders. Following Ixtlilxóchitl and Veytia, Brasseur stated that the kings of Texcoco adhered to a monotheistic philosophy, although this was not true of the majority of their subjects, who inclined more and more to Toltec idolatry.

The third volume of Brasseur's history, dealing with events from the fourteenth century to the arrival of the Spaniards, is the most satisfactory from a modern point of view. Sources for this period were more numerous, giving Brasseur some means of judging the veracity of the writings of the Texcocan historical school. A tone of healthy realism entered his work. Thus Brasseur rejected Ixtlilxóchitl's claim that Nezahualcóyotl and Nezahualpilli abhorred human sacrifice. "Whatever Ixtlilxóchitl may say, his forebear Nezahualcóyotl raised temples to Huitzilopochtli and offered human sacrifices to the god. The historian's kinship offers some excuse for his partiality." [15]

The third volume presents abundant information on every aspect of Aztec culture with a minimum of embellishment or distortion. Brasseur's concluding remarks were generous in their praise of Aztec institutions. Admitting the horror of human sacrifice and ritual cannibalism, he insisted that Aztec morality, as a whole, was superior to that of ancient Greece and Rome and even to that of many contemporary Asian nations. He compared favorably the mild Aztec treatment of slaves with the condition of slaves in contemporary Cuba and the United States. He conceded that the Aztec laws were severe and rigorous, but believed they were perfectly adapted to the character of the people for whom they were made. Polygamy existed in Aztec society, true, but it was an abuse peculiar to the nobility rather than a law of the society; the sanctity of marriage was as inviolable as among the Christian nations. Brasseur found the condition of women in Aztec Mexico to be admirable.[16]

Uncommonly perceptive and modern was Brasseur's view of Aztec society as a dynamic society in the throes of change on the eve of the Conquest. Just as the rise of the bourgeoisie undermined the foundations of the Ancien Régime and prepared the way for the French Revolution, so the emergence of the merchant class signaled the coming downfall of the Aztec Old Order. A new civilization was "advancing with ever increasing rapidity. To the feudalism of the nobles had succeeded a royal despotism which was in turn being undermined by the Third Estate; a league was being organized to overthrow Moctezuma's empire, just as other leagues had destroyed the various forms of government that preceded that empire; the Renaissance advanced with great strides, and there is every reason to believe that the peoples, weary of the military and religious tyranny of Mexico, would soon have wrested the scepter from its hands and, with the help of a new revolution, would have abolished in large part the abominations of its cult." [17]

The sanity and penetration often displayed by Brasseur in the *Histoire des nations civilisées* are difficult to reconcile with the wild and whirling words of the *Quatre Lettres*. Another distinguished Americanist, the historian Hubert Bancroft, offered this balanced judgment on Brasseur shortly after his death in 1874:

"Brasseur de Bourbourg devoted his life to the study of American primitive history. In actual knowledge pertaining to his chosen subjects, no man ever equalled or approached him. In the last decade of his life, he conceived a new and complicated theory respecting the origin of the American people, or rather the origin of Europeans and Asiatics from America, made known to the world in his *Quatre Lettres*. By reason of the extraordinary nature of the views expressed, and the author's well-known tendency to build magnificent structures on a slight foundation, his later writings were received, for the most part, by critics utterly incompetent to understand them, with a sneer, or what seems to have grieved the writer more, in silence. Now that the great Americanist is dead, while it is not likely that his theories will ever be received, his zeal in the cause of antiquarian science and the many valuable works of his pen will be better appreciated." [18]

The archaeological rediscovery of America caused less stir in England than on the Continent. The conservative English temper, distrustful of enthusiasms, discounted the advances postulated for the ancient Mexicans in the pages of Humboldt and Baradère. A reviewer of Humboldt's *Vues des cordillères* in the influential *Quarterly Review* conceded that the Indians had a calendar and a chronology, but could not "admit with our author that a nation so barbarous as the Mexicans had any knowledge of the causes of eclipses. . . ." Their picture writing, asserted the reviewer, "represented only the first and rudest efforts to record ideas." His scorn recalled the attitude of De Pauw: "We have dwelt but little, and that little will perhaps be thought too much, on those cycles and calendars, those chronologies and cosmogonies, extracted out of the —to us, at least—unintelligible daubings designated under the name of the 'Codices Mexicani.' To M. de Humboldt, however, they would appear to be of first-rate importance." [19]

The influence of Adam Smith, who had concluded that ancient Mexico and Peru were lamentably deficient in the means of production, contributed to a negative English attitude toward Indian civilization. A disciple of Smith, John R. McCulloch, regarded with complacence the subjugation if not the extermination of the Indian, since it "was indispensable to enable the foundation of a better order of things to be laid; and would therefore appear to be consonant to enlarged and just views of benevolence, as well as to expediency." Matters were not significantly better in Mexico and Peru, where, McCulloch conceded, some advances in civilization had been made. Even in those lands the condition of the people "was abject and wretched in the extreme." Crowds of slaves were sacrificed at the funeral ceremonies of important personages; at the great religious and state festivals "there was a wholesale butchery to the extent of thousands." Given these conditions, "it is impossible not to rejoice at the destruction of so sanguinary and atrocious a system." [20]

As one might expect, eulogy of the Indian in English circles was largely restricted to the liberal reformers, and especially to those English Jacobins whose mentality was "a curious compound of rationalistic romanticism and romantic rationalism."

William Godwin, in his essay on population, a refutation of the gloomy prognoses of Malthus, praised "this wonderful people," the Aztecs. Godwin regretted that the poor Mexicans had been "so subdued by the hardhearted avarice of their masters, that they felt no pleasure in recalling what Mexico had been, and the tales perhaps of revolving ages of glory that their infancy had heard. From an industrious and ingenious people, among whom astronomy had deposited her secrets, and the profoundest mysteries of policy and government were familiar, they sunk into a state of imbecility and helpless despondence, upon which the wild and active savage in the woods might look down with a well-founded sense of superiority." [21]

English interest in ancient Mexico grew sufficiently for a canny empresario to organize the first public exhibition of Mexican antiquities in London. He was William Bullock, a former jeweler who in 1812 moved to London and constructed an exhibition gallery in Piccadilly, then called the London Museum and later known as Egyptian Hall. Apparently scenting possibilities in the current Aztec vogue, Bullock visited Mexico in 1823 and spent six months in the country, returning with a considerable number of objects that he placed on exhibition in Egyptian Hall. They included plaster casts of the Calendar Stone, the Stone of Tizoc, and the statue of Coatlicue; models of the pyramids of Teotihuacán; and Mexican picture writings which he had acquired in Mexico on loan. On first seeing the Calendar Stone, Bullock described it in his travel account as "a striking proof of the perfection the

nation to which it belonged had attained in some of the sciences:—
few persons, even in the most enlightened cities of Europe, at the
present day, would be capable of executing such a work. . . ." [22]

The Calendar Stone then rested against the northwest wall of
the cathedral in Mexico City. Through the influence of Lucas
Alamán, Bullock obtained permission to erect a scaffold against the
cathedral and take an impression in plaster. The colossal Coatlicue,
having been exhumed from its burial place under a gallery of the
university for the benefit of Humboldt during his visit to Mexico,
had been buried once more, presumably to protect the unwary and
impressionable Indians against its evil influence. Through the intercession of Andrés del Río, professor of mineralogy, the statue was
dug up again to allow Bullock to make a plaster cast of it.

Londoners who visited the Mexican exhibition of 1824 could
obtain background information on ancient Mexico from a guide-
book prepared by Bullock. The text consisted principally of extracts from the letters of Cortés and Bernal Díaz' history; Bullock's own few comments were superficial. The naïve diffusionism
of his time was reflected in a statement that called attention to
"the close and striking resemblance which exists between the
antiquities of Mexico and Egypt. The mighty pyramid, the hiero-
glyphical writing, the sculptured stone, are almost alike; and their
kindred origin can hardly be doubted." [23]

It is difficult to assess the degree to which the exhibition stimulated interest in its subject. By this time the famous Lord Kingsborough had already fallen under the spell of the Aztec witchery.
Humboldt had expressed a wish for the publication of all known
Mexican codices. Between 1831 and 1846, at a cost of £32,000,
Kingsborough published nine oversize folio volumes containing
facsimile reproductions of all accessible codices by the Italian
draftsman Agostino Aglio. For five years Aglio labored at the
English lord's expense, three of them spent in making facsimile
drawings of codices in Continental collections, notably those of
Vienna, Rome, and Dresden. In addition, Kingsborough's volumes
included excerpts from manuscripts by Ixtlilxóchitl, Sahagún, and
Veytia, among others. "The preparation of his great work, Antiquities of Mexico, required all his attention, all his funds, and
eventually even his life," [24] for Kingsborough died of typhus in

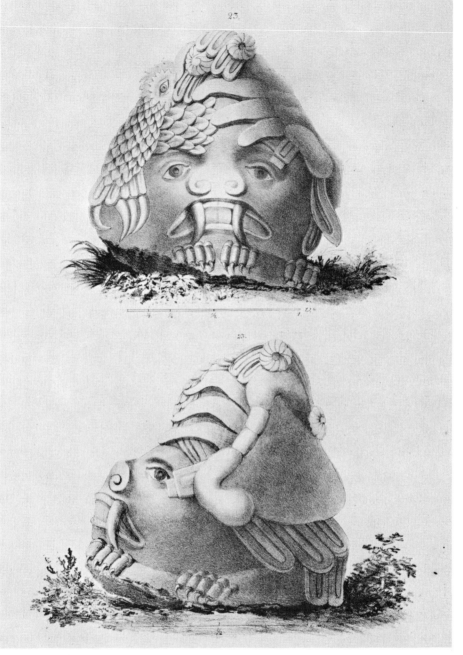

Monstrous head carved in high relief on a boulder discovered in the
vicinity of Quauquechúta [Puebla] during the Dupaix expeditions of 1805–
1808. Lithographed from a sketch by Luciano Castañeda. The head is
endowed with jaguar fangs and claws and garnished with weapons and
military insignia, including bow and arrows, quiver, breastplates, shield,
and eagle. Reproduced in Lord Kingsborough's *Antiquities of Mexico,*
Volume IV (London, 1831). Courtesy Department of Rare Books and
Special Collections, Princeton University Library.

7.

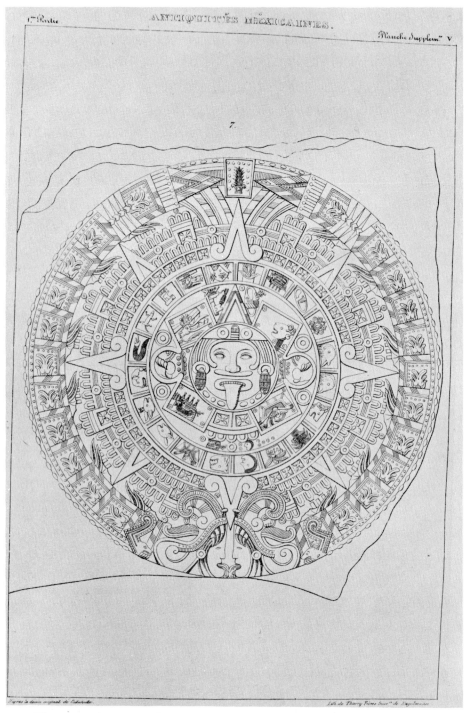

The Calendar Stone found in the Great Temple Square of México-Tenochtitlán. Lithographed from the drawing made by Luciano Castañeda and published by J.-H. Baradère in his *Antiquités mexicaines* (Paris, 1834). Courtesy Marquand Art Library, Princeton University.

the debtor's prison to which he was sent when he could not pay printers, paper manufacturers, and other creditors.

In one sense Kingsborough's place in our story is a marginal one, for Kingsborough's interest in Aztec civilization was secondary to his obsessive desire to prove that Mexico had been colonized by the Jews. "To this," wrote Prescott, "the whole battery of his logic and learning is directed. For this hieroglyphics are unriddled, manuscripts compared, monuments delineated." Prescott noted other serious defects of the work: its lack of order or arrangement, or of any effort to enlighten the reader as to the value or history of the respective documents. Even Kingsborough's "grand hypothesis, for which the work was concocted," was not presented in unified form, "but is huddled into notes, hitched on random passages of the text, with a good deal less connection than the stories of Queen Scheherazade, in the 'Arabian Nights,' and not quite so entertaining." Yet, wrote Prescott, Kingsborough "has brought together a most rich collection of unpublished materials to illustrate the Aztec, and in a wider sense, American antiquities; and . . . by this munificent undertaking, which no government, probably, would have, and few individuals could have, executed, he has entitled himself to the lasting gratitude of every friend of science." [25]

A substantial body of writings about ancient Mexico, both scholarly and fictional, appeared in the United States in the first half of the nineteenth century. This literary movement reached a climax in the 1840's with the contemporaneous publication of John Lloyd Stephens' *Incidents of Travel in Central America, Chiapas, and Yucatan* (1841), which introduced Americans to the splendor of Maya civilization; Prescott's *Conquest of Mexico* (1843); and Albert Gallatin's "Notes on the Semi-Civilized Nations of Mexico, Yucatan, and Central America" (1845).

Three general viewpoints on Aztec civilization can be discerned in this literature. One, distinctly favorable to the Aztecs, reflected both the strong influence of Clavigero, whose work was available in English translation in two editions (1806 and 1817), and that of Humboldt. Another viewpoint, skeptical about Aztec achievements and stressing the darker side of Aztec life, took for its point of departure the notion of an Indian racial type with more or less fixed limits of development. A third viewpoint, which somewhat ambiguously blended these attitudes, presented the Aztec as a mixture of highly civilized man and savage. This last viewpoint is best represented by the unquestioned masterpiece among these works, Prescott's *Conquest of Mexico*.

Thomas F. Gordon's *History of Ancient Mexico* (1832), the first book by an American writer devoted entirely to its subject, has fallen into an undeserved oblivion as a result of the fame and brilliance of Prescott's history. It is a well-written and detailed survey of Aztec history and civilization based in the first place on Clavigero and Humboldt, but it shows a wide and careful reading of all the important Spanish and Indian chroniclers. Rejecting "the spirit of vilification" in the writings of De Pauw and Robertson, Gordon declared that the Mexican nation must not be judged by the abased state to which Spanish policy had reduced it. In the words of Humboldt, "we must go back to the period when, governed by its own laws, it could display its proper energy."

Observing that the ancient Mexicans drew detailed maps, constructed cities, highways, dikes, canals, and immense, accurately designed pyramids, that they had populous cities, a complex feudal system, a large priesthood, a well-organized military, an elaborate system of political and social relations, and a pictorial writing which recorded and preserved their transactions, Gordon asked: "How can we deny them the merit of great intellectual civilization?" Like Clavigero, Gordon insisted that "while they [the ancient Mexicans] exceeded all other pagans in the cruelty of their superstition, their religious rites were distinguished by their peculiar and extraordinary decency." He assigned an equal distinction to the Aztec arts. "The language of their poetry was commonly brilliant and pure, figurative and agreeable; and its subject embellished, by comparisons with the most pleasing objects in nature." Gordon also cited the wall ornaments of the palace of Mitla to prove that "when not confined by superstition or established usage to particular forms, their artists were not destitute of taste." [26]

Some Americans of western pioneering background, who had dealt with North American Indians and to some extent studied their way of life, found it difficult to believe in the magnificent achievements attributed to the ancient Mexicans by Clavigero, Humboldt, and the French archaeological school.

In 1840, Lewis Cass, former governor of Michigan, a national political figure in the age of Jackson, and author of a number of Indian studies, wrote a review of Baradère's *Antiquités mexicaines* that broadened into an attack on the romantic interpretation of ancient Mexico and its sources.[27] The Spanish conquistadors, wrote Cass, were "rough soldiers, pushed forward by a dominant impulse, pursuing the path of conquest, and looking neither to the right hand nor the left." These adventurers credited the Indians with a level of civilization that "later and more cautious inquiries have in vain endeavored to discover."

Cass affirmed that "the general features . . . of that great branch of the human family, established upon the American continent, could not be misunderstood then, any more than they can be misunderstood now; and this race is so unchangeable in its habits, moral and physical, that we can readily recognize those great points of character and condition, which constituted as well its own identity as its circle of separation from the other descendants of our common progenitors."

That character and condition, as described by Cass, had almost no redeeming traits. "Indolent, improvident, revengeful, fierce; capable of bearing but incapable of forbearing; nomads, with some of the harshest features of nomadic tribes; placing their glory in the most barbarous and saguinary wars . . . ; in the very lowest stage of human existence, both with respect to material advantages, and to moral, social, and religious advancement; and, to add to all these evils, fascinated, as it were, within a ring, which they have not the wish to pass over—they seem incapable of appreciating their own condition, and inflexible in resisting the efforts which have been made for their amelioration."

The Spanish conquistadors, ironically commented Cass, seemed to have found two oases in "this great moral desert." Conceding that the Indians of Mexico and Peru had advanced beyond the level of the wandering tribes of North America, Cass charged that "a vein of exaggeration" ran through the accounts of the conquistadors and of the Spanish chroniclers who followed them. Cass objected that not one stone remained of the vaunted palaces and temples described in the chronicles. He was particularly severe with Clavigero, "the panegyrist rather than the historian of Mexico."

The recent discoveries of the ruins of Palenque, Mitla, and other sites left Cass generally unmoved. He had examined bas-reliefs in plaster brought from Palenque and now in the Royal Museum of Paris. "The impression they produced is far more feeble than we had anticipated from drawings and inscriptions. Certainly they are remarkable works when contrasted with the circumstances of their position. But they appear to us far inferior to the specimens of Egyptian architecture, with which Mr. Waldeck has compared them, and still further below the products of European art." Cass also deprecated "the extravagance of praise" accorded to the "palaces" of Mitla, praise that was not "calculated to gain the sober confidence of the reader."

Albert Gallatin's "Notes on the Semi-Civilized Nations of Mexico, Yucatan, and Central America" was an early scientific study of the languages, history, and cultural attainments of the peoples of Middle America. The word "semi-civilized" in the title suggests his point of view. Gallatin's skepticism was more restrained than Cass's almost belligerent incredulity. Behind the skepticism of both Cass and Gallatin lay the same conception of the Indian as a racial type with limited capacity for progress, a conception tinged with the inveterate hostility of the frontiersman for his Indian foe.

Gallatin conceded that the ancient Mexicans had made advances that raised their cultural level above that of "our own Indians," with "their almost unconquerable aversion to daily manual labor." But, like Cass, he found a large element of exaggeration in the writings of the Spanish and Indian chroniclers. Although Gallatin described Prescott's romantic masterpiece, published two years before, as "a permanent monument, equally honorable to himself and to the country," his harsh criticism of some of Prescott's sources implied serious reservations concerning portions of the work. Prescott, for example, had based a chapter on the "Golden Age of Texcoco" almost exclusively on the chronicle of Ixtlilxóchitl.

Gallatin called Ixtlilxóchitl "credulous and ignorant." "His principal object is to make [his] ancestors the sole legitimate emperors of the little world known to them." Yet Gallatin found Ixtlilxóchitl superior to the Spanish chroniclers who utilized him. Although he "may have ascribed to the later kings of Tezcoco much more

elevated and true notions of a Supreme Being than they enter-
tained, he does not insinuate that Christianity or Judaism had ever
penetrated into America, and does not attempt to identify St.
Thomas with Quetzalcoatl." Nor did he "bring the Chichimec,
Acolhua, and Aztecs directly from Asia into Mexico," as did
Boturini.

Gallatin had no patience with Veytia's credulity. He found
Clavigero's work superior in every respect, and commended him
especially for assigning no dates to the Texcocan kings before the
fifteenth century. It was regrettable that Clavigero's partiality for
the Indians made his history rather "the work of an advocate than
that of an impartial judge." [28]

Gallatin's skepticism systematically reduced the level of Aztec
cultural achievement. He disputed León y Gama's claim that the
ancient Mexicans intercalated twelve and a half days at the end
of the fifty-two year cycle. "The conjecture," argued Gallatin,
"rests solely on a single passage of Acosta." The elegant Indian
speeches and prayers in Sahagún's history aroused Gallatin's distrust. "The substance may be true, but several of the orations convey elevated and correct notions of a Supreme Being, which
appear to me altogether inconsistent with that which we know to
have been their practical religion and worship." He surmised that
a speech of an Aztec mother to her daughter contained post-
Conquest elements. "It is such as might have been taught fifty
years after the Conquest to an educated Christian Indian lady, an
imitation of the original form, with such corrections as the conversion from idolatry to Christianity rendered necessary." He even
hinted that the study of Aztec mythology and cosmogony through
the native codices was a waste of time. "Their mythology, as far
as we know it, presents a great number of unconnected gods,
without apparent system or unity of design. It exhibits no evidence
of metaphysical research or imaginative powers. Viewed only as
a development of the intellectual powers of man, it is, in every
respect, vastly inferior to the religious systems of Egypt, India,
Greece, or Scandinavia." [29]

Gallatin suggested that both the early Spanish chroniclers and
the eighteenth-century revisionists had erred, the ones on the side
of credulity and exaggeration, the others through an excessive
skepticism. He indicated that "some sober-minded and cautious

historians, such as Dr. Robertson, may have . . . denied to the
Mexicans the degree of knowledge and civilization which they had
actually attained." Gallatin himself clearly inclined toward the side
of caution. Completely rejecting Spanish statements on Indian pre-
Conquest populations, he expressed the opinion that the population of Middle America in pre-Conquest times must have been
"much less than the aggregate amount, at this time, of the pure
Indians and mixed races." [30]

Gallatin drew a balance sheet of the results of the conquest of
Mexico that was highly favorable to Spain. The Conquest had
ended the perpetual and destructive Indian intertribal wars; these
wars of extermination were succeeded by three hundred years of
internal peace. Agriculture became far more productive through
the introduction of iron tools, European grains, and above all of
domestic animals, making possible the substitution of animal for
human labor. Gallatin estimated that these improvements doubled
or tripled agricultural productivity. Conceding that the Conquest
and its sequel of Indian oppression formed "a sorrowful tale," he
paid generous tribute to the efforts of the Spanish clergy in behalf
of the natives. "The praise must be extended to all the Catholic
priests, whether Franciscans or Jesuits, monks or curates. All, from
the beginning, were, have ever been, and continue to be, the pro-
tectors and the friends of the Indian race."

This sweeping statement shows how selective Gallatin's skepticism could be. His pro-Spanish enthusiasm even led him to extoll
that bogyman of Protestant historians, Philip II. "It is due to the
Spanish government at home, and even to Philip the Second, to
acknowledge that the gross acts of injustice which had been committed in the years immediately following the conquest were in
many instances repaired as far as practicable; that freedom was
restored to the Indians; and that, though still an inferior class,
their situation was greatly ameliorated, and far preferable, during
the last two centuries of the Spanish dominion, to that in which
they were found by the Europeans." [31]

Pro-Indian and anti-Indian attitudes blend in Prescott's *Conquest
of Mexico*. Romantic artistic criteria required Prescott to assign a
suitable dignity to his Aztec protagonists and to portray in rich
colors the splendor and might of the Aztec Empire. On the other
hand, Prescott's romantic belief in progress and providence made

him design his work, in the words of David Levin, "to support a fundamental simple theme: the inevitable ruin of a rich but barbarous empire through its inherent moral faults; the triumph of 'civilization' over 'semi-civilization,' of Christianity (however imperfectly represented) over cannibalism; the triumph of Cortés' 'genius,' 'constancy,' and resourceful leadership over Montezuma's 'pusillanimity' and 'vacillation,' and then over Guatemozin's nobly savage but unscientific devotion to a doomed cause." [32] The conviction, which Prescott shared with Cass and Gallatin, that the Indian represented a racial type with a limited capacity for progress reinforced the basic anti-Indian feeling of the work.

Prescott told his story with the aid of an awesome quantity of sources. His Spanish correspondent and literary lieutenant abroad, Pascual de Gayangos, copied and sent him masses of manuscript material. Prescott also benefited by the timely appearance of the documentary collections of Kingsborough, Baradère, and Henri Ternaux-Compans,[33] supplementing Humboldt's work. Virtually no known manuscript or printed source on ancient Mexico escaped Prescott's search. At the ends of chapters he frequently inserted notes evaluating his most important sources; these notes, sometimes amounting to genuine essays, are almost invariably intelligent, perspicuous, and just.

Prescott gave a general view and assessment of Aztec civilization in the six chapters of the first Book of the *History*. Because of his distrust of the "extraordinary legends" told by Ixtlilxóchitl and Veytia concerning the Toltec and Chichimec periods, Prescott passed rapidly over the history of those early peoples. He contented himself with establishing that it was the Toltecs who laid the foundations of the civilization that met the eyes of the Spaniards on their arrival in the New World. The mysterious disappearance of the Toltecs was followed by the arrival of the rude Chichimecs, who were in turn succeeded by other groups, among whom Prescott singled out the Aculhuans and the Mexicans or Aztecs. The former were peculiarly fitted "by their comparatively mild civilization and manners" to receive the vestiges of civilization preserved among the surviving Toltecs; their flourishing capital of Texcoco "was filled with a numerous population, busily employed in many of the more useful and even elegant arts of a civilized community."

One notes, in passing, that despite Prescott's belief in progress, he appears to have no interest in an evolutionary or genetic approach to history; it never occurs to him to ask how these peoples made the difficult transition from nomadic or simple village society to urban life.

Prescott swiftly told of the struggles for supremacy among the states of the Valley of Mexico and the eventual rise of the Aztecs and the Triple Alliance, the instrument for the spread of Aztec power from the Atlantic to the Pacific.

Turning to describe the political, legal, and military institutions of the Aztecs, Prescott adopted without question the European terminology of king and emperor applied to the Aztec ruler by the Spanish chroniclers. He also accepted unquestioningly the existence of the "spacious palaces" of the monarchs, their numerous bodyguard, and a class of powerful nobles who held large estates by various systems of tenure. He doubted, however, that the Aztecs possessed a feudal system in the European sense. He had high praise for Aztec legal institutions, declaring that "the provision for making the superior judges wholly independent of the crown was worthy of an enlightened people." In the tradition of Clavigero, he wrote that the Aztec code "evinces a proper respect for the great principles of morality, and as clear a perception of these principles as is to be found in the most cultivated nations." [34]

Noting the immense importance of war and the military profession in Aztec life, Prescott observed that their great object was to gather human victims for the altars of the gods. He heightened the impression of a medieval society by asserting that the Aztecs had military orders and "a sort of knighthood, of inferior degree." He closed his discussion of "the civil and military polity of the Aztecs" by asserting that "the Aztec and Tezcucan races were advanced in civilization very far beyond the wandering tribes of North America."

In one of his few efforts to compare concretely the stage of development attained by the Aztecs with that of other societies, Prescott suggested that the level of political development achieved by the Aztecs was "perhaps not much short of that enjoyed by our Saxon ancestors, under Alfred"; but their social and intellectual state offered stronger comparison with Egyptian civilization. Asking himself how the ancestors of the listless and indolent Mexicans of his own day could have designed such an "enlightened polity," Prescott gave the answer of Clavigero. The modern Mexicans were a conquered race, as different as were the modern Egyptians and Greeks from their industrious and creative forebears.[35]

The civil and religious policies of the Aztecs were so closely blended, said Prescott, that the latter could not be understood without understanding the former. The Aztec religious system impressed him with its incongruity, "as if some portion of it emanated from a comparatively refined people, open to gentle influences, while the rest breathes a spirit of unmitigated ferocity." This fact made Prescott believe that the Aztecs had inherited from their predecessors—presumably the Toltecs—a milder faith on which they had grafted their own dark mythology. Prescott was gratified to find that the Aztecs possessed a Supreme Creator God, "invisible, incorporeal, one God, of perfect perfection and purity. . . ." Unhappily, the "idea of unity" was too simple or too vast for the Aztec understanding, and they sought relief in a multitude of deities who presided over natural phenomena and even the occupations of men.

After surveying the Aztec notion of the afterlife, their ceremonial, the role of the priesthood, Prescott ended the chapter on religion with a detailed discussion of Aztec human sacrifice, "their most striking institution and one that had the greatest influence in forming the national character." Prescott pondered the anomaly presented by the coexistence of this "revolting" institution with the many features of a civilized community that had characterized Mexican society. For a better understanding of the anomaly, Prescott asked his readers to reflect on the operations of the modern Inquisition in some of "the most polished countries in Europe." Some mitigating elements were discernible in Aztec human sacrifice, for it ennobled the victim and assured him of dwelling with the gods, whereas the Inquisition "branded its victims with infamy in this world, and consigned them to everlasting perdition in the next." [36]

Having rebuked Spanish fanaticism, Prescott discussed Aztec ritual cannibalism, declaring that it placed Aztec superstition far below the Christian. The Aztecs were not cannibals "in the coarsest sense of the term," since they ate human flesh not to satisfy appetite but from religious motives. Still, cannibalism must have "a fatal influence on the nation addicted to it. It suggests ideas so loathsome, so degrading to man, to his spiritual and moral nature, that it is impossible the people who practice it should make any great progress in moral or intellectual culture. The Mexicans furnish no exception to this remark." Casting aside his customary caution, Prescott insisted that the Toltecs "never stained their altars, still less their banquets, with the blood of man."

From this wonderful people the Aztecs had acquired all they had of science and art. All the Aztec advances were in "the social and mechanic arts, in that material culture—if I may so call it— the natural growth of increasing opulence, which ministers to the gratification of the senses." Indeed, in intellectual progress they were behind the Texcocans, "whose wise sovereigns came into the abominable rites of their neighbors with reluctance, and practiced them on a more moderate scale." By restricting Aztec progress to the material, sensual side of life, Prescott, in the words of David Levin, "fixed the inescapable limits of Aztec civilization"; by his stress on the debasing institutions of the Aztecs, Prescott furnished, in his own words, "the best apology for their conquest." [37]

From Aztec religion Prescott turned with relief to consider Aztec science: its hieroglyphics, mathematics, chronology, and astronomy. His discussion in general followed Clavigero and Humboldt. With admirable common sense, Prescott concluded that in the main the Indian achievements were made independently, "apart from those influences that operate in the Old World." Like the Egyptian writing, the Mexican was composed of three types of hieroglyphs—figurative, symbolic, and phonetic—but in the execution of the figures the Mexicans were much inferior to the Egyptians. Prescott agreed with Humboldt, however, that the Aztec writing seemed to be adequate to the needs of the nation, in its "imperfect state of civilization." Prescott mourned the alleged destruction of Mexican codices, "so many curious instruments of human ingenuity and learning," at the hands of Archbishop Zumárraga. Mexican attainments in literary culture, however, were surpassed by their mathematical and calendrical attainments. "We cannot contemplate the astronomical science of the Mexicans, so disproportionate to their progress in other walks of civilization, without astonishment." [38]

Prescott had the same high praise for the technical achievements of Aztec agriculture and industry. He observed with satisfaction the respect accorded to the various crafts and trades, and in particular the honors and distinctions allowed to the merchant. Was it not another of the Aztec anomalies that "trade should prove the path to eminent political preferment in a nation but partially civilized, where the names of soldier and priest are usually the only titles to respect?" The republican Prescott compared these attitudes favorably with the prejudices displayed in "some of the more polished monarchies of Europe," where useful labor caused more dishonor than a life of "idle ease or frivolous pleasure."

The same favorable tone marked Prescott's discussion of the Aztecs' domestic life and their educational system. Prescott again reflected on the incongruity between the "brutish usages" of the Aztecs and "the degree of refinement they showed in other things." This paradox, he concluded, could only be explained "as a result of religious superstition; superstition which clouds the moral perception, and perverts even the natural senses, till man, civilized man, is reconciled to the very things which are most revolting to humanity." [39]

Prescott devoted the last chapter of his introductory section to the "golden age of Tezcuco," a theme rich in romantic material and coloring, and one that provided in the "enlarged mind and endowments" of Nezahualcóyotl and his son Nezahualpilli an excellent foil to Aztec barbarism. Prescott let himself be guided through these two reigns by Ixtlilxóchitl, "uniformly commended for his fairness and integrity." Dropping the tone of ironic skepticism that he sometimes displayed toward the more fanciful statements of the early chroniclers, Prescott told the story as he found it, only warning his readers at the outset that he would not attempt to weigh the probability of the details, "which I will leave to be settled by the reader according to the measure of his faith."

Closely following Ixtlilxóchitl, Prescott presented Nezahualcóyotl's adventures with all the trappings of a romance of chivalry. At this point the narrative takes on the atmosphere of a historical novel by Sir Walter Scott, including its "medieval" dialogue. Thus Nezahualcóyotl, a hunted fugitive from the Tepanec usurper Maxtla, speaks as follows: " 'Would you not deliver up the prince, if he came in your way?' he inquired of a young peasant who was unacquainted with his person. 'Not I,' replied the other. 'What, not for a fair lady's hand, and a rich dowry beside?' rejoined the prince. At which the other only shook his head and laughed." [40]

Clouds of romance thickened about the king of Texcoco as Prescott described his patronage of the arts and sciences, the magnificence of his palaces, his exact justice, his liberality, and his poetic powers. For proof of the latter, Prescott cited the bogus "Otomí" poem first published by Granados. Naturally, a man of "the enlarged mind and endowments of Nezahualcóyotl" could not approve of the bloody sacrifices of the Aztecs and endeavored "to recall his people to the more pure and simple worship of the ancient Toltecs." Indeed, after some vacillation Nezahualcóyotl concluded that his idols of wood and stone were powerless and that all was the work of the all-powerful unknown God, Creator of the Universe. Prescott wrote in the same eulogistic vein of the king's son and successor Nezahualpilli. Unhappily, the Texcocans "were fast falling under the domination of the warlike Aztecs." [41]

It is unnecessary at this point to trace the story of the Conquest as told by Prescott. In his admirable book Professor Levin has shown how artfully Prescott organized that story as a study in dramatic contrasts: the major contrast is between Cortés, instrument of Providence and progress, wise, courageous, and resolute, and his antagonist Moctezuma, corrupted by power, luxury, and superstition, and doomed by his weakness and irresolution. Levin notes that a large majority of Prescott's pictures of Moctezuma "show him standing motionless or moving reluctantly toward some melancholy destination." "The characteristic image of Cortés, on the other hand, depicts him in energetic motion." Subordinate contrasts exist within each camp: Cuauhtémoc, model of savage virtue, faces Moctezuma; the scheming Governor Velásquez of Cuba and the corrupt Fonseca, Bishop of Burgos, oppose Cortés.

Levin also shows how consistently Prescott stacks the cards against the Indians, particularly in battle scenes in which Indian brute force is pitted against European science. "The rhetorical odds," remarks Levin, "are against the savage because of his superiority in numbers, his methods of fighting, his obedience to passion rather than discipline. Even when they fight courageously, a 'mob of barbarians' have little chance for praise in the account of a battle with 'the Christians.' For if they do not stand 'petrified with dismay,' they sound 'their hideous war-shriek' and rush 'impetuously' on the Christians. The eloquence, the resolution, the discipline, and the coolness of the European rarely fail in these conflicts with savage 'passion.' " For the Indian it only remains to make a good death, "for he has a natural aptitude for dying well." Even the cowardly Moctezuma recovers his spirit in time to make a good end. In defeat the Indian becomes eligible "for the sentimental treatment always accorded to vanishing races." [42]

Prescott's *Conquest of Mexico* scored an even greater triumph than his earlier *Ferdinand and Isabella*. He won election to the French Institute and the Royal Society of Berlin; congratulations poured in from such notables as Humboldt; and in the space of a month Prescott received one hundred and thirty favorable newspaper reviews.

Not all the verdicts were favorable, however. Among the most thoughtful and knowledgeable of the dissenting reviews was a trenchant essay by the radical transcendentalist Theodore Parker, published in the *Massachusetts Quarterly Review* for September, 1849. Parker severely criticized Prescott for his tendency to palliate Spanish misdeeds and to accept at face value the motives assigned to themselves by the Spaniards. Parker dismissed the argument that justified the Conquest by reference to the supposedly retrogressive, stationary character of Aztec society, a society incapable of further progress. "The Mexicans were a civilized people; the lands in the Valley of Mexico were as well cultivated as the lands in Granada, the garden of Europe; the natives had not stopped in their progress, as Mr. Prescott thinks the Moors had done in Spain, and their land therefore could not be claimed as a derelict of civilizations; on the contrary, they seem to have been in a state of rapid advance, as much so as the Spanish nation itself. The superior culture of the Spaniard gave him no right to those lands without indemnifying the individual owners—no more than the English have to China, or the Dutch to Turkey. . . ."

Prescott, commented Parker, often referred to Providence events that other men would assign to human agency. If Providence decreed that Mexico should be delivered over to another race, "in the same manner 'it was beneficently ordered by Providence' that merchant ships should be delivered over to Admiral Drake or Captain Kidd; that the Indians of Massachusetts should butcher the white men at Deerfield, and the whites should carry the head of King Philip on a pole into Plymouth and sell his family into slavery." [43]

A learned Mexican, José Fernando Ramírez, applied his vast knowledge of the sources for ancient Mexican civilization in his notes to the second Mexican edition (1845) of the *Conquest of Mexico*. Ramírez was generous in his praise of Prescott's book, but he complained of the author's "instinctive race prejudice" and his efforts to excuse or palliate Cortés' crimes. The prejudice, remarked Ramírez, so pervaded Prescott's history that only the most unskilled eye could miss it. Anticipating Levin's comments, Ramírez noted that Prescott alternately described the Indians as "barbarians" and "savages." These "barbarians" do not utter war cries like a civilized army, but emit "hideous war-shrieks"; they do not retreat, but precipitately "flee."

Ramírez also criticized Prescott's idealized picture of Toltec and Texcocan civilization. He drew on Prescott's own principal source, Ixtlilxóchitl, to prove that the Toltecs practiced human sacrifice; he cited other sources to show that Nezahualcóyotl and Nezahualpilli had done the same on an immense scale. Ramírez offered a sociological, developmental view of human sacrifice. He argued that human sacrifice, evolving out of the simple offerings of fruits and animals of the primitive Chichimec Indians, first appeared among the Toltecs and actually reached its peak in the "golden age of Texcoco." He also criticized Prescott's presentation of Aztec cannibalism. In an obvious effort to heighten the dramatic effectiveness of his description, Prescott had depicted this ritual as "a banquet teeming with delicious beverages and delicate viands, prepared with art and attended by both sexes, who, as we shall see hereafter, conducted themselves with all the decorum of civilized life." Citing the authoritative Sahagún, Ramírez easily demonstrated that the culinary refinements described by Prescott were imaginary, and that the preparation of the sacramental food was simplicity itself.[44]

The conservative, pro-Spanish Lucas Alamán displayed an equal sensitivity to Prescott's slights to the Aztecs. He disputed the epithet of "barbarians" used by Prescott, arguing that this name could not be fairly attached to a people who had not only a well-organized, complex governmental system of the kind described by

Prescott but also established laws, courts, and a technology capable of supplying not only necessities but luxuries. Only the religion of the Aztecs deserved to be called "barbarian." [45]

For the modern critic, the major weakness of Prescott's account of Aztec civilization is not the excusable factual error but its gross historical and psychological distortions, the absence of any serious effort to enter into the Aztec mind and society, the shallowness of its interpretation. This weakness is closely connected with the general mediocrity and conventionality of Prescott's thought, and more particularly with the romantic literary and philosophic conventions that determine the roles he assigned to Spaniards and Indians in the story of the Conquest. By substituting surface drama and color for serious analysis, by dissolving the complexity of the psychological makeup and motives of both sets of characters, these conventions inevitably introduced falseness and distortion into the picture. An obvious illustration is Prescott's easy acceptance, despite his own rules of historical criticism, of the highly colored tales of Ixtlilxóchitl about the elevated views and conduct of Nezahualcóyotl. The same conventions in effect barred Prescott from viewing Aztec human sacrifice and ritual cannibalism in the objective, sociological manner of Ramírez, and in general discouraged him from asking serious questions about Aztec society.

Even Prescott's style, graceful, stately, and clear as it frequently was, is not beyond reproach. Levin complains of a central weakness, "a surprising insensitivity to precise meaning," reflected in triteness of images and descriptive phrases; Parker had already made the same complaint, calling Prescott's figures of speech "commonplace."

Whatever its limitations of interpretation, method, and style, Prescott's survey of Aztec society illustrates his industry, his customary care and accuracy, and his mastery of romantic art. It has survived attacks from every quarter, and still dominates the conceptions of the layman, if not the specialist, concerning Aztec civilization.[46]

Prescott's *Conquest of Mexico* shows the thin dividing line between history and belles-lettres in the romantic era. The age produced a large number of poems, novels, paintings, and operas that dealt directly or indirectly with Aztec themes. Unfortunately, with some honorable exceptions, these creations had little to do with authentic romanticism; sentimentality and a superficial exoticism, devoid of passion or inspiration, were their salient characteristics. In Mexico there was a flowering of pseudo-Aztec poetry, most of which displayed these flaws.[47]

The best specimen of the genre is the volume of poems *Los Azteca* (1854), by José Joaquín Pesado. The work purported to contain translations of ancient Mexican poems, including some by King Nezahualcóyotl. In fact, Pesado knew no Indian languages and apparently utilized only the "Otomí" poem in Granados and some literal translations of Aztec texts made for him by Faustino Chimalpopoca. Chimalpopoca, however, protested that Pesado's verses had nothing in common with the texts he had given the poet. Pesado's Aztecs, writes one critic, are not Indians but "graceful Christian gentlemen and ladies of the nineteenth century, much disposed to give sound advice." [48] Pesado had a multitude of imitators, most of whom lacked entirely his talent for versification and good taste.

A more authentic romanticism appears in the Aztec poems of the highly gifted Cuban revolutionary poet José María Heredia, whose short life was closely linked to Mexico. Heredia first came to Mexico in 1819 with his father, an official of the Audiencia of Mexico City who died the following year. Returning to Cuba, Heredia joined the revolutionary underground, with the result that he was sentenced to perpetual exile in 1823. He departed for the United States, where he wrote his masterpiece "Niágara" (1823) and published his first collection of poetry (1825). Acting on an invitation by President Guadalupe Victoria, he returned to Mexico. There, active in politics and literature, he lived until his death in 1839.

Heredia's verses on Aztec themes illustrate the typical dualism of the romantic attitude toward Aztec civilization. Heredia was an incredible seventeen when he wrote "En el teocalli de Cholula" (1820), called by Marcelino Menéndez y Pelayo the best poem ever written by a Spanish American in the Spanish language. The poet, seated atop the immense pyramid-mound of Cholula, falls into slumber; in a dream he beholds a vast procession winding its way to the temple. He sees "amid the silent multitude of plumed leaders, the savage despot on his rich throne, adorned with feathers,

pearls, and gold." The procession advances to the sound of shell
trumpets to the place where wait "horrible priests, their faces and
clothes spattered with human blood." With a "profound stupor"
the enslaved people lower their faces to the dust, not daring to
look up to their lord, from whose "glittering eyes shine forth the
madness of power." The poet continues:

> Such were your monarchs, Anáhuac, such their pride;
> Their vile superstition and tyranny
> Into the abyss of nothingness have sunk.
> Yes, Death, that universal Lord,
> Impartially wounding the despot and the slave,
> Inscribes equality upon the tomb. . . .

Upon this immense pile, wrote the poet, "a most inhuman superstition once sat enthroned."

> It saw the thick vapor of the blood rise hot to the offended sky
>   and cast a funereal pall upon the sun;
> It heard the horrid cries with which the priests suppressed the
>   cries of pain.[49]

Here the Aztecs typified Oriental despotism, tyranny, and superstition, all detestable to the romantic liberal. Only two years later,
however, Heredia used the Aztecs to attack another tyranny—that
of Iturbide, the ambitious creole army officer who had installed
himself as emperor of Mexico. In an "Ode to the Inhabitants of
Anáhuac," Heredia invoked the shades of the "great Cuauhtémoc,"
Moctezuma, and the "magnanimous" Ahuítzotl, a ruler better
known to history for the brutality of his conquests. In Heredia's
poem these shades rise from their dusty tombs and fly about the
tyrant, hurling angry menaces that fill him with terror.[50]

The spirits of the Aztec kings again responded to Heredia's call
in "Las Sombras" (1825), a poem written in a time of growing
Mexican anger over the continued Spanish hold on the fort guarding the port of Veracruz. The poet, standing at night on the hill
of Chapultepec, first raises the shade of Moctezuma, who then
summons the shades of his successors Cuitláhuac and Cuauhtémoc;
presently they are joined upon the royal hill by the specters of
Atahualpa and other Indian monarchs, each of whom tells his story

of Spanish cruelty and perfidy. At dawn the shades scatter, while the hill resounds with their pitiful moans.[51]

The mighty Aztec dead could complain that Mexican romantic poets gave them no time for rest. The "Profecía de Guatimoc" (1839) of Ignacio Rodríguez Galván reflected the malaise that haunted the poet's short, tormented life and the wounds to his patriotism inflicted by foreign slights and threats to his country. The opening of the poem finds Galván by night on the wooded hill of Chapultepec, pleasure resort of the Aztec kings. The poet turns from bitter musings on his own woes to reflect on the sorrows of his country, humiliated by European powers and Texan rebels. He hopes to be heard by "the venerable shades of the kings who ruled Anáhuac, today the prize of birds of prey and wolves that tear at its bosom and heart." He invokes Cuauhtémoc. The warrior prince appears; he is richly dressed, adorned with gold and rich jewels, and wears a headdress of waving plumage. He holds a powerful club; a bow and quiver hang from his shoulders. The fire still plays beneath his feet, whose soles are burned to coals and covered with blood; shackles, fetters, and heavy chains are wound about his body; a halter is about his neck. The poet recognizes the work of Cortés.

Cuauhtémoc demands that the poet speak to him, "but in the language of the great Netzahualcóyotl!" When Galván replies, "I do not know it," the king exclaims: "Oh disgrace! Oh shame!" The poet calls upon Cuauhtémoc to return, to grasp again his powerful lance and make decrepit kings tremble at his voice. Cuauhtémoc replies: "My age is past: my people will never again raise their dark faces, pressed into filthy mud." He prophesies disaster for Mexico from implacable "English America" and Europe, the "sons of the East." Mexico's day of vengeance will come, not through the hand of man, but through divine intervention. In lines of Biblical grandeur Cuauhtémoc foretells the downfall of Paris and London. As the first morning light crosses the sky, amid tremblings of the earth and other awesome phenomena, the shade of Cuauhtémoc, transformed into a colossal phantasm, disappears.[52] The magnificent coloring of the poem, its authentic romantic agony, the restless alternation in the poet's mind between thoughts of his personal sorrow and the woes of his people, make it, in the words of Menéndez y Pelayo, "the masterpiece of Mexican romanticism."

The German poet Heinrich Heine treated the Aztec theme with startling novelty in the poem "Vitzliputzli" (Huitzilopochtli), composed between 1846 and 1852. The ballad begins with the departure of Cortés' expedition from Cuba and ends with the aftermath of the Noche Triste when Cortés broke out of Tenochtitlán with heavy loss of life. Heine left no doubt of his contempt for Cortés and the Spaniards, whose predatory cunning he contrasted with the generous Aztec hospitality and innocence.

> Bear me west to yonder castle
> That was hospitably given
> By the gracious Montezuma
> To his Spanish guests as lodging.
>
> And not food and shelter only
> Were with readiness accorded
> To these vagabonds and strollers;
> Presents rich and rare were added;
>
> Gifts of massive gold, and jewels,
> Fashioned cunningly, and gleaming,
> Witnessed also to the favor
> And the kindness of the monarch.
>
> This uncivilized, unlearned,
> Blind and superstitious heathen
> Still believed in faith, and fancied
> Hospitality was sacred.

The Spaniards kidnap the trusting Aztec monarch and make him a hostage for their safety. But fighting breaks out, and the Spaniards, besieged in their quarters,

> Thought with yearning of their country
> Where the pious bells were ringing,
> And in peace the Spanish hotch-potch
> On the cosy hearth was bubbling
>
> Thickly studded with garbanzos,
> With the sausages beloved,
> Little sausages of garlic
> Spluttering slyly underneath them.

The Spaniards fight their way out of the city and the survivors
rest on the shores of the lake. Meanwhile, in the Aztec capital:

> After battle's day of terror
> Comes the ghostly night of triumph;
> And in Mexico, exultant,
> Flare a hundred thousand lamps
>
> Lamps of joy and jubilation,
> Pitch-ring fires and pitch-pine torches
> Throw their harsh and gaudy daylight
> Upon palaces and temples.

The fires throw their light upon the temple of the idol Huitzilopochtli:

> There enthroned upon his altar
> Sits the mighty Vitzliputzli,
> Bloody war-god of the nation,
> Monster evil and misshapen
>
> But so droll is his exterior,
> So contorted and so childish,
> That, despite an inward shudder
> One is almost moved to laughter.

On the platform the high priest, Scarlet Jacket, prepares for the
sacrifice of the Spanish prisoners:

> 'Tis the high priest; he is whetting,
> With a smile, the knife, and leering,
> Squinting, leering, as he whets it,
> At the God who sits above him,
>
> Vitzliputzli knows the meaning
> Of the glances of his servant;
> Now he seems to twitch an eyelid,
> Now his lips are even moving.
>
> The musicians of the temple
> On the altar-steps are kneeling;
> Drummers, buglers, beating, blowing.
> What a rattling, what a tootling!

Across the waters of the lake, the Spaniards watch the death of their comrades as if from the pit of a vast playhouse.

> "Human Sacrifice" the title,
> Old the motive, old the fable;
> But as treated by the Christians,
> Less revolting is the drama.

> For, by transubstantiation,
> Into wine the blood is altered,
> And the body is a harmless
> Little wafer made of flour.

> But the game was rude and earnest
> As this savage people played it,
> 'Twas on human flesh they feasted,
> And the blood they drank was human.

> It was blue and undiluted
> Christian blood of long descent,
> That had never mingled basely
> With the blood of Moors or Hebrews.

That night, on the bloody roof of the temple, as the priests and laity lie snoring, Scarlet Jacket appeals to the god:

> "Bring destruction on our foemen,
> On those strangers who from distant
> And still undiscovered countries
> Hither sailed across the ocean

> "Wherefore left these men their country?
> Were they hungry, or blood-guilty?
> 'Stay at home and live by labor'
> Is a wise and good old proverb.

> "What, I wonder, are they seeking?
> With our gold they fill their pockets,
> And desire us to be happy
> After death, above in heaven."

The god gives a disconcerting reply. He proclaims the approaching fulfillment of the ancient prophecy

"Which predicts our land's destruction
By a dreadful bearded people
Who were one day to come flying
From the East on wooden birds

"Overthrown shall be my temple,
In its ashes I shall tumble.
I myself but smoke and ruin—
Never more shall any see me."

Still we have not seen the last of Huitzilopochtli. He will be
reborn to take an ironic revenge upon the destroyers of the Aztec
realm:

"Yet I shall not die—I cannot—
For we gods are like the parrots,
Live as long and moult as they do,
Moult like them and change our feathers.

"To the region they call Europe
To the country of my foes,
I will fly, and, having reached it,
Start a new career of glory.

"I will damn myself, and thenceforth
Be no longer god but devil;
As the foe of foes detested,
I will operate and labor,

"I will plague these Christian people,
Yes, with phantoms I will fright them,
They shall taste of hell beforehand,
And be always sniffing sulphur."

Huitzilopochtli will become a comrade of old Beelzebub and
Satan, of Belial and Ashtaroth. He calls upon Lilith, "sin's great
mother, slippery serpent," to instruct him "in the noble art of
lying," and ends with an assurance:

"My beloved Mexico!
Though I cannot save my country,
I can fearfully avenge her!
My beloved Mexico!" [53]

Heine's ironic romanticism was inimitable. The English poet Robert Southey wrote in a tamer, more conventional romantic vein. His long poem *Madoc* (finished in 1799 but not published till 1805) was based on an ancient legend that Madoc, a Welsh prince, had discovered and settled America in the thirteenth century. Southey placed the Welsh settlement in Florida, which he also supposed to be the legendary ancestral home of the Aztecs. The Aztecs had conquered their simpler Indian neighbors and forced them to yield up victims for their "foul idolatry."

Southey's sympathies were clearly with these vassals. He depicted them as amiable and virtuous children of nature, as opposed to the more civilized but ferocious Aztecs. The story centers on the struggle of Madoc and his Welsh followers to end the Aztec tyranny over their tributaries, the Hoamen. Madoc conquers, secures Aztec assent to an end of human sacrifice, and their reconciliation with the Hoamen. He then sails for Wales to announce that "beyond the Seas Madoc hath found his home"; he returns to find that the Aztecs have relapsed into their bloody ways and fomented rebellion against his mild rule. The complicated tale reaches its climax with Madoc's final victory over the Aztecs. He tells them they may stay and live under the new Christian order, but the youth of the tribe gather around their new king, who leads them away:

> To spread in other lands Mexitli's name,
> And rear a mightier empire, and set up
> Again their foul idolatry; till Heaven
> Making blind zeal and bloody avarice
> Its ministers of vengeance, sent among them
> The heroic Spaniard's unrelenting sword.[54]

Southey's attitude toward the Aztecs fluctuates uncertainly between detestation for their "foul idolatry" and admiration for their bravery and cultural accomplishments. A visit paid by Madoc to their capital of Aztlán gave Southey an opportunity to develop the theme of Aztec magnificence. The Aztlán which he describes as lying in "a beauteous plain, filled with stately towns and villages, cradled in mountains," of course had Tenochtitlán for its original. Southey, who knew better, could not resist the temptation to assign

Aztlán the medieval features of turrets, battlements, and "far-circling walls."

> A broad blue lake extended far and wide
> Its waters, darker beneath the light of noon.
> There Aztlan stood upon the farther shore;
> Amid the shade of trees its dwellings rose,
> Their level roofs with turrets set around,
> And battlements all burnished white, that shone
> Like silver in the sun-shine. I beheld
> The imperial city, her far-circling walls,
> Her garden groves, and stately palaces,
> Her temples mountain size, her thousand roofs;
> And when I saw her might and majesty,
> My mind misgave me then.

Combining reality and fantasy, Southey has Madoc conducted across the lake in a *chinampa:*

> We reached the shore:
> A floating islet waited me there,
> The beautiful work of man. I set my foot
> Upon green-growing herbs and flowers, and sate
> Embowered in odorous shrubs: Four long light boats
> Yoked to the garden, with accordant song
> And dip and dash of oars in harmony
> Bore me across the lake.[55]

Southey prided himself on the correctness of his details of Indian life, which he supported with copious notes based on Clavigero, Cortés, Bernal Díaz, Gómara, Torquemada, and other sources. Unfortunately his passion for accuracy does not compensate for the mediocrity of his verse, well made, often tuneful, but never inspired.

The romantic novel dealing with Aztec themes offers less interest than the poetry. We can pass rapidly over the hopelessly sentimental *Guatimozín, el último emperador de Méjico* (1846), by the Cuban poetess Gertrudis Gómez de Avellaneda. This novel had the honor of an English translation, published in Mexico, by one Mrs. William W. Blake. We must grant La Avellaneda a sincere effort to provide an accurate historical setting for the story, even to the employment of footnotes to document her statements; but the language and the postures of her characters are incredibly theatrical and stilted.

When Cuauhtémoc calls upon the gods to protect his wife and son, he says: "Protect his innocency, divine spirits! Protect this defenseless creature, and this tender mother who weeps at my feet! And if I am not destined to have the happiness of saving my country, grant me the glory of dying for it, and be ye the defender of the widow and orphan!" Indians and Spaniards alike conduct themselves with an impossible nobility. The Spanish soldiers doomed to die on the Aztec altars "presented themselves calm and tranquil for the horrible sacrifice, and even a scornful smile appeared on their lips in contemplating the singular aspect of their repugnant guard. . . ." [56]

By far the best specimen in the category of the Aztec novel is *Calavar; or The Knight of the Conquest, a Romance of Mexico* (1834), by the American novelist and playwright Robert Montgomery Bird. The book deserved the praise that greeted its appearance, for Bird not only took care to sketch an accurate historical background but managed to infuse a certain amount of life into his creation. Bird, who read Spanish fluently, consulted a large number of sources and diligently studied the history and geography of the area. Indeed, in his preface to the 1847 edition of the novel, he noted that it had been written in preparation for a projected history of Mexico, and therefore he had attempted to write it with the "strictest historical accuracy compatible with the requisitions of romance." [57]

The novel deals with the first phase of the conquest of Mexico; its hero is the young nobleman Amador and its heroine the mysterious Moorish maiden Leila. The intricate plot need not detain us; greater interest attaches to Bird's portrait of Aztec Mexico. His viewpoint, it quickly appears, owed much to Clavigero.

To launch his story, Bird used a well-worn device: he receives a manuscript from an eccentric Indian *cura* who introduces himself as a descendant of the Moctezumas, an Indian counterpart of the crusty, crotchety Scot types found in some novels of Scott. Cristóbal Johualicahuatzin is capable of sharp comments such as the following remark on the devastating effects of Spanish efforts to drain the lakes of the Valley: "The cutting through yonder hill of Nochistingo has given the last blow in a system of devastation; the canal of Huehuetoca has emptied the golden pitcher of Moteuczoma. It has converted the valley into a desert and will depopulate it. Men cannot live upon salt." The *cura* is also very knowledgeable about history and historians, as witness his remark on Robertson: "I could forgive you more readily, had you not named to me that infidel Scotchman, who calls the superb Moteuczoma a savage, and all the Tlatoani, the great princes and princesses, the people and all, barbarians! But what more could you expect of a heretic." [58]

Bird defended the Aztecs as ardently as his Indian spokesman when he interrupted his narrative to reflect on the character of Aztec society. He declared that the ancient Mexicans had made remarkable progress in the face of obstacles unknown in the Old World, such as the absence of useful domestic animals and the lack of iron. Nonetheless, Bird insisted, the Aztecs were in rapid forward movement at the time of the Conquest. "The discovery of even the properties of iron will soon follow the invention of an alphabet, however rude or hieroglyphic. The Mexicans could already record their discoveries. Without the aid of iron and domestic animals, they were advancing in refinement. Civilization had dawned, and was shedding a light, constantly augmenting, over their valleys." Aside from the defects of their religion, which, Bird believed, would eventually have been purged of its abominations, "the Mexican Empire was not far behind some of the monarchies of Europe in that method, purpose, and stability of institutions, both political and domestic, which are esteemed the evidences of civilization." [59]

Calavar carried the story of the Conquest only to the return of the Spaniards to Tlaxcala after their disastrous flight from the Aztec capital. In *The Infidel; or The Fall of Mexico* (1835), Bird brought the Conquest to its conclusion with a new set of characters. The historical narrative was again interwoven with a complicated intrigue, but this time the heroine was the lovely Zelahualla, Moctezuma's daughter, whom the Spanish hero converted, married, and carried back to Spain.

In *The Infidel*, Bird again defended the ancient Mexicans. He reserved his highest praise, however, for the kings and institutions of Texcoco. "The polished character of these barbarous chieftains, as the world has been taught to esteem them, may be better understood, when we know, that they sowed the roadside with corn for the sustenance of travelers, and the protection of husbandmen, built hospitals and observatories, endowed colleges and formed associations of literature and science, in which, to compare small things with great, as in the learned societies of modern Europe and America, encouragement was given to the study of history, poetry, music, painting, astronomy, and natural magic." [60]

Yet Bird's novels display the characteristic romantic ambivalence toward the Indian—that same ambivalence that we find in the histories of Prescott and the romances of Cooper, and that Bird's biographer calls "the dilemma of sympathy." On the one hand, Bird exalts the cultural works of the Indians, achieved with such scanty means; not only are they civilized but "they are patriots laudably defending their homelands, their wives and children and sacred altars, from the fierce, cruel, rapacious, untrustworthy invaders. Obviously the reader must sympathize with them." [61] But Bird knew very well that these virtuous patriots not only practiced human sacrifice on a large scale but ruled with an iron hand over their own subjects. Add to these considerations the pressures on Bird of his race and religion, not to speak of the taste of his readers. At all critical moments, therefore, Bird sided with the Spaniards, and presented the destruction of the Aztec Empire as divine retribution for its crimes against man and God.

The brilliant success of Prescott's *Conquest of Mexico* produced a new crop of novels with Mexican settings. In 1845 Edward Maturin published *Montezuma; The Last of the Aztecs*, dedicated to Prescott, to whose historical researches Maturin acknowledged his debt. In his introductory pages Maturin drew a picture of the Valley of Mexico as an Eden about to be despoiled by Spanish invaders. "Lakes slept in the amber beams of the morning sun, as with the conscious repose that their guardian spirits kept watch within their depths, and that their paradise retreat could never be ruffled by the storm or darkened by the cloud. On the bright bosom of each floated the chinampas, or gardens freighted with their glowing and perfumed treasures. . . . Far away stretched forests. . . . And there were also rich fields of grain, drooping with the weight of their own fertility, blending the treasures of their coming harvest with the teeming orchards and floating chinampas." Maturin mourned the fate awaiting the peaceful inhabitants of this idyllic spot. "Alas! Little did they deem their days of happy seclusion in that valley retreat were so rapidly drawing to a close." [62]

Maturin's romance was distinguished by the fact that all major characters, with the exception of Cortés, were Indian. In addition to the famous Malinche, they included an evil high priest who knew that his idols were lifeless blocks of wood and schemed to oust Moctezuma as king and usurp his throne with Spanish aid, an aged priestess who turned out to be Malinche's mother, and a heroic dwarf who turned out to be her sister. The novel ended in a Gothic riot of murder and suicide that almost emptied the stage. Presumably in the interests of moral purity, Malinche, "the Indian maid whose native simplicity of character was heightened by the spirit of the heroine," was married off to Cortés. Maturin sought to deepen the effect of historical authenticity by detailed descriptions of native dress and customs, liberally sprinkled with Indian terms. His work displayed all the faults of Bird's books— the stilted style, the absurd coincidences, the wooden characters— with none of Bird's merits.

The most preposterous in this series of Aztec novels by American authors was J. H. Ingraham's *Montezuma, the Serf, or the Revolt of the Mexitli*, also published in 1845. Ingraham, a prolific writer of potboilers, clearly intended to exploit commercially the interest in ancient Mexico aroused by Prescott's book. The total absurdity of this miserable tale is suggested by its references to knights in armor, gallant steeds, brazen chariots, virgins of the sun, and the like. It merits no further notice.

A work of more serious intent is W. W. Fosdick, *Malmiztic the Toltec; and the Cavaliers of the Cross* (1851). Fosdick avoided the "dilemma of sympathy" that weakened other novels dealing with the Conquest by making his hero a noble Toltec, free of the moral taint attached to the Aztecs. In his introduction Fosdick asserted that the territory ruled by the Aztecs had once belonged to the Toltecs, "a race that passed mysteriously away, leaving a multitude of documents which marked them as a mighty and wonderful people who never, according to historians, stained their altars with human blood, nor debased their banquets with the still more horrible custom of cannibalism." These Toltecs, Fosdick continued, "were in all probability, the founders of those vast cities whose solid superstructures of stone, and giant works of architecture, rival in beauty and magnificence, even in their ruins, the mighty wrecks which lie scattered in the desert sands of Egypt. . . ." [63]

Fosdick went on to give a reasonably accurate account of Mexican civilization on the eve of the Conquest, largely based on Prescott. He ended his survey with an implied rebuke to skeptics who discounted reports of Aztec magnificence. "In short, although their condition does not fill the modern European idea of civilization, yet it was in some respects a rival of oriental luxury and magnificence, and so far superior, in every regard, to the condition of the North American Indians, that any comparison between them is wholly out of the question. And the idea of their having emigrated from Asia has more fancy than fact for its foundation." [64]

Through the pages of the book stalks the stern, mysterious Malmiztic, last of the Toltecs, a convenient foil to the weak and irresolute Moctezuma. Malmiztic was "the living representative of that shadowy race whose works have outlasted memory and history!" His mental powers and learning are measureless; he is the chief authority in the empire in all relating to calendrical and mathematical science, and to all other arts. The Aztec priests abhor him, for he worships an unknown and invisible god and will not bow to any of the Aztec idols. To cap his virtues, Malmiztic is a temperance man; he refuses to drink a health to Moctezuma's sister Papantzin in alcoholic liquor, accepting only a "goblet full of pure, sparkling water."

Moctezuma's daughter Tecalco inevitably falls in love with Malmiztic, who converts her to monotheism with the aid of a manuscript left by Quetzalcóatl. Malmiztic's relations with the Aztecs reach a crisis when he intervenes to save the life of a Tlaxcalan warrior who has slain a succession of Aztec warriors in the gladiatorial sacrifice. Drawing a sword "of unknown metal and brilliancy," he fights off hundreds of foes, but is at last overcome and thrown into Moctezuma's dungeons. He escapes with the aid of Tecalco and his knowledge of alchemy and escorts Tecalco to a mountain cave containing the temple of the Invisible

God, the Cause of Causes. Later Malmiztic joins the Spaniards, the imperfect agents of Providence, and becomes Cortés' confidant and adviser.

The Toltec towers morally over the conquistador, who turns to him for solace and forgiveness. In the wilds of Guatemala Cortés tries to sleep after his execution of Cuauhtémoc and other Indian chiefs, but guilty dreams haunt his slumber. "Malmiztic," cries Cortés, "I am miserable! My evil deeds recoil and crush me like a mountain; horrors haunt me perpetually, and one word of forgiveness will be a balm to my burning soul!" Malmiztic's virtue is rewarded: the book ends with the Toltec and his bride inhabiting a palace on a "sweet little green isle" in a lake in the heart of Guatemala, "where cities of a forgotten people lay buried under the mould of ages." [65]

At least three plays dealing with the conquest of Mexico and the Aztecs were published in the United States in the 1840's and 1850's. I have examined the last in time, *Cortez the Conqueror, a Tragedy in Five Acts* (1857), by Lewis F. Thomas. In a preliminary "advertisement" the author claimed that the play had been read "by the late J. B. Booth, who gave it highest encomiums and intended to produce it, had he lived." Almost certainly, Booth was only being kind. The play is as extravagant in plot, as artificial in dialogue, as the worst of the novels here surveyed.

Romantic conventions had the same distorting effect on the Aztec image in the pictorial arts. Typical is the drawing of Moctezuma that adorned all the early editions of Prescott's *Conquest of Mexico*. The king is shown in a pensive pose, with an air of gentle melancholy; his features are European rather than Indian, with a small moustache over the upper lip; his dress only vaguely resembles Aztec clothing. This sentimental romanticism, joined to a classicist conception of beauty, influenced the treatment of Aztec themes by Mexican artists of the nineteenth century. In their paintings the Indian subjects usually bear a suspicious resemblance to Greek Apollos and Roman vestal virgins. [66]

There was no more ethnographic or psychological truth in the lithographs dealing with the conquest of Mexico produced on a mass scale by French engravers for the Spanish and Spanish American markets; the Mexican Indians in these pictures, with their theatrical poses and gestures, might as well be Arabs or ancient Romans. The same could be said of the pleasantly exotic music to the Aztec songs and dances in the opera *Fernand Cortez* by Gasparo Spontini, first staged in 1809, and highly praised by Hector Berlioz and Richard Wagner.[67]

CHAPTER TWELVE

Montezuma's Dinner

By mid-nineteenth century romanticism had almost exhausted its creative possibilities in Western politics, art, and thought. A time of relative political stability and burgeoning science and industry succeeded the age of romantic revolt. Over the new day presided a bourgeoisie for which Auguste Comte, high priest of the secular religion of positivism, had coined a fitting slogan: "Order and Progress." The spectacle of rapid scientific and economic advance, of man's growing mastery over nature, of European expansion over the planet, inspired euphoric moods in Western intellectuals. The eighteenth-century faith in progress revived, and scholars focused their attention on the dynamics of change. The rise of secularism, weakening religious authority and sanctions, encouraged scholars to disregard the limits set by Biblical chronology and dogma in reconstructing the stages in the history of the earth, of species, and of society. Anthropology emerged as an independent discipline, and the search for patterns and sequences in the early history of mankind produced the brilliant studies of Edward Tylor and Lewis H. Morgan.

The effect of these developments on the Western image of the Indian was mainly unfavorable. Since the romantic Noble Savage could not survive inspection by the impersonal light of the new evolutionist theories, he disappeared from the repertory of the social sciences, if not of literature. The evolutionists, as they regarded the Indian from the glorious height of European cultural superiority, tended to think of him as a being who had lost out in the struggle for existence, as a living fossil, as a datum to be studied, measured, described, and assigned to his lowly place in the grand evolutionary structure. The ethnocentrism, Victorian morality, and racism that formed part of the intellectual baggage of all the influential evolutionists of the late nineteenth century diminished the stature of the Indian. Edward Tylor argued that the white race was best endowed for civilized existence. Lewis H. Morgan, who believed that cultural traits were carried in the blood, maintained that the Indian lacked an essential passion, the desire for economic gain. Herbert Spencer frowned on efforts to impose civilization on "inferior races." [1] Anthropology presently sloughed off most of these prejudices and learned to view the Indian with more impartial and respectful eyes, but this reform began only in the late nineteenth century.

A case in point of the downgrading of Indian culture by evolutionist theory is Morgan's famous reconstruction of Aztec society. Thereby Moctezuma was reduced to a tribal chief, his palace to a communal dwelling, and the city of Tenochtitlán to a humble pueblo. In its essentials, the Morgan interpretation continued the attack on the romantic school of Indian history begun by Lewis Cass and Albert Gallatin.

The link between the old and new revisionism was the lawyer Robert A. Wilson, who joined the ranks of the skeptics with the appearance of his book, *Mexico and Its Religion* (1855). Wilson, like Morgan, was a resident of Rochester, New York; his father, he said, had lived among the Iroquois and had been adopted into the tribe; Wilson himself had lived in Seneca country and "there enjoyed a good opportunity of studying Indian character." [2] Wilson was patently a racist and bigot, anti-Negro, anti-Catholic, and anti-Spanish; appropriately enough he dedicated his book to the American (Know-Nothing) party.

His book early struck a note of belligerent incredulity in regard to the claims made for Aztec civilization by the Spanish and Indian chroniclers. He conceded that magnificent monuments of remote antiquity survived in Mexico and Central America, but believed that the long-vanished Toltecs had erected these structures. Citing surveys by United States military engineers, he insisted that temple-pyramids could not have been built on the soft earth in the waters of Lake Texcoco, rejected the possibility of floating gardens, and dismissed Cortés' accounts of large-scale military operations in the Conquest as the tales of a "great Münchhausen." The so-called pyramid of Cholula was "a shapeless mass of earth," and the city of the same name never existed, for "a city of forty thousand houses surely would leave some vestige or fragment." The so-called republic of Tlaxcala was nothing more than "an ordinary tribe of North American savages, obtaining their living, as other Indians did then and do now, by the cultivation of Indian corn and hunting, having the same crude form of government that is common to all the savage tribes of North America." The general similarity of Wilson's outlook to Morgan's position is suggested by the comment that the Tlaxcalans "had not yet reached that point of social organization at which the loose government of savages gives way to the despotism of the next stage of advancement, which we call *barbarism*." [3]

When Wilson's book appeared, Morgan had already published his important ethnographic study, *The League of the Ho-dé-no-sau-nee, or Iroquois* (1851), and was assembling the evidence needed to raise his conclusions on Iroquois kinship terminology and family structure to the level of a universal law. This research culminated in his *Systems of Consanguinity and Affinity of the Human Family* (1870). Understandably elated by his success in solving the problem of the social organization of the Iroquois, Morgan became convinced that the Iroquois were a model of Indian social organization. He was intensely annoyed, therefore, on reading Prescott's *Conquest of Mexico* in the 1850's, to find a portrait of Aztec society that was utterly contrary to the Iroquois model and its simplicity. Morgan concluded that the popular Prescott was a major obstacle to establishing American ethnology on a truly scientific basis. About the same time Morgan probably read Wilson's iconoclastic work. We have the testimony of Morgan's disciple, Adolph F. Bandelier, that Wilson's book "at least produced one good effect. It directed the attention of Lewis H. Morgan to the advantages to be derived from a critical study of documentary history for our understanding of the past, present, and future of the aborigines." [4]

In a paper read before the eleventh meeting of the American Association for the Advancement of Science in Montreal (1857), Morgan first spoke out on the Aztec theme. He affirmed that "the institutions of all the aborigines of this continent have a family cast. . . . They all sprang from a common mind, and, in their progressive development, have still retained the impress of their original elements, as is abundantly verified. The Aztecs were thoroughly and essentially Indian. . . . Differences existed, it is true, but they were not radical." Aztec civilization, according to Morgan, "simply exhibits a more advanced development of those primary ideas of civil and social life, which were common to the whole Indian family, and not their overthrow by the substitution of antagonistic institutions." Although Morgan had never visited Mexico and was only slightly acquainted with the Spanish chroniclers, he confidently asserted that if one could break "through the overlapping mass of fable and exaggeration, and bring to light the real institutions of the Aztecs, it would be found, there is every reason to believe, that their government was a hereditary oligarchy, very similar to that of the Iroquois."

Moctezuma, declared Morgan, was only one of a number of sachems who jointly administered the affairs of the tribe: Prescott had failed to understand the principles of Aztec social organization and rules of descent. For this reason he had given a mistaken explanation of why Moctezuma was succeeded in office by his brother Cuitláhuac, who was succeeded after his death from smallpox by his brother Cuauhtémoc. Unaware of the principle of succession in the female line, which the Aztecs shared with the Iroquois, Prescott had assumed that Moctezuma's son was set aside because of his illegitimacy. "Had the researches of this elegant writer brought him into contact with the real institutions of the Aztecs which controlled these questions of descent, he would have discovered, there is every reason to believe, that the people were divided into tribes [clans], with laws of descent precisely similar to those of the Iroquois." Morgan also rebuked Prescott for slighting the importance of the clan and communal landownership in Aztec society.[5]

Morgan's paper was published in the *Proceedings* of the American Association for the Advancement of Science (1858), in time for Wilson to cite it liberally in his *New History of the Conquest of Mexico* (1859). The work represented a full-scale effort to refute Prescott and his sources. In his foreword Wilson acknowledged his debt to Lewis Cass and especially to Albert Gallatin, "father of American ethnology." In the text he also paid his respects to Morgan. Wilson summarized the "fundamental laws of Indian society" as expounded by the master in his paper before the association. These laws, which included the principle of tribal organization, restrictions on marriage, descent in the female line, and communal ownership of land, had entirely escaped the notice of European authors, and were almost unknown to Americans, until Morgan brought them to light.[6]

Wilson's book, exuding brag, bluster, and ignorance at every pore, went far beyond his first work in the extravagance of its debunking claims. A second visit to Mexico, and careful inspection of the principal scenes of the Conquest, had shown Wilson the true value of the "historical romances" of Cortés and Bernal Díaz. Wilson now found that Cortés' narrative consisted of two parts. One was an accurate account of his adventures, consistent with the topography of the region, the other a mass of fictional material, "apparently borrowed from fables of the Moorish era, for effect in Spain. . . ." As for Bernal Díaz, Wilson had after much deliberation decided to denounce both him and his work as mythical. Moorish tales, Wilson repeatedly declared, were the principal mine from which the "fabulous histories" of the Spanish and Indian chroniclers were drawn. From that source Ixtlilxóchitl had obtained the material for "transforming his mud-built village of Tezcuco into the fabulous empire of his pretended ancestor, Nezahualcóyotl."

Equally fabulous were Spanish accounts of the "Aztec Empire," of the magnificence of its capital, of its teeming populations. Wilson easily disposed of the claims made for Aztec art and technology. The gold disc the size of a wagon wheel existed only in Cortés' imagination; the famous featherwork was only "that skillful arrangement of natural colors, in which the savage surpasses civilized man—the very wildness of his combinations being in fact the ground of his superiority." True, the monuments found in Central America and elsewhere in the area testified to a much higher culture, but Wilson had a new theory to explain away this inconvenient fact; his theory assigned those monumental structures to Phoenician colonizers whose empire had long ago risen and crumbled.[7]

By the extravagance of his claims and gross factual errors, Wilson damaged instead of aiding the revisionist cause. Morgan might well have prayed to be delivered from such allies as Wilson. In a devastating attack in the *Atlantic Monthly* (April–May, 1859), Prescott's learned literary secretary, John F. Kirk, demolished Wilson's pretensions to "correct" Prescott.[8]

Morgan continued to fret about the harm Prescott's book was doing to American ethnology. "The Mexican field," he wrote Francis Parkman in 1867, "is the one above all others that needs reworking, but the story has been so well told and so completely finished that it is next to impossible to overthrow the cunningly wrought fable." [9] In an article entitled "The Seven Cities of Cibola" Morgan dissected the Spanish sources to show that these fabled cities of the Southwest were mere pueblos, and their palaces only communal houses. In the same article he urged a study of the history of the Aztec confederacy; such a study would prove that the so-called Aztec king was merely a war chief, his palace a communal dwelling.[10] Morgan, engaged as he was in an ambitious effort to reduce mankind's early social evolution to the sway of law, evidently had not the time or qualifications to unravel the tangled problems of Mexican antiquity.

Up to this point (about 1870), the revisionist assault on the romantic view of Aztec society had had little success. The well-informed Brantz Mayer, in a book published by the Smithsonian Institution in 1856, took for granted the existence of civilized societies in ancient Mexico and Peru, and argued for their independent origin. He defended the Aztecs against the charge that their cruel human sacrifice proved their barbarism, and declared that "their architecture, laws, government, private life, and astronomical knowledge show that their social condition was much more refined than their faith." [11]

John D. Baldwin, author of a pioneering survey of American archaeology (1872), avoided reference to the highly respected Morgan but subjected Wilson to a blistering critique. He included Wilson's *New History* among "the curiosities of historical speculation," and called his notions "preposterous." He conceded that some of the Spaniards might have exaggerated for effect in Spain, but insisted that "we can see clearly that the Mexicans were a civilized people, that Montezuma's city of Mexico was larger than the present city, and that an important empire was substantially conquered when that city was finally conquered and destroyed. . . . It is not easy to understand how a denial of the Aztec civilization was possible." [12]

Instead of declining, the romantic interpretation of ancient Mexico reached a high-water mark of hyperbole in John W. Draper's best-selling *History of the Intellectual Development of Europe* (1863). Draper, professor of chemistry at New York University, wrote his book with the avowed purpose of impressing his readers with the conviction that "civilization does not proceed in an arbitrary manner or by chance, but that it passes through a determinate succession of stages, and is a development according to law." [13] The Aztec and Inca civilizations held special interest because they demonstrated that "similar ideas and similar usages make their appearance spontaneously in the progress of civilization of different countries, showing how little they depend on accident, how closely they are connected with the organization, and, therefore, with the necessities of man."

To make his point, Draper stressed the analogies alleged between Aztec civilization and civilizations of the Old World. He depicted the Aztec king as living in barbaric pomp, assisted by a privy council, and as having under him great lords who owed military service in return for the grant of land. The people lived in admirable order, subject to laws enforced by an independent judiciary. Caste distinctions did not exist. Draper believed that Aztec armies, in common with those of Europe, not only possessed standards and banners but "executed their evolutions to military music, and were provided with hospitals, army surgeons, and a medical staff." All this proved that "in the human hives of Europe, Asia, and America, the bees were marshalled in the same way, and were instinctively building their combs alike."

Unhampered by any pedantic urge to cite his sources, Draper combined familiar facts with prodigious claims for Aztec intellectual and artistic development. Aztec religion, like the Aztec political and military systems, appeared to imitate those of ancient Europe and Asia. "The common people had a mythology of many gods, but the higher classes were strictly Unitarian, acknowledging one almighty, invisible Creator." Aztec astronomy was so advanced that it had ascertained "the globular form of the earth and the obliquity of the ecliptic." Aztec agriculture was superior to that of Europe; "there was nothing in the Old World to compare with the menageries and botanical gardens of Huaxtepec, Chapultepec, Istapalapan, and Tezcuco." The refined, sophisticated society of Tenochtitlán resembled that of modern London and New York. "Like us, they had in their entertainments solid dishes, with suitable condiments, gravies, sauces, and desserts of pastries, confections, fruits, both fresh and preserved. They had chafing-dishes of silver or gold. Like us, they knew the use of intoxicating drinks; like us, they not unfrequently took them to excess; like us, they heightened their festivities with dancing and music."

The splendor of Texcoco moved Draper to write an ecstatic description. "The king's palace was a wonderful work of art. . . . Its harem was adorned with magnificent tapestries of featherwork; in its gardens were fountains, cascades, baths, statues, alabasters, cedar groves, forests, and a wilderness of flowers." Draper accepted the monotheism of the kings of Texcoco, citing the famous temple, "with a dome of polished black marble, studded with stars of gold, in imitation of the sky," dedicated to the omnipotent, invisible god." [14]

Carried away by pro-Indian enthusiasm and anti-Spanish bias, Draper proclaimed the Aztec and Inca cultures to be not only equal but in some respects superior to contemporary European civilization. "From Mexico and Peru a civilization that might have instructed Europe was crushed out." [15] Reading this overblown description of Aztec society, and recalling Draper's many thousands of readers, one finds it easier to understand Morgan's obsessive urge "to overthrow the cunningly wrought fable."

A second, more successful phase of the revisionist attack on the romantic school of Indian history began in the 1870's. In this second phase Morgan was joined by Adolph F. Bandelier, one of the most intriguing and complex figures in the history of American anthropology.[16] Bandelier was brought at the age of eight from Switzerland to southern Illinois by his well-to-do immigrant father, studied and traveled in Europe, and eventually devoted himself to a business career for which he was temperamentally unfit.

About 1870 he began to read intensively about ancient Mexico; a turning point came when he met Morgan in Rochester in December, 1873. Morgan, already a famous man, embodied for Bandelier the ideal to which he aspired: a life of scholarship and escape from the drudgery of business in the provincial world of southern Illinois. Morgan, in turn, recognized in the young man linguistic and research talents that he could utilize for his attack on Prescott's "cunningly wrought fable." In effect, Bandelier became Morgan's research assistant on the Aztec chapter in his masterpiece, *Ancient Society*. Their acquaintance soon ripened into a close friendship based not only on utility but on mutual respect and affection.

For Bandelier to be useful to Morgan he must be won over to the latter's ideas on ancient Mexico. Their early correspondence shows Bandelier respectful, even deferential, more than willing to be convinced, but troubled by the awkward discrepancies between the Spanish sources and Morgan's view of things. On December 20, 1873, Bandelier wrote Morgan that he could not help finding in Middle America, especially in Mexico, "a despotic barbarous monarchy, but still a monarchy, a political body, a state. . . ." [17] In a long letter of February 5–7, 1874, he still had some objections and reservations, being persuaded that in Mexico and Peru "power was consolidated, acknowledged, and exercised in a truly despotic manner," and he even defended Bernal Díaz' application of the term "palace" to certain Aztec buildings as "not so very improper, after all. . . ." [18]

By September of the same year Bandelier had begun to retreat. "More and more," he wrote Morgan, "I find the institutions of the Aztecs to be not of the monarchical kind, but, rather, as you have said, a military democracy." In a letter of April 20, 1876, he still demurred at some of the positions taken in an article that Morgan had written on "Montezuma's Dinner," finding Morgan's estimate of the population of ancient Mexico too low, and objecting to the lumping of Aztec architecture with that of the pueblos of New Mexico. On all major issues, however, he surrendered in a letter to Morgan dated January 4, 1877: "I want to take hold of the bull's horns, and dispose of feudalism, individual tenure of real estate, lordship, etc., at one fell blow." [19]

Bandelier's inability to find evidence in the sources of some elements required by Morgan's scheme, such as clans or gentes, caused him some anxious hours. At last he stumbled on the elusive gens in Torquemada. Bandelier had learned how to "wield" the Spanish sources. He wrote Morgan on August 4, 1876, that he "need not fear the influence of the Spanish authorities, I rather hope to prove to you that these can be wielded and used to advantage." [20]

While Bandelier was capitulating to Morgan, Hubert Howe Bancroft, across the continent in California, was bringing out his five-volume *History of the Native Races of the Pacific Coast* (1875–1876), the first fruit of a colossal enterprise planned to survey the history of Mexico, Central America, California, and the Northwest.[21] Bancroft was a self-made man, a businessman turned historian. In addition to great native talent and industry, Bancroft possessed a large fortune which he used to hire a staff of writers and researchers, whose work he supervised. He devoted the greater part of the second volume of the *Native Races* to the Aztecs, the remainder to the Maya. Despite the flaws inherent in Bancroft's factory system of literary production, and a tendency to follow Ixtlilxóchitl and Brasseur de Bourbourg too trustingly in the more remote phases of Nahua and Maya history, the volume was a remarkable work of synthesis, based on an impressive assemblage of sources.

Bancroft's conclusions on the veracity of the Spanish chroniclers, on the character of Aztec society, were diametrically opposed to those of Morgan. Conceding that the Spanish writers had exaggerated much of what they saw, for obvious reasons, Bancroft insisted that "to the truth of the greater part of their relations, testimony is borne by the unanimity of the authors, though this is partly owing to their copying each from the others; and more conclusively, by the architectural remains which survived the attacks of the ecclesiastical conquerors, and the golden and bejewelled ornaments of such exquisite workmanship as to equal if not surpass anything of the kind in Europe."

Aztec government was "monarchical and nearly absolute." An Oriental pomp and veneration surrounded the monarch, said Bancroft. Land was divided between the crown, the nobles, the temples, and the clans, but the greatest portion was held by the king and the aristocracy. Perhaps the strongest proof of the advanced nature of Aztec civilization was its calendar, "which, for ingenuity and correctness, equalled, if it did not surpass, the systems adopted by contemporaneous and Asiatic nations." Bancroft summed up his conclusions with the emphatic statement that "the Nahuas, the Mayas, and the subordinate and lesser civilizations surrounding them, [were] but little lower than the contemporaneous civilizations of Europe and Asia, and not nearly as low as we have been led to believe." [22]

Without naming Morgan or Wilson, Bancroft had refuted the principal revisionist contentions with regard to ancient Mexico. In his introduction to the same volume, Bancroft attacked the very foundations of the evolutionary scheme that Morgan was preparing to give the world. In 1875 Morgan delivered before the Detroit meeting of the American Association for the Advancement of Science a paper on "Ethnical Periods." This essay, slightly altered, became the first chapter of *Ancient Society*. Morgan divided human history into three major "ethnical periods"—savagery, barbarism, and civilization—each stage being correlated with certain "arts of subsistence" and a certain type of social organization. Leaving savagery undivided, Morgan divided the stage of barbarism again into "the Lower, Middle, and Upper Status." The invention of pottery seemed to Morgan the most effective criterion for determining the boundary line between savagery and barbarism. Groups in the "Middle Status" of barbarism were those village Indians, such as the Aztec and the Zuñi, who manufactured pottery in great quantities and many forms. To the "Lower Status" of barbarism Morgan assigned such "partially village Indians" as the Iroquois, Choctaws, and Cherokees, who made pottery on a smaller scale and in fewer forms. The distinguishing trait of the "Upper Status" of barbarism was the use of iron; civilization began with the phonetic alphabet and the use of writing.[23]

It is unclear whether Bancroft had read Morgan's paper when he wrote his introduction to the second volume of the *Native Races*, but it happened that his attack on fixed stages of human progress, defined by arbitrary technological criteria, applied perfectly to Morgan's scheme. Although Bancroft was himself an evolutionist, his critique anticipated to a remarkable degree the line of argument developed by post-Boasian foes of evolutionism and evaluative approaches to primitive culture in general. "The terms Savage and Civilized," wrote Bancroft, "as applied to races of men, are relative and not absolute terms. At best, these words mark only broad shifting stages in human progress; the one near the point of departure, the other farther on toward the unattainable end. . . . There are degrees in savagism, and there are degrees in civilization; indeed, though placed in opposition, the one is but a degree of the other. The Haidah, whom we call savage, are as much superior to the Shoshone, the lowest of Americans, as the Aztec is superior to the Haidah, or the European to the Aztec. Looking back some thousands of ages, we of today are civilized; looking forward through the same duration of time, we are savages."

Bancroft put his finger on the weakness of arbitrary technological criteria of cultural progress. He observed that it was no easy matter to tell where savagery ends and civilization begins. If the criteria of civilization were domestication of animals or knowledge of metallurgy and the arts, then the Eskimos were civilized, for they tamed reindeer, were skillful carvers, and used copper; if the criteria were agriculture, the building of houses of adobe, wood, and stone, and the manufacture of cloth and pottery, then the Pueblo Indians of New Mexico were civilized, yet clearly both the Eskimo and the Pueblo Indians ranked culturally below the Aztecs and the Maya.[24]

Morgan was soon given an opportunity for a rebuttal. Henry Adams, who felt of Bancroft's *Native Races* that "it would be a disgrace to let such a work go out as a measure of our national scholarship," invited Morgan to review the book for the *North American Review*. Morgan responded with a forty-page critique of the second volume, entitled "Montezuma's Dinner," published in the *North American Review* for April, 1876. A letter that Morgan wrote F. W. Putnam of Harvard at this time suggests the depth of his feeling against Bancroft and his book. Morgan lamented the lack of a science of American ethnology and asserted that "our first dead weight to be got rid of is the Aztec monarchy and the Aztec romance." Regard for the memory of Prescott had hitherto stayed Morgan's hand, but "the publication of Bancroft's *Native Races* alters the question. He has reiterated the worst exaggerations, their grossest absurdities, and added glosses in advance of all of them. This work and the commendation it is receiving is nothing less than a crime against ethnological science." [25]

As if to show his disdain for Bancroft's theorizing, Morgan took no notice of his critique of fixed-stage evolutionary schemes. The review opened on a note of sarcasm. Morgan derided Bancroft's presentation of "the high and mighty emperor of the Aztecs," whose subjects all told, according to Morgan, numbered nearly two hundred fifty thousand Indians, and "the great Aztec Empire, which covered an area as large as the whole state of Rhode Island." Indeed, Bancroft's book was filled with empires and kings, as "thick as blackbirds," not to speak of nobles, plebeians, and slaves. Bancroft had vested with "American prodigality" the aristocratic terminology of the Old World upon plain Indian sachems and war chiefs, and had gone beyond all previous writers in "fervor of imagination" and "recklessness of statement." The psychological roots of Bancroft's great illusion were "the eager, undefinable interest aroused by any picture of ancient society." Like the Spanish conquistadors of 1519, modern writers had had their imagination kindled by the revelation of the exotic Aztec society. "It caught the imagination and overcame the critical judgment of Prescott, our most charming writer; it ravaged the sprightly brain of Brasseur de Bourbourg; and it carried up in a whirlwind our author at the Golden Gate [Bancroft]." [26]

The favorable reviews of Bancroft's work in American journals proved to Morgan that "we have no science of American ethnology." He called on American scholars to explore a field of "unequaled richness and of vast extent," not from books but through a program of field work; he urged them "to visit the native tribes at their villages and encampments, and study their institutions as living organisms, their condition, and their plan of life. When this had been done from the region of the Arctic sea to Patagonia, Indian society will become intelligible, because its structure and principles will be understood." [27]

Morgan continued with an analysis (which gave his article its name) of Bancroft's description of the house in which Moctezuma resided, his so-called palace, and of Moctezuma's dinner, pictured by Bancroft as the banquet of a mighty emperor. By exposing the fictitious nature of the Spanish sources on which Bancroft's account was based, Morgan proposed to make a breach in "a vital section of the fabric of Aztec romance, now the most deadly encumbrance upon American ethnology." In words that seemed to echo a pas-

sage in William Robertson's *History of America*, Morgan stated
the premise "that the histories of Spanish America may be trusted
in whatever relates to the acts of the Spaniards, and to the acts
and personal characteristics of the Indians, in whatever relates to
their weapons, implements and utensils, fabrics, food, and raiment,
and things of a similar character. But in whatever relates to Indian
society and government, their social relations and plan of life, they
are totally worthless, because they learned nothing and knew
nothing of either. We are at full liberty to reject them in those
respects and commence anew, using any facts they may contain
which harmonize with what is known of Indian society." [28]

It was impossible to understand even such a simple event as
Moctezuma's dinner, asserted Morgan, without knowledge of certain institutions and customs that were "substantially universal in
the Indian family, and therefore existed, presumptively, among the
Aztecs." These institutions included organization in clans, phratries,
and tribes; communal ownership of land; the law of hospitality;
communal living; the custom of having but one prepared meal a
day, dinner. Applying these principles to the question at hand,
Morgan declared that one might reasonably suppose that Bernal
Díaz and other writers about the celebrated dinner found Moctezuma with his kindred in a "large joint-tenement house, containing
a hundred or more families united in a communal household." The
meal they witnessed was the single daily meal of the household,
prepared in a common kitchen, and distributed at the kettle. Each
person ate his portion from a clay bowl, without benefit of chair
or table. The rhapsodic accounts of Bernal Díaz and Cortés, followed by Prescott and Bancroft, presented a picture of Indian life
that was simply impossible. The window curtains of delicate tex-
ture, marble baths and porticos, floors of polished stone and marble,
wine cellars and secretaries—all were figments of the inspired Spanish imagination. "Whatever may be said by credulous and enthusiastic authors to decorate this Indian pueblo, its houses, and its
breech-cloth people cannot conceal the 'ragged Indian' therein by
dressing him in European costume." [29]

By way of illustration, Morgan cited some exaggerations of the
chroniclers. Bernal Díaz described Moctezuma as sitting in a low
chair at a table covered with a white cloth. Impossible, declared
Morgan, for the Aztecs had neither chairs nor tables. He grudg-

ingly conceded the possibility of a block of wood hollowed out
to make a stool or a seat, as described by Herrera, and of the use
of some sort of napkin, but he stood firm against a table or a table-
cloth. Morgan also found fanciful Cortés' mention of Moctezuma's
wine cellar and of the presence of secretaries at the dinner. The
wine cellar was remarkable for two reasons: first, because the level
of the streets and courts was only four feet above the level of the
water, making cellars impossible; and, second, because the Aztecs
had no knowledge of wine. Morgan found equally absurd Herrera's statement that three thousand Indians stood on guard while
Moctezuma ate, they dining only after the monarch had finished.
Morgan snorted at the idea of three thousand hungry Indians
patiently standing while their dinner grew cold upon the floor.
"No American Indian could be made to comprehend this picture.
It lacks the realism of Indian life, and embodies an amount of
puerility of which the Indian nature is not susceptible." [30]

Morgan's article made a stir and provoked favorable reactions
from several distinguished figures. "How you have gone for Bancroft," wrote Putnam, "you have taken his scalp clean off down
to his neck." Letters of approval also came from the historians
Francis Parkman and Henry Adams, and from the educator Henry
Barnard.[31]

Bandelier, meanwhile, was diligently working through the Spanish and Indian sources to provide Morgan with material for the
Aztec chapter in *Ancient Society*.[32] In this chapter Morgan attempted to demonstrate that the Aztecs were in the "Middle
Status" of barbarism, a stage whose character made impossible the
existence of an "Aztec empire." The Spaniards found in Mexico
a simple confederacy of three tribes, counterparts of which existed
throughout the continent. An elective council of chiefs, including
a war chief, administered the Aztec government. To this political
system Morgan assigned the name "military democracy."

The union of three tribes in a confederacy gave two of the four
members of what Morgan called the "organic social series." The
Spanish sources were unfortunately vague concerning the first and
the second members, the gens or clan and the phratry, but these
vague indications satisfied Morgan. The sole object of the confederacy was to extract tribute and victims for human sacrifice
from the vanquished, not to form a nation. It could not be other-

wise, since the tribal organization of the conquerors and the conquered excluded the possibility of the integration of alien clans into the Aztec tribe. Detracting from the importance of the Aztec conquests, Morgan declared that the Aztec sway did not extend a hundred miles beyond the Valley of Mexico. "Out of such limited materials the kingdom of Mexico of the Spanish chronicles was fabricated, and afterwards magnified into the Aztec empire of current history." [33]

Morgan had sketched an outline of Aztec social and political organization; it remained for Bandelier to plump the outline with enough documented detail to satisfy the requirements of modern scientific scholarship. After reading proof sheets of the Aztec chapter, Bandelier wrote Morgan that he was not too pleased with it, but no matter, he would sustain Morgan's position in a coming monograph. This was his study of Aztec warfare (1877), followed by one of Aztec land tenure (1878), and another of Aztec social organization and government (1879).[34] These monographs, revealing an immense amount of research and trailing gargantuan explanatory footnotes, had to inspire awe in all but the most skeptical readers. Since Bandelier was probably the only living American to have toiled through such massive works as those of Torquemada and Herrera, few could challenge the conclusion triumphantly stated by Bandelier in the closing lines of his third monograph, "that the social organization and mode of government of the ancient Mexicans was a military democracy, originally based upon communism in living." [35]

The imposing structure of Bandelier's research rested in fact on an unsound foundation, for he had manipulated or "wielded" the evidence to fit Morgan's preconceived ideas. This cavalier attitude toward the sources derived from a premise, first stated by Robertson, and adopted from him by Morgan and Bandelier, that the distortions of Aztec reality by Spanish chroniclers had what might be called semantic roots. "What in the first process of thinking was merely a comparative, became very soon a positive terminology for the purpose of describing institutions to which this foreign terminology never was adapted." Bandelier did not merely reserve the right to determine what it was that the Spanish chroniclers really saw. He ignored contradictory evidence, lifted phrases from their contexts, twisted the plain meaning of certain phrases, and asserted on his own authority facts that needed to be proved. In the United States of the 1880's, however, there was no scholar knowledgeable or interested enough to make the searching study required to expose Bandelier's faults. Accordingly, his monographs, supported by the immense prestige of Morgan, acquired an almost oracular authority. Typical was the unsigned comment of the influential *Nation* that Bandelier's paper on Aztec social organization was "one of the most learned and important contributions yet made to the history of primitive institutions." [36]

Bandelier had now found his life's work. In 1880, after a serious personal crisis terminated in a nervous breakdown, he cut himself loose from business forever. Through Morgan's influence the newly founded Archaeological Institute of America hired Bandelier to excavate in the Pueblo country of New Mexico; later he was to join the French Lorillard expedition to Yucatán. The Yucatán venture fell through, but Bandelier utilized the opportunity to study archaeological sites in central Mexico, including Teotihuacán, Cholula, Monte Albán, and Mitla. The sight of these imposing monuments did not shake Bandelier's faith in Morgan's doctrines. The Aztecs continued to be "the Iroquois of the South." Bandelier cited as proof of the tribal level of Mexican social organization the very success of the Aztecs in crushing pueblo after pueblo while others watched with indifference. It showed how loose intertribal relations were, *"how distant yet* were the conceptions of a state or a nation among the aborigines of Mexico." Bandelier also rejected the traditional romantic view of Tlaxcala as "a kind of Mexican Switzerland; as a free republic in the midst of despotically ruled communities." He found not the slightest fundamental difference between the social organization and government of Tlaxcala and those of other Mexican tribes; however, the Tlaxcalans were inferior in strategy and organizational capacity to the Aztecs, for "while the Mexicans, like the Iroquois, looked to strengthening their confederacy as the means of increase in power," the Tlaxcalans remains isolated, although the material for a powerful confederacy (Cholula and Huexotzinco) was within easy reach.[37]

Teotihuacán inspired no expressions of awe or respect in Bandelier. Instead he raised a doubt as to whether the famous pyramids were in fact man-made. In a letter to his Mexican friend Joaquín

García Icazbalceta he crowed over the fact that he had toppled Mitla from its pedestal and converted it into a simple pueblo like three others that he had found in its vicinity. About the same time he wrote Morgan that he had overcome the greatest problem of American archaeology, the great pyramid of Cholula. "Always have I been afraid of that monstrous pyramid, for I could not account for it." Now it was clear to him that it was built as "a place of refuge and last stand," "as a *communal work*, and all the stories about its being built in commemoration of gods or kings become superfluous to explain its fabrication. Rather than proving the high culture of the Cholulans, it proved the contrary, "for a people of high standing would have erected defenses on the outside, fortified local points to divide and distract the enemy." [38]

In Mexico City Bandelier inspected the Calendar Stone and found it so incorrectly shaped "as to render incredible the scientific knowledge that Gama ascribed to its makers." On a visit to the Museo Nacional the Coatlicue impressed him most disagreeably. "It is covered with carvings to overloading. However well executed some of them are when taken singly, their combination on the block is devoid of symmetry, and the mode of sculpture is very primitive." The general effect was "appalling"; the stone presented "a most hideous agglomeration of repulsive forms." Bandelier concluded that Mexican sculpture, while considerably above that of the northern village Indians, was not superior to the carvings in ivory and wood of the northwest Pacific coast.[39]

Bandelier's discussions with Mexican scholars had no appreciable effect on his ideas. Although Alfredo Chavero stated in his *Historia antigua y de la conquista* that Bandelier modified his views on ancient Mexico as a result of their talks,[40] no evidence of such a change appears in Bandelier's own writings. Probably the only Mexican historian who significantly influenced Bandelier during his Mexican tour was the conservative, pro-Spanish, anti-Aztec García Icazbalceta, with whom he had corresponded before coming to Mexico. García Icazbalceta may have played a part in Bandelier's decision while in Mexico to join the Catholic Church, a decision carried out in a secret ceremony at Puebla, July 31, 1881, with García Icazbalceta standing as sponsor. One reason for the secrecy may have been Bandelier's desire not to offend his patron, Lewis Morgan, who had a strong antipathy for the Catholic Church. Morgan died in December of that year. They had had eight years of friendship and collaboration.

On Bandelier's return to the United States at the end of 1881, he gave a number of addresses on Indian topics before historical societies. In these talks he appeared in a new role, that of ardent defender of Spain and her Indian policy. He also displayed a rabid hostility toward communism, both primitive and modern. In a lecture on "Kin and Clan," delivered before the Historical Society of New Mexico in 1882, Bandelier asserted that clan organization formed "the strongest, most efficacious, and most durable system of communism the earth has yet seen, and as such, the most powerful tyranny." This system, aggravated by a state of perpetual warfare, was the system the Spaniards found in Mexico. Bandelier represented Spanish policy-makers as grappling with a grave dilemma. "How to preserve the country and its inhabitants without forcing the latter across the chasm of divide, a leap, when they must invariably have been engulfed, since they lacked moral and mental strength to accomplish it." After a period of experimentation the counsels of the Church prevailed; and the Indian pueblos were permitted to govern themselves provided they kept peace with each other and adopted the Christian faith. "The results of it are apparent. For two hundred fifty years, at least, the Indians of Mexico, formerly in uninterrupted warfare, enjoyed the most profound, nay enervating peace, some savage tribes excepted." [41]

Bandelier enclosed the text of an address of similar tendency in a letter to García Icazbalceta. He hoped to have shown that "I am a good defender of the historical truth as concerns the Church. The intermediate position that I assume in religious matters is more useful to the Church than a show of public devotion." [42] The same themes appeared in Bandelier's paper, "The Romantic School in American Archaeology," read before the New York Historical Society in February, 1885. Gradually Bandelier's interests shifted from the Mexican field to other areas, especially the Andean archaeological zone.

The combined efforts of Morgan and Bandelier had secured victory for their ideas in the United States by the mid-eighties. They won that victory almost by default, through lack of serious opposition. The few Mexicanists in the United States capitulated almost without a struggle.

Daniel G. Brinton, who published extensively on Nahua and Maya literature and mythology, objected that Morgan and Bandelier had carried their doctrines too far, but accepted most of their premises. Brinton agreed, for example, that the government of the Mexican tribes "did not differ in principle from that of the northern tribes, though its development had reached a later stage." He also believed that all land in ancient Mexico was held by the gens and allotted to members for cultivation, and described Nezahualcóyotl's palace in Texcoco as a "communal house." [43]

The brilliant young anthropologist Mrs. Zelia Nuttall was another convert to the new theory. In 1886 she announced that a partial decipherment of the Borgia, Vatican, and Fejérváry codices had convinced her that these documents dealt, among other things, "with the details of a communal form of government, the existence of which has been suggested by some recent writers but not sufficiently proved to be generally accepted." She further affirmed that the Calendar Stone and the Sacrificial Stone were not what they had hitherto been considered, but rather recorded "the existence of communal property and of an equal division of general contributions into equal portions." [44]

If specialists such as Brinton and Nuttall meekly accepted the new dispensation in anthropology, amateurs in the field could be excused for doing the same. The historian John Fiske, popularizer of Darwin and Spencer, gave almost unqualified endorsement to the Morgan-Bandelier theory in his deservedly popular work, *The Discovery of America* (1892). In a long introductory section on "Ancient America," Fiske reviewed the literature and paid tribute to the pioneers of revisionism, Robertson, Gallatin, and Cass, but dismissed Wilson as "ignorant, uncritical, and full of wild fancies." It was Morgan, "whose minute and profound acquaintance with Indian life was joined with a power of penetrating the hidden implications of facts, so keen and so sure as to amount to genius," who had completed the revolution in historical interpretation. Morgan had seen the nature of the Spanish delusion. "He saw that what they mistook for feudal castles owned by great lords, and inhabited by dependent retainers, were really huge communal houses, owned and inhabited by clans, or rather by segments of overgrown clans." Fiske conceded that Morgan saw this so vividly "that it betrayed him now and then into a somewhat impatient and dogmatic manner of statement; but that was a slight fault, for what he saw was not the outcome of dreary speculation but of scientific insight."

Morgan's researches, added Fiske, had been fully sustained by the subsequent investigations of Bandelier, who joined to a "rare sagacity and untiring industry as a field archaeologist . . . such a thorough knowledge of Mexican literature as few men before him have possessed. Armed with such resources, Mr. Bandelier is doing for the ancient history of America work as significant as that which Mommsen has done for Rome, or Baur for the beginnings of Christianity." [45]

Yet Fiske was a writer of penetrating intelligence, and not devoid of critical spirit. After summarizing and accepting Morgan's three-stage scheme of social evolution, he cautioned his readers that "in all wide generalizations of this sort the case is liable to be somewhat unduly simplified." "The story of human progress is really not quite so easy to decipher as such descriptions would make it appear, and when we have laid down rules of this sort we need not be surprised if we now and then come upon facts that will not exactly fit into them." In such case, he observed, "it is best not to try to squeeze or distort the unruly facts, but to look and see if our facts will not bear a little qualification." Fiske offered some shrewd, good-humored comment on Morgan's dogmatic rejection, in "Montezuma's Dinner," of Aztec tables, chairs, secretaries, wine cellars, and wine. It was captious criticism of Morgan to chide Cortés for calling pulque "wine," when Morgan in the next breath called it "beer," pulque being neither the one nor the other. "And why is it 'hardly supposable' that pulque was used at dinner. Why should Mr. Morgan, who never dined with Montezuma, know so much more about *such things* than Cortés and Bernal Díaz, who did?" [46]

Another eminent historian, Justin Winsor, surveyed the dispute over "the so-called civilization of ancient Mexico and adjacent lands" in the monumental *Narrative and Critical History of America* of which he was editor. Although Winsor assumed an air of Olympian detachment, a guarded partiality for the revisionist school could be detected in his remarks. Winsor cited Robertson as the writer who first called attention to "the exaggerated and uncritical estimates of the older writers. . . ." Gallatin had been the first to recognize the "dangerous pitfalls of the pseudo-historical narratives" of the Indian chroniclers. In opposition to this trend stood Bancroft, who in the second volume of his *Native Races* "allied his opinion to those who most unhesitatingly accepted the old stories." Morgan had written the "most serious arraignment of these long-accepted views," and Bandelier's studies supported his interpretation. Noting the admiration expressed by Morgan and Bandelier for each other, Winsor drily commented that "this affectionate relation has very likely done something in unifying their intellectual sympathies." Winsor quoted copiously from Bandelier's articles in regard to moot points, but sometimes displayed a certain skepticism, as when he observed that Bandelier's argument against the use of the word "king" for Moctezuma was unconvincing. An implied doubt also appeared in Winsor's remark that Morgan inferred "communal living" from the data at his disposal, "although none of the early Spanish chroniclers mention such communism as existing." [47]

The Union Army officer, abolitionist, and historian Thomas Wentworth Higginson entered the dispute with an article on "The First Americans." He began by noting that a strong revisionist tide was sweeping over the interpretation of the ancient Indian cultures. He dated the beginning of that tide from the appearance of "Montezuma's Dinner." "The vast accumulation of facts in regard to the early American races then began to be classified and simplified; and with whatever differences of opinion as to details, the general opinion of scholars now inclines to the view which, when Morgan first urged it, was called startling and incredible." Higginson found Morgan's theory comparable in importance to that of Darwin's *Origin of Species*.

Despite this generous assessment, Higginson asked some sharp questions when he came to details. He concluded that Morgan's theory contained both strengths and weaknesses. The strength was that of "a strong, simple, intelligible, working hypothesis—not so much the best that has been offered as the first." Its principal weakness was that, "like many a promising theory in the natural sciences, it may prove to be only too simple, after all, and not quite adequate to account for the facts." Higginson complained that Morgan, "with all his great merits, had not always the moderation which gives such peculiar value to the works of Darwin."

In his search for perfect theoretical consistency Morgan ignored many difficulties and settled many points in an offhand manner. "There is something almost exasperating," continued Higginson, "in the positiveness with which he sometimes assumes as proved that which is only probable. Grant all his analogues of the gens and the communal dwelling, the fact is that in studying the Central American remains we are dealing with a race who had got beyond mere household architecture, and risen to the sphere of art, so that their attempts in this respect must enter into our estimate. In studying them from this point of view we encounter new difficulties which Mr. Morgan wholly ignores. The tales of the Spanish conquerors are scarcely harder to accept than the assumption that all the delicate beauty and all the artistic skill of the Yucatan edifices were lavished upon communal homes, built only to be densely packed with Indians 'in the Middle Status of Barbarism,' as Morgan calls them." [48]

No trace of the judicious approach that Higginson had used is visible in the unsigned review of the first volume of Bancroft's *History of Central America* in *The Nation*, January 25, 1883. Since the reviewer complained of Bancroft's failure to cite a bibliography by Bandelier, he may have been no other than Bandelier himself. The review also charged that Bancroft had failed to achieve his avowed ideal of writing scientific history. The book's grave fault consisted in its effort to perpetuate erroneous ideas about the condition of the American Indian at the time of the Conquest. In the face of the evidence supplied by recent criticism and exploration, Bancroft had preferred to rely on the "romances" of the early chroniclers and the "dreams" of John L. Stephens, holding out for the reality of an "Aztec Empire" and a Maya civilization with "the easy credibility of an earlier day." What had become of "all these marvels of a civilization worthy to be compared with that of Europe, over which the chroniclers so gloat? Who has ever seen anything that can properly be called a work of art that was indigenous to the continent?" The carvings and statues whose "delicate beauty" Higginson had praised were nothing more than "the uncouth, realistic work of half-barbarians." Their architecture was reduced to "the piling up of stones shaped by 'mere rule of thumb.'" All that was told about ancient Aztec civilization was a myth.[49]

Bancroft, who had followed the course of the dispute with growing irritation, gave vent to his wrath in a long essay, *The Early American Chroniclers* (1883). He professed to be startled that Morgan's speculations had been generally accepted by scholars, "that early American annals are by the light of this new theory transformed and to a great extent annulled, the eyes of the first comers having deceived them; that the aboriginal culture, politics, and religions, being not these but other things, as is clearly shown by the 'new interpretation,' the tales of the conquerors must accordingly be written anew, read and transformed by this new transforming light; that there never was an Aztec or a Maya Empire, but only wild tribes leagued like the northern savages; that Yucatan never had great cities, nor Montezuma a palace, but that as an ordinary Indian chief this personage had lived in the communal dwelling of his tribe; that we can see America as Cortés saw it, not in the words of Cortés and his companions, nor in the monumental remains of the south, but in the reflection of New Mexican villages, and through the mental vagaries of one man after the annihilation of facts presented by a hundred men. . . ."

Morgan, wrote Bancroft, allowed the chroniclers "to be right in whatever they say supporting his views; in all such statements as oppose his system they were in error." The "crotchets" of Morgan and his disciples Bancroft compared to the follies of "the poor, demented Lord Kingsborough" and the extravagances of Brasseur de Bourbourg, who, the more knowledge he brought to the subject, "the more confused he became."

As Bancroft renewed his attack on Morgan's evolutionary scheme for excluding the Aztecs from the precincts of civilization, he assailed the complacent assumptions of Western superiority implied in such schemes. What, he asked, was meant by "half-civilized, or quarter-civilized, or wholly civilized? A half-civilized nation is a nation half as civilized as ours. But is our civilized, fully civilized? Is there no higher culture, or refinement, or justice, or humanity in store for men than those formed on European models, which sanction coercion, bloody arbitrament, international robbery, the extermination of primitive peoples, and hide in society under more comely coverings all the iniquities of savagism." Again he insisted that civilization was not "a fixed condition, a goal attained, a complete and perfected idea or state." "Civilization and savagism are relative and not absolute terms. . . . The terms being rightly employed, there are no absolute savages and civilized peoples on the earth today; and when there are so many standards by which progress may be properly measured, is it wise to warp fundamental facts in dogmatically thrusting one people into the category of half civilized, and another but slightly different into that of one quarter savage?" [50]

Bancroft's view of civilization as a process, his stress on the shifting, evolving content and meaning of the term, was really not very different from Morgan's own vision of evolution as a continuous movement upward, illustrated by his reference in *Ancient Society* to "the next higher plane of society to which experience, intelligence and knowledge are steadily tending," or by his assertion that "a mere property career is not the final destiny of mankind, if progress is to be the law of the future as it has been of the past." [51]

Bancroft's essay did not attract much attention or change many minds. American intellectuals, dominated by evolutionism of the fixed-stage type, proud of having produced a Darwin in the person of Morgan, and smugly convinced, by and large, that they lived in the best of all times and places, were probably incapable of appreciating the force of Bancroft's arguments. His anti-imperialism, his denunciation of "international robbery" and "the extermination of primitive peoples," must have seemed empty rhetoric to some minds formed in the fashionable Spencerian mold. Justin Winsor, for example, complained of the offensive tone, the "bitter language," of *The Early American Chroniclers*, but ignored the substance of what Bancroft had to say. [52]

By 1900, however, the intellectual winds had begun to blow against Morgan and in favor of Bancroft. As clouds gathered on Western horizons, the nineteenth-century faith in science, technology, and progress began to wane. Materialist or technological interpretations of history became increasingly identified with Marxian socialism and thus acquired a subversive, heretical tinge. The new pragmatic, relativist, and historicist philosophies rejected rigid systems, universal laws, and the evaluation of one historical period or culture by the lights of another.

The movement away from Morganism in American anthropology received a marked impetus from Franz Boas, who came to the United States in 1888 and became curator for the Museum of Natural History in New York. Boas had been a junior colleague at the Berlin State Museum of Eduard Seler, the great scholar whose mission was to banish fantasy from Mexicanist studies. In 1896 Boas joined the faculty of Columbia University, where he taught ethnology for forty years. His influence on the development of the field was profound. He contributed to a process that was well under way and that Morgan himself had encouraged, the professionalization of anthropology as a discipline, with its own learned societies, journals, handbooks of method, and with a stress on field work.

More important was Boas' empiricism, his distrust of theory. Boas insisted that a particularist approach—the study of specific cultures in their particular historical context—was the most fruitful method of anthropological inquiry. A culture was a self-sufficient and homogeneous unit whose institutions and customs could not be understood except in their interrelations and in terms of the functions they performed. It followed that efforts to evaluate another culture were futile, since the standards employed must be subjective and irrelevant. The rejection of evaluation implied the equality of cultures, none being higher or lower than another. In the Boasian lexicon the terms "savagery," "barbarism," and the concept of evolutionary stages became virtually taboo. The implications of this egalitarian position could be awkward, as Leslie A. White has pointed out, since it declared "in effect that the culture of the Mayas was not higher than that of the Fuegians." [53] Yet in the context of that time, dominated by ethnocentric and racist stereotypes, the concept of the equality of cultures had a very salutary effect.

The rejection of Western standards as a yardstick for other cultures contributed, for example, to a growing appreciation of primitive art, hitherto regarded as crude and unimportant. William H. Holmes, second director of the Bureau of American Ethnology in the Smithsonian Institution, was a pioneer investigator of the problems of primitive art. His work helped not only to lift the shadow that Morgan and Bandelier had cast over the artistic achievements of ancient Mexico but to rehabilitate the early Mexican cultures in all respects.

Yet Holmes was a devoted follower of Morgan. In his paper "Contributions of American Archaeology to Human History," presented before the Congress of Americanists in Stuttgart, Germany, in 1904, Holmes accepted the three stages of savagery, barbarism, and civilization as "a scale on which the cultural achievements of any race or people in its struggle upward may be laid down," and added for good measure the stage of "pre-human development" at one end, and at the other, "the enlightened stage, reached as yet only by a limited number of nations." Holmes also accepted Morgan's dictum that in America "the high-water mark of culture barely reached the lower limit of civilization."

As soon as Holmes began to discuss the cultural achievements of the American barbarians, however, he displayed an enthusiasm that belied these disparaging distinctions. With respect to native sculpture, he wrote that "no people known to us has within the culture range of the Americans shown such versatility and power with the hammer and chisel, none that has embodied in stone a mythology so rich in imagery, including as it does forms of men, beasts, monsters, and cosmic phenomena in greatest variety." Holmes noted that a variety of metals were handled by the Indians "with a skill that astonished the conquerors," and observed that archaeology verified the statements of the Spanish historians. Of Indian ceramics he wrote that "the clay took on a multitude of forms in which were embodied a wide range of mythologic and esthetic concepts." [54]

Through intensive study of the materials, techniques, styles, and aesthetics of ancient Mexican art, Holmes acquired an expertise that enabled him to detect spurious antiquities in the national museums of Mexico and the United States, and to write a paper offering guidance in the identification of such spurious pieces.[55] His masterpiece, grand in scope but executed with painstaking attention to detail, was the *Archaeological Studies among the Ancient Cities of Mexico*. Part 2 of this work dealt with the monuments of Chiapas, Oaxaca, and the Valley of Mexico (1897). How different was Holmes's perspective from that of Bandelier, who had gazed on the same scenes some fifteen years before, is best shown by citing Holmes's first impressions of Monte Albán:

"In years of travel and mountain work I had met with many great surprises—such as that experienced on emerging suddenly from the forest-covered plateaus of Arizona into a full view of the Grand Canyon of the Colorado, or of obtaining unexpected glimpses of startling Alpine panoramas—but nothing had ever impressed me so deeply as this. The crest of Alban, one fourth of a mile wide and extending nearly a mile to the north, lay spread out at my feet. The surface was not covered with scattered and obscure piles of ruins as I had expected, but the whole mountain had been remodeled by the hand of man until not a trace of natural contour remained. There was a vast system of level courts inclosed by successive terraces and bordered by pyramids upon pyramids. Even the sides of the mountain descended in a succession of terraces, and the whole crest, separated by the hazy atmosphere from the dimly seen valleys more than a thousand feet below, seemed suspended in mid air. All was pervaded by a spirit of mystery, solitude, and utter desolation not relieved by a sound of life or a single touch of color." And Holmes exclaimed: "How striking must have been the effect when these pyramids were all crowned with imposing temples, when the great level plaza about them, 600 by 1,000 feet in extent, was brilliant with barbaric displays, and the inclosing ranges of terraces and pyramids were occupied by gathered throngs. Civilization has rarely conceived anything in the way of amphitheatric display more extensive than this." [56]

Holmes found the remains of Mitla "surpassingly interesting." In apparent reference to the recent downgrading of Indian culture, he wrote that Mitla confirmed the impression, "given by each great site in turn, that the pre-Spanish peoples had developed in certain lines, and especially in the temple building art, far beyond the stage of advancement ascribed by common estimate to the native races." Reflections on the engineering problems met and solved by the builders of Mitla led Holmes to conclusions about Indian political organization that were diametrically opposed to those of Morgan and Bandelier. "To transport masses of stone many tons in weight down a thousand feet of precipitous mountain face, accomplished by these stone age quarrymen, would be regarded as important undertakings even by our enterprising engineers of today. Their means and appliances were extremely simple, and much time must have been consumed in the work. In view of the vast results accomplished I believe we are warranted in assuming the employment of large numbers of men directed by a despotic power—a power not limited by the life of an individual but continued without break from generation to generation." [57]

Teotihuacán, wrote Holmes, "stands easily at the head of the ancient cities of Mexico." He affirmed that the people "were intelligent, enterprising, and powerful, and that their sway extended over a long period of time. Like the French archaeologist Désiré Charnay before him, Holmes noted that in addition to a ceremonial center the city contained a large residential area; he was also struck by the "singular absence of a warlike spirit." [58]

In his artistic judgments Holmes shared the traditional preference for Maya over Nahua sculpture. He observed that the sculpture of the highland peoples was generally limited to the making of single figures which rarely displayed any degree of realism. By contrast, Maya figures often displayed excellent proportions, and the skill and taste shown in the groupings of several figures indicated "advance toward higher planes of artistic development."

Holmes was far from denying artistic intent and value to the Nahua works. True, Nahua sculpture was largely of religious inspiration. "Whatever there is of grace and symmetry of form, whatever of elaboration and refinement, was, first of all, a tribute to the mysterious forces of nature personified in the various forms sculptured. Yet the influence of aesthetic notions was all-pervading; plain blunt statement was not enough; there was keen appreciation of the qualities of form regarded with favor by the highly cultured eye of the civilized world." Holmes cited the realization of the feathered serpent concept, "where every line of head, body, and feather embellishment is bold, graceful, and telling."

Among the Nahua sculptures Holmes saw no works "so colossal, so noble, so imbued with aesthetic feeling as . . . the great monoliths of Guatemala and Honduras." Yet, taking all points into account, he was inclined to place the figure of the goddess Coatlicue, "brutal and terrible as it is," very close to the head of the American list.[59] Nothing could better indicate the revolution in taste that was under way.

Holmes's book on the ancient cities of Mexico created serious difficulties for those who argued that Aztec civilization was only a little above the Iroquois cultural level. The beginnings of a revolt are suggested by the exasperated tone of an article on "Ancient Aztec Cities and Civilization" in *The American Antiquarian* in 1900. The author was Stephen D. Peet, former editor of the journal and a well-known writer on archaeological topics. The Spanish chroniclers, wrote Peet, did not stop to ask the history of the people before they gave the name "city" to the places they entered. Accepting the evidence of their senses, they applied the terms commonly used among them to the men and objects they saw. These names clearly showed that "there was a very different condition of things among the ancient Mexicans from that which prevailed among the northern tribes. Consequently the term *pueblo* should not be applied to the cities, nor *medicine lodge* to the temples, nor *council houses* to the palaces, nor *medicine men* to the priests, nor *tribal chiefs* to the kings." Peet cited Holmes's description of Monte Albán to prove that Spanish accounts of Aztec and Maya splendor, so often called "extravagant exaggerations" by critics, were in the main correct. He closed with copious citations from the Spanish chroniclers demonstrating the refinement, luxury, and grandeur of Aztec civilization.[60]

The reaction against the Morgan-Bandelier reconstruction of ancient Mexican society had begun, but the theory had a very tenacious hold on life. Although scholars gradually discarded its most extravagant claims, a substantial residue remained. As late as 1940 anthropologists of the eminence of George C. Vaillant and Robert Lowie accepted the validity of key elements in the Morgan-Bandelier doctrine. How the structure of that doctrine was dismantled in recent decades will be told in another chapter.

Before we leave this curious episode in the history of American anthropology, one caution is in order. The Morgan-Bandelier theory about ancient Mexico was more than a massive aberration that led American social science down a blind alley. Just as the romantic interpretation of Prescott and Brasseur de Bourbourg corrected the skeptical excesses of De Pauw and Robertson, so Morgan and Bandelier applied a needed astringent to the inflated portrayal of Aztec civilization in the romantic histories. Morgan's charge that Bancroft's book on *The Native Races* was filled with kings and empires "as thick as blackbirds" contained more than a kernel of truth. The stress of Morgan and Bandelier on the common elements in the cultures of such Indian groups as the Aztecs, the Pueblo Indians, and the Iroquois was in principle sound. Equally sound, in principle, was their conception of Indian development through stages defined by the level of social integration—to use modern terminology—and technological criteria. After an eclipse of half a century, Morgan's evolutionist strategy, purged of its rigidity and arbitrariness, has returned to anthropological favor and serves as the basis for new and sounder reconstructions of the process whose brilliant climax was Aztec civilization.

CHAPTER THIRTEEN

Farewell to Fantasy:
From Orozco y Berra to Seler

The Morgan-Bandelier reconstruction of Aztec society excited little interest outside the United States. Most foreign scholars apparently considered the theory too bizarre to take seriously; the reactions of the few who deigned to comment were usually unfavorable. Yet these scholars accepted Morgan's evolutionist premises. Indeed their own arbitrary application of sociological laws to the history of ancient Mexico produced some strange results.

By the end of the century, however, a new empiricist, inductive method had begun to drive the spirit of fantasy from the Mexicanist field. The German Eduard Seler and the Mexican Francisco del Paso y Troncoso pioneered in the movement to establish the study of ancient Mexico on rigorously scientific foundations. Their stress on a critical, comparative method and on mastery of the Indian languages in which the most authentic sources were preserved helped to found a school. Subjecting the sources to intensive analysis, they wrote monographs and commentaries on codices that heightened appreciation of Aztec culture by revealing the world of meaning and imagination hidden behind the esoteric language of codices, myths, prayers, and sculptures.

Two circumstances help to explain the general indifference of Mexican scholars to the Morgan-Bandelier theories. First, Mexican historians knew the sources too well to swallow the notion that Moctezuma's palace was a joint tenement house or that the Aztec government was democratic. Second, by 1850 the skeptical reaction against the romantic excesses of Mier and Bustamante had run its course. Mexico's political and intellectual climate after that date favored a revival of approving interest in her ancient civilizations.

The disasters suffered by Mexico during the dictatorship of Santa Anna caused a widespread revulsion against his conservative policies and spurred a gathering of all opposition forces. In 1855 a liberal revolt overthrew the dictator and ushered in the movement called the Reforma. Like the older liberalism of the 1830's, the Reforma sought to destroy feudalism and implant capitalism in Mexico.[1] Its ideology, however, was more spirited than the cool intellectual liberalism of José Luis Mora; it had closer links with the Indian masses, from which sprang such liberal leaders as Benito Juárez, Ignacio Ramírez, and Ignacio Altamirano. Moreover, with the Reforma came the rise of a flaming nationalism. A vast stock-taking of Mexico's natural and spiritual resources and intensive study of her past were among the ways in which nationalist sentiment was expressed. Liberal historians, in their search for traditions and precedents, naturally focused their gaze on the glories of ancient Mexico, and thus helped both to document the creative capacity of the ancient Mexicans and to restore the self-confidence of a nation badly shaken by the results of the Mexican War and other disasters.

An editorial note in the bulletin of the Instituto Nacional de Geografía y Estadística (1850) illustrates use of the splendor of ancient Mexico to improve the national image. The editor deplored the distorted picture of Mexico presented by foreign writers who knew only its recent turbulent history. In order to correct the record, he recalled the achievements of the ancient Mexicans: "A division of the year more exact than that of the Greeks and Romans; the use of ideographic writing and of maguey paper; maps of the country and of the lands traversed by their forebears; cities, roads, dikes, and canals; immense and precisely oriented pyramids; civil, military, and religious institutions—all this entitles the Mexicans to be regarded as the most cultured people the Spaniards found in the New World." [2]

In their enthusiasm for ancient Mexico, the liberal historians were akin to creole historians of the late colonial and revolutionary periods; but the new nationalist school, adhering to the positivist, scientific method of its founder, José Fernando Ramírez, avoided the mysticism and exaggerations of a Mier or a Bustamante. If one or another of the school sometimes strayed into fantasy, this usually resulted from an excess of scientism, from the desire to disclose the natural, historical roots of the most fanciful creations of the Indian mind. More sober than Mier, they never offered Aztec statecraft as a model for the Mexican republic or invoked the shades of Cuauhtémoc and Moctezuma to rejoice at the downfall of Santa Anna.

The debates of the Constitutional Convention of 1856 and 1857 reflect this realistic tendency of the generation of the Reforma in that they contain almost no allusions to ancient Mexico. Of perhaps only two such references in Francisco Zarco's massive collection of those debates, one was made by the radical Ignacio Ramírez, himself a full-blooded Indian. Ramírez recalled the diverse cultural traditions of the various Indian groups in a speech urging a territorial reorganization of Mexico: "The Tlaxcalan points with pride to the fields where stood the wall that separated him from the Mexican. The Yucatecan asks the Otomí if his forebears left monuments as admirable as those preserved at Uxmal. The cathedral nearby, gentlemen, that proud cathedral of which we are so vain, reflects less knowledge and talent than the humble stone preserving the Aztec calendar, which leans against it."

The pious moderate José María Lafragua, by contrast, evoked the horror of Aztec human sacrifice when he opposed inclusion in the Constitution of an article granting freedom of worship. Lafragua objected, perhaps not very seriously, that such tolerance might lead to the erection in Mexico City of not only a Lutheran church, a mosque, and a synagogue but also a *teocalli* that would be the scene of bloody sacrifices. He conceded that this was not very likely, but suggested that the Indians, if informed that they could practice their old religion, might next demand restoration of Cuauhtémoc's throne.[3]

For all its turbulence, the decade of the fifties produced a remarkable amount of research and publications on ancient Mexico. Under the moderate liberal government of 1848 to 1852, José Fernando Ramírez became director of the Museo Nacional and attempted a scientific reorganization of that institution. He also contributed to a monument of Mexican scholarship, the *Diccionario universal de historia y geografía* (1852–1953). Articles by Ramírez included a series of sketches of Aztec kings that displayed a lucid style and sound scholarship. An echo of the recent conflict with the United States appeared to sound in this comment on the life of Cuitláhuac: "The memory of Cuitláhuac, today forgotten like that of Cuauhtémoc, will be indelibly preserved in the pages of history, which presents the noble figures of two Mexican heroes towering over a generation of giants who knew how to die under the ruins and embers of their country and city." [4]

Exiled by Santa Anna on the eve of the dictator's downfall, Ramírez departed for Europe, where he remained until March, 1856, studying Mexican codices in private and public collections. He returned to find Mexico aflame with the Three Years' War between liberals and conservatives. Avoiding political activity, he devoted himself to educational work and research.

Amid the violence of war, other Mexican scholars also continued to lay a documentary base for the study of ancient and colonial Mexico. In 1857 and 1858, for example, Antonio García Cubas published reproductions of two Aztec migration maps, with commentary by Ramírez. In 1858 Joaquín García Icazbalceta published the first volume of his important *Documentos para la historia de México*.

Beaten in the field by the beginning of 1861, the conservatives called for help from the French Emperor Napoleon III. Napoleon, who had several motives for wishing to establish a sphere of influence in Mexico, responded favorably. Besides dispatching an expeditionary force, Napoleon mobilized French scientific and historical talent to study the geography, natural resources, and antiquities of his protectorate. His well-meaning puppet, the Emperor Maximilian, who was imposed on the Mexicans by French bayonets in 1864, found time amid his imperial concerns to reflect on the needs of Mexican culture. In 1865, by his order, the Museo Nacional was removed from its rooms in the University of Mexico to new quarters in the Palacio Nacional; here it remained until 1964. He also established a number of scientific commissions, two of which functioned effectively: the commission of Pachuca and the commission of the Valley of Mexico. The report of the former, directed by the engineer Ramón Almaraz, included a pioneer study of the pyramids of Teotihuacán.[5] Impressed by Maximilian's good will, cherishing the illusion of a stable and prosperous Mexico ruled by an enlightened monarch, two distinguished liberal historians, Ramírez and Manuel Orozco y Berra, accepted offices in the imperial regime.

A work published under the empire and dedicated to Maximilian showed that liberals had no monopoly on concern with the Indian, past and present. In 1864 Francisco Pimentel, an able philologist, published a study of the Indian problem. He began with a survey of ancient Mexican civilization in which he noted the numerous striking contradictions: between the barbarous Aztec religion and the Aztecs' "pure and generous morality"; between the supposed republicanism of Tlaxcala and the tyranny that prevailed elsewhere; between the scrupulous observation of international law in waging war and the custom of immolating innumerable victims on the Aztec altars; between the Aztecs' advances in astronomy and their lack of much more rudimentary arts.[6]

Pimentel conceded that Aztec morality was superior and that Aztec domestic customs were marked by an "exquisite urbanity"; Aztec women enjoyed all the rights due their sex. He hastened to add that he did not mean to imply that he mourned the passing of Aztec civilization. On the contrary, he argued that the defects of the Aztec system, "their barbarous religion, the despotism of their rulers, their cruel education, and their communism and slavery," were largely responsible for the degraded state of the modern Indian.

Pimentel's obsession with Aztec communism might lead the modern reader mistakenly to suppose that the specter haunting Europe had begun to haunt Mexico. The vigilant Pimentel noted that the Aztecs distributed food to the poor at their festivals. He triumphantly concluded: "There were poor people in Mexico, yet communism existed there, that communism which according to certain reformers offers a solution for misery." Pimentel's own solutions for the Indian problem closely resembled those of liberal writers on the subject: abolish Indian communal land tenure; let wealthy landowners sell surplus lands to the government for resale on easy terms to the Indians; encourage the coming of European immigrants who should provide models of industry and initiative for the Indians; spread European influence by encouraging race mixture between the Indians and such immigrants.[7]

The imperial experiment ended in tragedy. Napoleon III, faced with mounting difficulties in Mexico and at home, decided to cut his losses by liquidating the Mexican enterprise. Although Maximilian was urged by Napoleon to depart with the French troops, he, proclaiming Mexico his *patria*, chose to remain. He met his death before a Mexican firing squad in June, 1867. Ramírez left Mexico to spend his last years in Europe; he died in Bonn, Germany, in 1871. Orozco y Berra stayed on to suffer disgrace and sentencing to fines and imprisonment by a Juárez court, but was eventually pardoned and became sufficiently rehabilitated to rejoin the liberal intellectual élite.

Juárez, symbol of resistance to the foreign usurper, resumed the office of president in August, 1867. In the cultural field the new regime concentrated on educational reform; under the positivist Gabino Barreda, this reform aimed at the creation of an élite trained in the spirit of science rather than in metaphysics, an élite capable of laying the foundations of a bourgeois order. Despite the financial straits from which it suffered, the Juárez regime did not forget the Museo Nacional; 500 pesos monthly were assigned for its upkeep, and Gumesindo Mendoza was appointed its director.

Juárez had barely begun the task of reconstruction at his death in 1871. His successor, Sebastián Lerdo de Tejada, had to deal with a rising movement of protest which charged his government with violations of republican legality and of the Constitution of 1857. In 1876 a revolt brought Porfirio Díaz to power. The new regime continued and even increased support for the Museo Nacional. The first issue of the museum's *Anales* appeared in 1877, with articles on Aztec topics by Manuel Orozco y Berra and Gumesindo Mendoza. These essays were vigorously pro-Aztec in tone.

Orozco, in his article on the dedication of the Great Temple of Tenochtitlán, followed Ramírez in defending the Aztecs against the charge of cannibalism; in a paper on the Codex Mendoza he again supported Ramírez against Prescott, who had complained that Aztec hieroglyphic writing lacked clarity and precision.[8]

Mendoza, writing on the Aztec cosmogony, said he had found proof in the Vatican Codex that the ancient Mexicans, like the

Greeks, had conceived of four primordial elements. He maintained that the Codex depicted, among other things, the formation of suns and world out of the chaotic play of atoms and molecules. This proved to Mendoza that the ancient Nahuas had attained a level of culture as high as that of the foremost peoples of Old World antiquity. The Aztecs were equally advanced in the moral order. Mendoza conceded that their religion was polytheist, but perceived a gradual emergence of monotheist ideas. The coming of Cortés interrupted Aztec religious progress and deprived the Indians of their gods and their moral order. As a result the modern Indians were "pariahs practicing a gross idolatry, half Christian, half pagan." Mendoza expressed the hope that the Mexican government would comprehend its own true interest and attempt to uplift the Indian race so that it could march jointly with the mestizos along the road of progress.[9]

As the Porfiriato advanced, such mingling of social idealism with scholarship grew rare, and did not revive until the last decadent phase of the Díaz dictatorship. Mexican scholars learned to shun reference to current problems save in the most guarded and decorous way.[10] The massive drift of Porfirista policy in favor of native and foreign great landowners and against the Indian tended to make protest against that policy futile and possibly even dangerous. The ideologists of the regime justified the usurpation of Indian lands on the "scientific" grounds that the land should belong to those who could best exploit it. Indians who resisted such encroachments were charged with communism and "violations of public order."[11] Scholars found it more profitable to confine their attention to Indians who had been dead for a number of centuries. For its part, the Díaz regime regarded such academic activity benevolently, assigning funds for archaeological research and for the repair of monuments. This support gave Díaz the fame of being an enlightened statesman, attracted tourists, and directed the energies of able young men into harmless channels.

A high point in the exaltation of the Indian past under Díaz was the unveiling of a statue of Cuauhtémoc on the Paseo de la Reforma in the capital in 1887. The Jefe Supremo himself graced the occasion, and Francisco del Paso y Troncoso made an emotional speech in Náhuatl (translated into Spanish for the benefit of the greater part of the audience) in which he dealt with the

principal episodes in the last stand of the Aztecs. The Díaz regime
gave more proof of its interest in archaeology with the creation
in 1885 of the office of Inspector y Conservador de Monumentos
Arqueológicos. Unfortunately, this measure was tainted with corruption and favoritism. The man appointed to the office was
Leopoldo Batres, a crony of Díaz'. Some of the antiquities Batres
was supposed to protect he seems to have sold to foreigners. He
seriously botched the restoration of Teotihuacán, and in the restoration of Mitla had his own name carved in gold letters on a lintel
of the Hall of Columns! [12]

Not all the archaeological appointments of the Díaz period were
so unfortunate. In 1889 Francisco del Paso y Troncoso replaced
Jesús Sánchez as director of the Museo Nacional. The museum
and its *Anales* had already acquired a solid reputation for scholarship through the work of such men as Orozco y Berra and Alfredo
Chavero. Under Paso's direction the museum became the scene of
even more intense activity; from its press issued Náhuatl grammars,
reproductions of codices, and monographs. To the Columbian
Exposition of Madrid, 1892, the Mexican government sent a commission that included Joaquín García Icazbalceta, Alfredo Chavero,
and Paso y Troncoso. Mexico's tribute to Columbus included a
magnificent volume of colored reproductions of codices, designed,
in the words of Chavero, to give Europeans a synoptic view of a
great, though strange, civilization.[13] Aztec civilization was also
represented at Madrid by many antiquities, including plaster casts
of the great monoliths and the remains of the Boturini collection.

The last years of the Porfiriato were very productive in regard
to Mexicanist studies. Paso y Troncoso himself engaged in an
immense research activity. He passed many years in Europe in
search of archival sources for the history of ancient and colonial
Mexico; he photographed a large number of the documents he
found. Almost simultaneously with Eduard Seler, Paso recognized
the capital importance of the corpus of Sahagún materials dispersed
in various European repositories and undertook the gigantic task
of organizing, translating, and publishing these materials. Other
missions to Europe, like that of Antonio Peñafiel, sought to recover
for Mexico such collections of Mexican documents as that of
Aubin.[14]

The twilight years of the Porfiriato also saw a unique experiment in United States–Mexican intellectual cooperation. Franz Boas dreamed of establishing in Mexico a school of advanced archaeological studies where young Mexicans and North Americans could receive training in the method of scientific investigation, later going out to teach it to others. With the aid of several United States academic institutions and the Díaz government, the International School of American Archaeology got off to a faltering start in 1910. Eduard Seler was its first director, followed in 1911 by Boas, who was succeeded during the school's last two years by A. N. Tozzer and Manuel Gamio. Here budding archaeologists such as J. Alden Mason and Gamio received their first training in the method of stratigraphical investigation, then unknown in Mexico. The outbreak of revolution in 1910 disrupted the work of the school; in 1915 the hostility aroused in Mexico by Woodrow Wilson's order to attack Veracruz dealt it a deathblow.[15]

In the spectrum of attitudes Porfirista historians displayed toward Aztec civilization, admiration or even eulogy was certainly dominant; however, some men sharply dissented from this position, and even among the *indigenistas* various shades of opinion can be distinguished. These differences reflected not so much personal idiosyncrasies as ideological divisions within the Porfirista camp. The Porfiristas were a strangely assorted coalition that included old-time Juárez liberals, who wistfully clung to their libertarian ideals, ardent Catholic conservatives, and hard-boiled *científicos* contemptuous of democracy and convinced that the Indians were an inferior race.

A classic example of Porfirista historiography is the *Historia antigua y de la conquista de México* of Manuel Orozco y Berra. Forgiven for his collaboration with the Maximilian regime, and supported by a modest official salary, Orozco devoted the remainder of his life to the writing of this work. It was published in 1880 and 1881 at the expense of the Mexican government.

Orozco opened his work with a historical credo composed of Catholic orthodoxy, positivism, and nationalism. "I write under the influence of what I have seen, read, and calculated, always searching for truth and justice. I respect religion and trust in the road of progress which the Law imposed on humanity. I subordinate my ideas to these principles: God, country, and family."

In general, Orozco's historical method was the positivist, socio-logical method of Ramírez, which attempted to disclose the nat-ural, material roots of all historical phenomena, and explained all behavior and ideas, no matter how irrational they might seem in modern eyes, as the product of a given stage of social evolution. Orozco's treatment of Aztec myths is characteristic. Ramírez had long ago argued in his notes on Prescott's *Conquest of Mexico* that such myths, however absurd they might seem, were an important historical source because they illuminated, though in a distorted manner, actual historical events, natural catastrophes, and the Indian mode of thought. Orozco made much the same point. "Mythology," he wrote, "is not a subject of vain curiosity. It forms part of history, relating in an enigmatic manner great cataclysms and the feats of distinguished men."

Unfortunately Orozco's uncritical application of this principle, his dogged determination to get at the natural roots of the most poetic and fanciful creations of the native mind, produced some grotesque results. Thus he reduced the charming myth of the creation of the sun and the moon by the self-sacrifice of the gods to a symbolic version of an actual historical event, the replacement of the ancient religion of Teotihuacán by that of its supposed con-querors, the Toltecs. And Orozco related, with all the detail and matter-of-factness of a Brasseur de Bourbourg, precisely what had happened on the summits of the pyramids of Teotihuacán a thou-sand years before.[16]

Orozco's case demonstrates what the Morgan-Bandelier theories have already shown, that a supposed "scientific" approach to his-tory offers no guarantee against unwarranted speculation. The statement of León-Portilla that Orozco vigorously rejected all fantasy is hardly tenable.[17] Orozco's unappeasable urge to provide natural explanations for every Indian legend or belief repeatedly led him to construct what may be called scientific fantasies.

It is true that he rejected the tradition that Quetzalcóatl was one of several possible Saint Thomases on sound historical grounds, but he substituted an explanation that was only a little less fanciful. Assuming that the similarities between the Aztec and Christian religions could not be the result of simple chance, and noting that the Quetzalcóatl of Indian legend was white, bearded, and a civi-lizer, he concluded that he was an Icelandic missionary. According to Orozco, this man and his followers not only introduced Christian doctrines and rites into Mexico but also taught the Toltecs agriculture, metallurgy, and other arts. Unfortunately the Christian doctrines he had implanted soon lost their pristine purity as a result of the victory won by the cult of Tezcatlipoca and the admixture of pagan elements.[18] This is little more than the traditional version of Sigüenza, Veytia, Mier, and Bustamante, with the substitution of an Icelandic missionary for Saint Thomas.

Orozco followed Ramírez closely in his discussion of Aztec human sacrifice. This institution corresponded to a certain universal stage of human development; it represented, paradoxically enough, some material and moral progress over the previous stage. Orozco rebuked those sentimental philosophers who saw only the horror of human sacrifice and not its profound religious content. Moved by his ardent piety, Orozco went farther than Ramírez in his apologia for human sacrifice. Borrowing a thought from the Catholic philosopher Joseph de Maistre, he wrote that the offense of human sacrifice was nothing in comparison with the crime of atheism. "I prefer the human victim to the absence of God and his altar from the system of the atheist; for me the fetish of the African Negro contains more sound sense than the evasive and gloomy 'who knows?' of the skeptic." Orozco again employed Ramírez' sociological approach in his analysis of Aztec ritual cannibalism. He cautioned his readers not to construe his remarks as indicating approval, even remotely, of human sacrifice or cannibalism. "This is an explanation, not a defense." [19]

Orozco stressed the eclectic nature of Aztec religion as it was reflected in the diverse origins of the gods who swarmed in its pantheon. The Aztecs, observed Orozco, were not thinkers or philosophers; they were content to leave theological speculation to other peoples, whose gods and theogonies they freely borrowed. There was an old-fashioned flavor to Orozco's argument that the Aztec gods were morally superior to those of the Greeks and Romans. "Attentive to their duties, they had no time to waste in diversions; they were less poetic, but considerably more virtuous than the Greek deities. They did not busy themselves plotting incest, seducing maidens, or staining bridal beds." [20]

Orozco expressed the same approval of the Aztec laws and juridical system. The laws were harsh, but well adapted to a stiff-necked people who scorned physical suffering. The Aztec legal code was advanced, moderate, and just; it promoted respect for authority, the family, and property. In some respects, declared Orozco, it was very superior·to the codes of the barbarians who invaded Europe. Aztec slavery was more humane and rational than that of the Romans; by contrast with the barbarous Roman doctrine, the slave woman's child was free. This represented an enormous moral advance.[21]

Turning to Aztec culture, Orozco drew the conventional distinction between Texcoco and Mexico-Tenochtitlán. "Mexico was the Rome, Texcoco was the Athens of Anáhuac." Conventional, too, was Orozco's treatment of Aztec painting and sculpture. He insisted that Mexican drawing was incorrect, the contours of its figures angular and hard; the Aztec artist had no sense of proportion. On the other hand, Orozco defended the expressive power of Aztec picture writing and devoted long, erudite chapters to this subject and to the Náhuatl language.

Orozco's detailed survey of Aztec daily life, economic activity, and social classes (comprising the second book of the first volume) retains most of its original value. The discussion of Aztec social organization amounted to a massive refutation of the revisionist views of Morgan and Bandelier. With a wealth of documentation, Orozco demonstrated the existence of nobles, private estates, commoners, slaves, serfs, and, over all, a despotic ruler who was adored like a god. The privileged classes lived comfortably, the lot of the commoners was hard and laborious. With a Social Darwinist complacency, Orozco commented that the same conditions existed today, "from absolute necessity," in the most civilized nations.[22]

Orozco's *indigenista* fervor reached new heights when he came to describe the beauty and majesty of Tenochtitlán. He reproved skeptical writers with the acid remark: "This was no city of barbarians, resembling in the imaginations of some authors the disorderly and dirty villages of the redskins of our day." He took Alamán to task for expressing doubt about the grandeur of Tenochtitlán. Alamán had noted the absence of important Aztec ruins, whereas Rome, so often sacked and destroyed, possessed monuments of every kind. The comparison seemed to Orozco unjust and partisan. The conquerors of Rome, he argued, respected and sought to preserve the remains of ancient buildings; the conquerors of Mexico looked upon the Indian works with horror or contempt and destroyed them to make room for their own buildings.

Even casual excavation had brought to light "immense, beautifully sculptured fragments of porphyry and trachyte, representing monstrous symbolisms, votive stones, historical commemorations, astronomical calculations. These things reveal a civilization that was advanced, though different from the European: a city of great edifices, capable of housing those monoliths; solid foundations to support them; a certain grandeur in construction; many advances in architecture, mechanics, and ornament, all without the benefit of iron and machines. Mexico's ruins have produced enough fragments to prove that it was a great Indian city, but the white people have destroyed almost all of them." [23]

The last semblance of Orozco's vaunted impartiality disappeared in his account of the Conquest. His sympathies were entirely with the Aztec defenders of Tenochtitlán. The heroes of his narrative are Xiconténcatl, who counseled stubborn Tlaxcalan resistance to the Spanish invaders; Cuitláhuac, who advised against admitting the Spaniards into Tenochtitlán; and above all the gallant Cuauhtémoc, advocate of war to the end. In dark colors appear the ignoble Moctezuma, weak and superstitious, and the treacherous Texcocan Ixtlilxóchitl, traitor to his royal brother and to his people. In every question involving a decision on Spanish guilt—the massacre of Cholula, Moctezuma's death, Alvarado's assault on the Indian celebrants in the Great Square of Tenochtitlán—Orozco found for the Indian prosecution.

When the fighting ends, however, Orozco returns to his former posture of serene impartiality. Viewing the Conquest in the light of the long evolutionary process and the law of progress, he gave it his unqualified approval. "To wipe the Aztec religion from the face of the earth was an immense benefit; to replace it with Christianity was to make immense strides along the road of civilization. For us this conclusion is axiomatic, self-evident, clear as the sun at noon." Orozco went on, in the manner of Alamán, to recount the material and social advantages brought by the Conquest. They amounted to "an immense social revolution, whose major consequences included recovery by the *macehuales* of human dignity, whereas before they were reduced to the miserable condition of beasts of burden." Yet Orozco expressed wistful regret that amid the general shipwreck of ancient Mexican civilization some of its attainments had not been preserved: its astronomical lore, and the technical secrets that would explain the marvelous quality of its gold- and silverwork, its pottery, and its textiles. He closed by dismissing as hypothetical and futile the question of whether it would have been better for the Conquest to have been made by some other people than the Castilians. "The Castilians conquered America, and their conquest favored the progressive advance of humanity." [24]

In 1886 Alfredo Chavero published his own *Historia antigua y de la conquista*, the first volume of the large collaborative work *México a través de los siglos*, edited by Mariano Riva Palacio. Younger by some twenty years than Orozco, Chavero represented a more militant wing of the old liberal party. He had fought in that party's ranks from youth and shared with Juárez the privations of the northward retreat following the French intervention. His literary talents—for he was a poet and dramatist of the romantic school—gave his work a stylistic quality that Orozco's lacked. Chavero declared with excessive modesty that the contents of his book belonged entirely to historians who had preceded him.

It is true, as Rico González observes,[25] that Chavero sometimes does little more than paraphrase the material of his friend and mentor Orozco, but it is not the whole truth. The book is not merely Orozco served up in more palatable form. Chavero was a careful student of codices and manuscripts who edited works by Ixtlilxóchitl, Durán, and Muñoz Camargo, and published numerous essays on Aztec topics. He had his own judgments on problems ranging from the identity of Quetzalcóatl to the population of Tenochtitlán. Add to these differences the fact that his sociological interpretation was more sophisticated, that his *indigenismo* was more pronounced, and that a certain anticlericalism replaces the Catholic bias of Orozco.

Chavero opened with a survey of the sources and authorities for the history of ancient Mexico. He used an evolutionist, sociological yardstick to determine the value of these materials. He noted the importance of the picture writings, traditions, and legends of the Indians, and praised the friars who had preserved them. Ramírez, "founder of the method of writing history that we employ today," had made a signal contribution to the understanding of the Indian glyphs. Aztec sculptures of their gods also possessed much informational value, for "religious ideas enable us to comprehend the level of advancement and the social tendencies of a people." The sixteenth-century chroniclers were simple, truthful men who faithfully reproduced what they heard from the mouths of Indians or found in the picture writings. Unfortunately, they lacked critical sense, and attempted to link Mexican antiquity to Biblical traditions.

A critical spirit awakened in the seventeenth century, but the "religious and exaggerated ideas of the epoch" led men like Sigüenza y Góngora astray. Chavero was equally severe with Ixtlilxóchitl for crediting his forebears with a degree of culture incompatible with the time and social milieu in which they lived, and insisted that the two poems attributed by him to Nezahualcóyotl were spurious. The historiography of the eighteenth century displayed the weaknesses of its precedessor, "because the same social epoch continued," but evidence of some growth of critical spirit appeared in Clavigero's efforts to organize a chronology for Mexican history, to establish a logical succession of events.

At the end of the century, as if to inform historians that truth lay in the monuments, came the discovery of the Calendar Stone and other monoliths. Humboldt had charted new paths for the science of antiquity and initiated a judicious inquiry into the relations between the civilization of ancient Mexico and those of the Old World, but Chavero pointed out that this approach led to new exaggerations, as shown by Brasseur de Bourbourg, who, in his striving for originality, had invented a history that was all his own. Prescott, for all his learning, had committed serious errors in his history of the Conquest and failed to understand the character of the ancient Mexican civilization. A reform in historiography was needed, and the glory of initiating that reform fell to the lot of Ramírez, whose work was continued by his friend and disciple Orozco y Berra.[26]

Turning to the remote origins and early history of the Nahua race, Chavero displayed a spirit of "scientific fantasy" as riotous as that of Orozco. The Nahuas, he assured his readers, had come to Mexico by way of Atlantis. The legend of the four suns represented the great cataclysms that mankind had experienced. The

Nahuas retained a perfect memory of it, and the Indian codices were completely authentic sources of information on these disasters. In the Codex Vaticanus Chavero found a depiction of the Deluge. Not even the celebrated painting of Poussin gave such an adequate notion of that catastrophe. Chavero went on to affirm that the same Codex portrayed most precisely the second cataclysm, the coming of the Ice Age in which men lived in caves and died in great numbers in struggle with the elements and wild beasts. The monkeys shown in the Codex puzzled Chavero, as they had Orozco. Orozco had speculated that they symbolized the advent of the Negro race in Mexico. Chavero speculated, no less wildly, that they represented the appearance of the first apes, or perhaps the fact that men took refuge, like apes, in caves. In any case, Chavero found irresistible the argument that the four suns of the Nahuas were "cosmogonic ages, true catastrophes for the race, whose memory they preserved, indelibly engraved in the great library of the memory of this people." [27]

Chavero displayed an intense enthusiasm for the Indian mythology. Like Orozco, he regarded the legend of the creation of the sun and the moon as a symbolic account of the triumph of the Toltec religion over the older cult of Teotihuacán. Neither the Hindu Vedas nor Hesiod contained so lovely a legend, simultaneously historical and astronomical. Chavero spoke with the same tone of eulogy of the Nahua religious conceptions. Man's need to worship something superior to himself led the Nahuas to create a poetic religion that found its gods among the stars of the firmament, "that sublime temple of light and mysteries." They had conceived the idea of a supreme creator god, who was a pair, male and female. Chavero was sure that the early Nahuas never used human sacrifice. This was a later development that the Aztecs carried to a monstrous extreme. Nahua religious sculptures also drew Chavero's praise; he described the Coatlicue as the "most beautiful idol in the Museo Nacional." [28] He thus became the first commentator to apply the adjective "beautiful" to that awesome goddess.

On one point Chavero dissented sharply from his colleague Orozco y Berra. He rejected alike the older view that Quetzalcóatl was Saint Thomas and Orozco's idea that he was an Icelandic bishop who had found his way to America. "As a legend, the Christian Quetzalcóatl is an admirable type, but history cannot admit his existence. Quetzalcóatl was a Nahua priest, a religious reformer and founder of a numerous sect. He was a great pontiff, a great king." [29] By his rejection of an Old World origin for Quetzalcóatl, Chavero attested to his strong nationalism and the greater realism of his historical interpretation.

Along with Chavero's ardent *indigenismo* went a sharply defined evolutionist theory that suggests familiarity with the writings of Morgan, Tylor, and Spencer. For Chavero the history of a people was not so much the history of its kings and battles as the story of its social development, its causes, and "how on account of that development certain ideas dominate a people and constitute its special character." Chavero assigned the beginnings of Nahua civilization to northern Mexico, perhaps the region of the present states of Sonora and Sinaloa. The development of the early Nahuas in this region seemed to Chavero to recapitulate the evolution of the later Toltec and Aztec civilizations, heirs to the ancient Nahua culture. The history of this early people represented "the effort of a primitive people to attain the highest level of progress compatible with the social milieu in which it lived." They evolved a language that was a perfect instrument of expression, invented a system of writing, and "an original arithmetic of simple and surprising combinations." They developed an astral religion unstained by human blood. [30]

A farming race "by instinct," the Nahuas waged a struggle against nature that by degrees brought them from the communal dwelling to the city. Their early life was "communism and labor, whence spring fraternity and virtue." Presently they achieved comfort and even luxury. Society gradually became more complex. "To defend the fields watered with their sweat they turned into warriors, and the natural development of religion in the great centers gave rise to a priesthood." The inflexible "law of history" so dear to the evolutionists led to the emergence of castes, with a consequent decline of freedom but an increase in power. The arts appeared, and with them "an exquisite aesthetic taste." Science bloomed; a calendar was formed. Meanwhile agriculture continued to progress; irrigation canals instead of the natural overflow of rivers were used to water the fields. Industry and commerce flourished, and military power grew. Thus, Chavero concluded with

a rhetorical flourish, "the Nahuas attained the two expressions of
human greatness: power through force and riches, and happiness
through labor and virtue." [31]

The Toltecs, a branch of the Nahua family that also came from
the north, brought the accumulated cultural wealth of this ancient
people into central Mexico, according to Chavero; and upon the
fall of the Toltec empire the torch of Nahua culture was taken
up by new groups of invaders. One of these was the Mexica or
Aztecs, led by Tenoch, "one of those great spirits who have confidence in the future." Chavero gave the early founders of the
Aztec state a classical, heroic cast. Citing the eloquent speech made
by Itzcóatl on assuming the throne, he asserted that the grandeur
of speeches of this kind recalled the elevated language of the characters of Homer. "The greatness and glory that Moctezuma I gave
his nation caused the people to respect and regard him as a god."
But Chavero reproached Moctezuma I for his "superstition and
cruel fanaticism," which led, among other things, to the serious
political error of leaving free and immune from attack, in the
vicinity of Tenochtitlán, the cities of Cholula, Huexotzinco, and
Tlaxcala, although the Aztecs had a compact with these cities for
waging the sacred war of flowers. "So true is it that superstition
is the blackest blindfold for keeping out the light of reason." [32]

The most severe criticism that Chavero could level at the Aztecs
was their failure to develop a spirit of nationality, to unify the
peoples over whom they ruled. Their empire, he noted, consisted
in reality of a number of city-states, each of which ruled over a
number of smaller city-states. The Aztec conquests did not result
in permanent occupation and eventual unification of the victors
and the vanquished. Since their only link was tribute, there was
no common interest, and each tributary pueblo sought to shake
off the yoke of its master. The result was continual warfare.

Chavero's sociological method appears to best advantage in his
discussion of Aztec social organization and especially in his analysis of the results of the war of Atzcapotzalco. Here his work
marks a considerable advance over that of Orozco. In modern
fashion, Chavero stressed the importance of the war as a cause of
class divisions within Aztec society. He noted that Itzcóatl distributed land to successful warriors, whereas the *calpultin* merely
received some land for the support of the temples. Thus, power

shifted from the commoners to the warrior nobility as the latter became owners of private, hereditary estates.

Chavero praised Bandelier's studies for their erudition, but expressed disagreement with them on some fundamental points. Chavero's analysis of the complex tributary organization of the Aztec Empire led him to conclude that the Aztec Triple Alliance was certainly much more than a tribal confederacy on the lines of the Iroquois Confederacy. Basing himself on Zorita's *Breve y sumaria relación*, which he called "the key to the understanding of what may be called Mexican sociology," Chavero also disputed Bandelier's view of the internal organization of Aztec society. He conceded that at the founding of Tenochtitlán the essential principles of that society were tribalism and communism. Even before the critical turning point of the Tepanec War (1429), however, communism had been undermined by the difficult struggle for life; because of the scarcity of land and food, each family was forced to rely on its own labor for survival. The conquests of Itzcóatl, and the rise of private, hereditary estates for warriors in the conquered territory, had totally subverted the communal constitution. Moreover, the land tenure system of the *calpultin* was not truly communism, since the land was divided among householders who owned and worked their plots for life and could leave them to their sons. The existence of inheritable property clearly distinguished the Aztec land system from primitive tribal communism.[33]

Chavero questioned Bandelier's judgment that Aztec society was a military democracy in which all adult males had to render military service. On the contrary, argued Chavero, Aztec society was characterized by a high degree of division of labor. The *macehuales* or peasants served principally as porters in time of war, and there was a special, privileged warrior class, trained in the Calmécac for the duties of leadership. These things, wrote Chavero, indicated the existence of a class and even a caste system, of a state of affairs that had nothing in common with democratic ideas. Such ideas were "incompatible with the epoch and the social milieu in which the Aztecs lived." In addition to the warriors and the priesthood, there was a third privileged class, the *pochteca* or merchants, of mixed commercial-military character. He summed up: "Slavery, specialized labor by commoners, a *pochteca* class with its own jurisdiction, a warrior class subdivided by aristocratic degrees, a priestly class constituting a caste: these were the elements of Mexican society, a society so far removed from the liberty and equality of the tribe that it constituted instead a genuine despotism, such as Señor Orozco compares to that of the ancient Oriental states." [34]

Finally, Chavero took issue with Bandelier's conception of the role of the *calpulli* in the political life of Tenochtitlán. He denied the existence of a popular influence on Aztec government in its mature form and reduced the role of the heads of the *calpultin* to purely economic functions. He traced an evolution from government by popular assemblies to rule by an assembly of nobles, culminating in government by a small council presided over by a king with despotic powers. Chavero found nothing democratic in the procedure for selecting the Aztec king; a council, composed of members of the dynastic family, chose the new ruler from its own midst. [35]

In another area of debate, the character of Texcoco and its king Nezahualcóyotl, Chavero steered a middle course between total skepticism and the idealization of romantic historians. He agreed that Nezahualcóyotl was a superior being and a poet, but he insisted that the poems ascribed to him were apocryphal. As an "impartial historian," he felt compelled to say that Nezahualcóyotl was not the great man Ixtlilxóchitl made him out to be. Chavero recalled the king's cruelties, the irrefutable evidence that he practiced human sacrifice and worshiped Huitzilopochtli and Tláloc; he argued there was no evidence for Nezahualcóyotl's worship of a supreme god.

The stories of the schools of poetry, astronomy, music, and divination that Nezahualcóyotl was supposed to have founded aroused Chavero's distrust. "My apologies to the Texcocan Ixtlilxóchitl, but I have reasons for not believing his exaggerations." Chavero argued that the priesthood would never have tolerated such encroachment on their monopoly of the esoteric sciences; anyway, there were no facts to support Ixtlilxóchitl's claims. Chavero conceded, however, that Nezahualcóyotl had brought the Acolhua realm to a high point of cultural progress, filled Texcoco with magnificent temples and palaces, and turned the gardens of Texcotzingo, the royal pleasure retreat, into a true Eden.

Chavero devoted the last book of his history to "the grandeur and ruin of Mexico." He depicted shadows gathering about the

Aztec capital in its last decades. The Aztec blood thirst reached a climax in the frightful holocaust that attended the dedication of the Great Temple (1486). Under the second Moctezuma, who destroyed the remaining traditional limits on his power, the tendency toward royal despotism also attained its full height. Thus, reflected Chavero, the coming of the Spaniards found supreme power in the hands of a fanatical ruler, whose superstition stripped him of his natural valor, while fatalism relaxed his will and convinced him that resistance was useless. To Cortés' immense energy and calculating spirit he opposed "an incredible torpor." By the time Moctezuma determined to revolt against his destiny, it was too late. "The imperfect social organization of the empire left him isolated; the tributary peoples, who had no common interest with him, shook off his yoke, happy to be free from further contributions of sweat and blood; Anáhuac remained alone. . . ." Chavero's dramatic recital of the events of the Conquest ended with the surrender of Cuauhtémoc and his speech of surrender. "The afternoon was dying with a promise of storm, and amid clouds red as blood there sank forever behind the mountains the fifth sun of the Mexica." [36]

The great cycle of liberal historiography closed with the writings of Justo Sierra, who was loyal to the traditions of Juárez and the Reforma, yet served Díaz, persuading himself that the dictator was preparing Mexico to be free. Sierra, with no special interest in ancient Mexico, relied chiefly on Orozco y Berra and Chavero in the introductory chapter on Indian civilizations in his *Evolución política del pueblo mexicano* (1900–1902). There was no *indigenista* passion in Sierra's account; he viewed the Aztecs with a supreme detachment, from the civilized heights of the first years of the twentieth century. The achievements and shortcomings of Aztec culture he neatly balanced. Religion and war, each depending on the other, were the poles of the life of the empire. The contradictions of Aztec civilization, its grandeur and its terror, increased as the empire entered on its last days. "The cult of the gods assumed vast proportions; the coincidence of certain slaughters in the temples with the end of certain calamities so bloated the prestige of the cannibalistic gods that the sacrifices became massacres of entire pueblos, massacres which tinged the city and its inhabitants with blood; fumes of the stinking blood rose to the sky. This religious madness had to end; blessed be the sword or cross that stopped those bloody rites."

Yet, said Sierra, the priests who presided over those rites also supervised the construction of the Calendar Stone, a masterwork which summed up Aztec chronological and cosmological science with a precision not found among the ancient Egyptians, Chaldeans, and Chinese. The time of religious massacres was also the time of the "proud apogee" of Aztec culture. Sierra rebuked the detractors of Aztec civilization who, disregarding the testimony of the monuments and the conquistadors themselves, would reduce Tenochtitlán to a cluster of huts around a center of adobe houses in the shadow of an earthen pyramid eternally stained with blood.

Sierra drew a superb picture, touched with irony, of the poet-king Nezahualcóyotl. The chroniclers, perhaps influenced by Biblical traditions, had turned Nezahualcóyotl into a David: "The warrior-founder of his kingdom, a sinner who wept for his guilt, an erotic figure surrounded by beautiful women even in his old age, a sensual and melancholy poet, restless, weary, yearning for truth like a dilettante of our time or of the decadent days of the Roman Empire. These kings of Texcoco, Nezahualcóyotl-David and Nezahualpilli-Solomon, had intervened in all the problems of the life of Tenochtitlán and solved them: they saved the city from inundations, directed the construction of the aqueducts that brought sweet water to the capital, formed part of the college of electors who on the king's death chose his successor from among the princes of the royal family." Their refinement, their efforts to improve upon the Toltec legacy, might have produced great things if they, and not the superstitious Aztec rulers, had stood at the head of ancient Mexican civilization. On the other hand, Sierra paid tribute to the Aztec valor in the battle of Tenochtitlán and especially to the heroism of Cuauhtémoc, "the most beautiful epic figure in American history."

Sierra displayed no deep personal engagement with these long-past events. The questions of Spanish guilt or innocence, which so engaged Ramírez, Orozco, and Chavero, did not interest him. Even the pity he expresses for the doomed Aztecs reveals his detachment. "Poor Tenochca! If history stops to regard you with wonder, can we do less, we sons of the land that you sanctified with your suffering and patriotism?" The land for which they died would be reborn, but the rebirth would be the joint creation of the conquerors and the conquered. "From your blood and theirs, equally heroic, was reborn the nation that proudly adopted your name. . . ." [37]

Sierra's attempt to strike a balance between the dark and the bright sides of Aztec history and civilization did not appease some extreme anti-Indian, pro-Spanish elements in the Porfirista camp. Sierra's emphasis on the high cultural level of the Aztecs supported his position in the debate in progress about the advisability of educating the Indians. Rejecting the thesis of inherent Indian inferiority, Sierra argued that education could correct the seeming dullness and apathy of the Indians. This view was opposed by conservatives who maintained that the Indians were an inferior race incapable of benefiting from education of any kind. Such men closed their eyes to the glowing picture of Aztec culture painted by liberal historians and refused to believe that any civilization worthy of the name had existed in ancient Mexico.

Joaquín García Icazbalceta, a historian and great landowner of pure Spanish descent whose holdings had increased at the expense of neighboring Indian communities, adhered to such views. The editor of García Icazbalceta's letters explained his strong anti-Aztec position by reference to García's class and religious prejudices.[38] García developed that position in his major work, a life of Bishop Zumárraga. Here he insisted that the Aztecs had gained spiritually and materially from the Conquest. He would not enlarge on the benefits of being liberated from pagan error, for fear of provoking "the impious laughter of the gross materialism that suffocates us"; but even in external things the Indians had gained much. They paid no greater tribute after the Conquest than before; their new masters oppressed them less severely than the old ones.

The rapid decline of the Indian population was not principally due to Spanish cruelty, which had been exaggerated. Part of the responsibility for that decline García ascribed to that "mysterious law" by virtue of which an inferior race placed in contact with a superior one always dwindled away. Other causes were the great plagues, for which the Spaniards could not be held responsible;

and race mixture, especially the mixture with Spaniards who formed "the nerve of that society," its upper class which constituted its principal bulwark. Without that leadership the Indian mass could never raise itself from its prostration; it had been reduced to this state, not by the "Spanish yoke," but by the despotic rule under which the Indians had lived for ages.[39]

An influential Porfirista journalist, Francisco G. Cosmes, expressed even more searing scorn for the Mexican Indian. Cosmes rejected Sierra's claim that education could redeem the Indian, or that his intellectual faculties were the same as those of Europeans. Pre-Conquest Indian society was savage, for it lacked all those traits that justify the name of civilization. Everywhere in Mexico, Cosmes complained, he found educated people who were "ready to swear that the inhabitants of Tenochtitlán discovered the planetary system before Copernicus because there is in the Museum a sculptured stone whose hieroglyphics no one had been able to decipher exactly; to swear that Nezahualcóyotl was the father of poetry because a Spanish friar wrote down in weak verses some thoughts on life that he attributed to the king of Texcoco; to swear that the walls of the palaces of Mexico were covered with tapestries finer than Gobelins because they were featherwork (the smoke of the torches that lighted up Moctezuma's rooms must have played the devil with those tapestries!); and, in fine, to swear that the moral principles professed by the people of Anáhuac were superior to those of Christianity, notwithstanding the fact that the Indians practiced human sacrifice and ate the victims, obeying religious precepts that imposed cannibalism as a duty."

Cosmes jeered at the naïveté of people who believed that ancient Mexico had powerful empires, empires which, like the kingdom of Lilliput, stretched over three or four square leagues; or that no trace of Indian civilization survived because Bishop Zumárraga had destroyed it in a single bonfire. The yoke imposed by the Conquest could not have atrophied the intellectual faculties of the Indian, for there was no evidence that they had any before the Conquest. Cannibals and fetishists without the least notion of patriotism, the Aztecs practiced a most elementary agriculture and lived almost naked in the same miserable huts that their descendants still used.

Reviving an argument first employed by De Pauw, Cosmes declared that even Náhuatl, the most developed of the Indian languages, was characterized by a poverty of words and therefore relied on roundabout expressions and figures of speech to designate the most ordinary objects. A language that employed more metaphors than exact terms was one spoken by men of scanty intelligence, for the metaphor was the characteristic language of savages and children. The Indian languages also lacked the means of expressing general ideas.

Reviving still another traditional argument of the anti-Indian school, Cosmes alleged that the Indian lacked capacity for original thought or invention; he was reduced to servile copying or imitation of the things he saw. Even if one granted that the Indian brain was capable of reflecting upon and absorbing what it learned, the Indian lacked an indispensable condition for intellectual achievement: initiative and the desire to progress. "The Indian has only the passive force of inferior races, is incapable of actively pursuing the goal of civilization."

Cosmes exempted the mestizo from this harsh judgment. In the mestizo, his Spanish blood had instilled a special character that distinguished him from the Indian. "Our national spirit is a consequence of the union of two races, a union in which the *law of preponderance* in the *transmission of characters*, the name given in biology to the superior influence of the parents in the mental constitution of the child, speaks decidedly in favor of the Spanish type." The Indian provided only the raw material for that union, since his moral traits disappeared completely from the mestizo. Instead of Indian tenacity the mestizo had the mercurial Spanish nature; instead of the resignation and passivity that made the descendants of Moctezuma submit to every yoke, he had a turbulent temper. Only a few physical traits remained of the Indian background and these were steadily diminishing. "Intellectually and morally speaking," said Cosmes, "we are Spaniards, a trifle modified by our milieu." [40]

Ancient Mexico had again become a battleground for ideologists who in reality debated contemporary issues. It is gratifying that in this period, when racism exerted immense influence on Western thought, a majority of Mexican intellectuals, headed by the *maestro* Justo Sierra, rejected the racist views of a Cosmes or a Francisco Bulnes.[41] The liberal historians who affirmed the Aztec splendor were in effect defending the educability and creativity of the contemporary Indian. Their *indigenismo*, academic as it was, offered a point of departure for the integral, pragmatic *indigenismo* that arose during the great Revolution of 1910 and set as its goal the full integration of the Indian into the Mexican nation.

French scholarship, with its strong tradition of interest in ancient Mexico, welcomed the opportunity presented by Napoleon III's mobilization of scientific talent for the study of Mexican geography, history, linguistics, and archaeology during the French intervention in Mexico in the 1860's. Perhaps in conscious imitation of the researches that his illustrious relative had promoted on the banks of the Nile, Napoleon III instructed his able minister of public instruction, Victor Duruy, to organize a Commission Scientifique du Mexique to carry out similar studies.

Reporting to the Emperor on his compliance with this order, Duruy indicated his hopes for a fruitful archaeological activity: "The Mexico of Montezuma has almost wholly vanished; the expedition will provide us with the means of rediscovering it. Perhaps our travelers will find some of those rare Mexican or Yucatecan manuscripts that have escaped destruction. . . ." Recalling the discoveries made in Egypt in the time of the first Napoleon, Duruy expressed the hope that "the solitary landscapes of Mexico hold similar surprises for our savants." These savants would restore to life a "great and curious page of the annals of the world, a page which the ages have effaced, and our generation, so susceptible to the noble emotions of history, will see enlarged the horizon over which its thoughts may wander." [42] To the Third Committee of the commission, in charge of history, linguistics, and archaeology, Duruy appointed, among others, Brasseur de Bourbourg, Aubin, and the architectural historian Viollet-le-Duc.

The instructions of Jean-Baptiste-Louis, Baron Gros, to the persons who were to study the monuments in the vicinity of Mexico City prescribed in detail the reconnaissance to be made of the pyramids of Teotihuacán. The Baron, who had visited the site, found a considerable analogy between these pyramids and those of Egypt. The explorers should survey the site, establish the number of pyramids, their situation and proportions, determine the nature of the blocks of which they were formed and send some to Paris, excavate the interior galleries, and ascertain whether their ceilings were vaulted. They were to gather all the traditions preserved by the Indians of the vicinity, no matter how absurd or trivial those traditions might seem.[43]

Three volumes of reports on the commission's work, published from 1865 to 1867, contain the studies submitted to the body during its short life. The casual reader of these reports may not recall that the field work on which they were based was done under hazardous war conditions. In July, 1865, Colonel Louis-Toussaint-Simon Doutrelaine reported to the Third Committee on a reconnaissance that he had made of the ruins of Mitla. He sent drawings made on the spot; these drawings, he wrote, testified to the fidelity with which Dupaix and Castañeda had done their work. He took the occasion to warn the Committee against the "detestable drawings" of Mitla recently published in the United States by the Smithsonian Institution; these sketches were as crude as they were inaccurate.

The scholarly Colonel expressed admiration for the harmony of Mitla's complex of structures, the symmetry of their details, the meticulous artistry of their decorations. Doutrelaine had not escaped the diffusionist itch; he suggested that Mitla's structures displayed some notable resemblances to those of Nineveh, but did not positively claim an Asiatic origin for Zapotec civilization and architecture. Colonel Doutrelaine dispatched another learned paper concerning a recently discovered serpent's head of stone; this paper revealed his familiarity with the published material on ancient Mexico and his friendship with Orozco y Berra and other Mexican scholars with whom he had discussed archaeological questions.[44]

Under the same imperial auspices, Désiré Charnay explored parts of Mexico in 1857; his tour resulted in a publication consisting of an album of photographs and a volume of text, the greater part of which was devoted to a study of ancient Mexican architecture by Viollet-le-Duc. The principal interest of this curious essay derives from its racist-diffusionist interpretation of Mexican architecture, apparently influenced by the recent work of the Comte Joseph-Arthur de Gobineau, *Sur l'inégalité des races humaines* (1853–1855).

Viollet-le-Duc had convinced himself that the Aztecs were degenerate descendants of a mixture of white colonizers and the inferior native race of Mexico. He found proof of this in the imperfect Aztec picture writing, much inferior to the "phonetic writing" of the ancient Quichés and Toltecs; in the eloquence or "nebulous chatter" characteristic of Aztec literary style; and in their massive human sacrifices. Viollet-le-Duc found "every reason to believe" that some centuries before the Christian era Mexico and Central America were occupied by peoples chiefly of the yellow race, who had attained that level of material development of which the yellow races were capable; and that these people were then overrun and conquered by tribes of white people who came from the northeast and possessed a much higher capacity for civilization. It was this superior race that "raised those immense monuments which surprise us today by their grandeur and strangeness."

Viollet-le-Duc offered a sociological-racist interpretation of architectural style. Monumental architecture always originated under the same social conditions. In Mexico, as in India, Assyria, and Egypt, a conquering race imposed the task of constructing such monuments on the native peoples. The conquerors contributed their traditions, tastes, and special genius; the natives gave their labor and material resources. Construction processes offered a clue to the nationality of the builders. The absence of dry masonry in Mexico and Yucatán, the fact that mortar or plaster was employed everywhere, almost certainly proved that the builders had Turanian or Finnish blood in their veins. "Only Aryans and Semites," declared Viollet-le-Duc, "are capable of building in dry masonry"; but the indications, in the structure of buildings and certain architectural members, of a tradition of timber construction in Yucatán, gave evidence of a strong infusion of Aryan elements, for the use of carpentry was always associated with Aryan blood.[45] That these erratic speculations could be published and taken seriously suggests how powerful was the influence of racism in Western thought in the nineteenth century.

The terrible outcome of Napoleon III's intervention in Mexico did not dampen French scholarly interest in Mexican antiquity. Charnay returned to Mexico in 1880, under the joint auspices of the French and United States governments, to carry out an ambitious campaign of field work. This he recorded in a lively book, published in English translation in 1887 under the title *The Ancient Cities of the New World*. In his introduction the American editor, Allen Thorndike Rice, commended Charnay for his services in securing and transporting numerous casts of "the important palaces and temples of Central America now on exhibition in the museums of Paris and Washington." Oblivious of the teachings of Morgan and Bandelier, Rice declared that those monuments were of "surpassing grandeur," and regretted that "few Americans of our day have any adequate conception of the stately edifices of monumental Mitla or of Palenque, with its magnificent palace, its terraces and temples, its pyramids and sculptured ornaments. . . ." [46]

True to his time, Charnay had his own pet archaeological theory, constructed on the base of the familiar thesis that Toltec civilization was the fountainhead of all the high cultures of Mexico and Central America. In his reconstruction (which he found "beautifully simple") that civilization had arisen in the Valley of Tula, was transmitted following the disruption of the Toltec Empire to the peoples who invaded central Mexico, and was carried by Toltec emigrants to Central America, where it attained its highest development. According to Charnay, Aztec civilization represented a degenerate form of the higher Toltec culture, whose mild teachings the Aztecs had forgotten. Of greater importance were Charnay's energetic excavations at Tula, whose capital importance as a political and religious center he was the first to demonstrate, and at Teotihuacán, whose large extent and urban character his work helped to confirm.

Charnay's deservedly popular book was the best known of the many French studies of ancient Mexico in the second half of the nineteenth century.

The recognized leader of French Mexicanists and Americanists in general was E.-T. Hamy, curator of the Musée d'Ethnographie of Paris, editor of codices, and a prolific writer on a wide variety of topics. Hamy's thinking reflected the prevailing diffusionist trend, as did the writings of H. de Charencey, who was especially interested in tracing supposed connections between Asiatic and Mexican myths. [47]

Of more durable value was the monumental Náhuatl dictionary of Rémi Siméon. [48] Siméon was also joint translator with Denis

Jourdanet of Sahagún's *Historia general*. Their edition (based principally on Bustamante's defective text) was accompanied by profuse linguistic notes and a lengthy introduction by the two editors. Jourdanet contributed a general survey of Aztec civilization in which he placed the philosophical and religious thought of the Aztecs on an extremely high level. He discovered a certain pantheism in their religious beliefs, allegedly based on the belief that all things were one for all eternity with the Supreme Will from which they emanated. Noting that the Aztecs usually offered prayers to the one invisible, impalpable, and omnipresent God, Jourdanet affirmed that they were really monotheists or on the verge of becoming such.

He confessed to a feeling of regret that the short but brilliant Aztec career had ended so abruptly. Aside from their human sacrifice and ritual cannibalism, there was little in Aztec private life and customs that he could not endorse. Jourdanet speculated that the passage of time might gradually have cleansed Aztec religion of its aberrations. He was troubled, however, by evidence of the growth of luxurious tastes among the Aztecs, including the appearance of harems in the Oriental style; these traits seemed to be displacing the severe old morality and virtue. Moral decline, combined with mounting tribute demands upon the subject population, must have contributed to the crisis and destruction of the Aztec state. Jourdanet's brooding on the causes of the Aztec downfall may be related to the French search for the causes of their own stunning defeat at Prussian hands in 1870.

Siméon's essay was devoted to an appreciation of Sahagún and his work. In it he endorsed Jourdanet's favorable judgment of Aztec culture. Indeed, he criticized Sahagún for not stressing sufficiently the Aztec belief in a Supreme Being. Although Siméon acknowledged that Mexican polytheism was based on veneration of the forces of nature, he insisted that the majority of the divine names only symbolized the various forms in which the Aztecs perceived the supreme power. "From this to monotheism is not far." [49]

A French naturalist and archaeologist, Lucien Biart, wrote by far the best general survey of Aztec civilization available to Western readers in this period. Under the title *The Aztecs: Their His-*

tory, Manners, and Customs, it was quickly published in English translation (1887).

In a few severe lines Biart disposed of modern skeptics who would reduce the Aztecs to the level of the North American Indians. "The description of their political and private ethics, customs, and laws, gives the clearest idea of their intelligence, dignity, and wisdom, as well as the sanguinary aberrations, of the Aztec people. We have learned enough of this race, too often confounded with that of the heroes of James Fenimore Cooper, to understand that they could do something besides follow a trail, chase a buffalo (an animal unknown in the country subjugated by the Aztecs), and smoke the calumet, whose name and use was unknown to them."

Biart depicted an Aztec ruling class and court living in unheard-of luxury, a luxury that hid "the misery that naturally accompanies all despotic government. The king, the nobles, the priests, the officials, the privileged classes, lived in abundance; the people, bound to the soil, badly fed, without hope of seeing their condition improve, toiled to supply, not their own needs, but those of the great." Those inequalities, however, were to Biart the inevitable price of civilization. "Oppressor and oppressed: do not these two words, unfortunately, sum up the history of men in all ages, in all countries?" [50] Biart's book refuted in large and in detail the theory of Aztec tribal democracy and communism presented by Morgan and Bandelier.

That theory found no more acceptance in England than in France. The anthropologist Andrew Lang rudely dismissed Morgan's revisionist ideas as unworthy of notice: "it seems scarcely necessary to discuss Mr. Lewis Morgan's attempt to show that the Aztecs of Cortés' time were only on the level of the modern Pueblo Indians." Lang, however, had taken care to refute Morgan by pointing out that the Aztecs "were settled in what deserved to be called cities; they had developed a monumental and elaborately decorated architecture; they were industrious in the arts known to them, though ignorant of iron. . . . They were sedulous in agriculture, disciplined in war, capable of absorbing and amalgamating with conquered tribes." [51]

Long before the publication of Morgan's *Ancient Society*, the young Edward B. Tylor, traveling in Mexico with the ethnologist Henry Christy, had commented on the pyramids of Teotihuacán in a manner that directly contradicted the views of the American revisionist school. "Such buildings," he wrote, "can only be raised under peculiar social conditions. The ruler must be a despotic sovereign, and the masses of the people slaves, whose subsistence and whose lives are sacrificed without scruple to execute the fancies of the monarch, who is not so much the governor as the unrestricted owner of the country and the people. The population must be very dense, or it would not bear the loss of so large a proportion of the working class; and vegetable food must be exceedingly abundant in the country, to feed them while engaged in this unprofitable labor."

Tylor admitted that when he and Christy left England both doubted the accounts of the chroniclers, "believing they had exaggerated the numbers of the population and the size of the cities, from a natural desire to make the most of their victories, and to write as wonderful a history as they could, as historians are prone to do. But our examination of Mexican remains soon induced us to withdraw this accusation, and even made us inclined to blame the chroniclers for having had no eyes for the wonderful things that surrounded them." [52]

Tylor's Mexican journey, according to his biographer, was a turning point in his life, "from which can be definitely dated his devotion to the scientific study of man." More especially, Tylor discovered in Mexico apparent similarities between Old and New World cultures that aroused his curiosity and spurred him to seek for "principles of explanation that should bring the isolated culture of native America into organic touch with the rest of the world." [53] In his account of his Mexican travels, *Anahuac* (1861), Tylor appeared to waver between independent invention and diffusion to explain the puzzling Mexican analogies with Old World traits, finally assuming the cautious position that "we must wait for further evidence." [54]

Tylor's first major work, *Researches into the Early History of Mankind* (1865), frequently cited Mexican cultural features, usually to make a diffusionist point. Overlooking Humboldt's waverings and qualifications, Tylor insisted that the German scientist had offered evidence that "goes with great force that the civilization of Mexico and that of Asia have, in part at least, a common origin. . . . Of this evidence, the similarity of the chronological calendars is perhaps the strongest point." In an article on "Backgammon among the Aztecs" (1879), Tylor argued from the striking similarities between the Indian game of *pachisi* and the Aztec game of *patolli* that the latter probably had an Asiatic origin. Indeed, ever since his journey to Mexico he had held the view that "the higher art and life of the whole Central American district is most rationally accounted for by a carrying across of culture from Asia." [55]

Despite a marked tendency to offer diffusionist explanations for the presence of such traits as metallurgy in ancient Mexico, Tylor lavishly praised the Aztec achievement in this and other fields. Commenting on the "wonderful skill" of Aztec goldsmiths and silversmiths, Tylor declared that the few surviving specimens of this work showed that "the Spanish conquerors were not romancing in the wonderful stories they told of the skill of the native goldsmiths. I have seen a pair of gold eagle ornaments in the Berlin Museum which will compare almost with the Etruscan work for design and delicacy of finish." [56]

Tylor's point in his *Anahuac* about the relation between the monumental architecture of Teotihuacán and the productivity of ancient Mexican agriculture suggests a possible debt to the economic and environmentalist interpretation of the English historian Henry T. Buckle. In his world-ranging introduction to the *History of Civilization in England* (1857), Buckle offered Aztec Mexico and Inca Peru as illustrations of a universal law that subordinated early civilizations to their physical milieu. Buckle, who wrote from a militantly democratic, antifeudal point of view, argued that in Mexico and Peru, as in Egypt and India, soil and climate made "the national food cheap and abundant; hence the labour-market over-supplied; hence a very unequal division of wealth and power; and hence all the consequences which such an inequality will inevitably produce." What rice and dates were for Egypt and India, maize was for Mexico and Peru. Buckle conceded that there existed in those lands "an amount of knowledge, despicable indeed if tried by an European standard, but most remarkable if contrasted with the gross ignorance which prevailed among the adjoining and contemporary nations."

On the other hand, he complained that in Mexico and Peru, as in the ancient East, "there was the same inability to diffuse even that scanty civilization which they really possessed; there was the same utter absence of anything approaching the democratic spirit; there was the same despotic power on the part of the upper classes, and the same contemptible subservience on the part of the lower." In Mexico and Peru, the arts, especially those that catered to the luxurious tastes of the rich, had made considerable progress, "supplying evidence of the possession of unlimited wealth, and of the ostentatious prodigality with which that wealth was wasted."

Buckle roundly denied the conventional distinction made between the supposedly benevolent absolutism of the Inca and Aztec tyranny. "In the most essential particular for which history can be studied, namely, the state of the people, Mexico and Peru are the counterpart of each other. For though there were many minor points of difference, both were agreed in this, that there were only two classes—the upper class being tyrants, and the lower being slaves." Proof of the general discontent with Aztec rule was the aid the oppressed peoples gave the Spanish invaders. In both countries caste lines were strictly drawn. "This was the political symptom of that stationary and conservative spirit, which . . . has marked every country in which the upper classes have monopolized power." Buckle found in both that "frivolous waste of labor" that he had remarked in Egypt. "Long before the crises of their actual destruction," concluded Buckle, "these one-sided and irregular civilizations had begun to decay." [57]

Perhaps the most ambitious nineteenth-century effort to explain the cultural evolution of ancient America was the *History of the New World Called America* by the Oxford don Edward J. Payne. Only two volumes of this work had appeared by the time of Payne's death (1904). His total rejection of the Morgan-Bandelier theories on ancient Mexico is reflected in the fact that no reference to the relevant writings of those scholars appears in his text or copious footnotes; and certainly not from ignorance of their content.

The development of ancient Mexico and Peru Payne explained with the aid of a rigorous evolutionist scheme based on the familiar

Antonio Ruiz. *Sueño de la Malinche*. Signed and dated 1939. Oil on wood. 11 x 15½ in. (29.5 x 40 cm.). Coll. Inés Amor, Mexico City.

Young Toltec girl. Idealized representation based on 19th-century Indian types and Diego Durán's *Historia de las Indias de Nueva España*. From Désiré Charnay, *The Ancient Cities of the New World* (New York, 1887). Courtesy Marquand Art Library, Princeton University.

Indian king. Idealized representation based on Francisco Xavier Clavigero's *Storia antica del Messico*, Ramírez Ms., and Diego Durán's *Historia de las Indias de Nueva España*. From Désiré Charnay, *The Ancient Cities of the New World* (New York, 1887). Courtesy Marquand Art Library, Princeton University.

Mask of Xipe Totec, god of spring. Gray volcanic stone with traces of red paint. Height: 9 in. (22.8 cm.). Aztec civilization, from the Valley of Mexico (?), c. 1440–1521. British Museum, London. Once in the collection of the British ethnologist Henry Christy, who traveled in Mexico in 1856 and 1857 with Edward B. Tylor. Photograph courtesy Museum.

sequence of three stages, savagery, barbarism, and civilization. Technological progress and the struggle for existence were the decisive factors in social evolution. The rise of agriculture was a critical step in human advance, for it compelled the development of a warrior class to defend the tribe's stores of food. The formation of a warrior class implied the subordination of the peasantry to this group. Like the modern capitalist class, this ancient ruling class exerted a beneficial influence, for it "stimulated production, protected industry, and educated the labourer in spite of himself."

In Aztec Mexico, said Payne, the implied covenant between the master class and the plebeians was explicitly formulated in the agreement reached between warriors and commoners before the war of Atzcapotzalco; by this agreement the plebeians consented to serve the warriors if they gained the victory. By virtue of such implied covenants, the greater part of the land in both Mexico and Peru belonged to the warrior nobility and the gods. In Mexico these lands became hereditary estates, constituting a rudimentary feudalism. "The Spaniards rightly compared these proprietary estates, which seem to have usually comprised the greater part of the village lands, to the seigneuries or mayorazgos of Europe." Payne found "this remarkable analogy to a familiar element in the advancement of the Old World" entirely absent in Peru.

In the dispute over the origin of the ancient American cultures, Payne ranged himself firmly on the side of independent invention. His point of departure was the principle of psychic unity. "Mind is essentially the same in all varieties of man; the lowest American Indian thinks and reasons like ourselves." Payne applied a novel approach to the problem of American cultural origins: the structural analysis of language, regarded as an index of mental and cultural progress. After subjecting a Náhuatl passage from Chimalpahin to such analysis, Payne judged that Aztec civilization could not possibly have been an import from China or Japan. Literary Náhuatl "bears witness by its many defects, its continual redundancies, and its repetitions, to the backwardness of the language it employs and to the low mental cultivation which that language represented." He concluded that "the native Mexican was the language of a barbarism little removed from savagery."

Payne argued that the habit of ascribing everything American to Old World sources stemmed from the belief that the American

Indians were a type of men different from and lower than Old World people, hence "incapable of working out the problems of advancement for themselves." The chief blame for the popularity of diffusionist doctrines he laid to Humboldt, whose "crude speculations" he severely criticized. He also took Tylor to task for suggesting that the resemblances between Aztec *patolli* and the Indian *pachisi* game indicated a common origin. "Throwing and scoring are the essentials of all such games; and they have a natural tendency to assume the same form." One might as well argue, continued Payne, that the Mexican ball game *tlachtli*, because of certain similarities to tennis and soccer, had an Old World origin. He cited the Indians' success in cultivating every indigenous plant with food value as proof of their capacity for independent evolution. "To suppose that a race capable of this feat—the more astonishing the more closely it is examined—was incapable of counting 365 days to the year, and of bringing the game of 'throw and score' to the shape in which it existed in Mexico, is surely repugnant to reason." At the time of the Conquest, all the Mexican arts and sciences, including the calendrical and mathematical sciences, were in continuous progress. That advances were also taking place in their religion was proved by the development of "a simplified theology, and in some limited development of a true ethical system, based on conscience and the needs of society."

On the eve of the Conquest, then, Aztec energy still existed "in undiminished vigor." Payne speculated about the direction in which this energy was working. He perceived a tendency toward the emergence of a small barbarous kingdom, with Mexico as its capital and the two other members of the Triple Alliance, Tlacopan and Texcoco, reduced to mere dependencies. Aztec territorial enlargement, Payne believed, was limited by the existence of warlike tribes on the Aztec borders and by the need for having sources of sacrificial victims close at hand. However, there had been room for development within the bounds of the empire; many more tributary pueblos could have been formed. Looking beyond, Payne projected an expansion of Aztec foreign trade that might have taken in the whole Caribbean basis; Mexico might have become a rudimentary maritime power. On the other hand, no major advance in "the arts of life" or in "general mental progress" would likely have occurred. Indeed, he accepted the traditional view that in such respects Aztec culture represented a decline from the Toltec level.

Pondering the incongruities of Aztec human sacrifice and cannibalism, so "startling and perplexing" when compared with the many proofs of remarkable progress, Payne offered an economic explanation for those paradoxes. The Aztec system of perpetual war against neighboring peoples, ostensibly in order to secure victims for religious sacrifice, had as its real object the procurement of animal food for consumption by the privileged class. Religion provided a façade for this organized cannibalism; the real reason was the absence of large animals capable of affording a regular supply of food and labor power. "Hence human energy, in Mexico alone among advanced communities, was largely sustained by feeding on human flesh, and relied on forced human labour as its necessary auxiliary."

Comparing the Aztec and Inca empires, Payne dissented from the conventional preference for Inca over Aztec civilization. He rejected the "curious and widely spread misconception" that Inca rule represented some kind of socialism. "Nowhere have the distinctions of rank and the rights of property been more rigidly maintained than under the severe despotism of Peru: this so-called socialism, when examined, proves to be nothing but the forced common labour exacted from the peasantry. . . . Russia or Turkey might with equal propriety be quoted as examples of 'State Socialism.' " The Inca emperors were by habit and policy "brutal and sanguinary tyrants." By comparison with them, "the cannibal chiefs of Anahuac appear almost in the light of polished and civilized rulers."

Payne found Peruvian culture inferior in general to that of Mexico. He suggested various causes for this backwardness; one was Inca success in domesticating the llama, which obviated further effort; another was the cold climate of the Peruvian plateau, which may have made Inca brains more sluggish. For whatever reason, the Peruvians were far inferior to the Mexicans in the arts of reckoning time, writing, art, and even in religion; religion was more spiritual among the Aztecs when measured against the crass materialism of the Inca. On the other hand, the Inca were free from cannibalism; they practiced human sacrifice on a much smaller scale than the Aztecs; and they surpassed the Aztecs in the

size and complexity of their military and administrative organization. The latter enabled the Inca to overcome immense geographical difficulties and to establish a stable government over an area
much larger than the Aztec territory. In the last analysis, however,
Payne found little to choose between the two barbaric cultures.[58]

Germany, home of Humboldt, produced in Eduard Seler a figure
of equal or even greater importance than Humboldt for Mexicanist
studies. Like Franz Boas, Seler came to anthropology by way of
one of the physical sciences (botany), and this may help to explain
his insistence on rigorous study of details and his distrust of speculation. In 1885 he joined the staff of the Berlin Royal Museum of
Ethnology, directed by Adolf Bastian. In 1887 Seler made the first
of a series of archaeological journeys to Mexico. The subject of
ancient Mexican civilization soon absorbed him and continued to
be his ruling passion until his death in 1922. One story tells that
as he lay dying, in his delirium he called for a carriage to take him
to Mexico, while his hand traced hieroglyphic signs in the air.[59]

What Boas did for the discipline of anthropology in general,
Seler, it may be said, did for Middle American anthropology in
particular. Rejecting all speculation and fantasy, he insisted that it
was impossible to solve a problem—the meaning of a myth, for
example—without understanding its component elements. Such understanding could only be gained by the most intensive analysis
and comparison of the clues and information provided by Spanish
and Indian sources, native picture writings, sculptures, and ceramics. This comparative, critical method was most exacting; it
required a formidable mastery of the sources, documentary and
archaeological, and above all of the Indian languages in which,
Seler believed, the most authentic and reliable materials were preserved. His search for such materials led him unerringly to the
great corpus of Sahagún manuscripts that were gathering dust in
Madrid libraries, and he devoted almost thirty years to the translation of selected texts.

Seler's monographs and commentaries on codices set standards
of meticulous research that have not been surpassed. Writing in
1949, the dean of Mexican anthropologists, Alfonso Caso, observed
that Seler's major works, his commentaries on the codices of the
so-called Borgia group, "contain studies of permanent value which
it has not been possible to supersede and which form the solid

basis for subsequent investigations." An American specialist, H. B. Nicholson, recently endorsed Caso's judgment. Seler, Nicholson wrote, was "a genuine scholar in a previously poorly cultivated field; no earlier student had attempted anything like the thorough, determined attempt he undertook to explain the contents of the major members of the Borgia group." [60]

Seler's caution deterred him from writing a work of synthesis on ancient Mexican civilization. To suggestions that he write such a work, he invariably replied: "We do not yet know enough about these things." [61] From his writings, however, it is possible to reconstruct Seler's general views on the character of the civilizations of ancient Middle America.

To begin with, in the dispute concerning the origins of those civilizations, Seler in general sided with the advocates of independent invention. This attitude reflected his impatience with the extravagant theories of some diffusionists; it also suggests the influence of his teacher Adolf Bastian, whose doctrine of psychic unity Seler stated in the following words: "Where the customs and habits are similar, we shall . . . be obliged to consider this the result of a similar trend of the human mind, to ascribe it to a mode of thinking, which in the most different places and amid the most different conditions, travels the same paths, which sometimes seem very peculiar to ourselves."

Men naturally tended to assume that similar things must have a common origin. As a result, whenever notable analogies were found between Old and New World customs and institutions, the thought of a direct transfer immediately came to mind. Having pointed out the absurdity of some theories of transoceanic contact, Seler noted that many of the supposedly unique features of ancient Mexican civilization were found in more or less developed form among other Indian groups. These features included clan organization and religious concepts. The Feathered Serpent, for example, so prominent in the Aztec and Maya cults, was also held in honor by the Pueblo Indians. Even picture writing, often regarded as the distinctive achievement of Middle America, existed in rudimentary form among the North American Indians. Such arguments, ironically observed Seler, would not convince people who must have it that Christian missionaries or Buddhist priests brought the cross or the swastika to Mexico.[62]

In his battle against fantasy, Seler spared no feelings, gave no quarter. He did not hesitate to characterize a vast, mystical work by a respected American colleague, Zelia Nuttall, *Fundamental Principles of Old and New World Civilizations,* as "a tissue of more or less interesting speculations for which there is no real foundation whatever." With equal vigor he attacked debunkers who denied the historical reality of events and groups because they had become entangled with myth. Thus he proved the existence of a Toltec state with citations from Indian chronicles, refuting the efforts of the American anthropologist Daniel G. Brinton to explain the Toltecs away as mythical, fabulous beings.[63]

By his war on diffusionist fantasy Seler upheld belief in the reality of the creative capacity of the ancient Mexicans and the originality of their achievements. He depicted them as a people capable of making accurate astronomical observations and complex mathematical calculations, a people whose picture writings, sculpture, and prayers revealed a poetic imagination disciplined and controlled by a set of beliefs about the universe. They were a people moving toward greater heights of self-expression and mastery of their environment, and Seler regretted that they had not had "a couple of hundred years longer to develop [their] own peculiar civilization."

Seler's ideas on Aztec political and social organization owed nothing to Morgan or Bandelier. The clan or *calpulli* constituted the base of the Aztec political structure; but there existed a larger unit, the tribe, which included the clans, and which by forcible or peaceful incorporation of foreign clans had developed into a political body in the modern sense, that is, a state. At its head stood a king (*tlatoani*), selected by tribal and clan leaders from a family which had supplied the ruler from ancient times. In the conduct of political business and in his priestly duties, the ruler was assisted by a caste of nobles who held land by feudal tenure. "This social organization, displaying very sharp distinctions and degrees of rank, was also expressed in outward form, since the classes belonging to the higher rank and society, with the king at their head, not only wore more elaborate and expensive garments, corresponding to their larger income, but they had the exclusive right to wear a certain costly costume." [64]

Clearly, the teachings of Morgan and Bandelier on ancient Mexico had virtually no scholarly support on the Continent or in

England. A final piece of evidence is provided by the detailed bibliographic and interpretive survey of Mexicanist studies published by Seler's student Walter Lehmann in the *Archiv für Anthropologie* (1907). Lehmann made no reference to the theories or writings of Morgan and Bandelier. Reflecting the scientific revolution under way in Mexicanist studies, Lehmann wrote with severe caution that "the body of well-ascertained facts is absolutely insufficient to give anything like a connected view of the former state of things in Mexico." Proof of a related revolution in attitudes toward primitive art is Lehmann's expression of incredulous surprise that a writer of 1875, in the "presence of so many beautiful and highly artistic specimens" of ancient American art, could speak of the "absence of all plastic beauty in the creations of the indigenous American art." [65]

The revisionism of Morgan and Bandelier had no discernible influence on the portrayal of Aztec civilization in late nineteenth-century literature and art in either hemisphere. The continued dominance of romantic conventions is well illustrated by the very popular novel of Lew Wallace, *The Fair God, Or, The Last of the 'Tzins* (1873). How favorably Wallace regarded Aztec society is suggested by the book's motto, taken from Draper, proclaiming that the Conquest had crushed out "a civilization that might have instructed Europe."

Employing a familiar device of writers of romances, Wallace introduced his work as a translation of a chronicle by Ixtlilxóchitl. The story began on the eve of the Conquest and ended with the Noche Triste. Its crowded cast includes the historical figures of Cuauhtémoc, the book's true hero; Moctezuma, who has moments of nobility as well as of weakness; and Cortés, Alvarado, and Bernal Díaz, among the Spaniards. Wallace's debt to Scott and Bulwer-Lytton is evident in his style, dialogue, and plot, and in the general atmosphere he creates. Straight out of Scott's medieval novels is the bluff, honest soldier Hualpa, Cuauhtémoc's faithful retainer, who dies heroically in the Noche Triste. The story ends with Cuauhtémoc, organizer of the Spanish defeat, preparing to exemplify further "the qualities which had made him already the idol of his people and the hero of his race."

The "dilemma of sympathy," inescapable in a novel with an

infidel hero, Wallace attempted to solve by an improbable dialectic. The doomed Moctezuma prophesies the triumph of Christianity and the rise of the Mexicans to a place of splendor among the nations of the earth. Cuauhtémoc, in the interval of battle, looks to a future in which he may build a temple without images to the One Supreme God. Notwithstanding its anachronisms, its turgid dialogue, its Gothic absurdities, the book has a certain life and movement; the exciting battle scenes are especially well done.

Mexican novels in this period usually reflected the passions of the struggle over the Reforma. Of the works dealing with Aztec or Conquest themes, certainly the best was Eligio Ancona's *Los mártires del Anáhuac* (1873). Its title suggests its fervent *indigenismo*. Ancona took considerable pains to provide a solid, convincing historical framework for his story. Its historical figures include Cortés, cruel, cunning, and superstitious; the unhappy Malinche, fated to love an enemy of her race and to betray her country to foreigners; and the weak, vacillating Moctezuma. The chief fictional characters are Moctezuma's daughter Geliztli, beautiful despite the gold pendants that hang from her ears and lip; and her lover Tizoc, dedicated to the priesthood by a father's vow, but eager to become a warrior.

The story opens in the atmosphere of crisis that precedes the arrival of the Spaniards in Tenochtitlán. Tizoc, rejecting the argument that the bearded white strangers are Quetzalcóatl's emissaries, leaves for Tlaxcala to join Xiconténcatl in resistance to the Spaniards. Moctezuma, the "unworthy king of a great people," abjectly surrenders to the strangers. Ancona's novelistic anger rose to fever pitch as he described the burning of Cuauhpopoca and other Aztec chiefs by Cortés with Moctezuma's consent. "The fire had consumed all. But there was something that could not perish, that would never perish: the bloodthirst of the conquerors! The baseness of the king! The heroism of the victims!" [66] Geliztli, the "Judith of Anáhuac," prepares to give Cortés a sleeping potion that will put him in the power of the Aztecs, but the wily Cortés substitutes his cup for hers, rapes her in her sleep, and makes her pregnant. Nothing remains for Geliztli and her Aztec lover but to die in the last battles for Tenochtitlán.

If Ancona's Indianist passion and striving for historical accuracy gave his work a genuine vitality and pathos, the same cannot be said of *Amor y suplicio* (1873), by Ireneo Paz. This compound of stale romanticism and Catholic piety relates the rivalry of Cuauhtémoc and Xiconténcatl for the love of Otila, daughter of a Tlaxcalan lord. Otila's father frustrates both Indian suitors by giving her in marriage to the conquistador Velásquez de León. One sample will adequately indicate the style and tone of the book. Otila, fatally wounded by the vengeful Xiconténcatl, speaks: "Cuauhtémoc . . . I . . . am . . . dy . . . ing . . . yes . . . I . . . love . . . you. . . . Become a Christian that we may be joined . . . in . . . Heaven . . . kiss me so that I may die . . . happy. . . . Farewell . . . I love you . . . I love you!" [67]

Equally improbable is the story of *Nezahualpilli, el catolicismo en México* (1875), by Juan L. Tercero. Unctuous in style, interlarded with pious homilies, it tells of the conversion of Nezahualpilli, nephew of the king of that name, from a warrior prince into a Catholic missionary who gives up his love and the world to minister to the Indians on a distant frontier and dies in an odor of sanctity.

European novelists continued to exploit the rich vein of romantic material first opened up by Prescott. In *Montezuma's Daughter* (1893), H. Rider Haggard used again the device of a love affair between a white stranger and a native queen that he had so successfully employed in *King Solomon's Mines*.

The young Englishman Thomas Wingfield pursues a Spanish enemy to America and is cast away on the coast of Yucatán. Saved by Marina (Malinche) from being sacrificed, he is conducted by Cuauhtémoc to Tenochtitlán. There he meets and falls in love with Otomie, Moctezuma's daughter. Otomie's "eye was proud and full like the eye of a buck, her curling hair fell upon her shoulders, and her features were very noble, yet tender almost to sadness." The hero, startled by the grandeur and beauty of Tenochtitlán, describes it as "the mightiest city that ever I had seen." He is ushered into "a wondrous house, of which all the rooms were roofed with cedar wood, and its walls hung with richly colored cloths, and in that house gold seemed as plentiful as bricks and oak are with us in England." [68]

Thomas is chosen to impersonate Tezcatlipoca and be sacrificed in the annual festival in honor of the god, and Otomie marries him in order to share his fate. The timely arrival of Spanish attackers saves the lovers from death, and they escape to live an idyllic existence in the City of Pines, high in the mountains, until a Spanish expedition commanded by Bernal Díaz invades their refuge and captures the city. The claims of civilization are finally satisfied. Otomie, heartbroken by the death of her son at the hands of the evil García, conveniently commits suicide; Thomas, released by the generous Bernal Díaz, returns to England to marry a childhood sweetheart and, in his old age, to write the story of his adventures at the command of Queen Elizabeth. Haggard's sources of information were Prescott, Sahagún (in the French edition of Jourdanet and Siméon), and of course Bernal Díaz.

Haggard may also have borrowed some elements of his plot from a recently published boys' book by the prolific G. A. Henty, *By Right of Conquest; or, With Cortez in Mexico* (1891). Its young hero, Roger Hawkshaw, is cast ashore in Campeche on the eve of the Conquest, is befriended by the slave girl Marina, and is carried by Texcocan merchants to their city, "the centre of the education, science, and art of Anahuac." King Cacama helps Roger flee from the city to escape being seized and sacrificed by the priests of Tenochtitlán, "for the introduction of human sacrifice was a comparatively recent innovation in Tezcuco." Roger escapes the perils of the sacrificial stone and the battles of the Conquest to return to England with his Aztec princess Amenche in a conventional happy ending.

Henty had read his Prescott diligently. Frequently he interrupted the narrative to insert long sections on Aztec history and life, simply and clearly presented, in sufficient detail to give young readers a very adequate notion of Aztec culture. Henty's assessment of that culture was generally favorable. He wrote that Aztec religion was "a strange mixture of good and evil. The moral discipline enforced by it was excellent." In the traditional manner, he conjectured that this dual religion was the result of "the mixture of two peoples, the mild and gentle tenets of the Toltecs being adopted by the fierce Aztec invaders, who added to them their own superstitious and bloody rites." Under the dark side of Aztec religion lay "a system which, in point of morality, love of order and method, and a broad charity, was in no way inferior to that practiced among the Christian nations." Henty told of the supposed religious reforms of Nezahualcóyotl and Nezahualpilli, stressing Nezahualcóyotl's faith in "a God far greater than the idols of wood and stone worshiped by his subjects."

He applauded the "heroic constancy" of the Aztec last stand, comparing it to the defense of the city of Jerusalem against Titus. In the last analysis, however, "the fate of the Aztecs befell them because while a conquering people they had enslaved and tyrannized over the nations they subdued, extending them no rights or privileges, but using them simply as a means of supplying the pomp and luxury of the capital and of providing men for its wars." [69]

The dialogue form, so sparklingly used by Fontenelle to debate the merits of Aztec and European civilization, was revived for the same purpose by the Spanish intellectual and republican leader Francisco Pi y Margall, with the substitution of Cuauhtémoc for Moctezuma as the Aztec spokesman. The occasion for writing *Guatimozín y Hernán Cortés* was the erection of a statue to Cuauhtémoc in Mexico City (1887). This event had aroused criticism in Spain; the novelist Emilia Pardo Bazán, for example, complained that the Mexicans had seen fit to honor a "hairy, cannibalistic savage" instead of the civilizer Cortés. But Pi y Margall, an anti-imperialist who had favored granting Cuba her independence, thought differently. In *Guatimozín y Cortés* he took the side of the vanquished because "I think it is noble to defend one's country and ignoble to invade another's country. . . ." He hoped that the dialogue would illuminate the character of Nahua civilization and the character of the Conquest.

Into the mouth of Cortés the author put a severe indictment of Aztec society. Aztec culture bordered on barbarism, for it was still in the Stone or Copper Age. The Aztecs lacked horses, firearms, plows, vehicles of any kind, the compass, astrolabe, and ships. They had no coined money, no writing, being reduced to the use of symbols that could not precisely express abstract ideas. Their kings were tyrants, and worse still was the tyranny of the gods to whom they sacrificed masses of victims whose bodies they later consumed at repugnant banquets. Spain had the civilizing mission of putting an end to those evils, of admitting the light of Christianity, science, and industry into Mexico. The Spaniards, Soldiers of Christ who had just expelled the Moslems from their country, were singularly well endowed for this task.

domestic manners were singularly mild and polished, their laws remarkable, poesy was held in honor among them, their paintings and sculptures were very beautiful. Finally, they had attained an incredible degree of perfection in the mechanical arts and above all in astronomical science." Genin deplored that fanatical priests like Zumárraga had destroyed all that could remind the vanquished of their former grandeur. The *Poémes* consist of four sections: the Legends; the Mexica; the Conquest; and the Ruins. Although of little artistic merit, they reflect a considerable knowledge and skill, giving the reader faithful versified versions of Aztec myths, religious ideas, and history.

In the last decades of the century, Latin American poets, reacting against the outworn forms and ideals of romanticism, created the literary movement called Modernismo. Drawing on a variety of foreign sources, the Modernistas succeeded in forging a new, ornate poetry and prose, "entirely new, new in form and vocabulary and subject matter and feeling."

One of the movement's founders was the prodigiously gifted Nicaraguan poet Rubén Darío. If in the first escapist phase of his poetic career Darío peopled his verses with "satyrs, nymphs, centaurs, peacocks, and swans," in its second phase he gave voice to a virile public poetry that reflected a new concern with political and social themes. Darío's Americanism inevitably led to a search for symbols and themes in both the Spanish and the Indian past. These he regarded as the sources of a Latin American culture threatened by the aggressive expansionism of the United States.

Darío's explorations of the Indian past bore their first fruit in his *Cantos de vida y esperanza* (1905). In the poem "To Roosevelt" Darío flung a challenge to the United States, "future invader of that simple America that has Indian blood, that still prays to Jesus Christ and speaks Spanish." To the America of Theodore Roosevelt, Darío opposed "our America, which has had poets since the old times of Nezahualcóyotl," "the America of the Great Moctezuma and the Inca, the fragrant America of Christopher Columbus, Catholic America, Spanish America, the America where the noble Cuauhtémoc said: 'I am not on a bed of roses. . . .' "

In *El canto errante* (1907) Darío worked the vein of poetic material furnished by the legends and history of ancient Mexico. The poem *Tutecotzimi* opens with a striking archaeological image.

Digging into the soil of an ancient city,
the metal point of a pick encounters
a golden ornament, a sculptured stone,
an arrow, a fetish, a god of ambiguous form,
or the vast walls of a temple. My pick
is working in the soil of an unknown America.

May my poet's pick make harmonious sounds!
May it turn up gold and opals and rich fine stones,
a temple, or a broken statue!
And may the Muse divine the meaning of the
hieroglyphics.

The setting of *Tutecotzimi* is a valley in Guatemala, once the
home of the Pipil, a tribe of Nahua stock. The poet's imagination
re-creates "the strange life of a vanished people":

. . . the confused legend
becomes clear; the mountain where the ruins lie
reveals its secrets. The ancient trees recall
processions, battles, immemorial rites.
A cezontle sings. What does it sing?
A song that no one has ever heard before?
The cezontle has built its nest upon an idol.
(The Toltec women listened to that song,
and it delighted the proud prince Moctezuma.)
Meanwhile the panther rustles the dry leaves,
the green quetzal shows off its glorious plumage to the iris,
and the gods make sparkle the waters of the spring.
As evening falls, the bloody west
spreads out its barbarous cloak, and the vague wind
bears the musical speech of some vague lyre.

And Nezahualcóyotl, king and poet, sighs.

A procession winds its way to the royal palace before which
stands King Cuaucmichin. It is led by the poet Tekij, who has
"the light of visions glowing in his eyes." Tekij denounces King
Cuaucmichin for having shed Pipil blood in human sacrifice. The
poet relates the story of the Pipil. Long ago the Aztec King
Ahuítzotl sent five men to settle Guatemala, "without shields or

the royal bath somehow create the impression of a vanished grandeur.

Velasco's work was wholly untypical. Nothing less than a political and social revolution was needed to replace the prevailing artificiality with the archaeological realism of a Rivera or with the efforts of an Orozco or a Siqueiros to rise above realism in the depiction of the spirit of ancient Mexico.

CHAPTER FOURTEEN

The Return of Cuauhtémoc

In the twentieth century the West rediscovered the civilizations of ancient Mexico. As the archaeologist's spade unearthed the ruins of once populous cities, colossal structures and sculptures and jewels and pottery of exquisite artistry captured the popular imagination as well as the attention of scholars. Little by little, skillful reconstructions partially re-created and authenticated the splendor of Chichén Itzá, Monte Albán, and Teotihuacán.

These revelations of Indian talent and industry came to a West whose faith in itself had been shaken both by a World War and a great Depression and by the growing challenge of communism and anticolonialism. Western philosophy and social science reflected the loss of faith in reason, technology, and progress. Again, as in the Renaissance, another time of pervasive doubt, the primitivist yearning for a return to the presumed innocence and simplicity of the world's childhood became a potent influence in Western thought.

How far behind Europe had left the complacent assumptions of Western superiority nourished by the generation of Morgan and Tylor is evident in the assessments of Indian civilization by two German philosophers who wrote a century apart. Hegel, in his lectures on the philosophy of history (1822 to 1831), dismissed ancient America with a few scornful sentences containing echoes of De Pauw and Buffon: "Of America and its civilization, espe-

guise, came into being and soon accounted for the bulk of Mexico's agricultural production, sharing its profits with processing plants that often were subsidiaries of foreign companies. Meanwhile Indian and mestizo small landowners and ejidos starved for credit and other necessities. They lacked machinery, often did not have access to irrigation, and struggled to extract a living from soil that was frequently badly eroded. Worse still, landlessness and land-grabbing increased. "The situation," observes Fernando Benítez, was "not very different from what it was in the days of Porfirio Díaz. The latifundio of lands and peons has disappeared, with some exceptions, and has been openly replaced by the financial latifundio." [3]

Whereas the condition of the living Indians improved little, if at all, Mexican government and society continued to pay homage to their dead ancestors. Whether liberal or conservative, Mexican administrations looked favorably on anthropological studies. With modest official support, and in an atmosphere of widespread and sometimes emotional public interest in Mexico's Indian past, Mexican anthropology made large quantitative and qualitative advances. In addition to the old Museo Nacional, major centers of research were the Escuela Nacional de Antropología, established in 1942 in the Instituto Nacional de Antropología e Historia, and the Sociedad Mexicana de Antropología, founded under private auspices in 1937. The long roster of distinguished names includes Manuel Gamio, Miguel Othón de Mendizábal, Alfonso Caso, Wigberto Jiménez Moreno, Pablo Martínez del Río, Miguel Covarrubias. From Europe came other scholars who enriched Mexican anthropology with their work: Paul Kirchhoff, Juan Comas, Ángel Palerm, Pedro Armillas.

Beginning with Gamio's epoch-making excavations and reconstruction at Teotihuacán, Mexican archaeology moved from triumph to triumph. In 1931 came Caso's discovery of the famous Tomb 7 at Monte Albán, with its hoard of magnificent jewels and gold objects; in 1941, the discovery of impressive structures and colossal statues at Tula; in 1946, the find of the brilliant Maya frescoes at Bonampak. In the administration of President Adolfo López Mateos, construction was begun in the capital of an anthropological museum worthy of housing Mexico's Indian treasures; the museum, an imposing complex of marble and glass, fountains and gardens, with excerpts from Aztec poems and speeches engraved on its walls, opened in 1964.

The Mexican cult of ancient Mexico reflects above all an intense nationalism, the desire to accent that part of the national cultural heritage which is peculiarly Mexican, a justified pride in a great tradition of remote antiquity. As in the days of Don Porfirio, however, the cult has more pragmatic uses. It encourages an influx of tourists, it improves Mexico's image abroad, and at home it serves to conceal the continued tragic division of Mexico into two nations, no less than the official and private indifference to the plight of the living Indians.

Fernando Benítez has bluntly exposed the insincerity and shallowness of much of the current *indigenismo:* "The fact that we restored Teotihuacán or that Father Garibay labors to translate Aztec poems brings no benefit to the Indians, adds not a single tortilla to their daily diet. We adorn ourselves with their jewels, excavate the earth to turn up their ancient artifacts, but we stubbornly ignore their rags, protect the men who steal their lands, fail to punish their exploiters. . . . We have one attitude toward the dead Indians, a very different one toward the living. The dead Indians excite our admiration, stimulate a stream of tourists; the living Indians make us blush with shame, give a hollow ring to our fine words of progress and democracy." [4]

As the cult of the Indian past grew, the figure of Cuauhtémoc gained a transcendent significance, loomed titanic against the background of Mexican history. The "young grandfather," as the poet Ramón López Velarde called him, became the supreme symbol of the Calvary of the Mexican people, of its valor and steadfastness in struggle against oppressors, foreign and domestic. Poets and painters celebrated his heroism and martyrdom. In the continuing historical debate between the army of *indigenistas* and the shrinking force of *hispanistas,* he was the champion of the former, just as Cortés was the paladin of the latter. The emotive power of these names was nowhere so apparent as in the famous "battle of the bones."

On November 24, 1946, it was announced that skeletal remains believed to be those of Cortés had been unearthed in the Hospital de Jesús in the capital, and this identification was later confirmed by a commission that included experts from the Instituto Nacional

ested in Indian questions, and continues the Gamio tradition of combining study of the Indian past with practical efforts to incorporate the living Indians in modern civilization. Accepting the necessity and desirability of *mestizaje* and acculturation, writers of this school appraise the ancient Indian cultures realistically. They note the prodigious achievements but are not blind to the flaws and failures of the ancient Mexicans. A second *indigenista* tendency, represented by Eulalia Guzmán and her disciples, is violently anti-Spanish and idealizes Aztec Mexico beyond recognition. A third current of *indigenista* thought, identified above all with the archaeologist Laurette Séjourné, shows the strong influence of philosophical idealism and mystical psychological doctrines. Séjourné and her followers regard Teotihuacán as the luminous center of a great spiritual tradition which the Aztecs corrupted for their own predatory ends. Finally, there is the *hispanista* school, chiefly represented by the late Mariano Cuevas, S.J., and the late philosopher José Vasconcelos. Rabidly hostile to Indian culture and eulogistic of Spain and her work in America, these writers present, but less subtly and skillfully, the arguments of the nineteenth-century conservative historian Lucas Alamán.

Manuel Gamio was the founder of Mexican scientific *indigenismo*. His early career illustrates the transition from the academic archaeology of the nineteenth century to the alliance of archaeology and applied anthropology that characterizes the Mexican scene today. Gamio, who began to study archaeology at the Museo Nacional in 1906, went on to work under Boas at Columbia, and later, under Boas' direction, conducted important stratigraphic excavations in the Valley of Mexico. He early joined the movement for the redemption of the Indian that timidly emerged in the twilight years of the Porfiriato.[6] In an essay written in 1907 Gamio proclaimed the intellectual equality of the Indian and expressed a romantic sympathy for the suffering indigenes: "Poor, unhappy race! You fuse the might of the sturdy Tarahumara who fells cedars in the mountain, the Attic exquisiteness of divine Teotihuacán, the wisdom of the Tlaxcalan, the indomitable valor of the sanguinary Mexica. Why do you not stand erect, proud of your legend? Why do you not show to the world your Indian heritage?"[7]

The Revolution of 1910 enabled Gamio to replace this sentimental *indigenismo* with a concrete program of action in behalf of the Indian. In 1916 he published his classic book, *Forjando patria*. Here he argued that Mexico did not constitute a nation in the European sense, but was composed of numerous small nations, differing in speech, economy, social organization, and psychology. Only the redemption of the Indian, his incorporation in the modern world, could forge a true nation, a united people; this process required a thorough understanding of the Indian's past and of his present conditions of life. Gamio posed new tasks for the anthropologist. It was not enough to study and admire the achievements of the ancient Mexicans; anthropology must become functional, must ask what contribution it could make to the solution of contemporary Indian problems.[8]

In its nationalism, in its focus on the Indian as the key problem of Mexican reconstruction, Gamio's book was a text for the times. The Constitution of 1917 offered a blueprint for sweeping social changes; that same year Gamio secured the creation within the Secretaría de Agricultura y Fomento of a Dirección de Antropología. As chief of this office, Gamio planned a series of studies of key areas that would bring together the mass of data needed for a sound program of social reconstruction. The result of a pilot study he made of the Valley of Teotihuacán was a vast collaborative work (1922) describing in massive detail the past and present life and environment of the population of the valley.[9]

In his introduction, summarizing the findings of the study, Gamio systematically compared the present condition of the Indians of Teotihuacán with their state before the Conquest. The three stages of the history of the valley—preconquest, colonial, and modern—constituted an inverse or descending evolution. During the first and flourishing stage of their history, the Teotihuacanos made remarkable material and intellectual progress. The population was ten, twenty, or more times the number of inhabitants in 1917. Their architecture, sculpture, painting, ceramics, and other arts were of a high order of excellence. By the period 1917 to 1922, however, "the glorious architectural traditions of the people whose artisans had constructed the famous city of the pyramids" had disappeared. Hundreds of Indians lived in caves, the majority in huts of cactus, adobe, or volcanic stone. Of their once splendid industry, there remained only a "crude pottery, incomparably in-

he cited the recent monograph of Manuel Moreno on Aztec social organization to show that ancient Mexican society was divided into two basic classes—a privileged ruling class and the plebeians. Chávez paid special attention to the question of land tenure, noting that this question had aroused considerable scholarly interest in recent years, during which "erudition placed itself at the service of the Revolution, which from the first has sought a solution for our dreadful agrarian problem." The fact that in Aztec society communal land tenure coexisted with private land tenure proved to Chávez that that society had evolved past the tribal stage of organization, that there had emerged a state, "a centralizing entity in which the individual separates himself from the collective and becomes its master." By the time of the Conquest private property in land had made immense gains at the expense of communal land tenure. Otherwise it would be impossible to explain "the profound misery of the millions of *macehuales* who groaned under the yoke of priests and nobles." [15] Chávez' Marxist stress on class conflict and social inequalities could give little comfort to uncritical eulogists of Aztec society.

Such eulogists could derive no more satisfaction from the assessment of Aztec civilization by Alfonso Caso, dean of the present generation of Mexican anthropologists, in a brilliant work of synthesis, *El Pueblo del Sol* (1953). A brother of the distinguished philosopher and sociologist Antonio Caso, Alfonso early gave up the profession of the law in which he had been trained and devoted himself to the study of archaeology. The courses in Maya and Mexican archaeology taught at the Universidad Nacional in 1924 by Hermann Beyer especially stimulated his interest in the field and demonstrated the possibility of a rigorously scientific approach to its problems. Caso became the principal authority on pre-Cortesian Mixtec codices and history; one of his major triumphs was the spectacular discovery of Mixtec jewels at Monte Albán in 1931. Like Gamio and Mendizábal, Caso has combined archaeological research with a large practical activity in behalf of the Mexican Indian; he has been director since its founding (1948) of the Instituto Nacional Indigenista.

In *El Pueblo del Sol*, Caso focused his attention on Aztec religion, regarded as the driving force of Aztec civilization. Caso placed the Aztecs in the polytheistic stage of religious evolution, but discerned an effort on the part of the Aztec priesthood to reduce the numerous deities to multiple aspects of a small number of powerful gods. He conceded that a few individuals like Nezahualcóyotl had assigned primacy to a supreme invisible and impalpable god, but distinguished this development from monotheism. Caso described the cosmogonic foundations of Aztec religion, on which was based the compact between men and gods for their mutual support. War itself, wrote Caso, was a form of worship which fed the gods with the terrible nectar of life. All Aztec intellectual and artistic achievements were linked to this religious basis of Aztec civilization. As the masterpiece of Aztec art, Caso singled out the Coatlicue, which reflected "all the barbaric originality of a young and energetic people," and indeed surpassed "in expressive force the more refined creations of people like the Mayas, whose concepts of life and the gods were expressed in more serene forms." Caso defined the Aztec political system as "a religious theocracy in which the warrior was subordinate to the priest," in which the emperor himself and all other high officials were priests, products of the sacerdotal school, the Calmécac. On the other hand, said Caso, the mystical doctrine of a compact between men and gods also provided the Aztecs with their own kind of "Manifest Destiny," with a convincing rationale for striving for the continuous expansion of Aztec imperialism.

Caso described a cleavage in the Aztec soul: on the one hand, there was the energetic drive to power, expressed in the religious and imperialist ideal; on the other, a profound pessimism rooted in the belief in the inevitable destruction of the fifth sun that would bring the downfall of the world and mankind. According to Caso, this was "the fundamental contradiction in the Aztec culture."

If Caso regarded religion as the driving force of Aztec civilization, he also viewed it as "a fatal limitation" for the Aztecs and all other cultures of Mesoamerica. Religion had become a fetter on progress in art, science, and social organization, because religion had largely assumed the role that technical invention played in Western societies. "For the Indians of Mesoamerica sacrifice was the technical means that made the rain fall, the corn grow, an illness disappear, a father, husband, or son return safe from an expedition of war or commerce, or a wife give birth to a strong,

Frank Lloyd Wright. Charles Ennis house, Los Angeles. 1924. Concrete block construction. Photograph Ezra Stoller © Esto.

reducing ancient Mexican society to a lowly tribal level. Second, the current debate about the historical roots of and solutions for the burning agrarian problem drew attention to the nature of Aztec land tenure. Third, long before evolutionism revived in the United States, Mexican anthropology had a strong evolutionary bent and concerned itself with the problem of defining the level of social development attained by Mesoamerican civilization, with parallels between Old and New World cultural evolution, and with similar questions.

To the inquiry about the nature of Aztec society, Alfonso Caso made important direct and indirect contributions. Caso, who believed that Bandelier "exaggerated and distorted the social organization of the Aztecs at the time of the Conquest," encouraged one of his students at the Universidad Nacional, Manuel Moreno, to investigate the problem. The result was the first systematic effort to test Bandelier's premises against the evidence of the very Spanish and Indian sources Bandelier had used. In fine, Moreno concluded that Aztec society was neither a tribal nor a military democracy. The *calpulli*, he declared, was not a kinship unit at all; it was a simple territorial unit of the Aztec city, completely subordinate to the central Aztec government, which constituted a state in the essential meaning of the word. This state, according to Moreno, wielded power for the benefit of a few privileged classes to the prejudice of the majority of the Aztec people.[18]

Moreno had struck a serious blow at Bandelier's positions, although most United States anthropologists appeared blissfully unaware of the fact for at least a decade after the publication of Moreno's book. It remained to refine Moreno's solution to the problem, to correct its errors and oversimplifications. In 1949 the anthropologist Arturo Monzón published a book that attempted to do this. Monzón took an intermediate position on the key question of the *calpulli*. He regarded it as a clan that was ambilateral as concerned the rule of descent, and endogamous or with a tendency toward endogamy as concerned the rule of marriage. The Aztec clans, however, were not egalitarian clans of the Iroquois type, but were strongly stratified internally and in relation to each other, with indications that there existed one principal clan to which all the chiefs of the tribe belonged. In short, Aztec society combined kinship organization with a marked aristocratic charac-

atmosphere that a representative of the Mexican Chamber of Commerce in New York, himself pure white, could declare: "The ancient Mexicans had their own religion . . . their gods and their temples . . . and the first step taken by the Spanish soldiers and the Spanish priests upon gaining possession of the land, was to demolish the magnificent places of worship of the Mexican towns, and to erect Roman churches upon the débris. The idols and the icons were destroyed . . . and the Mexicans who were not killed were baptized en masse." [22]

Typical exponents of the extreme *indigenista* viewpoint are by no means uninformed amateurs, ignorant of the Spanish and Indian sources on Aztec civilization. Indeed, some have made serious contributions to Indian studies. Rubén Campos, poet and professor of folklore at the Universidad Nacional, published in 1936 a valuable pioneering anthology of Aztec literature. In his introduction Campos proclaimed that ancient Mexico was a land of peace and plenty, "an immense laboratory of labor." To prove its prosperity, Campos cited the testimony of conquistadors that because of the abundance of provisions a multitude of beggars swarmed in the city streets. Immediately grasping the damaging nature of this testimony, Campos hastened to remark that this was a typical Spanish exaggeration. Aztec law strictly forbade vagrancy; only cripples were allowed to beg for alms. Over this Aztec Eden presided the *teopixque*, a priesthood whose teachings formed a people unique among the nations of the earth. These wise old priests, declared Campos, had nothing in common with the modern clerical agitator in a cassock, "sent by the prelates into different areas to foment violence against constituted authorities with their speeches of hate." The striving for perfection inculcated by these priests pervaded all aspects of Aztec life, including the political institutions. The conquistadors, imposing the absolute rule of the Spanish king, wiped out all traces of popular sovereignty in a land that had enjoyed democratic rule.[23]

We have observed the archaeologist and historian Eulalia Guzmán in action in the "battle of the bones." With the same fervor that she applied to upholding the authenticity of the supposed remains of Cuauhtémoc, Doña Eulalia defended Moctezuma and condemned Cortés in an introduction to her edition of the Second Letter of Cortés. She dedicated this work to the memory of Moctezuma II, Cuitláhuac, Cuauhtémoc, and their heroic companions, "the seeds of our Mexican nationality." In her introduction Guzmán subjected the sources for the Conquest to a severe critique. The accounts of the conquistadors cannot be trusted because they confronted an alien world which they did not understand and therefore interpreted in terms of their own world, and because they unscrupulously falsified the facts to justify their conduct. The few available Indian and mestizo accounts are also defective, as a rule, because their authors had been indoctrinated with Spanish religious dogmas and because they were written in the shadow of Spanish power, making it impossible for the writers to tell the truth without fear of reprisal. As a result, the story of the Conquest that has come down to us is a tissue of lies and fantasies woven by Cortés, and embellished by Bernal Díaz with a multitude of fictional details such as the supposed battles with the Tlaxcalans—battles that never occurred, according to Guzmán.

What really happened, then? In Guzmán's reconstruction of the Conquest, Cortés, appearing on the shores of Mexico, gave himself out to be the messenger of a powerful king with messages for Moctezuma and asked to be received by the Aztec ruler. Moctezuma submitted the petition to the supreme council of the Confederation of Anáhuac, which granted Cortés' request. Moctezuma then issued orders to all the confederated states between Veracruz and Tenochtitlán to receive the strangers in peace. They were admitted as guests into Tenochtitlán. Once lodged in a royal palace, Cortés and his fellow conspirators kidnaped Moctezuma and all the other lords of the Confederation; they remained in captivity until death freed them from their sufferings. Guzmán denied to Cortés either bravery or intellectual capacity; he was lascivious, cunning, and greedy for power.

To complete the picture of Cortés' degeneracy, she cited the conclusions of a study of Cortés' bones made by herself and Dr. Alfonso Quiroz Cuarón in 1947: the conquistador suffered from dwarfism associated with congenital syphilis of the bones. Inevitably, an illustration reproduced a portion of Diego Rivera's historical mural in the Palacio Nacional, showing a cold, calculating Cortés with ferret's face, deformed knees, and a hunchback.

Guzmán's idyllic portrait of Aztec Mexico corresponded to this account of a trusting, guileless Moctezuma betrayed and destroyed

the revision of all textbooks that blackened his character, the erection of statues to him, and the destruction of all statues or other memorials to the "bandit" Cortés.

In the writings of Laurette Séjourné the mystique of ancient Teotihuacán replaces the mystique of Aztec Mexico. For this writer that great vanished city—which she, almost alone among archaeologists, identifies with the Tula of legend and history—was the home of a humanistic teaching, a great spiritual inheritance, which the Aztecs betrayed.

In her efforts to unlock the meaning of the hieroglyphs, pictures, and other objects discovered at Teotihuacán, Séjourné is guided by philosophical and psychological doctrines of a distinctly mystical nature. She reproves the majority of other anthropologists, including Eduard Seler, for allowing themselves to be led astray by "an excess of rationalism" in their interpretation of the ancient symbols. Her own reading of those figures discovers a constant Toltec preoccupation with the search for inner perfection and a striving for union with divinity. This reading rests for proof primarily on itself, that is, on the intuitive assumptions of the author, and seems to have little support in what we know of the stage of social and intellectual development achieved by the Teotihuacanos.

At the center of Séjourné's interpretation is her explanation of the Quetzalcóatl theme in Toltec history. She rejects efforts to find historical elements in the Quetzalcóatl legend. In Jungian language she asserts that "to wish to convert it into a fragment of history is to destroy it and deprive it forever of its vital content; because the myth, the most profound expression of the spirit, oversteps the boundaries of particular detail and always achieves the revelation of a fundamental eternal truth." For Séjourné, "the spiritual content of the Quetzalcóatl myth is self-evident; the anguish for his sin, his burning need for purification, and also the fire that converts him into light, reveal a religious doctrine closely related to those humanity has known elsewhere under various symbolic languages." Indeed, she finds that the Quetzalcóatl doctrine offers a vision of man strangely similar to that of such modern mystics as Julian Huxley and Teilhard de Chardin.[27]

Séjourné's interpretation requires her to prove that Teotihuacán civilization, as the embodiment of Quetzalcóatl's spiritual message, was free of the scourges of war and human sacrifice. This poses considerable difficulty in view of the growing evidence for the presence of militarism, human sacrifice, and ritual cannibalism at Teotihuacán.[28] Séjourné solves the problem by placing her own highly speculative construction on such evidence. Noting, for example, the appearance of jaguar and eagle knights in warlike attitudes in Teotihuacán frescoes, she explains that these represent ritual sacred battles "between heaven and earth, between Being and the Void." The portrayal of sacrificial knives and the act of splitting human hearts, which might suggest to more prosaic minds that human sacrifice existed in the home of Quetzalcóatl, instead symbolize for Séjourné "a high, holy and powerful concept" in which the sacrificial knife represents "the ceaseless search for spirituality which conscious man must undertake" and the heart "is an expression of man's mystic will to rise upward to God." [29]

Séjourné's key ideas, formulated more cautiously, appear in the writings of a leading student of ancient Mexican culture, Miguel León-Portilla. Like Séjourné, León-Portilla believes that the Aztecs degraded into a "mystico-militaristic" world vision "the spiritualist vision of the ancient times . . . the vision of the world of Quetzalcóatl." A corollary of this view is that within Aztec society, and upon its highest levels, there existed a secret coterie of poets and thinkers, men like Nezahualcóyotl, who rejected the Aztec message of "the darts and the shields" and through the way of "flower and song" attempted to revive the humanistic, monotheistic message of the great priest Quetzalcóatl.[30] To use a favorite phrase of the old positivist Alfredo Chavero, Séjourné and León-Portilla seem to assign to the ancient Mexicans ideas incompatible "with the social milieu in which they lived."

The conservative, pro-Spanish and anti-Indian literary tradition of Lucas Alamán revived in the polemical atmosphere of a post-revolutionary Mexico filled with wrangles between *indigenistas* and *hispanistas*. The tradition had relatively few supporters by contrast with the powerful phalanx of *indigenistas*, and it fought against the spirit of the times. After 1940, with the passing of the Church-State issue and the emergence of a political consensus based on the middle-of-the-road policies of post-Cárdenas governments, the conservative historiographic tradition lost influence. In its heyday, however, it could boast of two major figures, the Jesuit historian Mariano Cuevas and the many-faceted José Vasconcelos.

Cuevas' principal work was his *Historia de la iglesia en México*, certainly a partisan, tendentious book, but one that reveals a wide knowledge of printed and manuscript sources. The same uncompromisingly conservative spirit dominated his *Historia de la nación mexicana*. So old-fashioned were his views on ancient Mexico that they make his eighteenth-century coreligionist Clavigero appear to be a daring radical. Cuevas thundered against optimistic *indigenistas* who saw pre-Cortesian Mexico through rose-colored glasses. "Given the universal and intimate influence of their infernal religion, the peoples of Anáhuac were bound to be corrupted, despite the good natural character of its unhappy inhabitants." That religion was a compound of "superstition, vain prophecies, the most absurd, childish, and indecent theogonies, sacred drunkenness, and perfect cannibalism." A "bloody and ferocious Satanism" pervaded every aspect of Aztec life and society. It was improper to apply the terms "civilization," "empire," or even "political organization" to the Aztec state. The proper term was "tyranny, or the supreme abuse of authority." Cuevas grudgingly admitted, however, that Aztec statecraft was superior to what one might expect from "cannibals." [31]

The political and literary career of José Vasconcelos presents a paradox. As Secretary of Education under President Obregón, he launched bold new programs of popular education that probably owed something to the Soviet example. Soon, however, he moved into opposition to Obregón and his successor Calles, ran unsuccessfully for President in 1929 and, charging fraud, allied himself with right-wing, clerical opponents of the revolutionary regime. The man who had declared that "we are Indian, blood and soul; the language and civilization are Spanish," [32] became an ardent eulogist of Spain and an enemy of all things Indian. In his flamboyant autobiography the word Aztec serves as synonym for all that is barbarous and bloody. Victoriano Huerta's murder of Gustavo Madero in 1913 was an "Aztec ritual"; the revolutionary program of the agrarian reformer Emiliano Zapata was an example of "Aztec despotism"; Obregón's harsh suppression of the Adolfo de la Huerta revolt in 1924 was "Aztec cannibalism."

Vasconcelos defined his attitude toward ancient Mexico in the section on "México precortesiano" in his popular *Breve historia de México,* published in numerous editions since its first appearance in 1937. His discussion is sketchy and superficial, to say the least, being apparently based on use—but not very careful use—of one book, the *Historia de la América española* of the Mexican historian Carlos Pereyra. On Pereyra's authority, Vasconcelos upheld the "scientific school of Morgan" which claimed that the clan was the basis of Aztec society. But in his confused, garbled version of Pereyra's account Vasconcelos asserted that "clan life was only for the nobles," and that they alone received land from the clans. The informational value of this portion of the book is almost nil.

A few examples will suggest Vasconcelos' flair for sweeping statement and his political bias. "Moctezuma's despotism was worse than that found in the most degraded African state." "Women were little better than merchandise." "Yet there are agents of contemporary communism in Mexico and Peru who sigh for a return to the methods of Indian communism." Sometimes Vasconcelos makes use of Aztec material to point up a contemporary moral. Asserting that the forms employed in addressing Moctezuma ran the gamut of servility in all its nuances, Vasconcelos commented: "There still remains in the Mexican character a subconscious abjectness that makes it impossible to speak in the press of a public official without use of the 'Señor.' Señor Presidente. . . . Señor Gobernador. . . . Señor General. . . . Over our character still hangs the great weight of an Aztequismo which we have not been able to dispel." Vasconcelos proclaimed that the legend of Quetzalcóatl and his defeat symbolized the whole history of Mexico. Whenever a Mexican Quetzalcóatl emerged, he was destroyed politically or physically. The former was the fate of Lucas Alamán; the latter the destiny of Francisco I. Madero. "But we have known long, sterile, evil periods under the sign of Huichilobos the cannibal!" [33]

Vasconcelos adds little to the arsenal of arguments employed by critics of ancient Mexican civilization. On the other hand, the Aztec cultural heritage has never been so piquantly used to explain the general course of Mexican history, or assigned such a weight of negative symbolism. The validity of Vasconcelos' parallels and comparisons is, of course, another matter.

Bandelier's influence on United States scholars concerned with ancient Mexico suffered some decline in the first decades of the twentieth century. How tenacious was that influence is suggested by a study of Bandelier's theories (1917) by the Berkeley anthropologist T. T. Waterman. He began by noting the existence of two schools of thought about political and social organization in ancient Mexico. One school, consisting of Morgan and Bandelier, rejected the concept of an Aztec Empire, holding it was only a loose confederacy of democratic Indian tribes. These views, said Waterman, were supported "by the sentiments, if not the published writings, of most American ethnologists." The opposition, he conceded, consisted, "broadly speaking, of the other scholars who have written on the subject."

Waterman criticized some of Bandelier's methods, but concluded that "we are on firm ground in assuming with Bandelier that Mexican society, at the time of the Conquest, was still organized on a primitive clan basis." Waterman accepted as "perfectly obvious" Bandelier's position that "arguments cannot be based on the descriptive terminology of the Spanish authors of the sixteenth century, not even when these authors were eyewitnesses of what they described." With regard to specific points, Waterman concluded that "the Aztec war chief was probably well started on the way to becoming a king, but had not yet arrived," that "the ownership of land . . . was vested not in individuals but in the clan," and that Bandelier's point "that Spanish society was essentially feudal, while Indian society was essentially democratic, is . . . a good one." In fine, declared Waterman, "Bandelier may be regarded as finally confirming the most important of Morgan's conclusions." [34]

A survey of the relevant literature of the next two decades suggests that Waterman did not exaggerate when he stated in 1917 that most American ethnologists endorsed Bandelier's positions. As late as 1929 we find the very knowledgeable Marshall H. Saville writing that "the term 'king' is inappropriate in connection with the rulers of Mexico," and "similarly misleading is the term 'empire' which has come into general use to designate the native governments of ancient Middle and South America." [35]

Gradually, however, there emerged a tendency toward compromise that preserved much of Bandelier's general scheme while qualifying or revising it with respect to one or another detail. The highly respected archaeologist Herbert J. Spinden set the tone in his handbook *Ancient Civilizations of Mexico and Central America*. Noting the conflict between the traditional view of the Aztec ruler as absolute and that of more recent writers who held that tribal organization was essentially democratic, Spinden cautiously observed that "the truth doubtless lies between these extremes." Conceding that the great Aztec public offices were elective, he found a tendency to fill them from certain powerful families, thus laying the foundations of an aristocratic state. Spinden also questioned whether the *calpultin* were clans in the technical sense of exogamic kinship groups, and suggested they were military societies taking in all the men of the tribe.[36]

J. Eric Thompson, curator at the Field Museum of Chicago, inclined toward acceptance of Spinden's compromise solution in his excellent *Mexico Before Cortés* (1937). He suggested that the Aztec ruler might be compared to the chairman of a financial or industrial corporation. "His authority varied according to his personality, and that of the executive council." On the other hand, Thompson saw a threefold division of Aztec lands into *calpulli* land, private estates of nobles, hereditary and fully alienable, and land held in conquered territory by warriors, with reversion to the king.[37]

Perhaps the most striking example of Bandelier's continuing influence, because of the unexpected quarter in which we find it, is provided by the writings of the anthropologist Robert H. Lowie. In his *Primitive Society* (1920), Lowie subjected Morgan's evolutionary scheme to a systematic, sharp critique. Yet he conceded, apparently without troubling to examine the evidence, that Bandelier's claim that "feudal overlords were unknown in Mexico will probably stand"; Lowie also accepted Bandelier's argument for "the collective tenancy of land by the *calpulli* with mere usufruct by the individual families." He only questioned whether the *calpultin* were true clans in the technical sense, citing Spinden's suggestion that they were military societies. As late as 1937, in his *History of Ethnological Theory*, even as he scolded Morgan for the supposed aberrations of his classificatory scheme, Lowie admitted that Morgan's dogmatism "happened to yield a valuable by-product—the scrutiny of Spanish chronicles with their extravagant descriptions of an Aztec Empire."[38]

The disillusioned mood of United States intellectuals in the period between the two World Wars deserves mention as one of the causes for the continued hold of Bandelier's theories on American anthropology. The disillusioned recoil of these intellectuals from the failures of a capitalist, technological society heightened their appreciation for the supposed innocence and simplicity of primitive societies, past and present. Among the multiple reflections of this state of mind in American social science we may perhaps include Robert Redfield's *Tepoztlan* (1930), with its stress on the absence of competition and tensions in a Mexican village; the idealized portrayal of Inca civilization in the historical writings of Philip A. Means; and the enthusiasm for Maya civilization expressed in the books of Sylvanus G. Morley and J. Eric Thompson.

This neoromanticism provoked the Mexican anthropologist Pablo Martínez del Río to sarcastic comment. In their field work and monographs, he wrote, American scholars observed very high scientific standards, but when they published works of synthesis their admiration for the ancient Mexicans caused them to write incredible nonsense. By way of example he cited the *History of the Maya* (1931) by the Englishmen Thomas Gann and J. Eric Thompson. "Ah, they say, for those happy times before the coming of the white man! Ah, for the old, lazy, joyous, carefree life! . . . Ah culture, ah civilization, destined to disappear before that monstrosity imported from Europe, which is no civilization at all, but only a 'so-called' civilization. . . . As concerns Maya religion, we must not despair, for the author assures us that there still shine some golden grains of the old beliefs among the Christian 'chaff.' "

"What nonsense!" exclaimed Martínez del Río. "It is really incredible that scientists of indisputable merit should be so blind to reality!" [39]

This neoromanticism flaunts itself in the writings of two prominent American archaeologists, Edgar L. Hewett and George C. Vaillant. In his *Ancient Life in Mexico and Central America* (1936), Hewett proclaimed that the Indians "had no science, no nationalism, no church, but they had the fine culture values of religion, of community spirit, of confidence in nature. . . . Why exchange faith for skepticism? Known for unknown? Certainty for doubt? Serenity for perplexity? is the way the Indian would have considered it if left a free agent. Looking at the wreckage in our civilization, there is something to be said for the Indian's point of view." [40]

In conformity with this view of Indian life as characterized by "community spirit," by a fine simplicity, Hewett religiously followed Bandelier's assessment of the level of political and social organization attained by the Aztecs. "There is no excuse," wrote Hewett, "for perpetually handing on the glamorous, fantastic picture of Aztec life that every archaeologist knows to be misleading. Those attributes of European civilization—kings, counts, lords, palaces—were unknown to aboriginal America. The first European witnesses of the spectacular ceremonies of the Indians wrote of them in terms with which they were familiar, terms of European civilization. If for them we substitute chiefs, councils, headsmen, pueblos, we have a fairly accurate nomenclature in terms of Indian culture history." The houses of Tenochtitlán may have been more numerous, but otherwise were probably similar to the pueblos of New Mexico. Having so narrowly defined the bounds of Aztec cultural development, Hewett wistfully asked whether the Conquest had not interrupted an Indian unfolding whose climax was yet to come: "Who knows whether or not the apogee had been reached under the Aztec Confederacy of Moctezuma? Who knows what America might have brought forth in another thousand unmolested years?" [41]

Bandelier's influence also appears in attenuated form in the classic *Aztecs of Mexico* (1944) of George C. Vaillant. Let it be said that despite this and some other defects—notably Vaillant's error in identifying Teotihuacán with Tula—the book remains a brilliant, sensitive, and informative guide to Aztec civilization.

Bandelier supplied Vaillant with a theoretical framework for his vision of the Aztec social order as a harmonious collective in which the conflicts and tensions of modern capitalist society were unknown. "Mexican society," wrote Vaillant, "existed for the benefit of the tribe, and each member was supposed to do his part in preserving the community." In this society, "there was little to harass the individual intellectually or economically. Existence was subject to divine favor, and a man fared much as did his fellows. . . . An Aztec would have been horrified at the naked isolation of an individual's life in our Western world."

In the manner of Bandelier, Vaillant criticized the early Spanish chroniclers who, "conditioned by their medieval Spanish background, spoke of hereditary classes. In all probability, judging from Indian communities as a whole, there was *rank* but not *class* in a hereditary sense." However, since Vaillant recognized that land granted to warriors in conquered territory passed from father to son, it is difficult to understand why one should not call this warrior nobility a hereditary class. Vaillant's considerable knowledge of the facts sometimes got in the way of his theory. Thus he admitted that under conditions of growing population, "the priests and chiefs who lived off the public lands would be far better off than the ordinary citizen whose holding, generation by generation, tended to diminish." It is hard to reconcile this admission with the statement that "a man fared much as did his fellows." Vaillant himself recognized the difficulty of explaining the continual election of the highest tribal officers from the same family or lineage, "when democratic procedure obtained elsewhere." [42]

Aztec life, as seen by Vaillant, combined the advantages of a society based on the collective interest with the refinements of an advanced culture. "It is obvious that the Aztecs were no pitiable, craven savages. They lived upon variegated and delicious foods and dwelt in houses that were comfortable and airy. Their dress stimulated the exercise of merited self-satisfaction, not to be confused with the compensations of vanity. Their manner of life enabled them to take advantage of their personal aptitudes and exchange the products of their own creation for whatever they lacked. . . ." The measure of Aztec civilization could not be gauged solely by its technical achievements. "The arts and crafts transcend the products of Old World peoples at the same mechanical level. The spirit of the Aztec people, as exemplified in their religious art, soared to the lofty heights attained by the creators of all those ancient civilizations, like Egypt and Mesopotamia, whose monuments reflect the glory of their builders' religious devotion." In Aztec society Vaillant found none of those "socially sterile attitudes toward art which we have in our own culture," no term for "fine arts," no speculation about aesthetics, no creed of art for art's sake. [43]

Bidding a nostalgic farewell to the Aztecs, Vaillant held them up as teachers of valuable lessons to the Western world. "In this world, torn with hate and war, adrift without an anchor or compass with which to chart our course, we may well consider their example. The Indians worked together for their common good, and no sacrifice was too great for their corporate well-being. Man's strength lay in the physical and spiritual welfare of the tribe, and the individual was honored only inasmuch as he contributed to that communal good. The Indian civilization may have been powerless to resist the culture of the Western world, but it did not consume itself, as we are doing, in the expression of military power." [44]

That Vaillant, who knew the sources for Aztec society so well, should have shut his eyes so tightly to the abundant evidence of social cleavages and tensions within it, testifies to the power of emotive factors in the way we view the past. Vaillant's radiant vision of Aztec civilization undoubtedly reflects his profound discontent with the state of the world in which he lived, a discontent that may have contributed to his tragic death by suicide, at the height of his powers and his professional success, shortly after the publication of the *Aztecs of Mexico.*

The first United States scholar to question in a systematic way Bandelier's major premises was the anthropologist Paul Radin. His work on *The Sources and Authenticity of the History of the Ancient Mexicans* (1920) concentrated its attack on the skeptical approach to Indian sources that Morgan and Bandelier had made fashionable. Radin demonstrated with a wealth of examples that the ancient Mexicans had a true historical sense and produced "an amazing variety of types of histories" which yielded "a fair picture of the course of Nahua history, and more specifically of Aztec history, from approximately A.D. 100 to the time of the Conquest." On the evidence of these histories, Radin rejected most of the basic teachings of the Morgan-Bandelier school. He assumed a very ancient division of the Aztec tribe into nobles and commoners. The growing power of the tribal chief "must have crystallized these older, perhaps not unduly accentuated divisions, and formed them into true castes." The Tepanec War, "with the consequent rise to supreme importance of the military class and the problem of taking care of newly distributed alien lands, did the rest." Meanwhile the status of the ruler changed from that of elected chief to that of king. Another decisive event was the coming to the throne of Moctezuma II, who dismissed from his entourage all servants who were not of noble birth. However, Radin did not break completely with Bandelier's doctrines. He concluded that tribal interests were still paramount at the Conquest; true private property in land did not exist, since land reverted to the tribe when the owner left the community.[45]

Another early dissenter from Bandelier's views was A. L. Kroeber, one of the most perceptive anthropologists of his generation. In a time of exaggerated reaction against the excesses of nineteenth-century evolutionism, Kroeber upheld such notions as cultural ranking and higher and lower stages of social evolution. In his classic text, *Anthropology* (1923), Kroeber described the Mexican culture center as the peak of civilization in the New World. By the time of Cortés, the Aztecs had evolved beyond the stage of confederacy of the Iroquois type and had achieved "some sort of empire." This "straggling domain of subjected and reconquered towns and tribes" was governed by "a hereditary line of half-elected or confirmed rulers of great state and considerable power." Kroeber conceded that the Aztec Empire was "loose and simple, indeed, judged by Old World standards, but nevertheless an organized political achievement, in which the clans had disappeared or had been transformed into units of a different nature." Kroeber commented that Aztec human sacrifice, shocking as it might be, represented "the climax of American religious development." The practice was "a symptom of incipient civilization," not found among truly backward peoples. Had the Aztecs enjoyed a few thousand more years of undisturbed progress, human sacrifice would probably have been superseded as it had been in the Old World.[46]

The explicit or implied criticism of Bandelier by Radin and Kroeber does not seem to have significantly reduced the influence of his ideas in America. By a certain irony, it remained for Leslie A. White, the leading defender of Morgan's theories in the United States, to deflate the fame of both Morgan and Bandelier as authorities on ancient Mexico. In 1940 White published Bandelier's letters to Morgan. As is evident in previous chapters, these letters offered damaging testimony to the dubious tactics employed by Bandelier to make the sources fit Morgan's preconceived notions.

But White did more. In his long introduction he subjected Bandelier's views to a riddling critique. He noted that Bandelier had contradicted his own thesis by stating that "there were two very different classes within the area occupied by the tribe, enjoying each a very different quality of right." White also submitted a wealth of evidence—including support for the existence of a professional merchant class and currency, a servile class, property legislation, even a class of professional robbers—to demonstrate that Aztec productive forces, division of labor, and class antagonisms had reached a point of development incompatible with the communism of a tribal society. The concepts of territory and property, the criteria employed by Morgan to define a civil or political society, "were functioning as determining principles in Mexican society at the time of the Conquest." [47]

White's slashing attack on Bandelier joined with the parallel and contemporaneous efforts of Mexican scholars to end his influence over Mexicanist studies in the United States. Vaillant's Bandelier-oriented book, published in 1944, was the last of its kind.

Two major developments, broadly speaking, have determined the interpretation of Aztec society by United States scholars in the period since 1945. One is a vast accumulation of new data on Mesoamerican population, urbanism, industry, commerce, tribute, social classes, and the like. The other is a vigorous revival of evolutionist theory, stressing the interrelations between environment, technology, population, and social organization, and seeking to utilize the mass of new data for the construction of significant patterns or regularities. The vision of ancient Mexican society resulting from this integration of fact and theory is one of marked complexity. One recent writer, complaining of insufficient recognition of the great complexity of native Mesoamerican civilization, compared it to such Old World cultures as Old Kingdom Egypt, the Indus Valley Civilization of Northwest India, and Shang China. "We are dealing," he observed, "with one of the great early civilizations of mankind, whose essential genius was almost certainly autonomous, even if it might be conclusively demonstrated that some cultural elements diffused to the area from the outside, including the Old World." [48]

This viewpoint, it is safe to say, dominates the majority of recent United States writings on Mesoamerica, including such outstanding works of synthesis as Eric R. Wolf, *Sons of the Shaking Earth* (1959), Michael D. Coe, *Mexico* (1962), and William T. Sanders and Barbara J. Price, *Mesoamerica* (1968). Their rejection of Bandelier is total. All three regard Aztec society as being on the state level, with a sharp division into classes and a hereditary ruler who was in every sense an absolute king. Typical is Coe's emphatic comment: "It is utterly false that the Aztecs when first seen by the Spaniards were on the clan level of organization, without any kind of political power greater than that enjoyed by, say, an Iroquois chief. On the other hand, relics of a more simple kind of organization of human affairs certainly persisted in the administration of the empire." [49]

Recent United States Aztec studies offer few examples of the belligerently anti-Indian viewpoint typified in Mexico by the writings of Cuevas and Vasconcelos. A book which has some affinity with this school is R. C. Padden's *The Hummingbird and the Hawk* (1967). The title refers symbolically to what Padden regards as the central theme of the Conquest, the struggle between the Aztec god Huitzilopochtli and Cortés.

Padden's account of the course of Aztec history in general agrees with the interpretation of modern specialists for whom that history represents the rapid evolution of a tribal society based on communal land tenure into a class-structured, expansionist state headed by a despotic ruler. What distinguishes Padden's account is the element of sophisticated calculation, of long-range planning, that he introduces to explain this process. Padden believes that the myth of Huitzilopochtli as an all-powerful god who designated the Aztecs as his chosen people, and also the cosmogonal myth which made the survival of the universe depend on human sacrifice, were deliberately fabricated *after* the Aztecs had risen to imperial eminence. According to Padden, the architect of this ideology was the fifteenth-century Aztec general and gray eminence Tlacaélel. Across a gulf of five hundred years, Padden diagnoses him as a "brilliant psychopath." Padden admits that human sacrifice had existed on the Mexican plateau before the coming of the Aztecs, but "the calculated use of human sacrifice as a functional instrument of statecraft" was an Aztec innovation. The murderous Aztec doctrine was opposed by an older tradition, founded by Quetzalcóatl, whose religious system closely resembled Christianity, and whose followers sought to approximate "the founder's sublime moral sense and ethical code of conduct." This older tradition had its center in Texcoco, where a small group of progressive thinkers, including Nezahualcóyotl, promoted monotheism and recognized the Huitzilopochtli cult to be "a piece of barbarous fakery." [50]

At the Conquest, according to Padden, a serious socioeconomic crisis was in the making as a result of the growing concentration of land in noble and church hands and a parallel population explosion. The ruling class sought to solve the problem by resorting to human sacrifice on an unprecedented scale and by a renewed expansionist drive for land and tribute. The position of the commoners steadily deteriorated. In their anguish they turned increasingly to drink; alcoholism became so great a problem that the Aztec government applied the drastic remedy of making drunkenness a capital crime on the second offense (Padden seems to overlook the fact that the Aztec code prescribed death for a variety of seemingly trivial offenses). The most terrifying aspect of the situation, declared Padden, was the growing consumption of commoner flesh by the ravenous nobility. Padden asserts that Moctezuma had "fat and healthy unfortunates butchered daily for his table. His favorite dish, according to Bernal Díaz, was prepared from the flesh of young boys." [51]

Naturally, Padden concludes that the Conquest changed Indian life much for the better. He concedes that the Indians "found themselves just as bad off, if not worse, than they had been under the old regime," but "there was substantial change in one area of existence that greatly influenced all the others: they were no longer forced to see their children sacrificed or to fear their own demise on the slab; in the stead of Huitzilopochtli and his male-dominated regime of terror, they found a compassionate Mother Goddess who blessed and saved." Padden seems unaware that the Aztecs too had a mother goddess, represented as a mother carrying a child in her arms. Her cult, says Vaillant, was transferred to the Virgin by the early missionaries, "an act exemplifying their intelligent procedure in evangelizing the Aztecs." [52]

A curious aspect of Padden's book is the manner in which he purports to reveal in minute physical detail how historical figures

acted and reacted in certain situations. Padden knows, for example, that Moctezuma not only was angry but "trembling with
rage" on the return of his defeated troops from a war with Tlaxcala. Moctezuma, when he first met Cortés, "was perspiring under
his steady gaze." Later, writes Padden, Moctezuma "'in undis-
guised anguish . . . leaped to his feet and flung aside his robes"
to show Cortés that he was merely human, and "feverishly plucked
and grasped the flesh of his arms and breast" to the same end.[53]
Such imaginative reconstructions seem better suited to the writing
of historical fiction than of history.

In France, the strong tradition of Mexicanist studies, identified
with such prominent names as Baradère, Brasseur de Bourbourg,
Charnay, Hamy, and Eugène Boban, has been significantly enriched in our own time by the work of Jacques Soustelle. Besides
his contributions to an understanding of Aztec ideology, Soustelle
in 1955 published an important synthesis, translated into English
under the title, *The Daily Life of the Aztecs on the Eve of the
Spanish Conquest* (1961). In the best French scholarly tradition,
the book combines immense learning, breadth of interpretation,
and an elegant, vivacious style. The vision of Aztec society that
emerges is also characteristically French. Soustelle portrays the
grandeur, the nobility, the refined culture, of a great state that,
like France herself, had its hour of glory before misfortune toppled
it from its high estate.

Soustelle's eagerness to magnify the Aztec achievement, to pos-
tulate the utmost for Aztec civilization, is suggested by his discussion of the extent, population, and social organization of Tenochtitlán. To begin with, Soustelle extended the area of the city by
arguing that at the Conquest there existed a "Greater Mexico"
which included both Tenochtitlán and Tlatelolco. To this "Greater
Mexico" Soustelle assigned a population of between 560,000 and
700,000—an estimate far greater than those of other scholars.[54] But
he did not stop there. Assuming that many of the towns and villages on the mainland were no more than suburbs of Greater
Mexico, Soustelle saw "an enormous conurbation, which, having
spread itself on the shore, was now eating its way into the lake—
a vast urban area that embraced more than one million beings." [55]

Together with his stress on the large size and population of the Aztec capital went an insistence on the advanced, modern character of its political organization. Soustelle rejected the word "clan," commonly applied by American authors to the *calpulli*, in favor of the customary Spanish term, *barrio* or quarter. "In my opinion, the old Spaniards understood the facts better than the modern archaeologists. 'Clan' brings to mind various laws of marriage and lineage, or even a totem, and it seems to me less appropriate to the situation as it is known than 'quarter,' which stands for a territorial entity." Soustelle impatiently rejected Vaillant's definition of Tenochtitlán as "an American Indian tribal town." He observed that there was as much difference between Tenochtitlán and Taos as there was between the Rome of Julius Caesar and the Rome of the Tarquins. He also objected to Spengler's inclusion of the Aztec capital among those world cities which embodied the greatness and decadence of their cultures. On the contrary, wrote Soustelle, Tenochtitlán was "the young capital of a society in full development, of a civilization in full progression, and of an empire that was still in the making. The Aztecs had not reached their zenith; their rising star had scarcely passed the first degrees of its course." [56]

Soustelle reflected on the extraordinary rapidity of Aztec social evolution. In the short space of two centuries "tribal democracy had been replaced by an aristocratic and imperialistic monarchy." Wealth and luxury coexisted with misery. "Power no longer came from below, but from above: the new machinery of the state had absorbed the last traces of the democratic beginnings." There was a military nobility that possessed honors, lived in fine houses with many servants, and wore brilliant clothes and jewels. Soustelle insisted, however, that this was a nobility of merit, not of birth. The Spanish conquerors mistakenly compared the nobles who attended the Aztec emperor to the court nobility of Spain or France. "The court of the Aztec emperor was made up, not of hereditary magnates with great estates or inherited wealth, but of military or civil officials who enjoyed privileges that were attached to their offices."

Well aware, however, that private landed estates did exist in Aztec society, Soustelle went on to make a series of statements marked by less than perfect consistency. "Although in theory

property was still communal," he wrote, "in fact the land that had
been attributed by way of a life-interest to a *tecuhtli* was transmitted by him to his heirs, forming *pillali*, lands of the *pilli*, inheritable estates." In fact, "a private domain was building itself
up at the expense of the public domain." Again Soustelle insisted,
"it would be an exaggeration to say that the emperor and the dignitaries were great landed proprietors, for in fact an over-riding
law of communal possession was felt to exist: but it would be
equally mistaken to assert that this law alone was recognized in
practice." Soustelle offers no proof of the existence of this "over-
riding law of communal possession." [57] The ghost of Bandelier
seems to hang over these confusing lines.

On the other hand, Soustelle was emphatic on the point that
the Aztec ruler was a true king. "He was attended by all the outward show of monarchical power, and this show corresponded
exactly to the reality: nothing is more futile than the attempts of
certain modern scholars to deny this." Nor would Soustelle accept
Padden's view that the Aztec emperors were power-mad, bloodthirsty despots. "The fundamental ideas of the Aztec monarchy
are not without dignity; there is a sense of the public good, and
the feeling of a real unity between the rulers and the ruled. Furthermore, everything goes to show that the emperors took their
duties seriously." [58]

For Soustelle, religion was "the wonderfully powerful cement"
that bound the various elements of this society in which class enmity was beginning to appear, "in which the nature of ownership
was changing and in which the ideas of public service and of
private wealth were coming into hidden conflict." Human sacrifice
was the only response the Aztecs could conceive to "the instability
of a continually threatened world." Soustelle cited the testimony
of Indian informants that the relation between the sacrificer and
the victim was not one of dislike but "a kind of mystical kinship."
In religion, as in social and political life, Soustelle saw a striving
toward centralization and synthesis. "Just as the political institutions at the summit tended to grow stronger and to find the formation necessary for an imperial state, so the meditation of the
priests tended to bring order into this theological chaos. . . . A
syncretism was coming into being." This religious evolution had
not attained the level of monotheism.[59]

Soustelle closed his survey of Aztec civilization on a note of frank, fervent eulogy:

"Their culture, so suddenly destroyed, is one of those that humanity can be proud of having created. . . . At long intervals, in the immensity of the world's life and in the midst of its vast indifference, men joined together into a community bring something into existence that is greater than themselves—a civilization. These are the creators of cultures; and the Indians of Anáhuac, at the foot of their volcanoes, on the shores of their lake, may be counted among them." [60]

In Germany, Seler's pupils continued his tradition of painstaking, critical study and analysis of written and archaeological sources on ancient Mexico and of making available annotated translations of Indian documents. Walter Lehmann and Ernst Mengin, among others, concentrated on the field of translating and editing documents. Hermann Beyer, arriving in Mexico in 1908, sought to enrich and refine Seler's work on the cosmological and astronomical significance of codices, sculptures, and other native objects, dividing his attention between the Mexican highland and Maya areas. As professor of Mexican and Maya archaeology at the Universidad Nacional in the 1920's, Beyer showed the young Caso and other students that Mexican archaeology could be "a scientific discipline, based on facts, and not an assemblage of brilliant, purely imaginary hypotheses whose audacity was proportionate to the ignorance of their creators." A thick volume of essays constitutes Beyer's scientific legacy in the field of Aztec culture.[61]

Beyer left no synthesis containing his general vision of ancient Mexico. Another of Seler's pupils, Walter Krickeberg, wrote such a book for the German-reading public. His *Altmexikanische Kulturen* (1956) lacks the interpretive breadth and verve of Soustelle's book, but it is a work of solid learning and consistently up to date in its viewpoints. Krickeberg described the Aztec state as a complex, stratified society with a landowning nobility, commoners, merchants who monopolized foreign trade and acted as bankers, craft guilds, and a lower class of *mayeque, tamemes* or carriers, and slaves. It was idle, declared Krickeberg, to speak of popular representation in "a society as autocratic and aristocratic as the Aztec." [62]

From the age of William Robertson and Adam Smith to the day of Henry T. Buckle and Edward J. Payne, English writers had generally displayed a reserved or even hostile attitude toward ancient Mexican civilization. Under the warming influence of the new primitivism and relativism, this gave way to a respectful and even admiring outlook. In part, this change may have resulted from scholarly association of Aztec culture with the brilliant culture of the Maya. Alfred P. Maudslay investigated the imposing Maya ruins in the course of a series of expeditions and published his results in a magnificently illustrated work at the turn of the century.[63]

A rising interest in Aztec Mexico is suggested by the publication by the Oxford University Press of an excellent little primer on the subject, Lewis Spence's *The Civilization of Ancient Mexico* (1912). Although Spence was later drawn toward occultism and other esoteric matters, this book is sternly scientific in spirit. Recalling such "bibliographical monstrosities" as Brasseur de Bourbourg's ambitious history of the civilized peoples of Mexico and Central America, Spence cautioned that "Mexican history must not be treated as other histories, but as a series of unembellished facts." The book made heavy use of Seler for Aztec religion, and of Payne for social organization. Following Payne, Spence distinguished among communal *calpulli* lands, private estates of nobles, worked by serfs, and public lands applied to the support of Church and State. According to Spence, the Aztec monarchy was elective, with legislative power vested in the king, "but the possibility of a despotic government was minimized by the existence of an independent judiciary from whose decisions there was no appeal even to the throne."[64]

Spence had high praise for Aztec economic organization, noting the care taken to avoid soil exhaustion, the extensive use of irrigation, and the heavy penalties to prevent deforestation. Nahua metallurgy was also highly developed; failure to work iron was no argument against the native intelligence, for probably the "preparation [of iron] required so many processes to render it fit for use that it appeared to be a waste of labour to the Nahua. . . ." For the rest, Spence praised the refinement of the Aztec way of life, noting the luxury of their table, the respectful treatment of women, and the general courtesy and dignity of Aztec manners.[65]

Relying heavily on Seler, Spence described Aztec religion as a polytheism comparable in general to that of Greece, Rome, or Egypt, although he thought it probable that shortly before the Conquest "there was a general movement on the part of the ruling classes towards belief in monotheism." Human sacrifice constituted man's part in his covenant with the gods for their mutual support. At the base of Aztec ritual cannibalism was the doctrine of consubstantiation or oneness with the god to whom the victim was sacrificed.[66] Spence later devoted a book to *The Gods of Mexico* (1923). A specialist has recently described this work as "a useful summary, unique in English, wherein the author made a particular effort to introduce some classificatory order into a complex and often confusing subject." [67]

For encyclopedic knowledge of ancient Mexican culture, and for sympathetic, intelligent appreciation of its art, perhaps no English scholar of his time surpassed Thomas A. Joyce. His contribution to the popularization and understanding of Aztec art will be discussed separately. In his *Mexican Archaeology* (1914), Joyce devoted a series of chapters to Aztec civilization. The chapter on "Social System, War, Trade, and Justice" is especially valuable. Joyce defined the Aztec social sytsem in European feudal terms: a landed aristocracy who held their estates by feudal tenure, a military nobility who held land at the king's pleasure, *calpulli* freemen, rent-paying tenants, and serfs.

A leading English Mexicanist of our own day is Cottie A. Burland. A specialist in the study of codices, Burland wrote an attractive brief account of *Life and Art in Ancient Mexico* (1948) that reveals great knowledge and affection for its subject. The work is marred by the strong influence of Bandelier's theories, perhaps filtered through Vaillant.

The fault is even more glaring in Burland's *The Gods of Mexico* (1967), which covers much the same ground as Spence's book of the same title. Burland's account of Aztec social organization is exceedingly confused. Among the Aztecs, he tells us, "land was not owned by anybody. The Aztec concept was simply that the earth was a goddess, a divine being, superior to any human, and so could not be owned." Soon we are told, however, that "the great lords claimed dominion over towns and villages, and people paid tribute to them in return for protection." Quite naïvely,

Burland adds: "This was a very satisfactory arrangement in most cases: the nobleman had freedom from the ever pressing necessity of growing food and weaving cloth, so that he could look after the general welfare and organize military expeditions and other things beyond the competence of the normal village council. However, if there was a famine all classes suffered together." Even more incredible is Burland's description of the Aztec political system. The so-called emperor, we are told, was really the president of the Council of Four, which he must consult, and whose members "were confirmed by the popular acclamation of the warriors of the whole tribe." [68]

The chapters on religion proper contain other eye-opening statements. According to Burland, the Indian nobles "had not the heart" to tell Spanish priests such as Motolinía some of their more fantastic rituals. The Indian elders who assisted Sahagún in the preparation of his history "carefully prepared a standard version so that he received only such part of the inner mysteries of the religion as the people could agree on." Like Séjourné, Burland makes large use of Jung's psychological teachings to explain the Mexican mythology. In Burland's view, many or perhaps all of the Aztec gods were archetypal forms, "projections of the human unconscious personality." These projections must have been induced in the priests by such experiences as ceremonial abstinence, physical penance, the act of human sacrifice, and the taking of magical mushrooms and other herbs. The priests organized the chaotic, irrational material of their visions into a series of gods which they fitted into their ceremonial calendar. "So it came about that an orderly and rather frightening rational system was imposed upon material common to most of mankind when thrown up from the unconscious."

Using this psychological approach, Burland solves the problem of the identity of Quetzalcóatl; he is "an excellent symbol for the self." The story of his defeat symbolizes the progress of the human soul, "which conquers the powers of the unconscious and finally realizes that the conscious wealth and power of man is of little avail, that he must go forward to something higher, nothing less than the complete sacrifice of all his desires." [69]

To the same mystical school of thought belongs the English writer Irene Nicholson, whose debt to Laurette Séjourné is unmistakable. In her beautifully illustrated book *Mexican and Central American Mythology* (1967), Nicholson attempts to correct "the mistaken idea that the basic religion of Middle America was founded on human sacrifice and the tearing out of hearts. . . ." To Nicholson, as to Séjourné, it is clear that the "blood rituals and licensed homicide came later, and were a distortion of what must once have been an extraordinarily complete vision of the place of man and of organic life in the universe." Although she proposes to let "the religious, philosophical, and cosmological concepts speak for themselves," she accompanies the exposition of the Mexican myths with speculative glosses in the manner of Séjourné. Thus the myth of the successive transformations of the maiden Mayahuel is "the story of the transubstantiation of matter." Quetzalcóatl, in his aspect of the wind god, "represents spirit freed from matter"; and in his totality he is "a composite figure describing the many orders of matter in creation: a kind of ladder with man at the centre, but extending downward into animal, water, and mineral; and upward to the planets, the life-giving sun, and the god creators." [70]

In order here is a brief survey of recent developments in the interpretation of Aztec civilization in the Soviet Union and other socialist countries. Examination of the small amount of available material suggests that in the socialist camp, as in the United States, the tenacious hold of the Bandelier-Morgan theories has been the principal obstacle to obtaining a correct perspective on Aztec society. In the United States the chief reason for the hold of those theories on social science was the immense authority of Bandelier's scholarship. In the Soviet Union, on the other hand, Bandelier's name and work have been virtually unknown, though Morgan enjoys great prestige because of the intimate connection between his evolutionist scheme and the historical materialist theory of Marx and Engels.

As is well known, the fathers of scientific socialism received *Ancient Society* with enthusiastic approval. The work provided independent confirmation by a Yankee scholar with unimpeachable capitalist credentials of the Marxist explanation of the evolution from the stage of tribal communism to the stage of private property and the state. What is more, in the closing pages of his book Morgan had a prophetic vision of a higher, presumably socialist level of social development beyond that of private property and capitalism. In their satisfaction with the general conformity of Morgan's views on early social evolution to their own, Marx and Engels ignored the nonmaterialist elements in Morgan's thought. Unhappily, too, although Marx and Engels had a considerable grasp of the early history of Greece, Rome, and Germany, they knew almost nothing about ancient Mexico and so had to accept on faith the description of its society in Morgan's book, which we know was largely based on material supplied by Bandelier. Consequently, in his classic work, *The Origin of the Family, Private Property and the State in the Light of the Researches of Lewis H. Morgan* (1884), Engels accepted, lock, stock, and barrel, Morgan's assignment of the ancient Mexicans and Peruvians to the "middle stage of barbarism," down to the notion that "they lived in houses made like fortresses, made of adobe brick or of stone." [71]

If the Morgan-Bandelier theories held their own as late as the 1940's in the United States, even though scholars had easy access to the archaeological and documentary evidence that refuted those theories, it is not strange that their influence survived longer in the Soviet Union, especially in view of the intimate connection between those ideas and the ruling Marxist ideology. By the late 1950's, however, a decline of their influence was apparent. The discussion of Aztec social and political organization by B. I. Sharevskaya in the *Vsemirnaya istoria* (World History) of the Soviet Academy of Sciences, for example, reveals a critical spirit and partial rejection of Morgan's premises. "Polemically stressing the tribal elements in Aztec society," she wrote, "Morgan undoubtedly exaggerated their specific weight. The findings of modern investigations, especially in archaeology, testify that Aztec society of the sixteenth century was a class society, that private property and relations of subjection and domination existed; the state had arisen. Yet Aztec society indubitably preserved many survivals of the primitive-communal order." For Sharevskaya these "survivals" included communal ownership of land, with certain lands set aside for the support of the war chiefs, the priesthood, and the warriors. She also followed Morgan closely with respect to Aztec political organization. The Aztec capital, she believed, was composed of four quarters or phratries, each divided into five *calpultin*. Each *calpulli* was governed by a council of elected elders. These leaders and the heads of the phratries composed a supreme tribal council that included the principal war chief.[72]

Friedrich Katz, a professor at Humboldt University in East Germany, carried the Marxist revision of Morgan's view much farther in *Die sozialökonomischen Verhältnisse bei den Azteken im 15. und 16. Jahrhundert* (1956). The book reflects a wide acquaintance with and careful reading of the Indian and Spanish sources, as well as such modern monographs as those of Moreno and Monzón.

In summary, Katz sees Aztec society on the eve of the Conquest as the end result of an evolution through a series of stages. The first or tribal stage of social organization, resembling that of the Iroquois, was the one in which the Aztecs found themselves when they arrived in the Valley of Mexico. In this stage all land was owned by the tribe; there was no king, leadership was vested in clan elders, and important decisions were made by a popular assembly. Only after the founding of Tenochtitlán did the Mexicans choose a ruler, with prior consultation of the people by clan leaders. The second stage of "military democracy" (a term coined by Morgan and applied by Engels to similar stages among the ancient Greeks, Romans, and Germans) comprehended most of the fifteenth century. In this stage warfare caused growing social differentiation, with the rise of a military nobility who enjoyed life use of estates in conquered territory. The power of the war chief and ruler also grew, but was still limited by the supreme council (*tlatocan*), by the popular assembly, and by a colleague, the *cihuacóatl*, who shared authority with the war chief.

The third stage is one of transition to the state. Pressure for the establishment of private property in land becomes stronger; the warrior nobility demand the right to transmit their estates and privileges to their descendants and get their way in a more or less covert form. Simultaneously the warrior nobility annul the popular assembly and arrogate to themselves the power of deciding vital questions of war and peace. War also leads to the steady growth of a bureaucracy whose offices tend to become hereditary. Meanwhile the ruler becomes increasingly powerful and is surrounded with a growing pomp and veneration; Moctezuma II decrees that all public posts must be held by nobles. The outlines of a territorial state that is independent of and imposes its will upon the clans have emerged in Tenochtitlán and the adjoining territory.[73]

This brief summary does not do justice to the richness of Katz's argument or to his contributions to many specific problems of Aztec social and political organization. Leaving aside the Marxist theoretical framework and terminology, his reconstruction of the evolution of ancient Mexican society broadly agrees with that of modern Western scholars. In this area, at least, there seems to be developing some convergence of scholarly viewpoints, East and West.

CHAPTER FIFTEEN

The Plumed Serpent

In the twentieth century the star of Aztec culture has steadily risen in the firmament of world opinion. As new international artistic currents swept aside arbitrary canons of classical taste they made obsolete the traditional view that Aztec art was crude, imitative, and decidedly inferior to that of the Maya. By mid-century many artists and art critics were agreed that Aztec sculpture was one of the supreme glories of world art. Other specialists discovered that the Aztecs possessed a literature rich in expressive resources, in depth of thought and feeling. It was in this same period that painters, poets, and composers began to seek inspiration in the ancient heritage and to attempt a reconstruction of the material and spiritual face of the vanished Aztec world.

From the time of Dürer to that of Rodin—who envied the inimitable vigor of the well-known Aztec sculpture of the Eagle Knight [1]—artists and connoisseurs had praised Aztec artistic achievements. What they had applauded, however, were works that conformed to Western, naturalistic standards of beauty; they deplored the "monstrous" idols and the "stilted" drawing of the codices. The colossal basalt figure of Coatlicue that was found in 1790 on the site of the main temple of Tenochtitlán may serve as a touchstone of Western attitudes toward Aztec art. Before 1900 only two observers, both uncommonly artistic and gifted men, had ventured to praise the awesome earth goddess. One was Alfredo Chavero, who described her as the most beautiful idol in the Museo Nacional; the other was William H. Holmes, who placed the Coatlicue, "brutal and terrible as it is," very close to the head of the list of American sculptures. Far more typical was the complaint of the celebrated German art critic Karl Woermann that Indian sculptures suffered from "incompletion and a barbarian overloading." In other words, observes George Kubler, quoting this comment, "the nineteenth-century critic could not bring himself to credit the expressive strength of American Indian art, nor again could he rank it high by Occidental standards of verisimilitude. Faithful representation was for these critics the touchstone of value, and the representation to which they were accustomed is uncommon in ancient American art." [2]

By 1910, however, changes in the philosophical and artistic climate of the West combined to produce a more receptive attitude toward Aztec and all other so-called "primitive" art. The vogue of primitivism, the reaction against rationalism, and the rise of relativism all contributed to a revolution in artistic taste. [3] From the artists themselves came the decisive stimulus for a re-evaluation of primitive art. Their search for simplicity, sincerity, and faith, and for fresh new modes of expression, led to new appreciation of the artifacts of primitive peoples, which appeared to embody the qualities they sought. It was natural that the contemporary productions of Africa and Oceania should attract greater interest than the works of ancient Mexico, whose art implied a relatively high degree of formal complexity.

As early as 1889, however, Paul Gauguin, the leading spirit of European artistic primitivism, was copying Aztec sculpture at the Paris Exposition of that year. In a letter to Emile Bernard, Gauguin also wrote: "I saw in one of the illustrated papers a sketch of ancient Mexican dwellings; they too seem to be primitive and very beautiful. Ah, if one only knew the dwellings of those times, and if one could only paint the people who lived in them, it would be as beautiful as the work of Millet; I don't say in the matter of color, but with regard to character, as something significant, something one has a firm faith in." Herbert Read, citing this letter, calls attention to its twin assumptions: that what is primitive is beautiful and that it gives us faith, "faith in the significance of art, faith in humanity." [4]

By contrast with the abundant evidence of African influence on modern European art, however, reflections of Aztec influence are not numerous. Certainly the most striking example of the use of Aztec models is the work of the English sculptor Henry Moore. In the early 1920's Moore discovered and eagerly studied ancient Mexican sculpture in the collections of the British Museum. His tribute to this art has often been quoted. "Mexican sculpture, as soon as I found it, seemed to me true and right, perhaps because I at once hit on similarities in it with some eleventh-century carvings I had seen as a boy in Yorkshire. Its 'stoniness,' by which I mean its truth to material, its tremendous power without loss of sensitiveness, its astonishing variety and fertility of form-invention, and its approach to a full three-dimensional conception of form, make it unsurpassed in my opinion by any other period of stone sculpture." [5]

The critic John Russell finds a close affinity between Moore's earliest independent carving, the Portland stone *Mother and Child* (1922), and the British Museum's figure of Xochipilli, god of love and flowers and the arts. Comparing the quality of the two figures, Russell observes that "one has only to compare the relaxed eloquence of the pose in the Mexican figure, and the rich and confident handling of its lower legs, to see that Moore was still very much of a student. . . ." Robert Goldwater also remarks on several Moore heads that put "the round-face open-mouthed blank-eyed expression of the Aztec Xipe Totec [god of spring] into a semi-cubist handling of broken planes." The best-known sources of Mexican influence on Moore, however, are not Aztec but Toltec-Maya—the famous ritual Chacmools—source of his *Reclining Woman* (1929) and many other reclining figures. Goldwater finds additional Mexican influence in Alberto Giacometti's *Head* (1934–1935), "half of whose face shows only the skull," and he believes that "the compact shapes, rough surfaces, and animal forms of Aztec sculpture exerted a strong attraction for John Flannagan." [6]

On another artistic level, the English artist Keith Henderson made large and imaginative use of Aztec materials in his illustrations for the edition of Prescott's *Conquest of Mexico* published by Holt in 1922. In his preface Henderson wrote that this edition was the result of his obsession with the idea of making a picture book of the Conquest of Mexico. To master the material he spent weeks in study of the Aztec collections of the British Museum, being greatly aided by the curator, T. A. Joyce, who presided over those collections. "From cup-boards and cases the treasures of ancient Mexico (their very curves a shock of lovely surprise) one by one were brought out to be studied at leisure, as well as books such as the Codex Zouche, the Codex Borgia, the Codex Laud, the Codex Fejérváry-Mayer—superb pictorial achievements that every art student ought to investigate." [7]

Henderson's artistic plan for Prescott's book reflected a fine inventive spirit. In Book I, dealing with pre-Cortesian Mexico, "while Mexican art was as yet untainted by European influence," he annotated the pages with line drawings from native pictures. Beginning with Book II, Henderson imagined himself as having arrived with the Spaniards, "as a spy to begin with and eventually as a deserter." One does not know which to praise more highly, the charming, meticulously drawn figures taken from codices and other artifacts, in Book I, or the romantic, highly stylized portraits of Spaniards and Indians in action in the rest of the work, containing, in the words of T. A. Joyce, "the most correct interpretation of ancient Mexican costumes, ornaments, and warlike equipment which have yet supplemented the text of a history of that country."

Henderson also supplied notes indicating the sources of his native pictures, frequently adding a learned commentary. Complementing his preface, these notes displayed enthusiasm for the expressive power of ancient Mexican art. Similarly, T. A. Joyce, in his highly informative introduction, cited the evidence of the codices to refute Prescott's claim that the Egyptians "handled the pencil more gracefully than the Aztecs, were more true to the natural forms of objects. . . ." Joyce pleaded in Prescott's defense, however, "that only in the last few years has the indigenous art of America been rated at its proper value." [8]

Art critics and historians, following the lead of the artists, were soon discovering the beauties of primitive art. In 1920 appeared Roger Fry's *Vision and Design*, a book that Herbert Read has described as an "eye-opener" for the generation of artists of the 1920's. In his essay on "Ancient American Art" Fry noted that "recently we have come to recognize the beauty of Aztec and Maya sculpture, and some of our modern artists have even gone to them for inspiration." In retrospect, however, the essay seems curiously conventional in such judgments as, "The Aztecs carry on at a lower level the Maya art of sculpture," or, "The Aztecs had everything to learn from the Maya, and they never rose to the level of their precursors." [9]

Signs of the elevation of ancient Mexican art to the category of a major world art multiplied after 1920. They included the publication of the first studies devoted exclusively to the subject. In 1921 Walter Lehmann published his survey of *Altmexikanische Kunstgeschichte* in the series *Orbis Pictus*, under the general editorship of Paul Westheim; in 1927 T. A. Joyce issued his *Maya and Mexican Art*, which asserted that in certain respects Mexican relief sculpture was superior to that of Egypt or Mesopotamia, and that their pottery, "in technique, form, and ornament, surpassed the ceramic products of any other people ignorant of the potter's wheel, except that of the ancient Peruvians."

Another capital event was the exhibition of "The Ancient Arts of America" organized in the Pavillon de Marsan in Paris by Georges-Henri Rivière and Alfred Métraux in 1928. Henceforth, says Soustelle, it was recognized that the artistic creations of the ancient Americans, "strange or displeasing as they might be to a taste formed by the European tradition, were nevertheless worthy of being included in the common heritage of mankind." [10] Since that date, many exhibitions of ancient Mexican art treasures have been held; one of the most outstanding, for the variety and value of its objects, was that shown in Paris, Stockholm, and London in 1952 and 1953, and commemorated by two handsome books: *Mexique précolombien*, text by Paul Rivet, photographs by Gisèle Freund (Paris, 1954), and *Treasures of Mexican Art: Two Thousand Years of Art and Art Handicraft*, with informing notes by Sigvald Linné (Stockholm, 1956). Important recent exhibitions of pre-Columbian art in the United States include those held by the Museum of Primitive Art and the Metropolitan Museum of Art in New York City in 1969 and 1970. The fine 322-page catalogue of the 1970 exhibition, *Before Cortés: Sculpture of Middle America*, was prepared by Elizabeth Kennedy Easby and John F. Scott, with preface and foreword by Dudley T. Easby, Jr., and Thomas P. F. Hoving.

In Mexico the movement for the reevaluation of the ancient

Indian arts inevitably acquired a political and even revolutionary significance. To insist on the greatness of the old Indian arts was one way of asserting the value of one's own, one way of revolting against the tyranny of the pallid, lifeless French and Spanish academism over Mexican art during the last decades of the Porfiriato. Thus the revolution that overthrew Díaz inevitably generated an artistic upheaval, one of whose main tenets was the immense worth of the Indian cultural heritage that the arbiters of artistic taste under the Porfiriato had regarded with scorn.

It was fitting that perhaps the first great painting to emerge from the Revolution—Saturnino Herrán's moving *Nuestros Dioses* (1916–1918)—should assign a central place and a complex symbolism to the Coatlicue. Herrán depicted the agony of the Mexican people through a masterful synthesis of the old and the new gods, of Christ and Coatlicue. Christ is again crucified, this time on the body of the Mother of the Gods, who "simultaneously gives birth to him, lulls him to sleep, protects him. Pity, childbirth, and agony. The Indian past and the Christian past locked in an embrace eternally fatal for the present. . . ." [11]

It was fitting, too, that Manuel Gamio, founder of scientific *indigenismo*, should have pioneered in developing a scientific, experimental approach to the aesthetics of ancient Mexican art. In 1916, with the Revolution under way, Gamio conducted an experiment in art appreciation designed to test the validity of conventional judgments of Aztec art. He selected a number of individuals with Western cultural backgrounds and showed them fifteen to twenty archaeological objects. Some impressed the viewers as being artistic and pleasing; others elicited indifference or repulsion. The "artistic" items included the head of the Eagle Knight; those which aroused negative feelings invariably included the Coatlicue. Analyzing the reactions of his subjects, Gamio concluded that these reactions, favorable or unfavorable, were false, since the viewers unconsciously employed European aesthetic standards. They pronounced "artistic" those works which conformed to Occidental naturalistic ideals and "repulsive" those which failed to conform to classical ideals.

Thus the emotion of approval elicited by the head of the Eagle Knight was a "psychological fraud," said Gamio, since the apparent classical aspect of the sculpture did not correspond at all

to "the physicobiological-social milieu" in which it was carved
or to "the mental state" that presided over its creation. For the
Eagle Knight to evoke the proper aesthetic emotion, wrote Gamio,
the viewer must combine appreciation of its formal beauty with
comprehension of the idea that it expressed. That idea had nothing
in common with the ideas born under the skies of Greece or
medieval Europe. This sculpture projected "the immutability, the
repose, that Indian faces take on as they appear to slumber in pain
and pleasure alike, the cruel pride of the sons of Mexico, the
cosmopolis of that day, lord and mistress of a thousand regions
stained with blood and trembling with fear, the mental abstraction
produced by the religious milieu of bloody rites and voluntary
tortures, of eternal obsessive thaumaturgies, of mysterious cosmogonies. . . ." [12]

Gamio's experiment, with its relativist, historicist conclusions,
had effectively demonstrated the partiality, the one-sidedness of
judgments of ancient Indian art that were based on Occidental
classical standards. It remained for vanguard Mexican artists such
as Diego Rivera and David Alfaro Siqueiros to recognize the
relevance and kinship of the work of the ancient Indian artists to
the new artistic movements in Paris. Rivera and Siqueiros returned
home from Europe in the early 1920's, after thorough exposure to
cubism and other revolutionary new modes of expression.

Jean Charlot, French-born but with some Mexican ancestry, and
a member of that vanguard group, has described with typical
verve the shock of recognition of

the plastic pilgrim come from Paris to the National Museum of Mexico
City. But the Aztec pyramids, spheres, cubes, and cones, far from re-
taining, as did the cubist ones, a whiff of classroom dampness, were
cogs, pistons, and ball bearings that one suspected had cosmic functions.
They sublimated another fetish of Paris, the machine. Aztec theogonical
sculptures, Coatlicues, great serpent heads, sacrificial and calendar
stones suddenly appeared as classical pre-forms, illustrating the fiercely
rational trend that had just rid painting of all the bootblacks shooting
craps, the cardinals eating lobsters, and the naked women that passed
for art only a generation before.

Charlot, whose "rattles and hornbooks were the idols and Mexican manuscripts from my uncle Eugène Goupil's collection,"

amusingly shows how innocuous Europe's artistic experiments appeared in the light of the ancient Mexican art.

Just having known *calli*, the Aztec hieroglyph that signifies "house"— a cube of space contained in a cube of adobe—watered down the angular landscapes of Braque and Derain into little more than a mild departure from impressionism. The flat colors of the codices, with raw chromas paired in refined discord, could pass as the goal toward which the Matisse of "Music" and "Dance" took his first hesitant steps. The anatomies that Léger put together with ruler and compass were doubtless veering away from Bougereau, but still had far to go on their semimechanical legs to equal the frightfully abstract countenance of a Tlaloc or Tzontemoc. Idols combined the moroseness of a 1916 Derain with the mathematical innuendos of Juan Gris. A few were spared in the comparison: Picasso's evisceration of objects, for example, matched the fierceness of an Aztec ritual knifing.[13]

Not just a militant nationalism but rather their recognition of the "modernity" and expressive power of the ancient Indian art caused the vanguard artists to proclaim its value as a source of artistic inspiration. Even before he returned to Mexico, Siqueiros made a statement that has been described as the opening manifesto of the Mexican artistic renaissance (May, 1921): "Let us observe the works of our ancient people, our Indian painters and sculptors. . . . Our nearness to them will enable us to assimilate the constructive vigor of their work, in which there is clear knowledge of the elements of nature, and these things can serve as the point of departure." Characteristically, however, Siqueiros warned against "falling into lamentable archaeological reconstructions. . . . Let us not flee to 'archaic' motifs. We must live our marvelous dynamic age. We must love our modern machines." [14]

Rivera, on his return from Europe, expressed similar sentiments in an interview on July 28, 1921: "The search that European artists further with such intensity ends here in Mexico in the abundant realization of our national art. I could tell you much concerning the progress to be made by a painter, a sculptor, an artist, if he observes, analyzes, studies, Mayan, Aztec, or Toltec art, none of which falls short of any other art in my opinion." [15]

Of the three future giants of the Mexican artistic renaissance, only José Clemente Orozco rejected what he called the "Indian smallpox," "a disease that is making our politicians itch." Yet a reading of his *Autobiography* makes plain that Orozco's opposition to artistic as well as political *indigenismo*—an opposition rooted in a general aversion to demagogy, populist moods and postures, and perhaps in a certain *hispanidad*—implied no lack of admiration for the ancient Indian art. Orozco in his *Autobiography* recalls visiting the Museo Nacional with Charlot and studying the great Aztec sculptures. "We would talk for hours of that tremendous art which comes down to us and outstrips us, reaching out into the future." Charlot also notes that Orozco realized a "masterly fusion of ancient and present plastics and emotions in the Indian squatting before a blood-soaked *teocalli*, frescoed in 1926, in the main staircase of the Preparatoria. It was in the same year and in the same place that he blasted Indianism." [16]

Mexican art critics and historians lagged behind the artists in their comprehension and appreciation of the stature of ancient Mexican art. Justino Fernández' book *Coatlicue* provides a detailed, analytical survey of the progress of views in this field. Although art historians of the 1920's reflected the current revival of nationalist interest in Indian cultural achievements and praised the beauty of the ancient art, they retained much of the traditional bias in favor of Occidental, classical art.

Manuel G. Revilla, for example, found "well-proportioned" the colossal head of Coyolxauhqui, moon goddess and half sister of Huitzilopochtli, but complained that the artist had made her ugly by placing ornaments in her nose, cheeks, and chin. Revilla, writing in 1923, was convinced that as a result of the Conquest and the planting of "a new society with better germs of culture" there had appeared a superior Christian art, "more beautiful and finished than the native." [17]

The poet José Juan Tablada, a friend of Orozco's, wrote a history of Mexican art [18] that praised the head of Coyolxauhqui as "a masterful work, worthy of comparison with any Chinese, Egyptian, Indian, or Asiatic Greek piece," and called the Coatlicue, by reason of its skillful fusion of realistic elements into a fantastic yet harmonious unity and its impressive monumentality "an extraordinary work, unique in the world." Convinced that these masterpieces could not have been made by the Aztecs, cultural johnnies-come-lately with warlike, nomadic backgrounds, he assigned their creation to Toltec artists in the Aztec service; the term "Aztec art" he regarded as arbitrary. Equally conventional was Tablada's preference for Maya art, to which he turned with "mental relief" after consideration of the Aztec works.[19]

Justino Fernández credits Eulalia Guzmán with fostering a decisive advance in the comprehension and appreciation of Aztec art, citing an essay in which she stressed the artistic unity of the Mesoamerican cultures and defined their art as an expression of a magico-religious view of the world. Fernández also finds suggestive an essay by Edmundo O'Gorman in which this writer, turning the tables on Occidental aesthetic criteria, argued that monstrosity, as exemplified by the Coatlicue, represented the true spirit of art, reflecting a primordial mythical consciousness that is inherent in man and challenges the ordered, rational view of nature expressed in the Greek ideal of beauty. Fernández, while paying tribute to O'Gorman's ingenuity in his struggle against the tyranny of the classical ideal, objects that in the process he disposes of "one of the most prodigious arts of history." After all, writes Fernández, "the rational classical vision of the universe is as valid historically as is the mythical vision for men of other times and places."[20]

The historicist viewpoint with which Fernández is identified strongly colors Salvador Toscano's *Arte precolombino de México* (1944), a work hailed by Fernández as marking "the conquest of Indian art." Written five years before the brilliant young author's untimely death, no previous book had treated the subject so completely and systematically, and with such maturity and modernity of judgment. An introductory essay on "Indian Aesthetic" defined Toscano's artistic philosophy. "Artistic style," he wrote, "is the physiognomy, the form in which a culture expresses itself, its peculiar psychological expression; consequently there exists no criterion of universal validity that permits us to judge the art of different peoples in their historical development, for not even the Greek classical ideal—traditionally regarded as the highest achieved by humanity in the arts—can claim that title. There exist no barbarian and inferior arts, for artistic styles are neither better nor worse, but different. . . ."[21]

Toscano applied this historicist approach to Aztec sculpture. This art, he wrote, was "testimony of an implacable severity, a

dramatic sensibility, an austere conception of life. [The Aztecs']
sobriety and devotion, the pitiless harshness of their agricultural
gods, their profound religious sense of a Chosen People of the
Sun, passed over into their art and left an ineradicable stamp upon
it." The Coatlicue was "the most hallucinatory sculpture conceived
by the Indian mentality and a work of art that cannot be judged
with the serene canons of Greek art or with the pious elements
of Christian art; the goddess expresses the dramatic brutality of
Aztec religion, its solemnity and magnificence." [22]

In another study, *El arte antiguo* (1946), Toscano singled out
"sober realism, energetic carving, and dramatic traits" as the characteristics of Aztec sculpture and called the Coatlicue "the masterpiece of American sculpture." After these comments it is startling
to find Toscano complaining that Aztec art on the eve of the
Conquest had fallen into a "romanticism of the past" and often was
guilty of "servile imitation" and "naïve academism." Fernández
rightly asks how the people who created the Coatlicue and the
Calendar Stone could be charged with these faults. [23]

The versatile Miguel Covarrubias, artist, art historian, and anthropologist, brought his expert knowledge and artistic sensitivity
to bear on Aztec art in a major work of synthesis, *Indian Art of
Mexico and Central America* (1957). For Covarrubias the monumental Aztec art "reached the peak of the grandiose, and brilliantly
closed the epoch of pre-Spanish Indian art, not only by its heroic
proportions and masterful technique but also—and mainly—by its
sweeping plastic force, melodramatic sense, and individual and virile
style." Like Toscano, Covarrubias linked Aztec art to its social and
political milieu. Aztec art, he wrote, was "motivated by the reli-
gious-imperialist concept of its creators. It is a ferocious, necro-
philiac art, made to inspire religious awe and to impress the populace
with the greatness of the all-powerful state, whose philosophy is
conquest by the force of arms and whose religion is the cult of
death and blood. . . . Because it reflects faithfully the psychology
of the state, it cannot be understood without some knowledge of
the political structure, the religion, and the basic events of Aztec
history." [24]

Among recent works by Mexican and foreign scholars, Fernández finds only Paul Westheim's *Arte antiguo de Mexico* (1950) [25]
comparable to Toscano's in importance. Accepting Eulalia Guz-

mán's view of ancient Mexican art as an expression of a magico-religious world outlook, Westheim quotes approvingly from her essay: "The whole art is impregnated with a feeling of religion and magic. Its end is not imitation of the beautiful forms of nature, as in imitative art, but the representation of an idea, or of what surpasses the world of the senses, i.e. the religious." The decisive qualities of this art are for Westheim "the terrible and the sublime." "Beauty" was not an ideal of this artistic activity, and the emergence of this Western goal in works of the late periods and the Maya baroque represented "the incipient decadence and weakening of the creative powers, resulting, in all probability, from a decline in religious feeling and a change in the social structure." From this point of view, the Aztec head of the Eagle Knight, beautiful by Western standards, represents a decline, a decadence; "this work is no longer inspired by the visionary power that imparts a sacred note to the circle of jaguars and eagles in the cave of Malinalco." Realism was totally inadequate to express "in grandiose form . . . the representation that the collectivity develops of the myths and the gods." Therefore the ancient artist created "the formal idiom of a visionary expressionism that discards associative elements because they limit and paralyze the imagination, a cubico-geometric language, a language of signs, objective, exact, and of universal validity."

Fernández properly objects to Westheim's excessively narrow definition of beauty; however, Westheim's lines on the Coatlicue are among the best ever written on the subject. "It is monstrosity monumentalized to the sublime. The history of world art knows only one similar case, only one visionary creation where monstrosity has been shaped with identical vigor: Dante's Inferno." Westheim applies the term "surrealism" to the Coatlicue, not only because the Aztec sculptor was not bound to the Aristotelian precept that art must copy nature but also, especially, "in view of a certain affinity between the procedure used in the creation of the Great Coatlicue and the artistic method of today that surrealism resorts to. To a general contour that represents or suggests a human figure are incorporated, and not just added as decoration, foreign elements, extrahuman elements like serpentine heads, animal claws, etc." For the Aztec artist, cautions Westheim, these elements were in no sense unnatural or supernatural, but rather natural, part of his cosmic order; Westheim therefore describes the artistic attitude of ancient Mexico as "mythical realism."

Brilliant and moving is Westheim's description of the Coatlicue.

She, the earth goddess, mother of all that is created, determines the length of that intermezzo between two eternities that is called life, that brief moment given to the individual to walk in light. There is no conjuration to offset her acting; there are only periods of grace that can be wrung from her by force of adoration and constant sacrifices. . . . In that great Aztec work nothing is analyzed. None of the many legendary and frightful actions of the divinity is related. There is no story; there is no action. In majestic calm, immobile, impassive—a fact and a certainty—the goddess stands before the spectator: a monument, a symbol, a concept. And all the plastic resources—decorative and symbolic at the same time—all the details, represented with clarity and precision, the serpentine jaws and bodies, the human hearts and the severed hands, the animal claws: everything has the one purpose of accentuating and dramatizing the tremendous power of the earth goddess so that the spectator, i.e., the believer who devoutly approaches the image, re-creates it in his imagination.

In other Aztec sculptures, such as the Eagle Knight or the figure known as the *Sad Indian*, realistic elements, already contained in what Westheim calls the "surrealism" of the Coatlicue, strongly emerge, "repressing the magico-psychic forces that make that work such a grandiose expression of Aztec religiosity. Observation of reality, subjected to the architectonic, submitted to a formal discipline. In the literal sense of the word, this is not realism; it is a stylization that starts from the experience of the reality and that in certain works—like the head of Coyolxauhqui with its broad surfaces—recalls the art of India." The specific character of this developing Aztec style—its clarity and concision, "the base of realism without rhetoric, that nevertheless strives for a representative, monumental effect"—Westheim links to radical changes in the Aztec social structure and especially to the growing power of a military aristocracy that evidently exerted influence in artistic as well as political life. Citing a phrase coined by Wilhelm Worringer to describe Roman art, Westheim calls this Aztec art "an art of soldiers." The head of the Eagle Knight, in which the warrior's face appears through the open beak of the bird god, symbolizes the robust, predatory spirit of Aztec feudalism merged with a sense of religious mission.

Like Toscano, Westheim sees a decline in late Aztec art associated with the growth of luxury and refinement in the style of living. This refinement also found expression in art. "A trivial naturalism appears." In the reign of Moctezuma II Aztec ceramic art renounces "the great and sacred tradition: geometric ornamentation, symmetry, rhythmic repetition, linear abstraction. Imitation of nature becomes the fashion. . . ." For Westheim the "worldly grace" of this late Aztec art "is a symptom of decadence. Aztec art had been great and original when its wandering fantasy, powerful and barbarically bold, was absorbed by its meditation on life and death." [26]

Among other foreign commentators on Aztec art, special value may be assigned to the writings of two Americans, George C. Vaillant and George Kubler. Vaillant's *Aztecs of Mexico* Fernández commends for its conception of Aztec art as an expression of Aztec culture, for its effort to comprehend this art in terms of the Aztec vision of life and the universe. "The austerity of their life," wrote Vaillant, "led the Aztecs to attribute similar attitudes to their gods, and, as a result, the soft emotionalism so characteristic of European art is almost totally absent." Of the Coatlicue, he wrote that this "great statue in Mexico, whose head is twin serpents, whose necklace human hands and hearts, whose feet and hands are viciously armed with claws and whose skirt is a mat of writhing snakes, brings into a dynamic concentrate the manifold horrors of the universe." [27]

In a 1943 article on metropolitan Aztec sculpture, George Kubler affirmed that "among the great achievements of plastic art the world over, Aztec sculpture is to be accounted as one of the climactic events. . . ." In a larger, more recent work, *The Art and Architecture of Ancient America* (1962), Kubler again dealt with Aztec sculpture against a background of Aztec history and culture. Aztec sculpture, he believes, did not emerge as a distinct, identifiable style until after A.D. 1450. Drawing upon traditions and craftsmen from conquered regions, "it emerged as a new expression moulded by the sublime importance of human sacrifice and by the guilt-ridden conception of duty in Aztec life." The "primitive character of Aztec tribal life found its most tremendous expression" in the Coatlicue and the Yolotlicue, another gigantic stone figure of the earth goddess discovered in excavations for the Supreme Court Building. He cited one of the well-known figures of a woman in childbirth to illustrate the expressive power of Aztec sculpture. The figure simultaneously represents a deity giving birth to a time-period and a woman in childbirth—an act which the Aztecs equated with a warrior's capture of a sacrificial victim. "The figure was endowed by the sculptor with deeply expressive particulars conveying the pain and nausea of parturition. . . . The piece unites the domains of observation, of expression, and of calendrical ritual." "Expressive power was the distinctive attainment of Aztec sculptors," and Kubler notes that they vested animal and plant images with the greatest vitality, whereas human beings were usually shown in death or submissive postures. These attitudes expressed "the passive compliance of humans whose death was required in order that the gods might live to endow the earth with renewed vitality." [28]

Justino Fernández' own study of Coatlicue may be regarded as a climactic event in the inquiry into the aesthetics of ancient Mexican art. The first part of his book surveys the history of the process through the pertinent literature. The second part offers a critique of the process and identifies Fernández himself with "the new historical-humanist current" represented by Gamio, Eulalia Guzmán, O'Gorman, Toscano, Vaillant, Westheim, and above all Kubler. In the third and final part of his study Fernández proceeds to an intensive, detailed analysis of the formal and symbolic elements of the Coatlicue, regarded as an archetype of Aztec art. This analysis makes use of all the resources offered by archaeology as well as art criticism.

The Aztec sculptor, said Fernández, expressed with marvelous skill "a world of dynamic forms, but controlled, limited by the great fundamental structures: the cruciform and the pyramidal. . . . No 'pre-logical' mentality conceived Coatlicue; on the contrary, its structures are clearly logical and its forms are of a vigorous sensibility, highly imaginative. For us it has all the characteristics of a true and grandiose work of art."

In a rigorously thought out conception such as the Coatlicue, "of such profound religious meaning," continued Fernández, "none of its principal elements can originate in chance; each has a justification for being what and where it is." His analysis of the forms leads to the conclusion that fundamentally they derive neither from the geometric rigidity of the Teotihuacán water goddess Chalchihuitlicue nor from the "naturalism" of the Aztec head of the *Dead Warrior;* they are forms created expressly to embody a religious conception, the divinity Coatlicue. "The stupendous equilibrium achieved by the sculptor with all those elements, placed or composed in a certain order and in certain proportions, is what makes the forms emotional, synthetic, and pregnant with significance. They are forms born of plenitude, of a long creative experience, and of genius, which the Aztec people certainly had, especially in sculpture, where their originality and dramatic force appear magnificent."

From Fernández' exhaustive analysis of the symbolic content of these forms in terms of Aztec religious and mythological concepts, there emerges a recondite cosmological symbolism. In sum, Coatlicue "is the dynamic-cosmic force which gives life and is maintained by death in a struggle of contraries which is so necessary that its ultimate and radical meaning is war. . . . Thus the dramatic beauty of Coatlicue has ultimately a warlike meaning, life and death; and that is why it has a supreme, a tragic and moving beauty. For if the bloody Aztec religion, which gave coherence to Aztec life, gave the Coatlicue the meaning which it had for them, our contemplation and reflection upon it touch our own vital interests, inspire a sense of our own radical reality: the death that is in us." [29]

Inspired by nationalism and social revolutionary passion, Mexican artists in the half century after 1920 undertook the pictorial reconstruction of ancient Mexico, the Conquest, and indeed the whole sweep of Mexican history. In addition to the three giants— Rivera, Orozco, and Siqueiros—many talented painters have brilliantly evoked various aspects of ancient Mexican civilization. To attempt to survey their work would exceed the scope of this book; however an examination of the historical art of Rivera, Orozco, and Siqueiros will sufficiently illustrate how differences in personality, political philosophy, and artistic method produced very different interpretations and use of pre-Cortesian themes.

According to Rivera's biographer, Bertram Wolfe, Rivera returned from Europe in 1921 bringing with him "a highly sophisticated technique and sensibility, memories of a thousand great works he had seen in the cathedrals, palaces, and galleries of Europe, love for his native land, a determination to build his art on a fusion of his Paris sophistication with the plastic heritage of his people, and to paint for them on public walls." [30]

In the hectic Mexican atmosphere of the early 1920's, Rivera's *indigenismo* blossomed in exuberant, extravagant ways. According to Wolfe, he "began to idealize everything Aztec: daily life, ritual, cosmogony, way of waging war, even human sacrifice." From some hitherto unpublished Rivera papers dating from this period Wolfe cites a passage in which Rivera spoke of the Aztecs as a people "for whom everything, from the esoteric acts of the high priests to the most humble domestic activities, was so many rites of beauty; for whom rocks, clouds, birds, and flowers . . . were motives of delight and manifestations of the Great Material." Rivera was convinced that "what ingenious missionaries and holy historians believed to be polytheism [among the Aztecs] was only the marvelous plastification of natural forces, one in their unity and multiple in their infinity, beautiful always in their action favorable or unfavorable, positive or negative, always engenderers of life by birth—renovation; and death—transformation."

And Rivera went on to write a eulogy of Aztec sacrifice which could have been penned only in that superheated Mexican atmosphere of the early 1920's, charged with tension between *indigenistas* and *hispanistas.*

Never will the poor contemporary man of letters of criollo—that is, Catholic—mind, comprehend the joy and the moral clarity of the Sacrifice, mystic culmination, from which anaesthesia eliminated pain, for pain would destroy the magical efficacy of the act. After a purifying preparation with beautiful living for two years, after having left in the bellies of two virgins, two new lives in exchange for his own, the victim converted himself into the sacred book of the revealing entrails of the Macrocosm, and his heart, like a splendid bleeding flower, was offered to the Father Sun, irradiating center of all possibility of life. Or to the magnificent and beautiful Huitzilopochtli, of the beaks and wings of a bird who, in the Flowery War, gave to men the possibility of being more beautiful than the tigers or the eagles. Or to Tlaloc, of the great round eyes, possessor of the sacred waters generating life on the earth. All these were liberators from the end that comes by slow rotting, by the miserable condition of dissolving illness, or consumption by age, or slow reduction to total impotence—the highest good to which the mortal can attain who is incapable of preferring to these THE RITE OF SACRIFICE.

Rivera's Aztequismo blended somewhat incongruously with his emerging Marxian socialism. Wolfe quotes from another "long and chaotic manuscript" of this period which traced the evolution of the Mexican people and its art through history. In one passage Rivera startlingly fuses the symbolism of Christianity, of Aztec Flowery War, and of Soviet communism. Rivera declared that Mexican youth had discovered a great new star in the Mexican sky —"a great star which shines red and is five-pointed." On this star could be discerned "a hammer and sickle." "And emissaries have come saying that it is a presage of the birth of a new order and a new law, without false priests who enrich themselves, without greedy rich who make the people die though they might easily, on what they produce with their hands, live in love, loving the Sun and the flowers again, on condition of bringing the news to all their brothers in misery on the American continent, even though for that a new Flowery War might be needed." [31]

It was not Rivera, however, who pioneered in the pictorial rediscovery of ancient Mexico, or even of contemporary Mexico, for that matter. His first murals on the walls of the Escuela Preparatoria were painted in conformity with the mystical Pythagorean concepts and precepts of the Maecenas of the youthful Mexican artists, José Vasconcelos, Secretary of Education, who believed that "a heroic art could fortify the will to reconstruction." Accordingly Rivera painted a "great neo-classical composition on the theme of the Creation, an allegorical potpourri that purported to portray the formation of the Mexican race, but turned out to be a rationalist hymn to the origin of man and his intellectual powers, intoned in metaphors of all the religions. . . ." [32] The initiative in developing an authentic national muralist art was taken by five young men: Ramón Alva de la Canal, Fermín Revueltas, Emilio García Cahero, Fernando Leal, and Jean Charlot, who worked in the entrance hall and staircase of the Escuela Preparatoria; while Rivera painted in the auditorium. These young men gained the nickname "Dieguitos" because of the popular belief that they were Rivera's disciples and assistants. The

Eagle Knight. Andesite. Height: 14.8 in. (38 cm.). Aztec civilization, Valley of Mexico, 1300–1500. Museo Nacional de Antropología, Mexico. Photograph courtesy Instituto Nacional de Antropología e Historia, Mexico.

José Clemente Orozco. *The Departure of Quetzalcóatl*, 1932–1934. Fresco. From *An Epic of American Civilization*, Part I. Baker Library, Dartmouth College, Hanover, New Hampshire. Reproduced by permission of the Trustees of Dartmouth College.

José Clemente Orozco. *Head of Quetzalcóatl*. 1932–1934. Crayon. 32¼ x 24⅛ in. (82 x 61.8 cm.). Coll., The Museum of Modern Art, New York. Gift of the artist. Photograph courtesy Museum.

View of the Castillo, Chichén Itzá, Yucatán, looking between the inverted
serpent columns of the Temple of the Warriors, past a reclining Chacmool.
Photograph Irmgard Groth.

Henry Moore. Above: *Ideas for Metal Sculpture*. 1938. Pen and ink, wash. Coll. Sir Kenneth Clark. Photograph Soichi Sunami, courtesy The Museum of Modern Art, New York. Below: *Reclining Woman*. 1929. Brown Hornton stone. Length: 33 in. (83.8 cm.). Coll. Leeds City Art Galleries. Photograph courtesy Henry Moore.

David Alfaro Siqueiros. *Ethnography*. 1939. Duco on composition board.
48⅛ x 32⅜ in. (122.2 x 82.2 cm.). Abby Aldrich Rockefeller Fund. Coll.,
The Museum of Modern Art, New York. Photograph Sunami-Matisse.

Man with canine headdress. Coarse red clay with traces of white paint. Height: 29¾ in. (75.5 cm.). Acatlán region, Oaxaca (?). Late Protoclassic, c. A.D. 1–150. The Metropolitan Museum of Art, New York, J. M. Kaplan Fund. Photograph courtesy Museum.

The earth goddess Coatlicue. Basalt. Height: approx. 102⅜ in. (260 cm.).
Aztec civilization, near the Great Temple of México-Tenochtitlán, late 15th
century. Museo Nacional de Antropología, Mexico. Photograph courtesy
Instituto Nacional de Antropología e Historia, Mexico.

Dieguitos, according to Charlot, "exerted a lasting influence both on the form and on the content of the Mexican mural renaissance. The complete rerouting of Rivera's talents after his first mural suggested to Bertram Wolfe that the Byzantino-cubist *Creation* be labeled a false start. In fact, the nude or draped allegories brusquely gave way in Rivera's next work to folk themes steeped in Mexicanism, or rather in Indianism. This abrupt turnabout within a few months was made plausible by the spadework of the younger painters, who were facing Mexico squarely while the older master still squinted at Italian grandeur."

Charlot finds in Revueltas' *Devotion to the Virgin of Guadalupe* the first use of "the hieratic, white-clad Indian and the women wrapped in stylized rebozos that became the accepted ciphers of a Mexican mural alphabet." To Leal's *Pilgrimage of Chalma* he assigns precedence in a *costumbrista* accent on folk festivals and dances, picturesque clothes and customs. For himself Charlot claims priority in the painting of historical scenes. "The historical epic—theme of Rivera's Cuernavaca frescoes and the staircase of the National Palace—was treated years before in my 1922 'Massacre in the Main Palace,' which presented for the first time on a wall the personae of a drama—robot knights trampling upon Indian victims—that was to rate many an encore."[33]

Certainly Rivera changed his artistic course abruptly. In the following years he undertook a vast pictorial reconstruction of Mexican history from its beginnings to the present, within a framework of historical materialist theory, and with a clear didactic, inspirational aim—the aim of enabling the Mexican people to see where it had been and where it was going. The murals that he painted in the Palacio Nacional between 1929 and 1951 constitute his climactic achievement in this field. These murals re-create ancient Mexican civilization in immense detail, with the utmost archaeological veracity. In conformity with his Marxist outlook, Rivera devoted much attention to the material foundations of ancient Indian life, to the depiction of economic activity and technology. The crowning scene in this series is a panoramic view of Tenochtitlán, in which he conveys with marvelous coloring and stylized realism the teeming life of the great city.

Bertram Wolfe has written an appreciation of these murals whose ironic tone may tell as much about Wolfe's political prejudices as about Rivera's work. "The past, present and future of Mexico are presented in a dialectical march from the glories of primitive, pre-conquest Aztec 'tribal communism' through the valley of the shadow of Conquest, with its implantation of slavery, feudalism, and capitalism, and its class struggles . . . until Mexico climbs once more into the sunlit upland of Marxian communism." Reinforcing the implied charge of idealization and tendentiousness, Wolfe wrote: "In Diego's dream there is nothing modern civilized man can do which Aztec, Zapotec, and Mayan have not done more elegantly, intensely and skillfully. Men and women of graceful bodies, vestments, and movements, plant the corn, harvest the ear, grind the kernels, bake them into flat corn cakes in scenes which are a rhythmic dance of worship to the corn god. On sites of topographical distinction they erect their pyramid temples or bustling markets. Chieftain-priests don garments at once terrifying and beautiful for the performance of sacred rites. Before the temples, dancers dance their rounds, musicians play sweet, unheard music. Craftsmen weave, smelt, hammer, plait, make jewels of splendor. All these labors are pleasant and joyous, a rhythmic dance. Gentle rivers flow through idyllic land-scapes in which dark figures bathe, rhythmically wash clothes, separate bright gold from dark earth. Huntsmen draw their bows in poses of sheer grace, a grace possessed as well by the game they are about to slay. Over all presides the watchful *zopilote* or vulture, who takes upon himself the ungrateful task of scavenging to keep this world clean. . . ."

Wolfe notes that in the scenes of the Conquest, "rhythm, mood, and color change. Here the composition is crowded, the diagonals disturbing; the burden-bearers have lost their elegant outline, the rhythmic dance of labor has changed into a crushed, crowded, bowed shuffling of a chain-gang of slaves. . . ." Over this "evil scene" presides "the Cortés nobody knows," constructed, according to Wolfe, by Rivera's "wayward fancy and inventive malice" with the aid of Dr. Alfonso Quiroz Cuarón and Eulalia Guzmán, whose inquest into Cortés' remains showed that the conqueror was a poor deformed devil afflicted with congenital syphilis. (Rivera's portrait of Cortés bears no resemblance to the stately figure in the portraits made by Christoph Weiditz, probably from life, in 1529.) [34]

A critic who subscribed to Rivera's Marxist outlook might com-

plain of his failure to depict the evils that darkened the life of
ancient Mexico: the monumental scale of human sacrifice, the growing burdens of the tributary peoples, the oppression of the *mayeque*
class, the constant warfare. These omissions reflect Rivera's *indigenismo*, but they also seem to reflect a deliberate design to use the
immense constructive achievements of the ancient Mexicans to inspire pride in the cultural heritage of Mexico and persuade his
countrymen to have confidence in themselves and their future.

It is less than fair, however, to maintain, as Wolfe does, that
Rivera's portrait of Tenochtitlán depicts some kind of Aztec "tribal
communism." In fact, the great city of Rivera's mural contains no
trace of the "tribal communism" postulated by Morgan and Bandelier. Rivera portrays a highly organized, complex society, a
fascinating mixture of barbarism and civilization, with some very
modern vices. In the far distance we see the great Temple, topped
by the sanctuaries of Tláloc and Huitzilopochtli, its staircase omi-
nously tinged with blood. Rivera calls attention to the extreme
gulf between social classes by dressing nobles and officials in richly
ornamental clothing that contrasts with the plain garments of commoners; he suggests the complexity of economic life by constructing scenes of merchants bartering, a Totonac trader paying duties
with quills filled with gold dust. One scene features a lovely prosti-
tute—she bears the features of Rivera's wife, Frida Kahlo—surrounded by admirers who offer her exotic gifts. In another mural
of the series, depicting the legend of Quetzalcóatl, there are scenes
of Flowery War and preparation for human sacrifice.

To object to the marked contrast between the serene, festive
mood of pre-Cortesian scenes and the oppressive, violent atmosphere of Conquest and post-Conquest scenes is to quarrel with
Rivera's historical judgment—as he seeks to express it by artistic
means—that as a result of the Conquest the conditions of Indian
life changed for the worse in some important ways. This judgment,
of course, has respected scholarly authority behind it. As concerns
attitudes toward mass labor, for example, a modern historian,
Charles Gibson, observes that "a major change under Spanish rule
. . . was that Indian peoples lost the sense of joyous participation
and adopted an attitude of resignation." [35]

Leaving aside broad questions of interpretation, Rivera's historical art in general displays a great, almost obsessive concern with

factual accuracy. Rivera himself has written, in reference to the historical frescoes he painted at Cuernavaca in 1929: "I took care to authenticate every detail by exact research because I wanted to leave no opening for anyone to try to discredit the murals as a whole by the charge that any detail was a fabrication." A recent study of those frescoes affirms that Rivera's sources included such published and manuscript codices as the Lienzo de Tlaxcala, the Matrícula de tributos, Sahagún's Códice Florentino and his Primeros Memoriales, the Codex Mendoza, and Seler's writings, as well as a vast number of archaeological monuments and artifacts in the Museo Nacional and other sites and repositories.[36]

The historical art of José Clemente Orozco expresses a very different attitude toward Mexico's Indian past. A militant who took part in the armed struggles of the Revolution, a revolutionary artist who denounced capitalism and imperialism with all the power of a Goya, Orozco nevertheless rejected *indigenismo* as a political or artistic creed. In July, 1923, on the eve of launching his career as a muralist, he declared in an interview: "My one theme is *humanity*. My one tendency is *emotion* to a *maximum*. My means, the *real* and *integral* representation of bodies in themselves and in their inter-relation." [37]

In his *Autobiography*, Orozco attacked *indigenismo* as a creed which exacerbated racial antagonism. "It becomes as if Hernando Cortés and his soldiers had conquered Mexico only yesterday. At any given moment the Conquest looms more immediate than the forays of Pancho Villa. The attack upon the Great Teocalli, the Noche Triste, and the Destruction of Tenochtitlán did not take place early in the sixteenth century, but just last year." His rejection of *indigenismo* went so far as to carry Orozco into the *hispanista* camp. With an astounding disregard of Mexican realities, Orozco declared that indigenous races "are nothing but an item more in the Hispanic total, with the categorical rights of any other group. If we forgot the divisive topic of races, there would be no more need to speak of the lioness and her cubs, or the mother and her sons. We should all of us be the lion, and all of us Mother Spain, from Catalonia to Peru, from Chihuahua to Patagonia. . . ."

Orozco's opposition to *indigenismo*, and his *hispanista* leanings, help to explain his negative posture toward ancient Mexican civilization. In his *Autobiography* he indulges in savage satire at the expense of sentimental critics of the Conquest.

According to them the Conquest ought not to have taken place as it did. Instead of sending cruel and ambitious captains to the New World, Spain should have sent a great delegation of ethnologists, anthropologists, civil engineers, dentists, agronomists, Red Cross nurses, philosophers, philologists, biologists, art critics, mural painters, and learned historians. On reaching Veracruz the caravels should have unloaded carriages adorned with symbolical floral designs, with Cortés and his captains in one of them, carrying baskets of lilies and a great many other flowers and confetti and paper ribbons on the way to render homage to powerful Moctezuma and set up bacteriological, X-ray, and ultra-violet laboratories, a Department of Public Works, universities, kindergartens, libraries, and banking houses. . . . Alvarado, Ortiz, Sandoval, and other stout fellows should have been detailed to guard the ruins lest any least bit of the tremendous pre-Cortesian art be lost. . . . They should have respected the indigenous religion and left Huitzilopochtli standing. . . . Human sacrifice might have been encouraged further, and a great packing house built for human flesh, with a department to handle canning and refrigeration.[38]

This ferocious satire prepares us for the treatment of the Aztecs and the Conquest in Orozco's paintings. His early *Cortés and Malinche*, over the staircase of the Escuela Preparatoria, already defines his attitude toward the Conquest. The conqueror, a superb figure of a man, extends a protective hand toward a thoroughly Indian Malinche, and their union clearly represents the union of Spanish and Indian elements in a new Mexican synthesis. The monumental frescoes at Dartmouth College (1932 to 1934) spell out in detail Orozco's interpretation of ancient Mexican civilization. These frescoes offer an epic treatment of "the constructive and destructive forces which have moulded the patterns of life on this continent." The central theme is the myth of Quetzalcóatl. Part 1 deals with the god's coming. The first panel, *Migration*, depicts the primitive emigrants into Anáhuac, propelled by an irresistible nomadic impulse, advancing in wave after wave. Their faces are stolid, expressionless. The second panel, *Ancient Human Sacrifice*, portrays the most typical institution of this barbarous people. Nothing redeems the utter savagery of the rite. The sacrificial priests and the victim are adorned in brutal masks; over the scene presides an equally brutal mask of the god Huitzilopochtli. The next panel presents Aztec eagle and jaguar knights, cruel, arrogant, predatory. The third panel introduces Quetzalcóatl, a white-robed, blue-eyed sage, who first rouses the Indians from their mental and moral sleep. He is shown against "a lurid parade of the primitive gods across the sky"; these ugly and fantastic deities have elements vaguely allusive to known Aztec gods. Quetzalcóatl's figure rises above the pyramids of Teotihuacán, which Orozco, in conformity with then prevailing views, identifies as the home of his cult. The fifth panel, the *Pre-Columbian Golden Age*, pays tribute to the flowering of industry, art, and science under the aegis of Quetzalcóatl. In the sixth panel the forces of darkness regain their power and Quetzalcóatl departs on a raft of coiled serpents, promising to return in five hundred years in the company of other white gods to destroy the civilization of the faithless people who rejected his teachings and to establish a new civilization in its place.

Part 2 of the frescoes carries Orozco's epic from the Conquest to the present day. An introductory panel has Cortés in armor, sword in hand, standing amid a heap of slain bodies and the rubble of the destroyed Indian civilization. The handsome, bearded conqueror surveys the scene with a calm, intelligent gaze; nearby an austere priest supports and is supported by an immense cross. "In the figures of both Cortés and the priest," observes a commentator on Orozco's work, "are represented the mixture of positive and negative values inherent in the conquering European culture." In successive panels Orozco suggests modern analogues to the evils of Aztec society. Thus the twelfth panel, *Gods of the Modern World*, presents spectral academicians, dressed in the robes of famous universities, whose dead learning keeps the people in spiritual bondage, as did the frightful Aztec gods. The next panel, entitled *Modern Human Sacrifice*, shows an unknown soldier, covered by a composite national flag, while a pompous orator, to the sound of blaring trumpets, "pontificates at the solemn ritual glorifying the human sacrifice to the modern god of war." [39] Throughout the composition, then, Orozco assigns a negative significance to the Aztecs and their culture; he identifies the vanished Golden Age of ancient Mexico with the sway of the white, blue-eyed Quetzalcóatl, who looks more like a Greek sage than an Indian prophet.

If further evidence of Orozco's anti-Aztec outlook were needed, it is provided by two fresco lunettes in the Hospicio Cabañas in Guadalajara. One of these "recollections of Aztec days," as MacKinley Helm calls them, shows a group of ghoulish Indians gorging themselves in a cannibalistic feast before a huge pot from which protrude the feet of victims. Another depicts a wild dance by a group of masked and naked Aztecs whose bony ribs and musculature enhance their macabre appearance. By contrast, a panel of the Hospicio frescoes representing Cortés again interprets him sympathetically, although his armor "looks a little as though it had been manufactured in Detroit," and the massive bolts with which it is assembled add a striking, robot-like effect.[40]

Neither Rivera's idealizing tendency nor the anti-Aztec bias of Orozco appears in those rare works by Siqueiros that treat ancient Indian themes. Reaffirming in 1955 a viewpoint that he had announced as long ago as 1921, Siqueiros declared his opposition to folkloric and archaeological art with which Rivera is often identified. "I say we have had enough of pretty pictures of grinning peons in traditional Tehuana dress," Siqueiros told the press. "I say to hell with ox carts—let's see more tractors and bulldozers. Mexican art is suffering from primitivism and archaeologism." [41]

For Siqueiros, a socialist revolutionary artist, obsessed with the violence and injustice of the modern world, Aztec society has little contemporary relevance, perhaps no civic lesson except the lesson it offered in its death struggle of heroic resistance to foreign domination. The only figure out of Mexico's Indian past that Siqueiros celebrates is Cuauhtémoc, and that without any effort at archaeological veracity. A Siqueiros mural in the Palacio de Bellas Artes shows Cuauhtémoc mutely enduring Spanish torture; another presents the gallant youth, clad in Spanish armour, Aztec sword in hand, standing over a slain Spanish horse and rider. In *Cuauhtémoc Against the Myth* he is seen throwing an obsidian-tipped spear at an enormous Spanish horseman just as the latter hurls a sharpened cross upon him. Siqueiros has also done a portrait of Cuauhtémoc that is instinct with nobility and grace, yet completely free from sentimentality. "Siqueiros," says Justino Fernández, "is the only Mexican painter of our time who has given stature to the historical figure of Cuauhtémoc." [42]

Aztec literature gained increasing recognition in the half-century after 1920. Inspired by nationalist fervor and humanistic interest, scholars explored with growing scientific rigor the aesthetics, the techniques, and the meaning of Náhuatl literary expression. They discovered a literature marked by a surprising variety of forms, themes, and moods.

Appreciation of the Aztec literary achievement was by no means a new thing. Early friars such as Sahagún and Torquemada had extolled the rich and elegant imagery of Indian hymns and prayers. The current of praise ran strong in the judgments of creole nationalists such as Eguiara y Eguren and Clavigero. In the middle of the nineteenth century Prescott gave the English-speaking world its first taste of the beauties of Aztec poetry. Another American, the anthropologist Daniel G. Brinton, produced the first annotated collections of such verse in his *Ancient Náhuatl Poetry* (1887) and *Rig Veda Americanus* (1890). Unhappily, Brinton knew very little Náhuatl, and the failings of his translations were mercilessly exposed by Eduard Seler. Meanwhile José M. Vigil had discovered a collection of Náhuatl texts in the Biblioteca Nacional of Mexico; this source, of fundamental importance, was published by Antonio Peñafiel in facsimile edition with the title *Cantares en idioma mexicano* (1904). The illustrious Francisco del Paso y Troncoso, who passionately admired the charms of Náhuatl, of which he had a rare mastery, contributed to the creation of a documentary base by his publication of codices and other manuscript materials. Eduard Seler in Germany, Rémi Siméon in France, also added to the growing volume of texts. It was Seler who made the first scholarly and reasonably accurate translations of Náhuatl texts. Since his time the tempo of production of new texts has greatly quickened, as a direct result of the rise of important schools of Náhuatl linguistic and literary study in Mexico, Germany, and the United States.

The late Father Ángel María Garibay K. was long the acknowledged leader in the field of Náhuatl literary studies. His major work is the *Historia de la literatura náhuatl* (1953–1954). Volume I deals with the autonomous Indian production from about 1420 to 1521; Volume II deals with later works and what they reveal of the "trauma of the Conquest." In general, Garibay's viewpoint on the ancient native civilization is that of a scholarly *indigenista*, naturally tinged by his character of a Catholic priest and teacher of Scripture to the Indians. Garibay praises not only the clergy who helped to preserve the ancient literature but also Cortés, "a man of marvelous genius" who destroyed not only to conquer but to build. "The old social organization was destroyed. No matter how much we praise it, we cannot compare it to the Christian. . . . The multitude, which suffered the fate of all multitudes, did not greatly regret the loss of the past. No matter how hard the hand of the conquistador, harsher and, above all, much less intelligent, was the tyrant who had kept them in slavery." [43] This understandable partiality toward the Church and the Conquest is joined with a finely comprehending and appreciative attitude toward Aztec culture.

Garibay's book was the first large-scale, rigorously scientific exploration of a subject that swarmed with difficulties because of the obscure, hermetic character of much of the Náhuatl literary material; its meaning and aesthetic value can be unlocked only by patient investigation of Náhuatl expressive devices and the religious ideas and symbolism of the ancient Mexicans. He blazed a trail that others followed.

After Garibay, the most important living Mexican scholar in this field is Miguel León-Portilla, who studies the ancient literature from the viewpoint of its philosophical as well as its purely literary content and value. A number of his works are available in English versions; these include *The Broken Spears* (1962), an anthology of Indian and mestizo texts on the Conquest, his study of *Pre-Columbian Literatures of Mexico* (1969), and the especially valuable *Aztec Thought and Culture: A Study of the Ancient Náhuatl Mind* (1963). I have suggested my doubts about some of the conclusions drawn by León-Portilla from his reading of the native sources, but his *Aztec Thought and Culture* possesses indisputable merit. His *Trece poetas del mundo azteca* (1967) marks a further advance in the study in depth of Aztec literature; it not only brings together verses by thirteen Aztec poets but seeks to rescue them from anonymity, providing a respectable amount of biographical data for each. León-Portilla rightly asserts that today "Náhuatl literature transcends the limits of a purely scientific interest and has begun to be valued, together with other native artistic creations, from a point of view that searches for the meaning of the life experiences and ideas of men who, basically isolated from the Old World, were, in their own way, extraordinary creators of culture." [44]

The Anglo-Saxon world has also contributed to the discovery of Náhuatl literature in recent decades. A forgotten pioneer is the American scholar J. H. Cornyn, who published in 1930 *The Song of Quetzalcóatl*, a well-made, tuneful version of the legend, based on the Náhuatl texts of Sahagún, and employing the meter of Longfellow's *Hiawatha*. Arthur J. O. Anderson and Charles E. Dibble are now bringing to a close their monumental labor on an annotated English version of Sahagún's Florentine Codex, in course of publication since 1950. One of the few critical studies written outside Mexico is Irene Nicholson's *Firefly in the Night: A Study of Ancient Mexican Poetry and Symbolism* (1959). Although marred by a whole-hearted acceptance of Séjourné's peculiar mysticism, the book displays an infectious enthusiasm for its subject, adequately introduces the reader to Aztec poetic method, and presents some graceful English versions of Aztec poems, based on Garibay's Spanish translations of Náhuatl texts.

Mexican writers, as well as the artists, have explored the Indian past to enrich their repertory of thematic materials, symbols, and stylistic techniques. For obvious reasons, Cuauhtémoc has had a special attraction for the poets, and the image of the hero, his symbolic content, has naturally varied with the poet's artistic and political philosophy, and even with the decade in which he wrote.

An unfamiliar Cuauhtémoc appears in the intensely personal, frequently elliptical verse of Ramón López Velarde. The poet invoked Cuauhtémoc in the moving intermezzo of "Suave Patria" (1921) an intermezzo between two tender, teasing "acts" in which López Velarde describes and expresses his love for Mexico. The intermezzo opens: "Young grandfather: hear me praise you, the only hero of artistic stature." There are no heroics; the mood is subdued, tragic, compassionate. Upon the poet's spirit weighed the terrible losses and sufferings of the Mexican Revolution. He may have also been influenced, as Pedro de Alba suggests,[45] by the powerful *Nuestros Dioses* of the painter Saturnino Herrán, whose studio López Velarde visited almost daily. His Cuauhtémoc is a Man of Sorrows; he is also an instrument for the fusion of Spanish and Indian elements into a Mexican synthesis.

> Anachronistically, absurdly,
> The rosebush leans toward your nopal cactus. . . .

But the note most intensely sounded is that of suffering, of grief for:

> All that you suffered, the captive canoe,
> The terror of your children,
> The sobbing of your mythologies, the Malinche, the idols going down,
> And last of all, that you were torn from the curving breast of your empress
> As from a quail's breast.[46]

A more familiar Cuauhtémoc emerges from the passionate "Oda a Cuauhtémoc" (1924) of Carlos Pellicer. This poem is in the tradition of civic verse made celebrated by Rubén Darío and most recently by Pablo Neruda; it reflects the intense disquiet and anti-Yanquismo of Latin American intellectuals in the era of United States interventions in Central America and the Caribbean. Like the nineteenth-century Rodríguez Galván, Pellicer invoked Cuauhtémoc in a time of gathering storms for Mexico and the continent.

> Lord, so lovely was your will,
> That in the tragedy of your imperial months,
> The rhythm of the great stars accelerated.
> I think upon the moment,
> That was the most terrible of your sadness,
> When you sought alliances among the men of your race,
> And your cry was lost amid the forests. . . .

The poet brooded on the tragedy of the Conquest:

> The civilized monarchies of America fell;
> Tenochtitlán and Cuzco were their sculptured heads.

From the north came the threat of a new Conquest. Pellicer complained that "the men of the North pirate at will on the continent and in the islands, and snatch pieces of the sky." He asked:

> Will you again put our feet in the fire?
> Will you come with brutal hands
> From the mediocre, orderly, corpulent Yankeeland?
> Will you come with explosions and machines
> To rob, kill, and buy caciques with your endless money?

The poem ends with a final invocation of Cuauhtémoc:

> O Lord! O great king! Tlacatecuhtli!
> O solemn and tragic chief of men!
> O mild and ferocious Cuauhtémoc!
> Your life is an arrow that wounds the eyes of the sun
> And continues to climb in the sky,
> But in the crater of my heart
> Boils the faith that will save your peoples.[47]

In the calmer, more sedate Mexican atmosphere of recent times, public poetry of this kind has few followers. More common than invocation of Aztec heroism are graceful allusions to the presence of ancient Mexican motifs in the life of modern Mexico. Thus Pellicer, a great lover and connoisseur of the old Indian culture, observes in his "Discurso por las flores":

> The Mexican people has two obsessions:
> A liking for death and a love for flowers.
>
> Before we spoke Castilian,
> There was a day of the month consecrated to death;
> There was a strange war called flowery,
> And the altars spouted good luck with blood.
>
> The Calendar also registers a day of flowers.
> The day Xóchitl. Xochipilli bared himself for love of flowers.
> His legs, shoulders, knees, are covered with flowers.
> His hollow fingers hold flowers, forever fresh. In his mask
> Shines the profound smile of lovers.[48]

Another modern Mexican poet, Salvador Novo, pouring new wine into old bottles, has skillfully employed Aztec poetic imagery and technique for the expression of religious faith in "Ofrenda":

The Giver of Life,
He who is near and far,
Molded me from the bones rescued from the shades.
A drop of His blood
Became a flower in the heart I received from Him.
His glance, like a hook, raised the eyes to my face.

With face and heart, I was His guest;
Amply I lived in His house of emeralds.
His song and my song brought forth red flowers.
Fragrant necklaces bound my breast;
Birds filled my arms, stretched forth to seize the unseizable bird,
He of the gold and turquoise plumes,
The fugitive quetzal of the days.

My tongue, perforated with words,
Sucked honey in silence from the blue and yellow flowers.

My face withered,
Withered under the tenacious dust that clouds the gold of time,
That muddies the current
— sucker, vein, road, branch —
My heart folds its petals,
Folds and darkens its petals.

O Giver of Life!
O Lord who art far and yet within my blood,
The eyes that Thou gavest me
Contemplated happily the works of Thy hand;
My heart danced
The rhythm of Thy dawn still pale with stars,
The golden eagle over my head,
The flapping wings of coming night.

To Thy obsidian palace, O Giver of Life!
Admit one who was Thy guest on earth.
Silence my tongue,

Blind my eyes to Thy invisible grandeur,
May I leave here the songs,
The precious stones of friendship,
The flowers that Thy hands placed in mine.
Strip of its languid petals,
The heart Thou didst set to singing for a day,
Take back from it the drop of Thy divine blood.
I give it back to Thee,
I return it to Thee,
O Giver of Life,
Impregnated in the glory of having held Thine own! [49]

Pre-Cortesian themes have a strong appeal for Novo. The past and present riotously mingle in his madcap comedy in verse, *In Ticitezcatl o el espejo encantado*, in which the downfall of Quetzalcóatl is reenacted and Tezcatlipoca and Coatlicue reappear, the god as a tourist guide at Teotihuacán, the goddess as the aunt of an attractive anthropology student. Novo has also written a one-act play, *Cuauhtémoc*, which shows the hero in the posture of "Cuauhtémoc against the myth," vainly seeking to overcome Moctezuma's fatalism and the distrust and rancor of ancient tribal foes to whom he offers friendship and unity. Both pieces appear in a collection of Novo's plays, *In Ticitezcatl o el espejo encantado* (1966).

Novo again evokes Cuauhtémoc in his dialogue "Cuauhtémoc y Eulalia," (1970). On the road to Ixcateopan the anthropologist Eulalia Guzmán meets a youth who engages her in conversation. He questions the importance of the supposed discovery of Cuauhtémoc's bones. Cuauhtémoc's immortality is assured without the aid of those remains. "Cuauhtémoc will never die. The Spaniards could not kill him; no foreigner can kill him. Cortés, Maximilian, Wilson. . . . All pass away, all die. But Cuauhtémoc survives. They exploit him, rob him, whip him, cheat him, praise him, humiliate him, plunder his wealth, shanghai him to work on lands that once were his. But he will not die."

"What strange things you say," remarks Doña Eulalia. "Who are you, what's your name?" "Well," the youth replies, "you might, for example, call me . . . Cuauhtémoc." [50]

In prose as in verse, Mexican writers sought to evoke the aspect and spirit of the vanished Aztec civilization. The first important essay in this vein was Alfonso Reyes' *Visión de Anáhuac* (1915),

a distinguished expression of the reaction of a generation of Mexican intellectuals (of which Reyes was a leader) against the decadent, uninspired scientism that dominated the official philosophic
thought of the Porfiriato. Reyes' portrait of ancient Mexico bears
comparison with Rivera's panoramic vista of Tenochtitlán; like
that painting, it combines archaeological veracity with a tendency
to idealize, to pass over unpleasant realities. In truth, the essay is
not a historical reconstruction in a strict sense. It is a prose poem,
a genuine vision, a verbal canvas filled with exquisite coloring.
Reyes finds nothing ugly or disquieting in Aztec Tenochtitlán;
he vests both the city and its inhabitants with ideal beauty, dignity,
and charm:

The race has sensitive ears, and, at times, the talk is in whispers. One
hears melodious sibilants, flowing vowels and consonants that tend
to become liquid. The chatter sounds like music. Those *x*'s, those *tl*'s,
those *ch*'s, terrifying when we see them written, fall from the Indians'
lips with the sweetness of maguey syrup. . . . [The people] deck
themselves out gaily, for they are under the eyes of a great Emperor.
Tunics of red cotton, trimmed with gold, embroidered in black and
white, with feather appliqué or painted designs, come and go. The
dark faces have a smiling serenity, all manifesting a desire to please. . . .
The skins, the stones and metals, feathers and cotton fabrics mingle
their colors in one continual iridescence, and, lending the people their
quality and refinement, give them an air of delicate toys.

The pictorial, impressionist effect deepens in Reyes' account of
the human activity in the great marketplace as seen through the
eyes of a Bernal Díaz.

It turns the senses giddy, like a scene from Brueghel, where the material representations acquire a spiritual warmth. . . . The trays overflow with a paradise of fruit: balls of color, transparent ampoules,
clusters of lances, scaly pineapples, and hearts of leaves. The round
wooden trays of sardines are a glitter of silver and saffron, bordered
with fins and brush-fine tails. From a barrel emerges the bewhiskered,
astounded head of a huge fish. In the streets given over to falconry
sit the birds with thirsty beak, blue and red wings drooping like a half-
opened fan, clenched claws crooked like gnarled roots; hard round
eye unwinking. Farther along the heaps of legumes, black, red, yellow,
and white, all bright and oily. Then the venison stand, where, from

among the heaps of haunches and hoofs, emerge a horn, a muzzle, a flaccid tongue, while along the ground runs a dribble of blood that the sidling dogs lick up. . . . The breasts of the pottery vender are one with her dark wares. The arms move about in the clay as though it were their native element, shaping handles for the jugs and molding the red necks. About the belly of the jar run touches of black and gold which copy the collar that clasps her throat. The wide-bottomed pots seem to be seated, like the Indian woman, knees together and up-turned knees parallel. The water, oozing through the pores of the fragrant vases, sings to itself.

Then follows a description of Moctezuma's court, his palaces, diversions, gardens, and other evidence of the splendor of his state. A section on the poetry of ancient Mexico prematurely mourns its loss as irreparable. The essay ends on a note of emphatic assertion of the links between the ancient and modern Mexicans, of their community of spirit, of the subtle unnumbered ways in which the Indian historical heritage colored the modern Mexican's vision of his land.

We are linked to the race of yesterday, without entering into the question of blood, by a common effort to master our wild, hostile natural setting, an effort that lies at the very root of history. We are also linked by the far deeper community of the daily emotions aroused by the same natural objects. The impact of the same world on the sensibility engenders a common soul. But even if one refused to accept as valid either the one or the other, either the fruits of a common effort or the results of a common outlook, it must be allowed that the historical emotion forms a part of our modern life, and that without its glow our valleys and our mountains would be like an unlighted theater. The poet sees, as the moonlight shimmers on the snow of the volcanoes, the shade of Doña Marina outlined against the sky, pursued by the shadow of the Archer of Stars; or dreams of the copper axe on whose sharp edge the heavens rest; or thinks to hear, in the lonely desert, the tragic weeping of the twins the white-robed goddess bears upon her back. We must not ignore the evocation or turn our backs upon the legend. . . .[51]

The "historical emotion" of which Reyes speaks is especially associated with Cuauhtémoc, who challenges Mexican men of letters to write biographies worthy of the hero. Given the relative paucity of data, the works written to the present have been only in small part biography, the rest being history or imaginative reconstruction. Certainly the best existing lives are those by Hector Pérez Martínez and Salvador Toscano. Both works reflect the mature viewpoint of a scientific *indigenismo*, equally free from the uncritical eulogies of ancient Mexico of an Eulalia Guzmán and the exaltation of Cortés by a José Vasconcelos.

In the foreword to his *Cuauhtémoc* (1948), Pérez Martínez sets the tone by observing of the Conquest: "We have to do with an accomplished fact that discussion cannot alter. Those who disparage and condemn it, and those who justify and exalt it, both ignore its essential reality, one which touches us most intimately, the existence of Mexico as a mestizo country." The work reveals throughout a profound knowledge and understanding of the most recent discoveries in the field of Aztec archaeology, art, and literature. A brilliant opening chapter, "El imperio del sagrado," develops with great mastery the theme of the sway of religion over the Aztec mind, obsessed with life and death, with the instability of a world ever threatened with catastrophe; and Pérez Martínez shows how thoroughly Aztec art, literature, dance, and music were permeated with the spirit of this religion.

Into this fantastic world, "severe and fevered, mythical and supernatural," Cuauhtémoc was born. It is a world "governed by strange and mysterious powers: a world saturated with fantastic gods and rites that pervade life, give it meaning, and form the personal conduct of the individual, subjecting him to the mysterious spirit and destiny of the tribe. That is why Cuauhtémoc appears cold and prematurely dead in the studies that have sought to capture his being. For if we separate him from his environment, from that magical climate that was his by reason of descent and tradition, we strip him of all his attributes and leave him unexplained and nebulous, alien to the native spirit, which possesses in him one of its models."

Pérez Martínez' comments on the Aztec arts are penetrating. Writing in a time of full revaluation of those arts, he observed that Indian sculpture had long been scorned because of vain efforts to compare it with Western equivalents, because of failure to comprehend its essence. The hallmark of Western sculpture was its serenity, a peaceful sensuality that gave it its classical character.

Aztec sculpture, on the other hand, was possessed by the madness of myth and ritual; it contained an element of sexual exaltation, for it was obsessed with life and death.

Pérez Martínez offers a vivid illumination of the terrible dialectic of Aztec religion, war, and human sacrifice. "That vertigo of death pressed upon the Indian world and unhinged it. There emerged a bloody ritual, a magical conception of the universe, based on the continual rebirth and revitalization of Huitzilopochtli through the sanguinary orgies which he required to retain his power and immortality. But the Aztec did more than destroy life in order to feed the gods. The tornado rose to greater heights: a monstrous theophagy. . . . This cannibalism had a sacred purpose: man sank his teeth into the divine. Unable to bite the stone idol, the Aztecs magically changed it into flesh and devoured it in order to gain new force to apply to the mystery which they, divorced from the external world, had created."

This bloody routine and an increasingly brutal system of tribute and tribute collection produced its natural results. "The atmosphere of hate that surrounded the Aztecs slowly but fatally thickened." The spirit of resentment and revolt pervaded the empire; it was ripe for disintegration and conquest when Cortés arrived on its shores. To Cuauhtémoc fell the difficult task of preserving the Aztec domination.

The second part of the book begins with an attempt to reconstruct the stages of Cuauhtémoc's life before the arrival of the Spaniards: his birth, his education, his rise in the Aztec political and military hierarchy. The coming of the Spaniards and Cortés' progress toward the capital interrupt this life story. The meeting of Cortés and Moctezuma was more than a meeting of two men: "Two different worlds confronted each other." Pérez Martínez explains the passive and vacillating posture of Moctezuma toward the Spanish invasion in religious terms. "Moctezuma conceived of war as an urgent and magical activity needed to consolidate his Universe and the destiny of his people. But one cannot make war on a god, and this white man was an unexpected returning god! That is why Moctezuma postponed war in the hope of a more powerful intervention than that of his hand or voice: the intervention of the impenetrable gods."

Pérez Martínez contrasts this attitude with that of Cuauhtémoc.

"He was not dominated, as was Moctezuma, by that somewhat skeptical and fearful spirit that caused the Indian monarch to avoid his warlike obligations and the extermination of his enemies, although they were proposed by the noblest men of his court. Formed in struggle, always in contact with death, Cuauhtémoc felt growing within him the conviction that all that had happened was an ominous jest at the expense of the divinities, cloistered in the temples, who regarded impassively this downfall. Something had to happen. Huitzilopochtli, silent for centuries, would give the order for battle. It was necessary, therefore, to prepare the arrow, sharpen the knife, summon the chiefs of the soldiers of his domain, and give the signal. The enemies were there, a step away. War was imminent." With the slaughter of the celebrants at the great fiesta in honor of Huitzilopochtli—a slaughter that Pérez Martínez explains by Alvarado's fanaticism and his genuine suspicion that an uprising was being planned—the war that Cuauhtémoc and Alvarado had anticipated breaks out. And Cuauhtémoc enters history.

For Pérez Martínez, Cuauhtémoc represents the moving force in a despairing last effort to transcend the limits of the Aztec political and social order. Cuauhtémoc, the reformer, sought to implement "a policy of attraction, of unity of the different tribes. "He was doubtless the only Mexican *tecuhtli* or king who ever conceived the idea of forming a nationality." He simultaneously sought to humanize the tribal tradition. "Neither a despot nor a sanguinary ruler, he would not consume the human resources of his empire in sacrifices. He needed people to organize the resistance; he needed internal peace to attend to the imminent invasion. But his overtures met with no response. The Indian peoples considered each other strangers if not prospective victims. . . . Few towns, therefore, responded to Cuauhtémoc's call. The majority, like the Tarascans, sacrificed the Aztec emissaries; others mocked them and reported them to Cortés." [52]

Simply, with a continuous and convincing effort to enter the minds of both Indians and Spaniards, Pérez Martínez relates the defeat of Cuauhtémoc, his torture, and his martyrdom in Honduras. This poetic, sincere book, the fruit of ample research as well as profound emotion, makes a major contribution to the literary reconstruction of the Conquest. According to Wigberto

Jiménez Moreno, "we must not underestimate the influence exerted by this popular book, the bible, perhaps of many who supported the authenticity of the finds of Ixcateopan." [53]

Before his untimely death, Salvador Toscano had almost completed his own biography of Cuauhtémoc. In 1953 Rafael Heliodoro Valle published the book, adding a prologue and two concluding chapters.[54] Like Pérez Martínez' work, Toscano's *Cuauhtémoc* is free from ultra-*indigenista* rhetoric. Toscano notes, for example, that Cortés was the first admirer of the native arts. Toscano nonetheless displays a nostalgic regard for Aztec civilization; paraphrasing Spengler, he observes that that civilization did not die of senile old age, but was tragically assassinated. Yet this culture survived its death, the strangling of its creative forces; it injected its blood into the blood of the conquerors, tinged their language, molded their personality, transformed their tastes in food. The sixteenth century, wrote Toscano, expressed "the paradoxical struggle and communion of two forces," the Spanish and the Indian, fatally stricken, "yet agonizing with the magnificence of a thing that will not and should not die." Cuauhtémoc was the symbol of the Aztec culture in twilight.

In a series of sensitively written chapters, Toscano attempted to reconstruct Cuauhtémoc's life and milieu. The opening chapter, "The Nest of the Falling Eagle," describes the events surrounding his birth; successive chapters tell of the education of an Aztec prince and his initiation into the cult of the gods. Especially colorful is one entitled "A History Lesson," in which the author imagines Cuauhtémoc listening as the priests unfold the picture books and expound the tribal annals. The book goes on to relate the young Cuauhtémoc's rule as lord of Tlatelolco, then passes quickly to develop the crisis caused by the arrival of the Spaniards. With Pérez Martínez, Toscano sees a division arising between those Indian leaders who regarded Cortés as a god and counseled submission and those who insisted that the newcomers were men and urged war. Unlike Pérez Martínez, however, Toscano deals very harshly with Moctezuma. "A soft, cowardly sovereign, fearful of the strange gods, led his people along the road of ignominy." To this ignoble ruler Toscano opposes Cuauhtémoc, who rebelled "against the myth and fought against men." In the manner of Pérez Martínez, Toscano stresses the political genius and innovating spirit of Cuauhtémoc, a ruler who vainly sought to overcome ancient tribal enmities and form defensive and offensive alliances with the former foes and tributaries of the Aztecs.

Other biographers have attempted at least partially to rehabilitate Moctezuma. In 1943 Francisco Monterde published his *Moctezuma II, Señor del Anáhuac*. Like Pérez Martínez, Monterde makes large use of the newly available corpus of Náhuatl poetry to re-create the world of Moctezuma. In this muted, gently melancholic account Moctezuma emerges as a profoundly religious and cultured ruler, unaware until too late how heavily his sway has pressed upon his subjects, tortured by the prophecy of the return of Quetzalcóatl, and finally reconciled to submitting to the strangers, not from vulgar fear but from belief that this was the working out of destiny. In the end, moreover, he is shown as loyal and faithful to his tribal beliefs and traditions. Not only does he refuse to be converted to the new religion but, according to Monterde, he rejects the Spanish demand that he call upon his people to stop fighting. At this juncture a Spanish soldier stabs him and he is dragged unconscious to the rooftop and held erect while an Aztec noble speaks for him. He dies slain by stones thrown by his own people, to whom he has been loyal in his own fashion.[55]

Another biographer, Sara García Iglesias, has told with womanly sympathy and sensitivity the strange story of Moctezuma's daughter, Tecuixpo (Isabel Moctezuma), who was married in turn to Cuitláhuac, Cuauhtémoc, and three Spanish husbands, and who probably had a child by Cortés. In García's account, after endless humiliations at Spanish hands, Tecuixpo remains a devout Christian, declines to join in a conspiracy against Spanish rule, and ends her days a benefactor and protector of her own people.[56]

One effect of the literary neo-romanticism of the post-World War I era in the United States was to induce a revival of interest in the American past; and this again drew the attention of writers to ancient Mexico and its Conquest.

The excitement of discovery appears in "The Destruction of Tenochtitlan," one of a group of essays published in 1925 by the poet William Carlos Williams. It was written, says Horace Gregory, not to record American history but "to present its signs and signatures, its backward glances and, by implication, its warnings for the future." [57] In its poetic tone, delighted retailing of objects, and idealized vision of the Aztec capital and its inhabitants, Williams' essay strongly recalls Alfonso Reyes' *Visión de Anáhuac*. No doubt remains that the Spaniards destroyed a ravishingly beautiful civilization:

> Streets, public squares, markets, temples, palaces, the city spread its dark life upon the earth of a new world, rooted there, sensitive to its richest beauty, but so completely removed from those foreign contacts which harden and protect, that at the very breath of conquest it vanished. The whole world of its unique associations sank back into the ground to be reenkindled, never. Never at least, save in spirit; a spirit mysterious, constructive, independent, puissant with natural wealth; light, if it may be, as feathers; a spirit lost in that soil. Scarcely an element in the city's incredible organization but evidenced an intellectual vigor full of resource and delicacy which had given it distinction.

Williams cast an admiring, almost affectionate, regard on Moctezuma. By contrast with this impeccably civilized Indian ruler, Cortés appears a very boor. Citing Moctezuma's remark to Cortés: "You see that I am composed of flesh and bone like yourselves and that I am mortal and palpable to the touch," Williams observed: "To this smiling sally, so full of gentleness and amused irony, Cortez could reply nothing save to demand that the man declare himself a subject of the Spanish king forthwith, and that, furthermore, he should then and there announce publicly his allegiance to the new power." Clearly, the spiritual advantage was with Moctezuma.

Even in those actions which other historians regard as proof of Moctezuma's infamy and cowardice, Williams was determined to find evidence of redeeming traits. Noting that Moctezuma accepted the abolition of human sacrifice and himself assisted in the purification of the chapels, Williams wrote: "Whether or not this be evidence on the Aztec's part of weakness or the deepest forbearance, surely nothing like it for quiet flexibility of temper and retained dignity has ever been recorded. . . . Perhaps what we call forbearance was no more than the timidity which is an overwhelming agony of heart inspired by the sight of a resistless force aimed at our destruction. Still, if this be so, Montezuma has left no trace of cowardice upon the records. But weakling or genius, about the suave personality of this barbaric chieftain the liveliest, most airily expansive moods of the race did flower, just as the black permanence of tribal understanding stood rooted in the priesthood. Perhaps it was a conscious knowledge of this that inspired Montezuma in the present action."

Enraptured by his discovery of the Aztec splendor, Williams exclaimed: "Surely no other prince has lived, or ever will live, in such state as did this American cacique. The whole waking aspirations of his people, opposed to and completing their religious sense, seemed to come off in him and in him alone: the drive upward, toward the sun and stars. He was the very person of their ornate dreams, so delicate, so prismatically colorful, so full of tinkling sounds and rhythms, so tireless of invention. Never was such a surface lifted above the isolate blackness of such profound savagery. It is delightful to know that Moctezuma changed his clothes four times a day, donning four different suits, entirely new, which he never wore again; that at meals he was served in a great clean-swept chamber on mats upon the floor, his food being kept warm in chafing dishes containing live coals; that at meals he sat upon a small cushion 'curiously wrought of leather.' " [58]

Thus Williams created yet another variant or image of Moctezuma, a polished, all-too-civilized prince, capable of sallies of amused irony at Cortés' expense, in whose "suave personality" the "liveliest, most airily expansive moods did flower," and one who "left no trace of cowardice upon the records." In opposing the heavy-handed Cortés to the gracious, spiritual Moctezuma, this essay produces something of the atmosphere and theme of a celebrated neoromantic play of this period, Eugene O'Neill's *Marco Millions* (1928).

Another American poet of the 1920's, Hart Crane, dreamed of going to Mexico to write a poetic drama on Cortés and Moctezuma. Waldo Frank, a leading Latin American expert, helped to inspire the idea; in 1931 a Guggenheim grant gave Crane the opportunity to carry out his plan. "He was drawn to Mexico, there's no doubt," Frank later recalled. "He had read my *America Hispana*, and he wanted to do something on Montezuma. I don't say I was responsible for that; but I was an agent in it, because I was the one who had opened up to him the potentialities . . . of Mexico. . . . And I was afraid. I knew Mexico very well, and I knew how strong the death wish was in Mexico. I knew there

was a dark side to all that had come out of the Aztec civilization."
Knowing also Crane's propensities for strong drink, Frank made
him promise that he wouldn't drink alcohol for a month after
arriving in Mexico.[59]

Crane's most recent biographer points to the primitivist assumptions of his journey to Mexico. "He was looking for the sort of
thing D. H. Lawrence had been looking for. He wanted to discover a primitive Mexico—the world that had existed there before
the coming of the white man. If he could make such a discovery
he would feel grounded in the work he hoped to produce. . . .
He was after roots." [60]

Hart Crane passed nearly a year in Mexico, soaking in Mexican
atmosphere and traditions, and huge quantities of liquor. One of
his most exhilarating experiences was a visit to Tepoztlan during
the "yearly fiesta . . . of the ancient Aztec god of the district,
Tepoztécatl, whose ancient temple, though partially destroyed,
still commands a panorama of the whole valley from the top of
one of the surrounding palisades." With delight Crane listened to
the pagan sound of flute and drum played in honor of the god.
The divinity turned out to be the god of pulque, so Crane sampled
"the god's beverage in ceremonial quantities." Next day the fiesta
continued, with the addition of another drum, "this being the
ancient Aztec drum, pre-Conquest and guarded year after year
from the destruction of the priests and conquerors. . . . A large
wooden cylinder, exquisitely carved and showing a figure with
animal head, upright, and walking through thick woods—it lay
horizontally on the floor of the roof, resounding to two heavily
padded drum sticks before the folded knees of one of the Indians."
To Crane's indescribable satisfaction, one of the Indians who had
been playing it put the drum sticks in his hands and nodded toward the instrument. "You can't imagine how exciting it was,"
Crane later wrote, "to be actually part of their ritual." [61]

The words for his epic drama would not come. The historian
Lesley Byrd Simpson recalls a conversation with Crane in a Taxco
bar. "He told me what he was attempting to do: write a poem on
the Conquest of Mexico. He was up against it, for he couldn't read
Spanish with any fluency and had read precious little about the
subject. His notions were mostly taken from Prescott. I gave him

a lecture on bibliography (probably too long, but then we had a good deal to drink) and Hart got more and more restless and disputatious. His ideas about the early history of Mexico were completely naïve, according to my notions. I think I told him he couldn't write a decent poem on the history of the Conquest without knowing all there was to know about it. He said to hell with all that and left something in a huff." [62]

Crane never finished his poem on Cortés and Moctezuma. He died by throwing himself into the sea, April 27, 1932, on his way back to the States. Meanwhile Archibald MacLeish had completed a long poem on a similar subject, *Conquistador* (1932). Its narrator is Bernal Díaz del Castillo, whose viewpoint MacLeish adopts. There is much fine writing in MacLeish's characteristic declamatory style; however, the poet, purporting to view Tenochtitlán and its people through Bernal Díaz' eyes, sees them through a vague romantic haze, idealized and improbable. As in an adolescent's daydream, the Aztec girls are all tall, slender, "with strong breasts," and ever so willing. And the dark, brooding speech put in the mouth of Moctezuma in the moment of his seizure by the Spaniards seems more appropriate to a Greek king than an Indian emperor. In fine, the atmosphere of the Indian scenes and episodes is exotic rather than authentic.

Far more satisfying are the unpretentious verses on ancient Indian themes of Robert H. Barlow, who ended his short, brilliant life by suicide in Mexico City on New Year's day, 1951. Mexicanists know Barlow best for his contributions to Mesoamerican history and archaeology, including a major work, *The Extent of the Empire of the Culhua Mexica* (1949). Less known is the fact that he was a writer of fantasies, studied painting with Thomas Hart Benton and became "a not inconsiderable artist," and wrote poetry of some distinction. His poems, a majority of which dealt with Indian themes, have been collected and published in *Accent on Barlow: A Commemorative Anthology* (1962).

Avoiding efforts at historical reconstruction or direct imitation of Aztec style, Barlow deals with ancient Indian topics in a fresh, quizzical, impudent manner. The amusing "The Gods in the Patio" (the patio of the old Museo Nacional in Mexico City) opens:

Fifty bones of a murdered world are on view today at eleven. Guests will please smuggle cameras and check their tips. Have the gods herded into some cave, their clumsy joints all bent in the direction of flight: Is there a spider hanging its gourd in the Jar of Tlaloc, where rain once shook golden rings? Are all the Cholula plates broken?

There is the delightfully droll "The Chichimecs":

> The Chichimecs live to the north of us
> Eat prickly pears.
> They only catch rabbits, carry them folded in nets,
> And do not sing.
> And when a man dies, they say
> He had so-many rabbits, and
> so-many wives.
> Only the grass wrinkles our bellies,
> By the rivers.
> We scoop out fish with jade faces
> Who walk under our hands,
> And do not count our wives.

Another poem, entitled "Mythological Episode," makes playful reference to the mishap that cost Tezcatlipoca a foot:

> O that frog or flower that stealthily
> Snipped from the bone Black Tezcatlipoca's foot!
> Trapped with his hands full of magic, what could he do
> But wither a projected sun,
> Drop two or three eternities into his purse unwrought
> And leave us to make sacrifices forever?

"Warning to Snake Killers" tells of the horrid consequences of an impious act:

> Queerly walking by a slow and pagan clock
> Between the pyramid and church
> The god was surprised and killed on the stair of his ruined shrine.
> The Indian crushed the poison pod skull, he gathered the flowers
>   of the movable skin with a ten-cent knife and threw away
>   thirty tooth-colored bracelets.
> But the stamen tongue wrote a symbol in red beads.

He dreamed that night that Tláloc, in his heaven of the east
Peopled by those dead of dropsy, and all the colored shadows
  that have looked into rivers,
Turned an eye within his serpent mask
To the Messenger of the fourth rain-jar
And ordered mildew spread on all the village corn.[63]

Although historical novels with some Aztec background are
fairly numerous—one thinks of Salvador de Madariaga's *Heart of
Jade*, Samuel Shellabarger's *Captain From Castile*, and Alexander
Baron's *The Golden Princess*—none possesses sufficient literary
merit to warrant detailed analysis. Perhaps the intrinsic difficulty
of entering the heart and mind of a culture so alien as the Aztec
has deterred serious novelists from attempting the task.[64]

No diverting historical romance, but a fictional fantasy of deadly
serious intent is *The Plumed Serpent* of D. H. Lawrence. In this
work, set in the Mexico of the 1920's, the artistic recoil against
modern industrial society and its alienations reaches a strange
climax. The book also strongly suggests the wave of *indigenismo*
that then swept over Mexico. The novel resulted from D. H.
Lawrence's visit to Mexico and the mingled hope and repulsion
that Mexican life inspired in him. Beneath the fragile frosting of
the white man's world, Lawrence felt, writhed the "stone coiled
rattlesnake of Aztec eternity. The dove lays her eggs on his
flat head." In her excellent study of Lawrence's ideas, Mary Freeman attempts to summarize his reactions to Mexico: "Here dwelt
the god of sensuous fact, the god that, ignored or repudiated by
the Christian-industrial age, reached out from the unconscious to
divert the best-laid plans to the worst ends. The efforts of the
conquerors to make Mexico industrial or Christian had been . . .
futile." In the Indian "primeval assertion," in their sensuousness,
might be "the bud of a relationship destined to bloom into a new
world." Yet, writes Miss Freeman, "Indian sensuousness produced
no archaic heroes in a primitive paradise. If the European represented one extreme, the Indian, according to Lawrence, represented
another. The Indians were a fear-ridden, even though a stoic people;
their sensuousness abounded in both masochism and sadism. . . ."
Miss Freeman quotes Lawrence's far from flattering appraisal of the
ancient Indian cultures: "These old civilizations down here, they

never got any higher than Quetzalcoatl. And he's just a sort of feathered snake. Who needed the smoke of a little heart's blood now and then, even he."

Thus, says Miss Freeman, "*The Plumed Serpent* was written with a double motive: on the one hand to explore for the European those modes of living that he had so carefully denied, and, on the other, to suggest a move toward an indigenous Mexican renaissance. If Mexico should look to her roots in sensuous fact, Mexico should be drawn slowly from her primordial helplessness and fear—but in her own time and in her own way, not under the lash of European ideals. *The Plumed Serpent* sketched a political movement based on sensuous relationships, but on a level centuries behind the one that Lawrence recommended for Europe; Mexico should move toward articulation, while Europe should move away from it." [65]

The central Occidental figure of the novel is the forty-year-old Englishwoman Kate Leslie, world-weary and numb after the death of her second husband. From the first she is aware of the old primitive Mexico on which the white man's Mexico rests. "Superficially, Mexico might be all right: with its suburbs of villas, its central fine streets, its thousands of motor-cars, its tennis and its bridge parties. . . . Until you were alone with it. And then the undertone was like the low angry, snarling purring of some jaguar spotted with night. There was a ponderous, down-pressing weight upon the spirit: the great folds of the dragon of the Aztecs, the dragon of the Toltecs winding around one and weighing down the soul. . . ." And death was in the air. "Death to this, death to the other, it was all death! death! death! as insistent as the Aztec sacrifices."

Visiting the Museo Nacional, Kate "could not look at the stones . . . without depression and dread. Snakes coiled like excrement, snakes fanged and feathered beyond all dream of dread." Everywhere was the snake motif. "The ponderous pyramids of San Juan Teotihuacan, the House of Quetzalcoatl wreathed with the snake of all snakes, his huge fangs white and pure today as in the last centuries when his makers were alive. He has not died. He is not as dead as the Spanish churches, this all-enwreathing dragon of the horror of Mexico."

Through newspaper reports Kate learns of strange occurrences
at Lake Sayula (Chapala), where a man had arisen who claimed
to be the returned Quetzalcóatl. Kate "wanted to go to Sayula.
She wanted to see the big lake where the gods had once lived, and
where they were due to emerge. Amid all the bitterness that Mexico produced in her spirit, there was still a strange beam of wonder
and mystery, almost like hope. A strange darkly-iridescent beam
of wonder, of magic." Presently she learns of the existence of a
movement which proposes to restore the old Indian religion, in
the process solving all of Mexico's problems, economic and social
as well as spiritual. Its principal leader is don Ramón Carrasco,
who has assumed the role of Quetzalcóatl and surrounded himself
with an elaborate ritual drawn by Lawrence from the mythology
of Europe and Asia as well as Mexico. Ramón, who appears to be
Lawrence's spokesman, proclaims that the Mexican men "are like
trees, forests that the white men felled in their coming. But the
roots of the trees are deep and alive and forever sending up new
shoots. . . . And each new shoot that comes up overthrows a
Spanish church or an American factory. And soon the dark forest
will rise again and shake the Spanish buildings from the face of
America."

When it comes to solutions for Mexico's economic and social
problems, however, don Ramón's thought is as cloudy, as mystical,
as that of Lawrence himself. He will have nothing to do with the
current attack on the hacienda or the socialist critique of private
ownership of the means of production. He can only reply: "When
men seek life first, they will not seek land nor gold. The lands
will lie on the lap of the gods, where men lie. And if the old communal system comes back, and the village and the land are one,
it will be very good. For truly no man can possess land."

In spite of her impulse to flee, to return to England, Kate is irre-
sistibly drawn to and marries Cipriano Viedma, Ramón's lieutenant and surrogate in the role of Huitzilopochtli. It was "the black
fume of power which he emitted, the dark, heavy vibration of his
blood, which cast a spell over her." After a grotesque ritual trial,
Cipriano stabs to death three attackers of don Ramón in an execution with clear overtones of Aztec sacrifice. The movement headed
by Ramón assumes an increasingly fascist tinge, with special uni-
forms, unquestioning obedience to leaders, and the like. The story

ends on a curiously flat, unconvincing note, as if Lawrence himself had lost interest or belief in his utopian dream. Civil war breaks out between the men of Quetzalcóatl and his opponents. The President, a sympathizer with the movement, declares the Catholic Church illegal and has a law passed making the religion of Quetzalcóatl the national religion. This seems strangely discordant with Ramón's earlier claim that the movement must spread of itself; even more so is the decree that all priests must take an oath of allegiance to the new order or be exiled. Soon only "the white and blue and earth-colored serapes of Quetzalcoatl, and the scarlet and black of Huitzilopochtli were seen among the crowds." [66] To what final liberating end the movement comes Lawrence does not reveal.

The primitivism, the obsession with death and power, and the hysterical, overwrought tone that mark *The Plumed Serpent* are also features of one of Lawrence's most powerful but disturbing short stories, "The Woman Who Rode Away." Here Lawrence directly employs Aztec human sacrifice as the instrument of his symbolism. The story is set in a remote mining area of Chihuahua in northern Mexico. The American heroine is married to a mining engineer, a man "not exactly magical to her," a typical Western entrepreneur of Lawrence's repertory, without inner life. Moved by an irresistible impulse to escape her ennui, one day she carries out a "crazy plan"; she rides out of the little town to visit a tribe rumored to be descendants of Moctezuma; they are said to keep up the practice of human sacrifice. Even before she meets the Indians and they carry her off to their mountain haunts, she feels on "the silent, fatal-seeming slopes . . . like a woman who has died and passed beyond." The fate that awaits her is clearly announced by an Indian captor: "We know the sun, and we know the moon. And we say, when a white woman sacrifice herself to our gods, then our gods will begin to make the world again, and the white man's gods will fall to pieces." "What is extraordinary," observes one critic, "is the mixture of indifference and fascination with which the woman goes to her death, the supreme confidence that she seems to have in the knowledge that she is fulfilling her destiny." [67] As she lay passively on the stone, her outstretched arms and legs held by four Indians, the heroine knew that "the old man would strike, and strike home, accomplish the sacrifice and achieve the power. . . . The mastery that man must hold, and that passes from race to race." [68]

In marginal territory, between imaginative literature and scholarly writing, lie the biographies of Nezahualcóyotl and Moctezuma I by Frances Gillmor,[69] who brought to her work the experience of a novelist and long years of training in Náhuatl and Mesoamerican studies. It is an index of the progress of these studies in recent decades that Miss Gillmor was able to re-create the lives and times of these misty fifteenth-century figures in such impressive detail. The books rest on an immense documentary base of codex and chronicle materials; description of dress, ritual, and other material points relies on careful research in these sources. Miss Gillmor also uses the techniques of the historical novelist, turning the narrative of chronicles into direct conversations between historical personages and inventing dialogue between anonymous minor figures. Occasionally she goes so far as to fill in the detail of the moods, gestures, and actions of historical characters. The dying Nezahualcóyotl, for example, is made to recall the scenes of his life and recite various of his poems—including the so-called Otomí song that Father Garibay later found to be spurious. No doubt such freedoms are allowable in works of clear literary intent and flavor.

Small faults aside, these two books represent a remarkable effort to bring to life and make understandable in Western eyes the attractive figure of Nezahualcóyotl and the less attractive personality of Moctezuma I, "a militarist, an expansionist, a dictator." The second of these biographies, the life of Moctezuma I, seems to mark an advance over the first in its penetration of the dynamics of Aztec society, of the complex interplay between religion, trade, and territorial expansion, and in its capture of the subtleties of Aztec personal relations.

Recognition of the Aztec achievement in music and the dance understandably came last, for of all the Indian arts they were least accessible to Western senses. Prescott's judgment that nothing except "a rude minstrelsy scarcely deserving the name of music" preceded the coming of Cortés summed up professional critical opinion for more than half a century after the appearance of his book. As late as 1917 a faculty member of the Mexican Conservatorio Nacional de Música published a work entitled *El arte*

musical en México in which she condemned Aztec music as the
expression of the soul of a cruel and barbarous people and therefore unsuited to the refined tastes of Occidentals. "From the
exemplars of Aztec instruments preserved in the Museo Nacional
of Mexico, we may infer that the music of that people during the
pre-Conquest era was as barbarous and frightful as were the ceremonies in which their music was heard." Such instruments as the
conch shell, the rattle, and the Aztec *teponaztli* or horizontal cylin-
drical drum, she declared, were not "capable of producing either
alone, or in conjunction with each other, a graceful harmony; nor
of evoking a spiritual response in conformity with presently accepted standards of behavior; what these depraved sounds do
conjure up are instead scenes of unrelieved ferocity." [70]

The factors that led to a revaluation of Aztec music were the
same ones that helped to vindicate the Aztec plastic arts: the
growth of primitivism, nationalism, and more intensive systematic
study of the techniques and resources of Indian music-making.
By 1920 Stravinsky's *Sacre du Printemps* and Prokofieff's *Suite
scythienne* had legitimized and popularized so-called "primitive,"
"barbaric" music in the West. What Diego Rivera helped to accomplish for the ancient native plastic arts, the young composer
Carlos Chávez, his friend and collaborator for many years, achieved
in favor of the old Indian music. In a lecture or manifesto on
Aztec music, delivered in October, 1928, Chávez proposed a return
to pre-Cortesian musical ideals because that music "expressed what
is profoundest and deepest in the Mexican soul." In that music
Chávez found "a deep-seated and intuitive yearning for the minor
mode" and a pentatonic system which excluded any possibility of
modulation. Chávez maintained that "these aborigines avoided modulation (in our sense of the word) primarily because modulation
was alien to the simple and straightforward spirit of the Indian"—an
explanation whose primitivist, nationalist essence is unmistakable.
Chávez' lead was followed by many other Mexican composers.
As a result, "characteristics that previously had been looked upon
as basic faults and crude distortions in the indigenous music of
Mexico—its 'minor quality,' its 'monotony,' its 'simultaneous sound-
ing of different pentatonic melodies' that are out of tune with one
another in our way of thinking, its fondness for 'two or more
rhythms the beats of which never coincide'—came now to be
regarded as virtues." [71]

Since the appearance of Chávez' manifesto, archaeologists and musicologists have conducted extensive and intensive studies of pre-Conquest musical instruments and techniques. Robert Stevenson conveniently summarizes their findings in his excellent *Music in Aztec and Inca Territory* (1968). The net result of this research has been to increase the stature of the ancient Mexican music. "The musicians and artisans who created and played such remarkable instruments as the triple and quadruple flutes," remark Samuel Martí and Gertrude Kurath, "obviously had a profound knowledge of acoustics and of the harmonic series, and must have been acquainted with more than a primary five-tone scale. Not only did they know and practice this and other richer scales but they also practiced an embryonic harmony, as well as the traditional free heterophony that characterizes African and Asiatic ensembles." The same writers note, however, that Aztec formalism and hieraticism had a retarding effect on the development of Aztec music. The rigid patterns of Aztec ceremonial dances and music forbade the slightest deviation or mistake, and severe punishment was meted out to culprits. Aztec composers, therefore, "though acquainted with the more advanced instruments and scales of the people from the south and the Gulf of Mexico, continued to base their ceremonial music on a traditional five-tone scale. On the other hand, the instruments of older cultures, usually with five or more holes, produce richer scales and even three- and four-part chords. Thus we can affirm that the ceremonial dances and music of the Aztecs, like their art, had a hieratic, intense, and stylized character." [72]

Stevenson cautions against the tendency to inflate the qualities of Aztec music. "Some enthusiastic investigators contend that the Aztecs . . . consciously systematized modulation, worked out written schemes of rallentando-accelerando, crescendo-diminuendo, devised ostinato patterns, and hit on many other schemes that induce formal unity in music. . . . These recent attempts at draping Aztec music with so many victory flags run the danger of overplaying the hand. . . ." [73]

To appreciate the variety and complexity of Aztec musical resources was one thing; to attempt to re-create the spirit and effect of the old Indian music in modern composition was much more difficult, for no scores or any other manuscript sources existed. The young, nationalistic Carlos Chávez, in full revolt against a musical academism of strictly European inspiration, made an initial

contribution with a ballet, *El fuego nuevo* (1921). Its subject was
the ritual ceremony the Aztecs celebrated at the end of a fifty-two
year cycle. The progressive Secretary of Education, José Vasconcelos, had a part in promoting its composition, for he, at the suggestion of Pedro Henríquez Ureña, asked Chávez to compose a
ballet on an Aztec theme in connection with the celebration of
the centenary of Mexican independence in 1821. Chávez, who
from early childhood had heard and enjoyed native music during
vacations spent in remote corners of Tlaxcala, seized this opportunity to give a new orientation to Mexican music. He did not make
direct use of Indian thematic material, but sought rather to create
a personal musical language that would express the sober, laconic,
strongly rhythmic spirit of the Indian music. The ballet was scored
for a large orchestra, using Indian percussion instruments, and a
women's chorus. It was not produced until 1928.

Chávez had meanwhile composed another Indian ballet, *Los
Cuatro Soles* (1926), which attempted to evoke the emotions inspired in the Aztecs by their four suns or ages of earth, air, fire,
and water. Chávez again avoided direct use of Indian thematic
material, seeking instead to give symphonic expression to the peculiar qualities of Mexican Indian music—its austere, insistent, and
geometric character. This ballet was not produced until 1951.

Chávez' most "Aztec" composition is his *Xochipilli-Macuilxóchitl* (the name of the Aztec god of music), which he conducted at the Museum of Modern Art in New York City on May
16, 1940. Short as it is (about six minutes), it has a special interest
because of the seriousness of its effort to reconstruct the sound
and general effect produced by an Aztec instrumental ensemble.
To secure maximum authenticity, the players used reproductions
or modern adaptations of the ancient instruments; a trombone
approximated the sound of a conch shell. The principal role was
assigned to percussion instruments, including drums, rasps, and
rattles. According to Chávez' biographer, the piece creates a very
convincing impression; though "not of an absolute authenticity,
something that is impossible given the loss of pre-Conquest music,
it is still a forceful evocation of a world, a civilization profoundly
different from our own, and contains not the slightest concession
to a superficial exoticism. . . . Chávez himself has said that he did
not attempt a reconstruction of pre-Cortesian music but aimed

only to offer an impression of how the ancient Aztec music might have sounded." [74]

Since 1940 Chávez himself seems to have abandoned his former enthusiasm for the Indian sources of modern Mexican music. According to a spokesman for the younger group of Mexican composers, Joaquín Gutiérrez Heras, "the nationalist period ended abruptly in 1940, and all the worthwhile Mexican efforts at reconstruction preceded that cutoff date." [75] Robert Stevenson, reflecting on the future of Aztec musical research, believes that the vogue of Aztec or neo-Aztec music of the 1930's fulfilled the useful purpose of providing Mexican composers with real or supposed roots in their own past, with a proud musical heritage. "So far as practical results are concerned, it hardly matters whether such ideas on Aztec music as Chávez propagated were really accurate or not; they were accepted and believed, thereby fulfilling their purpose. Because they were indeed believed, Mexican musicians for the first time since 1821 succeeded in convincing *norteamericanos* that they deserved to be taken seriously. Scenes from the Aztec past are the culminating glory of Mexico's history, as Diego Rivera conceived them in his highly idealized versions of preconquest life painted for the National Palace. Mexican music profited for a few years from the same kind of idealizations." [76]

Dance ethnology is the most recent addition to the disciplines engaged in study of the Aztec cultural achievement. Employing a wealth of pictorial material, including codex illustrations, pottery, and other native artifacts, Samuel Martí and Gertrude Kurath have reconstructed in remarkably fine detail the dances of the Aztec and other Mesoamerican areas and have demonstrated the vital relationship of those dances to the religion, social structure, and mode of life of the ancient Mexicans.[77] In time the combined efforts of the dance ethnologists and musicologists may make it possible to reenact with mimic splendor the imposing communal dances performed in the spacious plazas of Tenochtitlán and other Aztec cities.

Afterword

For four and a half centuries ancient Mexico has been a battle-ground of ideas, and no end to the long quarrel over the nature of Aztec civilization is in sight. From the first, a quality of vehemence and involvement has tinged the works of men who dealt with the Aztec theme. In both its friends and its foes, the dramatic contrasts of Aztec culture have inspired strong emotion. Writers have tended to focus either on the dark or on the bright side of Aztec civilization; or—if they dwelled on both—to praise the one and condemn the other with equal passion. We sense that passion and involvement in the letters of Cortés, who could not find words to express the beauty of Aztec art; in the writings of pious Mendicants such as Las Casas, Durán, and Mendieta, who extolled the perfection of Aztec social and political institutions; and in the works of modern students such as Jacques Soustelle, who proclaims Aztec culture to be one of those that humanity can be proud of having created, and Robert Padden, who sees in Aztec Mexico only a mass of abject commoners terrorized by power-mad, cannibalistic despots. The provocative nature of the subject so inflamed some imaginations that it inspired speculative excesses. Carried away by the wonders of ancient Mexico, writers such as Boturini, Mier, and Brasseur de Bourbourg sometimes altogether left the realm of sober history to roam through an Indian world of illusion and fantasy.

The extreme diversity of views expressed by writers who drew upon much the same body of facts, and the passion they displayed, arose not only from the inherently controversial nature of the subject but from the premises and partialities they themselves brought to the subject. Inevitably, in debating the nature of Aztec society men debated contemporary issues—economic, social, and ideological.

Sometimes the class interests implicit in the debate emerge with perfect clarity. The virulently anti-Indian postures of sixteenth-century chroniclers such as Oviedo and Gómara, who defended the conquistadors and the encomienda, are cases in point. Group loyalties and aspirations also inspired the eulogies of Aztec culture by such Mexican creole historians of the colonial and independence periods as Mier and Clavigero, who resented European pretensions to superiority and constructed from Aztec materials a classical antiquity for their own rising class. Sometimes the divergent views appear to reflect different approaches to a purely European problem. We recall both the praise lavished on the Aztec polity by Voltaire and Carli, friends of enlightened despotism, and the severe criticism of Aztec tyranny by Montesquieu and Raynal, foes of French royal absolutism. Again, a writer's attitude may indicate his malaise, his feeling that the times are out of joint. Suggestive of such a frame of mind is the nostalgic contrast of Aztec solidarity with the anarchy of his own strife-filled time by the American archaeologist George C. Vaillant.

This persistent intrusion of contemporary issues into the debate over the Aztecs points to a conclusion: the impartiality or neutrality to which some historians aspire may be unattainable, no matter how remote from the present and its problems be the subject of historical inquiry.

To concede, with Karl Mannheim, that ideas are socially determined is not to deny the possibility of objectivity, of attaining relative historical truth. The movement of Western thought on the Aztecs suggests how the process of advancing the frontiers of historical knowledge, of refining or correcting historical ideas, actually works. In the long dispute over the nature of Aztec civilization, it is possible to distinguish a pattern. This may be described in Hegelian terms as a progress through the stages of thesis, antithesis, and synthesis, with advances in the Western grasp of Aztec civilization taking place through the clash of opposed ideas.

The point of departure of this process was the direct vision of Aztec society of such conquistadors as Cortés himself. If this vision was naïve, it was relatively undimmed by cultural bias. From the letters of Cortés emerged an image of a people of advanced culture, equal to Europeans in innate capacity, despite its flaws of paganism, human sacrifice, and cannibalism. The Mendicant chroniclers enriched this vision of Aztec civilization with a copious documentation and enhanced the Aztec prestige by using a comparative method that demonstrated the superiority of some Aztec institutions over those of ancient Greece and Rome. Antonio de Solís gave consummate literary expression to this assessment of Aztec society in his *Historia de la conquista de México*. This first, classic image of Aztec society dominated European thought on the subject during the greater part of the sixteenth and seventeenth centuries.

The skeptical reaction against this image that arose in the eighteenth century reflected the growth of a critical spirit and a genetic approach to history. The eighteenth century was also an age in which some European intellectuals, proud of their enlightened time, were complacently convinced of the superiority of the civilized man over the primitive. Hitherto doctrines of Indian inferiority had rested on such neomedieval notions as God's curse upon the Indians and the baneful influence of the American climate and constellations. The French naturalist Buffon provided a pseudo-scientific basis for these doctrines with his idea of America's geological immaturity. A crotchety Prussian curate, Cornelius de Pauw, exploited this idea and used the method of systematic historical doubt that Voltaire had made fashionable to demolish the structure of Aztec and Inca grandeur raised by the Spanish conquistadors and chroniclers.

The eighteenth-century reaction against the classic portrait of Aztec society reached its climax in William Robertson's *History of America*. Robertson examined the Aztecs within the framework of an evolutionary sequence of stages. Using essentially technological criteria, he made a painstaking effort to define the Aztec cultural level with precision. Despite its skeptical excesses, the eighteenth-century rationalist reaction performed a major service by correcting the naïve classic view of Aztec society as a simple analogue of Greek, Roman, or medieval societies. Robertson gave the study of ancient Mexico something it badly needed, a historical, genetic perspective.

Before the century ended, the Mexican Jesuit Clavigero, armed with immense erudition and a rationalist historical method, had mounted a powerful counteroffensive against the skeptics and revived the Aztec splendor in his *Historia antigua de México*. In restoring the classic vision of the Aztecs, however, Clavigero purged it of most of its naïveté, credulity, and mythologizing.

As the nineteenth century opened, the Herderian doctrine of the equality of cultures, the romantic impulse of sympathy with the vanquished, and romantic fascination with the exotic past, all helped to increase the popularity of the Aztecs. For all the ambiguity of its viewpoint, Prescott's *Conquest of Mexico* offers the finest example in style and scholarship of romantic transfiguration of the Aztecs. Yet, by allowing romantic literary and philosophical conventions to shape and color his historical portraiture, Prescott introduced distortions not unlike those of the classic vision into his picture of Aztec society. In some respects, therefore, Prescott's work represents a decline from the high scientific standard set by Robertson.

By mid-century the romantic fever had waned, and Prescott's image of Aztec society came under heavy attack from American writers who could not reconcile that image with their personal observations of Indian life in North America. The anthropologist Lewis H. Morgan, who had carefully studied Robertson, felt that Prescott's "cunningly wrought fable" was the main obstacle to the development of a science of American ethnology. Morgan offered the Iroquois as a model of Indian social organization to which he believed all Indian tribes, including the Aztecs, must conform. By the mid-1880's the ideas of Morgan and his lieutenant Bandelier had triumphed in the United States. In Mexico and Europe, however, the extravagance of those ideas caused them to be regarded with scant respect. Granting their scholarly faults, and the exaggeration of their stress on the simpler tribal and kinship elements in Aztec social organization, Morgan and Bandelier provided a needed corrective to the romantic excesses of Prescott and Bancroft. By reviving and updating Robertson's evolutionist scheme Morgan also created a potentially fruitful approach to the study of ancient Mexico.

By the first decades of the twentieth century the development of a rigorously scientific method that shunned grand theoretical schemes—a method associated above all with the name of Eduard Seler—had almost driven fantasy from the Mesoamerican field. Although Seler and his disciples were noted for their severe caution, their monographs and commentaries on codices gave firm support to the view of the Aztecs as a complex, class-structured society organized in a state, and to their stature as a gifted people of high artistic and intellectual achievement. Seler's influence, direct or indirect, was strong in Mexico. Here the Revolution of 1910–1917, accompanied by an upsurge of nationalism and *indigenismo*, led to the rise of a brilliant school of anthropology whose members often combined devotion to archaeology with a large interest in applied anthropology. The fieldwork and studies of the Mexican school, supplemented by the efforts of foreign scholars, have greatly expanded the historical horizons of Aztec civilization and supplied abundant new evidence of its complexity. In the same period intensive investigation of Aztec literature and art has amplified the vision of the Aztecs as a creative people who made distinctive contributions to the cultural legacy of ancient Mexico.

In both Mexico and the United States the past quarter-century has seen a strong revival of evolutionist theory that owes much to Morgan but is free from the rigidity and arbitrariness of Morgan's scheme. In the Mesoamerican phenomenon this new evolutionism has found an ideal field for the testing and illustration of its principles. From the resulting fusion of data and theory has emerged a consensus that Aztec civilization was one of the great early civilizations of mankind. Excavations in progress and to come, and further study of Aztec materials, will undoubtedly refine and deepen our grasp of the subject.

Meanwhile the paradoxes of the brilliant, tragic Aztec culture continue to intrigue Western man, whether layman or scholar. Perhaps one reason is that that culture mirrors our own contradictions and dilemmas, for the Aztec mixture of humanism and barbarism, and the introspective Aztec personality, haunted by doubts and fears, are not unfamiliar to us who live in the last third of the twentieth century.

Notes

Chapter One: The People of the Sun

1. George C. Vaillant, *The Aztecs of Mexico: Origin, Rise and Fall of the Aztec Nation* (Baltimore, Md.: Penguin Books, 1961), p. 268. Eric R. Wolf, *Sons of the Shaking Earth* (Chicago: University of Chicago Press, 1959), p. 149. Laurette Séjourné, *Burning Water: Thought and Religion in Ancient Mexico* (New York, 1960), p. 14. Ignacio Romerovargas Yturbide, "Las Instituciones," in *Esplendor del México antiguo*, 2 vols. (Mexico: Centro de Investigaciones Antropológicas de México, 1959), II, 756.

2. For a summary of the findings of recent research on the culture history of the Teotihuacán Valley, see William T. Sanders, *The Cultural Ecology of the Teotihuacán Valley* (University Park: The Pennsylvania State University, 1965), pp. 163–206.

3. Ignacio Bernal, *Mexico Before Cortez*, trans. Willis Barnstone (New York, 1963), p. 41.

4. Wolf, *Sons of the Shaking Earth*, p. 90.

5. See, however, for a vigorous challenge to this traditional "contrast of the peaceful Classic to the warlike Post Classic," and to other allegedly "outmoded viewpoints," William T. Sanders' review of Michael D. Coe's *Mexico* in the *American Anthropologist*, LXV (August, 1963), 972–974. It is conveniently reprinted in John A. Graham, ed., *Ancient Mesoamerica: Selected Readings* (Palo Alto, Calif., 1966), pp. 86–88.

6. Wolf, *Sons of the Shaking Earth*, p. 122.

7. Bernal, *Mexico Before Cortez*, p. 86.

8. Wolf, *Sons of the Shaking Earth*, p. 6.

9. The *Codex Ramírez*, in Paul Radin, *Sources and Authenticity of the History of the Ancient Mexicans*, University of California Publications in American Archaeology and Ethnology, XVII (Berkeley: University of California Press, 1920), p. 99.

10. Miguel León-Portilla, *Aztec Thought and Culture*, trans. J. E. Davis (Norman: University of Oklahoma Press, 1963), pp. 158–166. See also his *Los antiguos mexicanos* (Mexico, 1961), pp. 44–45, 89–92.

11. Bernardino de Sahagún, *General History of the Things of New Spain: Florentine Codex*, trans. from the Aztec into English, with notes and illustrations, by A. J. O. Anderson and C. E. Dibble (Salt Lake City: University

of Utah; and Santa Fe, N.M.: School of American Research, 1950–),
Book I, *The Gods* (1950), pp. 17–20.

12. Sherburne F. Cook, *The Historical Demography and Ecology of the
Teotlalpan* (Berkeley: University of California Press, 1949), p. 54.

13. Sherburne F. Cook, "Human Sacrifice and Warfare as Factors in the
Demography of Pre-Colonial Mexico," *Human Biology*, XVIII (May, 1946),
81–100.

14. Bernal Díaz del Castillo, *Historia verdadera de la conquista de la Nueva
España*, ed. Joaquín Ramírez Cabañas, 2 vols. (Mexico, 1960), I, 260–261.

15. Cited in León-Portilla, *Aztec Thought*, p. 141.

16. Sahagún, *General History of the Things of New Spain: Florentine
Codex*, Book VIII, *Kings and Lords* (1954), p. 54.

17. Diego Durán, *Historia de las Indias de Nueva España e islas de tierra
firme*, ed. Ángel María Garibay K., 2 vols. (Mexico, 1967), I, 209–210.

18. *Ibid.*, p. 200.

19. Sahagún, *General History of the Things of New Spain: Florentine
Codex*, Book III, *The Origin of the Gods* (1952), pp. 6–7.

20. The tump line was a sling formed by a strap slung over the forehead
or chest, used by Indians for carrying a pack on the back.

21. Sahagún, *General History of the Things of New Spain: Florentine
Codex*, Book VII, *The Sun, Moon, and Stars, and the Binding of the Years*
(1953), p. 24.

22. Cited in León-Portilla, *Aztec Thought*, p. 168.

23. *Ibid.*, pp. 172–173.

24. *Ibid.*, p. 173.

25. Sahagún, *General History of the Things of New Spain: Florentine
Codex*, Book VII, *The Sun, Moon, and Stars, and the Binding of the Years*
(1953), p. 23.

26. The title Quetzalcóatl was assigned to the two Aztec high priests.

27. An allusion to the sound produced by turning the dry, hard strips of
amate paper on which the codices were painted.

28. Cited in León-Portilla, *Aztec Thought*, pp. 18–19.

29. *Ibid.*, p. 18.

30. Sahagún, *General History of the Things of New Spain: Florentine
Codex*, Book I, *The Gods* (1950), p. 19.

31. *Ibid.*, Book VIII, *Kings and Lords* (1954), p. 39.

32. *Ibid.*, p. 29.

33. *Ibid.*

Chapter Two: The Aztec World View

1. George C. Vaillant, *The Aztecs of Mexico: Origin, Rise and Fall of the
Aztec Nation* (Baltimore, Md.: Penguin Books, 1961), p. 170.

2. Alfonso Caso, *The Aztecs, People of the Sun*, trans. Lowell Dunham
(Norman: University of Oklahoma Press, 1958), p. 11.

3. Vaillant, *Aztecs of Mexico*, p. 171.

4. Jacques Soustelle, *La Pensée cosmologique des anciens Mexicains* (Paris, 1940), p. 85, cited in Miguel León-Portilla, *Aztec Thought and Culture*, trans. J. E. Davis (Norman: University of Oklahoma Press, 1963), p. 57.

5. Jacques Soustelle, "Religion and the Mexican State," *Diogenes*, xxxiv (Summer, 1961), 9.

6. Wigberto Jiménez Moreno, "Filosofía de la vida y transculturación religiosa: La religión mexica y el cristianismo," *Boletín de Información, Seminario de Cultura Mexicana*, 2ª época, xix (September, 1962), 2.

7. León-Portilla, *Aztec Thought*, p. 84.

8. Hermann Beyer, "Das aztekische Götterbild Alexander von Humboldt's," in *Wissenschaftliche Festschrift zur Enthüllung des von Seiten S.M. Kaiser Wilhelm II, dem mexikanischen Volke zum Jubiläum, seiner Unabhängigkeit Gestifteten Humboldt-Denkmals . . .* (Mexico, 1910), p. 116.

9. Edward Tylor, *Religion in Primitive Culture* (New York: Harper and Row, Harper Torchbooks, 1958), p. 418.

10. Cited in Miguel León-Portilla, *Los antiguos mexicanos* (Mexico, 1961), p. 137.

11. Frances Gillmor, *Flute of the Smoking Mirror: A Portrait of Nezahualcóyotl, Poet-King of the Aztecs* (Albuquerque: University of New Mexico Press, 1949), p. 170n.

12. Cited in León-Portilla, *Aztec Thought*, pp. 64–65. For the complete Náhuatl and Spanish texts, with German translation, of the exchanges between the Indian spokesmen and the Franciscan missionaries, see Walter Lehmann, ed., *Sterbende Götter und Christliche Heilsbotschaft: Wechselreden indianischer Vornehmer und spanischer Glaubensapostel in Mexiko 1524* (Stuttgart, 1949).

13. León-Portilla, *Aztec Thought*, p. 7.

14. *Ibid.*

15. *Ibid.*, p. 6.

16. *Ibid.*, p. 74.

17. *Ibid.*, p. 131.

18. *Ibid.*, p. 79.

19. Notably in Garibay's great *Historia de la literatura náhuatl*, 2 vols. (Mexico, 1953–1954). (This is a work that richly merits translation into English.)

20. Cited in Michael D. Coe, *Mexico* (London, 1962), p. 168.

21. Cited in Garibay, *Historia de la literatura náhuatl*, i, 219.

22. *Ibid.*, p. 220.

23. Bernardino de Sahagún, *Historia general de las cosas de Nueva España*, ed. Ángel María Garibay K., 4 vols. (Mexico, 1956), ii, 62–63.

24. León-Portilla, *Los antiguos mexicanos*, p. 115.

25. Alonso de Zorita, *Life and Labor in Ancient Mexico: The Brief and Summary Relation of the Lords of New Spain by Alonso de Zorita*, trans. and ed. Benjamin Keen (New Brunswick, N.J.: Rutgers University Press, 1963), pp. 141–143.

26. Laurette Séjourné, *Burning Water: Thought and Religion in Ancient Mexico* (New York: Evergreen Books, 1960), p. 39.

27. León-Portilla, *Los antiguos mexicanos*, p. 105. León-Portilla asks: "Could Moctezuma II have been influenced by the ideas of men like Nezahualcóyotl and Nezahualpilli of Texcoco, and Tecayehuatzin and Ayocuan of Huexotzinco, who sought to renew the ancient Toltec concept with a religious and humane meaning, different from the warlike mysticism of the People of the Sun?" Such speculation concerning Moctezuma's possible lapse from orthodoxy seems to have little basis in fact. Far from wavering in his loyalty to the cult of human sacrifice, Moctezuma maintained it brilliantly; on one occasion alone during his reign, twelve thousand captives from the rebel province in Oaxaca were sacrificed to the war god. Vaillant, *Aztecs of Mexico*, p. 112.

28. Soustelle, "Religion and the Mexican State," p. 11.

29. *Ibid.*, p. 14.

30. Sahagún, *Historia general de las cosas de Nueva España*, ii, 140.

31. Soustelle, "Religion and the Mexican State," pp. 14–15.

Chapter Three: Europe Discovers the Aztecs

1. Bernardino de Sahagún, *Historia general de las cosas de Nueva España: Códice Florentino*, cited in Miguel León-Portilla, ed., *The Broken Spears*, trans. Lysander Kemp (Boston, 1962), p. 23.

2. *Ibid.*, p. 26.

3. *Ibid.*, pp. 30–31.

4. *Ibid.*, p. 41.

5. *Anonymous Manuscript of Tlatelolco*, cited in León-Portilla, *The Broken Spears*, pp. 137–138.

6. *The Life of the Admiral Christopher Columbus by His Son Ferdinand*, trans. and annotated Benjamin Keen (New Brunswick, N.J.: Rutgers University Press, 1959), p. 82.

7. Américo Castro, *The Structure of Spanish History*, trans. E. L. King (Princeton, N.J.: Princeton University Press, 1954), p. 87.

8. María Soledad Carrasco Urgoit, *El moro de Granada en la literatura (del siglo XV al XX)* (Madrid, 1956), p. 41.

9. Federico Gómez de Orozco studies the problem of authenticity of the Anonymous Conqueror in his introduction to the *Relación de algunas cosas de la Nueva España y de la gran ciudad de Temestitan Mexico, hecha por un gentilhombre del señor Fernando Cortés* (Mexico, 1961), pp. 23–33. He notes that the work contains numerous factual errors that its author could not have made if he had actually spent time in Mexico. Gómez de Orozco suggests that the *Relación* was compiled from the letters of Cortés and other sources, perhaps by the Spanish translator Antonio de Ulloa.

10. Fernando Cortés, *Cartas de relación*, in *Historiadores primitivos de Indias*, 2 vols. (Madrid, 1858), i, 1–153; and many other editions. English translation by F. A. MacNutt, *The Letters of Cortés*, 2 vols. (New York,

1908). Bernal Díaz del Castillo, *Historia verdadera de la conquista de la Nueva España*, ed. Joaquín Ramírez Cabañas, 3 vols. (Mexico, 1944); and many other editions. English translation by A. P. Maudslay, *The True History of the Conquest of New Spain*, 5 vols. (London, 1908–1916).

11. Cortés, *Cartas de relación*, in *Historiadores primitivos*, i, 21.

12. *Ibid.*, p. 24.

13. *Ibid.*, p. 34.

14. *Ibid.*

15. *Ibid.*, 115.

16. *Ibid.*, p. 34.

17. Pedro Henríquez Ureña, *Siete ensayos en busca de nuestra expresión* (Buenos Aires, 1928), cited in Benjamin Keen, ed., *Readings in Latin American Civilization* (Boston, 1955), p. 442.

18. Bernal Díaz, *Historia verdadera*, i, 349, 352.

19. *Ibid.*, ii, 83.

20. *Ibid.*, iii, 242. The same story is told by the Anonymous Conqueror in his *Relación*. Since the *Relación* first appeared in 1556, in the third volume of Giovanni Battista Ramusio's great travel collection, *Delle navigationi et viaggi*, Bernal Díaz, who was writing his book in 1568, may have taken this odd detail from Ramusio.

21. Bernal Díaz, *Historia verdadera*, iii, 250.

22. Cortés, *Cartas de relación*, in *Historiadores primitivos*, i, 10.

23. Francisco de Aguilar, *Relación breve de la conquista de la Nueva España*, in *The Conquistadors*, ed. and trans. Patricia de Fuentes (New York, 1963), pp. 163–164.

24. Anonymous Conqueror, *Relación de algunas cosas de la Nueva España y de la gran ciudad de Temestitan Mexico* . . . , p. 68.

25. English translation from the Latin by F. A. MacNutt, *De Orbe Novo, the Eight Decades of Peter Martyr d'Anghera*, 2 vols. (New York, 1912). The best Spanish edition is Pedro Mártir de Anglería, *Décadas del Nuevo Mundo*, trans. Agustín Millares Carlo and with an introductory essay "Pedro Mártir y el proceso de América" by Edmundo O'Gorman, 2 vols. (Mexico, 1964–1965). For the life of Martyr, see Jean-H. Mariéjol, *Pierre Martyr D'Anghera, sa vie et ses œuvres* (Paris, 1887). On Martyr as historian, see Alberto M. Salas, *Tres cronistas de Indias* (Mexico, 1959). John Howland Rowe stresses the anthropological importance of Martyr in "The Renaissance Foundations of Anthropology," *American Anthropologist*, lxvii (February, 1965), 1–20.

26. Peter Martyr, *De Orbe Novo*, MacNutt trans., ii, 41, 46.

27. "Relazione di Gasparo Contarini," in Eugenio Alberi, ed., *Relazioni dagli ambasciatori veneti al Senato*, 15 vols. (Florence, 1839–1863), Ser. 1, ii, 54.

28. For subsequent Mexican Indian visits and missions to Spain, see Howard F. Cline's article, "Hernando Cortés and the Aztec Indians in Spain," *Quarterly Journal of the Library of Congress*, xxvi (April, 1969), 70–90, which is illustrated with drawings of Indian subjects by the German

artist Christoph Weiditz. Also Charles Gibson, *Tlaxcala in the Sixteenth Century* (New Haven: Yale University Press, 1952), pp. 164–169.

29. Peter Martyr, *De Orbe Novo*, MacNutt trans., II, 38–39. Martyr's description of the Indians and objects sent by Cortés to Spain is supplemented by a letter from Giovanni Ruffo di Forli, Archbishop of Cosenza and apostolic nuncio at the Spanish court, to Francesco Chieregati. This letter reports that the youngest of the Indian men had learned some Spanish and acted as interpreter for the others, that they wore their hair long, had beards, and shaved themselves with stone razors. The king had presented them with fine garments of Spanish style, but the Archbishop obtained from them a description of their native dress. The Indians had been baptized by royal order, but the Archbishop suggested that unless they remained among Christians it might prove a waste of holy water, for the Indians showed little understanding of Christianity. Along with Martyr and Gaspar Contarini, Ruffo di Forli expressed his admiration for the beauty of the Aztec articles, particularly the featherwork. See Marcel Bataillon, "Les Premiers Mexicains envoyés en Espagne par Cortés," *Journal de la Société des Américanistes*, n.s., XLVIII (1959), 135–140. Henry R. Wagner published a translation of a Latin text of the same letter in the *Hispanic American Historical Review*, IX (August, 1929), 361–363.

30. Peter Martyr, *De Orbe Novo*, MacNutt trans., II, 202.

31. For the editions of Martyr's *Decades*, see the bibliographical essay by Joseph H. Sinclair in Pedro Mártir de Anglería, *Décadas del Nuevo Mundo*, Agustín Millares Carlo trans., I, 45–71.

32. For the editions of Cortés' letters, see José Toribio Medina, *Ensayo bio-bibliográphico sobre Hernan Cortés* (Santiago de Chile, 1952), and Henry Harrisse, *Bibliotheca Americana Vetustissima* (New York, 1866), pp. 215–219.

33. Henry R. Wagner, *The Rise of Fernando Cortés* (Berkeley, Calif.: The Cortés Society, 1944), p. xiii.

34. Cited in Harrisse, *Bibliotheca Americana Vetustissima*, p. 203.

35. For a study of the 1524 map of Tenochtitlán, see Manuel Toussaint, Federico Gómez de Orozco, and Justino Fernández, *Planos de la ciudad de México, siglos XVI y XVII* (Mexico, 1938).

36. Henry R. Wagner, "Three Accounts of the Expedition of Fernando Cortés, Printed in Germany Between 1520 and 1522," *Hispanic American Historical Review*, IX (May, 1929), 176–212.

37. *Ibid.*, p. 197.

38. Marshall H. Saville, *The Earliest Notices Concerning the Conquest of Mexico by Cortés* (New York, 1920).

39. *Ibid.*, pp. 26–30.

40. *Ibid.*, p. 35.

41. William Martin Conway, ed. and trans., *Literary Remains of Albrecht Dürer* (Cambridge: Cambridge University Press, 1889), p. 101.

42. Erwin Walter Palm, "Tenochtitlán y la ciudad ideal de Dürer," *Journal de la Société des Américanistes*, n.s., XL (1951), 59–66.

Chapter Four: The Aztecs and The Great Debate: 1

1. For a convenient brief summary of the positions taken in this controversy, see Silvio Zavala, *La filosofía política en la conquista de América* (Mexico, 1947). Venancio D. Carro, *La teología y los teólogos juristas españoles ante la conquista de América* (Salamanca, 1951), carefully examines the thought of leading figures in the controversy. Two important works in English are Lewis Hanke, *The Spanish Struggle for Justice in the Conquest of America* (Philadelphia, 1949), and his *Aristotle and the American Indians* (New York, 1959).

2. For a lucid exposition of the political, social, and legal views of four eminent Spanish theologians (Vitoria, Soto, Suárez, and Molina), see Bernice Hamilton, *Political Thought in Sixteenth-Century Spain* (Oxford: Oxford University Press, 1963).

3. On the subject of Spain's Indian policy, see especially Silvio Zavala, *La encomienda indiana* (Madrid, 1935); L. B. Simpson, *The Encomienda in New Spain* (Berkeley, 1950), and his *The Repartimiento System of Native Labor in New Spain and Guatemala* (Berkeley, Calif., 1938); José Miranda, *El tributo indígena en la Nueva España* (Mexico, 1952); and Charles Gibson, *The Aztecs under Spanish Rule* (Stanford, Calif., 1963).

4. John L. Phelan, *The Millennial Kingdom of the Franciscans in the New World: A Study of the Writings of Gerónimo de Mendieta (1525–1604)* (Berkeley: University of California Press, 1956), p. 54.

5. On the evolution of Las Casas' thought on Indian policy, see the brilliant essay of Juan Friede, "Las Casas y el movimiento indigenista en España y América en la primera mitad del siglo XVI," *Revista de Historia de América*, xxxiv (June, 1952), 339–411. Friede's essay contains a critique of Lewis Hanke's interpretation of Las Casas and the struggle over Indian policy. For a counter-critique of Friede by Hanke, see his article, "More Heat and Some Light on the Spanish Struggle for Justice in the Conquest of America," *Hispanic American Historical Review*, xliv (August, 1964), 293–340.

6. Carlos E. Castañeda, "Fray Juan de Zumárraga and Indian Policy," *The Americas*, v (January, 1949), 307.

7. Hanke, *Spanish Struggle for Justice*, pp. 96, 97.

8. Marcel Bataillon, "Vasco de Quiroga et Bartolomé de Las Casas," *Revista de Historia de América*, xxxiii (January, 1952), 85–95. Motolinía's letter to Charles V is found in *Colección de documentos para la historia de México*, ed. Joaquín García Icazbalceta, 2 vols. (Mexico, 1858–1866), i, 253–277; also, in partial translation, in Simpson, *The Encomienda in New Spain*, pp. 234–243.

9. *Cartas del licenciado Jerónimo Valderrama y otros documentos sobre su visita al gobierno de Nueva España*, ed. F. V. Scholes and E. A. Adams (Mexico, 1961), pp. 267–270.

10. Valderrama is cited in Miranda, *El tributo indígena*, p. 136.

11. *Cartas del licenciado Jerónimo Valderrama*, p. 46.

12. On the social changes of the sixteenth and seventeenth centuries in New Spain, see the fundamental work of Woodrow Borah, *New Spain's Century of Depression* (Berkeley, Calif.: 1951); the landmark study of François Chevalier, *La Formation des grands domaines au Mexique: Terre et société au XVIe–XVIIe siècles* (Paris, 1952); L. B. Simpson, *Exploitation of Land in Central Mexico in the Sixteenth Century* (Berkeley, Calif., 1956); and, again, Gibson's monumental *The Aztecs under Spanish Rule.*

13. The best recent edition is Gonzalo Fernández de Oviedo, *Historia general y natural de las Indias*, ed. Juan Pérez de Tudela Bueso, 4 vols. (Madrid, 1959).

14. John Howland Rowe, "The Renaissance Foundations of Anthropology," *American Anthropologist*, LXVII (February, 1965), 13.

15. Eduard Fueter, *Storia della storiografia moderna*, 2 vols. (Naples, 1944), I, 356. Alberto M. Salas, *Tres cronistas de Indias* (Mexico, 1959), p. 120. Oviedo, *Historia general y natural*, I, 111.

16. Oviedo, *Historia general y natural*, IV, 245–250.

17. Bartolomé de Las Casas, *Obras escogidas*, 5 vols. (Madrid, 1957–1958), V, 314.

18. The best edition and translation of Juan Ginés de Sepúlveda's treatise is by Ángel Losada, *Democrates segundo o de las justas causas de la guerra contra los indios* (Madrid, 1951).

19. *Ibid.*, pp. 35–38, 122; Las Casas, *Obras escogidas*, V, 315. For a careful summary of Sepúlveda's general argument, see Hanke, *Aristotle and the American Indians*, pp. 44–73.

20. Hanke, *Aristotle and the American Indians*, p. 76.

21. Francisco López de Gómara, *Historia de las Indias*, in *Historiadores primitivos de Indias*, 2 vols. (Madrid, 1858), I, 294.

22. Ramón Iglesia, *Cronistas e historiadores de la conquista de México* (Mexico, 1942), p. 152.

23. *Cortés: The Life of the Conqueror by His Secretary Francisco López de Gómara*, trans. and ed. L. B. Simpson (Berkeley, Calif., 1964), p. 174.

24. Iglesia, *Cronistas e historiadores*, p. 180.

25. Francisco López de Gómara, *Conquista de Méjico*, in *Historiadores primitivos de Indias*, 2 vols. (Madrid, 1858), I, 431.

26. *Ibid.*

27. On the reasons for the suppression, see Simpson's introduction to Gómara's *Cortés: The Life of the Conqueror*, pp. xvi–xvii.

28. Juan de Mariana, *Obras*, 2 vols. (Madrid, 1864–1872), II, 245. On Mariana's views on the Indian question, see José Cepeda Adán, "Una visión de América a fines del siglo XVI," *Estudios Americanos*, VI (November, 1953), 397–421.

29. Lewis Hanke and Agustín Millares Carlo, eds., *Cuerpo de documentos del siglo XVI sobre los derechos de España en las Indias y las Filipinas* (Mexico, 1943), p. cxxv.

30. Jorge Hugo Díaz-Thomé, "Francisco Cervantes de Salazar," in Ramón Iglesia, ed., *Estudios de historiografía de la Nueva España* (Mexico, 1945), pp. 17–41.

31. Francisco Cervantes de Salazar, *Crónica de la Nueva España* (Madrid, 1914), p. 32.

32. Gómara, *Conquista de Méjico*, in *Historiadores primitivos*, I, 442.

33. Cervantes de Salazar, *Crónica*, p. 47.

34. *Ibid.*, p. 741.

35. *Ibid.*, pp. 30–31.

36. Fernando Benítez, *Mexico after Cortés* (Chicago: University of Chicago Press, 1965), pp. 233–243, 238.

37. Juan Suárez de Peralta, *Noticias históricas de la Nueva España* (Madrid, 1878), pp. 3, 20–21.

38. Las Casas, who denounced the injustice of Negro slavery, owned Negro slaves as late as 1544. Hanke, *Aristotle and the American Indians*, p. 9.

39. Francisco de Terrazas, *Poesías*, ed. Antonio Castro Leal (Mexico, 1941), p. 87.

40. Baltasar Dorantes de Carranza, *Sumaria relación de las cosas de la Nueva España* (Mexico, 1902), p. 190.

41. *Ibid.*, pp. 34-35.

42. *Ibid.*, p. 17.

43. *Ibid.*, p. 9.

44. For a recent vitriolic attack on Las Casas, see Ramón Menéndez Pidal, *El Padre Las Casas: Su doble personalidad* (Madrid, 1963).

45. Manuel Giménez Fernández, *Bartolomé de Las Casas*, 2 vols. (Seville, 1953–1959). Lewis Hanke, *Bartolomé de Las Casas: An Interpretation of His Life and Writings* (The Hague, 1951), p. 21.

46. Fueter, *Storia della storiografia moderna*, I, 358. Sepúlveda is cited in Sir Arthur Helps, *The Life of Las Casas* (London, 1868), p. xi.

47. For an excellent demonstration of Las Casas' modernity of spirit, see Teresa Silva Tena, "El sacrificio humano en la *Apologética historia*," *Historia Mexicana*, XVI (January–March, 1967), 341–357. Collating Las Casas' description of Aztec human sacrifice with the parallel text of Motolinía's *Memoriales*, from which he drew his information, Silva Tena notes that he omitted all Motolinía's horrified comment, dispassionately regarding the ceremony as a *technique*, a religious rite. "He was perhaps the only Spaniard of his age," says Silva Tena, "who was capable of looking at native culture *from within*, that is, in the case of human sacrifice, from the standpoint of the Mexican religion and Mexican point of view."

48. Las Casas, *Historia de las Indias*, *Obras escogidas*, I, 112.

49. Alberto Pincherle, "La dignità dell'uomo e l'indigeno americano," in *Atti del Congresso Internazionale di studi umanistici* (Rome, 1952), p. 127. Friede, "Las Casas y el movimiento indigenista," pp. 383–384.

50. On Las Casas' anthropological methods and theories, see Hanke, *Bartolomé de Las Casas*, Chap. 3, "Bartolomé de Las Casas: Anthropologist"; and the introduction by Juan Pérez de Tudela Bueso to the *Apologética historia*, *Obras escogidas*, III.

51. Las Casas, *Obras escogidas*, III, 165.

52. *Ibid.*, pp. 206–208.

53. *Ibid.*, p. 224.

54. *Ibid.*, v, 333.

55. *Ibid.*, iv, 190.

56. Cited in Hanke, *Bartolomé de Las Casas*, p. 80.

57. Las Casas, *Obras escogidas*, iv, 434–445.

58. *Ibid.*, i, 213.

59. Alonso de Zorita, *Life and Labor in Ancient Mexico: The Brief and Summary Relation of the Lords of New Spain by Alonso de Zorita*, trans. and ed. Benjamin Keen (New Brunswick, N.J.: Rutgers University Press, 1963), p. 68.

60. Hoxie N. Fairchild, *The Noble Savage: A Study in Romantic Naturalism* (New York, 1928), p. 21.

61. Zorita, *Life and Labor in Ancient Mexico*, pp. 94–95.

62. *Ibid.*, p. 126.

63. *Ibid.*, pp. 130–132.

64. *Ibid.*, p. 152.

65. *Ibid.*, pp. 170–173.

66. *Ibid.*, pp. 173–174.

67. *Ibid.*, p. 203.

68. Jerónimo Román y Zamora, *Repúblicas de Indias: Idolatrías y gobierno en México y Perú antes de la Conquista*, 2 vols. (Madrid, 1897), i, 271–272.

Chapter Five: The Aztecs and the Great Debate: II

1. François Chevalier has studied the founding of the town of Puebla as an experiment, with Indian assistance, in the planting of Spanish communities of small farmers in New Spain. See his "Signification sociale de la fondation de Puebla de los Ángeles," *Revista de Historia de América*, xxiii (June, 1947), 105–130. The friars encouraged marriage between Spanish settlers and Indian women. Motolinía, who took an active part in the founding of Puebla, noted with approval that there were many mixed marriages in that town and elsewhere in New Spain. *Memoriales de Fray Toribio de Motolinía*, ed. Luis García Pimentel (Mexico, 1903), p. 112.

2. "Sir Thomas More in New Spain: A Utopian Adventure of the Renaissance," in Silvio Zavala, *Recuerdo de Vasco de Quiroga* (Mexico, 1965), p. 108. Sir Arthur Helps, *The Spanish Conquest in America*, 4 vols. (London, 1902), iii, 146.

3. Zavala, "Sir Thomas More in New Spain," p. 115.

4. Silvio Zavala has explored the thought of Vasco de Quiroga and its links with the Renaissance. His writings on the subject are conveniently collected in *Recuerdo de Vasco de Quiroga*, cited above. See also Raúl Villaseñor, "Luciano, Moro, y el utopismo de Vasco de Quiroga," *Cuadernos Americanos*, lxviii (March–April, 1953), 155–175. For the operation and history of the pueblo-hospitals of Santa Fe, see Fintan B. Warren, *Vasco de Quiroga and His Pueblo-Hospitals of Santa Fe* (Washington, D.C.: Academy of American Franciscan History, 1963).

5. Vasco de Quiroga, "Información en derecho," in *Don Vasco de Quiroga: Documentos,* ed. Rafael Aguayo Spencer (Mexico, 1939), pp. 380–386.
6. *Ibid.,* p. 316.
7. *Ibid.,* p. 308.
8. *Ibid.,* pp. 308–311.
9. Silvio Zavala, *Ideario de Vasco de Quiroga* (Mexico, 1941), pp. 29–31.
10. Motolinía, *Memoriales,* p. 303.
11. *Ibid.,* p. 264.
12. *Ibid.,* p. 314.
13. *Ibid.,* p. 303.
14. Alonso de Zorita, *Life and Labor in Ancient Mexico: The Brief and Summary Relation of the Lords of New Spain by Alonso de Zorita,* trans. and ed. Benjamin Keen (New Brunswick, N.J.: Rutgers University Press, 1963), p. 94. Motolinía, *Memoriales,* p. 283.
15. Motolinía, *Memoriales,* p. 258.
16. *Ibid.,* p. 176.
17. Cited by Zorita from a text by Motolinía in Zorita, *Life and Labor in Ancient Mexico,* p. 164.
18. Motolinía, *Memoriales,* p. 233.
19. *Ibid.,* p. 152.
20. *Motolinía's History of the Indians of New Spain,* trans. and ed. Elizabeth Andros Foster (Berkeley, Calif.: The Cortés Society, 1950), p. 216.
21. Motolinía, *Carta al Emperador,* ed. José Bravo Ugarte (Mexico, 1949), p. 52.
22. Wigberto Jiménez Moreno, *Fray Bernardino de Sahagún y su obra* (Mexico, 1938), p. 8. On Sahagún, see also Luis Nicolás d'Olwer, *Historiadores de América: Fray Bernardino de Sahagún (1499–1590)* (Mexico, 1952); and Donald Robertson, "The Sixteenth Century Mexican Encyclopedia of Fray Bernardino de Sahagún," *Journal of World History,* IX, 3 (1966), 617–627.
23. See the chapter on Sahagún in Luis Villoro, *Los grandes momentos del indigenismo en México* (Mexico, 1950).
24. Fray Bernardino de Sahagún, *Historia general de las cosas de la Nueva España,* ed. Ángel María Garibay K., 4 vols. (Mexico, 1956), I, 79.
25. *Ibid.,* p. 407.
26. Villoro, *Grandes momentos,* p. 40.
27. Sahagún, *Historia general,* I, 15.
28. *Ibid.,* p. 14.
29. *Ibid.,* p. 29.
30. *Ibid.*
31. *Ibid.,* p. 13.
32. *Ibid.,* III, 159.
33. *Ibid.,* p. 161.
34. *Ibid.,* p. 168.
35. Diego Durán, *Historia de las Indias de Nueva España e islas de tierra firme,* ed. José F. Ramírez, 2 vols. and Atlas (Mexico, 1867–1880), II, 71.

36. Fernando B. Sandoval, "La relación de la conquista de México en la *Historia* de Fray Diego Durán," in Ramón Iglesia, ed., *Estudios de historiografía de la Nueva España* (Mexico, 1945), p. 62.

37. Durán, *Historia*, I, 8.

38. *Ibid.*, II, 41, 60, 65.

39. *Ibid.*, p. 161.

40. *Ibid.*, pp. 225–226.

41. The best modern edition of Acosta's *Historia* is in *Obras del P. José de Acosta*, ed. Francisco Mateos, S.J. (Madrid, 1954).

42. *Ibid.*, pp. 477, 489–491.

43. On Acosta's originality and significance, see Theodore Hornberger, "Acosta's *Historia natural y moral de las Indias*," *Studies in English, 1939* (Austin: University of Texas, 1939), pp. 139–162.

44. Acosta, *Obras*, pp. 391–394.

45. *Ibid.*, pp. 182–183.

46. *Ibid.*, pp. 244–246, 241.

47. John L. Phelan traces the evolution of Mendieta's thought on the Indian question in his admirable book, *The Millennial Kingdom of the Franciscans in the New World: A Study of the Writings of Gerónimo de Mendieta (1525–1604)* (Berkeley: University of California Press, 1956).

48. *Ibid.*, pp. 102–104. Gerónimo de Mendieta, *Historia eclesiástica indiana*, ed. Joaquín García Icazbalceta (Mexico, 1870), p. 75.

49. Mendieta, *Historia*, pp. 112–120. Mendieta, Letter to Fray Francisco de Bustamante, in *Nueva colección de documentos para la historia de México*, ed. Joaquín García Icazbalceta, 5 vols. (Mexico, 1886–1892), I, 20–21.

50. Phelan, *Millennial Kingdom*, pp. 98, 60.

51. Gerónimo de Mendieta, "Consideraciones de Fray Hierónimo de Mendieta cerca de los indios de la Nueva España," in *Nueva colección de documentos para la historia de México*, ed. Joaquín García Icazbalceta, 5 vols. (Mexico, 1886–1892), V, 28–35.

52. On the Colegio de Santa Cruz, see Francis Borgia Steck, *El primer colegio de América, Santa Cruz de Tlatelolco, con un estudio del códice de Tlatelolco por R. H. Barlow* (Mexico, 1944); and the chapter on "Cultura literaria de los indios" in Ángel María Garibay K., *Historia de la literatura náhuatl*, 2 vols. (Mexico, 1953–1954), II, 209–233.

53. Charles Gibson has dispelled the confusion surrounding the identity of the chronicler in "The Identity of Diego Muñoz Camargo," *Hispanic American Historical Review*, XXX (May, 1950), 195–208. Magnus Morner and Charles Gibson, "Diego Muñoz Camargo and the Segregation Policy of the Spanish Crown," *Hispanic American Historical Review*, XLII (November, 1962), 558–567.

54. Charles Gibson, *Tlaxcala in the Sixteenth Century* (New Haven, 1952), p. 194.

55. Diego Muñoz Camargo, *Historia de Tlaxcala* (Mexico, 1870), p. 155.

56. *Ibid.*, p. 153.

57. *Ibid.*, p. 40.

58. *Ibid.*, pp. 135–136.

59. *Ibid.*, p. 149.

60. *Ibid.*, p. 150.

61. Juan Bautista Pomar, *Relación de Texcoco*, in *Nueva colección de documentos para la historia de México*, ed. Joaquín García Icazbalceta, 5 vols. (Mexico, 1886–1892), III, 1–69.

62. *Ibid.*, pp. 1–2.

63. *Ibid.*, pp. 5–7, 43.

64. *Ibid.*, pp. 15–16.

65. *Ibid.*, pp. 24–25.

66. *Ibid.*, pp. 53–55.

67. Garibay, *Historia*, II, 302. Fernando Alvarado Tezozómoc, *Crónica mexicana*, ed. Manuel Orozco y Berra (Mexico, 1878), p. 159.

68. Tezozómoc, *Crónica*, p. 330.

69. *Ibid.*, pp. 249–250.

70. Juan A. Ortega y Medina, "El indio absuelto y las Indias condenadas en las Cortes de la Muerte," *Historia Mexicana*, IV (April–June, 1955), 477–505.

71. Luis Zapata, *El primer poema que trata del descubrimiento del Nuevo Mundo*, ed. José Toribio Medina (Santiago de Chile, 1916), p. 62.

72. Francisco de Terrazas, *Poesías*, ed. Antonio Castro Leal (Mexico, 1941), p. xviii.

73. Gabriel Lasso de la Vega, *La Mexicana emendada y añadida por su mismo autor* . . . (Madrid, 1594), foll. 297–304.

Chapter Six: The Aztecs in Late Renaissance Thought, 1550–1600

1. Federico Chabod rightly observes that the intellectual repercussions of the discovery of the New World have received too little notice. See his *Machiavelli and the Renaissance* (New York: Harper and Row, Harper Torchbooks, 1965), p. 198.

2. Henri Hauser, *La Prépondérance espagnole (1559–1660)*, 3d ed. (Paris, 1948), p. 15.

3. Francisco López de Gómara, *La terza parte delle Historie dell'Indie, nella quale particolarmente si tratta dello scoprimento della provincia di Iucatan detta Nuova Spagna, e delle cose digne di memoria, fatte da Spagnuoli nella conquista della grande, e maravigliosa città di Messico, e delle altre provincie ad essa sottoposte* . . . (Venice, 1566), pp. vii–viii.

4. The full title of Volume III of Giovanni Battista Ramusio's book: *Terzo volume Delle navigationi et viaggi nel quale si contengono le navigationi al Mondo Nuovo, alli antichi incognito, fatte da Don Christoforo Colombo Genovese, che fu il primo à scoprirlo à i Re Catholici, detto hora le Indie occidentali, con gli acquisti fatti da lui, Et accresciuti poi da Fernando Cortese, da Francesco Pizzarro, & altri valerosi capitani, in diverse parti delle dette Indie, in nome della Ces. Maes. con lo scoprire la gran Città di Temistitan nel Mexico, dove hora e detto la Nuova Spagna, et la gran Provincia del*

Peru, il grandissimo fiume Maragnon, et altre città, regni, & provincie . . . (Venice, 1556).

5. Ptolemy's *Geografia cioè descrittione universale della terra* (Venice, 1597–1598), p. 203.

6. Michele Zappullo, *Historie di quattro principali città del mondo, Gerusalemme, Roma, Napoli, e Venetia . . . Aggiuntovi un compendio dell'istorie dell'Indie, & anche le tavole astronomiche, per maggior documento de lettori . . .* (Vicenza, 1603), pp. 377–378.

7. Giovanni Botero, *Relationi universali* (Venice, 1596), Part I, Book 4, pp. 200–201; Part IV, Book 3, p. 66.

8. Thomaso Porcacchi, *L'isole più famose del mondo descritte da Thomaso Porcacchi da Castiglione e intagliate da Girolamo Porro Padovano* (Venice, 1590), pp. 157–160.

9. Marco Allegri, "Girolamo Benzoni e la sua *Historia del Mondo Nuovo*," in *Raccolta di documenti e studi pubblicati dalla R. Commissione Colombina pel quarto centenario dalla scoperta dell'America*, Part V, Vol. 3 (Rome, 1894), pp. 149, 153.

10. Girolamo Benzoni, *History of the New World*, trans. W. H. Smyth (London: Hakluyt Society, 1857), pp. 57, 168, 47–50.

11. Rómulo D. Carbia, *Historia de la leyenda negra hispanoamericana* (Buenos Aires, 1943), p. 70.

12. Tommaso Campanella, "La Città del Sole," in *Scritti scelti di Giordano Bruno e di Tommaso Campanella* (Turin, 1965), p. 459.

13. Giordano Bruno, *The Expulsion of the Triumphant Beast*, trans. and ed. Arthur D. Imerti (New Brunswick, N.J.: Rutgers University Press, 1964), p. 250.

14. Girolamo Benzoni, *Histoire nouvelle du Nouveau Monde, contenant en somme ce que les Hespagnols ont fait iusqu'à présent aux Indes occidentales, & le rude traitement qu'ils font à ces povres peuples-là* (Paris or Geneva? 1579).

15. *Ibid.*, p. 215.

16. Bartolomé de Las Casas, *Tyranies & cruautez des Espagnols, perpetrees e's Indes occidentales, qu'on dit le Nouveau Monde; brievement descrites en langue castillane par l'Evesque Don Frere Bartelemy de Las Casas ou Casaus . . . fidelement traduictes par Jaques de Miggrode: pour servir d'exemple & advertissement aux XVII provinces du pais bas* (Antwerp, 1579).

17. *Ibid.*, fol. 7.

18. Lewis Hanke and Manuel Giménez Fernández, *Bartolomé de Las Casas: Bibliografía crítica y cuerpo de materiales para el estudio de su vida, escritos, actuación y polémicas que suscitaron durante cuatro siglos* (Santiago de Chile, 1954), pp. 207, 210.

19. Foreword to Francisco López de Gómara, *Voyages et conquêtes du Capitaine Ferdinand Courtois, es Indes occidentales* (Paris, 1588).

20. Jacques-Auguste de Thou, *Histoire universelle de Jacques-Auguste de Thou, avec la suite par Nicolas Rigault* (The Hague, 1740), pp. 29–30.

21. François de Belleforest, *Histoire universelle du monde* (Paris, 1572), pp. 275–276, 278.

22. *Ibid.*, p. 277.

23. Sebastian Münster, *La Cosmographie universelle de tout le monde*, 2 vols. (Paris, 1575), ii, 2128.

24. Ángel María Garibay K., *Historia de la literatura náhuatl*, 2 vols. (Mexico, 1953–1954), ii (1954), 48–49. See also Edouard de Jonghe, "*Histoire du Mechique:* Manuscrit français inédit du XVᵉ siècle," *Journal de la Société des Américanistes de Paris*, n.s., ii (1905), 1–41.

25. Fumée is cited in Jean Adhemas, *Frère André Thevet* (Paris, n.d.), p. 43. Gilbert Chinard, *L'Exotisme américain dans la littérature française au XVIᵉ siècle* (Paris, 1911), p. 85. Bernard G. Hoffman, *Cabot to Cartier: Sources for a Historical Ethnography of Northeastern North America, 1497–1550* (Toronto: University of Toronto Press, 1961), pp. 171–172. For other favorable views on Thevet's contribution to New World ethnography, see Manoel da Silveira Cardozo, "Some Remarks Concerning André Thevet," *The Americas*, i (July, 1944), 15–36.

26. André Thevet, *La Cosmographie universelle d'André Thevet, Cosmographe du Roy*, 2 vols. (Paris, 1575), ii, 997–998.

27. *Ibid.*, p. 991.

28. *Ibid.*

29. *Ibid.*, p. 997.

30. André Thevet, *Les Vrais Pourtraits et vies des hommes illustres grecz, latins, et payens, recueilliz de leur tableaux, livres, medalles antiques et modernes* (Paris, 1584), p. 378.

31. Thevet, *Les Vrais Pourtraits*, pp. 377–379. Thevet referred to a translation by Nicholas Pithou of Dionyse Settle's *True Reporte*, published under the title of *La Navigation du Capitaine Martin Frobisher Anglois, és regions de West & Nordwest, en l'année M.D. LXXVII* (Paris, 1578). In his preface, after describing "the miseries and calamities" inflicted upon the Indians by an unnamed power, the Protestant translator comforted himself and his readers with the thought that the "poor barbarians" need not fear the same issue from the voyages of the English nation, ruled by such a "humane, kindly, and God-fearing queen" as Queen Elizabeth.

32. Thevet, *Les Vrais Pourtraits*, pp. 645–646.

33. Abraham Ortelius, *Theatre de l'Univers, contenant les cartes de tout le monde. Avec une brieve declaration d'icelles* (Antwerp, 1587). Howard F. Cline has studied the Ortelius map of New Spain and its predecessors in "The Ortelius Map of New Spain, 1579, and Related Contemporary Material, 1560–1610," *Imago Mundi*, xvi (1962), 98–115.

34. Ortelius, *Theatre de l'Univers*, fol. 6. Cline, "The Ortelius Map," p. 102n, cites Arias Montanus.

35. Cornelis Koeman, *The History of Abraham Ortelius and the "Theatrum orbis terrarum"* (Lausanne, 1964), p. 34.

36. Ortelius, *Theatre de l'Univers*, fol. 2.

37. Chinard, *L'Exotisme américain*, pp. 48–79. Hoffman, *Cabot to Cartier*, pp. 151–153. Pantagruel's speech is cited in Howard M. Jones, *O Strange*

New World (New York, 1964), p. 36. See this work for a perceptive discussion of the early European image and "anti-image" of America and the American Indian.

38. Chinard, *L'Exotisme américain*, p. 117.

39. On Montaigne and Europe's "skeptical crisis," see Richard H. Popkin, *The History of Skepticism from Erasmus to Descartes* (Assen, Netherlands, 1960).

40. Chinard, *L'Exotisme américain*, pp. 196–197. Pierre Villey, *Les Sources et l'évolution des "Essais" de Montaigne*, 2 vols. (Paris, 1908), I, 137–138. Carlos Pereyra, "Montaigne y López de Gómara," *Escorial*, III (December, 1940), 227–236.

41. Villey, *Sources*, II, 313.

42. *The Complete Works of Montaigne*, trans. and ed. D. M. Frame (Stanford, Calif.: Stanford University Press, 1957), pp. 432–433.

43. *Ibid.*, p. 149.

44. Chinard, *L'Exotisme américain*, pp. 209–210.

45. Hoxie N. Fairchild, *The Noble Savage: A Study in Romantic Naturalism* (New York, 1928), p. 21.

46. Montaigne, *Works*, pp. 693–694.

47. *Ibid.*, pp. 694–695.

48. The full title of Nicolaus Hoeniger's translation of Benzoni's *Historia del Mondo Nuovo: Der newen Weldt und indianischen Königreichs, newe und wahrhaffte History, von allen Geschichten, Handlungen, Thaten, Strengem und ernstlichem Regiment der Spanier gegen den Indianern . . .* (Basel, 1579).

49. On De Bry's travel collections, see Armand Gaston Camus, *Mémoire sur la collection des "Grands et Petits Voyages"* (Paris, 1802).

50. Carbia, *Leyenda negra*, p. 73.

51. Bartolomé de Las Casas, *Narratio regionum indicarum per Hispanos quosdam devastatarum verissima: priùs quidem per Episcopum Bartholomaeum Casaum, natione Hispanum Hispanicè conscripta, & anno 1551. Hispali, Hispanicè, anno verò hoc 1598. Latine excusa* (Frankfurt am Main, 1598), "Praefatio ad Lectorem."

52. Franklin T. McCann, *English Discovery of America to 1585* (New York: Columbia University Press, 1952), pp. 115–116, 136.

53. Peter Martyr d'Anghera and others, *The Decades of the New Worlde*, comp. Richard Eden (London, 1555), "The Preface to the Reader."

54. Henry R. Wagner, *The Spanish Southwest, 1542–1794: An Annotated Bibliography*, 2 vols. (Albuquerque, N.M., 1937), I, 80.

55. Sir George Peckham, in *The Voyages and Colonising Enterprises of Sir Humphrey Gilbert*, ed. D. B. Quinn, 2 vols. (London: Hakluyt Society, 1940), II, 448–449.

56. *Ibid.*, p. 468.

57. David Powell, *The Historie of Cambria, Now Called Wales* (London, 1584), p. 228.

58. Richard Hakluyt, comp., *The Principall Navigations, Voiages and Discoveries of the English Nation*, ed. D. B. Quinn and R. A. Skelton, 2 vols. (Cambridge, 1965), II, 548, 552.

59. *The Original Writings and Correspondence of the Two Richard Hakluyts*, ed. E. G. R. Taylor, 2 vols. (London: Hakluyt Society, 1935), II, 212, 309–310.

60. *Ibid.*, p. 369.

Chapter Seven: The Baroque Vision of the Aztecs

1. Manuel Giménez Fernández and Lewis Hanke, eds., *Bartolomé de Las Casas, 1474–1566: Bibliografía crítica y cuerpo de materiales para el estudio de su vida, escritos, actuación y polémicas que suscitaron durante cuatro siglos* (Santiago de Chile, 1954), pp. 235–236. Antonio de León Pinelo, *Tratado de las confirmaciones reales* (Buenos Aires, 1922), p. 222.

2. Juan de Solórzano y Pereira, *Política indiana*, 5 vols. (Buenos Aires, 1930), I, 92–127 *passim*. For a convenient summary of Solórzano's views, see Silvio Zavala, *Servidumbre natural y libertad cristiana* (Buenos Aires, 1934), pp. 102–104. Antonio de León Pinelo, *El paraíso en el Nuevo Mundo*, 2 vols. (Lima, 1943), II, 5.

3. Antonio Domínguez Ortiz, *La sociedad española en el siglo XVII* (Madrid, 1963), p. 249.

4. Carlos Bosch García, "La conquista de la Nueva España en las *Décadas* de Antonio de Herrera y Tordesillas," in *Estudios de historiografía de la Nueva España*, ed. Ramón Iglesia (Mexico, 1945), pp. 148–153. See also the illuminating notes of Antonio Ballesteros y Beretta to Vol. v, dealing with the conquest of Mexico, of Antonio de Herrera y Tordesillas, *Historia general de los hechos de los castellanos en las islas y tierra firme del Mar Océano*, ed. Antonio Ballesteros y Beretta and others, 17 vols. (Madrid, 1934–1957).

5. Solís' letter to Carrera is cited in Luis A. Arocena, *Antonio de Solís, cronista indiano: Estudio sobre las formas historiográficas del Barroco* (Buenos Aires, 1963), p. 217.

6. Antonio de Solís, *Historia de la conquista de Méjico* (Buenos Aires, 1947), p. 229.

7. *Ibid.*, p. 457.

8. *Ibid.*, pp. 304, 69.

9. *Ibid.*, p. 198.

10. *Ibid.*, pp. 221–223.

11. *Ibid.*, p. 228.

12. Jorge Campos, "América en la obra de Cervantes," *Revista de Indias*, VIII (1947), 380. Marcos A. Morínigo, *América en el teatro de Lope de Vega* (Buenos Aires, 1946), p. 150.

13. Ángel Franco, *El tema de América en los autores españoles del siglo de oro* (Madrid, 1954), p. 393.

14. Morínigo, *América*, pp. 230, 232.

15. John L. Phelan, *The Millennial Kingdom of the Franciscans in the New World: A Study of the Writings of Gerónimo de Mendieta (1525–1604)* (Berkeley: University of California Press, 1956), p. 107. Juan de Torquemada, *Primera (Segunda, Tercera) parte de los veinte i un libros rituales i monarchía indiana*, 3 vols. (Madrid, 1723), iii, 280; ii, 566. Alejandra Moreno Toscano, *Fray Juan de Torquemada y su "Monarquía indiana"* (Xalapa, Mexico, 1963), p. 83.

16. Torquemada, *Monarchía indiana*, ii, 26.

17. *Ibid.*, Prologue to Book 6.

18. *Ibid.*, p. 115.

19. *Ibid.*, pp. 359, 371.

20. *Ibid.*, pp. 356, 359.

21. *Ibid.*, pp. 160–161, 486.

22. *Ibid.*, i, 379.

23. Miguel León-Portilla, introduction to Fray Juan de Torquemada, *Monarquía indiana* (Mexico, 1964), p. xxxiii. Another recent study speaks of Torquemada as "a skilled and careful historian, constrained only by some obvious usages and common attitudes of his age." Howard F. Cline, "A Note on Torquemada's Native Sources and Historiographical Methods," *The Americas*, xxv (April, 1969), 372–386.

24. Francisco Fernández del Castillo, "Fray Antonio de Remesal," in Antonio de Remesal, *Historia general de las Indias occidentales, y particular de la gobernación de Chiapa y Guatemala*, 2 vols. (Guatemala City, 1932), ii, 23, 30.

25. *Ibid.*, p. 20. On Remesal's life and work, see the "Estudio preliminar" with which Carmelo Sáenz de Santa María, S.J., introduces his edition of Remesal's history (2 vols., Madrid, 1964). Personal enmities, the creole-peninsular cleavage, and the conflict between the secular and regular clergy doubtless played a part in Remesal's misfortunes, as suggested by Fernández del Castillo and Father Sáenz, but the charges leveled against Remesal by Ruiz de Corral clearly indicate that attitudes on the Indian question were heavily involved. Murdo J. MacLeod reaches the same conclusion in his interesting paper, "Las Casas, Guatemala, and the Sad but Inevitable Case of Antonio de Remesal," *Topic: A Journal of the Liberal Arts* (Washington and Jefferson College), xx (Fall, 1970), 53–64.

26. Cited in Francisco Sánchez-Castañer, *Don Juan de Palafox, Virrey de Nueva España* (Zaragoza, 1964), p. 27.

27. Genaro García, *Don Juan de Palafox y Mendoza*, in *Documentos inéditos o muy raros para la historia de México*, 36 vols. (Mexico, 1905–1911), vii (1906), 28. Sánchez-Castañer, *Don Juan de Palafox*, p. 53.

28. Sánchez-Castañer, *Don Juan de Palafox*, pp. 176–193.

29. Agustín de Vetancurt, *Teatro mexicano* (Mexico, 1696), pp. 331–332.

30. *Ibid.*, pp. 48, 17.

31. *Ibid.*, p. 326.

32. Eli de Gortari, *Ciencia en la historia de México* (Mexico, 1963), p. 229.

33. Francisco Javier Clavigero, *Historia antigua de México*, ed. Mariano Cuevas (Mexico, 1964), p. 294.

34. Carlos de Sigüenza y Góngora, *Obras* (Mexico, 1928), pp. 34–35.

35. Carlos de Sigüenza y Góngora, *Paraýso occidental* (Mexico, 1684), foll. 2–5.

36. Sigüenza y Góngora, *Obras*, pp. 69–139.

37. Irving A. Leonard, *Don Carlos de Sigüenza y Góngora* (Berkeley: University of California Press, 1929), pp. 92–96.

38. Sigüenza y Góngora, *Obras*, p. 30.

39. Cited in Ramón Iglesia, "La mexicanidad de Don Carlos de Sigüenza y Góngora," *El hombre Colón y otros ensayos* (Mexico, 1944), pp. 141–142.

40. Arias de Villalobos, "México en 1623," in Genaro García, ed., *Documentos inéditos o muy raros para la historia de México*, 36 vols. (Mexico, 1905–1911), xii (1907), 123–281.

41. *Obras completas de Sor Juana de la Cruz*, ed. Alfonso Méndez Plancarte, 4 vols. (Mexico, 1951–1957), iii, 3–18.

42. *Ibid.*, pp. 193–196.

43. Charles Gibson, "The Aztec Aristocracy in Colonial Mexico," *Comparative Studies in Society and History* (The Hague), ii (January, 1960), 169–196.

44. Cristóbal del Castillo, *Migración de los mexicanos al país de Anauac: Fin de su dominación y noticias de su calendario*, trans. and ed. Francisco del Paso y Troncoso (Florence, 1908), p. 88.

45. Silvia Rendón in her introduction to Domingo Francisco de San Antón Muñón Chimalpahin, *Relaciones originales de Chalco Amaquemecan*, ed. and trans. Silvia Rendón (Mexico, 1965), p. 13.

46. *Ibid.*, pp. 75–76, 123.

47. *Ibid.*, p. 121.

48. *Obras históricas de Don Fernando de Alva Ixtlilxóchitl*, ed. Alfredo Chavero, 2 vols. (Mexico, 1891), i, 445–446.

49. *Ibid.*, ii, 15.

50. For a detailed study of this codex and its use by Ixtlilxóchitl, see Charles E. Dibble, ed., *Códice Xólotl*, introd. Rafael García Granados (Mexico, 1951). Ángel María Garibay K., *Historia de la literatura náhuatl*, 2 vols. (Mexico, 1953–1954), ii, 311.

51. Ixtlilxóchitl, *Obras*, ii, 301.

52. *Ibid.*, i, 419–420.

53. On this problem, see R. Trevor Davies, *Spain in Decline* (London, 1957), pp. 75–80.

54. Pedro Diego Luis de Motezuma, *Corona mexicana o Historia de los nueve Motezumas*, ed. Lucas de la Torre (Madrid, 1914), pp. 15–28, 49–52, 161–168, 364, 498.

55. *The Works of Francis Bacon*, 15 vols. (Boston, 1860), xiii, 197–198.

56. A record number of editions of Las Casas' *Brevísima relación*—27 in Dutch, Flemish, and French—appeared between 1578 and 1670 alone in the Netherlands. Italy had no translations of Las Casas before 1600; beginning in 1613, however, a steady stream of such translations issued from Venice, stronghold of liberal Catholicism and resistance to Spanish and Papal encroachments on her independence. On the publishing history of Las Casas'

writings, see Giménez Fernández and Hanke, eds., *Bartolomé de Las Casas, 1474–1566*, and the informative article of V. L. Afanasiev, "Literaturnoe nasledstvo Bartolome de Las-Kasasa i nekotorye voprosy istorii ego opublikovaniia," in I. R. Grigulevich, ed., *Bartolome de Las-Kasas: K istorii zavoevaniia Ameriki* (Moscow, 1966), pp. 180–220.

57. Samuel Purchas, *Hakluytus Posthumus, or Purchas, His Pilgrimes*, 20 vols. (London, 1905), xv, 413.

58. The best modern edition is the following: *Codex Mendoza: The Mexican Manuscript Known as the Collection of Mendoza and Preserved in the Bodleian Library, Oxford*, trans. and ed. James Cooper Clark, 3 vols. (London, 1938). For a discussion of artistic and technical aspects of this and related codices, see Donald Robertson, *Mexican Manuscript Painting of the Early Colonial Period: The Metropolitan Schools* (New Haven: Yale University Press, 1959).

59. Purchas, *Hakluytus Posthumus*, p. 412.

60. Athanasius Kircher, *Oedipus Aegyptiacus, hoc est universalis doctrinae hieroglyphicae instauratio*, 3 vols. (Rome, 1652–1654), iii, 28–36.

61. Hugo Grotius, *On the Origin of the Native Races of America . . .* , trans. from the Latin by Edmund Goldsmith (Edinburgh, 1884), pp. 10–18.

62. Joannis de Laet, *Notae ad dissertationem Hugonis Grotii: De origine gentium Americanorum* (Paris, 1643), pp. 23–40. Jean de Laet, *L'Histoire du Nouveau Monde* (Leyden, 1640); first Dutch edition, Leyden, 1625.

63. Told in Francesco Gemelli Carreri, *Giro del Mondo*, 6 vols. (Naples, 1700); and many other editions.

64. "*A Voyage Round the World*," in A. Churchill, *A Collection of Voyages and Travels*, 4 vols. (London, 1704), iv, 518, 523.

65. Marin Le Roy de Gomberville, *The History of Polexander: in Five Bookes, Done into English by William Browne* (London, 1647), p. 79.

66. See Philip A. Wadsworth, *The Novels of Gomberville: A Critical Study of Polexandre and Cythérée* (New Haven: Yale University Press, 1942).

67. *The Works of John Dryden*, ed. Sir Walter Scott, rev. and corrected George Saintsbury, 18 vols. (Edinburgh, 1882), ii, 331.

68. Louis I. Bredvold, *The Intellectual Milieu of John Dryden* (Ann Arbor: University of Michigan Press, 1934), p. 153.

69. *Works of John Dryden*, ii, 395–399.

70. Bernard de Fontenelle, *Fontenelle's Dialogues of the Dead* (London, 1707), pp. 188–194.

Chapter Eight: The Eyes of Reason: I

1. This view derives in large part from the myth of Rousseau's unqualified primitivism, a myth exploded long ago by Arthur O. Lovejoy in "The Supposed Primitivism of Rousseau's *Discourse on Inequality*," *Modern Philology*, xxi (August, 1923), 165–186; reprinted in A. O. Lovejoy, *Essays in the History of Ideas* (Baltimore: Johns Hopkins University Press, 1948), pp. 14–37.

2. Antonello Gerbi, *La disputa del Nuovo Mondo: Storia di una polemica, 1750–1900* (Milan, 1955), traces the history of this quarrel with learning, clarity, and wit. My citations are from the revised and enlarged Spanish edition: *La disputa del Nuevo Mundo: Historia de una polémica, 1750–1900* (Mexico, 1960).

3. Gilbert Chinard, *L'Amérique et le rêve exotique dans la littérature française au XVIIᵉ et au XVIIIᵉ siècle* (Paris, 1913), pp. 395–396.

4. Cited in J. B. Bury, *The Idea of Progress* (London, 1920), p. 167.

5. Basic studies of the subject are Jean Sarrailh, *L'Europe éclairée de la seconde moitiée du XVIIIᵉ siècle* (Paris, 1954); and Richard Herr, *The Eighteenth-Century Revolution in Spain* (Princeton, N.J.: Princeton University Press, 1958).

6. Herr, *The Eighteenth-Century Revolution in Spain*, p. 39.

7. Benito Gerónimo Feijóo, *Theatro crítico universal*, 9 vols. (Madrid, 1728), II, 283.

8. *Ibid.*, p. 279.

9. *Ibid.*, pp. 209–210.

10. José del Campillo y Cosío, *Nuevo sistema del gobierno económico para la América* (Madrid, 1789), pp. 54, 88–90.

11. Pedro Murillo Velarde, *Geographia histórica*, 10 vols. (Madrid, 1752), IX, 44–48.

12. José de Eguiara y Eguren, *Prólogos a la "Bibliotheca mexicana,"* ed. and trans. Agustín Millares Carlo, introd. Francisco Gómez de Orozco (Mexico, 1944), p. 55.

13. *Ibid.*, pp. 58–95.

14. See the informing sketch of Vico's philosophy by Patrick Gardner in *Encyclopedia of Philosophy*, 8 vols. (New York, 1967), and, for an excellent survey of his work and influence, the introduction by M. H. Fisch and Thomas G. Bergin to their translation of *The Autobiography of Giambattista Vico* (Ithaca, N.Y.: Cornell University Press, 1944).

15. Thomas G. Bergin and M. H. Fisch, trans. and ed., *The New Science of Giambattista Vico* (Ithaca, N.Y.: Cornell University Press, 1948), *passim*.

16. On Boturini, see the prologue of Manuel Ballesteros Gaibrois to *Papeles de Indias*, II, *Historia general de la América septentrional por el Caballero Lorenzo Boturini Benaducci*, Vol. VI of *Documentos inéditos para la historia de España* (Madrid, 1948); and J. Torre Revello, "Lorenzo Boturini Benaducci y el cargo de cronista de las Indias," *Boletín del Instituto de Investigaciones Históricas* (Buenos Aires), V (1926–1927), 52–61.

17. Mariano Veytia, "Discurso preliminar" to his *Historia del origen de las gentes que poblaron la América septentrional*, in Edward King, Viscount Kingsborough, *Antiquities of Mexico*, 9 vols. (London, 1830–1848), VIII, 166.

18. Lorenzo Boturini Benaducci, *Idea de una nueva historia general de la América septentrional* (Madrid, 1746), p. 7. The leader of the attack on Vico was a Dominican, G. F. Finetti, who, remark Fisch and Bergin, "saw more clearly than others that the *New Science*, however innocent in intent, was by no means innocuous in effect. To admit the feral state as the starting-point for the rise of humanity, and to make the development of humanity

a matter of internal dialectic, was to put the entire structure of Catholic thought in jeopardy." Fisch and Bergin, introduction to *Autobiography of Giambattista Vico*, p. 63.

19. Boturini, *Idea*, p. 69.

20. *Ibid.*, pp. 81–82.

21. *Ibid.*, p. 104.

22. *Ibid.*, p. 151.

23. Ballesteros Gaibrois, prologue to *Papeles de Indias*, II, xx.

24. *Ibid.*, p. liv.

25. *Ibid.*, p. 25.

26. Francisco Javier Clavigero, *Historia antigua de México*, ed. Mariano Cuevas (Mexico, 1964), pp. xxxi, 50–52. William H. Prescott, *The History of the Conquest of Mexico*, ed. J. F. Kirk, 3 vols. (Philadelphia, 1873), I, 162.

27. E.-T. Hamy, introduction to J.-M.-A. Aubin, *Mémoires sur la peinture didactique et l'écriture figurative des anciens Mexicains* (Paris, 1885), p. v.

28. Veytia, *Historia del origen* . . . , in Kingsborough, *Antiquities of Mexico*, VIII, 167.

29. *Ibid.*, p. 168.

30. Mariano Veytia, *Historia antigua de Méjico*, ed. C. F. Ortega, 3 vols. (Mexico, 1836), I, 165.

31. *Ibid.*, p. 254.

32. Víctor Rico González, *Historiadores mexicanos del siglo XVIII: Estudios historiográficos sobre Clavijero, Veytia, Cavo, y Alegre* (Mexico, 1949), pp. 84–97.

33. Du Tertre is cited in Geoffrey Atkinson, *Les Relations de voyages du XVIIᵉ siècle et l'évolution des idées* (Paris, 1924), p. 40.

34. Lescarbot is cited in Chinard, *L'Amérique et le rêve exotique*, p. 110.

35. Introduction to Louis Armand de Lom d'Arce, Baron de Lahontan, *Dialogues curieux entre l'auteur et un sauvage de bon sens qui a voyagé et mémoires de l'Amérique septentrionale* (Baltimore: Johns Hopkins University Press, 1938), p. 43.

36. Père Joseph-François Lafitau, *Mœurs des sauvages américains, comparées aux mœurs des premiers temps*, 2 vols. (Paris, 1724), I, 5–6.

37. *Ibid.*, p. 324.

38. Chinard, *L'Amérique et le rêve exotique*, p. 324.

39. Lafitau, *Mœurs des sauvages*, I, 49.

40. Wilhelm Windelband, *A History of Philosophy*, 2 vols. (New York: Harper and Row, Harper Torchbooks, 1958), II, 505.

41. Pierre Bayle, *Dictionnaire historique et critique*, 3d ed., 4 vols. (Rotterdam, 1724), II. 1689.

42. Henri-Abraham Châtelain, *Atlas historique, ou, nouvelle introduction à l'histoire, à la chronologie, & à la géographie ancienne & moderne. . . . Avec des dissertations sur l'histoire de chaque état par Mʳ Gueudeville*, 7 vols. (Amsterdam, 1705–1720), VII, 105–106.

43. J. F. Bernard, *The Religious Ceremonies and Customs of the Several Nations of the Known World Represented in Above an Hundred Copper-*

Plates, Designed by the famous Picart . . . , 7 vols. (London, 1731–1739), III, 53–58, 64, 151, 131.

44. Antoine Banier and Jean-Baptiste Le Mascrier, *Histoire générale des cérémonies, mœurs, et coutumes religieuses de tous les peuples du monde,* 7 vols. (Paris, 1741), VII, 82.

45. Antoine Touron, *Histoire générale de l'Amérique depuis sa découverte,* 14 vols. (Paris, 1769–1770), I, lviii–cii; II, 373.

46. Georges-Louis Leclerc, Comte de Buffon, *Histoire naturelle générale et particulière,* 43 vols. (Deux-Ponts, 1785–1787), XXXIV, 157–158.

47. Gerbi, *La disputa del Nuevo Mundo,* pp. 62–63.

48. Charles-Marie de La Condamine, *Relation abrégée d'un voyage fait dans l'intérieur de l'Amérique septentrionale* (Paris, 1745).

49. Buffon, *Histoire naturelle,* XXXIV, 75.

50. Buffon is cited in Gerbi, *La disputa del Nuevo Mundo,* p. 14n.

51. Buffon, *Histoire naturelle,* V, 140.

52. Franz Neumann in his introduction to Charles de Secondat, Baron de Montesquieu, *The Spirit of the Laws,* trans. Thomas Nugent, 2 vols. (New York, 1962), I, xxiv.

53. Montesquieu, *Œuvres complètes,* pref. Georges Vedel, présentation et notes Daniel Oster (Paris, 1964), p. 187.

54. *Ibid.,* pp. 941–942, 949.

55. *Ibid.,* p. 944.

56. For a general survey, see Jean David, "Voltaire et les Indiens d'Amérique," *Modern Language Quarterly,* IX (March, 1948), 90–103.

57. Voltaire, *Essai sur les mœurs et l'esprit des nations,* ed. René Ponceau, 2 vols. (Paris, 1963), I, 25.

58. Voltaire is cited in Gerbi, *La disputa del Nuevo Mundo,* p. 40.

59. Voltaire, *Essai,* I, 22–23; David, "Voltaire et les Indiens," pp. 97–99.

60. Richard A. Brooks, 'Voltaire and Garcilaso de la Vega," in *Studies on Voltaire and the Eighteenth Century,* ed. Theodore Besterman, Vol. XXX (Geneva, 1964), p. 190.

61. Voltaire, *Essai,* II, 346–361.

62. Jacques Proust, *Diderot et "l'Encyclopédie"* (Paris, 1962), pp. 521–522.

63. *Encyclopédie; ou Dictionnaire raisonné des sciences, des arts et des métiers.* . . . *Nouvelle impression en facsimile de la première édition de 1751–1780,* 35 vols. (Stuttgart, 1966–1967), X, 479–482.

64. John Lough, *Essays on the "Encyclopédie" of Diderot and D'Alembert* (London: Oxford University Press, 1968), pp. 147–152.

65. George Lyttelton, first Baron Lyttelton, *Dialogues of the Dead* (London, 1760), p. 61.

66. John Harris, *Navigantium atque itinerantium bibliotheca. Or, A Complete Collection of Voyages and Travels,* ed. John Campbell, 2 vols. (London, 1744–1748). John Campbell, *The Spanish Empire in America* (London, 1747). Edmund Burke, *An Account of the European Settlements in America,* 2 vols. (London, 1759).

67. Harris, *Navigantium atque itinerantium bibliotheca,* II, 113, 134.

Chapter Nine: The Eyes of Reason: II

1. Antonello Gerbi's *Disputa del Nuovo Mondo: Storia di una polemica, 1750–1900* (Milan, 1955) surveys in elaborate detail the debate provoked by De Pauw's anti-American doctrine. For an excellent summary of De Pauw's views, see Durand Echeverría, *Mirage in the West* (Princeton, N.J.: Princeton University Press, 1957), pp. 9–13. Echeverría suggests that De Pauw was influenced by a stay in the court of Frederick the Great, who strongly opposed emigration to the New World from his own realm, "to the extent of establishing a special agency at Hamburg to stop emigrants preparing to sail for America."

2. Cornelius de Pauw, *Recherches philosophiques sur les Américains.* . . . *Nouvelle édition augmentée d'une dissertation critique par Dom Pernetty, et de la défense de l'auteur des recherches contre cette dissertation,* 3 vols. (Berlin, 1774), I, 139–141.

3. *Ibid.,* II, 165–176.

4. Georges-Louis Leclerc, Comte de Buffon, *Histoire naturelle générale et particulière,* 43 vols. (Deux-Ponts, 1785–1787), XI, 239–240.

5. Hans Wolpe, *Raynal et sa machine de guerre: L'Histoire des Deux Indes et ses perfectionnements* (Stanford, Calif.: Stanford University Press, 1957).

6. Abbé Guillaume Raynal, *A Philosophical and Political History of the Settlements and Trade of the Europeans in the East and West Indies,* 3 vols. (London, 1776), II, 179–181. I have compared this translation of the 1774 edition with the text of the first edition (6 vols., Amsterdam, 1770).

7. Raynal, *A Philosophical and Political History,* II, 182, 194–195.

8. *Ibid.,* pp. 178, 174, 196.

9. *Ibid.,* pp. 169–170.

10. Antoine Hornot, *Anecdotes américaines, ou histoire abrégée des principaux événements arrivés dans le Nouveau Monde, depuis sa découverte jusqu'à l'époque présente* (Paris, 1776), pp. 128–135.

11. Louis Genty, *L'Influence de la découverte de l'Amérique sur le bonheur du genre-humain* (Paris, 1788), pp. 8–20.

12. Raynal, *A Philosophical and Political History,* II, 260–261.

13. For a detailed survey of the French writings on America in this period, see Silvio Zavala, *América en el espíritu francés del siglo XVIII* (Mexico, 1949).

On pages 51–56 of his book, Zavala summarizes the content of a book that I have not been able to consult: *Dissertation sur les suites de la découverte de l'Amérique, qui a obtenu en 1785 une mention honorable de l'Académie des Sciences, Arts, et Belles-Lettres de Lyon. Revue et corrigée pour le concours de l'année 1787.* . . . *Par un Citoyen, ancien Syndic de la Chambre du Commerce de Lyon.* 1787. Zavala's summary indicates that the author paid considerable attention to ancient Mexico. He had the customary high praise for Tlaxcala, whose struggle with the Aztecs he compared with that of Sparta against the Persians; but he was harshly critical of the despotic Moctezuma, who deferred in all things to a priesthood serving gods more cruel than those of Carthage. The author partially admitted the splendor of the Aztec Empire, but found it difficult to believe that there were one hundred thousand stores in a city whose private houses had no doors or windows, the majority containing no other furniture than a few mats and pots. Like Raynal, the author stressed that the majority of the population lived in extreme poverty. The sciences, arts, and industry were in a rudimentary stage of development. The navigation of the Aztecs was limited to the Lake of Mexico. They lacked iron and domestic animals. In many respects their culture was lower than that of the Greeks who destroyed Troy. It ranked far below that of the Chaldeans, Egyptians, and Phoenicians of the same era. The author paid the conventional tribute to the Incas, who, unlike the Aztecs, waged war to bring men from savagery to civilization.

14. Antonello Gerbi, *La disputa del Nuevo Mundo: Historia de una polémica, 1750–1900* (Mexico, 1960), pp. 97–100.

15. Gian Ricardo Carli, *Lettres américaines*, trans. Lefebvre de Villebrune, 2 vols. (Paris, 1788), I, 54–56.

16. *Ibid.*, pp. 167–181.

17. *Ibid.*, pp. 257–258, 283.

18. *Ibid.*, p. 345.

19. *Ibid.*, pp. 355–357.

20. *Ibid.*, pp. 363–400.

21. Francisco Javier Clavigero, *Storia antica del Messico*, 4 vols. (Cesena, 1780–1781), IV, 4.

22. For a good summary of the views on the Indian of the Scottish school of writers on society, see Roy Harvey Pearce, *The Savages of America* (Baltimore: The Johns Hopkins Press, 1953), pp. 82–91. For the larger aspects of the Scottish inquiry, see Gladys Bryson, *Man and Society: The Scottish Inquiry of the Eighteenth Century* (Princeton, N.J.: Princeton University Press, 1945).

23. Adam Ferguson, *An Essay on the History of Civil Society* [1767], 4th ed. (London, 1773), p. 194.

24. Adam Smith, *An Inquiry into the Nature and Causes of the Wealth of Nations*, ed. J. R. McCulloch (Edinburgh, 1863), pp. 93, 254–255.

25. Henry Home, Lord Kames, *Sketches of the History of Man*, 2d ed., 4 vols. (Edinburgh, 1778), III, 148, 157–181.

26. E. Adamson Hoebel, "William Robertson: An Eighteenth Century Anthropologist-Historian," *American Anthropologist*, LXII (August, 1960), 654.

27. William Robertson, *The History of America*, 2 vols. (London, 1777), I, 281–283.

28. *Ibid.*, p. 269.

29. *Ibid.*, pp. 270–271.

30. *Ibid.*, p. 272.

31. *Ibid.*, pp. 274–303.

32. Hoebel, "William Robertson," p. 655.

33. Juan Nuix, *Reflexiones imparciales sobre la humanidad de los españoles en las Indias* (Madrid, 1782), pp. 123–128.

34. José Cadalso, *Cartas marruecas* (Madrid, 1935), pp. 38–39, 42, 10.

35. Juan Pablo Forner. *Exequias de la lengua castellana* (Madrid, 1956), pp. 156–163.

36. Joseph Joaquín Granados y Gálvez, *Tardes americanas* (Mexico, 1778), p. 50.

37. *Ibid.*, pp. 73–75.

38. *Ibid.*, pp. 77–87.

39. Ángel María Garibay K., *Historia de la literatura náhuatl*, 2 vols. (Mexico, 1953–1954), I, 248.

40. Granados, *Tardes americanas*, pp. 191–196.

41. *Ibid.*, pp. 278–381.

42. *Ibid.*, p. 377.

43. On the Jesuit contributions to the Mexican Enlightenment, see Bernabé Navarro B., *La introducción de la filosofía moderna en México* (Mexico, 1948); and Bernabé Navarro B., *Cultura mexicana moderna en el siglo XVIII* (Mexico, 1964). In a personal communication (November 29, 1969), Professor Charles E. Ronan, S.J., cautions that the cultivation of the new sciences by the Jesuits "was just a significant but modest beginning." He cites the fact that "no Jesuit was allowed under pain of obedience, to teach the heliocentric system because of its apparent contradiction of Scripture." He believes that expansion of the modernist thrust was "only a matter of time, but the expulsion cut the movement short."

44. Francisco Javier Clavigero, *Historia antigua de México*, ed. Mariano Cuevas (Mexico, 1964), pp. 45–47.

45. *Ibid.*, pp. 50–51, 152–153, 446–447.

46. *Ibid.*, pp. 66, 190, 138–140.

47. *Ibid.*, pp. 417–418.

48. *Ibid.*, pp. 147, 573, 575, 578.

49. *Ibid.*, pp. 548–555.

50. *Ibid.*, pp. 229–230, 525–530, 537–542.

51. *Ibid.*, pp. 530–537, 544–548.

52. *Ibid.*, p. 47.

53. Charles E. Ronan, S.J., "Clavigero: The Fate of a Manuscript," *The Americas*, XXVII (October, 1970), 113–136.

54. William H. Prescott, *History of the Conquest of Mexico*, 2 vols. (New York, n.d.), p. 60.

55. John L. Phelan, "Neo-Aztecism in the Eighteenth Century and the Genesis of Mexican Nationalism," in Stanley Diamond, ed., *Culture in History: Essays in Honor of Paul Radin* (New York: Columbia University Press, 1960), pp. 760–770.

56. Pedro José Márquez, *Due antichi monumenti di architectura messicana* (Rome, 1804), pp. 3–4.

57. On the contributions of Alzate to the Enlightenment in eighteenth-century Mexico, see Navarro, *Cultura mexicana moderna en el siglo XVIII*,

pp. 167–185. For a general discussion of the scientific reform, see Eli de Gortari, *La sciencia en la historia de México* (Mexico, 1963), pp. 231–265.

58. José Antonio Alzate y Ramírez, *Descripción de las antigüedades de Xochicalco, dedicada a los señores de la actual expedición al rededor del orbe* (Mexico, 1791), pp. 1–23.

59. E.-T. Hamy, in his introduction to J.-M.-A. Aubin, *Mémoires sur la peinture didactique et l'écriture figurative des anciens Mexicains* (Paris, 1885), p. v.

60. Ignacio Bernal, "Humboldt y la arqueología mexicana," in *Ensayos sobre Humboldt* (Mexico, 1962), p. 123.

61. Antonio de León y Gama, *Descripción histórica y cronológica de las dos piedras . . .* , ed. Carlos María de Bustamante, 2d ed. (Mexico, 1832), Part ii, p. 210. Antonio de León y Gama, *Descripción histórica y cronológica de las dos piedras que se hallaron en la Plaza Principal de México* (Mexico, 1792), p. 116.

62. Luis Villoro, *Los grandes momentos del indigenismo en México* (Mexico, 1950), p. 132. Edmundo O'Gorman, ed., *Fray Servando Teresa de Mier: Selección* (Mexico, 1945), p. xv. Mier's definitive version of these events appears in an appendix to his *Historia de la revolución de Nueva España* [1813], 2 vols. (Mexico, 1922), ii, i–xliv.

63. On the image of the Indian in Spanish literature of this period, see Anthony Tudisco, "América en la literatura española del siglo XVIII," *Anuario de Estudios Americanos*, xi (1954), 565–585; and "The Land, People, and Problems of America in Eighteenth-Century Spanish Literature," *The Americas*, xii (April, 1956), 363–384.

64. A group of Aztec characters figures prominently in the large cast and intricate plot of *Les Incas*. They include the "sad remains of Moctezuma's family," headed by the brave and handsome Orizombo, who seek refuge in the Inca Empire after the conquest of Mexico. Orizombo relates to the horrified Inca ruler Huascar the story of Spanish treachery and cruelty. Orizombo has mixed feelings about his royal kinsman. "Moctezuma had virtues, he was sincere, generous, loyal. But all too often prosperity begets pride and indolence. Having forgotten that he was a man, Moctezuma forgot that he was king. His haughtiness and severity alienated his friends; his weakness and imprudence delivered him into the hands of a perfidious enemy and caused all his misfortunes." Orizombo and another Aztec character, his dear friend Telasco, are Nature's gentlemen, exemplary in deed and thought. Rebuked by the humanitarian Spaniard Molina because he rejoiced at the sight of a Spanish ship going down, Orizombo blushes for shame and says: "Pardon me, but I have suffered so much! I have seen my country suffer so much!" J.-F. Marmontel, *Les Incas, ou la destruction de l'Empire du Pérou*, 2 vols. (Paris, 1777), i, 70, 321.

65. Joel Barlow, *The Vision of Columbus* (Hartford, Conn., 1787), p. 77.

66. *Ibid.*, pp. 59–60, 62.

67. V. L. Parrington, *Main Currents in American Thought*, 3 vols. (New York, 1930), i, 384.

Chapter Ten: The Aztecs Transfigured: I

1. The historical essence of this age the Argentine statesman and writer Domingo F. Sarmiento brilliantly captured in his definition of romanticism as "that solemn and energetic protest against the categories in which the old social order had encased all creation." *Sarmiento en el destierro,* ed. Armando Donoso (Buenos Aires, 1927), p. 128.

2. William H. Prescott, *History of the Conquest of Mexico,* ed. J. F. Kirk, 3 vols. (Philadelphia, 1873), I, 52.

3. Antonio del Río, *Description of the Ruins of an Ancient City Discovered near Palenque, in the Kingdom of Guatemala, in Spanish America,* . . . trans. from the original ms. report of Captain Antonio del Río (London, 1822).

4. J.-H. Baradère, ed., *Antiquités mexicaines: Relation des trois expéditions du Capitaine Dupaix, ordonnées en 1805, 1806, et 1807, pour la recherche des antiquités du pays, notamment celles de Mitla et de Palenque* . . . , 2 vols. and atlas (Paris, 1834), I, 25.

5. *Ibid.*

6. *Ibid.,* p. 29.

7. *Ibid.,* pp. 32–33.

8. Benito María de Moxó, *Cartas mejicanas* (Genoa, 1837), p. 85.

9. *Ibid.,* pp. 214–215.

10. *Ibid.,* p. 72.

11. *Ibid.,* pp. 74–75.

12. *Ibid.,* p. 225.

13. For another assessment of Moxó's position on the Indians, see Antonello Gerbi, *La disputa del Nuevo Mundo* (Mexico, 1960), pp. 271–275.

14. Museo Nacional de Arqueología, Historia, y Etnografía, *Morelos: Documentos inéditos y poco conocidos,* 3 vols. (Mexico, 1927), II, 177.

15. See the discussion of its meaning in Prescott, *Conquest of Mexico,* I, 11n. Anáhuac has usually been taken to refer to the Valley of Mexico or to the whole central Mexican region between the Atlantic and Pacific Oceans. The German scholar Eduard Seler, however, believed that in Aztec times the name always referred to the rich coastal regions on the Gulf and the Pacific, for which Aztec trading expeditions departed. Eduard Seler, *Gesammelte Abhandlungen zur amerikanischen Sprach- und Alterthumskunde,* 5 vols. (Berlin, 1902–1923), II, 49.

16. Servando Teresa de Mier, *Historia de la revolución de Nueva España, antiguamente Anáhuac,* 2 vols. (Mexico, 1922), II, 287–290.

17. For a bibliography of Bustamante's publications, see Víctor Rico González, *Hacia un concepto de la conquista de México* (Mexico, 1953), pp. 41–53.

18. Carlos María Bustamante, *Mañanas de la alameda de México,* 2 vols. (Mexico, 1835), I, 108, 199.

19. Carlos María Bustamante, *Galería de antiguos príncipes mexicanos* (Puebla, 1821), pp. 11–12, 20.

20. Rico González, *Hacia un concepto de la conquista de México*, p. 38.

21. Bustamante is cited *ibid.*, pp. 32–33.

22. Carlos María Bustamante, ed., *Historia de las conquistas de Hernando Cortés, escrita en español por Francisco López de Gómara, traducida al mexicano y aprobada por verdadera por D. Juan Bautista de San Antón Muñón de Chimalpain*, 2 vols. (Mexico, 1826), II, 178.

23. For an acerbic survey of Bustamante as a historian, see Rico González, *Hacia un concepto de la conquista de México*, pp. 13–40. The only biography known to me is the unsatisfactory life by V. Salado Álvarez, *La vida azarosa y romántica de don Carlos María de Bustamante* (Madrid, 1933).

24. Bustamante, *Mañanas de la alameda*, I, 112, 195.

25. Wigberto Jiménez Moreno, *Fray Bernardino de Sahagún y su obra* (Mexico, 1938), p. 43.

26. Antonio de León y Gama, *Descripción histórica y cronológica de las dos piedras . . .* , ed. Carlos María de Bustamante, 2d ed. (Mexico, 1832), Part II, p. 89n.

27. Bustamante, *Mañanas de la alameda*, II, ii–lv; I, 19.

28. Ramón Mena, *La ciencia arqueológica en México desde la proclamación de la independencia hasta nuestros días . . .* (Mexico, 1911), p. 5.

29. On Waldeck's early career, see Howard F. Cline, "The Apocryphal Early Career of J. F. Waldeck, Pioneer Americanist," *Acta Americana*, V (October–December, 1947), 278–300.

30. There is a facsimile edition, with a foreword by Luis Castillo Ledón, *Colección de las antigüedades mexicanas que existían en el Museo Nacional y dieron a luz el Pbro. y Dr. Don Isidro Ignacio de Icaza y el Br. D. Isidro Rafael Gondra en 1827. Litografiadas por Federico Waldeck e impresas por Pedro Robert* (Mexico, 1927).

31. On Mora, see Charles A. Hale, *Mexican Liberalism in the Age of Mora, 1821–1853* (New Haven: Yale University Press, 1968).

32. José María Luis Mora, *Méjico y sus revoluciones*, 3 vols. (Paris, 1836), I, 65–66.

33. *Ibid.*, III, xi–xii.

34. *Ibid.*, p. viii.

35. Lorenzo de Zavala, *Ensayo histórico de las revoluciones de Mégico*, 2 vols. (Paris, 1831–1832), I, 2, 10. For an excellent survey of Zavala's ideas, see María de la Luz Parcero, *Lorenzo de Zavala: Fuente y origen de la reforma liberal en México* (Mexico, 1969).

36. Zavala, *Ensayo histórico*, I, 13.

37. See, however, Moisés González Navarro, *El pensamiento político de Lucas Alamán* (Mexico, 1952), a survey which serves to correct the traditional oversimplified picture of this conservative leader.

38. *Ibid.*, p. 90.

39. Lucas Alamán, *Disertaciones sobre la historia de la República Mejicana*, 3 vols. (Havana, 1873), I, 102–105.

40. Rico González has an unfriendly, hypercritical survey of Ramírez' historical work in *Hacia un concepto de la conquista de México*, pp. 139–152, with a useful bibliography.

41. Cited in Jaime Delgado, "Hernán Cortés en la poesía española de los siglos XVIII y XIX," *Revista de Indias*, IX (1948), 395–396.

42. Bustamante, *Mañanas de la alameda*, I, 19–20; II, 11.

43. Giacomo C. Beltrami, *Le Mexique*, 2 vols. (Paris, 1830), II, 87; I, 227–228.

44. Gerbi, *La disputa del Nuevo Mundo*, p. 258. For Herder's historical ideas, see F. M. Barnard, *Herder's Social and Political Thought* (London: Oxford University Press, 1965).

45. Johann Gottfried v. Herder, *Outlines of a Philosophy of the History of Man* [1784] (New York, 1966), pp. 155–161.

46. Juan A. Ortega y Medina in his introduction to Humboldt's *Ensayo político sobre el reino de la Nueva España* (Mexico, 1966), p. x.

47. Alexander de Humboldt, *Researches Concerning the Institutions and Monuments of the Ancient Inhabitants of America* . . . , trans. Helen Maria Williams, 2 vols. (London, 1814), I, 409.

48. *Ibid.*, pp. 4–6.

49. *Ibid.*, pp. 31.

50. *Ibid.*, pp. 31–32.

51. Humboldt, *Ensayo político*, p. 67.

52. Humboldt, *Researches*, I, 185.

53. *Ibid.*, pp. 35–36, 157.

54. *Ibid.*, 38.

55. *Ibid.*, pp. 166–167.

56. Ignacio Bernal, "Humboldt y la arqueología mexicana," in *Ensayos sobre Humboldt* (Mexico, 1962), pp. 131–132. Paul Kirchhoff, "La aportación de Humboldt al estudio de las antiguas civilizaciones americanas: Un modelo y un programa," in *Ensayos sobre Humboldt*, pp. 89–103. Miguel León-Portilla, "Humboldt, investigador de los códices y la cosmología náhuatl," in *Ensayos sobre Humboldt*, p. 147. Justino Fernández, in his prologue to Carlos Nebel, *Viaje pintoresco y arqueológico sobre la parte mas interesante de la República Mexicana en los años transcurridos desde 1829 hasta 1834* (Mexico, 1963), p. vii. Karl Nebel's book was one of the richly illustrated travel accounts that greatly increaseed Europe's interest in and knowledge of ancient Mexico in the romantic era. Justino Fernández has high praise for Nebel's drawings, whose subjects included the pyramid of Tajín, the ruins of Xochicalco, and the three great Aztec monoliths, the Stone of Tizoc, the Calendar Stone, and the Coatlicue. Fernández also praises Nebel's intelligent commentary on ancient Mexican architecture and sculpture. The work contained a letter by Nebel's countryman, Humboldt, in which he restated the views contained in the *Vues des cordillères* on the subject of ancient American art.

57. Humboldt, *Researches*, I, 200.

58. *Ibid.*, 47, 101.

59. *Ibid.*, p. 158. Marvin Harris, *The Rise of Anthropological Theory* (New York, 1968), p. 137.

60. Kirchhoff, "La aportación de Humboldt," in *Ensayos sobre Humboldt*, p. 103. Bernal, "Humboldt y la arqueología mexicana," in *Ensayos sobre*

Humboldt, p. 132. León-Portilla, "Humboldt, investigador de los códices," in *Ensayos sobre Humboldt*, p. 148.

Chapter Eleven: The Aztecs Transfigured: II

1. Charles-Etienne Brasseur de Bourbourg, *Esquisses d'histoire d'archaeologie, d'ethnographie, et de linguistique pouvant servir d'instructions générales* (Paris, 1864), p. 90. E.-T. Hamy, in his introduction to J.-M.-A. Aubin, *Mémoires sur la peinture didactique et l'écriture figurative des anciens Mexicains* . . . (Paris, 1885), p. vi.

2. J.-H. Baradère, ed., *Antiquités mexicaines: Relation des trois expéditions du Capitaine Dupaix, ordonnées en 1805, 1806, et 1807, pour la recherche des antiquités du pays, notamment celles de Mitla et de Palenque* . . . , 2 vols. and atlas (Paris, 1834), I, xi, 86–87.

3. On Baradère, see the sketch by Roman d'Amat in the *Dictionnaire de Biographie Française*, v (1951), pp. 159–160. Howard F. Cline, "The Apocryphal Early Career of J. F. Waldeck, Pioneer Americanist," *Acta Americana*, v (October–December, 1947), 279.

4. Aubin, *Mémoires*, pp. 5–6.

5. Auguste Génin, *Les Français au Mexique du XVIe siècle à nos jours* (Paris, 1933), p. 293. Alfredo Chavero tells the story of Aubin's search in "Boturini," *Anales del Museo Nacional* (Mexico), Época 1ª, III (1886), 243.

6. Génin, *Les Français au Mexique*, p. 243. Aubin, *Mémoires*, p. 8.

7. Charles-Etienne Brasseur de Bourbourg, *Histoire des nations civilisées du Mexique et de l'Amérique centrale durant les siècles antérieurs à Christophe Colomb*, 4 vols. (Paris, 1857–1859), I, xxxix.

8. Adrien de Longpérier, *Notice des monuments exposés dans la Salle des Antiquités au Musée du Louvre* (Paris, 1851), pp. 6–10.

9. Brasseur, *Histoire*, I, iii.

10. Charles-Etienne Brasseur de Bourbourg, *Quatre Lettres sur le Mexique* (Paris, 1868), p. 14.

11. Brasseur, *Histoire*, I, 33.

12. *Ibid.*, p. 47.

13. *Ibid.*, p. 254.

14. *Ibid.*, p. 253.

15. *Ibid.*, III, 297n.

16. *Ibid.*, p. 676.

17. *Ibid.*, p. 678.

18. Bancroft is cited in Robert Wauchope, *Lost Tribes and Sunken Continents* (Chicago: University of Chicago Press, 1962), pp. 48–49. For an excellent brief account of Brasseur's life and work, see Leo Deuel, *Testament of Time* (New York, 1965), pp. 511–541.

19. The review is cited in L. Kellner, *Alexander von Humboldt* (London, 1963), p. 99.

20. John R. McCulloch, *Treatises and Essays on Subjects Connected with Economical Policy* [1853] (New York, 1967), pp. 334–336.

21. Hoxie N. Fairchild, *The Noble Savage: A Study in Romantic Natural-ism* (New York: Columbia University Press, 1928), p. 171. William Godwin, *On Population: An Enquiry Concerning the Power of Increase of Mankind* [1820] (New York, 1964), pp. 60–61.

22. William Bullock, *Six Months' Residence and Travels in Mexico* (London, 1824), p. 334.

23. William Bullock, *A Description of the Unique Exhibition, Called Ancient Mexico: Collected on the Spot in 1823, by the Assistance of the Mexican Government, and Now Open for Public Inspection at the Egyptian Hall, Piccadilly* (London, n.d.), p. 3.

24. Deuel, *Testament of Time*, p. 507.

25. William H. Prescott, *History of the Conquest of Mexico*, ed. J. F. Kirk, 3 vols. (Philadelphia, 1873), I, 132.

26. Thomas F. Gordon, *History of Ancient Mexico*, 2 vols. (Philadelphia, 1832), I, 70–78, 81, 176, 345; II, 9.

27. Lewis Cass, *North American Review*, LI (October, 1840), 396–433. Cass had earlier attacked James Fenimore Cooper for idealizing the Indian in his novels. R. H. Pearce, *The Savages of America* (Baltimore: The Johns Hopkins Press, 1953), pp. 210–211.

28. Albert Gallatin, "Notes on the Semi-Civilized Nations of Mexico, Yucatan, and Central America," in *Transactions of the American Ethno-logical Society*, I (New York, 1845), 211.

29. *Ibid.*, pp. 89, 211, 35.

30. *Ibid.*, p. 211.

31. *Ibid.*, pp. 213–214.

32. David Levin, *History as Romantic Art* (Stanford, Calif.: Stanford University Press, 1959), p. 164.

33. Henri Ternaux-Compans, ed., *Voyages, relations et mémoires origi-naux pour servir à l'histoire de la découverte de l'Amérique*, 20 vols. (Paris, 1837–1841).

34. Prescott, *Conquest of Mexico*, I, 40.

35. *Ibid.*, p. 50.

36. *Ibid.*, p. 87.

37. *Ibid.*, pp. 87–89.

38. *Ibid.*, pp. 93, 126.

39. *Ibid.*, pp. 159–160.

40. *Ibid.*, p. 168.

41. *Ibid.*, p. 205.

42. Levin, *History as Romantic Art*, pp. 154–159, 169.

43. Theodore Parker, "Prescott's Conquest of Mexico," in *The American Scholar* (Boston, 1907), pp. 248–249, 266.

44. José Fernando Ramírez, "Notas i esclarecimientos a la historia de la conquista de México del Señor W. Prescott," in José Fernando Ramírez, *Obras*, 3 vols. (Mexico, 1898), I, 303–312, 440–449.

45. Guillermo H. Prescott, *Historia de la conquista de Méjico*, anotada por D. Lucas Alamán [1844], 2 vols. (Buenos Aires, 1944), I, 28n. The notes

of Ramírez and Alamán have been made available in the most recent and best Spanish edition of Prescott's work, *Historia de la conquista de México*, anotada por Don Lucas Alamán con notas críticas y esclarecimientos de Don José Fernando Ramírez y prólogo, notas y apéndices por Juan A. Ortega y Medina (Mexico, 1970).

46. The most recent biography of Prescott—the first in more than sixty years—is C. Harvey Gardiner, *William Hickling Prescott: A Biography* (Austin: University of Texas Press, 1969), based on a mass of published and manuscript materials, but lacking in critical spirit.

47. On this genre, see Daniel Wogan, "Cuatro aspectos de la poesía in-digenista," *Historia Mexicana*, II (April–June, 1953), 587–596.

48. *Ibid.*, p. 590.

49. José María Heredia, *Poesías completas*, 2 vols. (Havana, 1940–1941), II, 150–153.

50. *Ibid.*, pp. 49–53.

51. *Ibid.*, pp. 80–83.

52. Antonio Castro Leal, ed., *Las cien mejores poesías líricas mexicanas* (Mexico, 1967), pp. 110–126.

53. Heinrich Heine, *Works*, trans. Charles Godfrey Leland, 12 vols. (London, 1905), XI, 162–184.

54. Robert Southey, *Madoc* (London, 1805), p. 449.

55. *Ibid.*, p. 61.

56. Gertrudis Gómez de Avellaneda, *Cuauhtemoc, the Last Aztec Emperor*, trans. Mrs. Wilson W. Blake (Mexico, 1898), pp. 100, 237.

57. Cited in Curtis Dahl, *Robert Montgomery Bird* (New York, 1963), p. 74.

58. Robert Montgomery Bird, *Calavar; or The Knight of the Conquest, a Romance of Mexico*, 2 vols. (Philadelphia, 1834), I, xi–xvi.

59. *Ibid.*, p. 206.

60. Robert Montgomery Bird, *The Infidel; or The Fall of Mexico*, 2 vols. (Philadelphia, 1835), I, 14.

61. Dahl, *Robert Montgomery Bird*, p. 78.

62. Edward Maturin, *Montezuma; The Last of the Aztecs* (New York, 1845), pp. 8–9.

63. W. W. Fosdick, *Malmiztic the Toltec; and the Cavaliers of the Cross* (Cincinnati, 1851), p. vi.

64. *Ibid.*, p. xiii.

65. *Ibid.*, p. 354.

66. Justino Fernández, *Arte mexicano de sus orígenes a nuestros días*, 2d ed. (Mexico, 1961), p. 118.

67. For the links between the French romantic engravings featuring Cortés, Spontini's opera *Fernand Cortez*, and Marmontel's *Les Incas*, see the informative article by José Tudela, "Hernán Cortés en los grabados román-ticos franceses," *Revista de Indias*, IX (1948), 383–391.

Chapter Twelve: Montezuma's Dinner

1. On the racist views of four influential evolutionists, Darwin, Spencer, Morgan, and Tylor, see Marvin Harris, *The Rise of Anthropological Theory* (New York, 1968), pp. 118–141.

2. Robert A. Wilson, *A New History of the Conquest of Mexico* (New York, 1859), p. 78n.

3. Robert A. Wilson, *Mexico and Its Religion* (New York, 1855), pp. v, 99, 123–126, 186.

4. Adolph F. Bandelier, *The Romantic School of American Archaeology* (New York, 1885), p. 13. However, Bandelier does not make clear whether he is referring to Wilson's first book or the better-known *New History of the Conquest of Mexico*. Morgan himself partially endorsed the *New History*, declaring that the book, "notwithstanding its excesses, has running through it a vein of truth"; "The Seven Cities of Cibola," *North American Review*, cviii (April, 1869), 492n.

5. Lewis H. Morgan, "Laws of Descent of the Iroquois," American Association for the Advancement of Science, *Proceedings*, xi (1858), 132–148.

6. Wilson, *A New History*, p. 65.

7. *Ibid.*, pp. 97, 259, 332–333.

8. In Kirk's review of Wilson's *New History* in the *Atlantic Monthly*, iii (April, 1859), 518–525; (May, 1859), 633–645.

9. Morgan is cited in Carl Resek, *Lewis Henry Morgan, American Scholar* (Chicago: University of Chicago Press, 1960), p. 132.

10. Morgan, "Seven Cities of Cibola," pp. 457–498.

11. Brantz Mayer, *Observations on Mexican History and Archaeology, with a Special Notice of Zapotec Remains as Delineated in Mr. J. G. Sawkins's Drawings . . .* (Washington, 1856), pp. 12, 27n. Brantz had previously published two books containing considerable material on ancient Mexico, *Mexico as It Was and as It Is* (New York, 1844) and *Mexico, Aztec, Spanish, and Republican* (Hartford, Conn., 1853). This material was in large part based on observations made while he was attached to the United States legation in Mexico.

12. John D. Baldwin, *Ancient America* (New York, 1872), pp. 206–209.

13. John W. Draper, *History of the Intellectual Development of Europe*, rev. ed., 2 vols. (New York, 1896), ii, 392.

14. *Ibid.*, pp. 175–179.

15. *Ibid.*, p. 166.

16. On Bandelier, see the illuminating introduction by Leslie A. White, ed., *Pioneers in American Anthropology: The Bandelier-Morgan Letters, 1873–1883*, 2 vols. (Albuquerque: University of New Mexico Press, 1940). There is an unpublished biography by Edgar F. Goad, "A Study of the Life of Adolph Francis Alphonse Bandelier with an Appraisal of His Contribution to American Anthropology and Related Sciences" (Ph.D. dissertation, University of Southern California, Los Angeles, 1939).

17. White, ed., *Bandelier-Morgan Letters*, i, 113.

18. *Ibid.*, pp. 159–163.

19. *Ibid.*, pp. 174, 265–267; ii, 24.

20. *Ibid.*, p. 6.

21. On Bancroft, see John Walton Caughey, *Hubert Howe Bancroft, Historian of the West* (Berkeley: University of California Press, 1946).

22. Hubert H. Bancroft, *The Native Races of the Pacific Coast*, 5 vols. (San Francisco, 1875–1876), ii, 804–805.

23. Lewis H. Morgan, "Ethnical Periods," American Association for the Advancement of Science, *Proceedings*, xxiv (1875), 266–274.

24. Bancroft, *Native Races*, ii, 1–4.

25. Morgan's letter to Putnam is cited in Bernhard J. Stern, *Lewis Henry Morgan, Social Evolutionist* (Chicago: University of Chicago Press, 1931), pp. 115–116.

26. Lewis H. Morgan, *Montezuma's Dinner* [1876] (New York, 1950), pp. 12–15, 28.

27. *Ibid.*, pp. 15–16.

28. *Ibid.*, pp. 16–19.

29. *Ibid.*, pp. 19–20, 55–56.

30. *Ibid.*, pp. 56–63.

31. Stern, *Morgan*, pp. 117–122.

32. On Morgan's uncritical use of this material, see Charles Gibson, "Lewis Henry Morgan and the 'Aztec Empire,'" *Southwestern Journal of Anthropology*, iii (Spring, 1947), 78–84.

33. Lewis H. Morgan, *Ancient Society*, ed. Leslie A. White [1877] (Cambridge, Mass.: Harvard University Press, 1964), pp. 164–187.

34. White, ed., *Bandelier-Morgan Letters*, ii, 35–36. Adolph F. Bandelier, "On the Art of War and Mode of Warfare of the Ancient Mexicans," *Reports of the Peabody Museum*, x (1877), 95–166; "On the Distribution and Tenure of Land, and Customs in Respect to Inheritance among the Ancient Mexicans," *Reports of the Peabody Museum*, xi (1878), 385–448. Adolph F. Bandelier, "On the Social Organization and Mode of Government of the Ancient Mexicans," *Reports of the Peabody Museum*, xii (1879), 557–699.

35. Bandelier, "On the Social Organization and Mode of Government of the Ancient Mexicans," p. 699.

36. Bandelier, "On the Art of War and Mode of Warfare of the Ancient Mexicans," pp. 114–115. For an analysis of Bandelier's scholarship, see the unpublished Ph.D. dissertation of Clarissa P. Fuller, "A Reexamination of Bandelier's Studies of Ancient Mexico" (University of New Mexico, Albuquerque, 1950). *The Nation's* comment is cited in White, ed., *Bandelier-Morgan Letters*, ii, 69.

37. Adolph F. Bandelier, *Report of an Archaeological Tour in Mexico in 1881* (Boston, 1884), pp. 22–26, 31–32.

38. *Ibid.*, p. 44. Leslie A. White and Ignacio Bernal, eds., *Correspondencia de Adolfo F. Bandelier* (Mexico, 1960), p. 247. White, ed., *Bandelier-Morgan Letters*, ii, 232.

39. Bandelier, *Report of an Archaeological Tour*, pp. 54, 59, 771–778.

40. Alfredo Chavero, *Historia antigua y de la conquista*, I (1886), 568, in Vicente Riva Palacio, ed., *México a través de los siglos*, 5 vols. (Barcelona, 1886–1889).

41. In his extreme anticommunism, as in his pro-Catholic, pro-Spanish views, Bandelier was drawing away from the positions of his deceased master. Morgan regarded the emergence of private property as a milestone in the march of human progress, but admired "the liberty, equality and fraternity of the ancient gentes" and looked to the revival of those conditions in a higher form (*Ancient Society*, p. 467). He was blind to the reality of the bitter class struggles in the United States of his time, yet sympathized with the French Communards of 1871 and "saw the Commune as a footstep to the future." Resek, *Morgan*, p. 123. Adolph F. Bandelier, "Kin and Clan," a lecture delivered before the Historical Society of New Mexico, April 28, 1882 (Santa Fe, N.M., 1882).

42. White and Bernal, eds., *Correspondencia de Bandelier*, pp. 258–259.

43. Daniel G. Brinton, *The American Race* (New York, 1891), p. 130. Fuller, "A Reexamination of Bandelier's Studies of Ancient Mexico," p. 58.

44. Zelia Nuttall, "Preliminary Note of an Analysis of the Mexican Codices and Graven Inscriptions," American Association for the Advancement of Science, *Proceedings*, XXXV (1886), 325–327.

45. John Fiske, *The Discovery of America*, 2 vols. (Boston, 1892), I, 101–103.

46. *Ibid.*, pp. 32–33, 126–128.

47. Justin Winsor, ed., *Narrative and Critical History of the United States*, 8 vols. (Boston, 1884–1889), I, 169, 173–175.

48. Thomas Wentworth Higginson, "The First Americans," *Harper's Monthly Magazine*, LXV (August, 1882), 342–355.

49. *The Nation*, XXXVI (January 25, 1883), 85–87.

50. Hubert H. Bancroft, *The Early American Chroniclers* (San Francisco, 1883).

51. Morgan, *Ancient Society*, p. 467.

52. Winsor, ed., *Narrative and Critical History*, I, ix.

53. Leslie A. White, "Evolutionary Stages, Progress, and the Evaluation of Cultures," *Southwestern Journal of Anthropology*, III (Summer, 1947), 169.

54. William H. Holmes, "Contributions of American Archeology to Human History," *Smithsonian Miscellaneous Collections*, XLVII (1904–1905), 412–420.

55. William H. Holmes, "On Some Spurious Mexican Antiquities and Their Relation to Ancient Art," Smithsonian Institution, *Annual Report, 1886* (Washington, 1889), pp. 319–334.

56. William H. Holmes, *Archaeological Studies among the Ancient Cities of Mexico. Part II, Monuments of Chiapas, Oaxaca, and the Valley of Mexico* (Chicago, 1897), pp. 218–221.

57. *Ibid.*, pp. 229, 280.

58. *Ibid.*, pp. 289–290.

59. *Ibid.*, pp. 302–304.

60. Stephen D. Peet, "Ancient Aztec Cities and Civilization," *American Antiquarian*, XXII (January–November, 1900), 312–320.

Chapter Thirteen: Farewell to Fantasy: From Orozco y Berra to Seler

1. For an interpretation of the Reforma as an effort to establish a democratic capitalism in Mexico, see Walter V. Scholes, *Mexican Politics During the Juárez Regime, 1855–1872*, 2d ed. (Columbia: University of Missouri Press, 1969).

2. *Boletín del Instituto Nacional de Geografía y Estadística de la República Mexicana*, I, 2 (1850), 10n.

3. Francisco Zarco, *Historia del congreso constituyente, 1856–1857* [1856–1857] (Mexico, 1956), pp. 469, 630.

4. José Fernando Ramírez, "Cuitláhuac," in José Fernando Ramírez, *Fray Toribio de Motolinía y otros estudios* (Mexico, 1957), p. 257. Ramírez was undoubtedly contrasting the Aztec resistance with the performance of Mexican troops in the late war. Compare the text of a letter he wrote April 2–3, 1847: "The ancient Mexicans had more faith in Huitzilopochtli than we have in Jesus Christ. In spite of their fear and anguish they defended themselves against the intrepid conquistadors in a manner that makes us ashamed of the war we are waging against a gang of adventurers. The priests of those ancient Mexicans bore arms and perished beneath the ruins of their temples." José Fernando Ramírez, *Mexico During the War with the United States* (Columbia: University of Missouri Press, 1950), p. 114.

5. "Apuntes sobre las pirámides de San Juan Teotihuacán," in Ramón Almaraz, *Memoria de los trabajos ejecutados por la Comisión Científica de Pachuca en el año de 1864* . . . (Mexico, 1865).

6. Francisco Pimentel, *Memoria sobre las causas que han originado la situación actual de la raza indígena de México y medios de remediarla* (Mexico, 1864), pp. 67–68.

7. *Ibid.*, pp. 74–75, 25, 221–234.

8. Manuel Orozco y Berra, "Dedicación del Templo Mayor de México," *Anales del Museo Nacional de México*, Época 1ª, I (1877), 60–74. Manuel Orozco y Berra, "Códice Mendocino: Ensayo de descifración geroglífica," *Anales del Museo Nacional de México*, Época 1ª, I (1877), 120–186.

9. Gumesindo Mendoza, "Cosmogonía azteca," *Anales del Museo Nacional de México*, Época 1ª, I (1877), 340–353.

10. Some Mexican intellectuals did concern themselves with the plight of the Indian, to be sure, and even offered proposals for reforms that should relieve that plight; but these projects usually were of a Platonic, inoffensive kind (more elementary schools, homestead laws, etc.), and rarely touched the root problem of *latifundismo*. See T. G. Powell, "Mexican Intellectuals and the Indian Question," *Hispanic American Historical Review*, XLVIII (February, 1968), 19–36.

11. Leopoldo Zea, *Apogeo y decadencia del positivismo en México* (Mexico, 1944), pp. 82–83.

12. Zelia Nuttall exposed some of Batres' shady dealings in an article, "The Island of Sacrifices," published in the *American Anthropologist*, XII (April–June, 1910), 257–295. For a diverting account of her difficulties with Batres, see Ross Parmentier, "Glimpses of a Friendship," in June Helm, ed., *Pioneers of American Anthropology* (Seattle: University of Washington Press, 1966), pp. 87–147. Hermann Beyer offered a severe criticism of Batres' reconstruction of Teotihuacán in his article on "Arquitectura y escultura" in Manuel Gamio, *La población del valle de Teotihuacán*, 3 vols. (Mexico, 1922), I, Part 1, pp. 99–174.

13. *Homenaje a Cristóbal Colón: Antigüedades mexicanas publicadas por la Junta Colombina de México en el cuarto centenario del descubrimiento de América* (Mexico, 1892), p. vii.

14. See Silvio Zavala, *Don Francisco del Paso y Troncoso: Su misión en Europa* (Mexico, 1939). And, for Paso's contribution to the ordering and publication of Sahagún materials, Wigberto Jiménez Moreno, *Fray Bernardino de Sahagún y su obra* (Mexico, 1938) (offprint from Sahagún, *Historia general de las cosas de Nueva España*, 5 vols. (Mexico, 1938). Eugène Goupil tells of the defeat of Peñafiel's efforts to purchase the Aubin collection from its owner in his introduction to Eugène Boban, *Documents pour servir à l'histoire du Mexique*, 2 vols. and atlas (Paris, 1891), I, 10–12. The work is an illustrated annotated catalogue of the manuscripts collected by Aubin.

15. There is much interesting detail on the history of the school, involving Franz Boas, Zelia Nuttall, and Manuel Gamio, among others, in Ross Parmentier, "Glimpses of a Friendship," in Helm, *Pioneers of American Anthropology*, pp. 87–147.

16. Manuel Orozco y Berra, *Historia antigua y de la conquista de México*, 4 vols. (Mexico, 1960), I, 13–14.

17. Miguel León-Portilla makes this claim in his biographical sketch of Orozco, in Orozco's *Historia*, I, xxxviii.

18. Orozco, *Historia*, I, 86–88.

19. *Ibid.*, pp. 161–168.

20. *Ibid.*, p. 111.

21. *Ibid.*, pp. 229–230.

22. *Ibid.*, p. 306.

23. *Ibid.*. p. 259.

24. *Ibid.*, IV, 577–582.

25. Víctor Rico González, *Hacia un concepto de la conquista de México* (Mexico, 1953), p. 209.

26. Alfredo Chavero, *Historia antigua y de la conquista* (Mexico, 1886), pp. iv–lx.

27. *Ibid.*, pp. 77–81.

28. *Ibid.*, p. 102.

29. *Ibid.*, p. 382.

30. *Ibid.*, p. 117.

31. *Ibid.*, p. 158.

32. *Ibid.*, p. 563.

33. *Ibid.*, pp. 577, 578–579.

34. *Ibid.*, p. 612.

35. *Ibid.*, p. 639.

36. *Ibid.*, p. 911.

37. Justo Sierra, *Evolución política del pueblo mexicano* [1900–1902] (Mexico, 1950), pp. 24–30, 37.

38. Felipe Teixidor, ed., *Cartas de Joaquín García Icazbalceta a José Fernando Ramírez et al.* (Mexico, 1937), p. 36n.

39. Joaquín García Icazbalceta, *Don Fray Juan de Zumárraga* [1881], 4 vols. (Mexico, 1947), i, 221–232.

40. Francisco G. Cosmes, *La dominación española y la patria mexicana* (Mexico, 1896), pp. 1–82 *passim.*

41. Martin Stabb, "Indigenism and Racism," *Journal of Inter-American Studies*, i (October, 1959), 420.

42. *Archives de la Commission Scientifique du Mexique, publiés sous les auspices du Ministère de l'Instruction Publique*, 3 vols. (Paris, 1865–1867), i, 1–8.

43. *Ibid.*, pp. 137–138. See also, for French anthropological initiatives in Mexico, Juan Comas, *Las primeras instrucciones para la investigación antropológica en México: 1862* (Mexico, 1962).

44. *Archives de la Commission Scientifique du Mexique*, iii, 104ff.

45. Désiré Charnay, *Cités et ruines américaines . . . avec un texte par m. Viollet-le-Duc* (Paris, 1863), pp. 10–103 *passim.*

46. Désiré Charnay, *The Ancient Cities of the New World* (New York, 1887), p. xi.

47. Hamy published, with commentaries, facsimile editions of the Codex Borbonicus and the Codex Telleriano Remensis (Paris, 1899). His scattered Americanist essays are brought together in E.-T. Hamy's *Décades Americanae: Mémoires d'archaeologie et d'ethnographie américaines* (Paris, n.d.). For a typical Charencey effort to establish the Asiatic origin of Mexican myths, see *Le Mythe de Votan: Etude sur les origines asiatiques de la civilisation américaine* (Alençon, 1871). Still more imaginative was M.-E. Beauvois, who argued that the Knights Templars, persecuted in Europe, crossed over to Mexico, where they introduced Christianity and founded a state that still survived in the fifteenth century: "Les Templiers de l'ancien Mexique et leur origine européenne," *Le Muséon* (Louvain), n.s., iii (September, 1902), 187–234.

48. Rémi Siméon, *Dictionnaire de la langue nahuatl* (Paris, 1885).

49. Introduction to *Histoire générale des choses de la Nouvelle-Espagne par le R. P. Fray Bernardino de Sahagún.* Traduite et annotée par D. Jourdanet . . . et par Rémi Siméon (Paris, 1880).

50. Lucien Biart, *The Aztecs: Their History, Manners, and Customs* (Chicago, 1887), pp. 103, 195.

51. Andrew Lang, *Myth, Ritual, and Religion*, 2 vols. (New York, 1899), ii, 61–63.

52. Edward B. Tylor, *Anahuac; or Mexico and the Mexicans* (London, 1861), pp. 142–147.

53. R. R. Marett, *Tylor* (New York, 1936), p. 41.

54. Tylor, *Anahuac*, p. 244.

55. Edward B. Tylor, *Researches into the Early History of Mankind* (London, 1865), pp. 339–340. Edward B. Tylor, "Backgammon among the Aztecs," *Popular Science Monthly*, xiv (February, 1879), 499.

56. Tylor, *Researches*, p. 206.

57. Henry T. Buckle, *Introduction to the History of Civilization in England* (London, n.d.), pp. 62–67.

58. Edward J. Payne, *History of the New World Called America*, 2 vols. (London, 1892–1899), ii, 24, 56–57, 270, 297–299, 373–377, 544–552, 603–604; i, xiii–xiv.

59. Wigberto Jiménez Moreno, "Seler y las lenguas indígenas de México," *El Antiguo México*, vii (December, 1949), 21.

60. Alfonso Caso, "Influencia de Seler a las ciencias antropológicas," *El Antiguo México*, vii (December, 1949), 19. H. B. Nicholson, "A Note on *Comentarios al Códice Borgia*," *Tlalocan*, v, 2 (1966), 132.

61. Franz Termer, "Eduard Seler," *El Antiguo México*, vii (December, 1949), 46.

62. Eduard Seler, "On the Origin of the Ancient Mexican Civilizations," *Collected Works of Eduard Seler*, ed. J. Eric S. Thompson and Francis B. Richardson, 5 vols. (Cambridge, Mass., 1939), ii, Parts 1–2, pp. 1–6. Eduard Seler, "On the Origin of the Central American Civilizations," *Collected Works of E.S.*, ii, Parts 1–2, p. 13.

63. Eduard Seler, "Excavations on the Site of the Principal Temple in Mexico," *Collected Works of E.S.*, ii, Part 3, p. 195n.; Seler, "On the Origin of the Central American Civilizations," *Collected Works of E.S.*, ii, Parts 1–2, p. 16.

64. Eduard Seler, "Ancient Mexican Attire and Insignia of Social and Military Rank," *Collected Works of E.S.*, ii, Part 3, pp. 85–87.

65. Walter Lehmann, *Methods and Results in Mexican Research*, trans. Seymour de Ricci (from the original article in *Archiv für Anthropologie*, vi [1907], 113–168) (Paris, 1909), pp. 2, 98n.

66. Eligio Ancona, *Los mártires del Anáhuac*, 2 vols. (Mexico, 1873), ii, 25.

67. Ireneo Paz, *Amor y suplicio*, 2 vols. (Mexico, 1873) ii, 318.

68. H. Rider Haggard, *Montezuma's Daughter* (London, 1893), pp. 116–117.

69. G. A. Henty, *By Right of Conquest; or, With Cortez in Mexico* (New York, [1891]), pp. 151, 140–143, 429.

70. José María Roa Bárcena, *Leyendas mexicanas* (Mexico, 1862), p. 22.

71. Rubén Darío, *Obras completas*, 5 vols. (Madrid, 1950–1953), v, 878–879, 963–964, 978–986.

Chapter Fourteen: The Return of Cuauhtémoc

1. G. W. F. Hegel, *Lectures on the Philosophy of History*, trans. J. Sibree (London, 1890), p. 85.

2. Oswald Spengler, *The Decline of the West*, trans. and ed. C. F. Atkinson, 2 vols. (New York, 1926–1928), II, 43–44.

3. Fernando Benítez, *Los indios de México* (Mexico, 1967), pp. 29–30.

4. *Ibid.*, p. 47.

5. Interview with Eulalia Guzmán, *El Día* (Mexico), September 13, 1969. For a convenient summary of the dispute over the Cuauhtémoc find, see Wigberto Jiménez Moreno, "Los hallazgos de Ixcateopan," *Historia Mexicana*, XII (1962–1963), 161–181.

6. On the beginnings of this movement, see Guillermo Bonfil Batalla, "Andrés Molina Enríquez y la Sociedad Indianista Mexicana: El indigenismo en vísperas de la Revolución," *Anales del Instituto Nacional de Antropología e Historia*, XVIII (1965), 217–232. On the general development and ideology of Mexican *indigenismo*, see Juan Comas, *Ensayos sobre indigenismo* (Mexico, 1953); and Juan Comas, *La antropología social aplicada en Mexico: Trayectoria y antología* (Mexico, 1964).

7. Manuel Gamio, *Forjando patria* (*pro nacionalismo*) (Mexico, 1916), p. 32.

8. Gamio was the founder and leader for many years of what may properly be called the "official" school of Mexican *indigenistas*. The methods and goals of this school have recently come in for severe criticism from younger Mexican anthropologists who, though they recognize its good intentions, criticize its Indianist policy of "acculturation" and "integration" as tending objectively to the loss of Indian ethnic identity, to the disappearance of the Indian and the rejection of his right to autonomy, all in the interests of a bourgeois society that wishes to exploit the Indian more effectively by drawing him fully into the orbit of capitalist market and production relations. See the stimulating essays in Arturo Warman and others, *De eso que llaman antropología mexicana* (Mexico, 1970).

9. Manuel Gamio and others, *La población del Valle de Teotihuacán*, 3 vols. (Mexico, 1922).

10. Manuel Gamio, *Síntesis de la obra "La población del Valle de Teotihuacán,"* in Secretaría de Agricultura y Fomento, *Opiniones y juicios críticos sobre la obra, "La población del Valle de Teotihuacán"* (Mexico, 1924), pp. 47–65.

11. Miguel Othón de Mendizábal, *Las artes aborígenes mexicanas* (Mexico, 1922), p. 21.

12. Miguel Othón de Mendizábal, *Ensayos sobre las civilizaciones aborígenes americanas* (Mexico, 1924), pp. 128, 145–157.

13. Miguel Othón de Mendizábal, "Los problemas indígenas y su mas urgente tratamiento," in Juan Comas, *La antropología social aplicada en México: Trayectoria y antología* (Mexico, 1964), p. 144.

14. Mendizábal, *Ensayos*, pp. 244, 341.

15. Luis Chávez Orozco, *Historia de México (Época precortesiana)* (Mexico, 1934), pp. 205–207.

16. Alfonso Caso, *The Aztecs, People of the Sun*, trans. Lowell Dunham (Norman: University of Oklahoma Press, 1958), pp. 72, 90, 93–94, 96–97.

17. Ignacio Bernal, *Mexico Before Cortés*, trans. Willis Barnstone (New York, 1963), pp. 94–97, 123.

18. Manuel M. Moreno, *La organización política y social de los aztecas* (Mexico, 1931), pp. 81–82.

19. Arturo Monzón, *El calpulli en la organización social de los Tenochca* (Mexico, 1949).

20. Paul Kirchhoff, "Land Tenure in Ancient Mexico: A Preliminary Sketch," *Revista Mexicana de Estudios Antropológicos*, xiv (1954–1955), 351–361.

21. Alfonso Caso, "Land Tenure among the Ancient Mexicans," *American Anthropologist*, lxv (August, 1963), 863–878. The article originally appeared as "La tenencia de tierra entre los antiguos mexicanos," *Memorias del Colegio Nacional, México* (December, 1959), 29–54.

22. Cited in Ernest Gruening, *Mexico and Its Heritage* (New York, 1928), p. 81.

23. Rubén M. Campos, *La producción literaria de los aztecas* (Mexico, 1936), pp. 61–62, 71–74.

24. Eulalia Guzmán, *Relaciones de Hernan Cortés a Carlos V sobre la invasión de Anáhuac: Aclaraciones y rectificaciones . . .* (Mexico, 1958), pp. xxi–cxvii, *passim*.

25. Ignacio Romerovargas Yturbide, *Organización política de los pueblos de Anáhuac* (Mexico, 1957), p. 389.

26. Ignacio Romerovargas Yturbide, *Motecuhzoma Xocoyotzin o Moctezuma el magnífico y la invasión de Anáhuac*, 3 vols. (Mexico, 1963–1964).

27. Laurette Séjourné, *Burning Water: Thought and Religion in Ancient Mexico* (New York, 1960), pp. 54–55. Laurette Séjourné, *El universo de Quetzalcóatl* (Mexico, 1962), p. 133.

28. William T. Sanders and Barbara J. Price, *Mesoamerica: The Evolution of a Civilization* (New York, 1968), pp. 166–167.

29. Séjourné, *Burning Water*, pp. 113, 117.

30. Miguel León-Portilla, *Los antiguos mexicanos* (Mexico, 1961), pp. 46–47.

31. Mariano Cuevas, *Historia de la nación mexicana* (Mexico, 1940), pp. 81–83. Mariano Cuevas, *Historia de la iglesia en México*, 4 vols. (Mexico, 1927), i, 68.

32. Vasconcelos is cited in Gruening, *Mexico and Its Heritage*, p. 81.

33. José Vasconcelos, *Breve historia de México*, 5th ed. (Mexico, 1944), pp. 164–171.

34. T. T. Waterman, *Bandelier's Contribution to the Study of Ancient Mexican Social Organization* (Berkeley: University of California Press, 1917), pp. 249–250, 255, 274–276.

35. Marshall H. Saville, *Tizoc, Great Lord of the Aztecs, 1481–1486* (New York, 1929), p. 8.

36. Herbert J. Spinden, *Ancient Civilizations of Mexico and Central America*, 3d rev. ed. (New York, 1928), pp. 209–210.

37. J. Eric Thompson, *Mexico Before Cortés* (New York, 1937), pp. 99–100.

38. Robert H. Lowie, *Primitive Society* (New York: Harper and Row, Harper Torchbooks, 1961), p. 219. Robert H. Lowie, *History of Ethnological Theory* (New York, 1937), p. 55.

39. Pablo Martínez del Río, *Por las ventanas de la prehistoria* (Mexico, 1939), pp. 74–75.

40. Edgar L. Hewett, *Ancient Life in Mexico and Central America* (New York, 1936), p. xx.

41. *Ibid.*, pp. 67–68, 87, 77.

42. George C. Vaillant, *The Aztecs of Mexico: Origin, Rise and Fall of the Aztec Nation* (Baltimore, Md.: Penguin Books, 1961), pp. 119–129.

43. *Ibid.*, pp. 155–157.

44. *Ibid.*, p. 268.

45. Paul Radin, *The Sources and Authenticity of the History of the Ancient Mexicans* (Berkeley: University of California Press, 1920), pp. 6–8, 147–150.

46. A. L. Kroeber, *Anthropology* (New York, 1923), pp. 359–360, 370. Kroeber omitted these comments on Aztec government and religion from the drastically revised 1948 edition of his text.

47. Leslie A. White, ed., *Pioneers in American Anthropology: The Bandelier-Morgan Letters, 1873–1883*, 2 vols. (Albuquerque: University of New Mexico Press, 1940), I, 27–46.

48. H. B. Nicholson, "The Efflorescence of Mesoamerican Civilization: A Résumé," in Betty Bell, ed., *Indian Mexico Past and Present* (Los Angeles, Calif., 1967), pp. 65–66. For a suggestive comparative study of ancient Mesopotamia and ancient Mexico, with special emphasis on the role of irrigation agriculture in the evolution of the two areas, see Robert M. Adams, *The Evolution of Urban Society: Early Mesopotamia and Prehistoric Mexico* (Chicago, 1966).

49. Michael D. Coe, *Mexico* (New York, 1962), p. 164.

50. R. C. Padden, *The Hummingbird and the Hawk* (Columbus: Ohio State University Press, 1967), pp. 26–29.

51. *Ibid.*, p. 99. In point of fact, Bernal Díaz wrote, "I heard say (*oía decir*) that he was wont to eat the flesh of young boys"; but he seemed to cast doubt on the story by listing some of the innumerable meat and fish dishes served up for Moctezuma's table. Bernal Díaz del Castillo, *Historia verdadera de la conquista de México*, ed. Joaquín Ramírez Cabañas, 5th ed., 2 vols. (Mexico, 1960), I, 271.

52. Padden, *The Hummingbird and the Hawk*, p. 237. Vaillant, *The Aztecs of Mexico*, p. 177.

53. Padden, *The Hummingbird and the Hawk*, p. 167.

54. William T. Sanders and Barbara J. Price, for example, assign a minimum of sixty thousand and a maximum of one hundred and twenty thousand inhabitants. *Mesoamerica*, p. 151.

55. Jacques Soustelle, *The Daily Life of the Aztecs on the Eve of the Spanish Conquest* (New York, 1962), pp. 6–9.

56. *Ibid.*, pp. 7, 33–34.

57. *Ibid.*, pp. 37–39, 45, 81.

58. *Ibid.*, pp. 86, 90.

59. *Ibid.*, pp. 93, 99, 117, 119.

60. *Ibid.*, p. 244.

61. For a bibliographic survey of the accomplishments of the German and other national schools in this field, see Ernst Mengin, "Los resultados principales y fines de la filología azteca," *Actas y Memorias del XXXV Congreso Internacional de Americanistas, México, 1962,* 3 vols. (Mexico, 1964), III, 451–478. Alfonso Caso, "Nombres caléndricos de los dioses," *El México Antiguo,* IX (1961), 77. Hermann Beyer's Aztec studies are contained in the volume *Mito y simbolismo del México antiguo* (Mexico, 1965) (Vol. x of *El México Antiguo*).

62. Walter Krickeberg, *Las antiguas culturas mexicanas* (Mexico, 1961), p. 67.

63. Alfred P. Maudslay, *Biologia Centrali-Americana, Archaeology,* text and 4 vols. of plates (London, 1889–1902).

64. Lewis Spence, *The Civilization of Ancient Mexico* (Cambridge: Cambridge University Press, 1912), pp. 7, 97.

65. *Ibid.*, pp. 96–108 *passim.*

66. *Ibid.*, pp. 84–90 *passim.*

67. H. B. Nicholson, in the *American Anthropologist,* LXX (August, 1968), 821–823.

68. Cottie A. Burland, *The Gods of Mexico* (New York, 1967), pp. 51–52, 56.

69. *Ibid.*, pp. 60–62, 127, 129, 162–163.

70. Irene Nicholson, *Mexican and Central American Mythology* (London, 1967), pp. 28, 82.

71. On the use of Morgan's developmental scheme by Marx and Engels, see Marvin Harris, *The Rise of Anthropological Theory* (New York, 1968), pp. 246–249. Frederick Engels, *The Origin of the Family, Private Property and the State in the Light of the Researches of Lewis H. Morgan* (New York, 1942), pp. 21–22.

72. B. I. Sharevskaya, "Narodi Ameriki do nachala evropeiskoi kolonizatsii," in Akademia Nauk SSSR, *Vsemirnaya istoria,* IV (1958), 70–72.

73. Friedrich Katz, *Situación social y económica de los aztecas durante los siglos XV y XVI* (Mexico, 1966), pp. 173–179.

Chapter Fifteen: The Plumed Serpent

1. Salvador Toscano, *Arte precolombino de México y de la América central* (Mexico, 1944), p. 284.

2. George Kubler, *The Art and Architecture of Ancient America* (Baltimore, Md.: Penguin Books, 1962), p. 14.

3. On the sources of modern artistic primitivism, see Robert Goldwater, *Primitivism in Modern Art,* rev. ed. (New York, 1967).

4. Herbert Read, *A Concise History of Modern Sculpture* (New York, 1964), p. 48.

5. John Russell, *Henry Moore* (New York, 1968), p. 12.

6. *Ibid.*, p. 14. Goldwater, *Primitivism*, pp. 244–246, 14, 248n.

7. William H. Prescott, *The Conquest of Mexico*, illus. Keith Henderson, introd. T. A. Joyce, 2 vols. (New York, 1922), I, v–vi.

8. *Ibid.*, p. xxxii.

9. Roger Fry, *Vision and Design* (New York, n.d.), pp. 71–72.

10. Jacques Soustelle, *Mexico* (New York, 1967), p. 66.

11. Raquel Tibol, *Historia general del arte mexicano: Época moderna y contemporánea*, in Pedro Rojas, ed., *Historia general del arte mexicano*, 3 vols. (Mexico, 1962–1964), III (1964), 104.

12. Manuel Gamio, *Forjando patria (pro nacionalismo)* (Mexico, 1916), pp. 72–79.

13. Jean Charlot, *The Mexican Mural Renaissance, 1920–1925* (New Haven: Yale University Press, 1963), pp. 9–10.

14. Siqueiros is cited in Anita Brenner, *Idols Behind Altars* (New York, 1929), p. 242.

15. Rivera is cited in Charlot, *Mexican Mural Renaissance*, p. 11.

16. Orozco is cited *ibid.* José Clemente Orozco, *An Autobiography* (Austin: University of Texas Press, 1962), p. 87. Charlot, *Mexican Mural Renaissance*, p. 12.

17. Manuel G. Revilla, *El arte en México*, 2d ed. (Mexico, 1923), p. 29.

18. José Juan Tablada, *Historia del arte en México* (Mexico, 1927).

19. Tablada is cited in Justino Fernández, *Coatlicue, estética del arte indígena antiguo* (Mexico, 1954), p. 85.

20. Eulalia Guzmán, "Carácteres fundamentales del arte indígena," *México prehispánico* (Mexico, 1946), pp. 545–551. Edmundo O'Gorman, "El arte o de la monstruosidad," *Tiempo* (Mexico), no. 3 (March, 1940). Fernández, *Coatlicue*, p. 101.

21. Toscano, *Arte precolombino*, p. 3.

22. *Ibid.*, p. 277.

23. Fernández, *Coatlicue*, p. 107.

24. Miguel Covarrubias, *Indian Art of Mexico and Central America* (New York, 1957), pp. 315–316.

25. I quote from the English translation: Paul Westheim, *The Art of Ancient Mexico*, trans. Ursula Barnard (New York, 1965).

26. *Ibid.*, pp. 50–60 *passim*, 224–241 *passim*.

27. George C. Vaillant, *Aztecs of Mexico: Origin, Rise, and Fall of the Aztec Nation* (Baltimore, Md.: Penguin Books, 1961), pp. 161–163.

28. George Kubler, "The Cycle of Life and Death in Metropolitan Aztec Sculpture," *Gazette des Beaux Arts*, Ser. 6, XXIII (May, 1943), 257–268. Kubler, *Art and Architecture of Ancient America*, pp. 56–60.

29. Fernández, *Coatlicue*, pp. 215–216, 221, 266–267.

30. Bertram Wolfe, *The Fabulous Life of Diego Rivera* (New York, 1963), p. 3.

31. *Ibid.*, pp. 147–149.

32. Tibol, *Historia general del arte mexicano: Época moderna y contemporánea*, in *Historia general del arte mexicano*, Rojas, ed., III, 147.

33. Charlot, *Mexican Mural Renaissance*, p. 154.

34. Wolfe, *Fabulous Life of Diego Rivera*, pp. 368–369. See the Weiditz portraits of Cortés in Howard F. Cline, "Hernando Cortés and the Aztec Indians in Spain," *Quarterly Journal of the Library of Congress*, xxvi (April, 1969), 70–90.

35. Charles Gibson, *The Aztecs under Spanish Rule* (Stanford, Calif.: Stanford University Press, 1964), p. 220.

36. Diego Rivera, *My Art, My Life* (New York, 1960), p. 168; L. C. Stanton, "Some Sources and Uses of Pre-Columbian Art in the Cuernavaca Frescoes of Diego Rivera," *Actas y Memorias del XXXV Congreso Internacional de Americanistas, México, 1962*, 3 vols. (Mexico, 1964), iii, 439–449.

37. Orozco is cited in Alma M. Reed, *The Mexican Muralists* (New York, 1960), p. 46.

38. Orozco, *Autobiography*, pp. 108–110.

39. Albert I. Dickerson, ed., *The Orozco Frescoes at Dartmouth* (Hanover, N.H.: Dartmouth College, 1934), n.p.

40. MacKinley Helm, *Modern Mexican Painters* (New York, 1941), p. 84.

41. Siqueiros is cited in Wolfe, *Fabulous Life of Diego Rivera*, p. 431.

42. Fernández is cited in *Pinacoteca de los genios: David Alfaro Siqueiros* (Buenos Aires, 1965), n.p.

43. Ángel María Garibay K., *Historia de la literatura náhuatl*, 2 vols. (Mexico, 1953–1954), ii, 10.

44. Miguel León-Portilla, *Trece poetas del mundo azteca* (Mexico, 1967), p. 12.

45. Pedro de Alba, "Cuauhtémoc, el joven abuelo," *América Indígena*, vi (April, 1946), 133–137.

46. Ramón López Velarde, "Suave Patria," in Carlos Monsiváis, ed., *La poesía mexicana del siglo XX* (Mexico: Empresas Editoriales, 1966), pp. 278–283.

47. Carlos Pellicer, "Oda a Cuauhtémoc," *Material poético, 1918–1961* (Mexico: Universidad Nacional Autónoma de México, Empresas Editoriales, 1962), pp. 94–97.

48. Carlos Pellicer, "Discursos por las flores," in Carlos Monsiváis, ed., *La poesía mexicana del siglo XX* (Mexico: Empresas Editoriales, 1966), p. 387.

49. Salvador Novo, "Ofrenda," *Antología, 1925–1965*, ed. Antonio Castro Leal (Mexico, Editorial Porrúa, 1966), pp. 69–70.

50. Salvador Novo, "Cuauhtémoc y Eulalia," *Diálogos* (Mexico: Novaro, 1970), pp. 148–149.

51. Alfonso Reyes, "Vision of Anáhuac," in *The Position of America and Other Essays* (New York, 1950), pp. 9–30.

52. Hector Pérez Martínez, *Cuauhtémoc (Vida y muerte de una cultura)*, 2d ed. (Buenos Aires, 1956), pp. 9, 11–23, 35–37, 67–72, 112–113.

53. Wigberto Jiménez Moreno, "Los hallazgos de Ichcateopan," *Historia Mexicana*, vii (October–December, 1962), 165.

54. Salvador Toscano, *Cuauhtémoc*. Prólogo de Rafael Heliodoro Valle (Mexico, 1953).

55. With a poetic freedom not permitted the historian, Sergio Magaña

radically rehabilitates Moctezuma in his play *Moctezuma II* (1948). His Moctezuma is an enlightened ruler, dreaming of reform, who finds intolerable the arrogance of the clergy and the military orders, complains that their bloodlust has made the Aztecs universally hated, and believes that the gods prefer the peaceful sacrifice of flowers and fruit to human blood. He has replaced plebeians with nobles in his household to humble their aristocratic pride; he proposes to centralize power in his hands and reduce that of the Aztec barons. The so-called portents of his downfall Moctezuma ridicules as clumsy impostures and frauds. He would form a united front of Indian states to defend Tenochtitlán against the Spanish invaders, but the treason of his allies forces him to admit Cortés into his capital. The play was reprinted in *Panorama del teatro en México* (Mexico), 1 (July, 1954), 35–82.

56. Sara García Iglesias, *Isabel Moctezuma, la última princesa azteca* (Mexico, 1946).

57. William Carlos Williams, *In the American Grain* (Norfolk, Conn., n.d.), introduction.

58. *Ibid.*, pp. 27–38.

59. John Unterecker, *Voyager, a Life of Hart Crane* (New York, 1969), p. 650.

60. *Ibid.*, p. 652.

61. *Ibid.*

62. *Ibid.*, p. 695.

63. *Accent on Barlow, a Commemorative Anthology*, ed. Lawrence Hart (San Francisco, 1962), pp. 15–16, 23, 28. Quoted by permission of the editor.

64. The novels composing the Aztec trilogy of Dexter Allen, *Jaguar and the Golden Stag* (1954), *Coil of the Serpent* (1956), and *Valley of Eagles* (1957), reflect a serious effort to re-create the vanished world of Nezahualcóyotl and his contemporaries; they also reflect the author's wide reading in the sources. The effort cannot be called successful, not only because of anachronisms and incongruities—one character is shown reading poems from a codex and another keeps a journal—but because the medieval atmosphere, the individualistic psychology of the characters, and the unlikely plots, often told in flamboyant style, are quite unconvincing.

65. Mary Freeman, *D. H. Lawrence: A Basic Study of His Ideas* (Gainesville: University of Florida Press, 1955), pp. 178–182.

66. D. H. Lawrence, *The Plumed Serpent* (New York, 1926), p. 421.

67. Eugene Goodheart, *The Utopian Vision of D. H. Lawrence* (Chicago: University of Chicago Press, 1963), p. 132.

68. D. H. Lawrence, "The Woman Who Rode Away," *The Tales of D. H. Lawrence* (London, 1934), pp. 756–788.

69. Frances Gillmor, *Flute of the Smoking Mirror: A Portrait of Nezahualcóyotl, Poet-King of the Aztecs* (Albuquerque: University of New Mexico Press, 1949). Frances Gillmor, *The King Danced in the Marketplace* (Tucson: University of Arizona Press, 1964).

70. Alba Herrera y Ogazón, *El arte musical en México* (Mexico, 1917), p. 9, cited in Robert Stevenson, *Music in Aztec and Inca Territory* (Berkeley: University of California Press, 1968), p. 15.

71. *Ibid.*, p. 17.

72. Samuel Martí and Gertrude Prokosch Kurath, *Dances of Anáhuac* (Chicago, 1964), p. 174.

73. Stevenson, *Music in Aztec and Inca Territory*, pp. 4–5.

74. Roberto García Morillo, *Carlos Chávez: Vida y obra* (Mexico, 1960), p. 111.

75. Gutiérrez Heras is cited in Stevenson, *Music in Aztec and Inca Territory*, pp. 152–153.

76. *Ibid.*, p. 152.

77. In Martí and Kurath, *Dances of Anáhuac.*

Index

Acamapichtli, 189, 191–92
Acolhuas, 130, 353, 355, 430
Acolman, 20
Acosta, José de, 121, 223, 296, 340
  Clavigero on, 298
  De procuranda Indorum salute,
      121
  *Historia natural y moral de las In-
      dias,* 121–24, 145, 206, 211, 353
  Italian translation, 140
  selections in Purchas, 206
  influence of: on Botero, 141
    on Gueudeville, 244
    on Prévost, 249
    on Solís, 176, 178
    on Torquemada, 182
  Robertson on, 285
Adams, Henry: on Bancroft and
    Morgan, 391, 394
Africa: art, 510, 511
  fetishes, 421
  slave trade, 89, 286–87, 318, 345,
      348
Aglio, Agostino, 348
agriculture, 4, 9, 10, 15, 239, 320, 427,
    465
  Aztecs, 10, 13, 14, 15, 21, 22, 24, 26,
      87, 89

agriculture, Aztecs (cont.)
  18th century on: France, 267;
      Great Britain, 272–73, 273–74,
      282; Italy, 230, 269; Mexico,
      297; Spain, 286
  19th century on: Great Britain,
      441, 443; Italy, 328; Mexico,
      317, 434; Spain, 456; U.S., 354,
      359, 387, 388
  20th century on: Great Britain,
      502
  irrigation, 10, 57, 427, 466, 502
  soil erosion, 14, 466
  see also food; land
  Toltecs, 9, 239, 421
Aguilar, Francisco de: *Relación,* 56,
    62–63
Aguilar, Jerónimo de, 51
Ahuítzotl, 365
Alamán, Lucas, 321, 322, 324–25, 348,
    423
  *Disertaciones sobre la historia de la
      República Mejicana,* 325–26
  influence of, 485
    on Vasconcelos, 470
  Orozco y Berra on, 422
  on Prescott, 362–63
  on Zumárraga, 325

Alba, Pedro de, 536
alcoholism, *see* drinking
Allegri, Marco, 142–43
Almaraz, Ramón, 415
Altamirano, Ignacio, 412
Alva de la Canal, Ramón: Escuela
    Nacional Preparatoria, Mex-
    ico City, murals, 526–27
Alvarado, Pedro de, 50, 54, 119, 164,
    198, 317, 423, 451, 545
Alvarado Huanitzin, Diego de, 132
Alvarado Tezozómoc, Fernando, *see*
    Tezozómoc, Fernando Alva-
    rado
Alzate, José Antonio: *Gazetas de
    Literatura*, 300, 301–02, 312,
    313
influence on, of Clavigero, 302
American Anthropologist: Caso ar-
    ticle, 479
American Antiquarian: Holmes ar-
    ticle, 409
American Association for the Ad-
    vancement of Science: Mor-
    gan paper (1857), 383–84
Morgan paper (1875), 390
Amigos del País, 220
Anáhuac, 229, 232, 239, 293, 294, 317,
    319, 343, 344, 366, 422, 431,
    434, 447, 481, 482, 483, 486,
    501
Anales de Cuauhtitlán, *see* Codex
    Chimalpopoca
Anales de los Cakchiqueles, 341
Ancona, Eligio: *Los mártires del
    Anáhuac*, 452
Anderson, Arthur J. O.: edition of
    Sahagún's Florentine Codex,
    536
Anonymous Conqueror: account,
    56–57, 63, 140, 206
influence of, 140
    on Belleforest, 148–49
    on Porcacchi, 142
Antilles, 241
Aquinas, Thomas, Saint, 109
Arago, François, 339

Araucanians, 134
Arawaks, Aztecs compared with, 55
Archaeological Institute of America,
    396
archaeology (in Mexico):
    18th century: by Mexicans, 300–
        04, 312
    by Spanish, 312
    19th century: antiquities going
        abroad, 321, 327
    by French, 336–41, 414–15, 436–
        39
    by Germans, 330, 333, 335, 336
    by British, 347–49
    by Italians, 327–28
    by Mexicans, 314–16, 321–22,
        417, 418
    by Spanish, 313–14
    by U.S., 350, 352, 396
    20th century: by Mexicans, 465,
        466–67
    by U.S., 406–09
architecture and engineering, 407–
    08, 437, 439
Aztecs, 10, 14, 15, 21, 57, 58, 96,
    136
    18th century on: France, 267;
        Great Britain, 280, 283; Mex-
        ico, 297, 300, 301–02
    19th century on: Germany, 335,
        336; Great Britain, 441; Mex-
        ico, 314, 317, 322, 412, 422–
        23; U.S., 350, 381–82, 384–85,
        389, 397, 403
    Egyptians compared with, 96,
        183, 190, 192, 314, 335, 340–
        41, 348, 377, 436, 438, 492
    Greeks compared with, 96, 314
    irrigation, 10, 57, 427, 466, 502
    Phoenicians suggested as build-
        ers in Middle America, 384–
        85
    Romans compared with, 96, 136,
        422
Incas, 263
Maya, 6, 49, 438, 502, 513, 516
Olmecs, 5, 190, 192, 210

architecture and engineering (cont.)
  Toltecs, 5, 239, 381, 471
  see also pyramids; individual sites
Arias, Fray Joseph, 289
Arias Montanus, Benedictus, 155
Aristotle, 71, 94, 121–22
  on education of children, 125
  on political systems, 109
  "slaves by nature" theory, 71, 80–
    81, 86
Armillas, Pedro, 466
artisans and craftsmen, 15, 17, 20, 22–
  23, 60, 272, 279, 528; see also
  class structure and organization
arts and crafts:
  19th century on, 509–10; Great
    Britain, 444; Mexico, 427
  20th century on, 510–12, 567;
    France, 513; Germany, 451;
    Great Britain, 511–13; Mex-
    ico, 472, 513–33, 543; U.S.,
    513, 522–23
  Africa, 510, 511
  Aztecs, 20, 22, 23, 24, 47
    16th century on: Italy, 64;
      Spain, 60, 70
    18th century on: France, 267;
      Great Britain, 276, 281, 285;
      Mexico, 297–98
    19th century on: France, 339;
      Germany, 332–36; Mexico,
      314, 315–16; U.S., 350, 384,
      405, 406
    20th century: U.S., 492, 522
  exhibitions, 418, 510, 513
  Incas, 332–33, 444
  Oceania, 510
  Toltecs, 8, 314, 516
  see also individual fields
Aryans, 438
Assyrians, Aztecs compared with, 4,
  113, 438
astrology and divination, 17, 32, 40,
  116, 159
astronomy, see calendrical system
  and astronomy

Atahualpa, 123, 150, 253, 366
Atlantic Monthly: Kirk article, 385
Atlantis, 192, 210, 425
Atoloztli, 189
Atzcapotzalco, 9, 11, 26, 27, 131, 133,
  200, 428, 445
Aubin, J.-M.-A., 339–40, 418, 436
  Brasseur de Bourbourg on, 340
  Mémoire, 312, 340
Augustinians: missionaries, 73, 74;
  see also Mendicant orders;
  Roman Catholic Church
Avellaneda, Gertrudis Gómez de,
  see Gómez de Avellaneda,
  Gertrudis
Ávila Camacho, Manuel, 465
Ayocuan, 40
Aztlán, 197, 371–72

Bacon, Francis, 206, 220, 293
Baldwin, John D.: on Wilson, 385–
  86
Bancroft, Hubert Howe, 389, 566
  Adams on, 391, 394
  on Brasseur de Bourbourg, 345–
    46, 403
  The Early American Chroniclers,
    403–04
  History of Central America, 402
  History of the Native Races of the
    Pacific Coast, 389–91, 392
  Morgan review, 388, 391–94, 409
  influence of, on Brasseur de Bour-
    bourg, 389
  influence on, of Ixtlilxóchitl, 389
  on Kingsborough, 403
  and Morgan, 388–94 passim, 403,
    404, 409
  Winsor on, 401, 404
Bandelier, Adolph F., 387–89, 396–
  98, 402, 405, 406, 488–96, 500,
  505
  Burland on, 503
  Caso on, 477, 478–79
  Chavero on, 429, 430, 476–77
  on Díaz del Castillo, 388

Bandelier, Adolph F. (cont.)
  Fiske on, 400
  and García Icazbalceta, 396–97,
    398
  Hewett on, 491
  influence on, of Robertson, 395
  Kirchhoff opposed to, 478, 479
  Kroeber opposed to, 494
  on León y Gama, 397
  Lowie on, 409, 489
  monographs, 395–96
  Monzón opposed to, 477, 479
  Moreno opposed to, 477, 479
  and Morgan, 312, 382, 387, 388,
    389, 394–98, 494
  Radin on, 493
  "The Romantic School in Ameri-
    can Archaeology," 398
  Vaillant on, 409, 491, 492, 495
  Waterman on, 488
  see also Morgan-Bandelier theory
Banier, Abbé Antoine, 247
Baradère, Abbé Jean-Henri, 337–39,
    346, 498
  Antiquités mexicaines, 311, 313,
    337–38
  Cass review, 351–52
  influence of, on Prescott, 355
Barlow, Joel: The Vision of Colum-
    bus, 307–08
Barlow, Robert H., 551
  Accent on Barlow: A Commemo-
    rative Anthology, 551
  "The Chichimecs," 552
  The Extent of the Empire of the
    Culhua Mexica, 551
  "The Gods in the Patio," 551–52
  "Mythological Episode," 552
  "Warning to Snake Killers," 352–
    53
Barnard, Henry, 394
Baron, Alexander: The Golden Prin-
    cess, 553
Barreda, Gabino, 46
barter and exchange, 20, 24, 50
  16th century on: Spain, 84, 85, 102

barter and exchange (cont.)
  18th century on: Great Britain,
    272, 278, 283; Italy, 270; Mex-
    ico, 297
  see also trade
Bastian, Adolf, 335, 448
  influence of, on Seler, 449
Batres, Leopoldo, 418
Bayle, Pierre: Dictionnaire historique
    et critique, 243–44
Belleforest, François de: Cosmogra-
    phie (translation of Münster,
    Cosmography), 149, 153, 157
  Histoire universelle du monde,
    148–49
  influence on, of Anonymous Con-
    queror, 148–49
  Thevet on, 150, 152–53
Beltrami, Giacomo, 327–28
Benítez, Fernando, 88, 466, 467
Benzoni, Girolamo, 142
  Historia del Mondo Nuovo, 142–
    43, 154
    Chauveton translations, 144, 147,
      164
    Dutch translation, 162, 163
    Hoeniger translation, 163, 164
    selections in Purchas, 206
  influence of, on Hakluyt, 172
  influence on: of Gómara, 142, 143,
    153
    of Oviedo, 142
    of Peter Martyr, 142
  Las Casas opposed by, 142
  Solís on, 176
  Thevet on, 153
Bergin, Thomas G., 236
Berlioz, Hector, 329
Bernal, Ignacio: on Humboldt, 334,
    336
  Tenochtitlán en una isla, 476
  on Teotihuacán frescoes, 5–6
Bernard, Emile, 510
Bernard, J.-F.: Cérémonies et cou-
    tumes religieuses des peuples
    idolâtres, 245–47
Beyer, Hermann, 34, 474, 501

Bèze, Théodore de, 144
Biart, Lucien: *The Aztecs: Their History, Manners, and Customs* (English translation), 440–41
and Morgan-Bandelier theory, 441
Bird, Robert Montgomery, 376
Calavar; or The Knight of the Conquest, a Romance of Mexico, 373–74
The Infidel; or The Fall of Mexico, 374–75
influence on, of Clavigero, 373
Black Legend, 143, 163, 259, 265; *see also* individual writers
Blake, Mrs. William W., 372
Boas, Franz, 390, 405, 419, 448
Gamio as pupil, 470
on Morgan, 404–05
Boban, Eugène, 498
body decoration and deformation, 12, 16, 27, 65, 68, 135
Boesnier: *Le Mexique conquis,* 306
Bonampak, 466
Booth, J. B., 378
Bordone, Benedetto, see *Libro de Benedetto Bordone*
Borgia Codex, *see* Codex Borgia
Bosch García, Carlos, 175
Botero, Giovanni: influences on, 141
Relationi universali, 141–42, 250
Boturini Benaducci, Lorenzo, 227–28, 233, 235, 236, 238, 291, 317, 318, 340, 418, 563
Clavigero on, 235, 236, 294–95, 298
Gallatin on, 353
Historia general de la América septentrional, 233, 234–35, 237
Idea de una nueva historia general de la América septentrional, 228–33, 234, 235–37
influence of: on Brasseur de Bourbourg, 342
on Robertson, 277
influence on, of Vico, 227, 228, 230, 231, 234, 235–36

Boturini Benaducci, Lorenzo (cont.)
manuscript collection, 227, 228, 232, 233–34, 235, 236, 339
Prescott on, 235, 236
Brahe, Tycho, 189
Brasseur de Bourbourg, Abbé Charles-Etienne, 311, 312, 341, 409, 436, 498, 563
on Aubin, 340
Bancroft on, 345–46, 403
Chavero on, 425
Histoire des nations civilisées du Mexique et de l'Amérique centrale, 342–45
on Humboldt, 337
influence of, on Bancroft, 389
influence on: of Boturini, 342
of Veytia, 344
of Vico, 342
on Ixtlilxóchitl, 344–45
Morgan on, 392
Quatre Lettres sur le Mexique, 342, 345, 346
Spence on, 502
Braun, Georgius: *Civitates orbis terrarum,* 165
Brazil: Lery on, 150–51, 157
Montaigne on, 157–58, 160, 255
Ronsard on, 157
Thevet on, 150–51
Voltaire on, 255
Breton, Guillaume le, 147
Brinton, Daniel G., 399
Ancient Náhuatl Poetry, 534
on Morgan-Bandelier theory, 399
Rig Veda Americanus, 534
Seler on, 534
Brooke, Henry: *Montezuma,* 306
Bruno, Giordano, 172
Spaccio de la bestia trionfante, 144
Bry, Jean Israel de, 163
Grands Voyages, 164, 165
Bry, Jean Théodore de, 163
Grands Voyages, 164, 165
Bry, Théodore de, 163–64
Grands Voyages, 164, 165
Solís on, 176

Buckle, Henry T., 502
  History of Civilization in England, 443–44
Buffon, Georges-Louis Leclerc, Comte de: *Histore naturelle*, 249–50, 251, 289, 463, 565
  influence of, 271, 273, 275
    on Kames, 273
    on Robertson, 275
    on De Pauw, 260, 263
  Voltaire on, 254
Bullock, William, 347–48
Bulnes, Francisco, 435
Burke, Edmund: *An Account of the European Settlements in America*, 257, 259
Burland, Cottie A., 503
  The Gods of Mexico, 503
  Life and Art in Ancient Mexico, 503
Burriel, Andrés Marcos, 234
Bustamante, Carlos María, 303, 318–21, 322, 326, 327, 412, 421, 440, 479
  Galería de los príncipes mexicanos, 318
  influence on, of Mier, 318, 320
  Mañanas de la alameda de México, 318
  Mora on, 323
  Zavala on, 324

Cabot, Sebastian, 167
Cacama, 200
Cadalso, José, 286–87
Cakchiqueles, Anales de los, *see* Anales de los Cakchiqueles
Calderón de la Barca, Pedro, 176
Calendar Stone (Stone of the Sun):
  Bandelier on, 397
  cast by Bullock displayed in London, 347–48
  Cosmes on, 434
  discovery, 302, 425
  León y Gama on, 302–03, 321
  Nuttall on, 399
  Sierra on, 432

calendrical system and astronomy:
  Aztecs, 17, 18, 24, 25, 32–33, 40, 136, 144, 207
    16th century on: France, 152
    17th century on: Italy, 209–10; Mexico, 190, 192
    18th century on: France, 256; Germany, 262; Great Britain, 274, 282; Italy, 229, 234, 235, 271; Mexico, 224, 290, 301, 302–03
    19th century on: Germany, 330, 335, 450; Great Britain, 347, 443, 446; Mexico, 315, 324, 412, 415, 424, 427, 434; Spain, 456; U.S., 353, 358, 385, 387, 389–90, 397
    20th century on: Germany, 501; Great Britain, 504; Mexico, 432
    Egyptians compared with, 192, 229, 256, 335, 432
    Greeks and Romans compared with, 412
    Tonalámatl, 32, 224, 339
    Xiuhámatl, 18
  Maya, 6
  Olmecs, 5
  Toltecs, 229, 232, 239, 294–95, 343
Calles, Plutarco Elías, 464, 486
Calmécac, 17, 18, 46, 47, 475
calpulli, see class structure and organization
Calvin, John, 150
Campanella, Tommaso, 143
  La Città del Sole, 143–44
Campbell, John: *The Spanish Empire in America*, 257, 259
Campeche, 232
Campilla y Cosío, José del, 222–23
Campos, Rubén, 480
Canada (New France), 241
  Voltaire on, 255
cannibalism, 5, 12, 179, 243
  Aztecs, 12, 47
    16th century on, 172; France, 149; Great Britain, 167, 169;

cannibalism, Aztecs, 16th century on (cont.)
    Italy, 65, 66, 140; Mexico, 89, 128, 135; Spain, 60, 61, 63, 70, 82, 83, 85, 101, 115
    17th century on: Mexico, 196
    18th century on: Mexico, 296; Spain, 222, 305
    19th century on: France, 345, 440; Great Britain, 447; Mexico, 315, 325, 362, 416, 421, 434; Spain, 455; U.S., 355, 357–58, 362, 363
    20th century on: Great Britain, 503; Mexico, 486; U.S., 497
    Toltecs, 5, 485
canoes, 14, 85, 297
Carbia, Rómulo, 143, 164
Cárdenas, Lázaro, 465
Caribs, 79, 287, 289
    Aztecs compared with, 55, 122, 247, 297
Carli, Gian Ricardo, 268, 564
    influence of, on Clavigero, 271, 297
    influence on: of Herrera, 269, 271 of Laet, 271
    Lettere americane, 268–71, 314–15
    on De Pauw, 269, 270–71
Carranza, Venustiano, 464
Carrera, Alonso, 176
Carthaginians, Aztecs compared with, 221, 296, 322
Cartier, Jacques: influence of, on Rabelais, 157
Carvajal, Micael de: Las Cortes de la Muerte, 134
Casas, Bartolomé de Las, see Las Casas, Bartolomé de
Caso, Alfonso, 32, 47, 466, 468, 469, 474, 476, 477, 501
    on Bandelier, 477, 478–79
    influence of, on Bernal, 476
    Monte Albán excavations, 466, 474
    El Pueblo del Sol, 474–76
    on Seler, 448–49
Caso, Antonio, 474

Cass, Lewis, 312, 351, 355, 381
    Baradère, review of, 351–52
    on Clavigero, 351
    Fiske on, 399
    influence of, on Wilson, 384
Castañeda, Luciano, 313, 321, 437
    published by Baradère, 311, 313, 337–38
Castillo, Cristóbal del, 196
Catherine de Médicis, Queen of France, 150
Cempoala, 63
Centéotl, 296
ceramics, see pottery and ceramics
ceremonies and rituals, 12, 27–28, 29, 41
    16th century on: France, 153, 159; Spain, 96, 103, 118–19
    18th century on: Mexico, 318
    19th century on: Spain, 456
    see also cannibalism; human sacrifice; religion
Cervantes de Salazar, Francisco, 85–86, 127, 188
    Crónica de la Nueva España, 86–88, 88–89, 91, 92
    plagiarism of Gómara, 86, 87, 175
    plagiarism by Herrera, 175
Cervantes Saavedra, Miguel de, 179
Chacmool (sculpture), 511
Chalchihuitlicue, 524
Chalco, 40, 41, 42–43, 131
    history of, by Chimalpahin, 196, 197–98, 232
Chaldeans, Aztecs compared with, 224, 229, 432
Champollion, Jean-François, 341
Chapultepec, 15, 183–84, 365, 366, 387
Charencey, H. de, 439
Charlemagne, 305, 343
Charles II, King of Spain, 176, 202
Charles III, King of Spain, 219, 281, 293, 312
Charles IV, King of Spain, 313

Charles V, Holy Roman Emperor, 51, 56, 69, 72, 79, 82, 106, 186, 277
  and Cortés, letters from (*Cartas de relación*), 3, 53, 57–60, 61, 63, 64, 66–67, 69, 70, 87, 101, 140, 142, 148, 149, 155, 156, 165, 169, 176, 277, 348, 372, 480–81, 563, 565
  and Cortés, treasure sent by, 51, 52, 53, 59, 63–66, 69, 168
  and Motolinía, letter from, 74–75, 110, 114
  policy toward Indians, 74, 75, 81, 84, 124, 174
Charlot, Jean, 515–16, 517
  Escuela Nacional Preparatoria, Mexico City, murals, 526–27
  on Orozco, 517
  on Rivera, 527
Charnay, Désiré, 408, 437, 438, 498
  The Ancient Cities of the New World (English translation), 438–39
Chateaubriand, Vicomte François-René de, 338
  Génie du Christianisme, 339
Châtelain, Henri-Abraham, 244
Chauveton, Urbain, 144–46, 156
  Benzoni translated by, 144, 147, 164
    Thevet on, 153
  on Gómara, 144–45, 147
  influence on, of Las Casas, 144, 146
Chavero, Alfredo, 128, 418, 424, 432, 485
  on Bandelier, 429, 430, 476–77
  on Brasseur de Bourbourg, 425
  on Clavigero, 425
  on Coatlicue sculpture, 426, 509–10
  Historia antigua y de la conquista, 397, 424–31
  on Humboldt, 425
  influence of, on Sierra, 431
  influence on: of Orozco y Berra, 424

Chavero, Alfredo, influence on (cont.)
  of Zorita, 429
  on Ixtlilxóchitl, 424, 425, 430
  México a través de los siglos, 424
  on Orozco y Berra, 425, 426–27, 428, 430
  on Prescott, 425
  on Ramírez, 424–25
  on Sigüenza, 425
Chávez, Carlos, 558–61
  Los Cuatro Soles, 560
  El fuego nuevo, 560
  Xochipilli-Macuilxóchitl, 560
Chávez Orozco, Luis, 473–74
Cherokees, 390
Chichén Itzá, 463
Chichimecs, 9–10
  Boturini on, 231, 232, 353
  Clavigero on, 294
  Ramírez on, 362
  Robertson on, 282
  Veytia on, 240, 355
  see also Texcoco
Chicomecóatl, 116
Chile, 134
Chilpancingo, Congress of, 317
Chimalpahin, Francisco de San Antón Muñón, 189, 196–97, 319, 445
  Relaciones originales de Chalco Amaquemecan, 196, 197–98, 232
Chimalpopoca, Codex, *see* Codex Chimalpopoca
Chimalpopoca Galicia, Faustino, 341, 364
China: Aztecs compared with, 122, 310, 332, 432, 445, 495, 517
  as origin of Incas, 208
Chinard, Gilbert, 151, 157, 160, 241
Choctaws, 390
Cholula, 12, 20, 96, 116, 203, 292, 344, 428
  pyramid, 239, 295, 382, 396, 397
  Spanish conquest, 53, 57–58, 164, 423
Christy, Henry, 442

chronology, *see* calendrical system and astronomy
Cieza de León, Pedro, 243
Cisneros, Cardinal Francisco Jiménez de, *see* Jiménez de Cisneros, Cardinal Francisco
civil servants, *see* public officials
clan, *see* class structure and social organization
class structure and social organization, 10, 15, 16–17, 20–27
  16th century on: Mexico, 129
  Spain, 60, 99, 111–12, 120, 564
  18th century on: Great Britain, 276, 278, 279
  Italy, 231, 269
  19th century on: France, 441
  Germany, 449, 450
  Great Britain, 444, 445
  Mexico, 422, 428–29
  U.S., 359, 383, 384, 385, 386, 388–89, 392–96 *passim*, 398
  20th century on: France, 499, 500
  Germany, 501
  Great Britain, 502, 503, 504
  Mexico, 474, 476, 477–78, 479, 482, 487, 528, 529
  U.S.S.R. and East Germany, 506–08
  U.S., 488–96 *passim*
  artisans and craftsmen, 15, 17, 20, 22–23, 60, 272, 279, 528
  clan (*calpulli*), 20–21, 27
    18th century on: Great Britain, 278
    19th century on: Germany, 450; Mexico, 428, 429, 430
    20th century on: France, 499; Great Britain, 502, 503; Mexico, 477, 478, 479; U.S.S.R., 507; U.S., 489
  commoners, 15, 16, 17, 19, 21–22, 24, 26, 27
    16th century on: Spain, 56, 80, 83, 103, 109
    18th century on: France, 265; Great Britain, 278, 279, 280
    19th century on: Germany, 332; Great Britain, 445; Mexico, 422, 428–29
    20th century on: Germany, 501; Mexico, 474, 478, 479, 482–83, 529; U.S., 497
  entertainers, 15, 22, 28, 129, 528
  merchants, 12, 15, 16, 17, 22, 23–24, 27, 46, 359, 429, 501
  nobility, 15, 16, 17, 18, 19, 21, 24, 26, 27, 47
    16th century on: Spain, 56, 59, 96
    18th century on: Great Britain, 278, 279, 280; Italy, 269
    19th century on: Germany, 332, 450; Mexico, 422; U.S., 356, 389
    20th century on: France, 499; Germany, 501; Great Britain, 502, 503, 504; Mexico, 474, 477, 478, 479, 482–83, 529; U.S., 497
  priests, 13, 15, 16, 17, 24–26, 27, 34, 46
    16th century on: Spain, 56, 59, 62
    18th century on: Italy, 269
    19th century on: Germany, 332; Mexico, 429–30; U.S., 350
    20th century on: Mexico, 474, 475, 476, 480; U.S.S.R., 506
  public officials, 13, 15, 17, 26, 27, 46, 269, 478, 499; *see also* nobility *above*
  serfs (*mayeque*), 16, 26, 279, 422, 478, 479, 501, 503
  slaves, 15, 19, 27
    16th century on: Mexico, 131; Spain, 80, 98–99
    17th century on: Spain, 181
    18th century on: Great Britain, 279
    19th century on: France, 345; Great Britain, 347; Mexico, 415, 422, 429

class structure, slaves (cont.)
  20th century on: Germany, 501;
    Mexico, 479
  warriors, 11, 13, 15, 16, 17, 26, 27,
    46
  16th century on: Spain, 56
  17th century on: Mexico, 198;
    Spain, 178
  18th century on: France, 243,
    266
  19th century on: Great Britain,
    445; Mexico, 428, 429; U.S.,
    350, 356
  20th century on: France, 499;
    Great Britain, 503, 504; Mex-
    ico, 475; U.S., 492, 493
  land given to, 11, 13, 26, 428–29,
    445, 450, 489, 493, 506, 507
  see also nobility above
Classic period, 5–7, 40, 43–44, 237
Clavigero, Francisco Javier, 135, 208,
    240, 293, 301, 486, 534
  on Acosta, 298
  on Boturini, 235, 236, 294–95, 298
  Cass on, 351
  Chavero on, 425
  Gallatin on, 353
  Historia antigua de México (in-
    cluding Disertaciones; origi-
    nally Storia Antica del Mes-
    sico), 225, 271, 293–300, 313,
    314–15, 364, 566
  translations, 299, 349
  influence of, 349, 350
    on Alzate, 302
    on Bird, 373
    on Gordon, 350
    on Herder, 329
    on Prescott, 299, 356, 357, 358
    on Southey, 372
  influence on: of Carli, 271
    of Sigüenza, 190, 295
    on De Pauw, 294, 296, 297, 298,
      299
    on Robertson, 298
    on Solís, 295
    on Torquemada, 295

clothing, see dress
Coatlicue: in Herrán painting, 514,
    536
  Mier's identification of with Vir-
    gin Mary, 304
  sculpture of, 302, 509
    Bandelier on, 397
    Caso on, 475
    cast by Bullock displayed in
      London, 347, 348
    Chavero on, 426, 509–10
    Fernández on, 523–24
    Holmes on, 408, 510
    Kubler on, 522–23
    León y Gama on, 303
    O'Gorman on, 518
    reactions to, in 20th century
      Mexico, 514, 515
    Tablada on, 517
    Toscano on, 519
    Vaillant on, 522
    Westheim on, 520–21
Coci, Jorge, 67
Codex Borgia, 399, 449, 512
Codex Chimalpopoca (Anales de
    Cuauhtitlán), 341
Codex Fejérváry-Mayer, 399, 512
Codex Laud, 512
Codex Mendoza, 150, 207
  Dutch translation, 207
  French translation, 207
  Hakluyt's ownership of, 170–71,
    206
  Humboldt on, 332
  Lok translation, 170–71
  Orozco y Berra on, 416
  De Pauw on, 261–62
  Purchas' ownership and publica-
    tion of, 171, 190, 206, 207, 281
  Rivera influenced by, 530
  Thevet's ownership and use of,
    150, 152, 206
Codex Troano, 341–42
Codex Vaticanus, 399, 416–17, 426
Codex Xólotl, 199
Codex Zouche, 512

Códice Florentino (Florentine Codex): English version by Anderson and Dibble, 536
  as Rivera source, 530
  see also Sahagún, Bernardino de
Coe, Michael D.: Mexico, 496
Columbian Exposition (Madrid; 1892), 418
Columbus, Christopher, 55, 60, 64, 70, 156, 157, 166
  in Barlow poem, 307, 308
  in Darío poem, 460–61
Comas, Juan, 466
commoners, see class structure and social organization
Comte, Auguste, 380
Congress of Americanists: Holmes paper, 406
Constitution of Mexico (1917), 471
Constitutional Convention (Mexico) (1856–1857), 413
Contarini, Gaspar, 64–65, 70
Cooper, James Fenimore, 375, 441
Copernicus, Nicolaus, 189
Córdoba, Francisco Hernández de, 49–50
Córdoba, Gonzalo Fernández de, 50
Cornyn, J. H.: The Song of Quetzalcóatl, 536
Cortés, Hernando, 4, 50–54, 60, 72–73, 80, 85
  Acosta on, 123–24
  in Ancona novel, 452
  in Barlow poem, 308
  Belleforest on, 148
  Bustamante on, 319
  Cadalso on, 287
  and Charles V, letters to (Cartas de relación), 3, 53, 57–60, 61, 63, 64, 66–67, 69, 70, 87, 101, 140, 142, 148, 149, 155, 156, 165, 169, 277, 348, 563, 565
  Guzmán edition, 480–81
  influence of: on Porcacchi, 142; on Solís, 176; on Southey, 372
  and Charles V, treasure sent to, 51, 52, 53, 59, 63–66, 69, 168
  Chavero on, 431

Cortés, Hernando (cont.)
  Chimalpahin on, 198
  Durán on, 119
  Eden on, 168
  Fiske on, 400
  on Fontenelle play, 215–16, 305
  in Fosdick novel, 378
  Garibay on, 535
  Gómara on, 82–83, 159, 319
  Granados on, 292
  Guzmán on, 480, 481, 482, 483
  Hakluyt on, 172
  Harris on, 258
  in Heine poem, 367
  Ixtlilxóchitl on, 200
  in Lasso de la Vega work, 135–36
  in Maturin novel, 376
  Mier on, 317
  and Moctezuma II, 9, 45, 47, 51, 52, 53–54, 59, 81, 164, 186
  on Moctezuma II, 59, 149, 393, 394
  Montesquieu on, 252, 253–54
  Morgan on, 393, 394
  Motezuma, Father, on, 203–04, 205
  Nuix on, 286
  in Orozco murals, 531, 532, 533
  Ortelius on, 155
  Palafox on, 186, 187
  De Pauw on, 262
  Peter Martyr on, 168
  in Pi y Margall dialogue, 455, 456, 457
  in Piron play, 306
  portrait of: owned by Thevet, 150 by Weiditz, 528
  Prescott on, 355, 360
  and Quetzalcóatl myth, 9, 51–52, 186, 483
  Ramírez on, 136
  in Rivera mural, 481, 528
  Robertson on, 277, 282, 284, 285
  Romerovargas Yturbide on, 483–84
  in Saavedra Guzmán work, 135
  skeletal remains found, 467–68, 481
  Solís on, 176
  in Spontini opera, 379

Cortés, Hernando (cont.)
  and Tecuixpo, 547
  in Terrazas poem, 135
  Thevet on, 154–55
  Torquemada on, 184
  Vega on, 180
  Wallace novel, 451
  Williams on, 548, 549
  Wilson on, 382, 384
  in Zapata work, 134–35
  Zavala on, 324
  Ziletti on, 139
  Zorita on, 101–02
Cortés, Don Martín, 82, 86, 88
Cosmes, Francisco G., 434–35
cosmogony (cosmic myths), 12, 30–
  33, 40–41
  19th century on: France, 342–44;
    Mexico, 416–17, 425–26; Spain,
    456; U.S., 353
  20th century on: Mexico, 475;
    U.S., 496
  see also myths and legends
courier system, 280, 285
couvade, 243
Covarrubias, Miguel, 466, 519
  Indian Art of Mexico and Central
    America, 519
Coyolxauhqui (sculpture), 517, 521
Cozumel, 50, 51
craftsmen, see artisans and craftsmen
Crane, Hart, 549–51
  influence on, of Prescott, 550
Cravaliz, Agostino de: Gómara
  translated by, 139, 158
creoles (in Mexico), 88, 89, 90, 117,
  188, 192, 195–96, 198, 223,
  260–61, 292–93, 301, 322
  land taken from, 72, 76, 77, 78, 87–
    88, 90, 196, 198, 222, 291–92
  see also Indians (as theme) and
    Indians, attitudes toward, en-
    tries under Mexico; national-
    ism
Cristero rebellion, 479
Cromberger, Juan, 66

Cruz, Sor Juana Inés de la, 193, 229
  El cetro de José, 195
  El divino Narciso, 193–95
Cuauhtémoc, 54, 87, 152, 177, 200,
  212, 322, 355, 360, 383, 423, 431
  in Avellaneda novel, 372–73
  Cervantes on, 87
  controversy over supposed re-
    mains, 468–69, 480
  in Rodríguez Galván poem, 366,
    537
  Gómara on, 87
  in Heredia poems, 365
  interest in, in 20th century Mex-
    ico, 467–69, 536, 542–43
  in Jerningham poem, 306, 307
  in López Velarde poem, 536–37
  Montesquieu on, 253
  in Novo works, 540
  in Pellicer poems, 537–38
  Pérez Martínez biography, 543–46
  in Pi y Margall dialogue, 456, 457
  Sierra on, 432
  Sigüenza on, 192
  in Siqueiros paintings, 533
  statue of, Mexico City, 417–18,
    455, 457, 468, 469
  and Tecuixpo, 547
  Toscano on, 543, 546–47
  in Wallace novel, 451, 452
Cuauhtitlán, Anales de, see Codex
  Chimalpopoca
Cuba: attitudes toward Indians, 19th
  century, 364–66, 372–73
  slavery, 345
Cuetlaxtla, 231
Cuevas, Mariano, 299, 470, 486, 496
  Historia de la iglesia en México,
    486
  Historia de la nación mexicana,
    486
Cuitláhuac, 54, 365, 383, 414, 423,
  483, 547
Culhuacán, 9
Culiacán: map (1579), 155
Cuzco, 123, 160

dance, *see* music and dance
Darío, Rubén, 458–61, 537
  El canto errante, 458
  Cantos de vida y esperanza, 458
  "To Roosevelt," 458
  Tutecotzimi, 458–60
Dartmouth College: Orozco frescoes, 531–33
Darwin, Charles, 399, 401, 422
Dead Warrior (sculpture), 524
deities: Aztecs, 10, 11–12, 19, 20, 21, 30–34, 35, 36–38, 43
  16th century on: Spain, 115, 116
  17th century on: Spain, 182
  18th century on: Italy, 230; Mexico, 296
  19th century on: Mexico, 315, 421, 426
  20th century on: Great Britain, 503; Mexico, 431, 482
  Greeks compared with, 91, 182, 226, 230, 296, 416–17, 421, 482
  Romans compared with, 91, 116, 182, 230, 296, 421
  Olmecs, 5
  Toltecs, 8
  see also cosmogony; religion; individual deities
Departamiento de Asuntos Indígenas, Mexico, 465
Descartes, René, 173, 189, 220, 252, 293
Díaz, Porfirio (and period), 416, 417, 418–19, 431, 433, 434, 466, 467, 470, 472, 514, 541
Díaz del Castillo, Bernal: Bandelier on, 388
  Fiske on, 400
  in Forner satire, 287–88
  Guzmán on, 481
  Historia verdadera de la conquista de la Nueva España, 14, 57, 60–61, 63, 70, 348, 497
  influence of: on Haggard, 454
    on Solís, 176
    on Southey, 372
  Morgan on, 393

Díaz del Castillo, Bernal (cont.)
  in Wallace novel, 451
  Wilson on, 384
Díaz-Thomé, Jorge Hugo, 86
Dibble, Charles E.: edition of Sahagún's Florentine Codex, 536
Diderot, Denis, 217
  Encyclopédie, 218, 257
Didot (publisher), 338
Dienz, Diego, 69
disease, *see* epidemics and disease
divination, *see* astrology and divination
Dominicans: missionaries, 73, 74, 76, 143; *see also* Mendicant orders; Roman Catholic Church
Dorantes, Andrés, 89
Dorantes de Carranza, Baltasar, 89–90
  Sumaria relación de las cosas de la Nueva España, 90–92
Doutrelaine, Louis-Toussaint-Simon, 437
Draper, John W., 451
  History of the Intellectual Development of Europe, 386–87
dress, 13, 15–16, 165
  16th century on:
    Germany, 165
    Mexico, 135
    Spain, 66, 85
  17th century on:
    Netherlands, 208, 209
    Spain, 179–80
  18th century on:
    France, 265
    Mexico, 292
  19th century on:
    Germany, 450
    Spain, 456
    U.S., 393
  20th century on:
    Mexico, 529
    U.S., 492
drinking, 27
  16th century on:
    France, 149, 159

drinking, 16th century on (cont.)
    Great Britain, 171
    Italy, 140, 141
    Mexico, 129
    Spain, 61, 63, 80, 83, 88, 101, 111,
        117, 118, 121, 125
    17th century on:
        Spain, 174, 187, 188
    18th century on:
        Mexico, 290, 294
        U.S., 387, 394, 400
    20th century on:
        Mexico, 486
        U.S., 497
Dryden, John: *The Indian Emperor*,
    212–14, 305, 316
    influence of, on Brooke, 306
Dupaix, Guillermo, 313–14, 316, 321,
    437
    published by Baradère, 311, 313,
        337–38
Durán, Diego, 19–20, 78, 118, 424,
    563
    *Historia de las Indias de Nueva-
        España e islas de tierra firme*,
        118–21
    influence of, on Moxó, 315
    influence on, of Las Casas, 119
Durand de Villegagnon, Nicholas,
    157
Dürer, Albrecht, 69–70, 509
Duruy, Victor, 436
Du Vivier, Gérard, 156
Dwight, Timothy: *America*, 308–09

Eagle Knight (sculpture), 514–15
    Rodin on, 509
    Westheim on, 520, 521–22
Easby, Dudley T., Jr., 513
Easby, Elizabeth Kennedy, 513
Eden, Richard: *The Decades of the
        New Worlde*, 166–68, 170
    influence on, of Gómara, 166
    Treatyse of the Newe India, 166
education, 17–18, 24, 26, 207

education (cont.)
    16th century on:
        Spain, 78, 87, 97, 112, 117, 120,
            125
    17th century on:
        Spain, 178
    18th century on:
        France, 244, 248, 256
        Mexico, 291
    19th century on:
        Mexico, 415, 434
        Spain, 456
        U.S., 359
    20th century on:
        Mexico, 433, 465
    Calmécac, 17, 18, 46, 47, 475
    Colegio de Santa Cruz de Tlate-
        lolco, 114, 118, 126–27, 291
    Real y Pontificia Universidad de
        México, 85
    Telpochcalli, 17, 21, 46
Eguiara y Eguren, Juan José de, 208,
    534
    Bibliotheca mexicana, 223, 224–25
    influence of, on Robertson, 277
    influence on, of Sigüenza, 225
Egyptians:
    Aztecs compared with, 102, 136,
        281, 310, 332, 342, 356, 443,
        444, 495
    architecture, 96, 183, 190, 192,
        314, 335, 340–41, 348, 377, 436,
        438, 492
    calendrical system and astron-
        omy, 192, 229, 256, 335, 432
    hieroglyphs and picture writing,
        64, 152, 190, 207–08, 231, 271,
        315, 335, 348, 358, 512
    religion, 353, 503
    sculpture, 348, 352, 513, 517
    Incas compared with, 443, 444
    Indians compared with, 314, 322,
        513
    suggested as antecedents of Aztecs
        and Olmecs, 192, 210
Ekholm, Gordon F., 334
Elizabeth I, Queen of England, 171

encomienda system, 72–76 *passim*,
82, 88, 90, 92, 93, 110, 121,
124, 564
Encyclopédie, 218, 257
Engels, Friedrich: and Morgan's
Ancient Society, 505, 506, 507
*The Origin of the Family, Private
Property and the State in
Light of the Researches of
Lewis H. Morgan*, 506
engineering, *see* architecture and en-
gineering
Enríquez, Martín, 122
Ensenada, Marqués de, 234
epidemics and disease, 118, 124, 126,
132, 141, 163, 174, 294, 433
introduced by Spanish, 132, 145
Erasmus, Desiderius, 80
Ercilla y Zuñiga, Alonso de: *La
Araucana*, 134
influence of, 135, 136
Escóiquiz, Juan de: *México con-
quistada*, 305–06
Escuela Nacional de Antropología,
466
Eskimos, 391
Etruscans, Aztecs compared with,
322, 331, 443

Fairchild, Hoxie N., 100, 160
Farcy, Charles, 338
farming *see* agriculture
featherwork, 13, 16, 20, 24, 27, 28,
42, 47
16th century on:
Mexico, 91, 133, 135, 136
Spain, 51, 59, 64, 65, 66, 94–96
17th century on:
Spain, 179–80
18th century on:
France, 256
Great Britain, 258
Mexico, 292, 294
19th century on:
Mexico, 434
U.S., 384

Feijóo y Montenegro, Benito Gerónimo, 220–22, 223
De Pauw on, 261
Theatro crítico, 261
Fejérváry-Mayer Codex, *see* Codex
Fejérváry-Mayer
Ferdinand V, King of Castile (II of
Aragón), 73, 75, 82, 105
Ferdinand VI, King of Spain, 219,
234
Ferguson, Adam, 272, 275
Fernández, Justino: *Coatlicue*, 517,
519, 523–24
on Gamio, 523
on Guzmán, 518, 523
on Humboldt, 334
on Kubler, 523
on O'Gorman, 518, 523
on Siqueiros, 533
on Toscano, 518, 523
on Vaillant, 522, 523
on Westheim, 523
Fernández de Córdoba, Gonzalo, 50
Fernández de Oviedo y Valdés,
Gonzalo, *see* Oviedo y Val-
dés, Gonzalo Fernández de
Fisch, M. H., 236
Fiske, John, 399
The Discovery of America, 399–
400
Flannagan, John, 511
Florentine Codex, *see* Códice Florentino; Sahagún, Bernardino de
Fonseca, Juan Rodríguez de, 67, 360
Fontenelle, Bernard de: *Dialogues
des Morts*, 215–16, 257, 305, 455
food, 16–17
16th century on:
Italy, 141
Spain, 85
18th century on:
Great Britain, 274, 282
Mexico, 290
Spain, 286
19th century on:
Mexico, 325
U.S., 387, 393

food (cont.)
    20th century on:
        U.S., 492
    see also agriculture
Forner, Juan Pablo: Exequias de la
    lengua castellana, 287–89
Fosdick, W. W.: Malmiztic the Tol-
    tec; and the Cavaliers of the
    Cross, 376–78
France: and Brazil, 150–51
    Enlightenment and philosophes,
        141, 217–18, 252, 268, 315
    Indians, attitudes toward:
        16th century, 138, 144–62; trans-
            lations into English, 169; trans-
            lations from Italian, 144, 147;
            translations from Spanish, 66,
            67, 138, 146–47
        17th century, 208–09, 210–12,
            215–16; translations from Eng-
            lish, 207; translations from
            Spanish, 179
        18th century, 141, 217–19, 240–
            57, 263–68, 306–07
        19th century, 311, 312, 336–46,
            378–79, 414–16, 436–41, 510;
            translations from Spanish, 313
        20th century, 498–501, 513
    and Mexico, 414–15, 416, 436–38
    archaeology, 19th century, 336–
        41, 414–15, 436–39
    and New France, 241
    Treaty of Cateau-Cambrésis, 139
    and West Indies, 166
Franciscans:
    missionaries, 73, 74, 76, 180, 181,
        241, 354
    Colegio de Santa Cruz de Tla-
        telolco, 114, 118, 126–27, 291
    debate with Aztec priests, 25,
        36–37, 41, 110, 114
    see also Mendicant orders; Roman
        Catholic Church
Frank, Waldo: on Crane, 549–50
Frederick IV, Count Palatine of the
    Rhine, 165
Freeman, Mary: on Lawrence, 553–
    54

French Revolution, 345
frescoes, see painting
Freund, Gisèle: Mexique précolom-
    bien, 513
Friede, Juan, 93–94
Frisi, Paolo: on De Pauw, 268
Frobisher, Martin: Thevet on, 154
Fry, Roger: Vision and Design, 512–
    13
Fueter, Eduard, 79, 93
Fumée, Martin: Gómara translated
    by, 147, 158
    on Thevet, 151

Galileo Galilei, 189
Gallatin, Albert, 312, 355, 381
    on Boturini, 353
    on Clavigero, 353
    Fiske on, 399
    influence of, on Wilson, 384
    on Ixtlilxóchitl, 352–53
    on León y Gama, 353
    "Notes on the Semi-Civilized Na-
        tions of Mexico, Yucatan, and
        Central America," 349, 352–54
    on Prescott, 352
    on Robertson, 502
    on Sahagún, 353
    on Veytia, 353
    Winsor on, 400–01
Galucci, Giovanni Paolo, 140
Galván, Ignacio Rodríguez, see
    Rodríguez Galván, Ignacio
Gálvez, José de, 289
gambling, 19–20, 28, 209
games and sports, 19–20, 28, 136–37,
    140, 158, 443, 446
Gamio, Manuel, 419, 464–65, 466,
    469, 470–71, 473
    art appreciation, experiments in,
        514–15
    Boas as teacher, 470
    Fernández on, 523
    Forjando patria, 471
    Teotihuacán, study of, 465, 466,
        471–72

Gann, Thomas: *History of the Maya*, Martínez del Río on, 490

García Cahero, Emilio: Escuela Nacional Preparatoria, Mexico City, murals, 526–27

García Cubas, Antonio, 414

García Guerra, Bishop, 199

García Icazbalceta, Joaquín, 124, 130, 418, 433
and Bandelier, 396–97, 398
Documentos para la historia de México, 414
Zumárraga, biography of, 433–34

García Iglesias, Sara: Tecuixpo, biography of, 547

Garcilaso de la Vega (el Inca):
Comentarios reales de los Incas, 198, 206, 219, 267
English translation in Purchas, 206
influence of, 307
on Voltaire, 254, 255

Garibay K., Ángel María, 40, 132, 150, 199, 291, 467, 534, 557
Historia de la literatura náhuatl, 534–35
Irene Nicholson's use of translations, 536
Pre-Columbian Literatures of Mexico, 535

Gassendi, Pierre, 189

Gauguin, Paul: on Aztec sculpture, 510

Gayangos, Pascual de, 355

Gemelli Carreri, Francesco, 209
Giro del mondo, 209–10
influence of, on Prévost, 249
De Pauw on, 262
and Sigüenza, 209, 210

Génin, Auguste, 339
Poèmes aztèques, 457–58

Genty, Louis, 266–67

Gerbi, Antonello, 328

Germans: Aztecs compared with, 226
human sacrifice, 145

Germans (cont.)
suggested as antecedents of Aztecs, 208, 209

Germany:
Indians, attitudes toward:
16th century, 68, 69, 163–65; translations from Italian, 163, 164; translations from Spanish, 66–67, 138
18th century, 260–63; translations from English and Spanish, 299
19th century, 311, 328–36, 367–71, 448–50, 463–64
20th century, 451, 464, 501, 534
and Mexico, archaeology in 19th century, 330, 333, 335, 336
Peace of Augsburg, 163
and Venezuela, 222

Giacometti, Alberto: *Head* (1934–1935), 511

Gibson, Charles, 529

Gilbert, Sir Humphrey, 169

Gillmor, Frances: biographies of Moctezuma I and Nezahualcóyotl, 557

Giménez Fernández, Manuel, 92

Ginés de Sepúlveda, Juan, *see* Sepúlveda, Juan Ginés de

Gobineau, Comte Joseph-Arthur de:
Sur l'inégalité des races humaines, 437

gods, *see* deities

Godwin, William, 347

Goethe, Johann Wolfgang von, 328

gold and silver (including goldwork and silverwork):
Aztecs, 20, 27, 28
16th century on: France, 161; Italy, 65; Mexico, 133, 135; Spain, 51, 52, 54, 59, 60, 68, 69, 84
18th century on: France, 256, 267; Great Britain, 281; Mexico, 294, 297–98; Spain, 221, 222

gold and silver, Aztecs (cont.)
   19th century on: Great Britain,
     443; Mexico, 424; U.S., 384,
     387
   Maya, 49, 50
   Mixtecs, 466
   taken by Spanish, 84, 145–46, 154,
     167, 168–69, 188, 222
   see also metalwork
Goldwater, Robert, 511
Gómara, Francisco López de, 34, 82,
   91, 101, 113, 179, 188
   Chauveton on, 144–45, 147
   in Forner satire, 287
   Historia de las Indias (including
     Conquista de México), 77, 82–
     84, 87, 89, 141, 159, 206, 250,
     319, 325, 564
     Breton translation, 147
     Cervantes de Salazar plagiarism
       of, 86, 87, 175
     Cravaliz translation, 139, 158
     Fumée translation, 147, 158
     Italian translations, 139
     Nicholas translation, 168, 170
   influence of, 140, 170
     on Benzoni, 142, 143, 153
     on Botero, 141
     on Eden, 166
     on Gueudeville, 244
     on Lasso de la Vega, 136
     on Montaigne, 158, 159, 160
     on Muñoz Camargo, 127
     on Porcacchi, 142
     on Prévost, 249
     on Raynal, 264
     on Saavedra Guzmán, 135
     on Solís, 176
     on Southey, 372
     on Thevet, 152
     on Zapata, 134–35
     on Zappullo, 140
Gomberville, Marin Le Roy de:
     Polexandre, 210–12
Gómez de Avellaneda, Gertrudis:
     Guatimozín, el último em-
     perador de Méjico, 372–73

Gondra, Isidro Rafael, 321, 341
Góngora y Argote, Luis de, 201
Gordon, Thomas F.: History of An-
     cient Mexico, 350
Goupil, Eugène, 515
government, see political organiza-
   tion
Granados y Gálvez, Joseph Joaquín:
     Tardes americanas, 289–92,
     300, 313, 364
Great Britain:
   exploration and colonization, in-
     terest in, 166–72 passim
   Indians, attitudes toward:
     16th century, 166–72; transla-
       tions from French, 169; trans-
       lations from Spanish, 138,
       166–68
     17th century, 206, 212–14; trans-
       lations into Dutch, 207; trans-
       lations into French, 207; trans-
       lations from Spanish, 179, 206
     18th century, 210, 257–59, 270–
       85, 306–07; translations from
       Spanish, 299, 312
     19th century, 312, 346–49, 371–
       72, 441–48, 453–55
     20th century, 502–05, 511–13,
       536, 553–57
   and Mexico, archaeology in 19th
     century, 347–49
   slave trade, 286
   and Spain, 166, 169, 172, 228, 257
   and West Indies, 166
Greeks:
   Aztecs compared with, 77, 79, 94,
     96, 98, 102, 116, 161, 190, 199,
     241, 242, 243, 276, 289, 290,
     291, 294, 302, 331, 332, 345,
     464, 518, 564
   architecture, 96, 314
   barter and exchange, 270, 297
   calendrical system, 412
   cannibalism, 296
   deities and religion, 9, 182, 226,
     230, 296, 353, 416–17, 421, 482,
     503

Greeks, Aztecs compared with (cont.)
language, 226, 298, 324, 428
myths, 230–31, 416–17, 426, 482
painting, 136
philosophy, 40, 97–98
political system, 482
portrayal in 19th century Mexican art, 378
sculpture, 316, 333, 515, 517
warfare and weapons, 221, 268, 287
Incas compared with, 307, 331–32
Indians educated in tradition of, 114, 126–27
Gregory, Horace, 547–48
Grijalva, Juan de, 49, 50
Gros, Baron Jean-Baptiste-Louis, 436–37
Grotius, Hugo, 208, 209
Guadalajara: Hospicio Cabañas, Orozco frescoes, 533
Guadalupe, see Virgin of Guadalupe
Guatemala, 143, 232, 408
Guatemozin, see Cuauhtémoc
Güémez de Horcasitas, Juan Francisco, Conde de Revillagigedo, 237
Gueudeville, Nicolas, 241, 242, 244–45
influences on, 244, 245
Gutiérrez, Rodrigo: El senado de Tlaxcala, 461
Gutiérrez Heras, Joaquín, 561
Guzmán, Eulalia, 468, 469, 470, 480–82, 528, 543
on Díaz del Castillo, 481
Fernández on, 518, 523
influence of, on Romerovargas Yturbide, 482, 483
in Novo work, 540
on Sahagún, 482
Westheim on, 519–20

hacienda, 76–77, 292, 465–66
Haggard, H. Rider: King Solomon's Mines, 453
Montezuma's Daughter, 453–54

Haidah, 391
Hakluyt, Richard, 164, 166, 170–72
Codex Mendoza owned by, 170–71, 206
influence on: of Benzoni, 172
of Las Casas, 172
Peter Martyr edited by, 172
The Principall Navigations, Voiages and Discoveries of the English Nation, 171–72
and Raleigh, 170, 172
and Thevet, 170, 206
Hamy, E.-T., 236, 439, 498
on Humboldt, 337
Hanke, Lewis, 93
Harris, John, 257–59
influence on, of Solís, 258
on Las Casas, 258
Harris, Marvin, 335–36
Hauser, Henri, 139
Hawks, Henry, 171
Hegel, Georg Wilhelm Friedrich, 38, 463–64, 564
Heine, Heinrich: "Vitzliputzli," 367–71
Heine-Geldern, Robert, 334
Helm, MacKinley, 533
Henderson, Keith, 511–12
Henríquez Ureña, Pedro, 560
Henry III, King of France, 144
Henty, G. A.: By Right of Conquest; or, With Cortez in Mexico, 454–55
Herder, Johann Gottfried von, 311, 566
influence of, on Humboldt, 330
influence on, of Clavigero, 329
Outlines of a Philosophy of the History of Man, 328–29
Heredia, José María, 364–66
"En el teocalli de Cholula," 364–65
"Niágara," 364
"Las Sombras," 365
Hernández de Córdoba, Francisco see Córdoba, Francisco Hernández de
Hernández Portocarrero, Alonso, 63

Herrán, Saturnino: *Nuestros Dioses*, 514, 536

Herrera y Tordesillas, Antonio de, 175
  Historia general de los hechos de los castellanos en las islas y tierra firme del Mar Océano, 175–76, 283, 394, 395
  influence of: on Carli, 269, 271
  on Prévost, 249
  on Solís, 176
  on Voltaire, 254
  Morgan on, 394

Hesiod, 426

Hewett, Edgar L.: *Ancient Life in Mexico and Central America*, 490–91
  on Bandelier, 491

Hidalgo, Miguel, 316, 317

hieroglyphic writing, *see* picture writing

Higginson, Thomas Wentworth: "The First Americans," 401
  on Morgan, 401–02

Hispaniola, 50, 72, 75

Hoefnagel, Joris, 165

Hoeniger, Nicolaus: Benzoni translated by, 163, 164

Hohenberg, Franz: *Civitates orbis terrarum*, 165

Holbach, Paul-Henri, Baron d', 218, 257, 300

Holmes, William H., 405
  Archaeological Studies among the Ancient Cities of Mexico, 406–09
  on Coatlicue sculpture, 408, 510
  "Contributions of American Archaeology to Human History," 406
  Morgan-Bandelier theory, 405, 406, 407

Homer, 428

Homes, Henry, Lord Kames: *Sketches of the History of Man*, 273–75

Honduras, 271, 408

Hornot, Antoine, 265–66

Hoving, Thomas P. F., 513

Huaxteca: map (1579), 155

Huaxtepec, 387

Huehuetéotl, 33

Huehuetlapan, 229

Huehuetlatolli (Speeches of the Ancients), 44, 47, 125, 184

Huémac, 9, 342–43

Huemantzin, 232, 239

Huerta, Adolfo de la, 486

Huerta, Victoriano, 486

Huexotzinco, 40, 41, 44, 131, 396, 426

Huichilobos, 487

Huitzilopochtli, 10, 11–12, 21, 33, 41, 46, 54, 115, 116, 133, 182, 191, 198, 202, 230, 256, 257, 296, 319, 344, 430, 476, 496, 497, 529, 544, 545
  Blue Tezcatlipoca identified with, 31–32, 34
  in Heine poem, 367–70
  Jesus identified with, 304
  statue eaten in communion ceremony, 193, 194–95, 295

human sacrifice, 179, 196, 243, 255, 343, 344–45, 426, 496, 505
  Aztecs, 4, 12, 13, 14, 24, 27, 28, 31, 41, 43–47 *passim*
  16th century on, 172; France, 149, 153, 159; Great Britain, 169, 170; Italy, 65, 140, 145, 146; Mexico, 91, 128, 131, 133; Spain, 60, 61, 62, 68, 70, 77, 78, 82, 85, 87, 96–97, 101, 112
  17th century on: Mexico, 196; Netherlands, 208
  18th century on: France, 249, 256, 257; Italy, 226; Mexico, 296, 301, 413; Spain, 287, 305
  19th century on: France, 345, 438, 440; Great Britain, 347, 446, 447; Mexico, 315, 317, 325, 362, 363, 415, 421, 426, 434; Spain, 455, 456; U.S., 356, 357, 363, 385

human sacrifice, Aztecs (cont.)
20th century on: France, 500; Great Britain, 503; Mexico, 431, 473, 482, 525–26, 529, 544; U.S., 494, 496, 497
Germans and Franks, 145
Incas, 255, 447
Olmecs, 5
Spanish, 182
Toltecs, 5, 8, 343–44, 362, 485
Humboldt, Alexander von, 311, 329–36, 338, 340, 341, 346, 348, 355
Bernal on, 334, 336
Brasseur de Bourbourg on, 337
Chavero on, 425
Essai politique sur le royaume de la Nouvelle Espagne, 330, 334
Fernández on, 334
Hamy on, 337
influence of, 349, 350
on Gordon, 350
on Prescott, 355, 358
influence on, of Herder, 330
Kirchhoff on, 334, 336
León-Portilla on, 334
Ortega y Medina on, 329, 332
on De Pauw, 330
Payne on, 446
on Pichardo, 339
picture writing, interest in, 330, 332, 333, 336, 340, 346, 348, 358
on Raynal, 330
on Robertson, 330
Tylor on, 442–43
Vues des cordillères et monuments des peuples indigènes de l'Amérique, 330, 334, 336, 346
Hurtado de Toledo, Luis: Las Cortes de la Muerte, 134
Huxley, Julian, 484

Iglesia, Ramón, 83
Incas, 4, 160, 257
Acosta on, 122, 123
architecture, 263
art, 332–33, 444

Incas (cont.)
Aztecs compared with, 122, 123, 211, 219, 226, 229, 246, 247–48, 251, 253, 254, 255, 263, 269–70, 272, 273, 276, 284, 297, 331, 332–33, 340, 346, 347, 351, 385, 386, 388, 443–45, 447–48, 464
Bacon on, 206
Bandelier on, 388
Bernard on, 246
Boturini on, 229
Buckle on, 443–44
Buffon on, 251, 263
Carli on, 268, 269, 270
Cass on, 351
Chinese origin suggested, 208
Clavigero on, 297
Draper on, 286, 387
Egyptians compared with, 443, 444
Enlightenment view of, 219
Garcilaso de la Vega on, 198, 206, 219, 267
Genty on, 267
in Gomberville romance, 211
Greeks compared with, 307, 331–32
Hegel on, 464
human sacrifice, 255, 447
Humboldt on, 331, 332–33
Kames on, 273, 274–75
McCulloch on, 347
Mayer on, 385
Means on, 490
Montesquieu on, 253
De Pauw on, 261, 262, 267
Payne on, 444–45, 447–48
political system, 206, 219, 253, 269, 275, 331, 388, 444
pottery, 513
quipu, 229
Raynal on, 267–68
religion, 270, 274, 275, 304, 347, 447
Smith on, 272, 346
Vico on, 226

Incas (cont.)
  Viracocha identified with Saint
    Thomas, 304
  Voltaire on, 254, 255
India, Aztecs compared with, 332,
    353, 426, 438, 443, 446, 517,
    521
Indians (as theme in art, music, and
    literature):
  16th century:
    France, 156–57
    Mexico, 90, 91, 135
    Spain, 134–35
  17th century:
    France, 210–12, 215–16
    Great Britain, 212–14
    Mexico, 193–95
    Spain, 179–80
  18th century:
    France, 306–07
    Great Britain, 257
    Spain, 305–06
    U.S., 307–09
  19th century, 363–64
    Cuba, 364–66, 372–73
    Germany, 367–71
    Great Britain, 371–73, 453–55
    Italy, 379
    Latin America, 458, 460
    Mexico, 364, 378, 452–53, 457–
      58, 461–62
    Spain, 455
    U.S., 373–78, 451–52
  20th century, 509
    Great Britain, 553–57
    Mexico, 462, 465, 514, 515–16,
      517, 524–47, 558–61
    U.S., 547–53, 557
Indians, attitudes toward:
  16th century, 130–72
    France, 66, 67, 138, 144–62
    Germany, 66, 67, 68, 69, 138,
      163–65
    Great Britain, 138, 166–72
    Italy, 56–57, 63–67 passim, 69,
      70, 79, 85, 139–44, 147, 162,
      163, 164

Indians, attitudes toward, 16th cen-
    tury (cont.)
    Mexico, 88–92, 127–34, 135–37,
      564
    Netherlands, 67, 138, 162–63
    Spain, 55–64, 66–88, 92–127,
      134–35, 137–40, 146–47, 162–
      63, 166–68, 564
  17th century, 90, 92, 172–216
    France, 179, 207–09, 210–12,
      215–16
    Great Britain, 179, 206, 207,
      212–14
    Italy, 179, 209–10
    Mexico, 187–205, 564
    Spain, 174–87, 206, 216
  18th century, 217–309, 565–66
    France, 141, 217–19, 240–57,
      263–68, 306–07
    Germany, 260–63, 299
    Great Britain, 210, 257–59, 270–
      85, 299, 306–07, 312
    Italy, 255–57, 268–70
    Mexico, 219, 223, 224–25, 237–
      40, 289–304, 564
    Spain, 220–24, 285–89, 299, 305–
      06, 312
    U.S., 307–09
  19th century, 304–05, 310–462, 566
    Cuba, 364–66, 372–73
    France, 311, 312, 336–46, 378–79,
      414–16, 436–41, 510
    Germany, 311, 328–36, 367–71,
      448–50, 463–64
    Great Britain, 312, 346–49, 371–
      72, 441–48, 453–55
    Italy, 327–28, 379
    Mexico, 313–27, 364, 378, 411–
      31, 433–35, 452–53, 457–62
    Spain, 299, 313, 455
    U.S.S.R., 505–06
    U.S., 299, 312, 349–63, 373–78,
      380–404, 451–52, 534, 566
  20th century, 463–562, 567
    France, 498–501, 513
    Germany, 451, 464, 501, 534
    Great Britain, 502–05, 511–13,
      536, 553–57

Indians, attitudes toward, 20th century (cont.)
 Mexico, 431–33, 435–36, 464–87, 513–47, 557–61, 567
 U.S.S.R. and East Germany, 506–08
 U.S., 404–10, 488–98, 505, 513, 522–23, 534, 536, 547–53, 557
Indus Valley civilization, Aztecs compared with, 495
Ingraham, J. H.: *Montezuma, the Serf, or the Revolt of the Mexitli*, 376
Ingrams, David, 169
Instituto Indigenista Interamericano, 465
Instituto Nacional de Antropología e Historia, Mexico, 465, 466, 467–68
Instituto Nacional de Geografía y Estadística, Mexico, 412
Instituto Nacional Indigenista, Mexico, 474
International School of American Archaeology, 419
Ipalnemohuani, 34, 482
Iroquois: Aztecs compared with, 297, 383, 396, 408, 410, 429, 477, 496
 Morgan on, 382, 383, 390, 566
Isabella I, Queen of Castile and Léon, 73, 105
Italy:
 Indians, attitudes toward:
  16th century, 56–57, 63–67 *passim*, 69, 70, 79, 85, 139–44; translations from Dutch, 162, 163; translations into French, 144, 147; translations into German, 163, 164; translations from Spanish, 66, 67, 138, 139, 140
  17th century, 209–10; translations from Spanish, 179
  18th century, 225–37, 268–70, 299; translations from Spanish, 299
  19th century, 327–28, 379

Italy (cont.)
 and Mexico, archaeology in 19th century, 327–28
 and Spain, 139
Iturbide, Agustín de, 365
Itzcóatl, 11, 428, 429
Ixcateopan: church, supposed remains of Cuauhtémoc, 468, 469, 546
Ixtlilxóchitl (brother of Cacama), 200, 423
Ixtlilxóchitl, Fernando de Alva, 35, 198–99, 232, 317, 322, 348
 Brasseur de Bourbourg on, 344–45
 Chavero on, 424, 425, 430
 Gallatin on, 352–53
 Historia chichimeca, 199–200, 352–53, 355
 influence of: on Bancroft, 389
  on Prescott, 352, 355, 359, 362, 363
  on Veytia, 238, 240
 manuscript collection, 190, 191
 Relación décimotercera, 200–01
 Relaciones, 199
 Wilson on, 384
Izaguirre, Leandro: *El suplicio de Cuauhtémoc*, 461
Iztapalapan, 58, 387

Jalisco, 110
Japan, Aztecs compared with, 445
Jaucourt, Louis de: *Encyclopédie*, 257
Jerningham, Edward: *The Fall of Mexico*, 306–07
Jesuits, 217
 missionaries, 121, 241, 354
  accounts by, 241, 242, 293–301
 see also Roman Catholic Church
jewelry, *see* ornament and jewelry
Jews: Aztecs compared with, 183
 suggested as antecedents of Aztecs, 119, 121, 145, 147, 192, 231, 349
Jiménez de Cisneros, Cardinal Francisco, 73

Jiménez Moreno, Wigberto, 321, 466, 468, 469
on Pérez Martínez, 545–46
Johnson, Samuel, 306
Joseph II, Holy Roman Emperor, 268
Jourdanet, Denis: Sahagún edited by, 439–40, 454
Journal des Savants: Río article, 341
Joyce, Thomas A., 503, 512
Maya and Mexican Art, 513
Mexican Archaeology, 503
on Prescott, 512
Juan, Jorge, 234
Juan Diego, 227, 304
Juárez, Benito, 412, 416, 424, 431
Jung, Carl, influence of, 484, 504

Kahlo, Frida, 529
Kames, Lord, *see* Home, Henry, Lord Kames
influence on, of Buffon, 273
on Montesquieu, 274
Kant, Immanuel, 311
Katz, Friedrich: *Die sozialökono-mischen Verhätnisse bei den Azteken im 15. und 16. Jahr-hundert,* 507–08
King, Edward, Viscount Kingsbor-ough, 337, 348–49
Antiquities of Mexico, 238, 311, 348, 349
Bancroft on, 403
Prescott on, 349, 355
Kino, Father Eusebio Francisco, 189
Kircher, Athanasius: *Oedipus Ae-gypticus,* on picture writing, 190, 207–08, 261, 298
Kirchhoff, Paul, 466
Bandelier theory, 478, 479
on Humboldt, 334, 336
Kirk, John F., 385
Krickeberg, Walter: *Altmexikan-ische Kulturen,* 501
Kroeber, A. L.: *Anthropology,* 494

Kubler, George, 510, 522
The Art and Architecture of An-cient America, 522–23
Fernández on, 523
Kurath, Gertrude Prokosch, 559, 561

labor, 72, 73, 78, 88, 124, 181, 183, 316, 427, 465, 466, 529
Aztecs, 17, 21, 22, 23
16th century on: Spain, 103
17th century on: Mexico, 197–98
18th century on: Great Britain, 279, 280
19th century on: Great Britain, 443, 444, 447; Mexico, 429; U.S., 397
20th century on: Mexico, 478, 479, 480
see also class structure and or-ganization, serfs and slavery
encomienda system, 72–76 *passim,* 82, 88, 90, 92, 93, 110, 121, 124, 564
mita (in mines), 79, 121, 163
repartimiento system, 75–76, 77
see also slavery; Spain, land and labor
La Condamine, Charles-Marie de, 250–51
Laet, Jean de: *Histoire du Nouveau Monde,* 209
influence of, on Carli, 271
on Náhuatl language, 208–09
Solís on, 176
Lafitau, Joseph-François: *Mœurs des sauvages amércains comparées aux mœurs des premiers temps,* 242–43, 245, 275
Lafragua, José María, 413
Lahontan, Baron de, Louis-Armand de Lom d'Arce: *Dialogues curieux entre l'auteur et un sauvage de bon sens,* 241, 242, 244

land, 399, 415, 417, 465, 466, 477
Aztecs, 13, 21, 26
  16th century on: Mexico, 89; Spain, 81, 83, 87–88
  18th century on: Great Britain, 278
  19th century on: Germany, 332, 450; Great Britain, 445; Mexico, 428–29; U.S., 383, 384, 389, 393, 395
  20th century on: France, 499–500; Great Britain, 502, 503; Mexico, 474, 477, 478, 482; U.S.S.R. and East Germany, 506, 507; U.S., 488, 489, 493, 496, 497
  chinampas, 10, 15, 297, 320
  communal land, 21, 278, 383, 384, 393, 428, 429, 482, 488, 500, 502, 506
  for warrior nobles, 11, 13, 26, 428–29, 445, 450, 489, 493, 506, 507
  ejidos, 466
  encomienda system, 72–76 *passim*, 82, 88, 90, 92, 93, 110, 121, 124, 564
  hacienda, 76–77, 292, 465–66
  latifundio, 466
  reforms, 464
  repartimiento system, 75–76, 77
  see also Spain, land and labor
Landa, Diego de: *Relación de las cosas de Yucatán*, 341
Lang, Andrew: on Morgan-Bandelier theory, 441
language, *see* Náhuatl; Quiché
Las Casas, Bartolomé de, 73–74, 89, 92–94, 101, 116, 156, 162, 169, 173, 182, 184, 206, 250, 563
  Apologética historia, 94–98
  Brevísima relación de la destruición de las Indias, 134, 139, 143, 154, 173
    Dutch translations, 162–63
    English translation, 206

Las Casas, Bartolomé de, *Brevísima relación . . .* (cont.)
    Iodocus a Winghe illustrations, 164
    Miggrode translation, 146–47; into English by "M.M.S.," 169; into German and Latin, 164; Thevet on, 153–54
  Entre los remedios (English translation), 206
  Harris on, 258
  influence of, 78, 81, 108, 119, 146–47, 206, 220, 289
    on Chauveton, 144, 146
    on Durán, 119
    on Hakluyt, 172
    on Mier, 317
    on Palafox, 186
    on Román y Zamora, 103
    on Touron, 248
    on Voltaire, 254, 256
    in Jerningham poem, 306
  León Pinelo on, 173–74
  opposition to, 74–78 *passim*, 80, 81, 84, 97, 105, 146, 164, 173–74
    Benzoni, 143
    Escóiquiz, 305
    Mora, 323
    Motolinía, 74–75, 110
    Quiroga, 74
    Solís, 176–77
    Thevet, 154
    Valderrama, 76
    Zumárraga, 74
  Remesal biography, 185
  and Sepúlveda, debate (*Aquí se contiene una disputa*), 74, 80–81, 92, 93, 97, 98, 146, 164, 206, 217
    English translation, 206
    in Forner satire, 287–89
  Tratado sobre los indios que se han hecho esclavos, 98–99
  Venezuelan scheme criticized, 143
Lasso de la Vega, Gabriel: *Cortés valeroso* (*La Mexicana*), 135–36

Lasso de la Vega, Gabriel (cont.)
  influence on, of Gómara, 136
Laud Codex, *see* Codex Laud
law, *see* legal system
Lawrence, D. H., 4, 550, 553–57
  The Plumed Serpent, 553–56
  "The Woman Who Rode Away,"
    556–57
Leal, Fernando: Escuela Nacional
    Preparatoria, Mexico City,
    murals, 526–27
legal system, 229, 231, 240
  Aztecs, 18, 19, 20, 27, 207
    16th century on: Mexico, 88–89,
      130; Spanish, 56, 59, 78, 81, 86,
      87, 101, 102, 103–04, 111, 113,
      121, 125
    17th century on: Spain, 178, 183
    18th century on: France, 244,
      247, 248, 265, 266, 267; Great
      Britain, 280; Mexico, 290, 294,
      297
    19th century on: France, 345;
      Mexico, 317, 363, 421–22;
      U.S., 356, 386
    20th century on: U.S., 497
    Spanish, 74, 75, 80, 81, 105–06, 107,
      108, 143, 185, 188
Lehmann, Walter, 501
  Altmexikanische Kunstgeschichte,
    513
  Archiv für Anthropologie, 451
  on Morgan-Bandelier theory, 451
Le Mascrier, Abbé Jean-Baptiste, 247
León Pinelo, Antonio de, 174
  on Las Casas, 173–74
León-Portilla, Miguel, 535–36
  *Aztec Thought and Culture: A
    Study of the Ancient Náhuatl
    Mind*, 535
  The Broken Spears, 535
  on Humboldt, 334
  influence on, of Séjourné, 485
  on Orozco y Berra, 420
  on philosophy and religion, 11,
    25–26, 34–35, 38, 39, 40–41, 45,
    485

León-Portilla, Miguel (cont.)
  on Torquemada, 184
  Trece poetas del mundo azteca,
    535–36
León y Gama, Antonio de, 339, 340
  Bandelier on, 397
  *Descripción histórica y cronológ-
    ica de las dos piedras*, 301,
    302–04, 312, 313, 318, 321
  Gallatin on, 353
Lerdo de Tejada, Sebastián, 416
Lery, Jean de: on Brazil, 150–51, 157
  influence of, on Montaigne, 157–
    58
Lescarbot, Marc, 241
  Histoire de la Nouvelle France,
    241
Levin, David: on Prescott, 355, 358,
    360–61, 363
Libro di Benedetto Bordone, 68
Lienzo de Tlaxcala, 530
Linné, Sigvald: *Treasures of Mexi-
    can Art: Two Thousand Years
    of Art and Art Handicraft*,
    513
Livy, 324, 326
Locke, John, 246
Lok, Michael: Codex Mendoza trans-
    lated by, 170–71
London: Mexican antiquities dis-
    played, 347, 348
Longpérier, Adrien de: *Notice des
    monuments exposés dans la
    Salle des Antiquités au Musée
    du Louvre*, 340–41
López de Cerrato, Alonso, 143
López de Gómara, Francisco, *see*
    Gómara, Francisco López de
López Mateos, Adolfo, 466
López Velarde, Ramón, 467, 536–37
  "Suave Patria," 536
Lowie, Robert H.: *History of Eth-
    nological Theory*, 489
  Morgan-Bandelier theory, 409, 489
  Primitive Society, 489
Lucian: *Saturnalia*, 107–08

Lyttleton, George, first Baron Lyttleton: *Dialogues of the Dead*, 257
Lytton, Edward George Earle Lytton Bulwer-, first Baron Lytton, 451

McCulloch, John R., 346–47
MacLeish, Archibald: *Conquistador*, 551
MacNutt, F. A., 166
Madariaga, Salvador de: *Heart of Jade*, 553
Madero, Francisco I., 464, 487
Madero, Gustavo, 486
Madoc, 170, 371
  Quetzalcóatl identified with, 170
  in Southey poem, 371–73
Magellan, Ferdinand, 166
Magini, Giovanni Antonio, 140
Maistre, Joseph de, 421
Malinalco, 520
Malinche, 51, 204, 376, 452, 533
Malthus, Thomas Robert, 347
Manco Capac, 307
Mandeville, Sir John, *see Travels of Sir John Mandeville*
Mannheim, Karl, 564
maps, 13, 229, 233, 350, 412, 414
  Cortés, 67–68, 69–70, 115, 142
  Gemelli Carreri, 209
  Hoefnagel, 165
  Ortelius, 155
  Porcacchi, 142
  Ruscelli, 155
  Savorgnani, *see above* Cortés
Mariana, Juan de: *Historia de España*, 84–85
Marmontel, Jean-François: *Les Incas, ou La Destruction de l'Empire du Pérou*, 267, 307
Márquez, Pedro José, 293
  Due antichi monumenti di architectura messicana, 300–01, 312
marriage customs, 18, 112, 135, 153, 345, 384, 477
Martí, Manuel, 223–24, 225

Martí, Samuel, 559, 561
Martín, Benito, 67
Martínez del Río, Pablo, 466, 469, 490
Marx, Karl, 162
  and Morgan's *Ancient Society*, 505, 506
Marxism, influence of, 404, 473–74, 486, 505–08, 526, 527, 528–29
Mary Tudor, Queen of England, 166
Mason, J. Alden, 419
Massachusetts Quarterly Review: Parker essay, 361
mathematics:
  Aztecs:
    16th century on: Italy, 141
    18th century on: Italy, 271; Mexico, 291, 298, 303–04
    19th century on: Germany, 450; Great Britain, 446; Mexico, 315, 322, 427; U.S., 358
  Maya, 6
  Toltecs, 229
Matrícula de tributos, 530
Maturin, Edward: *Montezuma: The Last of the Aztecs*, 375–76
Maudslay, Alfred P., 502
Mauro, Lucio, 139
Maximilian, Archduke of Austria and Emperor of Mexico, 414, 415, 416
Maxtla, 200, 359
Maya, 6–7
  architecture, 6, 49, 438, 502, 513, 516
  Bancroft on, 389, 390, 391
  calendrical system, 6
  frescoes, 466
  Fry on, 512–13
  games, 19
  Gann and Thompson on, 490
  gold, 49, 50
  Holmes on, 408
  Joyce on, 513
  mathematics, 6
  Maudslay on, 502
  Morley on, 490

Maya (cont.)
  myths, 399
  picture writing, 341–42, 399, 438
  religion, 449
  sculpture, 6, 408, 475, 511, 512–13
  Spanish Conquest, 49–50
  Stephens on, 349
  trade, 6
Mayahuel, 505
mayeque, see serfs
Mayer, Brantz, 385
Means, Philip A., 490
medicine: Aztecs, 158, 224, 256, 270,
  291, 386
  Toltecs, 232
Mendicant orders, 77–78, 124, 126,
  187
  studies of Indian past, 78, 126–27,
    175, 180, 181–82, 183, 188, 190,
    248, 292, 296, 314, 315, 316,
    563, 565
  see also Augustinians; Dominicans;
    Franciscans
Mendieta, Gerónimo de, 124, 180,
  563
  "Consideraciones de Fray Hieróni-
    mo de Mendieta cerca de los
    indios de la Nueva España,"
    125–26
  Historia eclesiástica indiana, 124–
    25, 181
  influence of, on Torquemada, 181,
    182, 184
Mendizábal, Miguel Othón de, 466,
  472–73
Mendoza, Antonio de, 143, 197; *see
  also* Codex Mendoza
Mendoza, Gumesindo, 416–17
Menéndez y Pelayo, Marcelino, 364,
  366
Mengin, Ernst, 501
merchants, *see* barter and exchange;
  class structure and social organization; trade
Mesopotamia: Aztecs compared
  with, 492

Mesopotamia (cont.)
  Mexican sculpture compared with,
    513
mestizos, 195–96, 198, 436, 464, 465–
  66, 480; *see also* Indians (as
  theme) and Indians, attitudes
  toward, entries under Mexico;
  nationalism
metalwork:
  16th century on:
    France, 145
    Italy, 141
    Spain, 84, 85
  18th century on:
    France, 252
    Great Britain, 272, 273
    Mexico, 297
  19th century on:
    Great Britain, 441, 443
    Mexico, 324, 325, 423
    U.S., 354, 390
  20th century on:
    Great Britain, 502
    U.S., 406
  see also gold and silver
Métraux, Alfred, 513
Mexico City:
  Biblioteca Nacional, 534
  Convento de San Francisco, 339
  Escuela Nacional Preparatoria,
    murals, 465, 517, 526–27, 531
  Grito de Dolores, 327
  Museo Nacional, 313, 321, 337,
    413, 414, 416, 418, 466–67, 515,
    517
    19th century publications, 321–
      22, 416, 418
  Palacio de Bellas Artes, 461
    Siqueiros mural, 533
  Palacio Nacional, 414
    Rivera mural, 4, 481
  riots (1692), 192–93
  Smith on, 272
  statue of Cuauhtémoc, 417–18,
    455, 457, 468, 469
  town council (*cabildo*), 74, 82, 86
Michoacán, 74, 106, 283

Mier, Servando Teresa de, 240, 304, 305, 317, 412, 413, 421, 479, 563, 564
Historia de la revolución de Nueva España, antiguamente Anáhuac, 317–18, 326
influence of, on Bustamante, 318, 320
influence on, of Las Casas, 317
Miggrode, Jacques de:
Las Casas translated by, 146–47
English translation by "M.M.S.," 169
German and Latin translations, 164
Thevet on, 153–54
Minaya, Bernardino de, 144
Mitla: Bandelier on, 397
bas-relief wall ornaments, 314, 333, 335, 350
Cass on, 352
Doutrelaine on, 437
excavations, 19th century, 313, 314, 321, 327, 338, 418, 437
Holmes on, 407–08
Humboldt on, 333, 335
Rice on, 439
Mixcóatl, 7
Mixtecs, 466, 474
"M.M.S.": *The Spanish Colonie . . .* (translation of Miggrode's translation of Las Casas), 169
Moche Indians, 243
Moctezuma I, 47, 428
Gillmor biography, 557
Moctezuma II, 12, 14, 16, 45, 54, 56, 173, 320, 322, 424, 508
Acosta on, 123
in Ancona book, 452
Bancroft on, 393
in Barlow poem, 307
Belleforest on, 149
Benzoni on, 154
in Brooke work, 306
Carli on, 269, 270
Chavero on, 431
Clavigero on, 296–97

Moctezuma II (cont.)
and Cortés, 9, 45, 47, 51, 52, 53–54, 59, 91, 164, 186
treasure, 51, 52, 53, 59, 63–66, 69, 168
Cortés on, 59, 149, 393, 394
court, 27–29, 56
death, 54, 119, 292, 483
Díaz del Castillo on, 61, 393
in Dryden play, 212–14
Durán on, 119
in Fontenelle play, 215–16, 305
in Fosdick novel, 377
in Gomberville romance, 210–12
Gueudeville on, 244–45
Guzmán on, 480–81, 481–82, 483
Harris on, 258–59
Hawks on, 171
in Heredia poems, 365
Herrera on, 394
in Ingraham book, 376
Las Casas on, 96, 154
in Maturin novel, 375–76
Monterde biography, 547
Montesquieu on, 253
Morgan on, 381, 383, 392–94
Motezuma, Father, on, 203–05
Motolinía on, 113
Muñoz Camargo on, 129
Ortelius on, 155
Padden on, 497, 498
Palafox on, 186
Peckham on, 170
Pérez Martínez on, 544, 545
in Piron play, 306
Powell on, 170
Prescott on, 355, 360, 361, 393
illustration, 378
Quiroga on, 109
Radin on, 494
Robertson on, 279–80, 282
Romerovargas Yturbide biography, 183–84
Sahagún on, 49
Sepúlveda on, 81
Solís on, 177–78, 284, 295
Soustelle on, 47

Moctezuma II (cont.)
  Thevet on, 150, 154–55
  Toscano on, 546
  Vetancurt on, 189
  in Wallace novel, 451, 452
  Williams on, 548–49
Moctezuma, Diego Luis de, 205
Moctezuma, Francisca de, 132
Moctezuma, Isabel: García Iglesias
    biography, 547
Modernismo (literary movement),
    458, 460
Molina, Alonso de: *Vocabulario*, 209
Montaigne, Michel de, 138, 156–62,
    172, 173, 255
  Apology for Raymond Sébond,
    158–59
  on Brazil, 157–58, 160, 255
  Essais, 158
  influence on, of Gómara, 158, 159,
    160
  On Cannibals, 160
  On Coaches, 160–61
Monte Albán, 6–7
  Dupaix on, 313
  excavations, 19th century, 313, 396
  excavations, 20th century, 463
    by Caso, 466, 474
    Holmes on, 406–07, 409
  pyramids, 407
Montejo, Francisco de, 63
Monterde, Francisco: *Moctezuma II,
    Señor de Anáhuac*, 547
Montesquieu, Charles de Secondat,
    Baron de, 252–54, 264, 564
  Kames on, 274
Monzón, Arturo, 477–78, 479
  on Bandelier, 477, 479
Moore, Henry, 511
  Mother and Child (1922), 511
  Reclining Woman (1929), 511
Moquihuix, 231
Mora, José María Luis, 322–23, 325,
    412
  on Bustamante, 323
  influence on: of De Pauw, 323
    of Robertson, 323

Mora, José María Luis (cont.)
  Las Casas opposed by, 323
  Méjico y sus revoluciones, 323
  on Quiroga, 323
More, Thomas: *Utopia*, 106, 108, 157
Morelos, José María, 316, 322
Moreno, Manuel, 474, 477, 479
  on Bandelier, 477, 479
Morgan, Lewis H., 276, 312, 380, 381,
    382, 387, 398, 404, 405, 410,
    427, 463, 505–07
  Adams on, 391, 394
  American Association for the Ad-
    vancement of Science, papers,
    383, 384, 390
  Ancient Society, 390, 394–95, 404
    Engels and Marx on, 505–06
  and Bancroft, 388–94 *passim*, 403,
    404, 409
  and Bandelier, 312, 382, 387, 388,
    389, 394–98, 494
  Boas on, 404–05
  on Brasseur de Bourbourg, 392
  on Díaz del Castillo, 393
  Fiske on, 399–400
  on Herrera, 394
  Higginson on, 401–02
  influence of, 567
    on Wilson, 383–84
  influence on, of Robertson, 395,
    566
  Lang on, 441
  *The League of the Ho-dé-no-sau-
    nee*, 382
  "Montezuma's Dinner" (review of
    Bancroft), 388, 391–94, 409
    Fiske on, 400
    Higginson on, 401
  on Prescott, 382, 383, 385, 388,
    391, 392, 393, 566
  "The Seven Cities of Cibola," 385
  *Systems of Consanguinity and Af-
    finity of the Human Family*,
    382
  Vasconcelos on, 487
  on Wilson, 382

Morgan-Bandelier theory, 312, 398,
    409–10, 420, 450–51, 505, 506,
    529, 566
  Biart, 441
  Brinton, 399
  Chávez Orozco, 473
  Fiske, 399, 400
  Holmes, 405, 406, 407
  Lang, 441
  Lehmann, 451
  Lowie, 409, 489
  Nuttall, 399
  Orozco y Berra, 422, 476–77
  Payne, 444
  Radin, 493–94
  Seler, 450
  Vaillant, 409, 491, 492, 495
  White, 494–95
  Winsor, 401
  see also Bandelier, Adolph F.
Morley, Sylvanus G., 490
Motezuma, Pedro Diego Luis de, 201
  Corona mexicana, o Historia de
      los nueve Motezumas, 201–05
Motolinía (Fray Toribio de Bena-
      vente), 78, 87, 103, 105, 110–
      14, 119, 126, 180, 296, 328, 468,
      504
  Charles V, letter to, 74–75, 110,
      114
  Historia de los indios de la Nueva
      España, 110
  influence of: on Robertson, 277,
      285
    on Zorita, 99
  Las Casas opposed by, 74–75, 110
  Memoriales, 83, 110–11
Moxó, Benito María de, 314, 316
  Cartas mejicanas, 314–16
  influence on, of Durán and Saha-
      gún, 315
  on Voltaire, 315
Münster, Sebastian:
  Cosmography
    Belleforest translation, 149, 153,
        157; Thevet on, 150, 152–53
    Eden translation, 166

Münster, Sebastian, Cosmography
    (cont.)
    Thevet on, 152
Muñoz, Juan Bautista, 233
Muñoz Camargo, Diego, 127, 131,
    424
  Historia de Tlaxcala, 78, 127–30,
      175
  Herrera plagiarism of, 175
  influence on, of Gómara, 127
Murillo Velarde, Pedro: Geographía
    histórica, 223
music and dance, 13, 18, 28
  16th century on:
    France, 158
    Italy, 141
    Mexico, 130, 136
    Spain, 54, 108, 118
  18th century on:
    Great Britain, 274
    Mexico, 290
  19th century on:
    U.S., 387, 557
  20th century on:
    Mexico, 529, 557–61
    U.S., 550
  entertainers, 15, 22, 28, 129, 528
myths and legends, 45, 399, 406, 439,
    457–58, 505
  16th century on:
    Great Britain, 170
    Mexico, 132
  18th century on:
    Italy, 230–31, 234, 236
    Mexico, 238
  19th century on:
    Germany, 335
    Mexico, 420, 424, 425–26
    U.S., 353, 386
  20th century on:
    Great Britain, 504
  Greeks compared with, 230–31,
      416–17, 426, 482
  see also cosmogony; Quetzalcóatl;
      Thomas, Saint

Náhuatl (language and texts), 18, 22–23, 38–39, 40, 41–45, 54–55, 90
  16th century on:
    Italy, 141
    Mexico, 129, 196
    Spain, 4, 12, 19, 25, 36–37, 81, 123, 125
  17th century on:
    Germany, 208
    Spain, 184, 190, 534
  18th century on:
    France, 208–09
    Germany, 262, 298
    Great Britain, 274
    Italy, 226, 227, 229, 231–36 *passim*, 239
    Mexico, 290–91, 294, 298, 534
  19th century on:
    France, 339–40, 439
    Great Britain, 445
    Mexico, 324, 422, 427, 434–35
    U.S., 350, 534
  20th century on, 411, 534
    Germany, 534
    Great Britain, 536
    Mexico, 534–36, 547
    U.S., 534, 536
  Greek compared with, 226, 298, 324, 428
  Hebrew compared with, 231
  Huehuetlatolli, 44, 47, 125, 184
  Latin compared with, 298, 324
  see also myths and legends
Napoleon Bonaparte: in Egypt, 436
Napoleon III, Emperor, 414, 416, 436, 438
The Nation: on Bancroft, 402
  on Bandelier, 396
nationalism (in Mexico):
  16th century, 77, 92, 129, 130, 136–37, 188
  18th century, 225, 240, 293, 301, 311
  19th century, 322, 324, 325–26, 412–13, 452

nationalism (in Mexico) (cont.)
  20th century, 466–73, 476, 479, 525, 530–31, 543, 553, 567
  see also Revolution of 1910; War of Independence
Negroes, 426; *see also* Africa; slavery
Neruda, Pablo, 537
Netherlands:
  Indians, attitudes toward:
    16th century: translations from Italian and Spanish, 67, 138, 162–63
    17th century, 208, 209; translations from English, 207; translations from Spanish, 179
  and Spain, 162, 163, 248
Neumann, Franz, 252
New France (Canada), 241
New York City:
  Metropolitan Museum of Art, exhibition (1970), 513
  Museum of Modern Art, Chávez concert, 560
  Museum of Primitive Art, exhibition (1969), 513
New York Historical Society: Bandelier paper, 398
Newfoundland, 169, 170
Newton, Isaac, 220
Nezahualcóyotl, 10, 40, 240, 294, 344, 362, 399
  Chavero on, 425, 430
  Gillmor biography, 557
  Henty on, 454–55
  Ixtlilxóchitl on, 200, 384, 425, 430
  laws, 101, 290, 360
  Pomar on, 130–31
  Prescott on, 359, 360, 363
  Sierra on, 432
  supreme god, belief in, 35, 41, 45, 360, 430, 455, 475, 485, 497
  verse attributed to, 38, 225, 291, 360, 364, 425, 430, 434, 557
Nezahualpilli, 101, 130–31, 183, 225, 294, 344, 359, 360, 362, 432
Nicholas, Thomas: *The Pleasant Historie of the Weast India,*

Now Called New Spayne
(translation of Gómara), 168,
170
Nicholson, H. B.: on Seler, 449
Nicholson, Irene, 504
*Firefly in the Night: A Study of
Ancient Mexican Poetry and
Symbolism*, 536
influence on, of Séjourné, 504–05,
536
*Mexican and Central American
Mythology*, 505
Niza, Marcos de, 150, 152
nobility *see* class structure and or-
ganization
Noble Savage, concept of Indian as,
55, 60, 70, 85, 100, 156, 271–
72, 275, 306, 380
rejected in Enlightenment, 217–18,
246
Norsemen: suggested as antecedents
of Aztecs, 208
North American Review: Morgan
review, 391–94
Northwest Passage, 168
Novo, Salvador, 539–40
Cuauhtémoc, 540
"Cuauhtémoc y Eulalia," 540
*In Ticitezcatl o el espejo encan-
tado*, 540
"Ofrenda," 539
Nueva Galicia: map (1579), 155
Nuix, Juan: *Reflexiones imparciales
sobre la humanidad de los
españoles en las Indias*, 286
Nuttall, Mrs. Zelia, 399
*Fundamental Principles of Old
and New World Civilizations*,
Seler on, 450

Obregón, Álvaro, 464, 465, 486
Obregón, José: *El descubrimento
del pulque*, 461
Oceania, art of, 510
O'Gorman, Edmundo, 304
Fernández on, 518, 523

Olmecs, 4–6
architecture, 5, 190, 192, 210
Egyptian origin suggested, 192,
210
picture writing, 5, 192
Olmedo, Bartolomé de, 119
Olmos, Andrés de, 124, 126, 150,
152, 180, 184
influence of, on Zorita, 99
Ometéotl, 34
Ometochtli, 129
Ometochtzin, Carlos, 130
O'Neill, Eugene: *Marco Millions*,
549
Opochtli, 189, 296
origin, theories of:
from Asia, 121, 145, 229, 238, 314,
328, 334–35, 353, 425, 442, 443,
449
by Egyptians, 192, 210
from Europe, 149, 192
by Germans (Norsemen), 208, 209
by Jews, 119, 121, 145, 147, 192,
231, 349
ornament and jewelry: Aztecs, 12,
16, 27, 65, 68, 91, 135, 389
Mixtecs, 466, 474
Orozco, José Clemente, 462, 516–17,
524, 530–33
Autobiography, 517, 530–31
Charlot on, 517
Dartmouth College, frescoes, 531–
33
Escuela Nacional Preparatoria,
Mexico City, murals, 531
Helm on, 533
Hospicio Cabañas, Guadalajara,
frescoes, 533
Orozco y Berra, Manuel, 132–33,
415, 416, 418, 419, 432, 437
on Alamán, 422
Chavero on, 425, 426–27, 428, 430
*Historia antigua y de la conquista
de México*, 419–24, 426
influence of: on Chavero, 424
on Sierra, 431

Orozco y Berra, Manuel (cont.)
  influence on, of Ramírez, 416, 420,
    421, 425
  León-Portilla on, 420
  Morgan-Bandelier theory opposed,
    422, 476–77
Ortega, C. F., 238
Ortega y Medina, Juan A.: on Hum-
    boldt, 329, 332
Ortelius, Abraham, 155
  Theatrum orbis terrarum, 155–56
Othón de Mendizábal, Miguel, *see*
    Mendizábal, Miguel Othón de
Otomí, 282, 478
  verse attributed to, 291, 364, 557
Otumba, 108
Ovando, Nicolás de, 93
Oviedo y Valdés, Gonzalo Fernán-
    dez de, 78–79, 113, 179, 564
  in Forner satire, 287
  *Historia general y natural de las
    Indias*, 78, 79–80, 206, 250
    Breton on, 147
    English translation, 168
    Ramusio summary, 140
  influence of, 140
    on Benzoni, 142
    on Botero, 141
    on Hakluyt, 172

Padden, R. C.: *The Hummingbird
    and the Hawk*, 496–98, 500,
    563
painting: Aztecs, 52, 136, 183, 190,
    267, 297, 422
  Maya, 466
  Mexico, 19th century, 378, 461–62
  Mexico, 20th century, 462, 465,
    514, 515–16, 517, 524–33
  Olmecs, 5
  Toltecs, 5, 471, 485
  see also picture writing
Palafox de Mendoza, Juan de, 185–
    87, 220, 289, 290
  De la naturaleza de los indios, 186,
    221
  influence on, of Las Casas, 186

Palenque: Cass on, 352
  Dupaix on, 314
  excavations, 18th century, 312, 341
  excavations, 19th century, 313, 321,
    327, 338, 352
  Rice on, 439
Palerm, Ángel, 466
Palm, Erwin Walter, 69–70
Pánuco, 61, 63, 342
Papantla, *see* Tajín
Papantzin, 295, 377
Pardo Bazán, Emilia, 455
Paredes, Conde de, 191
Paris:
  Louvre:
    monograph on Aztec archaeol-
      ogy, 340–41
    Palenque reliefs, 352
  Pavillon de Marsan, exhibition
    (1928), 513
Paris Exposition (1889), 510
Parker, Theodore: on Prescott, 361–
    62, 363
Parkman, Francis, 385, 394
Parrington, V. L., 308
Paso y Troncoso, Francisco del, 196,
    411, 417–18
Paul, Saint, 102
Pauw, Cornelius de, 293, 328
  and Buffon, 260, 263
  Carli on, 268, 270–71
  Clavigero on, 294, 296, 297, 298,
    299
  on Feijóo, 261
  Frisi on, 268
  on Gemelli Carreri, 262
  Genty on, 266, 267
  Humboldt on, 330
  influence of, 271, 285, 289
    on Mora, 323
    on Nuix, 286
    on Raynal, 264, 265
    on Robertson, 275, 277, 284
    on Smith, 272
  *Recherches philosophiques sur les
    Américains*, 260–63, 267, 268,

Pauw, Cornelius de (cont.)
289, 299, 309, 312, 314, 315,
346, 350, 409, 434, 463, 565
on Solís, 262
Payne, Edward J., 502
*History of the New World Called
America*, 444–48
on Humboldt, 446
influence of, on Spence, 502
on Morgan-Bandelier theory, 444
on Tylor, 446
Paz, Ireneo: *Amor y suplicio*, 452–53
peasants, *see* class structure and social
organization, commoners
Peckham, Sir George, 169–70
Pedrarias Dávila (Pedro Arias de
Ávila), 79
Peet, Stephen P.: "Ancient Aztec
Cities and Civilization," 409
Peñafiel, Antonio, 418
Cantares en idioma mexicano, 534
Pellicer, Carlos: "Discurso por las
flores," 538; "Oda a Cuauhté-
moc," 537–38
Pérez Martínez, Hector: *Cuauhté-
moc*, 543–46, 547
Jiménez Moreno on, 545–46
Peru, 72, 75, 138, 174, 253
gold and silver, 168–69, 188
Herder on, 329
Humboldt on, 331
see also Incas
Pesado, José Joaquín, 364
Petén, 6, 7
Peter Martyr, 79
Decades, 64, 65–66, 70, 79, 85
Breton on, 147
*De nuper sub D. Carolo Repertis
insulis*, 66
De Orbe Novo, 66
Eden, translation in, 166–68, 170
Hakluyt edition, 172
MacNutt translation, 166
Ramusio summary, 140
Willes translation, 168, 170
influence of: on Benzoni, 142
on Rabelais, 157

Pereyra, Carlos: *Historia de la
América española*, 487
Phelan, John L., 124, 125, 181
Philip II, King of Spain, 76, 124, 166,
173, 181, 205, 298
Gallatin on, 354
Philip III, King of Spain, 175
Philip IV, King of Spain, 185, 186
Philip V, King of Spain, 219, 228
philosophy, 17, 18, 25–26, 38–41, 97–
98, 116, 137, 290, 440
Greeks compared with, 40, 97–98
Phoenicians: suggested as builders
in Middle America, 384–85
Pichardo, José Antonio: Humboldt
on, 339
picture writing, 190
Aztecs, 19, 23, 25, 34
16th century on: France, 152,
158; Italy, 64; Mexico, 130,
132; Spain, 81, 87, 102, 118,
119
17th century on: Germany, 190,
207–08, 261, 298; Italy, 209;
Mexico, 190, 191, 197; Spain,
181
18th century on: Germany,
261–62, 346; Great Britain,
277, 278, 281–82; Italy, 229,
231; Mexico, 224, 225, 298
19th century on: Germany, 330,
332, 333, 335, 336, 340, 346,
348, 358, 449, 450; Great Britain, 346, 347, 348–49; Mexico,
315, 412, 416–17, 418, 422,
424–25, 426, 427, 434; Spain,
455, 456; U.S., 349, 350, 353,
358, 399, 416
20th century on: Great Britain,
512; Mexico, 516, 530
destruction of, 12, 102, 130, 277,
358
Egyptian compared with, 64,
152, 190, 207–08, 231, 271, 315,
335, 348, 358, 512
Maya, 341–42, 399, 438

picture writing, Aztecs (cont.)
  Mixtecs, 474
  North American Indians, 449
  Olmecs, 5, 192
  Toltecs, 231, 294, 438, 484
  Zapotecs, 6
  see also Codex
Pimentel, Francisco, 415
Pincherle, Alberto, 93
Pínotl, 49, 50
Piron, Alexis: *Fernand Cortez ou
    Moctezuma*, 306
Pi y Margall, Francisco: *Guatimozin
    y Hernán Cortés*, 455–57
Pius IV, Pope, 142
Pizarro, Francisco, 124
plagues, *see* epidemics
political system:
  Aztecs, 13, 27–29, 207
    16th century on: France, 148;
      Spain, 56, 59, 86, 87, 99, 100,
      109, 110, 122, 125, 126, 137
    17th century on: Spain, 177, 178,
      183
    18th century on: France, 219,
      253, 255, 257, 264–65; Ger-
      many, 262; Great Britain, 274,
      279–80, 284–85; Italy, 230, 232,
      269–70; Mexico, 239, 296–97;
      U.S., 307
    19th century on: Germany, 330;
      Mexico, 362, 415, 428, 430;
      U.S., 350, 385, 389, 393, 395,
      399
    20th century on: France, 500;
      Great Britain, 504; Mexico,
      475, 477, 482–83, 486, 487, 519
    Greeks and Romans compared
      with, 48
  Incas, 206, 219, 253, 269, 275, 331,
    388, 444
Polo de Ondegardo, Juan, 122
Pomar, Juan Bautista, 78, 130
  Relación de Texcoco, 130–32
Popocatépetl, 29
Popol Vuh, 341

population estimates: after Conquest,
    76, 132, 272, 323, 433–34, 471
  before Conquest, 265, 282–83, 286,
    323, 324, 354, 388, 392, 442,
    471, 498
  human sacrifice suggested as re-
    sponse to overpopulation, 14,
    497
Porcacchi, Thomaso: *L'isole più
    famose del mondo*, 142
Portugal, 146
pottery and ceramics, 4, 406, 513
  Aztecs, 15, 20, 22, 23, 256, 322, 390,
    424
  Incas, 513
  Toltecs, 471
Powell, David: *Historie of Cambria*,
    170
precious stones, 4, 20, 24, 28, 59, 166
Prescott, William H., 311, 320, 325,
    361, 375, 534
  Alamán on, 362–63
  on Boturini, 235, 236
  Chavero on, 425
  Conquest of Mexico, 312, 349, 350,
    354–61, 378, 409, 557, 566
    Henderson illustrations, 511–12
    Ramírez notes to second Mexi-
      can edition, 327, 362, 363, 420
  Ferdinand and Isabella, 361
  Gallatin on, 352
  influence of, 375, 376, 377
    on Crane, 550
    on Haggard, 453, 454
    on Henty, 454
  influence on: of Baradère, 355
    of Clavigero, 299, 356, 357, 358
    of Humboldt, 355, 358
    of Ixtlilxóchitl, 352, 355, 359,
      362, 363
  Joyce on, 512
  on Kingsborough, 349, 355
  Levin on, 355, 358, 360–61, 363
  Morgan on, 382, 383, 385, 388, 391,
    392, 393, 566

Prescott, William H. (cont.)
    Parker on, 361–62, 363
    on Robertson, 285
    on Veytia, 355
    and Wilson, 384, 385
Prévost, Abbé Antoine-François, 248–49
    Carli on, 271
    Histoire générale des voyages, 248, 249
    influences on, 249
Price, Barbara J.: *Mesoamerica*, 496
priests, *see* Calmécac; class structure and social organization; religion
Prokofieff, Sergei: *Suite scythienne*, 558
Protestantism, 138, 150, 163
Ptolemy: *Geography*, Magini's adaptation of, 140
public officials, 13, 15, 17, 26, 27, 46, 269, 478, 499; *see also* class structure and social organization
Puebla: Biblioteca Palafoxiana, 186
    Colegio de San Pedro, 186
Pueblo Indians, 391, 410, 441, 449
Puente, Juan de la, 223
Purchas, Samuel:
    Codex Mendoza purchased and published by, 171, 190, 206, 207, 281
    Hakluytus Posthumus, or Purchas, His Pilgrimes, 171, 206
    influence of: on Gueudeville, 244
    on Prévost, 249
Putnam, F. W., 391, 394
pyramids, 412
    Bullock on, 348
    Cholula, 239, 295, 382, 396, 397
    Dupaix on, 314
    Egyptian compared with, 436
    Gordon on, 350
    Humboldt on, 335
    Monte Albán, 407
    Tajín, 314

pyramids (cont.)
    Teotihuacán, 5, 190, 192, 210, 347, 396, 415, 436–37, 442, 443, 471

Quarterly Review: review of Humboldt, 346
Quetzalcóatl, 5, 8, 44, 45, 46, 51, 53, 115, 239, 296, 424, 427, 479, 485, 497, 504, 505
    Cortés identified with, 9, 51–52, 186, 483
    Icelandic missionary identified with, 420–21, 426
    Madoc identified with, 170
    myths and legends, 8–9, 31, 33, 47, 49, 170, 186, 342, 343–44, 426–27, 484
    in Orozco fresco, 532–33
    Saint Thomas identified with, 192, 238–39, 240, 295, 304, 318, 320, 352, 420, 421, 426
    White Tezcatlipoca identified with, 31, 34
Quevedo, Francisco de: in Forner satire, 287
Quiché: texts, 341, 342, 438
Quiroga, Vasco de, 74, 105–07
    Información en derecho, 107–10
    Mora on, 323
Quiroz Cuarón, Dr. Alfonso, 481, 528

Rabelais, François, 151, 153
    Gargantua, 157
    influences on, 157
    Pantagruel, 157
Radin, Paul: *The Sources and Authenticity of the History of the Ancient Mexicans*, 493–94
Raleigh, Sir Walter: and Hakluyt, 170, 172
Ramírez, Gerónimo, 136–37
Ramírez, Ignacio, 412, 413
Ramírez, José Fernando, 326–27, 413, 415, 416, 432
    Chavero on, 424–25

Ramírez, José Fernando (cont.)
  *Diccionario universal de historia y
    geografía*, 413–14
  influence of, on Orozco y Berra,
    416, 420, 421, 425
  Prescott, *Conquest of Mexico*,
    notes on, 327, 362, 363, 421
Ramusio, Giovanni Battista: *Delle
    navigationi e viaggi*, 139–40
Raynal, Abbé Guillaume, 218, 564
  in Forner satire, 287
  Genty on, 266
  *Histoire philosophique et politique
    des établissements et du com-
    merce dans les Deux Indes*,
    263–65, 267–68, 314
  Humboldt on, 330
  influence of, on Robertson, 284
  influence on: of Gómara, 264
    of De Pauw, 264, 265
Read, Herbert, 510, 512
Real y Pontificia Universidad de
    México, 85
Redfield, Robert: *Tepoztlan*, 490
Reforma, 412–13, 452
religion, 5, 6, 7, 35
  17th century on:
    Mexico, 196
  18th century on:
    France, 241–47
    Italy, 236, 238
    Mexico, 238–39
  19th century on:
    France, 342, 343, 344–45
    Germany, 449
    Mexico, 417, 427
  20th century on:
    Great Britain, 505
    Mexico, 472, 475–76
  Aztecs, 13, 17, 18, 21, 23, 33, 34–38,
    43, 45, 46, 47–48
    16th century on: France, 153,
      158–59, 161; Italy, 140, 145;
      Mexico, 128, 130, 131, 137;
      Spain, 60, 62, 91, 113, 118, 123,
      125, 126

religion, Aztecs, 16th century on
    (cont.)
    17th century on: Mexico, 193–
      95; Spain, 176, 178–79, 182–83,
      184
    18th century on: France, 248,
      257, 265; Great Britain, 275,
      285; Italy, 270; Mexico, 240,
      291, 295–96, 301; U.S., 307
    19th century on: France, 440;
      Germany, 336, 449; Great
      Britain, 446, 447, 454; Mexico,
      325, 363, 415, 417, 421, 423,
      425, 426; Spain, 456, 457; U.S.,
      350, 353, 357, 359, 386–87
    20th century on: France, 500;
      Great Britain, 503, 504; Mex-
      ico, 431–32, 474–76, 482, 485,
      486, 544
    Calmécac, 17, 18, 46, 47, 475
    Egyptians compared with, 353,
      503
    Greeks compared with, 353, 482,
      503
    Romans compared with, 103, 503
    vestal virgins, 191
  Incas, 270, 274, 275, 304, 347, 447
  Maya, 449
  Olmecs, 5
  Toltecs, 8, 35, 44, 45, 46, 238, 343,
    344, 357, 358, 360, 420, 426
  see also cannibalism; ceremonies
    and rituals; cosmogony; dei-
    ties; human sacrifice; Roman
    Catholic Church
Remesal, Antonio de, 185
Renaissance, *see* Indians, attitudes
    toward, 16th century
Rendón, Silvia, 197
repartimiento system, 75–76, 77
Revilla, Manuel G., 517
Revillagigedo, Conde de, *see*
    Güémez de Horcasitas, Juan
    Francisco, Conde de Revilla-
    gigedo

Revolution of 1910 (Mexico), 436, 464, 470, 567
Revueltas, Fermín: Escuela Nacional Preparatoria, Mexico City, murals, 526–27
Reyes, Alfonso: *Visión de Anáhuac*, 540–43, 548
Ribera, Juan de, 65
Rice, Allen Thorndike, 439
Rico González, Víctor, 240, 424
Río, Andrés del, 348
Río, Antonio del, 312, 341
rituals, *see* ceremonies and rituals
Riva Palacio, Mariano, 424
Rivera, Diego, 462, 515, 516, 524–30, 558
    Charlot on, 527
    Cuernavaca, frescoes, 527, 530
    Escuela Nacional Preparatoria, Mexico City, murals, 526, 527
    influence on, of Seler, 530
    Palacio Nacional, Mexico City, murals, 4, 481, 527–29, 541, 561
    Wolfe on, 524–26, 527–28, 529
Rivet, Paul: *Mexique précolombien*, 513
Rivière, Georges-Henri, 513
Roa Bárcena, José María: *Leyendas mexicanas*, 457
Robertson, William, 502
    on Acosta, 285
    Clavigero on, 298
    Fiske on, 399
    in Forner satire, 287
    Gallatin on, 354
    History of America, 210, 275–85, 312, 314, 315, 350, 393, 409, 565–66
    History of the Reign of the Emperor Charles V, 275
    Humboldt on, 330
    influence of: on Bandelier, 395
        on Mora, 323
        on Morgan, 395, 566
        on Nuix, 286

Robertson, William (cont.)
    influence on: of Boturini, 277
        of Buffon, 275
        of Eguiara y Eguren, 277
        of Motolinía, 277, 285
        of De Pauw, 275, 277, 284
        of Raynal, 284
        of Torquemada, 277, 285
        of Zorita, 277, 278, 285
    Prescott on, 285
    on Solís, 284
    Winsor on, 400
Rodin, François-Auguste-René, 509
Rodríguez Galván, Ignacio: "Profecía de Guatimoc," 366, 537
Roman Catholic Church: Cortés on, 59
    Enlightenment view of, 219, 220, 252
    Indians, attitudes toward (16th century), 71–78, 138
    Indians as Christians, 62, 106, 123, 132, 398, 416, 480
    Inquisition, 139, 173, 220, 357
    Las Casas on, 98
    in Mexico, Church-State issue, 479–80, 485
    Motezuma, Father, on, 203
    Papal grant of America to Spain, 71, 172
    Portuguese missionaries, 146
    Spanish missionaries, 25, 36–37, 41, 62, 73, 74, 78, 106–07, 110, 113–18, 121–27, 130, 134, 175, 180, 181, 186, 241, 293
        16th century on: France, 145, 146, 148–49, 153; Germany, 163, 165; Great Britain, 172; Italy, 140–44 *passim*
        18th century on: France, 242; Mexico, 291, 304
        19th century on: Mexico, 323; U.S., 354
    see also Augustinians; Dominicans; Franciscans; Jesuits; Mendicant orders

Román y Zamora, Jerónimo, 103–04
  influence on, of Las Casas, 103
Romans:
  Aztecs compared with, 77, 79, 94,
    96, 97, 98, 102, 116, 161, 177,
    190, 191, 199, 242, 276, 289,
    291, 294, 331, 345, 464, 565
  architecture, 96, 136, 422
  calendrical system, 412
  deities and religion, 91, 103, 116,
    182, 230, 296, 421, 503
  language, 298, 324
  political system, 482
  portrayal in 19th century art,
    378, 379, 461
  sculpture, 316
  slavery, 107, 422
  warfare and weapons, 221, 252,
    274, 287
  Indians educated in tradition of,
    114, 126–27
Romerovargas Yturbide, Ignacio,
  482–84
  influence on, of Guzmán, 482, 483
Rondeau, José, 316
Ronsard, Pierre de, 156
  Discours contre Fortune, 157
Roosevelt, Theodore: in Darío poem,
  458
Rousseau, Jean-Jacques, 275, 306
Ruiz de Corral, 185
Ruscelli, Girolamo, 155
Russell, John, 511

Saavedra Guzmán, Antonio de: El
  peregrino indiano, 135
Sacrificial Stone, see Stone of Tizoc
Sad Indian (sculpture), 521
Sahagún, Bernardino de, 4, 49, 78,
  114, 126, 127, 180, 296, 418,
  534
  Burland on, 504
  Cornyn's study of manuscripts,
    536
  Florentine Codex: English ver-
    sion, 536
    as Rivera source, 530

Sahagún, Bernardino de (cont.)
  Gallatin on, 353
  Guzmán on, 482
  Historia de las cosas de la Nueva
    España, 24, 25, 36–37, 114–18,
    119, 182, 224, 318, 321, 322,
    325, 348, 362
  Jourdanet and Siméon edition,
    439–40, 454
  influence of: on Haggard, 454
    on Moxó, 315
  Primeros Memoriales, 530
  Seler's study of manuscripts, 418,
    448
Salas, Alberto M., 79
Salvatierra, Conde de, 186
Sánchez, Jesús, 418
Sanders, William T.: Mesoamerica,
  496
Santa Anna, Antonio López de, 338,
  412, 413, 414
Santibáñez, Condesa de, 227
Saville, Marshall H., 488
Savorgnani, Pietro, 67–68, 69–70, 142
Saxons, Aztecs compared with, 356
Scandinavians, Aztecs compared
  with, 353
Scholasticism, 38, 71, 93, 219–20, 293
Scott, John F., 513
sculpture, 4, 406, 408, 466, 510
  Aztecs, 183–84, 302
  18th century on: Mexico, 297
  19th century on, 509–10; Ger-
    many, 450; Mexico, 315–16,
    322, 422, 423, 426; U.S., 397,
    425
  20th century on, 509; Great
    Britain, 511, 512–13; Mexico,
    514–21 passim, 523–24, 543–
    44; U.S., 408, 522–23
  Egyptians compared with, 348,
    352, 513, 517
  Greeks compared with, 316, 333,
    515, 517
  Romans compared with, 316
  Maya, 6, 408, 475, 511, 512–13
  Olmecs, 5

sculpture (cont.)
Toltecs, 5, 471, 511
Scythians, Aztecs compared with, 296
Séjourné, Laurette, 44–45, 470, 484–85, 504
influence of: on León-Portilla, 485
on Irene Nicholson, 504–05, 536
on Seler, 484
Seler, Eduard, 405, 411, 419, 448–50, 567
on Brinton, 534
Caso on, 448–49
influence of, 501, 567
on Rivera, 530
on Spence, 502, 503
influence on, of Bastian, 449
Morgan-Bandelier theory, 450
H. B. Nicholson on, 449
Sahagún manuscripts studied, 418, 448
Séjourné on, 484
Sepúlveda, Juan Ginés de, 80–82, 83, 91, 101, 174
and Las Casas, debate, 74, 80–81, 92, 93, 97, 98, 146, 164, 206, 217
in Forner satire, 287–89
serfs (mayeque), 16, 26, 279, 422, 478, 479, 501, 503; see also class structure and social organization
Seville, 179
sexual practices, 243, 260
Aztecs, 18–19
16th century on, 172; France, 149, 153, 156; Great Britain, 171; Italy, 140, 141; Spain, 59, 61, 62, 63, 83, 85, 87, 101, 111, 121
17th century on: Spain, 184
18th century on: France, 250, 273; Great Britain, 273, 275; Spain, 222
19th century on: France, 440
Sharevskaya, B. I., 506–08

Shellabarger, Samuel: Captain from Castile, 553
Shoshone, 391
Sierra, Justo, 431, 435
Evolución política del pueblo mexicano, 431–33
Sigüenza y Góngora, Carlos de, 189–93, 207, 208, 229, 291, 317, 421
Chavero on, 425
Ciclografía mexicana, 190, 210
and Gemelli Carreri, 209, 210
Genealogía de los emperadores mexicanos, 189
influence of: on Clavigero, 190, 295
on Eguiara y Eguren, 225
on Veytia, 240
Paraýso occidental, 190–91
Phoenix of the West . . . , 192
Theatro de virtudes políticas, 191–92
treatise on comets, 189
silver, see gold and silver
Siméon, Rémi, 534
Náhuatl dictionary, 439
Sahagún edited by, 439–40, 454
Simpson, Lesley Byrd: on Crane, 550–51
Siqueiros, David Alfaro, 462, 515, 516, 524, 533
Cuauhtémoc Against the Myth, 533
Fernández on, 533
Palacio de Bellas Artes, Mexico City, mural, 533
Sixtus V, Pope, 298
slavery:
Africa, 89, 286–87, 318, 345, 348
Aristotle's "slaves by nature" theory, 71, 80–81, 86
Aztecs, see class structure and social organization
Cuba, 345
Great Britain, 286
of Indians, by the Spanish, 72, 75, 77, 79, 89, 98, 107, 143
U.S., 345

Smith, Adam, 502
  influence of, 346
    on McCulloch, 346
  influence on, of De Pauw, 272
  Wealth of Nations, 272–73, 274
social organization, *see* class struc-
    ture and social organization
Sociedad Mexicana de Antropología,
  466
Solís y Ribadeneyra, Antonio de, 176
  on Benzoni, 176
  on De Bry, 176
  Clavigero on, 295
  Genty on, 266
  *Historia de la conquista de Méx-
    ico*, 176–79, 201, 203, 216, 287,
    565
  Hornot on, 266
  influence of, 305
    on Escóiquiz, 305, 306
    on Gueudeville, 244, 245
    on Harris, 258
  influences on, 176
  Jaucourt on, 257
  on Laet, 176
  Las Casas opposed by, 176–77
  De Pauw on, 262
  Robertson on, 284
  Voltaire on, 256–57
Solórzano y Pereira, Juan de: *Polít-
    ica indiana*, 174
Soustelle, Jacques, 32–33, 45–47, 498,
  513, 563
  *The Daily Life of the Aztecs on
    the Eve of the Spanish Con-
    quest*, 498–501
  on Spengler, 499
  on Vaillant, 499
Southey, Robert: *Madoc*, 371–72
  influences on, 372
Spain, 154, 172, 174, 201, 222
  archaeology in Mexico, 312, 313–
    14
  Black Legend, 143, 163, 259, 265
  and Chile, 134
  Conquest, 14, 47, 48, 51–56

Spain (cont.)
  diseases introduced to New
    World, 132, 145
  during Enlightenment, 219–20,
    289, 301
  gold and silver from New World,
    84, 145–46, 154, 167, 168–69,
    188, 222
  and Great Britain, 166, 169, 172,
    228, 257
  and Guatemala, 143
  and Hispaniola, 50, 72, 75
  human sacrifice, 182
  Indians, attitudes toward:
    16th century, 55–64, 66–88, 92–
      127, 134–35, 137–40, 146–47,
      162–63, 166–68, 564; transla-
      tions into Dutch, 67, 138, 162–
      63; translations into English,
      138, 166–68; translations into
      French, 66, 67, 138, 146–47;
      translations into German, 66–
      67, 138; translations into Ital-
      ian, 66, 67, 138, 139, 140
    17th century, 174–87, 216; trans-
      lations into English, 179, 206;
      translations into French, 179;
      translations into Italian, 179
    18th century, 220–24, 285–89,
      305–06; translations into Eng-
      lish, 299, 312; translations into
      Italian, 299
    19th century, 455; translations
      into English, 299; translations
      into French, 313
  and Italy, 139
  land and labor, 72–78, 87–88, 90,
    196, 198, 222, 291–92
  composición, 174
  encomienda system, 72–76 *pas-
    sim*, 82, 88, 90, 92, 93, 110, 121,
    124
  repartimiento system, 75–76, 77
  slavery, 72, 75, 77, 79, 89, 98,
    107, 143, 345
  laws and legal system, 74, 75, 80,

Spain (cont.)
  81, 105–06, 107, 108, 143, 185,
    188
  Moors, 56
  and Netherlands, 162, 163, 248
  Papal grant of America to, 71, 172
  and Peru, 72, 75, 138, 174, 252
  tribute demanded by, 72, 73, 75,
    76, 77, 80, 83–84, 89, 109, 124,
    174, 196, 198, 292
  and Venezuela, 143
  warfare and weapons, 52, 53, 54,
    91, 109, 161, 187, 253, 268–69,
    274
    horses used, 52, 137, 161, 187,
      253, 269, 274
  and West Indies, 72, 73, 75, 77–78,
    223
  see also Roman Catholic Church;
    War of Independence
Spartans, Indians compared with,
    241, 242
Spence, Lewis: The Civilization of
    Ancient Mexico, 502–03
  The Gods of Mexico, 503
Spencer, Herbert, 381, 399, 404, 427
Spengler, Oswald: Decline of the
    West, 464, 546
  Soustelle on, 499
Spinden, Herbert J.: Ancient Civili-
    zations of Mexico and Central
    America, 489
Spontini, Gasparo: Fernand Cortez,
    379
sports, see games and sports
Stafford, Sir Edward, 170
Stephens, John Lloyd: Incidents of
    Travel in Central America,
    Chiapas, and Yucatan, 349, 402
Stevenson, Robert: Music in Aztec
    and Inca Territory, 559, 561
Stone of the Sun, see Calendar Stone
Stone of Tizoc (Sacrificial Stone),
    302, 303, 321, 347, 399
Stravinsky, Igor: Sacre du Prin-
    temps, 558

Suárez de Peralta, Juan: Noticias
    históricas de la Nueva España,
    88–89, 91, 92

Tabasco, 51
Tablada, José Juan, 517–18
Tacuba, 280
Tajín: excavations, 18th century,
    300, 301
  pyramid, 314
Tapia, Andrés de: Relaciones, 56
Tapia, Bernardino Vásquez de, see
    Vásquez de Tapia, Bernardino
Tarascans, 12
Tecamachalco, 40
Tecayehuatzin, 40, 44
Techotlalatzin, 240
Tecuixpo (Isabel Moctezuma):
    García Iglesias biography, 547
Teilhard de Chardin, Pierre, 484
Telpochcalli (House of Youth), 17,
    21, 46
Tenayuca, 232
Tenoch, 428
Tenochtitlán, 9, 10, 13, 41, 44, 46,
    49, 131, 200, 232
  architecture and city planning,
    14–15, 19, 58, 59, 67, 69–70,
    148, 167–68, 183, 256, 280–81,
    283
  in Barlow poem, 307–08
  Bordone on, 68
  Chavero on, 424, 429, 430
  Cortés sketch and description, 58–
    60, 67–68, 69–70, 101, 142,
    148, 165
  Díaz del Castillo on, 14, 60
  Draper on, 387
  Eden on, 166, 167–68
  Great Temple, 33, 416, 431, 529
  in Haggard novel, 453
  Hoefnagel engraving of, 165
  market, 20, 58, 60, 148, 256
  Montaigne on, 160
  Morgan on, 381
  Münster on, 152

Tenochtitlán (cont.)
  as name, 208, 239
  Orozco y Berra on, 422, 423
  Ortelius description, 155
  Peter Martyr on, 66, 168
  Porcacchi on, 142
  in Prévost book, 249
  Raynal on, 264
  in Reyes essay, 541–42
  in Rivera mural, 4, 527–29, 541
  Robertson on, 280, 283, 285
  Sierra on, 432
  Solís on, 266
  Soustelle on, 498–99
  in Southey poem (as Aztlán),
    371–72
  Spanish Conquest, 52, 53, 54, 58,
    81, 119, 123, 175, 177, 187, 200,
    203, 205, 317, 432
  Spengler on, 464, 499
  Thevet on, 152
  Vaillant on, 499
  Voltaire on, 255–56
  Ziletti on, 139
Teoamoxtli, 232, 239, 294–95, 343
Teotihuacán, 5–6, 7
  architecture, 5, 239, 471
  Brasseur de Bourbourg on, 343–44
  excavations, 17th century, 190, 192
  excavations, 19th century, 418,
    436–37, 439
  excavations, 20th century, 463
    Gamio study, 465, 466, 471–72
  frescoes, 5, 471, 485
  Gemelli Carreri on, 210
  Holmes on, 408
  in Orozco fresco, 532
  Orozco y Berra on, 420
  pottery, 471
  pyramids, 5, 471
    Almaraz on, 415
    Bandelier on, 396
    French study (19th century),
      436–37
    Gemelli Carreri on, 210
    model displayed in London, 347

Teotihuacán, pyramids (cont.)
    Sigüenza on, 190, 192
    Tylor on, 442, 443
  sculpture, 5, 471
  Séjourné on, 484–85
  Tula identified with, 484, 491
  Veytia on, 239
  see also Toltecs
Tepanecs, 191, 200, 359, 429, 493
Tepeaca, 282
Tepoztécatl, 550
Tercero, Juan L.: Nezahualpilli, el
    catolicismo en México, 453
Ternaux-Compans, Henri, 355
Terrazas, Francisco de, 90, 91, 135
    Nuevo Mundo y Conquista, 135
Tertre, Jean-Baptiste du, 241
Texcoco, 9–14 passim, 20, 27, 35, 40,
    41, 101, 111, 201, 232, 240, 280,
    294, 301, 317, 399, 446, 497
  Bird on, 374–75
  Brasseur de Bourbourg on, 344
  Chavero on, 430
  Draper on, 387
  Ixtlilxóchitl on, 199–200, 352–53,
    355
  Pomar on, 130–32
  Prescott on, 355, 356, 358, 359–60
  Sierra on, 432
  temple, 183, 387
  see also Chichimecs; Nezahual-
    cóyotl
Texcotzingo, 430
textiles, 15, 20, 85, 133, 256, 424
Tezcatlipoca, 8, 30, 31–32, 34, 43, 46,
    51, 54, 115, 116, 182, 196, 230,
    304, 344, 421
  Black Tezcatlipoca, 31, 34, 552
  Blue Tezcatlipoca (Huitzilopocht-
    li), 31–32, 34
  Red Tezcatlipoca (Xipe Totec),
    31, 34
  White Tezcatlipoca (Quetzal-
    cóatl), 31, 34
Tezozómoc, Fernando Alvarado, 78,
    132
    Crónica mexicana, 132–34

Thévenot, Melchisédec, 207
Thevet, André, 149–55, 156
  on Belleforest's translation of Münster, 150, 152–53
  on Benzoni, 153
  Codex Mendoza owned by, 150, 152, 206
  Cosmographie du Levant, 150
  Cosmographie universelle, 150, 151–53, 157
  on Frobisher, 154
  Fumée on, 151
  and Hakluyt, 170, 206
  influence on, of Gómara, 152
  Las Casas opposed by, 154
  on Miggrode, 153–54
  on Münster, 152
  Les Singularitez de la France antarctique, 150–51
  Les Vrais Portraits et vies des hommes illustres grecz, latins, et payens, 150, 154–55
Thomas, Saint (in Mexico), 231, 291, 304
  Mier on meeting with Virgin of Guadalupe, 304, 317
  Quetzalcóatl identified with, 192, 238–39, 240, 295, 304, 318, 320, 352, 420, 421, 426
  Viracocha identified with, by Incas, 304
Thomas, Lewis F.: Cortez the Conqueror, a Tragedy in Five Acts, 378
Thompson, J. Eric: History of the Maya, 490
  Mexico Before Cortés, 489
Thou, Jacques-Auguste de, 147–48
Three Years' War (Mexico), 414
Tirso de Molina, 179
Tizoc, Stone of, see Stone of Tizoc
Tlacaélel, 11, 45, 496
Tlacopan, 11, 13, 27, 131, 232, 446
Tláloc, 5, 33, 46, 51, 182, 430, 482, 529
Tlalocan, 38, 290
Tlaltecuhtli, 43

Tlatelolco, 231, 498
  Colegio de Santa Cruz, 114, 118, 126–27, 291
Tlaxcala, 12, 96, 116, 127, 131, 201, 268, 282, 301, 428, 481
  Bandelier on, 396
  Bustamante on, 319
  Herrera on, 283
  Moxó on, 316
  Muñoz Camargo on, 78, 127–30, 175
  Pimentel on, 415
  Solís on, 177
  Spanish Conquest, 53, 54, 57, 60, 127, 128, 187, 205, 286, 287
  Wilson on, 382
Tlaxcala, Lienzo de, 530
Tloque Nahuaque, 34
"Toltec" (artist or craftsman), 22–23
Toltecs, 7–9, 342, 447, 479
  agriculture, 9, 239, 421
  architecture, 5, 239, 381, 471
  art, 8, 314, 516
  Boturini on, 229, 231, 232, 294–95
  Brasseur de Bourbourg on, 343–44
  Brinton on, 450
  calendrical system, 229, 232, 239, 294–95, 343
  cannibalism, 5, 485
  Charnay on, 439
  Chavero on, 426, 428
  Clavigero on, 294–95
  Dupaix on, 314
  in Fosdick novel, 376–78
  frescoes, 5, 471, 485
  human sacrifice, 5, 8, 343–44, 362, 485
  mathematics, 229
  medicine, 232
  Orozco y Berra on, 420, 421
  picture writing, 231, 294, 438, 484
  pottery, 471
  Prescott on, 355, 357, 358, 360
  religion, 8, 35, 44, 45, 46, 238, 343, 344, 357, 358, 360, 420, 426

Toltecs (cont.)
  sculpture, 5, 471, 511
  Séjourné on, 484–85
  Seler on, 450
  Teoamoxtli, 232, 239, 294–95, 343
  trade, 6
  Veytia on, 238, 239–40, 355
  Wilson on, 381
  see also Teotihuacán
Tonalámatl, 32, 224, 339
Tonantzín, Virgin of Guadalupe
  identified with, 318–19
Topiltzin, 8, 9, 239, 343
  see also Quetzalcóatl
Toral, Francisco de, 114
Toribio de Benavente, Fray, see
  Motolinía
Torquemada, Juan de, 34, 180, 184,
  185, 187–88, 239, 340, 389, 534
  Clavigero on, 295
  influence of: on Robertson, 277,
    285
    on Southey, 372
    on Vetancurt, 187
  influence on: of Acosta, 182
    of Mendieta, 181, 182, 184
  León-Portilla on, 184
  Monarchía indiana, 180–84, 224,
    395
Torre, Lucas de la, 201
Toscano, Salvador, 522
  El arte antiguo, 519
  Arte precolombino de México,
    518–19
  on Cuauhtémoc, 543, 546–47
  Fernández on, 518, 523
Totonacs, 53, 63, 295
Touron, Antoine, 247–48
Toussaint, Manuel, 469
Tovar, Juan de, 122
Tozzer, A. N., 419
trade, 6, 247
  Aztecs, 12, 20, 24
    16th century on: France, 158,
      162; Italy, 141; Spain, 58, 60,
      81, 84, 85, 88

trade, Aztecs (cont.)
    18th century on: Great Britain,
      279; Italy, 269, 270
    19th century on: Great Britain,
      446; Italy, 328; Mexico, 317,
      318; Spain, 456; U.S., 359
    20th century on: Mexico, 473
  merchants, 12, 15, 16, 17, 22, 23–
    24, 27, 46, 359, 429, 501
  weights and measures, 20, 84, 85,
    141
  see also barter and exchange
Travels of Sir John Mandeville, 151
tribute demands:
  by Aztecs, 12, 13, 21, 47, 52
    17th century on: Mexico, 197–
      98
    18th century on: Great Britain,
      280
    19th century on: Germany, 332;
      Mexico, 429
    20th century on: Great Britain,
      503; U.S., 497
  by Spanish, 72, 73, 75, 76, 77, 80,
    83–84, 89, 109, 124, 174, 196,
    198, 292
Troano Codex, see Codex Troano
Tula, 7, 8, 9, 116, 197, 232, 239, 343,
  344, 473, 484
  excavations, 439, 466
Tylor, Edward B., 35, 380, 381, 427,
  442, 463
  Anahuac, 442, 443
  "Backgammon among the Aztecs,"
    443
  Payne on, 446
  on Humboldt, 442–43
  Researches into the Early History
    of Mankind, 442–43
Tzapotlaténan, 296

Union of Soviet Socialist Republics:
  Indians, attitudes toward,
    505–507
United States of America:
  Indians, attitudes toward:
    18th century, 307–09

U.S.A., Indians, attitude toward
(cont.)
19th century, 312, 349–63, 373–
78, 380–404, 451–52, 534, 566;
translations from Spanish, 299
20th century, 404–10, 488–98,
505, 513, 522–23, 534, 536,
547–53, 557
and Mexico, 418–19, 537
archaeology, 350, 352, 396, 406–
09
El Universal, 327
Upper Peru, 316
Uxmal, 327

Vaillant, George C., 490, 493, 564
Aztecs of Mexico, 491–93, 495,
497, 522
on Bandelier, 409, 491, 492, 495
Fernández on, 522, 523
influence of, 503
influence on, of Morgan-Bandelier
theory, 409, 491, 492, 495
Soustelle on, 499
Valderrama, Jerónimo, 76, 86
Valencia, Martín de, 110
Valeriano, Antonio, 180
Vasconcelos, José, 486, 496, 526
Breve historia de México, 487
influence on: of Alamán, 471
of Pereyra, 487
on Morgan, 487
as Secretary of Education, 465,
486, 526, 543, 560
Vásquez de Tapia, Bernardino, 56
Vatican Codex, *see* Codex Vaticanus
Vega, Garcilaso de la, *see* Garcilaso
de la Vega
Vega Carpio, Lope de, 179, 180
La conquista de México, 180
*La mayor desgracia de Carlos V y
hechicerías de Argel,* 180
Velasco, José María: *Baño de Neza-
hualcóyotl,* 461–62
Velásquez, Diego, 49, 50–51, 67, 367
Venezuela, 143, 222

Veracruz (Villa Rica de la Vera
Cruz), 9, 51, 62, 63, 277, 365,
419
Vespucci, Amerigo, 166
influence of, on Rabelais, 157
Vetancurt, Agustín de, 190, 192
influence on, of Torquemada, 187
Teatro mexicano, 187–89
Veytia, José de, 228
Veytia, Mariano, 228, 237–40, 317,
318, 339, 348, 421
Gallatin on, 353
influence of, on Brasseur de Bour-
bourg, 344
influence on: of Ixtlilxóchitl, 238,
240
of Sigüenza, 240
Prescott on, 355
Vico, Giambattista, 236
influence of: on Boturini, 227, 228,
230, 231, 234, 235–36
on Brasseur de Bourbourg, 342
Nuova scienza, 225–27, 229–30,
232, 235, 238, 243
Victoria, Guadalupe, 364
Vigil, José M., 534
Villalobos, Arias de, 193
Villey, Pierre, 158
Villoro, Luis, 114, 304
Viollet-le-Duc, Eugène-Emmanuel,
436, 437–38
Viracocha, Saint Thomas identified
with, 304
Virgin Mary: Coatlicue identified
with, 304
mother goddess cult identified
with, 497
Virgin of Guadalupe: Boturini on,
227, 228
Mier on meeting with Saint
Thomas, 304, 317
Tonantzín identified with, 318–19
Virginia, 169
Vivier, Gérard du, 156
Voltaire, 217, 218, 252, 263, 299, 564,
565
on Buffon, 254

Voltaire (cont.)
  Essai sur les mœurs, 254–57
  influence on: of Garcilaso de la
    Vega, 254, 255
    of Herrera, 254
    of Las Casas, 254, 256
  Moxó on, 315
  on Solís, 256–57

Wagner, Richard, 379
Waldeck, Jean-Frédéric-Maximilien,
    Baron de, 321–22, 337, 352
  *Voyage archaeologique et pittor-
    esque dans la Province de Yu-
    catan,* 338–39
Wallace, Lew: *The Fair God, Or,
    The Last of the 'Tzins,* 451–52
Walsingham, Sir Francis, 169
warfare, 3, 4, 11, 12–13, 17, 21, 30, 31,
    41, 43–47 *passim,* 207
  16th century on:
    France, 149, 159
    Great Britain, 169
    Italy, 66
    Mexico, 133
    Spain, 60, 96, 98–99, 135, 137
  17th century on:
    Spain, 177, 187
  18th century on:
    France, 252–53, 255, 256
    Great Britain, 258, 274, 282
    Mexico, 297
    Spain, 287, 305
  19th century on:
    Great Britain, 441, 446, 447
    Mexico, 318, 415, 428
    Spain, 456
    U.S., 351, 354, 356, 360–61, 386,
      395
  20th century on:
    East Germany, 507
    Mexico, 431, 475, 476, 544
  Greeks compared with Aztecs,
    221, 268, 287
  Romans compared with Aztecs,
    221, 252, 274, 287

warfare (cont.)
  see also Spain, warfare and weap-
    ons; weapons
War of Independence (Mexico),
    311, 313, 316–17, 412
warriors, *see* class structure and so-
    cial organization
Washington: Smithsonian Institu-
    tion, 437
Waterman, T. T.: on Bandelier, 488
weapons, 7
  Aztec, 12, 13
  16th century on: Spain, 65, 91,
    135, 137
  18th century on: France, 252,
    255; Italy, 268
  19th century on: U.S., 393
  see also Spain, warfare and weap-
    ons
Weiditz, Christoph, 528
West Indies: encomienda system, 72,
    73, 75
  France and Great Britain, 166
Westheim, Paul, 513
  Arte antiguo de México, 519–22
  Fernández on, 523
  on Guzmán, 519–20
White, Leslie A.: on Boas, 405
  on Morgan and Bandelier, 494–95
Willes, Richard: *The History of
    Travayle in the West and
    East Indies,* 168, 170
Williams, William Carlos: "The De-
    struction of Tenochtitlan,"
    547–49
Wilson, Robert A., 381
  Baldwin on, 385–86
  on Díaz del Castillo, 384
  Fiske on, 399
  influence on: of Cass, 384
    of Gallatin, 384
    of Morgan, 383–84
  on Ixtlilxóchitl, 384
  Mexico and Its Religion, 381–82
  Morgan on, 382
  *New History of the Conquest of
    Mexico,* 383–85

Wilson, Robert A. (cont.)
and Prescott, 384, 385
Winghe, Iodocus a, 164–65
Winsor, Justin: on Bancroft, 401, 404
on Gallatin, 400–01
on Morgan-Bandelier theory, 401
Narrative and Critical History of America, 400–01
on Robertson, 400
Woermann, Karl, 510
Wolf, Eric R.: *Sons of the Shaking Earth*, 6, 496
Wolfe, Bertram: on Rivera, 524–26, 527–28, 529
Wolpe, Hans, 263
Worringer, Wilhelm, 521
writing, *see* Náhuatl; picture writing

Xiconténcatl, 324, 423, 452, 453
Xipe Totec, 34, 511
Red Tezcatlipoca identified with, 31, 34
Xiuhámatl (Books of the Years), 18
Xiutecuhtli, 34, 230
Xochicalco: excavations, 18th century, 300, 301–02
excavations, 19th century, 313, 321, 327
Xochipilli, 511
Xólotl, 232, 294
Xólotl Codex, *see* Codex Xólotl

Yohualli-Ehécatl, 34
Yolotlicue, 523
Yucatán, 6–7, 49, 344, 438
Ruscelli map (1561), 155

Zapata, Emiliano, 486
Zapata, Luis: *Carlos famoso*, 134–35
Zapotecs, 6
Zappullo, Michele, 140–41
Zarco, Francisco, 413
Zavala, Lorenzo de, 322, 323
on Bustamante, 324
Ensayo histórico de las revoluciones de Mégico, 323–24
Ziletti, Giordano, 139
Zorita, Alonso de:
Breve y sumaria relación de los señores de la Nueva España, 99–103, 111, 112
Herrera plagiarism of, 175
influence of: on Chavero, 429
on Robertson, 277, 278, 285
influences on, 99
Zouche Codex, *see* Codex Zouche
Zumárraga, Juan de, 106, 130, 277, 358, 434, 458
Alamán on, 325
García Icazbalceta biography, 433–34
Las Casas opposed by, 74
Zuñi, 390

ABOUT THE AUTHOR

Benjamin Keen is professor emeritus of Latin American history at Northern Illinois University. He is the author of *David Curtis De Forest and the Revolution of Buenos Aires* and the editor and translator of *The Spain of Ferdinand and Isabella*, by Jean Hippolyte Mariéjol, *The Life of the Admiral Christopher Columbus by His Son Ferdinand*, and *Life and Labor in Ancient Mexico*, Alonso de Zorita's *Brief and Summary Relation of the Lords of New Spain*. Mr. Keen is a graduate of Muhlenberg College and did his graduate work at Lehigh University and Yale University. He has previously taught at Yale University, Amherst College, West Virginia University, and Jersey City State College.